DØ770935

DATE DUE

DEMCO 38-296

Microsoft

MCSE

Exam 70-221

Designing a Microsoft® Windows® 2000 Network Infrastructure

Training Kit

IT Professional

A Division of Microsoft Corporation
One Microsoft Way
Redmond, Washington 98052-6399

Library of Congress Cataloging-in-Publication Data
MCSE Training Kit : Designing a Microsoft Windows 2000 Network Infrastructure / Microsoft Corporation.
        p. cm.
    Includes index.
    ISBN 0-7356-1133-5
    1. Electronic data processing personnel--Certification.   2. Microsoft software--Examinations--Studey guides.   3. Computer networks--Examinations--Study guides. 4. Microsoft Windows (Computer file)   I. Title: Desigining a Microsoft Windows 2000 network infrastructure. II. Microsoft Corporation.

    QA76.3 .M3283   2001
    005.7'13769--dc21   00-066238

Printed and bound in the United States of America.

1 2 3 4 5 6 7 8 9   QWT   6 5 4 3 2 1

Distributed in Canada by Penguin Books Canada Limited.

A CIP catalogue record for this book is available from the British Library.

Microsoft Press books are available through booksellers and distributors worldwide. For further information about international editions, contact your local Microsoft Corporation office or contact Microsoft Press International directly at fax (425) 936-7329. Visit our Web site at mspress.microsoft.com. Send comments to *tkinput@microsoft.com*.

Active Directory, FrontPage, JScript, Microsoft, Microsoft Press, Outlook, Visual Basic, Visual C++, Visual J++, Windows, and Windows NT are either registered trademarks or trademarks of Microsoft Corporation in the United States and/or other countries. Other product and company names mentioned herein may be the trademarks of their respective owners.

Unless otherwise noted, the example companies, organizations, products, people, and events depicted herein are fictitious. No association with any real company, organization, product, person, or event is intended or should be inferred.

Acquisitions Editor: Thomas Pohlmann
Project Editor: Michael Bolinger

Author: Doug Steen

Body Part No. X08-04947

Contents

About This Book

Welcome to *MCSE Training Kit—Designing a Microsoft Windows 2000 Network Infrastructure.* This kit prepares you to analyze the business and technical requirements of an organization and then create a networking services design that provides an appropriate solution by using Windows 2000. In addition, you will learn how to evaluate existing designs and recommend solutions to improve the security, availability, and performance characteristics of the existing network.

This course supports the Microsoft Certified Systems Engineer program.

Note For more information on becoming a Microsoft Certified Systems Engineer, see the section titled "The Microsoft Certified Professional Program," later in this introduction.

Each chapter in this book is divided into lessons, activities, labs, and reviews. Lessons include discussions of the key design decisions and then provides examples of how you would make those design decisions. The activities and labs are designed to allow you to apply the design decisions discussed within a chapter. At the end of each chapter, a set of review questions are presented to illustrate alternative solutions, and pose hypothetical situations, and test your knowledge of the chapter material.

Content and labs are written in a scenario format to help you develop the soft skills required for the MCSE certification. The scenarios are incorporated into each chapter and provide a "real world" example of how design decisions are made.

The scenarios in the chapter content are brief and focus only on the design decision that you're currently reading. In some instances, multiple scenarios are presented for a design decision to illustrate why you would choose an alternative solution.

The scenarios in the activities focus on the design decision discussed in the previous lessons in the chapter. The scenarios in the activities allow you to see how multiple design decisions interact with each other and let you create a portion of a complete solution.

Finally, the lab scenarios provide an overall picture of an organization and let you create a complete solution for the organization. You must apply all the design decisions in the chapter to create the design for the organization depicted in the lab scenario.

Intended Audience

This book was developed for the information technology (IT) professional who

- Is a network designer (network architect, senior support professional, or consultant)

Or

- Wants to become a network designer (architect)

Or

- Plans to take the Microsoft Certified Professional Exam 70-221, Designing a Microsoft Windows 2000 Network Infrastructure

Prerequisites

This course requires that students meet the following prerequisites.

- A minimum of one year's experience implementing, administering, and configuring network operating systems, including Novell NetWare, UNIX, Macintosh networks
- Gained their experience in environments that have the following characteristics:
  - Supported users range from 200 to 26,000+
  - Physical locations range from 5 to 150+
  - Typical network services and applications include file and print, database, messaging, proxy server or firewall, dial-in remote access, virtual private networking (VPN), desktop management, and Web hosting
  - Connectivity needs include connecting individual offices and users at remote locations to the corporate network and connecting corporate networks to the Internet
- Successful completion of the following four core exams for the Microsoft Windows 2000 MCSE track is recommended:
  - Exam 70-210: Installing, Configuring, and Administering Microsoft Windows 2000 Professional
  - Exam 70-215: Installing, Configuring, and Administering Microsoft Windows 2000 Server
  - Exam 70-216: Implementing and Administering a Microsoft Windows 2000 Network Infrastructure
  - Exam 70-217: Implementing and Administering a Microsoft Windows 2000 Directory Services Infrastructure

Or completion of the following exam:

  - Exam 70-240: Microsoft Windows 2000 Accelerated Exam for MCPs Certified on Microsoft Window NT 4.0

Reference Materials

You might find the following reference materials useful.

- Microsoft Corporation. *MCSE Training Kit—Microsoft Windows 2000 Server*. Redmond, Washington: Microsoft Press, 2000.
- Microsoft Corporation. *MCSE Training Kit—Microsoft Windows 2000 Active Directory Services*. Redmond, Washington: Microsoft Press, 2000.
- Microsoft Corporation. *MCSE Training Kit—Microsoft Windows 2000 Network Infrastructure Administration*. Redmond, Washington: Microsoft Press, 2000.
- Windows 2000 white papers and case studies, available online at *http://www.microsoft.com/windows2000/library/*.

About the Supplemental Course Materials CD-ROM

The Supplemental Course Materials compact disc contains a set of the worksheets in electronic form that may be used in conjunction with the lab sections of this book. See the Readme.txt file in the CD root directory for instructions on how to view and print these worksheets. For more information regarding the contents of this CD-ROM, see the section of this introduction titled "Getting Started."

Features of This Book

Each chapter opens with a "About This Chapter" section, which prepares you for completing the chapter.

▶ **The chapters are then divided into lessons, activities, and labs.**

The "Review" section at the end of the chapter allows you to test what you have learned in the chapter's lessons.

The Appendix, "Questions and Answers," contains all the book's questions and corresponding answers.

Notes

Several types of notes appear throughout the lessons.

- Notes marked **Tip** contain explanations of possible results or alternative methods.
- Notes marked **Important** contain information that is essential to completing a task.
- Notes marked **Note** contain supplemental information.
- Notes marked **Caution** contain warnings about potential problems to look out for.

Conventions

The following conventions are used throughout this book.

Notational Conventions

- *Italic* in sentences indicates an important term, concept, or information. *Italic* is also used for book titles and URLs.
- Names of files and folders appear in Title caps.
- File name extensions appear in all lowercase.
- Acronyms appear in all uppercase.
- Icons represent specific sections in the book as follows:

Icon	Represents
	A hands-on activity or lab. You should perform the activity or lab to give yourself an opportunity to use the skills being presented in the lesson. The answers to the activity questions are in the Appendix, "Questions and Answers," at the end of the book. Completed sample lab design worksheets are on the Supplemental Course Materials CD-ROM in the Completed Worksheets folder.
	Chapter review questions. These questions at the end of each chapter allow you to test what you have learned in the lessons. The answers to the review questions are in the Appendix, "Questions and Answers," at the end of the book.

Fictitious Name Conventions

The content of this training kit requires the use of fictitious company and domain names in fictitious scenarios. This training kit makes every effort to avoid using domain names that represent live Web sites. To accomplish this, each domain name illustrated in the book for fictitious companies uses the nonexistent top-level domain.msft rather than the standard ones of .com or .net. In reality, domain names should represent an organization's identity.

Chapter and Appendix Overview

This self-paced training course combines notes, hands-on activities and labs, professional interviews and worksheets, and review questions to teach you how to evaluate and create networking services designs. Typically, you will use this course by completing the chapters in sequence, from beginning to end. However, you can choose a customized track and complete only the sections that interest you. (See the next section, "Finding the Best Starting Point for You," for more information.) If you choose the customized track option, see the "Before You Begin" section in each chapter. Any labs or chapter that require preliminary work or study from preceding chapters refer to the appropriate chapters.

The book is divided into the following chapters.

The "About This Book" section contains a self-paced training overview and introduces the components of this training. Read this section thoroughly to get the greatest educational value from this self-paced training and to plan which lessons you will complete.

Chapter 1, "Introduction to Networking Services Design," introduces the technologies that comprise a networking services design. In addition, the chapter describes how to create a successful networking services design. Read this chapter to learn what technologies are available and to learn a method for approaching the creation of networking services design.

Chapter 2, "Networking Protocol Design," identifies the design decisions in creating a foundation for the networking services by using Transmission Control Protocol/Internet Protocol (TCP/IP). Many of the networking services utilize TCP/IP exclusively as a transport protocol. Read this chapter to learn how to create TCP/IP designs that will support the Windows 2000 networking services that will, in turn, support your applications.

In Chapter 3, "Multiprotocol Network Design," the discussion turns to the design decisions for other transport protocols, including Internetwork Packet Exchange (IPX), AppleTalk, and System Network Architecture (SNA) protocols. Read this chapter to determine how to create multiprotocol designs to provide integration between systems that use IPX, AppleTalk, and SNA protocols.

Chapter 4, " IP Routing Designs," discusses how to utilize the Internet Protocol (IP) routing capabilities in the Routing and Remote Access feature in Windows 2000. Read this chapter to learn how to create edge of network and internal IP routing designs.

In Chapter 5, "Multiprotocol Routing Designs," the content focuses on how to create routing solutions for IPX and AppleTalk protocols by using the Routing and Remote Access feature in Windows 2000. Read this chapter to determine how to create multiprotocol solutions for edge of network and internal routing solutions.

Chapter 6, "Proxy Server in Internet and Intranet Designs," covers how to provide Internet connectivity by using Microsoft Proxy Server 2.0. Read this chapter to create secure Internet connectivity solutions that scale to large designs and are accessible to users a high percentage of time.

In Chapter 7, "NAT in Internet and Intranet Designs," Internet connectivity is revisited with the NAT protocol in Routing and Remote Access as the technology used to create the solutions. Read this chapter to create Internet connectivity solutions for small offices or home offices (SOHOs).

Chapter 8, "DHCP in IP Configuration Designs," describes how to automate and manage the IP configuration of your network by using the Dynamic Host

Configuration Protocol (DHCP) implementation in Windows 2000. To create designs that reduce IP administration and common IP configuration errors, read this chapter.

Chapter 9, "DNS in Name Resolution Designs," presents the design decisions in creating a Domain Name System (DNS) solution for Windows 2000 networks. DNS is crucial to the proper deployment of Active Directory, Internet connectivity, and extranet connectivity. Read this chapter to learn how to create designs to support Active Directory and to integrate with DNS running on other operating systems (such as Windows NT 4.0 and UNIX).

In Chapter 10, "WINS in Name Resolution Designs," the decisions for creating Network Basic Input Output System (NetBIOS) name resolution designs are presented. Although Windows 2000 no longer requires NetBIOS for file and print services, many applications and earlier versions of Windows operating systems require NetBIOS. Read this chapter when you must create networks that incorporate applications that rely on NetBIOS or that must integrate with versions of Windows operating systems prior to Windows 2000.

In Chapter 11, "Dial-Up Connectivity in Remote Access Designs," the remote access solutions for organizations that want to control every aspect of their remote access connectivity is discussed. Dial-up remote access is the only remote access solution that allows an organization to control all aspects of its remote access design. Read this chapter when you must create solutions for organizations with these requirements.

In Chapter 12, "VPN Connectivity in Remote Access Designs," another type of remote access solution is discussed. Organizations that are willing to outsource the dial-up portion of their remote access solution can utilize virtual private networking (VPN) to provide secured remote connectivity to their private network. Read this chapter to provide remote access solutions when the organization wants to outsource the dial-up portion of its remote access solution, but doesn't want to enter into an agreement with any individual provider.

In Chapter 13, "RADIUS in Remote Access Designs," the remote access solutions are extended by providing enhanced security, administration and management to dial-up or VPN remote access solutions. Organizations might want to outsource their dial-up connectivity while enforcing certain security measures (such as caller-ID or callback). Read this chapter to determine how to provide these enhanced security features, and to reduce the administration and management of all remote access solutions.

Chapter 14, "Monitoring and Managing a Microsoft Windows 2000 Network," discusses the strategies for monitoring and managing the networking services after they are deployed in your network. Read this chapter to identify the critical applications in your network, the networking services that support the critical applications, and how to ensure the networking services are always operating at optimal efficiency to support the critical applications.

Finally, Chapter 15, "Networking Services Design Optimization," discusses the strategies for optimizing your networking services design for applications or to reduce the number of servers in your design. Read this chapter to determine which combinations of networking services can be combined on a single server and how to ensure that applications are supported by the networking services in your designs.

The Appendix, "Questions and Answers," lists all the activity and review questions from the book and shows the suggested answers.

The glossary lists and defines the acronyms and terminology utilized in this book. Read this section to locate the definition for any unfamiliar acronyms or terms.

Finding the Best Starting Point for You

Because this book is self-paced, you can skip some lessons and revisit them later. Use the following table to find the best starting point for you.

If You	Follow This Learning Path
Are preparing to take the Microsoft Certified Professional exam 70-221, Designing a Microsoft Windows 2000 Network Infrastructure	Read the "Getting Started" section later in this introduction. Then work through Chapters 1 through 15 in order.
Want to review information about specific topics from the exam	Use the "Where to Find Specific Skills in This Book" section that follows this table.

Where to Find Specific Skills in This Book

The following tables provide a list of the skills measured on certification exam 70-221, Designing a Microsoft Windows 2000 Network Infrastructure. The table provides the skill and where in this book you will find the lesson relating to that skill.

Note Exam skills are subject to change without prior notice and at the sole discretion of Microsoft.

Analyzing Business Requirements

Skill Being Measured	Location in Book
Analyze the existing and planned business models	
Analyze the company model and the geographical scope. Models include regional, national, international, subsidiary, and branch offices	See the "Making the Decision" and "Applying the Decision" sections for each design topic in each chapter
Analyze the company model and the geographical scope. Models include regional, national, international, subsidiary, and branch offices	See the "Making the Decision" and "Applying The Decision" sections for each design topic in each chapter

Analyze company processes. Processes include information flow, communication flow, service and product lifecycles, and decision-making	See the "Making the Decision" and "Applying the Decision" sections for each design topic in each chapter

Analyze the existing and planned organizational structures

Consider management model; company organization; vendor, partner, and customer relationships; and acquisition plans	See the "Making the Decision" and "Applying the Decision" sections for each design topic in each chapter

Analyze factors that influence company strategies

Identify company priorities	See the "Making the Decision" and "Applying the Decision" sections for each design topic in each chapter
Identify the projected growth and growth strategy	See the "Making the Decision" and "Applying the Decision" sections for each design topic in each chapter
Identify relevant laws and regulations	See the "Making the Decision" and "Applying the Decision" sections for each design topic in each chapter
Identify the company's tolerance for risk	See the "Making the Decision" and "Applying the Decision" sections for each design topic in each chapter
Identify the total cost of operations	See the "Making the Decision" and "Applying the Decision" sections for each design topic in each chapter

Analyze the structure of IT management

Consider type of administration, such ascentralized type or decentralized; funding model; outsourcing; decision-making process; and change-management process	See the "Making the Decision" and "Applying the Decision" sections for each design topic in each chapter

Analyzing Technical Requirements

Skill Being Measured	**Location in Book**

Evaluate the company's existing and planned technical environment and goals

Analyze company size and user and resource distribution	See the "Making the Decision" and "Applying the Decision" sections for each design topic in each chapter
Assess the available connectivity between the geographic location of worksites and remote sites	See the "Making the Decision" and "Applying the Decision" sections for each design topic in each chapter
Assess net available bandwidth and latency issues	See the "Making the Decision" and "Applying the Decision" sections for each design topic in each chapter

Analyze performance, availability, and scalability requirements of service	See the "Making the Decision" and "Applying the Decision" sections for each design topic in each chapter
Analyze data and system access patterns	See the "Making the Decision" and "Applying the Decision" sections for each design topic in each chapter
Analyze network roles and responsibilities	See the "Making the Decision" and "Applying the Decision" sections for each design topic in each chapter
Analyze security considerations	See the "Making the Decision" and "Applying the Decision" sections for each design topic in each chapter

Analyze the impact of infrastructure design on the existing and planned technical environment

Assess current applications	See the "Making the Decision" and "Applying the Decision" sections for each design topic in each chapter
Analyze network infrastructure, protocols, and hosts	See the "Making the Decision" and "Applying the Decision" sections for each design topic in each chapter
Evaluate network services	See the "Making the Decision" and "Applying the Decision" sections for each design topic in each chapter
Analyze TCP/IP infrastructure	See the "Making the Decision" and "Applying the Decision" sections for each design topic in each chapter
Assess current hardware	See the "Making the Decision" and "Applying the Decision" sections for each design topic in each chapter
Identify existing and planned upgrades and rollouts	See the "Making the Decision" and "Applying the Decision" sections for each design topic in each chapter
Analyze technical support structure	See the "Making the Decision" and "Applying the Decision" sections for each design topic in each chapter
Analyze existing and planned network and systems management	See the "Making the Decision" and "Applying the Decision" sections for each design topic in each chapter

Analyze the network requirements for client computer access

Analyze end-user work needs	See the "Making the Decision" and "Applying the Decision" sections for each design topic in each chapter

Analyze end-user usage patterns	See the "Making the Decision" and "Applying the Decision" sections for each design topic in each chapter

Analyze the existing disaster recovery strategy for client computers, servers, and the network

Designing a Windows 2000 Network Infrastructure

Skill Being Measured	Location in Book
Modify and design a network topology	**Chapter 2: Lessons 1-4**
Design a TCP/IP networking strategy	
Analyze IP subnet requirements	Chapter 2: Lesson 2
Design a TCP/IP addressing and implementation plan	Chapter 2: Lesson 2
Measure and optimize a TCP/IP infrastructure design	Chapter 2: Lesson 4
Integrate software routing into existing networks	Chapter 4: Lessons 1-4
Integrate TCP/IP with existing WAN requirements	Chapter 4: Lessons 1-4
Design a DHCP strategy	
Integrate DHCP into a routed environment	Chapter 8: Lesson 1 Chapter 8: Lesson 2
Integrate DHCP with Windows 2000	Chapter 8: Lesson 1 Chapter 8: Lesson 2
Design a DHCP service for remote locations	Chapter 8: Lesson 1 Chapter 8: Lesson 2
Measure and optimize a DHCP infrastructure design	Chapter 8: Lesson 4
Design name resolution services	
Create an integrated DNS design	Chapter 9: Lesson 1 Chapter 9: Lesson 2
Create a secure DNS design	Chapter 9: Lesson 3
Create a highly available DNS design	Chapter 9: Lesson 4
Measure and optimize a DNS infrastructure design	Chapter 9: Lesson 4
Design a DNS deployment strategy	Chapter 9: Lessons 1-4
Create a Windows Internet Name Service (WINS) design	Chapter 10: Lessons 1-4
Create a secure WINS design	Chapter 10: Lesson 3
Measure and optimize a WINS infrastructure design	Chapter 10: Lesson 4
Design a WINS deployment strategy	Chapter 10: Lessons 1-4
Design a multiprotocol strategy	
Protocols include IPX/SPX and SNA	Chapter 3: Lessons 1-4 Chapter 5: Lessons 1-3

Design a Distributed file system (Dfs) strategy

Design the placement of a Dfs root	Chapter 14: Lesson 1
	Chapter 15: Lesson 1
Design a Dfs root replica strategy	Chapter 14: Lesson 1
	Chapter 15: Lesson 1

Designing for Internet Connectivity

Skill Being Measured	Location in Book
Design an Internet and extranet access solution	**Chapter 4: Lessons 1-4**
Components of the solution can include proxy server, firewall, routing and remote access, Network Address Translation (NAT), connection sharing, Web server, or mail server.	Chapter 5: Lessons 1-4
	Chapter 6: Lessons 1-4
	Chapter 7: Lessons 1-4
Design a load-balancing strategy.	Chapter 4: Lesson 4
	Chapter 5: Lesson 4
	Chapter 6: Lesson 4
	Chapter 8: Lesson 4
	Chapter 9: Lesson 4
	Chapter 10: Lesson 4
	Chapter 11: Lesson 4
	Chapter 12: Lesson 4
	Chapter 13: Lesson 4
	Chapter 15: Lesson 3

Designing a Wide Area Network Infrastructure

Skill Being Measured	Location in Book
Design an implementation strategy for dial-up remote access	
Design a remote access solution that uses Routing and Remote Access	Chapter 11: Lessons 1-4
	Chapter 12: Lessons 1-4
	Chapter 13: Lessons 1
	Chapter 11: Lessons 1-4
Integrate authentication with Remote Authentication Dial-In User Service (RADIUS)	Chapter 13: Lessons 1-4
Design a virtual private network (VPN) strategy	**Chapter 12: Lessons 1-4**
Design a Routing and Remote Access routing solution to connect locations	**Chapter 4: Lessons 1-4**
Design a demand-dial routing strategy	Chapter 4: Lesson 2

Designing a Management and Implementation Strategy for Windows 2000 Networking

Skill Being Measured	Location in Book
Design a strategy for monitoring and managing Windows 2000 network services.	
Services include global catalog, Lightweight Directory Access Protocol (LDAP) services, Certificate Services, DNS, DHCP, WINS, Routing and Remote Access, Proxy Server, and Dfs.	Chapter 14: Lessons 1-2
Design network services that support application architecture	Chapter 15: Lesson 1
Design a plan for the interaction of Windows 2000 network services such as WINS, DHCP, and DNS	Chapter 4: Lesson 1 Chapter 5: Lesson 1 Chapter 6: Lesson 1 Chapter 7: Lesson 1 Chapter 8: Lesson 1 Chapter 9: Lesson 1 Chapter 10: Lesson 1 Chapter 11: Lesson 1 Chapter 12: Lesson 1 Chapter 13: Lesson 1 Chapter 15: Lessons 1-3
Design a resource strategy	
Plan for the placement and management of resources	Chapter 15: Lessons 1-3 See the "Making the Decision" and "Applying the Decision" sections for each design decision in each chapter.
Plan for growth	Chapter 15: Lessons 1-3 See the "Making the Decision" and "Applying the Decision" sections for each design decision in each chapter.
Plan for decentralized resources or centralized resources	Chapter 15: Lessons 1-3 See the "Making the Decision" and "Applying the Decision" sections for each design decision in each chapter.

Getting Started

This self-paced training course contains activities and labs to help you learn about designing Microsoft Windows 2000 networking services. The focus of this self-paced training course is design, so the activities and labs that you complete will require you to evaluate the requirements of an organization and then create a design that meets the organization's requirements.

Software Requirements

A copy of the 120-day evaluation edition of Microsoft Windows 2000 Advanced Server isn't required to do the activities and labs in this course.

Caution   The 120-day Evaluation Edition of Windows 2000 Advanced Server provided with this training isn't the full retail product and is provided only for training purposes. Microsoft Technical Support doesn't support this evaluation edition. For additional support information regarding this book and the CD-ROMs (including answers to commonly asked questions about installation and use), visit the Microsoft Press Technical Support Web site at http://mspress.microsoft.com/support/. You can also e-mail TKINPUT@MICROSOFT.COM or send a letter to Microsoft Press, Attn: Microsoft Press Technical Support, One Microsoft Way, Redmond, WA 98502-6399.

Setup Instructions

The following information is a checklist of the tasks you need to perform to prepare your computer to install the evaluation software. If you don't have experience installing Windows 2000 or another network operating system, you might need help from an experienced network administrator. As you complete a task, mark it off in the check box. Step-by-step instructions for each task follow.

☐ Create Windows 2000 Advanced Server setup diskettes.

☐ Run the Windows 2000 Advanced Server Pre-Copy and Text Mode Setup Routine.

☐ Run the graphical user interface (GUI) mode and gathering information phase of Windows 2000 Advanced Server Setup.

☐ Complete the Installing Windows Networking Components phase of Windows 2000 Advanced Server Setup.

☐ Complete the hardware installation phase of Windows 2000 Advanced Server Setup.

Note   The installation information provided will help you prepare a computer with the evaluation software. It isn't intended to teach you installation.

Installing Windows 2000 Advanced Server

Install Windows 2000 Advanced Server on a computer with no formatted partitions. During installation, you can use the Windows 2000 Advanced Server Setup program to create a partition on your hard disk, on which you install Windows 2000 Advanced Server as a stand-alone server in a workgroup.

▶   **To create Windows 2000 Advanced Server setup diskettes**

Complete this procedure on a computer running MS-DOS or any version of
Windows with access to the Bootdisk directory on the Windows 2000 Advanced
Server installation CD-ROM. If your computer is configured with a bootable
CD-ROM drive, you can install Windows 2000 without using the Setup disks.
To complete this procedure as outlined, bootable CD-ROM support must be dis-
abled in the BIOS.

Important   This procedure requires four formatted 1.44-MB disks. If you use
diskettes that contain data, the data will be overwritten without warning.

---

1. Label the four blank, formatted 1.44-MB diskettes as follows:
   ▪ Windows 2000 Advanced Server Setup Disk #1
   ▪ Windows 2000 Advanced Server Setup Disk #2
   ▪ Windows 2000 Advanced Server Setup Disk #3
   ▪ Windows 2000 Advanced Server Setup Disk #4

2. Insert the Microsoft Windows 2000 Advanced Server CD-ROM into the
   CD-ROM drive.

3. If the Windows 2000 CD-ROM dialog box appears prompting you to install
   or upgrade to Windows 2000, click No.

4. Open a command prompt.

5. At the command prompt, change to your CD-ROM drive. For example, if
   your CD-ROM drive name is E, type **e:** and press Enter.

6. At the command prompt, change to the Bootdisk directory by typing **cd
   bootdisk** and pressing Enter.

7. If you're creating the setup boot diskettes from a computer running
   MS-DOS or a Windows 16-bit operating system, type **makeboot a:** (where
   A: is the name of your floppy disk drive) and press Enter. If you're creating
   the setup boot diskettes from a computer running Microsoft Windows NT or
   Windows 2000, type **makebt32 a:** (where A: is the name of your floppy disk
   drive), and then press Enter. Windows 2000 displays a message indicating
   that this program creates the four setup disks for installing Windows 2000. It
   also indicates that four blank, formatted, high-density floppy disks are
   required.

8. Press any key to continue. Windows 2000 displays a message prompting you
   to insert the disk that will become the Windows 2000 Setup Boot Disk.

9. Insert the blank formatted diskette labeled Windows 2000 Advanced Server
   Setup Disk #1 into the floppy disk drive and press any key to continue. After
   Windows 2000 creates the disk image, it displays a message prompting you
   to insert the diskette labeled Windows 2000 Setup Disk #2.

10. Remove Disk #1, insert the blank formatted diskette labeled Windows 2000 Advanced Server Setup Disk #2 into the floppy disk drive, and press any key to continue. After Windows 2000 creates the disk image, it displays a message prompting you to insert the diskette labeled Windows 2000 Setup Disk #3.

11. Remove Disk #2, insert the blank formatted diskette labeled Windows 2000 Advanced Server Setup Disk #3 into the floppy disk drive, and press any key to continue. After Windows 2000 creates the disk image, it displays a message prompting you to insert the diskette labeled Windows 2000 Setup Disk #4.

12. Remove Disk #3, insert the blank formatted diskette labeled Windows 2000 Advanced Server Setup Disk #4 into the floppy disk drive, and press any key to continue. After Windows 2000 creates the disk image, it displays a message indicating that the imaging process is done.

13. At the command prompt, type **exit** and then press Enter.

14. Remove the disk from the floppy disk drive and the CD-ROM from the CD-ROM drive.

▶   **To run the Windows 2000 Advanced Server pre-copy and text mode setup routine**

It's assumed for this procedure that your computer has no operating system installed, the disk isn't partitioned, and bootable CD-ROM support, if available, is disabled.

1. Insert the disk labeled Windows 2000 Advanced Server Setup Disk #1 into the floppy disk drive, insert the Windows 2000 Advanced Server CD-ROM into the CD-ROM drive, and restart your computer.

   After the computer starts, Windows 2000 Setup displays a brief message that your system configuration is being checked, and then the Windows 2000 Setup screen appears.

   Notice that the gray bar at the bottom of the screen indicates that the computer is being inspected and that the Windows 2000 Executive is loading, which is a minimal version of the Windows 2000 kernel.

2. When prompted, insert Setup Disk #2 into the floppy disk drive and press Enter.

   Notice that Setup indicates that it's loading the hardware abstraction layer (HAL), fonts, local specific data, bus drivers, and other software components to support your computer's motherboard, bus, and other hardware. Setup also loads the Windows 2000 Setup program files.

3. When prompted, insert Setup Disk #3 into the floppy disk drive and press Enter.

   Notice that Setup indicates that it's loading disk drive controller drivers. After the drive controllers load, the setup program initializes drivers appropriate to support access to your disk drives. Setup might pause several times during this process.

4. When prompted, insert Setup Disk #4 into the floppy disk drive and press Enter.

   Setup loads peripheral support drivers, like the floppy disk driver and file systems, and then it initializes the Windows 2000 Executive and loads the rest of the Windows 2000 Setup program.

   If you're installing the evaluation version of Windows 2000, a Setup notification screen appears, informing you that you're about to install an evaluation version of Windows 2000.

5. Read the Setup Notification message and press Enter to continue.

   Setup displays the Welcome To Setup screen. Notice that, in addition to the initial installation of Windows 2000, you can use Windows 2000 Setup to repair or recover a damaged Windows 2000 installation.

6. Read the Welcome To Setup message and press Enter to begin the installation phase of Windows 2000 Setup. Setup displays the License Agreement screen.

7. Read the license agreement, pressing Page Down to scroll down to the bottom of the screen.

8. Select I Accept the Agreement by pressing F8.

   Setup displays the Windows 2000 Server Setup screen, prompting you to select an area of free space or an existing partition on which to install Windows 2000. This stage of setup provides a way for you to create and delete partitions on your hard disk.

   If your computer doesn't contain any disk partitions (as required for this exercise), you will notice that the hard disk listed on the screen contains an existing unformatted partition.

9. Make sure that the Unpartitioned space partition is highlighted and then type **c.**

   Setup displays the Windows 2000 Setup screen, confirming that you've chosen to create a new partition in the unpartitioned space and informing you of the minimum and maximum sizes of the partition you might create.

10. Specify the size of the partition you want to create (at least 2048 MB) and press Enter to continue.

    Setup displays the Windows 2000 Setup screen, showing the new partition as C: New (Unformatted).

Note Although you can create additional partitions from the remaining unpartitioned space during setup, it's recommended that you perform additional partitioning tasks after you install Windows 2000. To partition hard disks after installation, use the Disk Management console.

---

11. Make sure the new partition is highlighted and press Enter.

    You're prompted to select a file system for the partition.

12. Use the arrow keys to select Format The Partition Using The NTFS File System and press Enter.

    The Setup program formats the partition with NTFS. After it formats the partition, Setup examines the hard disk for physical errors that might cause Setup to fail and then copies files to the hard disk. This process takes several minutes.

    Eventually, Setup displays the Windows 2000 Advanced Server Setup screen. A red status bar counts down for 15 seconds before Setup restarts the computer.

13. Remove the Setup disk from the floppy disk drive.

    Important   If your computer supports booting from the CD-ROM drive and this feature wasn't disabled in the BIOS, the computer could boot from the Windows 2000 Advanced Server installation CD-ROM after Windows 2000 Setup restarts. This will cause Setup to start again from the beginning. If this happens, remove the CD-ROM and then restart the computer.

14. Setup copies additional files and then restarts your machine and loads the Windows 2000 Setup Wizard.

▶   **To run the GUI mode and gathering information phase of Windows 2000 Advanced Server setup**

This procedure begins the graphical portion of Setup on your computer.

1. On the Welcome To The Windows 2000 Setup Wizard page, click Next to begin gathering information about your computer.

   Setup configures NTFS folder and file permissions for the operating system files, detects the hardware devices in the computer, and then installs and configures device drivers to support the detected hardware. This process takes several minutes.

2. On the Regional Settings page, make sure that the system locale, user locale, and keyboard layout are correct for your language and location, and then click Next.

   Note   You can modify regional settings after you install Windows 2000 by using Regional Options in Control Panel.

   Setup displays the Personalize Your Software page, prompting you for your name and organization name. Setup uses your organization name to generate the default computer name. Many applications that you install later will use this information for product registration and document identification.

3. In the Name field, type your name; in the Organization field, type the name of an organization; then click Next.

Note   If the Your Product Key screen appears, enter the product key, located on the sticker attached to the Windows 2000 Advanced Server, Evaluation Edition, CD sleeve bound into the back of this book.

Setup displays the Licensing Modes page, prompting you to select a licensing mode. By default, the Per Server licensing mode is selected. Setup prompts you to enter the number of licenses you have purchased for this server.

4. Select the Per Server Number of concurrent connections button, type **5** for the number of concurrent connections, and then click Next.

Important   Per Server Number of concurrent connections and 5 concurrent connections are suggested values to be used to complete your self-study. Use a legal number of concurrent connections based on the actual licenses you own. You can also choose to use Per Seat instead of Per Server.

Setup displays the Computer Name And Administrator Password page.

Notice that Setup uses your organization name to generate a suggested name for the computer.

5. In the Computer Name field, type **server1**.

Windows 2000 displays the computer name in all capital letters regardless of how it's entered.

Warning   If your computer is on a network, check with the network administrator before assigning a name to your computer.

---

6. In the Administrator Password field and the Confirm Password field, type **password** (all lowercase) and click Next. Passwords are case-sensitive, so make sure you type **password** in all lowercase letters.

For the labs in this self-paced training kit, use password for the Administrator account. In a production environment, always use a complex password for the Administrator account (one that others can't easily guess). Microsoft recommends mixing uppercase and lowercase letters, numbers, and symbols (for example, Lp6*g9).

Setup displays the Windows 2000 Components page, indicating which Windows 2000 system components Setup will install.

7. On the Windows 2000 Components page, click Next.

You can install additional components after you install Windows 2000 by using Add/Remove Programs in Control Panel. Make sure to install only the components selected by default during setup. Later in your training, you will be installing additional components.

If a modem is detected in the computer during setup, Setup displays the Modem Dialing Information page.

8. If the Modem Dialing Information page appears, enter an area code or city code and click Next.

   The Date And Time Settings page appears.

Important   Windows 2000 services perform many tasks whose successful completion depends on the computer's time and date settings. Be sure to select the correct time zone for your location to avoid problems in later labs.

---

9. Enter the correct Date and Time and Time Zone settings, and then click Next.

   The Network Settings page appears and Setup installs networking components.

▶ **To complete the installing Windows networking components phase of Windows 2000 Advanced Server setup**

Networking is an integral part of Windows 2000 Advanced Server. There are many selections and configurations available. In this procedure, basic networking is configured. In a later exercise, you will install additional network components.

1. On the Networking Settings page, make sure that Typical Settings is selected, and then click Next to begin installing Windows networking components.

   This setting installs networking components that are used to gain access to and share resources on a network and configures Transmission Control Protocol/Internet Protocol (TCP/IP) to automatically obtain an IP address from a DHCP server on the network.

   Setup displays the Workgroup or Computer Domain page, prompting you to join either a workgroup or a domain.

2. On the Workgroup or Computer Domain page, make sure that the button No, This Computer Isn't On A Network or Is On A Network Without A Domain is selected, and that the workgroup name is WORKGROUP, and then click Next.

   Setup displays the Installing Components page, displaying the status as Setup installs and configures the remaining operating system components according to the options you specified. This takes several minutes.

   Setup then displays the Performing Final Tasks page, which shows the status as Setup finishes copying files, making and saving configuration changes, and deleting temporary files. Computers that don't exceed the minimum hardware requirements might take 30 minutes or more to complete this phase of installation.

   Setup then displays the Completing The Windows 2000 Setup Wizard page.

3. Remove the Windows 2000 Advanced Server CD-ROM from the CD-ROM drive, and then click Finish.

   Windows 2000 restarts and runs the newly installed version of Windows 2000 Advanced Server.

▶ **To complete the hardware installation phase of Windows 2000 Advanced Server setup**

During this final phase of installation, any Plug and Play hardware not detected in the previous phases of Setup will be detected.

1. At the completion of the startup phase, log on by pressing Ctrl+Alt+Delete.

2. In the Enter Password dialog box, type **administrator** in the User Name field and type **password** in the Password field.

3. Click OK.

   If Windows 2000 detects hardware that wasn't detected during Setup, the Found New Hardware Wizard screen displays, indicating that Windows 2000 is installing the appropriate drivers.

4. If the Found New Hardware Wizard screen appears, verify that the Restart The Computer When I Click Finish check box is cleared and click Finish to complete the Found New Hardware Wizard.

   Windows 2000 displays the Microsoft Windows 2000 Configure Your Server dialog box. From this dialog box, you can configure a variety of advanced options and services.

5. Select I Will Configure This Server Later, and then click Next.

6. From the next screen that appears, clear the Show This Screen At Startup check box.

7. Close the Configure Your Server screen.

   You have now completed the Windows 2000 Advanced Server installation and are logged on as Administrator.

Note To properly shut down Windows 2000 Advanced Server, click Start, choose Shut Down, and then follow the directions that appear.

Caution If your computers are part of a larger network, you *must* verify with your network administrator that the computer names, domain name, and other information used in setting up Windows 2000 Advanced Server as described in this section don't conflict with network operations. If they do conflict, ask your network administrator to provide alternative values and use those values through-out all the activities and labs in this book.

The eBook

The CD-ROM also includes an eBook that you can view on-screen using Microsoft Internet Explorer 4.01 or later.

► **To use the eBook**

1. Insert the Supplemental Course Materials CD-ROM into your CD-ROM drive.
2. Select Run from the Start menu on your desktop, and type **D:\Ebook\Setup.exe** (where D is the name of your CD-ROM disk drive).

   This installs an icon for the online book in your Start menu.
3. Click OK to exit the Installation Wizard.

Note   You must have the Supplemental Course Materials CD-ROM inserted in your CD-ROM drive to run the eBook.

Sample Readiness Review Questions

With this Training Kit, Microsoft provides 180 days of unlimited access to 25 practice test questions for Exam 70-221, Designing a Microsoft Windows 2000 Network Infrastructure. The exam preparation questions are a subset of practice test questions offered in the *MCSE Readiness Review—Exam 70-221: Designing a Microsoft Windows 2000 Network Infrastructure* book developed by Microsoft and MeasureUp, a Microsoft Certified Practice Test Provider.

To use these questions, create a free user account at *http://mspress.measureup.com* and register with the key provided on the sticker attached to the Supplemental Course Materials CD-ROM sleeve near the back of this book. If you encounter any problems accessing the questions, please call MeasureUp's customer service team at (678) 356-5050.

The Microsoft Certified Professional Program

The Microsoft Certified Professional (MCP) program provides the best method to prove your command of current Microsoft products and technologies. Microsoft, an industry leader in certification, is on the forefront of testing methodology. Our exams and corresponding certifications are developed to validate your mastery of critical competencies as you design and develop, or implement and support, solutions with Microsoft products and technologies. Computer professionals who become Microsoft certified are recognized as experts and are sought after industry-wide.

The MCP program offers the following certifications, based on specific areas of technical expertise.

- **Microsoft Certified Professional (MCP)**   An individual who has demonstrated in-depth knowledge of at least one Microsoft operating system. Candidates may pass additional Microsoft certification exams to further qualify their skills with Microsoft BackOffice products, development tools, or desktop programs.

- **Microsoft Certified Systems Engineer (MCSE)**   An individual who is qualified to effectively plan, implement, maintain, and support information systems in a wide range of computing environments with Microsoft Windows NT Server and the Microsoft BackOffice integrated family of server software.

- **Microsoft Certified Database Administrator (MCDBA)**   An individual who derives physical database designs, develops logical data models, creates physical databases, creates data services by using Transact-SQL, manages and maintains databases, configures and manages security, monitors and optimizes databases, and installs and configures Microsoft SQL Server.

- **Microsoft Certified Solution Developer (MCSD)**   An individual who is qualified to design and develop custom business solutions with Microsoft development tools, technologies, and platforms, including Microsoft Office and Microsoft BackOffice.

- **Microsoft Certified Trainer (MCT)**   An individual who is instructionally and technically qualified to deliver Microsoft Official Curriculum through a Microsoft Certified Technical Education Center (CTEC).

Microsoft Certification Benefits

Microsoft certification, one of the most comprehensive certification programs available for assessing and maintaining software-related skills, is a valuable measure of an individual's knowledge and expertise. Microsoft certification is awarded to individuals who have successfully demonstrated their ability to perform specific tasks and implement solutions with Microsoft products. Not only does this provide an objective measure for employers to consider, but it also provides guidance for what an individual should know to be proficient. And as with any skills-assessment and benchmarking measure, certification brings a variety of benefits: to the individual, and to employers and organizations.

Microsoft Certification Benefits for Individuals

As a MCP, you receive many benefits.

- **Industry recognition of your knowledge and proficiency with Microsoft products and technologies**

- **A Microsoft Developer Network (MSDN) subscription**   MCPs receive rebates or discounts on a one-year subscription to the Microsoft Developer Network (*http://msdn.microsoft.com/subscriptions/*) during the first year of certification. (Fulfillment details vary, depending on your location; please see your Welcome Kit.) The rebate or discount amount is U.S. $50 for MSDN Library.

- **Access to technical and product information direct from Microsoft through a secured area of the MCP Web site**   Go to *http:// www.microsoft.com/trainingandservices/* and then expand the Certification node from the tree directory in the left margin. Finally, select the "For MCPs Only" link.

- **Access to exclusive discounts on products and services from selected companies**   Individuals who are currently certified can learn more about exclusive discounts by visiting the MCP secured Web site. Go to *http:// www.microsoft.com/trainingandservices/* and then expand the Certification node from the tree directory in the left margin. Next, select the "Form MCPs Only" link) and then select the "Other Benefits" link.

- **A MCP logo, certificate, transcript, wallet card, and lapel pin to identify you as a Microsoft Certified Professional to colleagues and clients**   Electronic files of logos and transcript may be downloaded from the MCP secured Web site upon certification. Go to *http://www.microsoft.com /trainingandservices/* and then expand the Certification node from the tree directory in the left margin. Finally, select the "Form MCPs Only" link.

- **Invitations to Microsoft conferences, technical training sessions, and special events**

- **Free access to *Microsoft Certified Professional Magazine Online,* a career and professional development magazine**   Secured content on the *Microsoft Certified Professional Magazine Online* Web site includes the current issue (available only to MCPs), additional online-only content and columns, an MCP-only database, and regular chats with Microsoft and other technical experts.

An additional benefit is received by Microsoft Certified System Engineers (MCSEs).

- **A 50 percent rebate or discount off the estimated retail price of a one-year subscription to *TechNet* or *TechNet Plus* during the first year of certification**   (Fulfillment details vary, depending on your location. Please see your Welcome Kit.) In addition, about 95 percent of the CD-ROM content is available free online at the *TechNet* Web site (*http://www.microsoft.com /technet/*).

Microsoft Certification Benefits for Employers and Organizations

Through certification, computer professionals can maximize the return on investment in Microsoft technology. Research shows that Microsoft certification provides organizations with

- Excellent return on training and certification investments by providing a standard method of determining training needs and measuring results

- Increased customer satisfaction and decreased support costs through improved service, increased productivity, and greater technical self-sufficiency

- Reliable benchmarks for hiring, promoting and career planning
- Recognition and rewards for productive employees by validating their expertise
- Retraining options for existing employees so they can work effectively with new technologies
- Assurance of quality when outsourcing computer services

To learn more about how certification can help your company, see the back-grounders, white papers, and case studies available at *http://www.microsoft.com /trainingandservices/* (expand the Certification node from the tree directory in the left margin, and then select the "Case Studies" link). Here is what you will find

- A white paper, MCSE Criterion Validity Study White Paper, Oct. 1998, that evaluates the Microsoft Certified Systems Engineer certification (SysEngrCert.doc 339 KB)
- Compaq Case Study (Compaq.doc 85 KB)
- CrossTier.com Case Study (CrossTier.doc 246 KB)
- Extreme Logic Case Study (Extreme Logic.doc 74 KB)
- Financial Benefits to Supporters of Microsoft Professional Certification, IDC White Paper (1998wpidc.doc 948 KB)
- Lyondel Case Study (lyondel.doc 20 KB)
- Prudential Case Study (prudentl.exe 74 KB self-extracting file)
- Stellcom Case Study (stellcom.doc 72KB)
- Unisys Case Study (Unisys.doc 48 KB)

Requirements for Becoming a Microsoft Certified Professional

The certification requirements differ for each certification and are specific to the products and job functions addressed by the certification.

To become a MCP, you must pass rigorous certification exams that provide a valid and reliable measure of technical proficiency and expertise. These exams are designed to test your expertise and ability to perform a role or task with a product, and are developed with the input of professionals in the industry. Questions in the exams reflect how Microsoft products are used in actual organizations, giving them "real world" relevance.

Microsoft Certified Product Specialists are required to pass one operating system exam. Candidate may pass additional Microsoft certification exams to further qualify their skills with Microsoft BackOffice products, development tools, or desktop applications.

Microsoft Certified Systems Engineers are required to pass a series of core Microsoft Windows operating system and networking exams, and BackOffice technology elective exams.

Microsoft Certified Database Administrators are required to pass three core exams and one elective exam that provide a valid and reliable measure of technical proficiency and expertise.

Microsoft Certified Solution Developers are required to pass two core Microsoft Windows operating system technology exams and two BackOffice technology elective exams.

Microsoft Certified Trainers are required to meet instructional and technical requirements specific to each Microsoft Official Curriculum course they are certified to deliver. In the United States and Canada, call Microsoft at (800) 636-7544 for more information on becoming a Microsoft Certified Trainer or visit *http://www.microsoft.com/trainingandservices/* (expand the Certification node from the tree directory in the left margin, and then select the "MCT" link). Outside the United States and Canada, contact your local Microsoft subsidiary.

Technical Training for Computer Professionals

Technical training is available in a variety of ways, with instructor-led classes, online instruction, or self-paced training available at thousands of locations worldwide.

Self-Paced Training

For motivated learners who are ready for the challenge, self-paced instruction is the most flexible, cost-effective way to increase your knowledge and skills.

A full-line of self-paced print and computer-based training materials is available directly from the source—Microsoft Press. Microsoft Official Curriculum courseware kits from Microsoft Press are designed for advanced computer system professionals and are available from Microsoft Press and the Microsoft Developer Division. Self-paced training kits from Microsoft Press feature print-based instructional materials, along with CD-ROM based product software, multimedia presentations, lab exercises, and practice files. The Mastering Series provides in-depth, interactive training on CD-ROM for experienced developers. They're both great ways to prepare for Microsoft Certified Professional (MCP) exams.

Online Training

For a more flexible alternative to instructor-led classes, turn to online instruction. It's as near as the Internet and it's ready whenever you are. Learn at your own pace and on your own schedule in a virtual classroom, often with easy access to an online instructor. Without ever leaving your desk, you can gain the expertise you need. Online instruction covers a variety of Microsoft products and technologies. It includes options ranging from Microsoft Official Curriculum to choices available nowhere else. It's training on demand, with access to learning resources 24 hours a day. Online training is available through Microsoft Certified Technical Education Centers.

Microsoft Certified Technical Education Centers

Microsoft Certified Technical Education Centers (CTECs) are the best source for instructor-led training that can help you prepare to become a Microsoft Certified Professional. The Microsoft CTEC program is a worldwide network of qualified technical training organizations that provide authorized delivery of Microsoft Official Curriculum courses by Microsoft Certified Trainers to computer professionals.

For a listing of CTEC locations in the United States and Canada, visit *http:// www.microsoft.com/CTEC/default.htm.*

Technical Support

Every effort has been made to ensure the accuracy of this book and the contents of the companion disc. If you have comments, questions, or ideas regarding this book or the companion disc, please send them to Microsoft Press using either of the following methods:

E-mail:
TKINPUT@MICROSOFT.COM

Postal Mail:
Microsoft Press
Attn: *Designing a Microsoft Windows 2000 Network Infrastructure*
Editor
One Microsoft Way
Redmond, WA 98052-6399

Microsoft Press provides corrections for books through the World Wide Web at the following address:

http://mspress.microsoft.com/support/

Please note that product support isn't offered through the preceding mail addresses. For further information regarding Microsoft software support options, please visit *http://www.microsoft.com/support/* or call Microsoft Support Network Sales at (800) 936-3500.

For information about ordering the full version of any Microsoft software, please call Microsoft Sales at (800) 426-9400 or visit *http://www.microsoft.com.*

CHAPTER 1

Introduction to Networking Services Design

About This Chapter

Organizations rely on up-to-the-minute data about their customers, their vendors, their employees, and other information. All of this data is managed by the organization's information services. As a network designer, you're responsible for creating solutions that will provide the information to these organizations.

This chapter answers questions such as:

- What is a networking services design?
- What is the difference between a networking services design and a network design?
- What portions of Microsoft Windows 2000 can be used to create a networking services design?
- Where does design fit in the overall network deployment cycle?
- What constitutes a successful networking services design?

Before You Begin

Before attempting a Windows 2000 networking services design, you should

- Have a solid foundation in current networking technologies and an awareness of the future trends in these technologies

- An overall understanding of the networking services included in Windows 2000
- The experience or soft skills required to interview individuals, collect information, and translate that information into design requirements

Lesson 1: Windows 2000 Networking Services Overview

This lesson provides an overview of networking services design, based on Microsoft Windows 2000 Advanced Server. This lesson describes the scope of a networking services design in the solutions you create.

After this lesson, you will be able to

- Distinguish networking services from the networking infrastructure
- Identify the features provided by a networking services design
- List the networking services provided by Windows 2000
- Describe the solutions that each networking service provides in a design

Estimated lesson time: 20 minutes

Networking Services Within a Network

A network consists of all the hardware and software components required for connectivity between devices within your organization and with other organizations. The hardware components in your network (such as computers, network interface cards, cabling, phone lines, routers, and hubs) provide the physical connections running from device to device. The software components in your network include the communications protocols and services needed to exchange data between physically *connected* devices.

Once your network is in place, you can place file servers, print servers, database servers, Web servers, messaging servers, and other application servers on your network. These servers support the applications run by the users in your organization. But all of these applications are built on the foundation you create in your networking services design.

Figure 1.1 illustrates the relationship between networking services and the remainder of your total solution. Networking services run on the communications protocols and physical networking hardware within your network. These networking services extend the physical network, provide name resolution, enhance network security, and aid in the management of your network.

In this book, you learn about evaluating and creating networking services designs. Your networking services designs depend on the physical network designs. The scenarios, practice exercises, and examples in this book assume the physical network is already in place.

Note This book discusses network protocols as they relate to networking services, including routing. However, a complete discussion of the networking protocols is beyond the scope of this book.

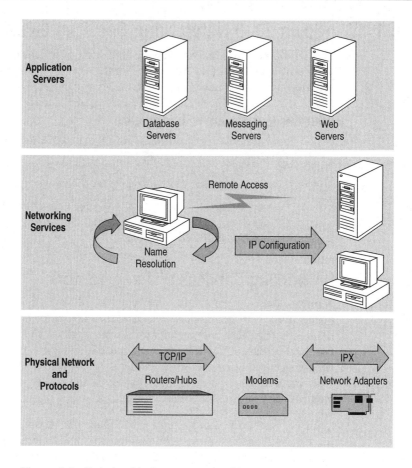

Figure 1.1   Relationship between networking services in a solution

Within your design, networking services can provide

Multiprotocol support   Many of your networking services designs will be based on networks running multiple protocols, such as Transmission Control Protocol/Internet Protocol (TCP/IP), Internetwork Packet Exchange/Sequenced Packet Exchange (IPX/SPX), Appletalk, and Systems Network Architecture (SNA). Your design must accommodate these protocols and provide connectivity for the protocols between the appropriate network segments.

Multiprotocol routing between network segments   Unless an organization's network is very small, you need to provide routing between network segments. You can use the Routing and Remote Access feature in Windows 2000 to isolate networks with different topologies, reduce traffic on individual network segments, and secure portions of your network.

Enhanced network security   Many organizations will require that your designs include strong security to protect confidential data. You can use Internet Protocol Security (IPSec) and Virtual Private Networks (VPN) to provide authentication of users and encryption of data transmitted within the organization's private network or over public networks.

Connectivity for private network and Internet Web-based applications
When an organization needs to run Web-based applications within its private network or on the Internet, your networking services design must provide the appropriate connectivity. You can use Microsoft Proxy Server 2.0, Network Address Translation (NAT), and Routing and Remote Access to provide the connectivity while protecting the resources and confidential data within the organization.

Automatic IP configuration   As the number of IP devices grows within an organization, your design needs to allow centralized management of IP configuration. You can include Dynamic Host Configuration Protocol (DHCP) in your design to manage the IP configuration for the organization.

Name resolution   Your networking services design must provide users, and the applications that the users run, with recognizable names that can be used to access resources. You can use Domain Name System (DNS) and Windows Internet Name Service (WINS) to resolve these recognizable names to IP addresses.

Remote user access   A majority of the designs you create must support users who aren't directly connected to the organization's private network. These users will be performing their job functions remotely and will require remote access to the organization's resources. You can solve these remote access problems by using Routing and Remote Access to provide direct dial-up modem connectivity or VPN connectivity over the Internet.

Networking services management   After your networking services design is implemented, the operations staff and network administrators of the organization are responsible for managing the networking services in your design. You can reduce the cost of managing your design by using the automatic monitoring and management features found in Windows 2000.

Networking Services in Windows 2000

Not all of your networking services designs will require all the Windows 2000 networking services. You must analyze the needs of an organization and optimize your design by including only the appropriate services. Figure 1.2 illustrates a typical network and the networking services that support the users and applications for an organization.

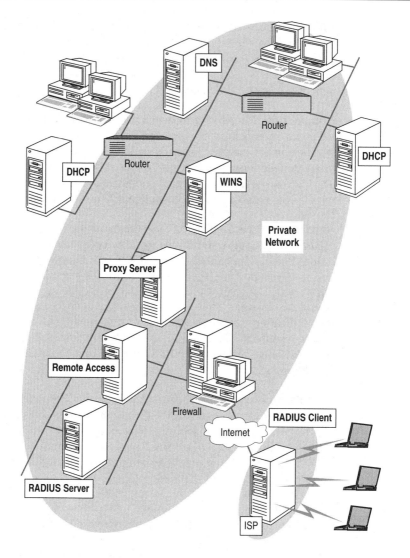

Figure 1.2   Illustration showing placement of the networking services

Routing and Remote Access Routing

Routing and Remote Access provides a full-featured multiprotocol router. You can include Routing and Remote Access in your designs to provide routing within private networks and between locations.

The routing features provided by Routing and Remote Access include

- Multiprotocol support for IP, IPX, and AppleTalk
- IP unicast routing by using

- ▪ Open Shortest Path First (OSPF) IP routing protocol
- ▪ Routing Information Protocol (RIP), versions 1 and 2, IP routing protocol
- ■ IP multicast routing by using Internet Group Membership Protocol (IGMP) router and IGMP proxy modes
- ■ Demand-dial routing over dial-up wide area network (WAN) links
- ■ VPN support for Point-to-Point Tunneling Protocol (PPTP)
- ■ VPN support for Layer Two Tunneling Protocol (L2TP)
- ■ IP and IPX packet filtering
- ■ DHCP Relay Agent for IP
- ■ Media support, including Ethernet, Token Ring, Fiber Distributed Data Interface (FDDI), asynchronous transfer mode (ATM), Integrated Services Digital Network (ISDN), T-Carrier, Frame Relay, xDSL, cable modems, X.25, and analog modems

NAT

Routing and Remote Access NAT is a protocol found in Routing and Remote Access that provides a simple connectivity to the Internet. Include NAT in your designs when you need to provide Internet connectivity while securing Internet user access to private network resources.

You can use the NAT service to hide private network IP addresses from public networks by translating the private network addresses to public addresses. NAT can reduce IP address registration costs by letting you use private IP addresses in the private network and translating to a small number of public IP addresses. Include NAT in your design when the organization wants to hide the internal network structure and reduce the risk of attacks against internal systems.

The NAT protocol in Routing and Remote Access provides

- ■ Address translation to support private IP addressing schemes
- ■ Automatic IP configuration to DHCP clients
- ■ DNS name-resolution proxy to DNS clients

Microsoft Proxy Server 2.0

Microsoft Proxy Server 2.0 allows organizations to control the exchange of information between their private network and the Internet. You can include Proxy Server like a firewall in your design to protect the private network. In addition, using Proxy Server in your design improves the performance of Internet access through existing connections. You can also enhance the availability of your Proxy Server solution by including Proxy Server arrays.

DHCP

DHCP is a Request for Comments (RFC) standard that allows DHCP servers to manage dynamic allocation of IP addresses and other related IP configuration information to DHCP-enabled clients on your network. DHCP reduces the complexity and amount of administration required in the configuration of TCP/IP hosts.

Every computer in your network design must have a unique computer name and IP address. When you move a computer from one subnet to a different subnet, you must change the IP address and other configuration information. By including DHCP in your design, you can dynamically reconfigure the clients.

DNS

DNS is an RFC standard name resolution service that allows computers on your network to register and resolve DNS domain names. Users and applications use the DNS domain names to locate and access resources offered by other computers on your network or other networks, such as the Internet.

DNS provides a distributed database for registering and querying of fully qualified domain names (FQDN) for computers within your network. Include DNS in your design to resolve FQDNs to IP addresses and IP addresses to FQDNs.

The DNS service in Microsoft Windows 2000 Server provides

- An RFC-compliant DNS name server
- Interoperability with other DNS server implementations
- Integration with Active Directory, WINS, and DHCP services
- RFC-compliant dynamic zone updates
- Incremental zone transfers between DNS servers

WINS

In the designs you will create, you include client computers and applications that require NetBIOS over TCP/IP support (NetBT). These client computers and applications require that you provide NetBIOS name to IP address name resolution. Include WINS in your design to provide NetBIOS name to IP address name resolution.

WINS provides a distributed database for automatically registering and querying NetBIOS names for computers on your network. Include WINS in designs that require NetBIOS name resolution in an IP routed environment.

Routing and Remote Access

Routing and Remote Access provides remote user access to the resources in your organization's private network. Include Routing and Remote Access in your designs when you must provide dial-up and VPN remote access connectivity to users.

The features provided by Routing and Remote Access include

- Multiprotocol support for IP, IPX, and AppleTalk
- VPN support for PPTP and L2TP
- Media support, including Ethernet, Token Ring, Fiber Distributed Data Interface (FDDI), asynchronous transfer mode (ATM), Integrated Services Digital Network (ISDN), T-Carrier, Frame Relay, xDSL, cable modems, X.25, and analog modems

RADIUS

Remote Authentication Dial-In User Service (RADIUS) protocol allows you to authenticate remote access users by using network access servers (NASs) that are located outside the organization's private network. RADIUS is widely used by Internet service providers (ISPs) so that organizations can outsource their dial-up remote access to the ISP.

In your designs, you place the RADIUS client, typically a dial-up server provided by the ISP, outside the organization's private network. You place the RADIUS server within the private network to provide authentication by using user accounts that are maintained by the organization.

Include Routing and Remote Access in your designs to provide RADIUS client functionality. Include Internet Authentication Service (IAS) in your design to provide RADIUS server functionality.

Lesson 2: Network Deployment Process

This lesson provides you with an overview of the network deployment process.

After this lesson, you will be able to

- Describe the three phases of the network deployment process
- Describe the portions of the network deployment process that are performed during each phase
- Identify the individuals involved in each development process

Estimated lesson time: 10 minutes

Phases in the Network Deployment Process

Each deployment process you participate in will be comprised of three phases, shown in Figure 1.3: the design phase, the implementation phase, and the management phase.

Depending on your role in the network deployment process, you might be involved in all three phases. The focus of this book is your role in the design phase of the network deployment process. In this lesson, you learn about all three phases so you can clearly define your role in the design phase of the network deployment process.

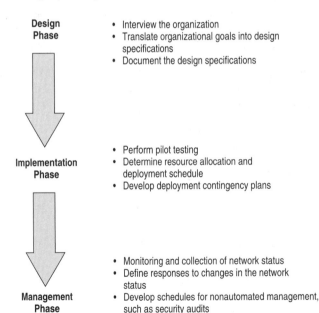

Design Phase
- Interview the organization
- Translate organizational goals into design specifications
- Document the design specifications

Implementation Phase
- Perform pilot testing
- Determine resource allocation and deployment schedule
- Develop deployment contingency plans

Management Phase
- Monitoring and collection of network status
- Define responses to changes in the network status
- Develop schedules for nonautomated management, such as security audits

Figure 1.3   The phases in the network deployment process

Design Phase

As the designer, you make a number of essential decisions during the design phase. During this phase, you collect all relevant information about the existing network, determine what service improvements the organization is considering, and, most important, how the organization expects to benefit from these network enhancements.

Throughout this book, you find suggestions and recommendations on the information that you must collect so you can create your designs. You take the information you collect from the organization and translate the organization's goals into design specifications. Finally, you document the design specifications in your formal design.

In some cases, an organization might present you with conflicting goals. For example, an organization might require your design to provide high-speed remote access at a low cost. These two design requirements, high-speed remote access and low cost, might be exclusive to one another. During the design phase of your projects, be prepared to have the organization rank its goals in order of importance.

Implementation Phase

After you complete the design phase, you need to prepare for the implementation phase of the deployment process. During this phase of the process, if you're involved, you perform pilot testing to ensure that the design specifications can be obtained.

Typically you implement the changes in the network in small increments, only making changes to a controlled number of existing servers and workstation computers. Throughout the conversion to your new design, you must have contingency plans in place so you can return the network to the last properly operating state.

Management Phase

During the management phase of the network deployment process, if you're involved, you begin the day-to-day collection of network status. During the design phase, you work with administration and operations staff to develop a management plan.

The management plan you develop must specify what types of network status are to be collected. Your management plan must also specify what actions will be taken if the network characteristics significantly differ from the design specifications.

Your management plans must include schedules for collecting network status that can't be obtained automatically. For example, you might have a server cluster within your design. Your management plan must include periodic testing of the server cluster to ensure proper operation if one of the cluster nodes fails.

Personnel Responsible for Each Phase

Over the network deployment process, you work with other individuals who are closely involved in the process. As the network designer, you're the central figure in the design phase activities. During the implementation phase, members of the information services team work with you while pilot testing your design.

Once your design has been tested, the information services team creates a timetable for the deployment of the network. Once the network changes are deployed, you work with the administrators and operations staff to create a management plan that ensures that the network will continue to function within the design specifications.

Figure 1.4 illustrates the team responsibilities in the deployment process. Each phase of the deployment process has different individuals or teams that are primarily responsible for their design phase. However, in each phase, the responsible team members for that phase interact with the other teams to ensure ease of transition from one phase to the next.

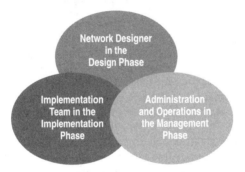

Figure 1.4   Overlapping of responsibilities during the deployment process

For example, as the networking services designer, your primary responsibility occurs during the design phase. During the design phase, you interact with team members who are responsible for the implementation and management phase. Conversely, during the implementation and management phases, the team members responsible for their respective phase interact with you as they interpret your design.

Design Responsibilities

During the design phase, the networking services designer analyzes the business goals of the organization and the existing network environment. Based on this information, the designer creates a design specification for the network enhancements.

The designer interacts primarily with individuals in the organization who are responsible for setting business priorities and for integrating any network changes into the existing environment. In addition to the design specification, the designer helps create deployment and management specifications.

Beyond creating the networking services design, your responsibilities include

- Designing a pilot test program
- Providing the order in which the networking services will be upgraded
- Identifying the essential networking services that require close monitoring and management

Implementation Responsibilities

During the implementation phase of the deployment process, the implementation team in charge of upgrading the network has the principal responsibility. Often, the implementation team works with you, as the designer, on the schedule for upgrades and changes to the network.

You must be available during the implementation phase to answer questions about the network design. Upon completion of the implementation phase you must make any design changes that occurred, based on the actual implementation.

The responsibility of the implementation team includes

- Conducting the pilot test and collecting the results of the test
- Implementing new servers or upgrading existing servers in the network
- Keeping users informed about changes in the network, including any scheduled network outages
- Providing users with any necessary training

Management Responsibilities

As the implementation phase of your project is nearing completion, the management staff, such as network administrators and operations staff, starts monitoring the network. You work with the management staff to ensure that the specifications in the design are reflected in the actual network. The management staff needs input from you as they develop monitoring and management tools, including how to determine which critical networking services to monitor.

The responsibility of the management staff includes

- Collecting the status of the networking services
- Evaluating the status of the networking services to ensure that the network is functioning properly
- Responding to changes in the networking services status so that the design specifications continue to be achieved

Lesson 3: Aspects of a Networking Services Design

In this lesson, you learn the aspects that you use as you evaluate and create networking services designs.

After this lesson, you will be able to

- Identify the aspects of a networking services design
- Describe how to achieve the aspects of a networking services design

Estimated lesson time: 20 minutes

Networking Services Design Aspects

As Figure 1.5 summarizes, the business goals of your organization define requirements that your networking services design must achieve. You need to translate the business goals into design requirements and then create a design that fulfills those requirements.

The networking services you include in your design will provide essential services in the overall solution. This essential aspect of these services is the primary reason for implementing the networking services. For example, you include DNS in your design because you need to support Active Directory directory service in your organization.

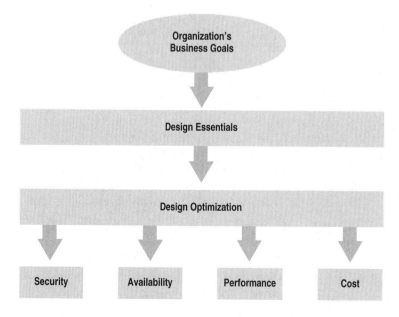

Figure 1.5 The aspects of a networking services design

After your design meets the essential requirements, you can optimize your design based on the business goals of the organization. Based on the requirements that you determine from the business goals, you can optimize your design from the aspect of security, availability, performance, or cost.

You can use these design aspects as a checklist while you're

- **Translating your business goals into design requirements**   As you interview the organization and collect the requirements for your design, be sure that you ask the organization which of these design aspects is important in the success of its business goals.

- **Creating and refining your design**   You can use the design aspects to ensure that your design fulfills the requirements of the organization's business goals.

- **Evaluating existing designs**   As a network designer, you will often evaluate existing network designs. Once you determine that the design you're evaluating provides the essential services, you can evaluate how well the existing design meets the security, availability, performance, and cost aspects of the organization's business goals.

The chapters in this book are structured so you can examine the essential design aspects, and then the optimization design aspects. Most of the technologies you examine in this book have a separate lesson that discusses the security aspects of that technology. Availability, performance, and cost are often combined under a common lesson for most technologies you examine. Because of the book's structure, you can use this book as a reference while you're creating your designs.

Essential Design Aspects

The essential aspects of your design are the most important aspects because they are the reason you included the technology in your design. In addition, the essential aspects of your design are the foundation on which all the other design aspects are built.

For example, consider the scenario in Figure 1.6 in which you're evaluating a design created by a consulting company. You observe that IP routers are included in the design to exchange data between two locations over the Internet. The router in Location B has a DSL interface to connect to the Internet. The ISP expects the organization to connect to its DSL modem by using an Ethernet interface.

As a result, the router at Location B isn't able to connect to the Internet and route packets between locations. Because the routers aren't able to exchange packets, you determine that the design, created by the consulting company, doesn't fulfill the essential aspects of the design.

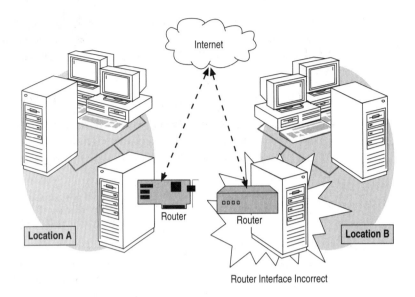

Figure 1.6   Scenario where the essential aspects of the design are incorrect

Any failure to meet the essential aspects of your design makes the other design aspects irrelevant. In the scenario in Figure 1.6, you might observe that the consulting company specified that both routers be configured to use IPSec to secure data transmissions between locations. Unfortunately, because the routers are unable to communicate, the IPSec data encryption performs no useful purpose.

You can assume the same conclusion about the other optimization aspects. At this point in your evaluation, the availability, performance, or cost of the situation aren't a significant factor in the design until you resolve the existing problems.

Security Design Aspects

After you establish the essential aspects of your design, you can turn your attention to the security aspects. The security aspects of your design ensure the confidentiality of data. Your design is secure when only authorized users are granted access to confidential data.

For example, the scenario in Figure 1.7 shows the essential design changes you suggested to the consulting company. Now you note that the consultants have designated 128-bit encryption for all data passed between the locations. The routers at Location A and Location B both specify 3DES encryption. Location A is in a country to which the US government restricts the export of 3DES encryption technology.

Because the router at Location A can't encrypt data by using 3DES encryption, you determine that the consulting company's design doesn't fulfill the security

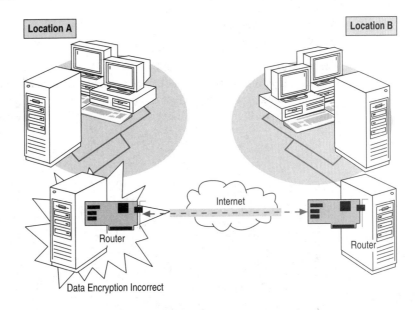

Figure 1.7 Scenario where the security aspects of the design are incorrect

aspects of the design. Depending on the security requirements of the organization, you can recommend it use an encryption algorithm that is approved for use in the country in which Location A resides.

Based on the security requirements of the organization, you might determine that any encryption below 3DES is unacceptable. You must review the mandatory requirements for 3DES with the organization and determine whether the requirement is essential to the success of the solution. This is an example of when you need to prioritize the goals of the organization.

If the organization is unwilling or unable to change their requirements for 3DES, as the designer you must do one of the following:

- Obtain special waivers to export 3DES to the country in question
- Inform the organization that its goals are unobtainable

Note in this example that although the design achieves the essential design aspects, the failure to achieve the security aspects can invalidate the entire design.

Availability Design Aspects

Consider availability in each of the designs you evaluate or create. The availability aspects of your design ensure that users can access the data on the private network. Your design is considered more available when users can access the data on the private network a higher percentage of time.

The scenario in Figure 1.8 indicates that the Internet connection on the router in Location B is unreliable. The telephony connection to the Internet experiences frequent outages. As you collect the design requirements, you must include the unreliability of the Internet connection when evaluating availability.

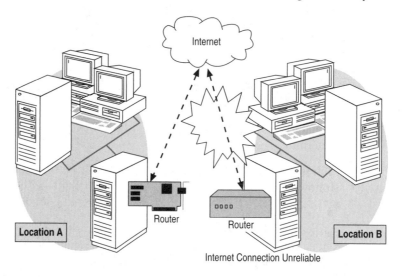

Figure 1.8   Scenario for which the Internet connection is unreliable and negatively affects the availability aspects of the design

Depending on the availability requirements of the organization, you can recommend it install a redundant Internet connection or install a more reliable Internet connection. If the organization doesn't place high importance on availability, you must at least notify the organization of the effects the unreliable connection will have on your overall design.

As with security, note that the availability aspects of your design don't directly affect the essentials of your design. Place as much emphasis on the availability aspects of your design as required by the organization and the applications run by the users in the organization.

Performance Design Aspects

The performance aspects of your design are the most difficult to quantify because performance is largely a user perception. The most important information to include in the performance aspects for your design is how the performance is to be measured.

Your design must clearly define measurable thresholds of data transmission rates or response times you can use to verify that your design meets the organization's requirements. During pilot testing and during implementation, you can use those defined data rates and response times to ensure that your design meets the requirements.

Consider the scenario illustrated in Figure 1.9. After your design is implemented, the organization contacts you regarding slow response times when accessing resources across the routed Internet connection. As you examine the design, you discover that the organization has added six messaging applications since the initial deployment of your design.

You discover that your design is performing within the specification in your design for the data transmission rates. Based on the performance requirements of the organization, you might determine that the existing performance is unacceptable. Again, you must prioritize the goals of the organization so you can determine how to best address the performance issues.

To resolve the performance requirements, as the designer you must do one of the following:

- Install a faster Internet connection at Location B
- Reduce the amount of traffic between locations generated by the messaging applications

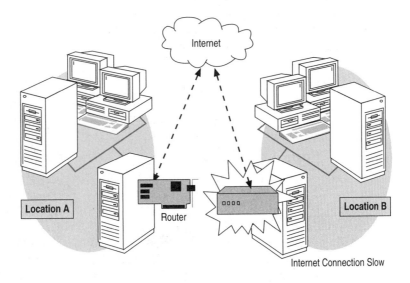

Figure 1.9 Scenario for which the performance aspects of the design are unacceptable

Usually, an increase in performance in your design doesn't necessarily affect the essential networking services, the security of the services, or the availability of the services. However, as you increase in performance in your design, you almost always increase the cost associated with implementing your design.

Cost Design Aspects

In every design, you're constrained by cost. Usually organizations allocate a budget for network improvements. Your design must achieve the requirements specified by the organization while the cost associated with implementing your design must be within the guidelines of the budget.

Your design is considered cost effective when it provides essential networking services that are secure, available, and that perform within specifications, while remaining below budgeted cost. While creating or evaluating designs, remember to optimize your design to reduce the overall cost.

In most networking services design, you can significantly affect the cost of your design by making small reductions in cost over a large number of instances within your design. For example, reducing the cost of 128MB memory within a single server has minimal impact on the cost of your design. Reducing the cost of 128MB memory across 1,500 servers or workstations has a significant impact on the cost of your design.

The scenario illustrated in Figure 1.10 has an Internet connection at each location. You're reviewing a design proposal created by a consulting company. In the proposal, you discover that the consulting company has proposed the installation of T1 leased lines at each location.

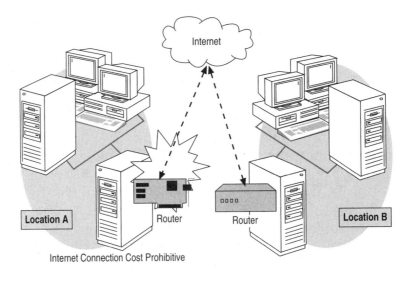

Figure 1.10   Scenario where the cost aspects of the design are prohibitive

You find out that many locations within the organization are in remote geographic areas. The cost associated with installing T1 leased lines is significantly higher than in metropolitan areas. As a result, the number of T1 leased lines will cause the design to be overbudget.

As with the other aspects, you must prioritize the goals of the organization so you can determine how to best address the cost issues. If the organization requires T1 data rates between locations, the organization will need to increase the budget for the deployment of the new T1 leased lines.

Unlike the other design aspects, cost affects all aspects of the design. You might need to scale back the essentials, the security, the availability, or the performance aspects of the design to achieve the budgetary requirements of the organization.

Review

The following questions are intended to reinforce key information in this chapter. If you're unable to answer a question, review the lesson and then try to answer the question again. You can find answers to the questions in the Appendix, "Questions and Answers."

1. You're participating in a meeting with other members of the information services department in your organization. The meeting is the first for a new deployment project that your organization is starting. The members of the team are introducing themselves and describing the part they will play in the deployment project. As the networking services designer, how do you define networking service and your role in the deployment project?

2. A multinational organization has locations in 22 countries around the world. Currently, the locations are connected via a network of point-to-point leased lines. You're responsible for creating a solution for the organization that will connect the locations over the Internet. The organization is very concerned about the confidentiality of the data transmitted between locations. The organization will be using Active Directory as its directory service. In addition, the organization has a number of users who work remotely. Which Windows 2000 networking services do you include in your design?

3. You're creating a networking services design for an organization. The organization has a mission-critical e-commerce site that Internet-based users will access. The majority of the organization's revenue is derived from the e-commerce site. Customers make purchases on the site 24 hours per day, seven days per week. The sales department of the organization wants customers to complete a purchase in fewer than 30 seconds after they submit the purchase. What design aspects do you suspect are a high priority for the organization? Why are those design aspects important?

CHAPTER 2

Networking Protocol Design

About This Chapter

The network designs you create will be comprised of many operating systems and hardware platforms. Your design must transparently connect these operating systems and hardware platforms. Your network design must provide connectivity for these heterogeneous networks.

Many of the network designs you create will be based on Transmission Control Protocol/Internet Protocol (TCP/IP). As a result, you must provide TCP/IP designs that can connect devices within the private network and to the Internet. Your design must protect confidential data, ensure that users can access TCP/IP-based resources, and provide application responses within the requirements of the organization.

Note A full discussion of TCP/IP is beyond the scope of this book. For more information on TCP/IP, see *Microsoft Windows 2000 TCP/IP Protocols and Services Technical Reference* (Redmond, Washington: Microsoft Press, 2000).

This chapter answers questions such as:

- When must TCP/IP be included in the design?
- How can confidential data transmitted over TCP/IP be secured?
- How can the design be optimized to ensure users can always get access to private network resources?
- What design optimizations ensure the optimal performance for TCP/IP?

Before You Begin

Before you begin, you must have an overall understanding of

- Network technologies (including Ethernet, Token Ring, hubs, switches, and concentrators)
- The common TCP/IP configuration parameters (such as IP address, subnet mask, or default gateway)
- Routed networks (including subnets, network segments, routers, and IP switches)

Lesson 1: Designs That Include TCP/IP

This lesson presents the requirements and constraints, both business and technical, that identify the instances when TCP/IP is required in your network design.

After this lesson, you will be able to

- Describe the role of TCP/IP in the Microsoft Windows 2000 architecture
- Identify the requirements and constraints, both business and technical, that must be collected to create a TCP/IP network design
- Identify the design decisions required to create a TCP/IP network design
- Evaluate scenarios and determine when the TCP/IP implementation in Windows 2000 is an appropriate solution
- Evaluate scenarios and determine which capabilities and features of the TCP/IP implementation in Windows 2000 are appropriate

Estimated lesson time: 20 minutes

TCP/IP in Windows 2000

You can provide TCP/IP connectivity by using TCP/IP implemented in Windows 2000. Because TCP/IP is integral component of Windows 2000, you can connect any computer running Microsoft Windows 2000 Server, Microsoft Windows 2000 Advanced Server, or Microsoft Windows 2000 Datacenter Server to a TCP/IP-based network.

Figure 2.1 illustrates the portion of the TCP/IP suite you examine in this chapter.

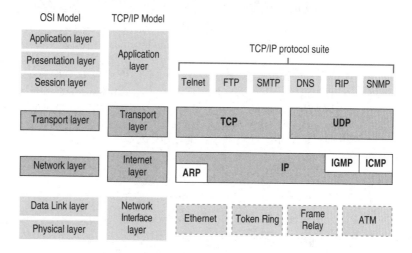

Figure 2.1   The portion of the TCP/IP protocol suite discussed in this chapter

Your TCP/IP network protocol design focuses on the transport and network layers of the International Standards Organization (ISO) model. You'll examine some of the layers above the transport layer, such as Domain Name System (DNS), Simple Network Management Protocol (SNMP), and Routing Information Protocol (RIP), in later chapters.

In Figure 2.2, you can see that TCP/IP is implemented in Windows 2000 as a Transport Driver Interface (TDI) transport driver. The TCP/IP TDI transport driver resides between the TDI layer and the Network Driver Interface Specification (NDIS) layer.

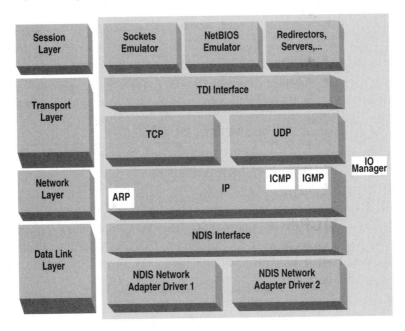

Figure 2.2   How TCP/IP is implemented in Windows 2000

The networking services you run on Windows 2000 can communicate with TCP/IP by using the NetBIOS or Windows Sockets application interfaces. The TCP/IP configuration of the computer affects the operation of the networking services running on the computer. As a result, your networking services design depends on your TCP/IP network design.

TCP/IP Design Requirements and Constraints

Before you create your TCP/IP network design, you must gather the requirements and constraints, both business and technical, of the organization. As you create your design, you make design decisions based on the requirements and constraints you collect.

The list of the design requirements and constraints that you collect includes

- Characteristics of the data transmitted through each network segment, including:
    - The amount of data transmitted through each network segment
    - The confidentiality of the data transmitted through each network segment
- Plans for future network growth
- Characteristics of the existing TCP/IP network including:
    - IP address range allocated to the organization
    - Number of existing network segments
    - Routing protocols in use
- Response times for applications that access resources through the network
- Acceptable percentage of time that users require access through the network

TCP/IP Design Decisions

After you determine the requirements and constraints, both business and technical, you can apply the information you gathered to make routing design decisions.

To create your routing design, you must decide the

- IP addressing scheme, public or private, to be used within the organization
- IP subnet mask configuration for use within the organization
- Variable Length Subnet Masks to use within the organization's private network
- Classless Interdomain Routing usage within the IP address range assigned to the organization
- Authentication and encryption algorithms that you'll use to protect your confidential data
- Criteria that you'll use to create TCP/IP filters
- Methods for improving the availability and performance in your design

The lessons that follow in this chapter provide the information required to make specific TCP/IP design decisions.

TCP/IP in Networking Services Designs

The first decision you must make when creating your TCP/IP network design is to determine whether TCP/IP is required in your design. The applications and networking services in your network determine whether your design requires TCP/IP.

Making the Decision

Table 2.1 lists the network components that require TCP/IP and why the components require TCP/IP.

Table 2.1   Network Components That Require TCP/IP

If Your Network Includes	TCP/IP Is Required Because
Web servers	The HTTP and FTP protocols used by Web servers are based on TCP/IP
Active Directory directory service	Active Directory is based on Lightweight Directory Access Protocol (LDAP) and uses DNS for name resolution, both of which require TCP/IP
UNIX or other operating systems	Common transport protocol used for interoperabilityon these operating systems is TCP/IP
Internet connectivity	Internet and all Internet protocols are based on TCP/IP
DNS name resolution	DNS name resolution is based on TCP/IP
Line Printer Daemon (LPD) and Line Printer Remote (LPR) printers	LPD and LPR printers are based on TCP/IP

Applying the Decision

In Figure 2.3, you see a scenario that illustrates the network components that require TCP/IP as the networking protocol. When your existing network or your proposed network solution includes any of these network components, you must consider TCP/IP in your networking services design.

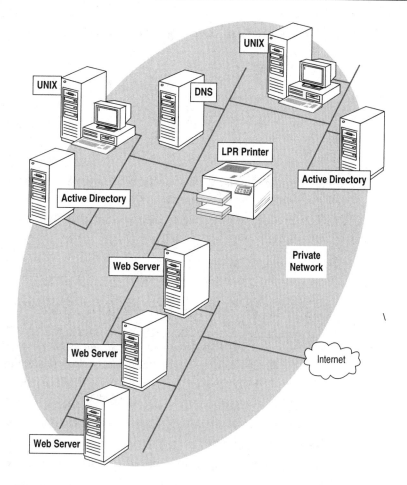

Figure 2.3   The networking components that require TCP/IP

Lesson 2: Essential TCP/IP Design Concepts

After this lesson, you will be able to

- Identify the essential IP configuration information
- Determine the appropriate IP addressing scheme for a given number of network segments and hosts
- Determine the appropriate subnet mask for a given number of network segments and hosts
- Determine the influence of Variable Length Subnet Masks (VLSM) on networking services designs
- Determine the influence of Classless Internet Domain Routing (CIDR) on networking services designs

Estimated lesson time: 45 minutes

Essential IP Configuration Information

Your networking services designs must conform to the TCP/IP configuration of the Windows 2000–based computers running the networking services. Most of the networking services you include in your design, such as DNS, Dynamic Host Configuration Protocol (DHCP), Windows Internet Name Service (WINS), or Remote Authentication Dial-In User Service (RADIUS), require TCP/IP as the transport protocol.

Making the Decision

For each Windows 2000 computer in your networking services design, you must supply

- **An IP address**   All devices on your TCP/IP network require an IP address that falls within the IP address range of the private network. The IP address of a device uniquely identifies the device on your network.

- **A subnet mask**   Each device on your TCP/IP network requires a subnet mask. Hosts, routers, and IP switches use the subnet mask to determine the appropriate route path for IP packets. Configure the subnet mask to divide the IP address range of the private network for the appropriate number of subnets and hosts per subnet.

- **A default gateway, in some instances**   Most IP devices on your TCP/IP network, including servers, desktop computers, and printers in your network design, require a default gateway. Typically, routers and IP switches don't require a default gateway.

Applying the Decision

In Figure 2.4, you see a scenario that illustrates the devices on your network that require IP configuration. For devices that have more than one interface, such as routers or network address translators, you must provide the IP configuration for each interface.

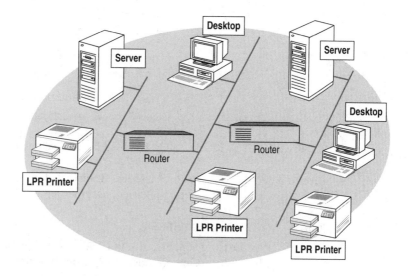

Figure 2.4   The devices on your network that require IP configuration

IP Addressing Scheme

The IP addressing scheme in your networking services designs can be based on private or public IP addresses. You can create an IP addressing scheme comprised of only public IP addresses. An IP addressing scheme that contains private IP addresses requires a minimal number of public IP addresses to support Internet connectivity.

All IP addressing schemes are *based* on the original class-based IP addresses listed in Figure 2.5. You can use these class-based IP addresses in public and private IP addressing schemes.

You can create a unicast IP addressing scheme with an IP address range from Class A, B, or C. Create a multicast IP addressing scheme with an IP address range from Class D. Avoid creating an IP addressing scheme based on Class E addresses because these addresses are reserved for experimental use.

Note   Classless-based IP address schemes, based on VLSM and CIDR, are discussed later in this lesson.

Class	Starts With	Possible Subnets	Possible Hosts
A	1-127	1-4,194,304	2-16,777,215
B	128-191	1-16,384	2-65,535
C	192-223	1-64	2-255
D	224-239	Reserved for multicast addresses.	
E	240-254	Reserved for experimental addresses.	

Figure 2.5   Class-based IP addresses used in all IP addressing schemes

A subset of IP addresses from Classes A, B, or C is designated for use as private IP addresses. Unless otherwise specified, assume that an IP address is public.

Public IP Addressing Schemes

In a public IP addressing scheme, all the IP addresses in your design are registered with an Internet service provider (ISP) or an Internet registry. Each device on your private network is assigned a public IP address.

Making the Decision

When you create networking services designs based on public IP addressing schemes, you must

- **Obtain a public IP address range from an Internet registry or ISP**
  The Internet Corporation for Assigned Names and Numbers (ICANN) is the organization that is ultimately responsible for the assignment of your IP addresses. Typically, you *purchase* a range of IP addresses from an ISP who reports to ICANN.

Note   ICANN has taken responsibility for IP address management that was previously managed under U.S. government contract by the Internet Assigned Number Authority (IANA).

- **Select an IP address range with enough addresses to accommodate all your network interfaces**   Each device that connects to your private network requires at least one IP address. Remember to include the IP addresses used by virtual private network (VPN) connections.

- **Consider the incremental cost of each IP address that you obtain from an Internet registry**

- **Ensure that no network address translation (NAT) is required**   The Internet connectivity performance in your design is improved because the latency introduced by the device that performs NAT is not present.

- **Security of the private network depends on firewalls and router filters** Assigning public IP addresses within your private network potentially exposes any network device to the Internet. The firewalls and routers within your design prevent Internet-based users from accessing confidential resources within your private network.

Applying the Decision

In Figure 2.6, you see a scenario where the private network provides public IP addresses for all network devices. For networking services designs that use public IP addresses, connect the private network to the Internet through a router or firewall.

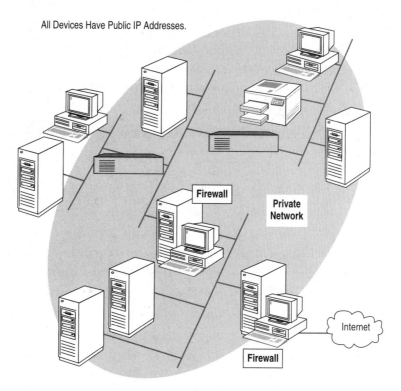

Figure 2.6 IP addressing scheme with only public IP addresses

Tip   Because all devices on the private network are assigned public addresses, your design doesn't need to provide NAT. However, your design may include Microsoft Proxy Server 2.0 to provide caching of Web content.

Private IP Addressing Schemes

In a private IP addressing scheme, your design includes private and public IP addresses. You assign private IP addresses to the devices within your private network. You assign public IP addresses to the devices that connect to public networks, such as the Internet.

The table in Figure 2.7 lists the IP address ranges available to you as private IP addresses. Select the private IP address range that meets the requirements of your organization.

To select the appropriate IP address range for your organization, determine the maximum number of

- Subnets required in your network
- IP hosts, or IP devices, on any subnet

Note   Request for Comments (RFC) 1918 lists 10.0.0.0/8, 172.16.0.0/12, and 192.168.0.0/16 as available IP addresses for you to use in private IP addressing schemes. 169.254.0.0/16 is reserved by IANA for Automatic Private IP Addressing (APIPA). You can use 169.254.0.0/16 for your private IP addressing schemes if you disable APIPA on the computers running Microsoft Windows 98 and Windows 2000 in your network.

The IP address ranges listed in Figure 2.7 are in CIDR notation. You can use Table 2.2 to relate each of the IP address ranges to their respective CIDR designation and their respective pre-CIDR designation.

Address Range	Possible Subnets	Possible Hosts
10.0.0.0/8	1-4,194,304	2-16,777,215
172.16.0.0/12	1-262,144	2-1,048,575
169.254.0.0/16	1-16,384	2-65,535
192.168.0.0/16	1-16,384	2-65,535

Figure 2.7   Table listing the IP address ranges available for private IP addressing schemes

Table 2.2   IP Address Ranges in CIDR Notation

Address Range	CIDR Designation	Pre-CIDR Designation
10.0.0.0/8	24-bit address block	Single Class A network number
172.16.0.0/12	20-bit address block	16 contiguous Class B network numbers
169.254.0.0/16	16-bit address block	Single Class B network number
192.168.0.0/16	16-bit address block	256 contiguous Class C network numbers

You can use these IP address ranges on networks that support CIDR and pre-CIDR addressing schemes. The types of routers and IP switches in your private network determine the addressing scheme your network can support.

Note   Consult the documentation for the routers and IP switches in your private network for further information about the IP addressing schemes that are supported.

Table 2.3 lists the same IP address ranges in pre-CIDR notation.

Table 2.3   IP Address Ranges in Pre-CIDR Notation

Starting IP Address	Ending IP Address	Default Subnet Mask
10.0.0.0	10.255.255.255	255.0.0.0
172.16.0.0	172.31.255.255	255.255.0.0
169.254.0.0	169.254.255.255	255.255.0.0
192.168.0.0	192.168.255.255	255.255.255.0

Note   Because the IP address ranges 172.16.0.0 and 192.168.0.0 are actually comprised of contiguous Class B and Class C network numbers, your private network must use VLSM to take full advantage of the subnet and host ranges listed in Figure 2.7.

Making the Decision

When you create networking services designs based on private addressing schemes, remember to

- **Obtain a public IP address range from an Internet registry or ISP to connect your network to the Internet**   Although the majority of your private network devices use private IP addresses, you must provide public IP addresses for all devices that don't reside behind the network address translator.

- **Select a private IP address range that supports the maximum number of subnets and hosts per subnet in your private network**

Note   Select a private IP address range that supports the current *and future* requirements of your network. If there is any uncertainty, select the 10.0.0.0/8 private IP address range to adequately provide for *any* IP addressing requirements for your organization.

- **Reduce the number of IP devices that are directly connected to the Internet**   Because each IP address that you obtain from an Internet registry incurs an incremental cost, assign public IP addresses to devices only when they must communicate directly with the Internet. Examples of devices that must connect directly to the Internet include

  - Network address translators
  - Routers
  - Firewalls
  - VPN remote access servers
  - Web or Internet-based application servers

- **Include NAT capability in your design**   You must provide a NAT device to map private IP addresses on your private network to public IP addresses.

- **Take advantage of the enhanced network security afforded by NAT devices**   Because the network address translator translates all IP addresses within your private network, Internet-based users and computers receive IP packets only from the network address translator. The resources in your private network can't be directly accessed from the Internet. As a result, the majority of your network configuration is obscured to Internet-based users and computers because they can't directly access any resources behind the network address translator.

Applying the Decision

Figure 2.8 presents a design that provides private IP addresses for devices within the private network. When using private IP addresses in your network, include a network address translator, such as Microsoft Proxy Server 2.0 or the NAT protocol in Routing and Remote Access, in your networking services design. The network address translator maps the private IP addresses in your network to one or more public IP addresses.

Note   Your network design must include public IP addresses, as illustrated in Figure 2.8, for any devices that connect directly to the Internet.

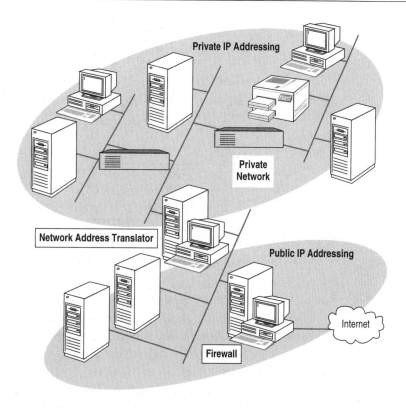

Figure 2.8   IP addressing scheme with private and public IP addresses

IP Subnet Mask

The IP subnet mask in your networking services design determines the portion of the IP address used for routing and the portion used for host identification. The portion of your IP address used for routing is called the *network prefix* (also known as the *network number* in pre-CIDR terminology). The portion of your IP address used for identifying a specific host, or device, on a specific subnet is called the *host number*.

Creating network segments adds an additional portion to your IP address called a *subnet number*. The subnet number is the portion of your IP address that uniquely identifies a subnet within your private network. Figure 2.9 illustrates how the subnet mask that you assign divides an IP address.

Making the Decision

When creating a subnet mask by using class-based addresses, consider that

- **The network prefix portion of the subnet mask is fixed**   Without CIDR, you can't modify the network prefix portion of the subnet mask. See the section on CIDR later in this lesson for a further discussion of CIDR.

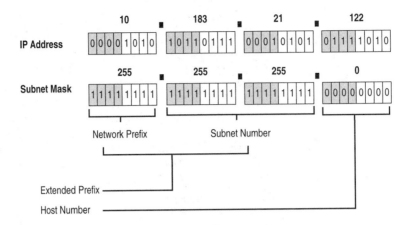

Figure 2.9   How a subnet mask divides an IP address

- **As you increase the subnet number portion of the subnet mask, you decrease the corresponding host number portion**   You must prioritize the importance of more subnets or more hosts per subnet. When creating an IP subnet mask, remember to include sufficient growth potential for subnets and hosts per subnet.

- **The IP address class limits the maximum number of subnets and maximum number of hosts per subnet**   The network prefix portion of the IP subnet mask is fixed. As a result, the portion of the IP address that you can use for identifying network segments and hosts is the remaining portion of the address.

  For example, a subnet mask design based on a Class A address provides you with 24 bits of address that you can assign to network segments or hosts. A subnet mask design based on a Class C address provides you with 8 bits of address that you can assign to network segments or hosts.

Note   You can use CIDR and VLSM to treat a consecutive range of IP network numbers, such as three Class C network numbers, as a single IP network number.

Applying the Decision

Figure 2.10 illustrates how IP subnet masks affect the number of subnets and number of hosts per subnet. The network prefix portion of your subnet mask is based on the IP address class and is fixed at 8 bits. In this example, your subnet number is set at 16 bits. You can determine the maximum number of subnets by raising 2 to the number of bits assigned to the subnet number ($2^{16} = 65,536$).

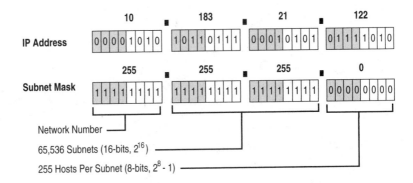

Figure 2.10   Example of how IP subnet masks affect the number of subnets and number of hosts per subnet

Note   When your network designates subnet broadcasts as all 1s or all 0s, you must subtract two available subnets from the total number of subnets. Networks based on Open Shortest Path First (OSPF) and RIP v2 routing protocols use all the 1s and all 0s in the subnet number. If the network in the previous example prevented the use of all 1s or all 0s in the subnet number, your subnet design provides a maximum of 65,534 subnets ($2^{16} - 2 = 65,534$).

You can determine the maximum number of hosts per subnet by raising 2 to the number of bits assigned to the host number minus one ($2^8 - 1 = 255$). You must subtract one available host address to allow for subnet broadcasts (when the host address is all 1s or 255).

Note   When your network designates subnet broadcasts as all 1s or all 0s, you must subtract two available host addresses. If the network in the previous example used all 1s or all 0s to designate subnet broadcasts, your subnet design provides 254 hosts per subnet ($2^8 - 2 = 254$).

Figure 2.11 illustrates how the maximum number of subnets and maximum number of hosts per subnet changes with each new subnet mask. Notice that the number of maximum subnets decreases as the maximum number of hosts per subnet increases.

Tip   You can download a number of free IP calculators from the Internet. With these IP calculators, you can determine your subnet mask without performing binary arithmetic.

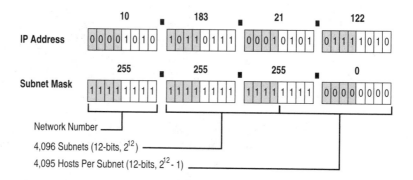

Figure 2.11   Second example of how IP subnet masks affect the number of subnets and number of hosts per subnet

Default Gateway

You must specify a default gateway in your IP configuration for IP-based devices other than routers, IP switches, and NAT devices. Devices on your network use the default gateway IP configuration setting to determine where to forward IP packets that are destined for other network segments.

Making the Decision

Select a router as the default gateway for a subnet when

- The router is the only router on the subnet
- Most IP traffic destined for other subnets goes through that router

Applying the Decision

Figure 2.12 illustrates a design that includes three subnets (Subnet A, Subnet B, and Subnet C) connected by two routers (Router 1 and Router 2). On each subnet, you must designate a default gateway. The default gateway for each subnet is responsible for forwarding packets to other subnets or to other routers on the same subnet.

Table 2.4 lists each subnet in the example, the default gateway for each subnet, and why that default gateway was selected.

Table 2.4   Designating Default Gateways for Subnets A, B, and C

On This Subnet	This Is the Default Gateway	Because
Subnet A	Interface in Router 1 that is connected to Subnet A	Router 1 is the only router connected to Subnet A
Subnet B	Interface in Router 1 that is connected to Subnet B	Subnet A is the most common destination for packets from Subnet B

Table 2.4 *(continued)*

On This Subnet	This Is the Default Gateway	Because
Subnet C	Interface in Router 2 that is connected to Subnet C	Router 2 is the only router connected to Subnet C

Routers use Internet Control Message Protocol (ICMP) to inform computers and other routers when a better route path is available. In the example scenario in Figure 2.12, there are two routers on Subnet B. Router 1 is the default gateway for Subnet B. Router 1 will use ICMP to inform the computers on Subnet B that Router 2 provides a better route to Subnet C.

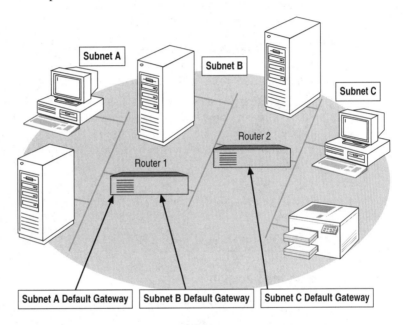

Figure 2.12   An example of default gateway settings in a network

Consider the following sequence when a computer on Subnet B sends an IP packet destined for Subnet C.

1. The computer on Subnet B checks the local route table and determines that the destination IP address resides on a different subnet.

2. The computer looks in the local route table and determines that Router 1 is the default gateway for the local subnet.

3. The computer on Subnet B forwards the packet to Router 1.

4. Router 1 looks in the local route table and determines that Router 2 provides the best route to Subnet C.

5. Router 1 sends an Internet Group Membership Protocol (IGMP) message to the computer on Subnet B and informs the computer that Router 2 will provide the best route.

6. The computer on Subnet B forwards the packet to Router 2.

7. The computer on Subnet B makes an entry in the local route table that designates Router 2 as the proper route path for all packets destined for Subnet C.

Variable Length Subnet Masks

You may create networking services designs for networks that have a large number of subnets. Without Variable Length Subnet Masks (VLSM), as the number of subnets in your network increases

- **Routing table entries increase**   Each subnet in your network requires a routing table entry. For example, a network comprised of 200 subnets requires a minimum of 200 routing table entries for each router.

- **Wasted IP addresses increase**   The distribution of IP addresses across all subnets in your network will not be equal. Your subnet mask must be large enough to support the maximum number of hosts per subnet, plus future growth. Subnets with fewer than the maximum number of hosts per subnet waste IP addresses.

   For example, a subnet configured to support 255 hosts per subnet that only has 75 hosts wastes the other 180 IP addresses.

Note   Subnetting is described in RFC 950. VLSM is described in RFC 1009.

Making the Decision

To determine the configuration of the VLSM masks in your design

- Arrange the routers in your organization in a hierarchical structure

- At the highest level of the router hierarchy, assign subnet masks that allocate the least number of bits for the subnet number

- At each level in the router hierarchy, assign more bits in the subnet mask for the subnet number than in the previous level in the hierarchy

- At the lowest level in the router hierarchy, ensure that the subnet mask allows the maximum number of hosts per subnet to be supported

Applying the Decision

Figure 2.13 illustrates a network design with routers arranged in a hierarchical structure. In a non-VLSM subnet mask configuration, all subnet masks are identical.

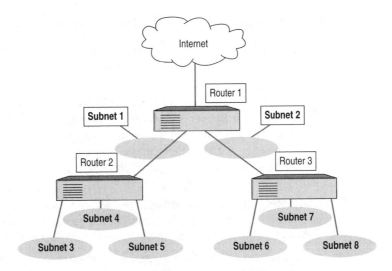

Figure 2.13   Hierarchical organization of routers within an organization

Each router in this network contains a route entry for each of the eight subnets. Although this number doesn't negatively affect your network at this size, consider the effect when you have 1,500 subnets in your private network. Without VLSM, your routers need to manage and update all 1,500 route entries at each router.

Assume that the subnet for your organization, depicted in Figure 2.13, has a fixed-length subnet mask that allows 127 hosts per subnet. Table 2.5 lists each subnet, the number of hosts per subnet, the number of hosts per subnet that are allocated, and the number of unused IP addresses per subnet.

Table 2.5   Number of Unused IP Addresses in Example Without VLSM

Subnet	Hosts Per Subnet	Allocated	Unused IP Addresses
Subnet 1	2	127	125
Subnet 2	2	127	125
Subnet 3	54	127	73
Subnet 4	115	127	12
Subnet 5	108	127	19
Subnet 6	73	127	54
Subnet 7	48	127	79
Subnet 8	66	127	61
Total number of unused IP addresses			**548**

VLSM solve routing table and IP addressing problems by

- **Aggregating routing table information**   VLSM allow routers to combine the routing information for routers lower in the router hierarchy to a single route entry.

  In the scenario depicted in Figure 2.13, Router 2 can aggregate the routing information for Subnet 3, Subnet 4, and Subnet 5. Router 2 can then send one routing table entry to Router 1. Router 3 can aggregate Subnet 6, Subnet 7, and Subnet 8 so that a single route entry can be sent to Router 1. Now Router 1 contains only two routing table entries, instead of eight separate routing table entries.

- **Adjusting the number of hosts per subnet on a subnet-by-subnet basis** VLSM allow you to create hierarchical layers in your router design. Each layer can allocate only the number of subnets required at each layer.

  In the scenario depicted in Figure 2.13, Router 1 only has two directly connected subnets. You can configure VLSM to permit a maximum of four subnets immediately below Router 1 (two more than required to allow for growth).

  Router 2 and Router 3 each have three directly connected subnets beneath them. You can configure VLSM for Router 2 and Router 3 to allow a maximum of four subnets immediately below Router 1 (one more than required to allow for growth).

Assume that your organization, as depicted in Figure 2.13, has implemented a VLSM strategy. Table 2.6 lists each subnet, the current number of hosts per subnet, the number of hosts per subnet that are allocated, and the number of unused IP addresses per subnet.

Table 2.6   Reduced Number of Unused IP Addresses in Example by Using VLSM

Subnet	Hosts Per Subnet	Allocated	Unused IP Addresses
Subnet 1	2	4	2
Subnet 2	2	4	2
Subnet 3	54	64	10
Subnet 4	115	127	12
Subnet 5	108	127	19
Subnet 6	73	127	54
Subnet 7	48	64	16
Subnet 8	66	127	61
Total number of unused IP addresses			**176**

By using VLSM in your network design, you can significantly reduce the number of unused IP addresses. The difference between using fixed and VLSM subnet masks as illustrated in Figure 2.13 can result in a reduction of the total unused IP addresses by 372.

Figure 2.14 illustrates a design in which the routers in the organization are arranged hierarchically. At the top of the hierarchy, assign the least number of bits to the subnet number.

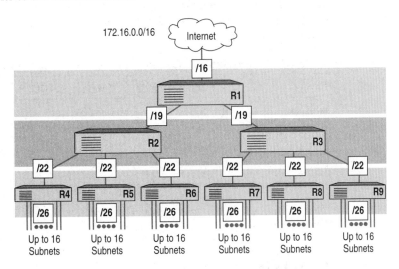

Figure 2.14   VLSM IP subnet mask configuration in a hierarchical router structure

To properly implement VLSM on your network

- **Arrange your routers hierarchically**   Arranging routers hierarchically takes advantage of routing table entry aggregation and reduces the number of unused IP addresses. In the scenario in Figure 2.14, Routers R4, R5, and R6 support up to 48 subnets. With VLSM, R2 uses a single route entry for R4, R5, and R6.

- **Assign more bits at the current level than to the level immediately above**   In the scenario in Figure 2.14, Routers R7, R8, and R9 assign /26 to the subnet masks of the 48 subnets that they support. /26 is an appropriate VLSM subnet mask because the level immediately above R7, R8, and R9 assigned /22 to the subnet mask. Anything less than /23 is inappropriate.

- **Ensure that the VLSM subnet mask assigned at the lowest level in the hierarchy supports the maximum number of hosts per subnet**   In the scenario in Figure 2.14, the /26 VLSM subnet mask must accommodate the largest number of hosts on any of the subnets supported by Routers R4 through R9.

You can calculate the number of subnets supported at each level in the hierarchy by raising 2 to the power of the difference between the subnet masks of the previous and current levels.

For example, to calculate the maximum number of subnets supported by Router R3, subtract 19 (R1 level) from 22 (R3 level), to obtain 3. Then you raise 2 to the third power. This indicates that Router R3 can support up to 8 subnets.

Table 2.7 lists each level in the VLSM scenario presented in Figure 2.14, the CIDR notation for the subnet mask at that level, and the number of subnets supported by the mask.

Table 2.7   VLSM Subnet Mask and the Number of Subnets in Figure 2.14

Level	Subnet Mask	Number of Bits	Number of Subnets
Internet	/16	0	1
R1	/19	3	8
R2 – R3	/22	3	8
R4 – R9	/26	4	16

Note To use VLSM in your networking services design, all routers must support either OSPF or RIP v2 routing protocols.

Classless Interdomain Routing

When you apply to an ISP or an Internet registry for a block of IP addresses, you're typically not assigned a Class A or Class B network number. In the class-based addressing scheme, almost all Class A and Class B network numbers have already been assigned. In addition, because Class C network numbers support only a maximum of 255 hosts, organizations must typically be assigned multiple Class C network numbers.

Classless Interdomain Routing (CIDR) addresses the limitations of the class-based addressing scheme by

- **Replacing the Class A, B, or C network number with a network-prefix**
  Your routers use the entire network-prefix, rather than the first three bits of the IP address, to determine the routing and subnet information. As a result, you can design networks based on your requirements, rather than the standard 8-bit, 16-bit, or 25-bit network numbers associated with class-based addressing.

- **Aggregating multiple routing table entries into a single routing table entry**   Routers report the aggregate, single routing table entry to routers higher in the router hierarchy.

Making the Decision

CIDR is very similar in concept to VLSM. You typically implement VLSM within your private network. Your Internet registry or ISP typically implements CIDR.

Because CIDR is very similar to VLSM, the decisions you must make regarding CIDR are the same. For more information on the decisions you must make for CIDR, see the VLSM "Making the Decision" section earlier in this lesson.

Note   CIDR is documented in RFCs 1517, 1518, 1519, and 1520.

Applying the Decision

Figure 2.15 presents a scenario in which an ISP owns a block of IP addresses that it plans to distribute among four organizations. The ISP assigns a portion of the block of IP addresses to each organization. Each organization can further subdivide its IP addresses internally with VLSM.

Notice that the subnet masks are assigned hierarchically, just as with VLSM. In this scenario, assume that Organization A requires eight address blocks, where each address block is as large as a single Class B address block (/16). The ISP assigns a block of IP addresses that provide Organization A with enough addresses by using a /13 subnet mask.

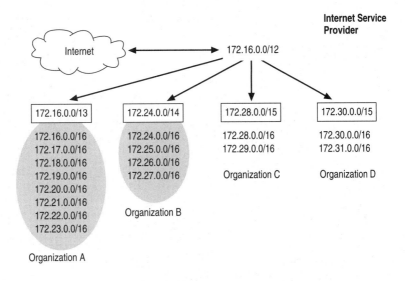

Figure 2.15   Illustration of how an ISP can divide a class-based IP address between four organizations by using CIDR

By subtracting the number of bits in the subnet mask assigned to Organization A (13) from the number of bits in the subnet mask that Organization A required (16 for a Class B address), you determine that Organization A has three bits of subnetting remaining. Raising 2 to the number of subnetting bits remaining ($2^3 = 8$) indicates that Organization A can divide its assigned address block into eight address blocks, where each is as large as a single Class B. You can perform the same calculations for Organizations B, C, and D.

Note To use CIDR in your networking services design, all routers in your organization must support OSPF or RIP v2 routing protocols.

Activity 2.1: Evaluating a TCP/IP Network Design

In this activity, you are presented with a scenario. To complete the activity:

1. Evaluate the scenario and determine the design requirements

2. Answer questions regarding design recommendations

Figure 2.16 provides a diagram of an electronics field service firm. The field service firm has a central office (located in Memphis), 15 regional offices (located throughout North America), and 2,200 field engineers who work from their homes. The field service firm repairs electronic equipment such as computers, printers, point-of-sale equipment, and other electromechanical devices.

Figure 2.16   Diagram of the electronics field service firm offices

The regional offices are connected to the central offices by point-to-point leased lines. The field engineer home offices are connected to their respective regional office by using dial-up modems, Digital Subscriber Line (DSL), or Integrated Services Digital Network (ISDN) connections.

Requests for service are received at the regional offices. The field engineers are notified of the service request by alphanumeric pager, wireless handheld PCs, and e-mail. After completing the service request, the field engineers update the status of the service request by their wireless handheld PC or one of the computers in their home office.

Currently, the field service firm has servers in the central office that support a Web site. The Web site allows customers to place service requests and to check on the status of their service request. The central office and the regional offices access the Web site to enter service requests received by telephone. In addition, the regional offices can check on the status of the field engineers to determine when customers will receive service.

Answer the following questions concerning your design recommendations. You can find answers to the questions in the Appendix, "Questions and Answers."

1. The field service firm is migrating from a Novell NetWare environment to Windows 2000. The firm plans on using Active Directory for directory services. The central office and regional offices communicate within each office and over the point-to-point connections by using the Internetwork Packet Exchange (IPX) protocol. Currently, the servers that support the Web site and the e-mail servers are the only computers that run TCP/IP. The central office and regional offices communicate with the Web site by using an IPX to TCP/IP gateway, such as Microsoft Proxy Server 2.0. What recommendations do you make to the firm?

2. The field service firm decided to use a public IP addressing scheme. You're in the process of obtaining public IP addresses for the firm. The preferred ISP can allocate you a block of IP addresses by using CIDR. How does the use of CIDR and public IP addressing affect your TCP/IP network design?

3. After examining the proposal for the public IP addresses from the ISP, the field service firm is concerned about the associated costs. How can you modify your TCP/IP design to reduce the costs and how will the design modification affect your design?

4. You want to reduce the number of unused IP addresses on each subnet within the firm. In addition, you want to reduce the routing information exchanged between offices over the point-to-point lines. How can you accomplish these design goals and how do these new goals affect your design?

Lesson 3: TCP/IP Data Protection

After this lesson, you will be able to

- Identify when Internet Protocol Security (IPSec) or VPN is appropriate for protecting TCP/IP data transmissions
- Describe how IPSec protects TCP/IP data transmissions
- Describe how VPN protects TCP/IP data transmissions
- Describe how TCP/IP filtering protects Windows Sockets–based applications

Estimated lesson time: 60 minutes

IPSec and VPN in TCP/IP Data Protection

In every networking services design you create, you need to protect the confidentiality of some of the data transmitted on the organization's network. Your networking services design can play a significant role in protecting the confidential data. Internet Protocol Security (IPSec) and virtual private networking (VPN) are two of the mechanisms that protect confidential data.

IPSec is an extension to the TCP/IPs that exist in your network. IPSec is also an Internet Engineering Task Force (IETF) draft that is implemented in Windows 2000. You can protect confidential data within your private network or across the Internet using IPSec.

Making the Decision

Select IPSec to protect confidential data on your network when

- Protecting specific servers or resources that contain confidential data
- Designing a network for computers running Windows 2000, or other operating systems that support IPSec
- Providing end-to-end data encryption to meet your organization's requirements

---

Note   Currently, Windows 2000 is the only Microsoft operating system that supports IPSec.

You can include VPN in any design that includes computers running Macintosh, UNIX, Microsoft Windows 95, Windows 98, Microsoft Windows NT 4.0, and Windows 2000 operating systems.

Select a VPN to protect confidential data on your network when

- Protecting an entire subnet that contains confidential data

- Supporting a mixture of operating systems
- Protecting data in an IP or IPX Point-to-Point Protocol (PPP) packet
- Providing point-to-point data encryption to meet the requirements of your organization

Note For more information, see "Virtual Private Networking and IPSec" in the Windows 2000 Resource Kit.

Applying the Decision

Figure 2.17 illustrates the application of IPSec on your private network. The desktop computer on Segment C accesses resources managed by the restricted server on Segment A. You can encrypt the data being transferred between the desktop computer and the restricted server by using IPSec.

When you select IPSec for data encryption, you encrypt the data for the entire path between the desktop computer and the restricted server. When you encrypt data from the desktop computer to the restricted server, you provide *end-to-end* data encryption. The data encryption is transparent to Router 1 and Router 2.

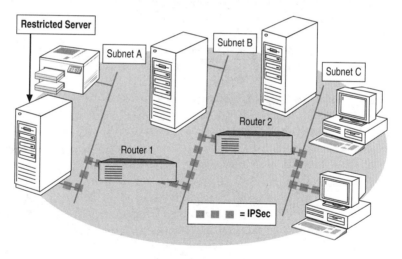

Figure 2.17 IPSec encryption of confidential data in your private network

You typically use VPN in remote access solutions, as illustrated in Figure 2.18. In these situations, you connect remote users to your private network with VPN remote access servers. The remote users connect to the Internet through an ISP. When connected to the ISP, remote users can establish a *secure connection* to your private network by establishing a VPN connection.

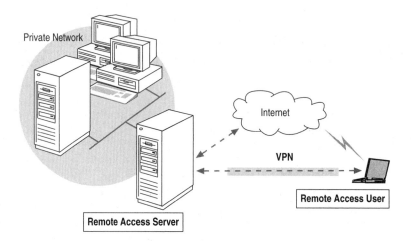

Figure 2.18   A typical use of VPN in remote access solutions

Figure 2.19 illustrates how you can create an isolated portion of your private network, referred to as a *screened subnet* or demilitarized zone (DMZ). You can place servers that manage confidential data on the screened subnet.

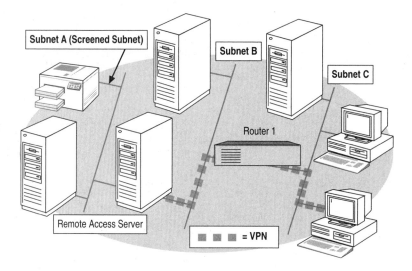

Figure 2.19   Creating a screened subnet in your private network by using VPN

Like the scenario presented in Figure 2.16, the desktop computer on Subnet C accesses resources managed by the restricted server on Subnet A. Use a VPN to encrypt data being transferred between the desktop computer and the remote access server.

When you select a VPN for protecting confidential data, you're protecting all devices on the screened subnet. You protect the data for the entire path between the desktop computer and the remote access server. When you encrypt data from the desktop computer to the remote access server, you provide *point-to-point* data encryption. The data encryption is transparent to Router 1. The remote access server acts as the router between Subnet A and Subnet B.

TCP/IP Data Protection with IPSec

After you have selected IPSec to protect your confidential data, you must select the level of data protection your organization wants. IPSec performs *machine authentication*, meaning IPSec authenticates the IPSec device, computer, or router and not the user running applications on the device. IPSec establishes a *security association* (SA) prior to the exchange of data between computers in your network.

Figure 2.20 illustrates the sequence of events that must occur before the secure exchange of confidential data.

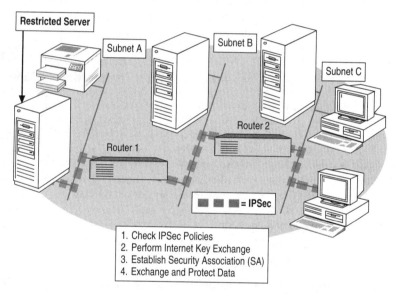

1. Check IPSec Policies
2. Perform Internet Key Exchange
3. Establish Security Association (SA)
4. Exchange and Protect Data

Figure 2.20   The sequence of events between two computers that protect data by using IPSec

To securely exchange data using IPSec, the two computers must

- **Check IPSec policies**   When the two computers attempt to create a SA, they examine their own IPSec policies to determine whether a SA can be established.

- **Perform Internet Key Exchange**   The computers must identify each other by a source (such as Active Directory directory service or an X509 certificate server) that both computers trust. After they have mutually identified each other, the computers negotiate identity and encryption algorithms.

- **Establish the SA**   The computers exchange public keys and complete the SA.
- **Exchange and protect data**   The computers exchange data and protect the data by using the identity and encryption algorithms negotiated in step 2. IPSec periodically (after a given number of transmitted packets) regenerates public keys to update the SA.

You can customize IPSec to protect your confidential data based on the level of data protection your organization wants. You can create a different level of data protection between any two computers (or routers). Or you can use the same level of data protection for all computers and routers on the network.

To specify the level of data protection required

1. Select an existing IPSec policy or create a custom IPSec policy
2. Choose IPSec transport mode or IPSec tunnel mode
3. Identify the method that the two computers, or routers, will use to mutually identify each other
4. Determine whether integrity checking or data encryption is required
5. Select the appropriate algorithms for identity checking and data encryption

IPSec Policies

Specify IPSec policies in your design so the appropriate computers can protect confidential data. IPSec policies are the mechanism you use to customize the security of your confidential data. The IPSec policies you include in your design must protect confidential data. However, your IPSec policies must allow authorized users access to servers and applications.

Making the Decision

Within an IPSec policy, you can specify one or more IPSec rules. For each IPSec rule, you can specify

- A filter that identifies the IP traffic managed by the rule. You can base the filter on the source or destination
    - DNS name
    - IP address or IP address range
    - TCP port number, User Datagram Protocol (UDP) port number, or port number range
    - IP number
- IPSec transport mode or IPSec tunnel mode
- Authentication method
- Identity algorithms
- Encryption algorithms

Setting the IPSec tunnel or tunnel mode, authentication method, identity algorithms, and encryption algorithms are discussed later in this lesson.

Select the appropriate IPSec protection of your data by

- Using an existing IPSec policy without modification
- Modifying one of the existing IPSec policies
- Creating a completely new IPSec policy

The default IPSec policies you can include in your design are

- **Client (Respond Only)**   This policy enables the computer to respond appropriately to requests for secured communications. Select this policy for computers that don't secure communications for the majority of the time.
- **Server (Request Security)**   This policy enables the computer to accept unsecured traffic, but always attempt to secure additional communications by requesting security from the original sender. Select this policy for computers that secure communications for the majority of the time, but will allow unsecured communications if the other computer is not IPSec-enabled.

Note   Because you can require IPSec on individual TCP or UDP ports, a server might require IPSec for specific applications, but not require IPSec for all other traffic.

- **Secure Server (Require Security)**   This policy accepts unsecured, incoming communications, but secures all outgoing traffic. Select this policy for computers that require secure communications.

Applying the Decision

In Figure 2.21, the server on Subnet B is assigned the server policy because the server communicates with IPSec-enabled and non-IPSec-enabled computers. In Figure 2.21, the computer on Subnet C is assigned the client policy because the computer communicates with IPSec-enabled and non-IPSec-enabled computers. In Figure 2.21, the restricted server on Subnet A is assigned the secure server policy because the server contains sensitive data. The restricted server communicates only with IPSec-enabled computers.

After you have selected your IPSec policies, you can assign the policies to

- Active Directory organizational units (OUs)
- User accounts
- Group accounts
- Computer accounts

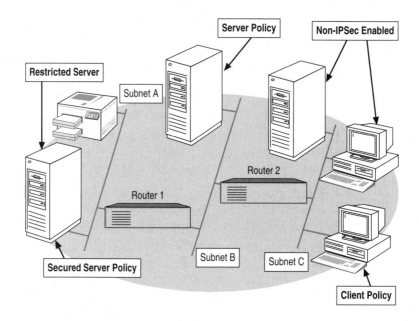

Figure 2.21   An example of the default IPSec policies in TCP/IP data protection

When you assign IPSec policies in Active Directory, an order of precedence exists. Table 2.8 lists policy types and what policy types they override.

Table 2.8   IPSec Policy Types and Overrides

Policy Container	Override
Domain policies	All local policies
OU policies	Domain policies
Child OU policies	Parent OU policies

The scenario in Figure 2.21 illustrates how the IPSec policies can be used. Consider the following sequence that describes the interaction between the client and server policies.

1. The desktop computer (with the client policy) on Subnet C attempts to access a shared folder managed by the server (with the server policy) on Subnet B.

2. The server on Subnet B receives the request, checks the active IPSec policies (server policy), and sends back a reply that requests IPSec.

3. The desktop computer on Subnet C receives the request for IPSec, checks the active IPSec policies (client policy), and accepts the request for IPSec.

4. The server and the desktop computer establish an SA.

5. The desktop computer can access the shared folder managed by the server.

When your design includes non-IPSec-enabled computers, you must consider how the IPSec policies respond to non-IPSec-enabled computers. Based on the scenario depicted in Figure 2.20, the following sequence describes the interaction between a non-IPSec-enabled desktop computer and server policies.

1. The non-IPSec-enabled desktop computer on Subnet C attempts to access a shared folder managed by the server (with the server policy) on Subnet B.

2. The server on Subnet B receives the request, checks the active IPSec policies (server policy), and sends back a reply that requests IPSec.

3. The desktop computer on Subnet C receives the request for IPSec, but has no concept of IPSec, so the desktop computer discards the request.

4. After a period of time, the server times out and resends IPSec request.

5. After a fixed number of retries, the server aborts the attempt to establish an SA and responds with an unsecured reply.

6. The desktop computer can access the shared folder by using unsecured communication.

In Figure 2.21, the interaction between the non-IPSec-enabled desktop computer on Subnet C and restricted server on Subnet A is similar to the previous example. However, when the restricted server times out, the server does *not* respond. From the desktop computer's perspective, the restricted server appears to be disconnected from the network.

Note   For more information on creating and configuring IPSec policies, see Windows 2000 Help.

IPSec Transport Mode and IPSec Tunnel Mode

You can protect confidential data by using IPSec in *transport mode* or *tunnel mode*. You specify the IPSec mode you want to use in an IPSec rule within an IPSec policy. Each IPSec rule can support only one IPSec mode.

Making the Decision

When you use IPSec transport mode, you protect data between an IPSec-enabled device (typically a computer) and any number of IPSec-enabled devices (multiple end points). IPSec transport mode allows you to provide end-to-end protection of confidential data.

When you use IPSec tunnel mode, you protect data between an IPSec-enabled device (typically a computer) and one *peer* IPSec-enabled device (single endpoint). IPSec tunnel mode allows you to provide point-to-point protection of confidential data.

Although you can use IPSec tunnel mode to protect confidential data between routers, L2TP/IPSec provides enhanced security. Unless you're constrained by support for L2TP/IPSec, use L2TP/IPSec for all router-to-router tunneling solutions. For more information, see Chapter 4, "Lesson 3: Data Protection on Unsecured Segments."

Applying the Decision

Figure 2.22 illustrates a scenario in which IPSec transport mode protects transmitted confidential data. The desktop computer on Subnet C exchanges data with the servers on Subnets A, B, and C. Because the desktop computer must communicate with *multiple* IPSec-enabled servers, IPSec transport mode is the appropriate choice.

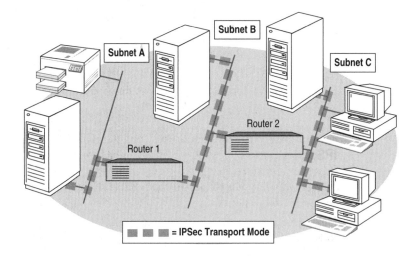

Figure 2.22   Scenario in which confidential data is protected by using IPSec transport mode

Note   In the scenario depicted in Figure 2.22, a separate SA exists between the desktop computer and each server.

Figure 2.23 illustrates a scenario in which you protect transmitted confidential data using IPSec tunnel mode. The router at Location A exchanges data with the router at Location B over the Internet. Because the routers communicate only with each other, IPSec tunnel mode is the appropriate choice.

Include IPSec tunnel mode to protect confidential data when

- Your design requires interoperability with other routers that don't support L2TP/IPSec or PPTP VPN tunneling technology
- The requirements of your organization include router-to-router tunneling

Note   IPSec tunnel mode is not supported for client remote access VPN scenarios. Instead, use L2TP/IPSec or PPTP for client remote access VPN.

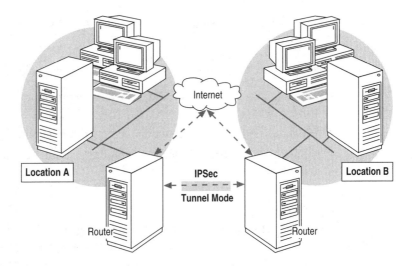

Figure 2.23   Scenario in which confidential data is protected by using IPSec tunnel mode

IPSec Authentication

For each IPSec rule, you must select an IPSec authentication method. IPSec authentication occurs when IPSec-enabled devices establish an SA.

Making the Decision

Select IPSec authentication so that IPSec-enabled devices can identify each other. You can create IPSec authentication solutions with

- Kerberos version 5
- X509 version 3 certificates
- A preshared key (password)

Select Kerberos for IPSec authentication when the organization

- Wants to protect confidential data within their private network
- Has an existing Active Directory or Kerberos infrastructure

---

Note   The Kerberos tickets for the desktop computer and the server must exist in the same Active Directory domain or a trusted domain.

Select X509 certificates for IPSec authentication when the organization

- Wants to protect confidential data within its private network or between trusted networks
- Has an existing public key infrastructure (PKI)

- When other organizations with a common, trusted certificate authority (CA) are involved

Select preshared keys for IPSec authentication when the organization

- Wants to protect confidential data within its private network or between trusted networks
- Has no existing PKI or Active Directory infrastructure
- Wants to connect remote locations before installing domain controllers at the remote location

Applying the Decision

Figure 2.24 illustrates a scenario in which your organization chooses Kerberos version 5 for IPSec authentication. The desktop computer on Subnet C and the server on Subnet A use Kerberos tickets in Active Directory directory service to verify the identity of each other. Because this authentication method is based on Kerberos and Active Directory, the source and destination computers must be connected to the same private network.

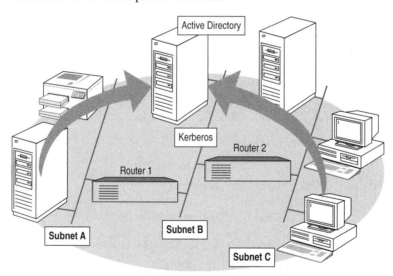

Figure 2.24   Using Kerberos as the IPSec authentication method

Figure 2.25 illustrates a scenario in which your organization uses X509 certificates for IPSec authentication. The router in Organization A and the router in Organization B use X509 certificates, from an Internet-based CA, to verify the identity of each other. Because this authentication method is based on X509 certificates, the source and destination IPSec devices can reside within the same private network or in different private networks.

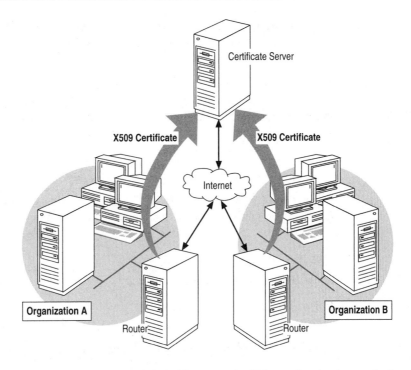

Figure 2.25   Using X509 certificates as the IPSec authentication method

Figure 2.26 illustrates a scenario in which your organization uses preshared keys (passwords) for IPSec authentication. The router in Location A and the

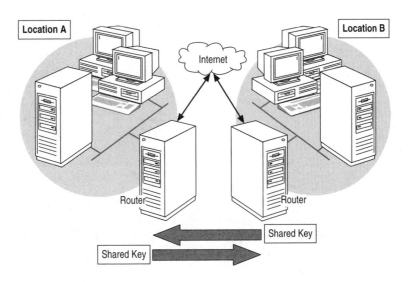

Figure 2.26   Using preshared keys as the IPSec authentication method

router in Location B are assigned the *same* preshared key. When the routers at Location A and Location B establish an IPSec SA, they authenticate one another by exchanging the preshared key.

Router 1 (at Location A) receives the preshared key of Router 2 (at Location B). Router 1 verifies that the preshared key received from Router 2 matches the preshared key assigned to Router 1. With preshared key authentication, the source and destination IPSec devices can reside within the same private network or in different private networks.

IPSec Integrity Checking

You can use IPSec to ensure that the integrity of your confidential data is maintained. IPSec performs integrity checking with the IPSec Authentication Header (AH) protocol.

Making the Decision

Select IPSec integrity checking, using the AH protocol, when you

- Don't want to encrypt data
- Want to prevent modification of the data
- Want to ensure the identity of the source and destination computer

Select the identity algorithm used by the IPSec AH protocol to sign the IP packet. Table 2.9 lists the possible identity algorithms, their key length, and when to include the algorithm in your design.

Table 2.9   Selecting Identity Algorithms

Use	Key Length	To
Message Digest version 5 (MD5)	128-bit	Reduce the processor and memory overhead associated with cryptography
		Comply with Internet standards
Secure Hash Algorithm (SHA)	160-bit	Provide the strongest possible identity algorithm
		Comply with Federal Information Processing Standards (FIPS) that are used by the U.S. government

Applying the Decision

Figure 2.27 illustrates an IP packet that has been *digitally signed* using the IPSec AH protocol. When the IPSec AH signs an IP packet, a checksum is calculated for the entire IP packed and saved in the AH. If *any* portion of the IP packet is changed, the checksum is no longer valid.

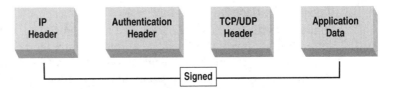

Figure 2.27   Illustration of an application data and IP packet that is digitally signed by using the IPSec AH protocol

---

Note   Because network address translators modify the IP header, TCP/UDP header, and application data, you can't use the AH protocol in solutions where the IP packets must pass through a network address translator.

IPSec Data Encryption

You can also use IPSec to encrypt your confidential data using the IPSec Encapsulating Security Payload (ESP) protocol.

Making the Decision

Select IPSec data encryption, using the ESP protocol, when you want to

- Prevent unauthorized viewing of the data

- Prevent modifications to the data

- Ensure the identity of the source and destination computers

You can also select the encryption algorithm used by the IPSec ESP protocol to encrypt the IP packet itself. Select one of the same identity algorithms that are used by the IPSec AH protocol.

Table 2.10 lists the encryption algorithms and when to include the algorithm in your design.

Table 2.10   Encryption Algorithms

Use	To
Data Encryption Standard (DES)	Reduce the processor and memory overhead associated with cryptography Provide the lowest level of encryption when the physical network is secured Encrypt data in all countries
56 bit-DES	Reduce the processor and memory overhead associated with cryptography Provide a medium level of encryption Encrypt data in most countries
3DES (Triple DES)	Provide the highest level of encryption on unsecured networks Encrypt data within the United States and Canada

Applying the Decision

Figure 2.28 illustrates an IP packet that has been signed and encrypted by the IPSec ESP protocol. Unlike the AH protocol, only the ESP header, application data, ESP trailer, and ESP authentication portion of the IP packet are signed. In addition, this protocol encrypts only the application data and the ESP trailer.

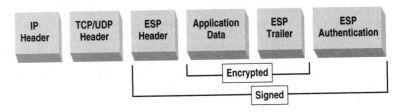

Figure 2.28   Illustration of an application data and IP packet that is signed and encrypted using the IPSec ESP protocol

TCP/IP Data Protection with VPN

After selecting VPN to protect your confidential data, you must determine the level of data protection your organization wants. VPN enhances TCP/IP security by requiring *user authentication*. VPN authenticates the user running applications on the computer. The user can be either a user running applications on the private network or a remote access user. Scenarios that call for remote access user solutions are discussed further in Chapter 12, "VPN in Remote Access Designs."

When implementing VPN for router-to-router solutions, VPN authenticates the routers through a user account. You create the user account specifically for router authentication. Scenarios including VPN in router-to-router solutions are discussed further in Chapter 4, "IP Routing Designs."

You can customize VPN to protect your confidential data based on the level of data protection your organization wants. You can create a different level of data protection between any two computers (or routers). Or you can use the same level of data protection for all computers and routers.

Making the Decision

To specify the level of data protection required for VPN, you must

- Choose between PPTP tunnels or L2TP tunnel
- Determine whether integrity checking or data encryption is required
- Select the appropriate algorithms for identity checking and data encryption

Note   Although data encryption is usually associated with VPN, you can use VPN to provide only integrity checking.

Applying the Decision

Figure 2.29 illustrates a scenario in which your organization uses VPN for data protection between Location A and Location B. A VPN tunnel is created between the routers at both locations. The VPN tunnel protects *all* data transmitted between Location A and Location B.

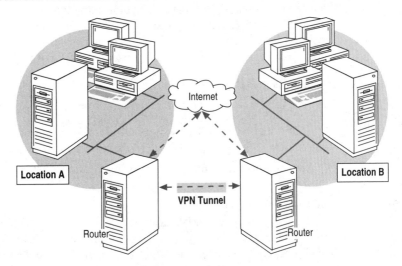

Figure 2.29   Physical representation of a router-to-router scenario that uses VPN for data protection

The VPN tunnel protects confidential data by performing router authentication (identity checking), preventing data modification (data integrity), and preventing unauthorized viewing of the data (data encryption).

Figure 2.30 provides a logical representation of the VPN tunnel presented in the scenario in Figure 2.29. To the remainder of the computers, network devices, and

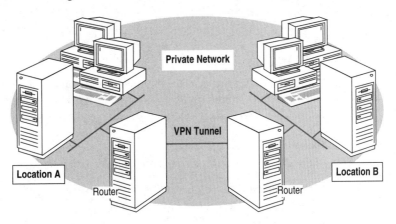

Figure 2.30   Logical representation of a router-to-router scenario that uses VPN for data protection

users, the VPN tunnel joins Location A and Location B into a single private network. The VPN tunnel is transparent to the computers, network devices, and users in either location.

PPTP Tunnels

You can base your TCP/IP data protection solution on Point-to-Point Tunneling Protocol (PPTP). PPTP is a de facto industry standard tunneling protocol that first appeared in Windows NT 4.0. PPTP is the more established and mature tunneling protocol supported by VPN and is an extension of Point-to-Point Protocol (PPP).

Making the Decision

Include PPTP in your network design to protect your confidential data when

- Your network includes a variety of operating systems, such as Windows 95, Windows 98, Windows NT 4.0, Windows 2000, Macintosh, or UNIX
- Your routers and remote access servers support PPTP

Applying the Decision

Figure 2.31 illustrates an IP packet that is protected by PPTP. The IP datagram (the PPP payload) that contains the confidential data is *encapsulated* inside the PPTP packet. The Generic Routing Encapsulation (GRE) header and the IP header preface the PPP payload. The GRE header provides packet identification and sequencing within the tunnel. The IP header contains the source and destination IP addresses of the tunnel endpoints.

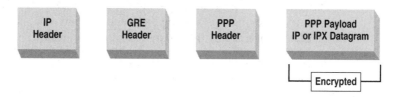

Figure 2.31   The format of an IP packet protected by PPTP

L2TP Tunnels

If supported by your network, you can base your TCP/IP data protection solution on Layer Two Tunneling Protocol (L2TP). L2TP is a draft RFC-based tunneling protocol that will likely become the industry standard.

Making the Decision

Include L2TP to protect your confidential data when

- Your network is comprised of computers running Windows 2000 or other operating systems that support L2TP
- Your routers and remote access servers support L2TP

Note   Currently, the only Microsoft operating system that supports L2TP is Windows 2000. However, many third-party router, network switch, and operating system vendors support L2TP.

Applying the Decision

Figure 2.32 illustrates an IP packet that is encapsulated using L2TP. Unlike PPTP, L2TP provides no native data protection. L2TP depends on IPSec to provide data integrity checking and encryption.

Figure 2.32   The format of an IP packet that is encapsulated using L2TP without integrity checking or encryption

Figure 2.33 illustrates an IP packet that is encapsulated by L2TP and protected by the IPSec ESP protocol. IPSec protects the L2TP packet exactly like a normal IP packet (see Figure 2.27).

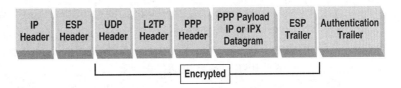

Figure 2.33   The format of an IP packet that is encapsulated by L2TP with IPSec ESP protocol

Note   Although integrity checking and encryption aren't required in L2TP, include protection of any confidential data that is transmitted across public networks.

VPN Authentication Protocols

You can use VPN to provide *identity checking* between a remote access computer and a remote access server as part of a remote access solution or between routers as part of a router-to-router solution.

Making the Decision

The VPN authentication protocols you can include in your design are

- **Password Authentication Protocol (PAP)**   PAP provides unprotected, clear text authentication. Include PAP as your authentication protocol when

- You must support a variety of routers or operating systems that remotely access your network

- Clear text authentication doesn't invalidate the security requirements of your organization

- **Shiva Password Authentication Protocol (SPAP)**   SPAP provides encrypted authentication and always sends the password in the same reversibly encrypted form. As a result, SPAP is susceptible to replay attacks, where a malicious user captures the packets of the authentication process and replays the responses to gain authenticated access to your intranet. Include SPAP as your authentication protocol when

  - You must support Shiva remote access clients or Shiva remote access servers

  - Susceptibility to replay attacks doesn't invalidate the security requirements of your organization

- **Challenge Handshake Authentication Protocol (CHAP)**   CHAP provides encrypted authentication using a challenge-response that provides one-way MD5 hashing (encryption) on the response. CHAP doesn't allow users to change their passwords while logging on. Include CHAP as your authentication protocol when

  - You must support a variety of routers or operating systems that remotely access your network

  - One-way encryption of the response doesn't invalidate the security requirements of your organization

  - Users aren't permitted to change their passwords while logging on

- **Microsoft Challenge Handshake Authentication Protocol (MS-CHAP)**   MS-CHAP provides encrypted authentication and is a derivative of CHAP. Wherever possible, MS-CHAP is consistent with standard CHAP. The response packet MS-CHAP returns to the user is in a format specifically designed for Windows 95, Windows NT 4.0, Windows 2000, and later networking products. MS-CHAP allows users to change their passwords while logging on. Include MS-CHAP as your authentication protocol when

  - You must support a variety of Microsoft operating systems that remotely access your network

  - Users can change their passwords while logging on

- **Microsoft Challenge Handshake Authentication Protocol version 2 (MS-CHAP v2)**   MS-CHAP v2 is an enhanced version of MS-CHAP. MS-CHAP v2 improves security by

  - Authenticating both endpoints of the tunnel with one-way, mutual authentication

  - Generating a separate key for transmitted and received data

Include MS-CHAP v2 as your authentication protocol when

- You must support computers running Windows 2000 that remotely access your network

- You must provide mutual authentication between routers or between remote access computers and remote access servers

- Users can change their passwords while logging on

- **Extensible Authentication Protocol (EAP)**   EAP is an extension to PPP. EAP provides support for a number of authentication schemes including token cards, one-time passwords, public key authentication using smart cards, or certificates. Windows 2000 supports

  - **EAP-MD5 CHAP**   EAP-MD5 CHAP provides security equivalent to CHAP, but the challenges and responses are sent as EAP messages. You can use EAP-MD5 CHAP to test EAP interoperability.

  - **EAP-TLS**   EAP-Transport Level Security (TLS) is used in certificate-based security environments. EAP-TLS is supported only on computers running Windows 2000 that are members of a mixed-mode or native-mode domain. Remote access servers or routers running stand-alone Windows 2000 don't support EAP-TLS.

Table 2.11 summarizes when you may implement EAP-MD5 CHAP and EAP-TLS as your authentication protocol.

Table 2.11   Using EAP-MD5 CHAP and EAP-TLS

Choose EAP-MD5 CHAP for	Choose EAP-TLS for
Computers running Windows 2000 that remotely access your network	Computers running Windows 2000 that remotely access your network
Computers running Windows 2000 that provide routing services	Network supporting smart card or certificate-based authentication
Third-party routers and other devices that require EAP-MD5 CHAP authentication	

Applying the Decision

Figure 2.34 illustrates a scenario in which three locations are connected over the Internet. The routers connecting the three locations are running Windows 2000 and Routing and Remote Access. Because the routers are Windows 2000–based to enhance security, the routers authenticate each other by using MS-CHAP v2. MS-CHAP v2 is the only authentication protocol that supports mutual authentication.

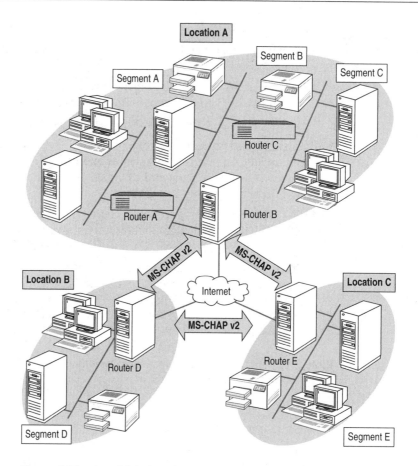

Figure 2.34   A multiple location scenario that illustrates VPN authentication

VPN Encryption Protocols

You can use VPN to provide encryption of data between the remote access computer and remote access server as part of a remote access solution or between routers as part of a router-to-router solution.

Making the Decision

The VPN authentication protocols you can include in your design are

- **Microsoft Point-to-Point Encryption (MPPE)**   MPPE provides data encryption for PPTP tunnels. MPPE provides two levels of encryption. You can select

  - 40-bit MPPE data encryption when you want to reduce the memory and processor resource overhead

  - 40-bit MPPE for data encryption in countries where export restrictions prevent stronger data encryption algorithms

- 128-bit MPPE data encryption when you want to provide the strongest data encryption possible

- 128-bit MPPE data encryption in countries where export restrictions allow stronger data encryption algorithms

- **IPSec Encryption Algorithms**   IPSec provides data encryption for L2TP tunnels. You can use any IPSec data encryption algorithm. For more information on IPSec data encryption, see the section on IPSec encryption earlier in this lesson.

Applying the Decision

Figure 2.35 illustrates a scenario in which three locations are connected over the Internet. You want to protect any confidential data transmitted over the Internet. The routers connecting the three locations are running Windows 2000 and Routing and Remote Access service. You also want the strongest security possible for the data transmitted between the routers.

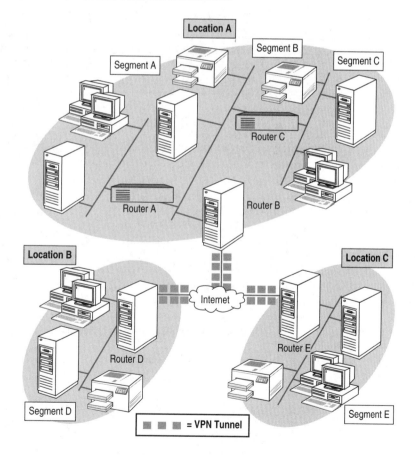

Figure 2.35   A multiple location scenario that illustrates VPN encryption

In this case, you can use L2TP, IPSec, and 3DES to provide the strongest possible security. 3DES provides the strongest data encryption available to Windows 2000. When you're using 3DES for data encryption, L2TP and IPSec are also required because PPTP tunnels support only MPPE.

TCP/IP Data Protection with TCP/IP Filters

TCP/IP filters can protect data transmitted by TCP/IP Windows Sockets–based applications. You can use the TCP/IP filters in Windows 2000 to limit the TCP and UDP ports that applications can utilize.

Making the Decision

Include TCP/IP filters in your design to

- Filter inbound TCP/IP traffic; TCP/IP filters don't apply to IP traffic that is forwarded between interfaces
- Provide data protection when other TCP/IP filtering, such as Routing and Remote Access or Proxy Server filtering, is not present

---

Note Because Windows 2000 Server and Windows 2000 Advanced Server include Routing and Remote Access, don't include TCP/IP filters in any solution based on these versions of Windows 2000.

Figure 2.36 illustrates the relationship between TCP/IP applications, TCP/IP filters, Routing and Remote Access filters, and Proxy Server filters. TCP/IP filters exist immediately beneath the Windows Sockets layer. As a result, TCP/IP filters can't affect routing or other activities that occur at layers *beneath* the TCP/IP filters.

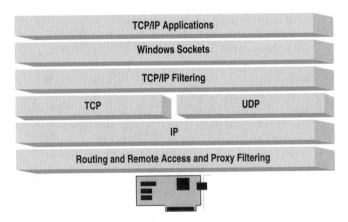

Figure 2.36   The relationship between TCP/IP applications, TCP/IP filters, Routing and Remote Access filters, and Proxy Server filters

You can create TCP/IP filters based on TCP port numbers, UDP port numbers, and IP numbers.

Note The default TCP/IP filters block all inbound traffic. Enabling TCP/IP filters can restrict the proper operation of networking services.

Routing and Remote Access and Proxy Server filters exist at the lowest layer in the TCP/IP stack. Therefore, Routing and Remote Access and Proxy Server filters affect *all* IP traffic. For more information on Routing and Remote Access filters, see Chapter 4, "IP Routing Designs." For more information on Proxy Server filters, see Chapter 6, "Proxy Server in Internet and Intranet Designs."

Note Whenever possible, use Routing and Remote Access and Proxy Server filters instead of TCP/IP filters.

Applying the Decision

Figure 2.37 illustrates an organization that has a Web server and a File Transfer Protocol (FTP) server. Internet-based users access the Web and FTP servers, located behind the organization's firewall.

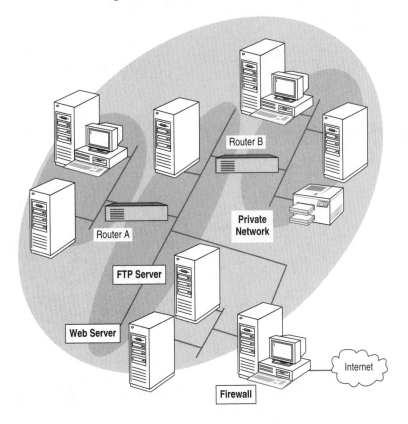

Figure 2.37 Scenario that illustrates the use of TCP/IP filters

You can specify the criteria for the TCP/IP filter on the Web server to allow only Hypertext Transfer Protocol (HTTP) traffic. You can also specify the criteria for the TCP/IP filter on the FTP server to allow only FTP traffic.

Lesson 4: TCP/IP Optimization

After this lesson, you will be able to
- Improve the availability of a TCP/IP network design
- Improve the performance of a TCP/IP network design

Estimated lesson time: 15 minutes

Improving TCP/IP Availability and Performance

After you establish the essentials of your TCP/IP design and secure your design, you can focus on optimizing the availability and performance of your design. Most strategies used to improve TCP/IP availability also improve TCP/IP performance. Conversely, strategies adopted to improve TCP/IP performance improve TCP/IP availability.

Making the Decision

You can improve TCP/IP availability and performance by

- Replacing nonpersistent connections with persistent connections. Nonpersistent connections, such as dial-up connections, affect
  - Availability when the line is busy
  - Availability and performance because of the delay in establishing the connection
- Adding additional connections; additional connections affect
  - Availability because the additional connection acts as a redundant path if the primary connection fails
  - Performance because the additional connection adds increased bandwidth between route paths if the primary route path is saturated
- Adding additional routers; additional routers affect
  - Availability when additional routers provide redundancy if the primary router fails
  - Performance when the additional router increases bandwidth between route paths

Applying the Decision

Figure 2.38 illustrates a scenario before optimization for availability and performance. Router 1 connects Location A to Location B by using a persistent Internet connection. Router 2 connects Location B to Location A by using a nonpersistent Internet connection.

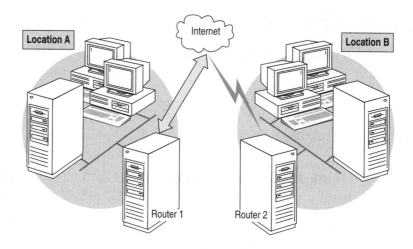

Figure 2.38   Scenario before availability and performance optimization

Figure 2.39 illustrates the previous scenario after optimization for availability and performance. The optimizations for availability and performance include

- Adding Routers 3 and 4 to Location A and Location B respectively
- Upgrading the connection at Location B to a persistent connection
- Adding additional connections at Locations A and B

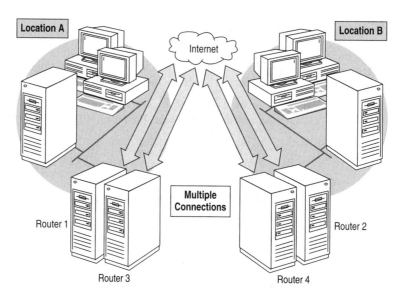

Figure 2.39   The previous scenario after availability and performance optimization

Activity 2.2: Completing a TCP/IP Design

In this activity, you are presented with a scenario. To complete the activity:

1. Evaluate the scenario and determine the design requirements

2. Answer questions and make design recommendations

In Figure 2.40, you see a diagram of the electronics field service firm offices presented earlier in this chapter. A year after the initial deployment of your design, the field service firm wants to replace the point-to-point connections between the offices. The firm wants to connect the offices together using the Internet.

Figure 2.40   Diagram of the electronics field service firm offices

Answer the following questions concerning your design recommendations. You can find answers to the questions in the Appendix, "Questions and Answers."

1. As the consultant, what recommendations do you make to migrate the firm from point-to-point connections to Internet-based connections?

2. The management of the field service firm is concerned about confidential data transmitted over the Internet. The firm wants to ensure that the strongest possible security is used. How can you address these security concerns?

3. An independent consulting firm has proposed the use of IPSec tunnel mode to protect the confidential data transmitted over the Internet. How do you respond to the recommendations proposed by the consulting firm?

4. After migrating to Internet-based connectivity between offices, the users in the regional offices are experiencing slower response time. The firm has verified that the Web servers aren't the source of the reduction in response time. How can you modify your design to improve the response time of the users in the regional offices?

Lab: Creating a TCP/IP Network Design

After this lab, you will be able to

- Evaluate a scenario and determine the design requirements
- Create a TCP/IP network design based on the design requirements

Estimated lab time: 45 minutes

In this lab, you're the director of information services for a cruise line and are responsible for creating a TCP/IP network design. The cruise line has a central reservation location, 18 seaport facilities, and 15 cruise liners.

To complete this lab:

1. Examine the networking environment presented in the scenario, the network diagrams, the business requirements, business constraints, and the technical requirements and constraints

2. Use the worksheet for each location to create your TCP/IP network design (you can find completed sample design worksheets on the Supplemental Course Materials CD-ROM in the Completed Worksheets folder)

3. Create, eliminate, or replace existing networking devices and network segments when required

4. Ensure that your design fulfills the business requirements, constraints, and technical requirements of the scenario by

   - Assigning the appropriate network address numbers on each network segment

   - Optimizing your design to provide the security, availability, performance, and affordability

Note To reduce the length of time spent on this lab, create a TCP/IP network design for the reservation location, one of the seaports, and one of the cruise liners.

Scenario

A cruise ship line is migrating its network to Windows 2000. The cruise line maintains a fleet of 15 luxury cruise ships and has a central reservation center where agents take reservations for cruises. The cruse line operates out of 18 seaports where the vessels dock and customers board.

Figure 2.41 provides a high-level overview of the cruise ship line's network. Each seaport facility is connected to the Internet by a T1 line. The company's reservation center, which is located in Miami, is connected to the Internet by a T3 line. Figure 2.42 illustrates the existing network at the company's reservation center.

Figure 2.41   Overview network diagram of the cruise ship line

In addition to reservations made at the cruise ship line's reservation center, each seaport facility can also take reservations. Each seaport facility connects to thereservation center over the Internet. Figure 2.43 shows each seaport facility's network. (For the purposes of this lab, assume that all seaports have the same network configuration.)

Each cruise ship has a primary microwave connection to the Internet. In addition, every cruise ship has a satellite connection that acts as a redundant Internet connection if the microwave connection fails. Because of the costs associated with the satellite connection, the satellite connection is for cruise ship personnel's use exclusively. Passengers may access the Internet through the microwave connection to the Internet at business centers located on each cruise ship. Figure 2.44 shows each cruise ship's network. (For the purposes of this lab, assume that all cruise ships have the same network configuration.)

The cruise ships receive passenger manifests, baggage, and e-mail messages from the reservation center. In addition, each cruise ship maintains a maintenance and inventory system that the ship personnel use to manage the maintenance and parts inventory for the cruise ship. The restaurant and food services on the cruise ships also maintain an inventory of food and beverage items they require. The food services group orders the necessary items at its next port before the cruise ship docks.

Business Requirements and Constraints

The cruise ship line has a number of requirements and constraints based on the business model of the company. As you create your TCP/IP network design, ensure that your design meets the business requirements and stays within the business constraints.

To achieve the business requirements and constraints, your design must

- Utilize the existing hardware and operating systems in each seaport facility and cruise liner. These facilities include
    - Baggage check-in and reservation kiosks at each seaport
    - Reservation and baggage computers for use by cruise line personnel at each seaport
    - Business centers on each cruise liner for use by passengers
    - Ship operations computers for use by ship personnel
- Provide Internet access to each reservation agent
- Support Active Directory as the directory services for the cruise line
- Provide an Internet presence hosted on Web servers in the reservation center
- Ensure that connectivity between the individual seaport facilities and the reservation center is available 24 hours a day, 7 days a week
- Ensure that the baggage check-in and reservation kiosks are available during normal hours of operation
- Ensure that cruise ship personnel and passengers can, by default, access the Internet through the microwave connection
- Ensure that cruise ship personnel can access the Internet through the satellite connection if the microwave connection fails

Technical Requirements and Constraints

The applications that run on each seaport and cruise ship network require internal connectivity, as well as connectivity with other seaport facilities and cruise ships and with the reservation center. These applications run on computers used by the reservation agents, baggage handlers, and cruise ship personnel, and on computers used in the reservation and baggage kiosks.

The existing physical network, hardware, and operating systems place certain technical requirements and constraints on your design. As you create your TCP/IP network design, ensure that your design meets the technical requirements and stays within the technical constraints.

To achieve the technical requirements and constraints, your design must

- Secure the private networks of the cruise line's reservation center, seaports, and cruise ships
- Provide network addressing for each network segment
- Protect all data transmitted over the Internet by using the strongest encryption and identity checking possible
- Utilize 172.16.0.0/16 to assign public addresses
- Utilize 10.0.0.0/8 to assign private IP addresses

Note   For the purposes of this lab, treat the private IP address range 172.16.123.0/24 as a public address.

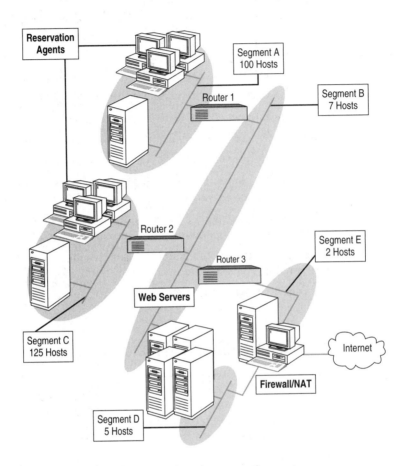

Figure 2.42   Existing network at the reservation center

Design Worksheet – Reservation Center (for Figure 2.42)

Segment	Protocols and addressing	Comments
	Network number: _____ ❑ VPN <table><tr><th>Authentication</th><th>Tunnel Type</th><th>Encryption</th></tr><tr><td>❑ MS-CHAP ❑ MS-CHAP v2 ❑ EAP-TLS</td><td>❑ PPTP ❑ L2TP</td><td>❑ 40-bit MPPE ❑ 128-bit MPPE Complete IPSec section</td></tr></table> ❑ IPSec <table><tr><th>Mode</th><th>Authentication</th><th>Identity</th><th>Protection</th><th>Encryption</th></tr><tr><td>❑ Transport ❑ Tunnel</td><td>❑ Kerberos ❑ X509 ❑ Preshared key</td><td>❑ MD5 ❑ SHA</td><td>❑ Identity (AH) ❑ Identity and Encryption (ESP)</td><td>Not required ❑ DES ❑ 56-bit DES ❑ 3DES</td></tr></table>	
	Network number: _____ Default gateway: _____	
	Network number: _____ Default gateway: _____	
	Network number: _____ Default gateway: _____	
	Network number: _____ Default gateway: _____	
	Network number: _____ Default gateway: _____	

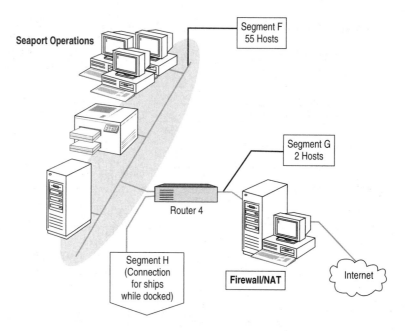

Figure 2.43   Existing network at seaports (assume that all seaports have the same network configuration)

Design Worksheet – Seaport (for Figure 2.43)

Segment	Protocols and addressing					Comments
	Network number: _____					
	❑ **VPN**					
		Authentication	Tunnel Type	Encryption		
		❑ MS-CHAP	❑ PPTP	❑ 40-bit MPPE		
		❑ MS-CHAP v2		❑ 128-bit MPPE		
		❑ EAP-TLS	❑ L2TP	Complete IPSec section		
	❑ **IPSec**					
		Mode	Authentication	Identity	Protection	Encryption
		❑ Transport	❑ Kerberos	❑ MD5	❑ Identity (AH)	Not required
		❑ Tunnel	❑ X509	❑ SHA	❑ Identity and Encryption (ESP)	❑ DES
			❑ Preshared key			❑ 56-bit DES
						❑ 3DES
	Network number: _____ Default gateway: _____					
	Network number: _____ Default gateway: _____					
	Network number: _____ Default gateway: _____					

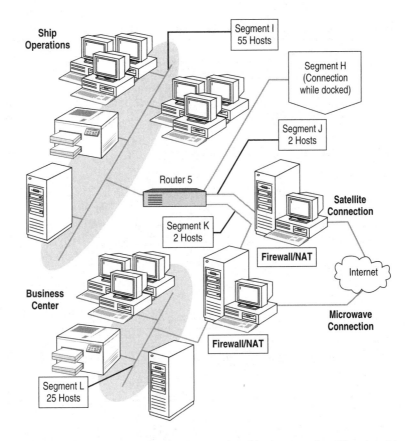

Figure 2.44 Existing network on a cruise ship (assume that all cruise ships have the same network configuration)

Design Worksheet – Cruise Ship (for Figure 2.44)

Segment	Protocols and addressing	Comments
	Network number: _____	
	❑ **VPN**	
	❑ **IPSec**	
	Network number: _____	
	❑ **VPN**	
	❑ **IPSec**	
	Network number: _____ Default gateway: _____	
	Network number: _____ Default gateway: _____	
	Network number: _____ Default gateway: _____	
	Network number: _____ Default gateway: _____	

VPN (first section)

Authentication	Tunnel Type	Encryption	
❑ MS-CHAP	❑ PPTP	❑ 40-bit MPPE	
❑ MS-CHAP v2		❑ 128-bit MPPE	
❑ EAP-TLS	❑ L2TP	Complete IPSec section	

IPSec (first section)

Mode	Authentication	Identity	Protection	Encryption
❑ Transport	❑ Kerberos	❑ MD5	❑ Identity (AH)	Not required
❑ Tunnel	❑ X509	❑ SHA	❑ Identity and Encryption (ESP)	❑ DES
	❑ Preshared key			❑ 56-bit DES
				❑ 3DES

VPN (second section)

Authentication	Tunnel Type	Encryption	
❑ MS-CHAP	❑ PPTP	❑ 40-bit MPPE	
❑ MS-CHAP v2		❑ 128-bit MPPE	
❑ EAP-TLS	❑ L2TP	Complete IPSec section	

IPSec (second section)

Mode	Authentication	Identity	Protection	Encryption
❑ Transport	❑ Kerberos	❑ MD5	❑ Identity (AH)	Not required
❑ Tunnel	❑ X509	❑ SHA	❑ Identity and Encryption (ESP)	❑ DES
	❑ Preshared key			❑ 56-bit DES
				❑ 3DES

Review

The following questions are intended to reinforce key information in this chapter. If you're unable to answer a question, review the lesson and then try to answer the question again. You can find answers to the questions in the Appendix, "Questions and Answers."

1. An organization is preparing to migrate its network to Windows 2000. You're responsible for designing the networking services design for the organization. The organization has 3,200 users located in 25 offices throughout the world. What information do you need to collect to create your design?

2. You're creating a networking services design for a multinational organization with locations in London, New York, Madrid, Paris, and Tokyo. The organization has recently connected the locations together over the Internet. As a result, the organization is concerned about protecting data transmitted between locations. What can you do to ensure the integrity and confidentiality of the data transmitted over the network?

3. You're the director of information services for a university. The students, faculty, and the administration share the same physical TCP/IP-based network. However, the computers that contain the student registration, accounting, and budgetary information are connected to the same network segment. The faculty and administration must be able to access the confidential information. The students must not be able to access confidential data transmitted within the network. How do you ensure that these requirements are met in your design?

4. Your services have been retained as a consultant to a marketing company that has five regional offices. The marketing company uses Web-based applications to record marketing information collected by the representatives in the company. The marketing company is experiencing slow response times when running the Web-based applications. In addition, the company is experiencing outages during periods of peak usage. What can you do to ensure that the requirements of the company are met in your design?

C H A P T E R   3

Multiprotocol Network Design

About This Chapter

Modern networks must support a large variety of operating systems and network protocols. Users who run these operating systems and network protocols must transparently access the same resources within the organization. Your networking services designs must support the variety of operating systems and network protocols.

In the network designs you create, you need to integrate your networking services, especially remote access and routing services, with other networking protocols. The networking protocols that you'll commonly integrate with network services are the Internetwork Packet Exchange (IPX), AppleTalk, and System Network Architecture (SNA) protocols.

Note   A full discussion of the IPX, AppleTalk, and SNA protocols is beyond the scope of this book. For more information on the IPX, AppleTalk, and SNA protocols, see *Microsoft Encyclopedia of Networking* (Redmond, Washington: Microsoft Press, 2000).

This chapter answers questions such as:

- What networking protocols must be included in the design?
- How can confidential data transmitted over the networking protocols be secured?
- How can the design be optimized to ensure users can always get access to private network resources?
- What design optimizations ensure the optimal performance for network protocols?

Before You Begin

Before you begin, you must have an overall understanding of

- Network technologies (including Ethernet, Token Ring, hubs, switches, and concentrators)
- The common transport protocol configuration for Internet Protocol (IP), Internetwork Packet Exchange (IPX), AppleTalk, and Data Link Control (DLC) (such as IP address, subnet mask, or default gateway for IP)
- IP, IPX, and AppleTalk routed networks (including subnets, network segments, routers, and IP switches)
- DLC bridged networks (including network segments, bridges, and Media Access Control (MAC) layer switches)

Lesson 1: Designs That Include Multiple Protocols

This lesson presents the requirements and constraints, both business and technical, which identify the instances when the IPX, AppleTalk, or SNA protocols are required in your network.

After this lesson, you will be able to

- Describe the role of IPX, AppleTalk, and SNA in the Microsoft Windows 2000 architecture
- Identify requirements and constraints, both business and technical, that must be collected to create a multiprotocol design
- Identify the design decisions required to create a multiprotocol network design
- Evaluate scenarios and determine when the IPX, AppleTalk, or SNA protocol implementation in Windows 2000 is an appropriate solution

Estimated lesson time: 20 minutes

IPX, AppleTalk, and SNA Protocols in Windows 2000

As you evaluate and create networking services designs, consider the network protocols that you'll include in your design. Typically, the network protocols already exist within the organization and you must ensure your design integrates with and supports these protocols.

You can provide connectivity to IPX, AppleTalk, and SNA protocol-based networks by using the corresponding protocols implemented in Windows 2000. Because IPX, AppleTalk, and SNA protocols are integral components in Windows 2000, you can connect any computer running Microsoft Windows 2000 Server, Microsoft Windows 2000 Advanced Server, or Microsoft Windows 2000 Datacenter Server to networks based on these protocols.

Figure 3.1 illustrates the portions of the IPX, AppleTalk, and SNA protocols that you examine in this chapter. Your multiprotocol design will focus on the transport and network layers of the International Standards Organization (ISO) model.

Note   The Data Link Control (DLC) protocol is the primary SNA protocol implemented in Windows 2000 that is covered in this chapter.

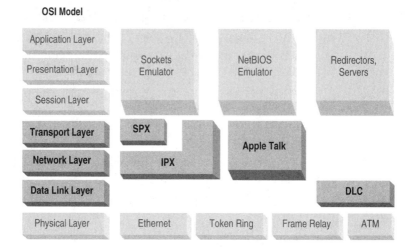

Figure 3.1   The network protocols discussed in this chapter

In Figure 3.2 you can see that IPX, AppleTalk, and DLC are implemented in
Windows 2000 as Transport Driver Interface (TDI) transport drivers. The TDI
transport drivers reside between the TDI layer and the Network Driver Interface
Specification (NDIS) layer.

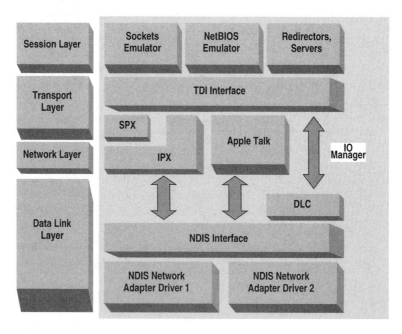

Figure 3.2   How IPX, AppleTalk, and DLC are implemented in Windows 2000

Table 3.1 lists each network protocol and describes how applications, such as networking services, can communicate with the respective protocol.

Table 3.1   How Applications Communicate with Network Protocols

Communicate With	By
IPX	The Windows Sockets and NetBIOS application interfaces
AppleTalk	Directly accessing the TDI layer for AppleTalk
DLC	Directly accessing the TDI layer for DLC

Multiprotocol Design Requirements and Constraints

Before you create your multiprotocol network design, you must collect the requirements and constraints of the organization. As you create your design, you make decisions based on the requirements and constraints, both business and technical, provided by the organization.

Table 3.2 lists each protocol and the respective requirements and constraints that you collect.

Table 3.2   Requirements and Constraints That Must Be Determined for Each Protocol

For	You Need to Determine
All protocols	Quantity of data transmitted through each network segment
	Confidentiality of the data transmitted through each network segment
	Number of network segments
	Plans for future growth
	Response times for applications that access resources through the network
	Acceptable percentage of time that users require access through the network
IPX	Number of devices that require internal IPX network numbers
	Network numbers in use by the organization
	IPX frame types in use by the organization
AppleTalk	Zones and network numbers in use by the organization
	Number of devices that exist on each network segment
SNA	Proximity of DLC-based devices, such as printers, to users that access the devices
	Media Access Control (MAC)-layer bridges or source routing bridges within the organization
	Connectivity options available to the mainframe, front-end processor, or minicomputer

Multiprotocol Design Decisions

Make your multiprotocol design decisions based on the organization's requirements and constraints. Your design must ensure that all of the organization's requirements are met. In addition, ensure that your design doesn't exceed any of the constraints, such as cost, that are mandated by the organization.

Table 3.3 lists each protocol and the respective design decisions you must make.

Table 3.3   Network Protocols and Design Decisions

For	You Must Decide
IPX	IPX network number addressing scheme
	IPX frame types in use by the organization
	Methods for protecting any confidential data transmitted over public networks
AppleTalk	Network numbers or network number range addressing scheme
	Zones to be used for organizing resources within the network
SNA	Connectivity requirements for the mainframe
	Network segments, routers, MAC-layer bridges, or source routing bridges between the terminal emulation clients and the mainframe

IPX in Multiprotocol Designs

Before you create a multiprotocol network design that includes IPX, determine whether IPX is required in your design. After you have determined that IPX is required, you can make further decisions regarding the integration of IPX in your design. IPX design concepts are discussed further in Lesson 2, "IPX Design Concepts," in this chapter.

Making the Decision

Determine whether your design requires IPX by examining the file servers, print servers, routers, and other network devices that your design must include. Table 3.4 lists the network devices you can use to identify when IPX is required and why the devices require IPX.

Table 3.4   When and Why IPX/SPX Is Required

If Your Network Includes	IPX/SPX Is Required Because
NetWare file servers	NetWare 3.x and 4.x file servers can be accessed only by IPX
NetWare print servers	NetWare print servers can be accessed only by IPX
NetWare Directory Services	NetWare 4.x servers that run NetWare Directory Services require IPX
NetWare application servers	NetWare 3.x and 4.x servers that support client/server applications can be accessed only by IPX
IPX routers	The presence of IPX routers implies that devices, other than the ones listed in this table, require IPX

Applying the Decision

Figure 3.3 illustrates the network devices in a complete solution that requires IPX as a networking protocol. When your existing network or your proposed network solutions include any of these network devices, you must consider IPX in your networking services design.

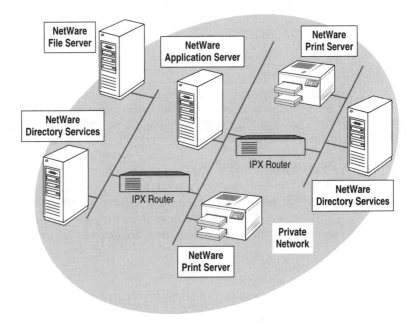

Figure 3.3   Scenario that illustrates the network devices that require the IPX protocol

AppleTalk in Multiprotocol Designs

Determine whether AppleTalk is required in your multiprotocol design. Once you have determined that AppleTalk is required, you can make further decisions regarding the integration of AppleTalk in your design. See Lesson 3, "AppleTalk Design Concepts," later in this chapter, for a further discussion of AppleTalk design concepts.

Making the Decision

You can determine whether your design requires AppleTalk by examining the file servers, print servers, routers, and other network devices that your design must include. Table 3.5 lists the network devices you can use to identify when AppleTalk is required and why the devices require AppleTalk.

Table 3.5   When and Why AppleTalk Is Required

If Your Network Includes	AppleTalk Is Required Because
AppleShare file servers	AppleShare file servers require AppleTalk protocol
AppleTalk printers	AppleTalk-based printers require AppleTalk protocol
LocalTalk networks	LocalTalk networks use the AppleTalk transport protocols exclusively
AppleTalk routers	The presence of AppleTalk routers implies that some devices require the AppleTalk protocol

Note   Macintosh computers refer to Ethernet and Token Ring as EtherTalk and TokenTalk respectively. Any networks where you observe the use of the terms EtherTalk and TokenTalk are probably based on the AppleTalk protocol.

Applying the Decision

Figure 3.4 illustrates the network devices in a complete solution that require AppleTalk as a networking protocol. You must consider AppleTalk in your networking services design when your existing network or your proposed network solutions include any of these network devices.

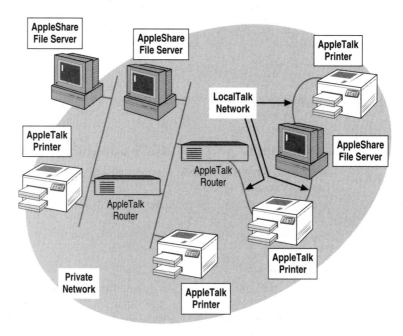

Figure 3.4   Scenario that illustrates the network devices that require the AppleTalk protocol

SNA in Multiprotocol Designs

Before you create a multiprotocol network design that includes Systems Network Architecture (SNA), you must determine whether SNA or SNA-specific protocols are required in your design. After you have determined that SNA is required in your design, you can make further decisions regarding the integration of SNA in your design. SNA design concepts are discussed further in Lesson 4, "SNA Design Concepts," later in this chapter.

Making the Decision

You can determine whether your design requires SNA by examining the mainframes, minicomputers, terminal emulators, print servers, gateways, and other network devices that your design must include. You can connect most SNA devices to your network by using Transmission Control Protocol/Internet Protocol (TCP/IP) or Data Link Control (DLC). This lesson focuses on the use of DLC in an SNA solution. For more information on creating TCP/IP network designs, review Chapter 2, "TCP/IP Network Design."

Table 3.6 lists the network devices you can use to identify when SNA is required and why the devices require SNA.

Table 3.6   When and Why DLC Protocol Is Required in an SNA Solution

If Your Network Includes	DLC Protocol Might Be Required
Mainframe computers	To access mainframe computers when TCP/IP can't be used
AS/400 computers	To access AS/400 computers (required)
Front-end processors	To access front-end processors (required)
3270/5250 gateways	To connect to mainframe and AS/400 computers using 3270 and 5250 gateways, respectively
3270/5250 terminal emulation	To connect directly to AS/400 and mainframe computers using 3270 and 5250 terminal emulation software, respectively
DLC printers	To access DLC-based printers (required)
MAC layer bridges	To support routing for some devices using SNA protocols; SNA protocols are not routable, so a MAC-layer bridge implies the presence of some devices that require DCL

Note   Many SNA solutions now use TCP/IP to communicate directly from 3270/5250 gateways and terminal emulators. Review the specifications of your gateway and terminal emulators for details.

Applying the Decision

Figure 3.5 illustrates the network components in a complete solution that requires SNA protocols. Integrate SNA in your networking services design when your existing network or your proposed network solutions include any of these network components.

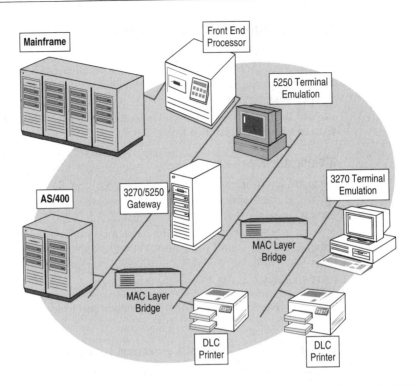

Figure 3.5   Scenario that illustrates the network devices that require the DLC protocol

Lesson 2: IPX Design Concepts

After this lesson, you will be able to

- Evaluate a physical network and create an IPX addressing design
- Create solutions where IPX networks have more than one IPX frame type
- Create solutions where IPX networks are connected over IP-routed networks by IPX/IP tunnels
- Create solutions where IPX data transmissions are protected by virtual private network (VPN) tunnels
- Create solutions where IPX networks exchange data with IP networks using Microsoft Proxy Server

Estimated lesson time: 30 minutes

IPX Addressing Design

As with an IP network, you must create a valid IPX addressing design for data to be properly exchanged on IPX-routed networks. As the complexity of the physical network increases, the complexity of your IPX addressing design also increases.

Making the Decision

All the devices on your IPX network require an IPX address. Figure 3.6 illustrates an IPX Internetwork address. An IPX Internetwork address is comprised of the following.

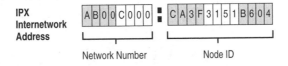

IPX Internetwork Address

| A | B | 0 | 0 | C | 0 | 0 | 0 | : | C | A | 3 | F | 3 | 1 | 5 | 1 | B | 6 | 0 | 4 |

Network Number   Node ID

Figure 3.6   Illustration of an IPX Internetwork address

- **Network number**   The network number is an eight-digit hexadecimal number that uniquely identifies a network segment. Network numbers must be unique within your IPX Internetwork. You must assign a network number to
  - Each physical network segment in your network
  - Each file server, print server, or application server that advertises its services by Service Advertising Protocol (SAP)
- **Node ID**   The node ID is a 12-digit hexadecimal number that uniquely identifies a host computer on a network segment. Node IDs must be unique within an IPX network number.

Note   Node IDs are typically assigned automatically. For Ethernet, Token Ring, and other network types, the node ID is the MAC address of the network adapter.

Each file server, print server, and application server requires an *internal* IPX network number. An internal IPX network number is the *logical* IPX network number used by applications (such as file servers, print servers, database servers, or other application servers) running on that computer.

Internal IPX network numbers create a virtual network segment that allows client computers to direct IPX traffic to a specific application running on a specific server. All applications running on a server share the same IPX network number, but have unique node IDs, as is the case for network interfaces. Unlike network interfaces, however, these applications automatically allocate their own unique node ID.

Note   All IPX devices connected to the same physical network segment must assign the same IPX network number to the interfaces connected to the network segment.

Applying the Decision

Figure 3.7 illustrates the devices on your IPX network that require IPX network numbers. Segments A, B, and C each require a unique *physical* IPX network number.

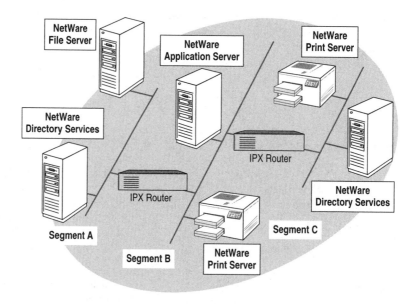

Figure 3.7   Illustration of the devices in an IPX Internetwork that require IPX network numbers

Figure 3.8 illustrates the proper assignment of IPX network numbers. Each network segment, file server, print server, and application server is assigned a network number. Networks 2, 4, 7, 9, 10, 12, and 15 are physical network segments. The remaining network numbers are assigned to internal IPX network numbers.

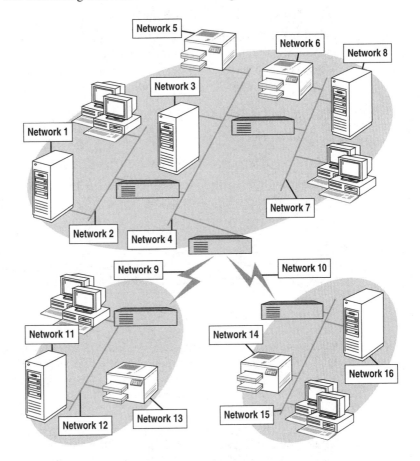

Figure 3.8   Illustration showing the proper assignment of network numbers in an
IPX network

Note The network number is automatically assigned to client computers by the
routers, print servers, and file servers attached to the same network segment.

When creating your IPX network number design, create *meaningful* network
numbers. You can create IPX network number schemes by assigning network
numbers that indicate

- Geographic location, such as a campus, building, floor, or wing
- Computer or operating system, such as UNIX, Macintosh, or Windows–based
  systems

- Relationship to other network protocols, such as IP; for example, you can create an IPX network number of 10110 that corresponds to an IP network number, 10.1.1.0

Determining IPX Frame Types

Select the IPX frame types for your network so that IPX-based devices can communicate with one another. You can enable Microsoft Windows 95, Microsoft Windows 98, Microsoft Windows NT 4, and Windows 2000 to automatically detect the IPX frame type and prevent IPX frame type configuration errors.

Making the Decision

You should select

- Ethernet_II when the Ethernet MAC frames contain Ethernet II protocol numbers
- Ethernet_802.3 when supporting NetWare 3.x and older versions
- Ethernet_802.2 when supporting NetWare 4.x and newer versions
- Ethernet_ SNAP when supporting Macintosh computers that use IPX

Note   Your network can use IPX frame types other than the default. For example, NetWare 4.x servers can be configured for Ethernet_II IPX frame types.

By default, computers running Windows 95, Windows 98, Windows NT 4.0, and Windows 2000 access Microsoft file and print services by using NetBIOS over IPX (NBIPX). You can configure Windows 95 and Windows 98 computers to access resources on other computers through *direct hosting*. Direct hosting allows Windows 95 and Windows 98 computers to access Microsoft file and print services on computers running Windows NT 4, and Windows 2000 without NetBIOS.

Note   You can support direct hosting on Windows 95 and Windows 98 only as client computers. Windows NT 4.0 and Windows 2000 support direct hosting only as file and print servers.

As you incorporate the IPX frame types into your IPX network design

- **Provide IPX routing between different IPX frame types on the same network segment**   To provide connectivity between IPX-based devices that use different IPX frame types, use an IPX router to forward packets between the two devices.
- **Minimize the number of IPX frame types in use**   IPX-based network devices that use different IPX frame types can't communicate directly with each other. By reducing the number of IPX frame types, you can reduce the load on routers in your network.

- **Use automatic IPX frame type detection** Eliminate the manual configuration of the IPX protocol by allowing Windows 2000 to automatically detect the IPX frame type. However, if your network includes more than one IPX frame type on the same network, explicitly specify the IPX frame type that you want.
- **Avoid IPX direct hosting** As previously mentioned, direct hosting depends on the operating system. Other desktop operating systems, application servers, and print servers might not be able to access file and print resources on a server that supports only direct hosting.

Applying the Decision

Figure 3.9 illustrates a network that has multiple IPX frame types. Segments 2, 4, and 5 support a single IPX frame type within each network segment. You don't need to provide IPX routing within Segments 2, 4, and 5 because of different IPX

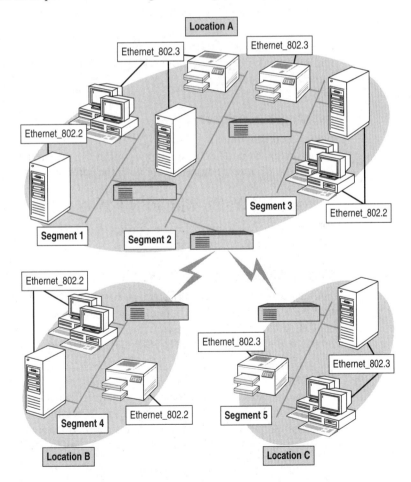

Figure 3.9 Illustration showing a network with multiple IPX frame types

frame types. However, Segments 1 and 3 support more than one IPX frame type on a network segment. You need to provide IPX routing *within* Segment 1 and 3.

Connecting IPX Networks over IP Routed Networks

Many organizations that use IPX in their local private network connect locations over the Internet. You can encapsulate IPX packets inside Point-to-Point Tunneling Protocol (PPTP) or Layer Two Tunneling Protocol (L2TP) tunnels. Once you have encapsulated the IPX packets, they can be transmitted through any IP-routed network.

Making the Decision

Select IPX encapsulation in PPTP or L2TP packets

- When the organization has an existing IP-routed infrastructure
- To reduce costs by using the Internet for connectivity

Note   You can also use Routing and Remote Access to tunnel IPX traffic from remote access clients, through an IP-routed VPN connection, to a remote access server.

Applying the Decision

Figure 3.10 illustrates the use of IPX encapsulation in your private network. Locations A, B, and C communicate within the private network using IPX. Routers B, D, and E communicate with the Internet using IP.

Protect IPX Traffic with VPN Tunnels

IPX has no native support for data protection. Instead, you must protect confidential data with VPN data encryption.

Making the Decision

You can use any of the data protection methods available to VPN to protect IPX traffic encapsulated in VPN tunnels. For more information on protecting confidential data by using VPN, review the information in Chapter 2, "Networking Protocol Design," Lesson 3 "TCP/IP Data Protection."

Applying the Decision

Figure 3.11 illustrates how to protect data in IPX packets transmitted over public networks with VPN tunnels. Routers A and B establish a VPN tunnel between Locations A and B. Because the data transmitted between the locations is encapsulated in IP packets, you can encrypt the data by any VPN encryption method.

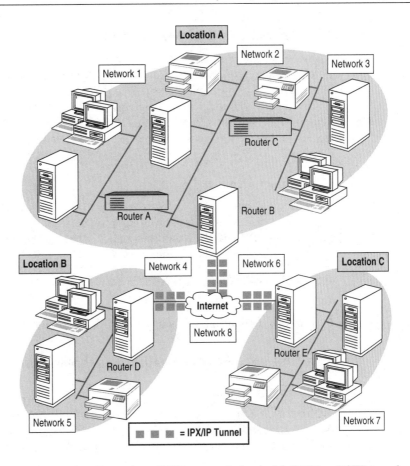

Figure 3.10 Illustration of IPX encapsulation inside PPTP or L2TP tunnels

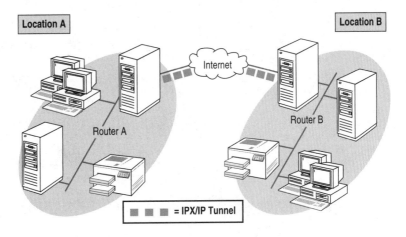

Figure 3.11 Illustration of how to protect data in IPX packets transmitted over public networks with VPN tunnels

IPX Network and IP Network Interoperability

Many networking services designs created for existing IPX networks require access to IP networks. You can create an IPX to IP gateway with Microsoft Proxy Server 2.0. By using the Microsoft Proxy Server Client software, you can access IP-based networks and servers from any IPX-based desktop computers running Windows 95, Windows 98, Windows NT 4.0, or Windows 2000. For more information on Proxy Server, see Chapter 6, "Proxy Server in Internet and Intranet Designs."

Making the Decision

You can use Proxy Server to create an IPX to IP gateway when you're unable, or the organization is unwilling, to migrate the network to IP. In addition, you can include both IPX and IP within the organization, but the routers required by your design will be more expensive.

Include Proxy Server as an IPX to IP gateway in your network design when you want

- IPX-based clients and servers on the private network to access Internet-based resources
- Internet-based users to access IPX-based resources on the private network

Applying the Decision

Figure 3.12 illustrates a scenario that uses Proxy Server in an IPX private network to interoperate with IP networks. The private network is comprised of network segments that include only IPX. The proxy server connects the IPX-based private network to the Internet.

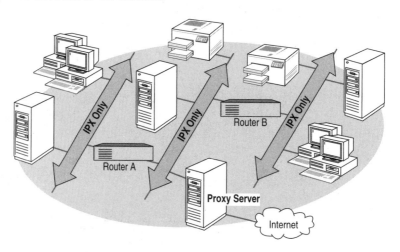

Figure 3.12   Scenario where Proxy Server connects an IPX-based network to the Internet

Activity 3.1: Evaluating a Networking Protocol Design

In this activity, you're presented with a scenario. To complete the activity:

1. Evaluate the scenario and determine its design requirements

2. Answer questions regarding your design recommendations

Figure 3.13 illustrates a scenario for a structural engineering consulting firm. The engineering firm's central office is located in Winnipeg, with branch offices in Vancouver, Toronto, and Montreal. Servers in the central office host the company's Web site. The Web site describes the services provided by the firm and provides a list of projects managed by the firm.

Figure 3.13   Structural engineering consulting firm scenario

Currently, the firm is running Microsoft Windows 2000 Professional and Windows 2000 Server on desktop and server computers respectively. The firm has selected Active Directory to provide directory services.

The engineering firm has acquired another structural engineering firm. The central office for the acquired engineering firm is in Calgary, with branch offices in Edmonton and Halifax.

The Calgary office has 65 administrative and support personnel. The Edmonton and Halifax offices each have 7 administrative and support personnel. The Calgary, Edmonton, and Halifax offices each support 250 to 300 engineers that work in the field. None of the new offices are connected to one another. The

Calgary, Edmonton, and Halifax offices all have NetWare 4.2 file and print servers.

Answer the following questions concerning your design recommendations. You can find answers to the questions in the Appendix, "Questions and Answers."

1. As a consultant to the engineering firm, you're responsible for creating the networking services design. What network protocols must your design include and why are the network protocols required?

2. The engineering firm wants to connect all locations to the Winnipeg central office so the engineers can access Web-based project management and time and billing software. However, the firm wants to migrate the new offices to IP over the next year. As the consultant, what recommendations do you make to the firm?

3. The engineering firm transmits confidential customer information between offices. The offices are connected to each other by using the Internet. The engineering firm wants to use the strongest data encryption possible. What security recommendations do you make to the firm?

Lesson 3: AppleTalk Design Concepts

After this lesson, you will be able to
- Evaluate a physical network and create an AppleTalk addressing design
- Evaluate network resources and create an AppleTalk zone design

Estimated lesson time: 20 minutes

AppleTalk Addressing Design

Many of the networking services designs that you create will include Macintosh computers. All Macintosh computers can use the AppleTalk Phase 2 protocol to communicate between computers and printers.

Note   You can also connect Macintosh computers and printers to your network with TCP/IP. When your network is based on TCP/IP, to reduce network complexity, consider converting Macintosh computers and printers to use TCP/IP instead of AppleTalk.

AppleTalk addressing is similar to IP addressing because AppleTalk addresses are *logical* addresses. In fact, AppleTalk networks use AppleTalk Address Resolution Protocol (AARP) to resolve AppleTalk addresses to MAC addresses in the same manner that IP networks use Address Resolution Protocol (ARP) to resolve IP addresses to MAC addresses.

Making the Decision

Figure 3.14 illustrates an AppleTalk address. An AppleTalk address is comprised of the following.

- **Network number**   The network number is a 16-bit decimal number that uniquely identifies an entire network segment or a portion of a network segment. Network numbers must be unique within your AppleTalk network. The AppleTalk network number is also known as *network range* or *cable range*. You must assign
  - At least one network number to each physical network segment in your network

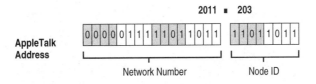

Figure 3.14   Illustration of an AppleTalk address

    ■ Additional network numbers for every 253 devices on the same network segment

---

Note   When a network segment currently contains or will contain more than 253 devices, you must assign additional AppleTalk network numbers to a network segment. Ethernet and Token Ring networks can support more than 253 devices on a single network segment. As a result, any Ethernet or Token Ring network segments that contain more than 253 devices requires additional network numbers.

- **Node ID**   The node ID is an 8-bit decimal number that uniquely identifies a host computer within a network number. The node ID is automatically assigned within a network number. AppleTalk Phase 2 supports no more than 253 hosts within a network number.

Applying the Decision

Figure 3.15 illustrates a scenario that includes a TokenTalk network segment, an EtherTalk network segment, and a LocalTalk network segment. This design requires at least three network numbers, one for each network segment. You might require additional network numbers for the TokenTalk and EtherTalk network segments if either segment contains more than 253 devices.

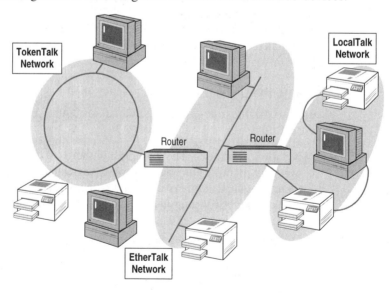

Figure 3.15   Scenario showing network numbers in an AppleTalk network

When creating an AppleTalk addressing scheme

- **Base the length of your network number range on the number of nodes you expect on the physical network**   In the scenario depicted in Figure 3.15, if you assign 1024-1099 to the EtherTalk network segment, you can place up to 19,228 nodes, (1024-1099)*253, on the EtherTalk network segment. If you assign 1400-1450 to the TokenTalk network segment, you can place up to 12,903 nodes, (1450-1400)*253, on the TokenTalk network segment.

- **Assign network numbers that leave room for expansion**   In the scenario depicted in Figure 3.15, if you assign 1024-1099 to the EtherTalk network segment, assign 1400-1450 to the TokenTalk network segment. You can use the range between 1100-1399 for future expansion on the EtherTalk network segment.

- **Network numbers are essentially arbitrary, but must be unique**   In the scenario depicted in Figure 3.15, if you assign 1024-1250 to the EtherTalk network segment and 1200-1450 to the TokenTalk network segment, you have an *overlap* of network number ranges.

Note Unlike EtherTalk and TokenTalk networks, LocalTalk networks support only a single network number.

AppleTalk Zone Design

Users locate network resources within an AppleTalk network by using AppleTalk zones. AppleTalk zones are very similar to Windows 2000 domains, sites, organizational units, or workgroups.

Making the Decision

Create AppleTalk zones to group resources together so users can easily locate network resources.

As you create your AppleTalk zone design

- **Base zones on geographic, departmental, business division, or other logical groupings**   Create an AppleTalk zone design that is meaningful to the users in the organization. Specify zone names that represent logical groupings of computers within the organization. Avoid creating cryptic or arbitrary zone-naming conventions.

- **Optimize the number of zones**   Ensure that the number of zones is the minimum number of zones required. As the number of zones increases, users need to look through more zones to find network resources.

  In addition, zone information must be propagated throughout the entire network. As the number of zones increases, the quantity of information exchanged between AppleTalk routers increases.

- **Remember that an AppleTalk zone is a grouping of one or more network numbers**   An AppleTalk zone can be comprised of one or more network numbers. However, a network number can't belong to more than one zone.

Applying the Decision

All the devices on your AppleTalk network belong to a zone. Figure 3.16 shows how you can group resources into AppleTalk zones. The resources in Zone 1 are most commonly used by one department or division. Zones 2 and 3 contain resources that are used by other departments, divisions, or groups of users.

AppleTalk zones are grouped by the network numbers assigned to the resources. In the scenario presented in Figure 3.16, Zone 1 contains resources from Segments A and B. All the resources on Segment A can have the same network number. The resource that belongs to Zone 1 on Segment B must be a different network number from the resources that belong to Zone 2.

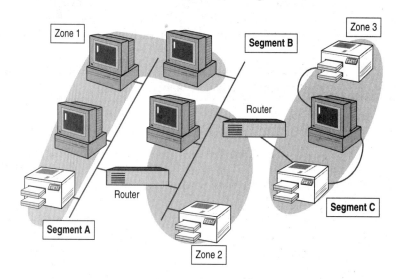

Figure 3.16   Scenario showing zones in an AppleTalk network

Lesson 4: SNA Design Concepts

After this lesson, you will be able to

- Evaluate a physical network and create an SNA network protocol design
- Create SNA network protocol designs that use TCP/IP for SNA connectivity

Estimated lesson time: 10 minutes

SNA Network Protocol Design

Although many organizations are currently transitioning from mainframe-based and minicomputer-based environments, many designs that you create will include SNA network protocols. The SNA protocol that is common to most SNA networks is the DLC protocol.

Making the Decision

DLC is a nonroutable network protocol that exists at the data link layer in the ISO model. DLC packets are transmitted between network segments by using *source-routing* bridges or MAC layer bridges. MAC layer bridges allow more network traffic to propagate between network segments than source-routing bridges.

Note   In addition to providing SNA connectivity to front-end processors, mainframes, or AS/400 computers, DLC can provide connectivity to network printers.

You can integrate DLC into your network by

- Including routers that can perform bridging as well as routing functions
- Locating users and the resources the users must access on the same network segment to eliminate the need for bridging
- Installing SNA gateways, such as Microsoft SNA Server, to reduce the number of network segments that require DLC

Applying the Decision

Figure 3.17 illustrates a network that uses DLC to communicate with the AS/400 and front-end processor. Bridges A and B pass the DLC packets between the network segments. The terminal emulation software and printer drivers communicate directly with their respective devices using DLC.

Note   Ensure that all DLC devices are on the same network segment or on network segments that are connected with source routers or MAC layer bridges.

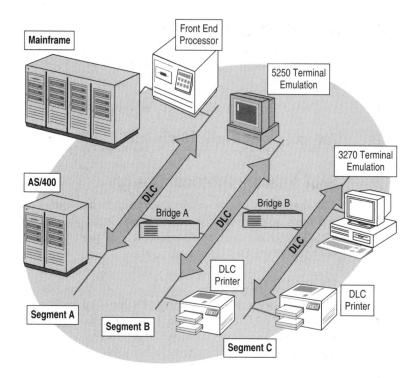

Figure 3.17   Illustration of a network that uses the DLC network protocol for SNA and network printer connectivity

SNA and TCP/IP Integration

In most instances, you don't want to support a bridged network environment unless the number of network nodes is extremely small. As more network nodes are added, the amount of unnecessary traffic sent between network segments increases accordingly. You can integrate an SNA-based network with TCP/IP to reduce the unnecessary traffic between network segments.

Making the Decision

You can integrate SNA-based devices with TCP/IP by

- **Connecting SNA-based devices through an SNA gateway, such as Microsoft SNA Server**   Integrate SNA-based devices with TCP/IP by using an SNA gateway when

  - The management and operations staff of the mainframe or AS/400 is unable or unwilling to use a protocol other than DLC

  - You can upgrade DLC-based printer interfaces to Line Printer Remote (LPR)-based printer interfaces

  - The cost of adding a 3270/5250 gateway is less than the cost of adding TCP/IP to the front-end processor, mainframe, or AS/400

Note You can create a similar solution using IPX instead of IP. Most 3270/5250 gateway products support both IPX and IP.

- **Installing TCP/IP on the front-end processor, mainframe, or AS/400** Integrate SNA-based devices with TCP/IP by installing TCP/IP on the devices when

  - The management and operations staff of the mainframe, front-end processor, or AS/400 is able to use a protocol besides DLC

  - The cost of adding IP to the front-end processor, mainframe, or AS/400 is less than a 3270/5250 gateway solution

  - You can upgrade DLC-based printer interfaces to LPR-based printer interfaces

Note There are many other issues to consider when using a 3270/5250 gateway in an SNA solution. For more information on designing SNA connectivity solutions, see the Microsoft SNA Server deployment and support Web site at *http://www.microsoft.com/sna.*

Applying the Decision

Figure 3.18 illustrates a scenario in which DLC is used only on Segment A. Segments B and C use IP to communicate between network segments. The DLC interfaces in the printers have been upgraded to LPR interfaces to support IP.

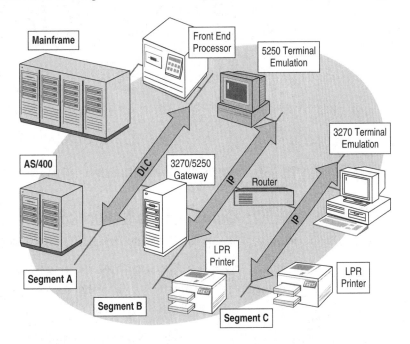

Figure 3.18 Scenario in which IP and DLC coexist on the same network

The 3270/5250 SNA gateway that connects Segments A and B translates the SNA traffic from the IP portion of the network to the DLC portion of the network. The terminal emulation software encapsulates SNA packets inside the IP packets. The SNA gateway removes the SNA packets from the IP packets and forwards them to the AS/400 and front-end processor.

Figure 3.19 illustrates a scenario in which IP is used on all network segments. The DLC interfaces in all printers have been upgraded to LPR interfaces to support IP. In addition, IP has been added to the AS/400 and to the front-end processor.

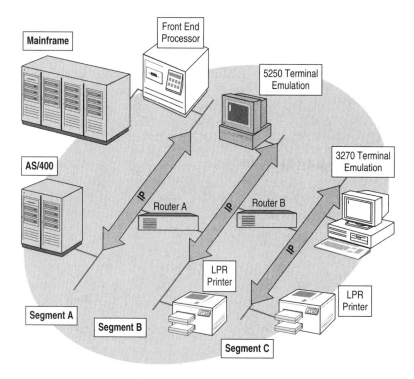

Figure 3.19   Scenario in which the entire network is based on IP

Activity 3.2: Completing a Network Protocol Design

In this activity, you're presented with a scenario. To complete the activity:

1. Evaluate the scenario and determine its design requirements

2. Answer the questions regarding your design recommendations

Figure 3.20 illustrates a scenario for the structural engineering consulting firm presented earlier in this chapter. A year after the initial implementation of your network design, the firm acquires yet another company with several additional offices. The Calgary office obtains an AS/400 to support accounting, billing, and job estimation.

Figure 3.20   Structural engineering consulting firm scenario with additional locations

Answer the following questions concerning your design recommendations. You can find answers to the questions in the Appendix, "Questions and Answers."

1. The management at the Winnipeg office must access the applications running on the AS/400 in the Calgary office. Because the number of employees in Calgary is small, the network consists of a single, nonrouted Ethernet network segment. The users at the Calgary office connect to the AS/400 using DLC. How can you provide management access to the AS/400?

2. While you're creating your design, you find out that a number of Macintosh-based computers and printers exist at the Halifax office. How does the presence of the Macintosh-based computers and printers affect your design?

Lab: Creating a Multiprotocol Network Design

After this lab, you will be able to

- Evaluate a scenario and determine the design requirements
- Create a multiprotocol network design based on the design requirements

Estimated lab time: 45 minutes

In this lab, you're a consultant hired to create a multiprotocol network design for a museum. The museum has a central administrative office and five separate museums in a campus setting.

To complete this lab:

1. Examine the networking environment presented in the scenario, the network diagrams, the business requirements and constraints, and the technical requirements and constraints

2. Use the worksheet for each location to assist you in creating your multiprotocol network design (you can find completed sample design worksheets on the Supplemental Course Materials CD-ROM in the Completed Worksheets folder)

3. Create, eliminate, or replace existing networking devices and network segments when required

4. Ensure that your design fulfills the business requirements and constraints, and the technical requirements and constraints, of the scenario by

   - Including the appropriate protocols on each network segment

   - Assigning the appropriate network address numbers on each network segment

   - Optimizing your design to provide the security, availability, performance, and affordability

Note   To reduce the length of time for this lab, create a multiprotocol network design only for the central office and two of the museums.

Scenario

A foundation that manages a group of museums is restructuring its network (shown in Figure 3.21) in preparation for deploying Windows 2000. The foundation has a central office (shown in Figure 3.23) for the administration and management of the museums. The foundation manages a Museum of Natural History (shown in Figure 3.25), an American History Museum (shown in Figure 3.25), an Aerospace Museum (shown in Figure 3.25), a Museum of Art (shown in Figure 3.26), and a Museum of Modern Art (shown in Figure 3.26).

A 100Mbps Ethernet fiber-optic network connects the museums to the foundation's central office. A T1 line at the central office connects the foundation to the Internet. Figure 3.22 illustrates the hierarchical router structure of the foundation.

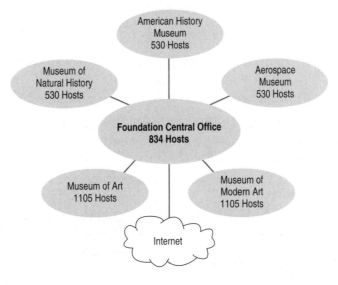

Figure 3.21   Overview network diagram of the foundation that manages the museums

In addition to the funding received through the foundation, each museum receives individual grants and funding. As a result, each museum has different hardware and operating system platforms.

The network in each museum supports

- The museum curators and docents that work in the individual museums
- Interactive displays and kiosks that museum visitors use while visiting the museum

Business Requirements and Constraints

The foundation has a number of requirements and constraints that are based on the business model of the foundation. As you create your multiprotocol design, ensure that it meets the business requirements and stays within the business constraints.

To achieve the business requirements and constraints, your design must

- Utilize the existing hardware and operating systems in each museum. As a result

- The interactive displays, exhibits, and kiosks at the Museum of Art and the Museum of Modern Art use Macintosh computers that were provided by a corporate grant

- The file and print servers used by the museum curators and docents at the Museum of Natural History, the American History Museum, and the Aerospace Museum are NetWare 4.2 servers that were donated to the museums

- The mainframe computer at the central office runs applications that manage the foundation's financial information and catalogs the artifacts currently on exhibit at the museums

- Provide Internet access to all museum curators and docents

- Support Active Directory as the directory service for the foundation

- Provide an Internet presence for the foundation that is hosted on the Web servers in the central office

- Provide access to the mainframe computer to all museum curators and docents

- Ensure that connectivity between the individual museums and the central office is available 24 hours a day, 7 days a week

- Ensure that the interactive displays, exhibits, and kiosks are available during normal museum hours of operation

Technical Requirements and Constraints

The applications that run within each museum require connectivity within each museum, with other museums, and with the foundation's central office. These applications run on the computers used by the museum curators and docents, and on computers used in interactive exhibits or kiosks.

The existing physical network, hardware, and operating systems place certain technical requirements and constraints on your design. As you create your multiprotocol design, ensure that your design meets the technical requirements and stays within the technical constraints.

To achieve the technical requirements and constraints, your design must

- Retain the existing connectivity to the mainframe in the central office (currently direct 3270 coaxial connections) so users can connect to the mainframe throughout the network

- Isolate the foundation's private network from the Internet

- Include only the protocols that are required on each network segment

- Include only TCP/IP on the museum backbone (Segment F)

- Provide network addressing for each protocol on each network segment

- Utilize the existing TCP/IP address, 172.16.0.0/16, which is assigned to the foundation

Note For the purposes of this exercise, treat the private IP address range
172.16.0.0/16 as a public address.

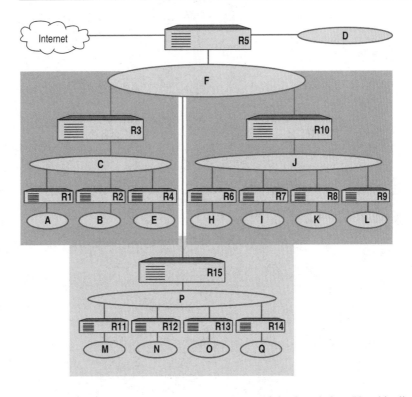

Figure 3.22   The hierarchical router structure of the foundation. Use this diagram as
you develop the IP, IPX, and AppleTalk network numbering schemes.

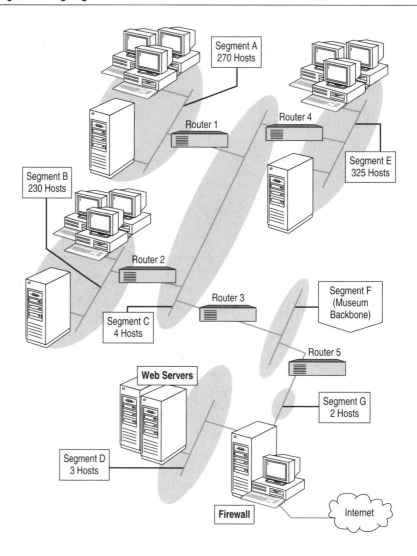

Figure 3.23   The existing network at the foundation central office. In addition to the devices illustrated here, there is a front-end processor and a mainframe computer. The front-end processor and the mainframe computer are illustrated in Figure 3.24

Design Worksheet – Foundation Central Office (for Figure 3.23)

Segment	Protocols and addressing	Comments
	❏ TCP/IP, Network number: _____ ❏ IPX, Network number(s): _____ ❏ AppleTalk, Network Range: _____ ❏ DLC	
	❏ TCP/IP, Network number: _____ ❏ IPX, Network number(s): _____ ❏ AppleTalk, Network Range: _____ ❏ DLC	
	❏ TCP/IP, Network number: _____ ❏ IPX, Network number(s): _____ ❏ AppleTalk, Network Range: _____ ❏ DLC	
	❏ TCP/IP, Network number: _____ ❏ IPX, Network number(s): _____ ❏ AppleTalk, Network Range: _____ ❏ DLC	
	❏ TCP/IP, Network number: _____ ❏ IPX, Network number(s): _____ ❏ AppleTalk, Network Range: _____ ❏ DLC	
	❏ TCP/IP, Network number: _____ ❏ IPX, Network number(s): _____ ❏ AppleTalk, Network Range: _____ ❏ DLC	
	❏ TCP/IP, Network number: _____ ❏ IPX, Network number(s): _____ ❏ AppleTalk, Network Range: _____ ❏ DLC	

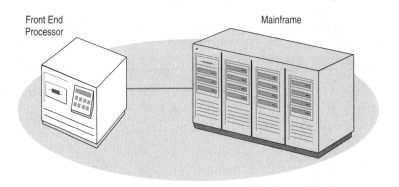

Figure 3.24   The mainframe and front-end processor at the foundation central office. Currently, users connect to mainframe by using coaxial terminal emulation cards and a separate coaxial cabling system.

Design Worksheet – Central Office Mainframe (for Figure 3.24)

❏ **Install MAC layer bridges in parallel with all routers.**	
	Reason for choosing this solution:
❏ **Install a 3270/5050 gateway.**	
	Reason for choosing this solution:
	Connect the mainframe side of the gateway to:
	Connect the network side of the gateway to:
❏ **Add TCP/IP to the mainframe computer.**	
	Reason for choosing this solution:
	Connect the mainframe directly to:

Complete the following worksheet by

1. Selecting one of the solutions
2. Justifying your solution
3. Specifying the design information required by the solution

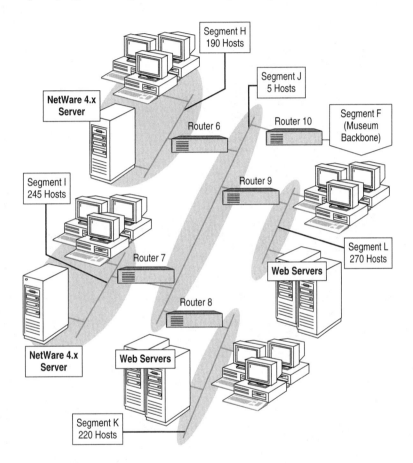

Figure 3.25   The existing network at the Museum of Natural History, the American History Museum, and the Aerospace Museum. For the purposes of this lab, assume that all these museums have the same network configuration.

Design Worksheet – Museum of Natural History (for Figure 3.25)

Segment	Protocols and addressing	Comments
	☐ TCP/IP, Network number: _____ ☐ IPX, Network number(s): _____ ☐ AppleTalk, Network Range: _____ ☐ DLC	
	☐ TCP/IP, Network number: _____ ☐ IPX, Network number(s): _____ ☐ AppleTalk, Network Range: _____ ☐ DLC	
	☐ TCP/IP, Network number: _____ ☐ IPX, Network number(s): _____ ☐ AppleTalk, Network Range: _____ ☐ DLC	
	☐ TCP/IP, Network number: _____ ☐ IPX, Network number(s): _____ ☐ AppleTalk, Network Range: _____ ☐ DLC	
	☐ TCP/IP, Network number: _____ ☐ IPX, Network number(s): _____ ☐ AppleTalk, Network Range: _____ ☐ DLC	

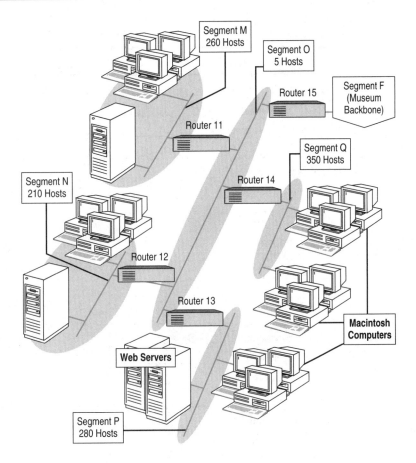

Figure 3.26   The existing network at the Museum of Art and the Museum of
Modern Art. For the purposes of this lab, assume that all these
museums have the same network configuration.

Design Worksheet – Museum of Modern Art (for Figure 3.26)

Segment	Protocols and addressing	Comments
	❑ TCP/IP, Network number: _____ ❑ IPX, Network number(s): _____ ❑ AppleTalk, Network Range: _____ ❑ DLC	
	❑ TCP/IP, Network number: _____ ❑ IPX, Network number(s): _____ ❑ AppleTalk, Network Range: _____ ❑ DLC	
	❑ TCP/IP, Network number: _____ ❑ IPX, Network number(s): _____ ❑ AppleTalk, Network Range: _____ ❑ DLC	
	❑ TCP/IP, Network number: _____ ❑ IPX, Network number(s): _____ ❑ AppleTalk, Network Range: _____ ❑ DLC	
	❑ TCP/IP, Network number: _____ ❑ IPX, Network number(s): _____ ❑ AppleTalk, Network Range: _____ ❑ DLC	

Review

The following questions are intended to reinforce key information in this chapter. If you're unable to answer a question, review the lesson and then try to answer the question again. You can find answers to the questions in the Appendix, "Questions and Answers."

1. Your organization wants to integrate Windows 2000 into its existing network. Your organization uses Active Directory for directory services. The network is comprised of a variety of operating systems including Windows 95, Windows 98, Windows NT 4.0, NetWare 4.x, UNIX, and Macintosh operating systems. What information do you need to collect to determine the influence of these operating systems on your networking services design?

2. You're creating a networking services design for your network that is comprised of Windows 2000 computers and Macintosh computers. Your organization has a number of locations. Each location has a number of networking segments. What information must you collect to determine the network protocol design?

3. You're creating a networking services design for an organization. The organization is comprised of 15 locations. Each location has a number of network segments that are connected by Token Ring source routing bridges. The organization has a number of mission-critical applications that run on an AS/400. All desktop computers connect directly to the AS/400 by using DLC. The network operations and support staff informs you that as the network has grown, the network utilization has increased dramatically. The organization plans to deploy Windows 2000 over the next 36 months. How can you address the network utilization concerns, while maintaining connectivity to the AS/400 and supporting the Windows 2000 deployment?

CHAPTER 4

IP Routing Designs

About This Chapter

The networks you design will likely include many network segments. Remote locations are connected over wide area networks (WANs), and because of current trends in connectivity, most of these WANs communicate over the Internet. Your networking services designs must therefore provide connectivity for these networks.

Because most networks are based on Transmission Control Protocol/Internet Protocol (TCP/IP), you must provide IP routing designs that can connect network segments and locations. To transmit sensitive information between these network segments and locations, your design must provide data security.

This chapter answers questions such as:

- In what situations are the IP routing services provided by Microsoft Windows 2000 appropriate for your design?
- Which routing protocols can minimize network route paths while reducing the network traffic required to manage IP routing tables?

- How can confidential data be transmitted securely between network segments and locations?
- How can you ensure that IP packets are always delivered when transmitted between network segments and locations?
- How can you optimize the aggregate data transfer rate between network segments and locations?

Before You Begin

Before you begin, you must have an overall understanding of

- Network technologies (including Ethernet, Token Ring, hubs, switches, and concentrators)
- The common transport protocol configuration for Internet Protocol (IP) (such as IP address, subnet mask, or default gateway for IP)
- IP routed networks (including subnets, network segments, routers, and IP switches)
- The common methods for managing unicast IP routing tables (such as static entries, autostatic routing, or dynamic routing protocols)
- Multicast IP routing including Internet Group Membership Protocol (IGMP)
- Router security technologies (including protocol filtering and router identification)
- Tunneling protocols (including how packets are encapsulated in tunnels and how tunnels are established)

Lesson 1: Designs That Include IP Routing

This lesson presents the requirements and constraints, both business and technical, that identify the IP routing services in Windows 2000 as a solution.

After this lesson, you will be able to

- Describe the role of IP routing in the Windows 2000 architecture
- Identify the business and technical requirements and constraints that must be collected to create an IP routing design
- Identify the IP routing design decisions
- Evaluate networking scenarios and determine when the IP routing services provided by Windows 2000 are an appropriate solution
- Evaluate networking scenarios and determine which capabilities and features of Windows 2000 IP routing services are appropriate

Estimated lesson time: 30 minutes

IP Routing in Windows 2000

Because Routing and Remote Access is an integral feature of Windows 2000, any computer running Microsoft Windows 2000 Server, Microsoft Windows 2000 Advanced Server, or Microsoft Windows 2000 Datacenter Server can provide IP routing for your network.

All TCP/IP devices in your network can participate in IP routing because each device maintains a routing table. Figure 4.1 illustrates the TCP/IP devices involved in IP routing.

Consider the following scenario in which a source host wants to send an IP packet to the destination host.

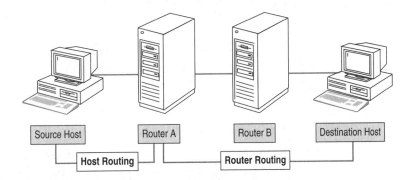

Figure 4.1   The role of various TCP/IP devices in IP routing

1. The source host determines the IP address of the destination host.

2. The source host examines its local routing table and determines that the destination host can be reached through Router A.

3. The source host sends the IP packet to Router A.

4. Router A examines its local routing table and determines that the destination host can be reached through Router B.

5. Router A forwards the IP packet to Router B.

6. Router B examines its local routing table and determines that the destination host can be reached directly.

7. Router B forwards the IP packet to the destination host.

Each of the devices in the preceding scenario participates in the routing between the source host and the destination host. The routing that occurs between the source host and Router A is known as *host routing*. The routing that occurs between Router A, Router B, and the destination host is known as *router routing*.

All TCP/IP devices must support host routing to send IP packets in an IP-routed network. Microsoft Windows 95, Microsoft Windows 98, Microsoft Windows NT 4.0, Windows 2000, UNIX, Macintosh, and other operating systems support host routing.

Hardware routers, hardware IP switches, and other hardware-based devices support router routing. The Routing and Remote Access feature in Windows 2000 provides software-based router routing.

In this chapter, you learn how to create router routing solutions with Windows 2000. To successfully create IP routing designs, you must be familiar with general routing theory and IP routing protocols.

Note   In this book, unless otherwise specified, IP routing always refers to the IP routing provided by Windows 2000. In this chapter, unless otherwise specified, IP routers are Windows 2000–based IP routers.

IP Routing Design Requirements and Constraints

Before creating a routing design, evaluate the requirements and constraints, both business and technical, of the organization. You make design decisions based on the requirements and constraints.

The list of the design requirements and constraints that you collect includes

- Characteristics of the data transmitted through the router, including
  - The amount of data transmitted through the router
  - The confidentiality of the data transmitted through the router
- Plans for future network growth

- Characteristics of existing routers including
  - Router placement
  - WAN connections in use
  - Routing protocols in use
- Response times for applications that access resources through the router
- Acceptable percentage of time that users require access through the router

IP Routing Design Decisions

To create your routing design, you must choose the

- Types of connections, persistent or nonpersistent, that each router must support
- Connection technologies, including T1, Public Switched Telephone Network (PSTN), Integrated Services Digital Network (ISDN), Digital Subscriber Line (DSL), or X.25 for each router
- Dynamic routing protocols or static routing table entries for each router
- Multiple route paths and multiple routers to improve availability and performance
- Criteria that you'll adopt to filter packet traffic
- Authentication and encryption algorithms to protect confidential data

The lessons that follow in this chapter provide the information required for you to make specific IP routing design recommendations.

Edge of Network Scenario

The most common scenario for IP routing in Windows 2000 uses an *edge of network* design. An edge of network design connects your private network to a public network, such as the Internet.

Making the Decision

When you create designs that require edge of network routers, the routers must

- **Prevent unauthorized access to private network resources**   Routing and Remote Access IP filters and virtual private network (VPN) technology prevent unauthorized access by authenticating routers and encrypting data.
- **Provide access to public network or Internet resources**   Routing and Remote Access supports Internet standards, Internet drafts, and other industry standards.
- **Protect confidential data transmitted over the public network or the Internet**   The VPN technologies in Routing and Remote Access protect confidential data by providing router identity, data integrity, and data encryption.
- **Connect to a variety of WAN technologies**   Routing and Remote Access can route IP packets over any network interface supported by Windows 2000.

Applying the Decision

Figure 4.2 illustrates a design that connects your private network to the Internet. The edge of your private network is where you connect to the Internet, in this case at Routers C and D. All network segments behind Routers C and D (Segments A, B, and C) are considered part of your private network.

Routers A and B are examples of *internal* routers. Typically, internal routers require no features other than the ability to provide IP routing. Routers A and B both reside within the private network and, in this case, aren't required to encrypt data or to identify one another.

The added security and WAN connectivity options of edge of network routers increase the cost of the routers. As a result, you can use routers without the enhanced features of Routing and Remote Access for internal routers.

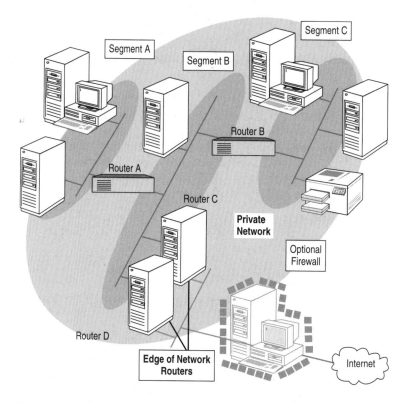

Figure 4.2   A scenario in which IP routers are used to connect a private network to the Internet

The firewall shown in Figure 4.2 is optional in your design when

- **The routers support point-to-point communications**   When you use the routers for point-to-point communications, such as connecting two or more locations, the endpoints are known. You can restrict the router so the router communicates only with the known endpoints. In addition, you can encrypt the data transmitted between the known endpoints.

- **Router filters provide sufficient security**   You can restrict the traffic Routing and Remote Access transmits and receives with IP routing filters. IP routing filters allow you to create filters that discard unauthorized traffic.

Note   IP routing filters and data encryption are discussed further in Lesson 3, "Data Protection on Unsecured Segments," in this chapter.

Multiple Location Scenario

You can identify a multiple location scenario when you connect multiple locations together over a public network, such as the Internet. You create your multiple location design based on the assumption that the locations belong to the same organization or to trusted partner organizations.

You can connect remote locations by using point-to-point leased lines or by using the Internet. Either connectivity option requires you to protect confidential data transmitted between locations.

Making the Decision

When you create designs that connect multiple locations over public networks, each router must

- **Meet all the requirements of an edge of network design**   All the Routing and Remote Access features used in an edge of network scenario are required in the multiple location scenario.

- **Authenticate routers**   Routing and Remote Access can authenticate routers and VPN tunnels with

    - User account authentication managed by the organization. For additional security, you can authenticate users accounts in Active Directory directory service

    - Machine certificates based on Kerberos V5 tickets, X509 certificates, or a preshared key

Applying the Decision

Figure 4.3 illustrates a scenario in which IP routers connect multiple locations over the Internet. At the edge of each location's network, you place a router (Routers B, D, and E) that connects the location to the Internet. Each location is a superset of the edge of network scenario.

With a multiple location design, you're extending the private network of each location to include the other locations. Routers B, D, and E are responsible for seamlessly connecting each location. Each router protects any confidential data exchanged between locations by providing router identity, data integrity, and data encryption.

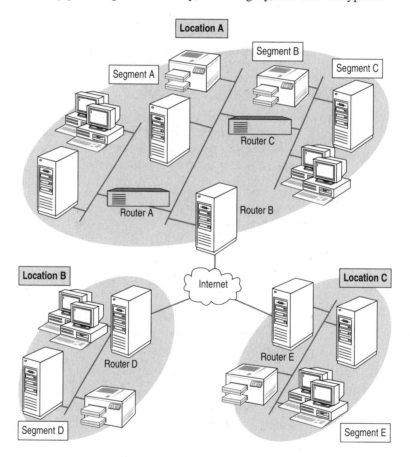

Figure 4.3   A scenario in which IP routers are used to connect multiple locations together over the Internet

Single Location Scenario

When your situation includes a single location comprised of multiple network segments, you can apply the design principles found in the single location scenario. The single location scenario is appropriate when you want to connect multiple network segments within your private network and connect your private network to the Internet.

Making the Decision

Select Routing and Remote Access as your single location design solution to reduce cost. If a computer running Windows 2000 is required for other functions, in addition to routing, you can reduce the implementation cost by incorporating IP routing onto the same computer.

A single location design solution is most appropriate for small organizations or branch offices of a larger organization. The design decisions of the single location scenario are the same as the edge of network design.

Applying the Decision

Figure 4.4 illustrates a scenario in which IP routers connect multiple network segments within a location and connect the private network to the Internet. Router A provides internal routing between Segments A, B, and C. In addition, Router A connects the private network to the Internet.

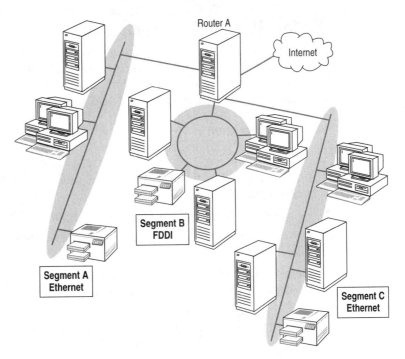

Figure 4.4 A scenario in which IP routers are used to connect multiple network segments together within a location and to the Internet

Lesson 2: Essential IP Routing Design Concepts

This lesson discusses the requirements, constraints, and design decisions that are essential when creating an IP routing design. Your design should provide essential IP routing so the router can transmit IP packets between different network segments.

After this lesson, you will be able to

- Determine the appropriate placement of routers in an IP routing design
- Identify the appropriate design specifications for each router interface
- Select the appropriate method for maintaining unicast routing tables
- Determine the appropriate instances for including an Internet Group Membership Protocol (IGMP) multicast proxy
- Determine the appropriate instances for including a Dynamic Host Configuration Protocol (DHCP) Relay Agent

Estimated lesson time: 60 minutes

Placing Routers in the Network Design

In Lesson 1 of this chapter, you examined scenarios that depicted the placement of routers within a network. The scenarios illustrated that you can place routers at the edge of your private network (edge of network routers) or within your private network (internal routers).

Making the Decision

You place routers in your design to

- Connect network segments with dissimilar local area network (LAN) or WAN technologies
- Reduce network traffic between network segments
- Prevent unauthorized network traffic between network segments by using IP filters
- Prevent unauthorized access to confidential data transmitted over public networks by using encryption and authentication

Applying the Decision

Figure 4.5 illustrates a scenario with internal and edge of network routers. Routers A and C are internal routers, while Routers B, D, and E are edge of network routers. The requirements and constraints for internal routers and edge of network routers are different.

For the purposes of this scenario, assume that

- The existing network segments are optimized to localize traffic within each network segment
- The organization isn't concerned about the security of packets within each location

Table 4.1 lists the reasons for placing internal routers and edge of network routers in your design and discusses the appropriateness of the reason in the scenario.

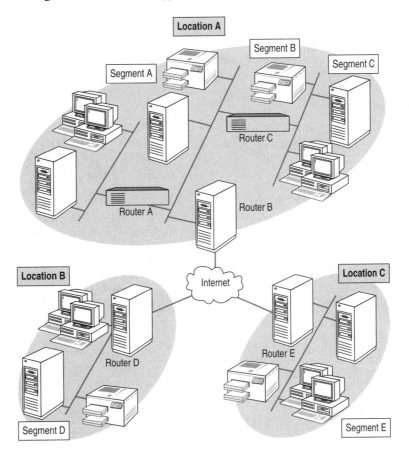

Figure 4.5 Multiple location scenario that shows internal and edge of network router placement

Table 4.1   When to Place Internal Routers or Edge of Network Routers in Your Design

Place Routers in Your Design to	Internal Routers (Routers A and C)	Edge of Network Routers (Routers B, D, and E)
Connect network segments with dissimilar LAN or WAN technologies	**Inappropriate** The network segments (Segments A, B, and C) aren't dissimilar technologies	**Appropriate** The router interfaces connected to the Internet are connecting dissimilar technologies
Reduce network traffic between network segments	**Appropriate** You want to reduce the traffic between Segments A, B, and C	**Appropriate** You want to reduce the traffic between locations
Prevent unauthorized network traffic between network segments by using IP filters	**Inappropriate** The organization isn't concerned about unauthorized traffic within each location	**Appropriate** The organization wants to block unauthorized traffic from the Internet
Prevent unauthorized access to confidential data transmitted over public networks by using encryption and authentication	**Inappropriate** The organization isn't concerned about unauthorized viewing of confidential data within each location	**Appropriate** The organization wants to prevent unauthorized viewing of confidential data transmitted between locations

The IP routing provided by Routing and Remote Access can be used as an internal router or an edge of network router. Routing and Remote Access meets all the requirements for an edge of network router. As a result, you can use Routing and Remote Access to provide a cost-effective solution.

Routing and Remote Access has features that exceed the requirements for internal routers. As a result, the cost associated with using Routing and Remote Access as an internal router might be too expensive. As a result, consider using lower cost, hardware routers as internal routers.

Figure 4.6 illustrates a scenario where Routing and Remote Access provides IP routing for private network segments and connectivity to the Internet. The requirements for Router A in this scenario are the same as the edge of network routers (Routers B, D, and E) in the scenario illustrated in Figure 4.5.

Place the router in the network so the router directly connects to Segments A, B, and C and to the Internet. By reducing the number of routers in your design, you can reduce the total cost of ownership associated with your routing design.

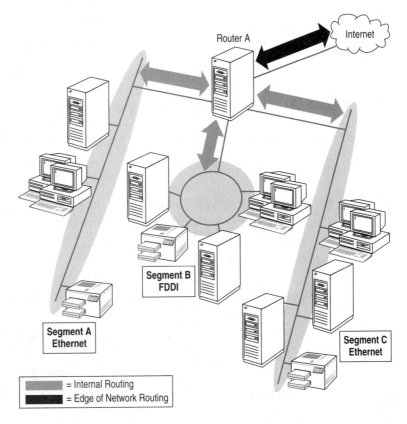

Figure 4.6   Single location scenario that illustrates the placement of a router
that provides internal and edge of network routing

Integrating Routers into an Existing Network

Most routers in your designs will have at least two network interfaces. The router
interfaces provide connectivity between the routers and the network segments in
your design.

For each interface in each router in your design, you must specify

- The IP configuration information, including the IP address and subnet mask
- The type of connection between the router interface and the network, such as
  persistent or nonpersistent
- The level of authentication, filtering, and encryption

Note   You can create a router that has a single network interface card (NIC) with
two IP addresses bound to the same interface. With this arrangement, you can
route IP packets between the two IP addresses on the same interface. Use this
method to consolidate two IP subnets on one network segment.

Router Interface IP Address Specifications

You must specify a fixed IP address and subnet for each router interface in your design.

Making the Decision

Select the IP address from the IP address range of the subnet to which the interface is directly connected. The subnet mask you assign to the router interface must match the subnet mask of the subnet to which the interface is directly connected.

Note   Most TCP/IP network designs establish standards for IP address assignment. For example, many standards reserve the values between 1 and 99 in the last octet of an IP address for routers and other network devices. As you create a design, review any existing standards in the organization.

Applying the Decision

Figure 4.7 illustrates the interfaces required in the single location scenario. For each of the interfaces, you must supply an IP address and a subnet mask.

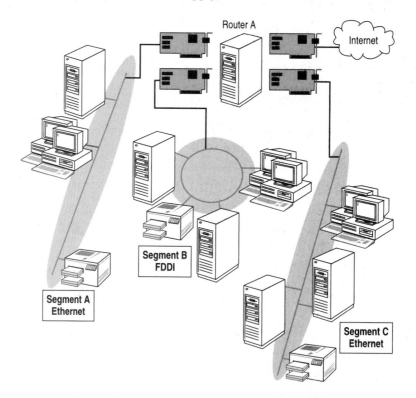

Figure 4.7   Scenario that illustrates the number of network interfaces in a router that provides internal and edge of network routing

Table 4.2 lists each network segment, the IP address range and subnet mask for the network segment, and the IP address and subnet mask assigned to the interface that connects to the network segment.

Table 4.2   Network Segments and IP Address Ranges/Subnet Masks

Network Segment	Network Segment IP Address Range/Subnet Mask	Router Interface IP Address/ Subnet Mask
Internet	10.0.0.0/8	10.0.0.1/8
A	10.0.0.0/16	10.0.0.2/16
B	10.1.0.0/16	10.1.0.1/16
C	10.2.0.0/16	10.2.0.1/16

Note   Although 10.0.0.0/8 is actually a reserved private IP address range, for the purposes of this example, assume that 10.0.0.0/8 is a valid public IP address range.

Router Interface Connection Specifications

You must specify the router interface connection for each router interface in your design. You must also specify the technology and the persistence of each router interface.

Making the Decision

The router interface connection must match the network segment technology to which the interface is directly connected. The persistence of the router interface is based on physical and VPN connections.

Table 4.3 lists the router interface types you can specify in Routing and Remote Access and the reasons for selecting the interface type.

Table 4.3   Reasons for Choosing Specific Router Interface Types

Select This Interface Type	When the Interface
LAN	▪ Appears to Routing and Remote Access as a LAN adapter ▪ Supports persistent connections ▪ Includes technologies such as Ethernet, Token Ring, Fiber Distributed Data Interface (FDDI), T1, or T34
Demand-dial	▪ Appears to Routing and Remote Access as a demand-dial adapter ▪ Supports nonpersistent connections ▪ Requires authentication (such as VPNs) or connection initiation procedures (such as DSL or ISDN) ▪ Incurs incremental costs for the amount of time the interface is active (such as ISDN)

Applying the Decision

Figure 4.8 illustrates the router interface connections required in the multiple location scenario. For each interface in each router, you must determine the router interface type.

For the purposes of this scenario, assume that

- The network segments (Segments A, B, C, D, and E) within each location are 100Mbps Ethernet
- Each location is directly connected to the Internet by using a T1 connection
- Any confidential data transmitted between locations must be protected

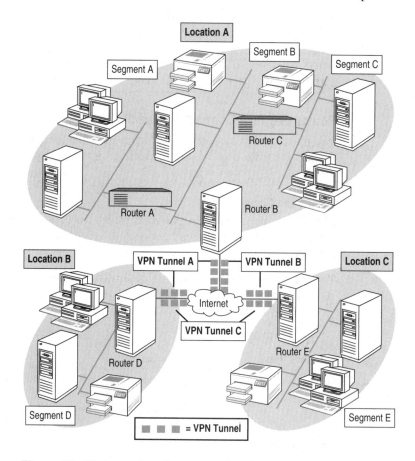

Figure 4.8   The router interface connections in routers that provide edge of network routing

Table 4.4 lists each router interface, the interface type and persistence, and reason for selecting the interface type and persistence.

Table 4.4   Reasons for Selecting Specific Router Interface Type and Persistence

For This Router and Interface		Select This Interface Type and Persistence	Reason
Router A	Segment A	LAN, persistent	Ethernet LAN connection
	Segment B	LAN, persistent	Ethernet LAN connection
Router B	Segment B	LAN, persistent	Ethernet LAN connection
	Internet	LAN, persistent	Dedicated T1 connection
	VPN Tunnel A	Demand-dial, nonpersistent	VPN tunnels require authentication
	VPN Tunnel B	Demand-dial, nonpersistent	VPN tunnels require authentication
Router C	Segment B	LAN, persistent	Ethernet LAN connection
	Segment C	LAN, persistent	Ethernet LAN connection
Router D	Segment D	LAN, persistent	Ethernet LAN connection
	Internet	LAN, persistent	Dedicated T1 connection
	VPN Tunnel A	Demand-dial, nonpersistent	VPN tunnels require authentication
	VPN Tunnel C	Demand-dial, nonpersistent	VPN tunnels require authentication
Router E	Segment E	LAN, persistent	Ethernet LAN connection
	Internet	LAN, persistent	Dedicated T1 connection
	VPN Tunnel B	Demand-dial, nonpersistent	VPN tunnels require authentication
	VPN Tunnel C	Demand-dial, nonpersistent	VPN tunnels require authentication

Router Security Options

You can assign a different level of security to each interface on each router. You can also customize the security of your design to meet the requirements of the organization.

Making the Decision

For each interface that transmits confidential data over public networks, your design must

- Authenticate the routers that exchange the confidential data
- Encrypt the confidential data
- Prevent unauthorized access to private network resources

Applying the Decision

The scenario in Figure 4.8 protects the confidential data transmitted between locations over the Internet by using a VPN connection. You can also protect confidential data by using Internet Protocol Security (IPSec). For more information on securing router-to-router traffic, see Lesson 3, "Data Protection on Unsecured Segments," in this chapter.

Unicast Routing

The routers in your design must determine how to forward broadcast, multicast, and unicast IP traffic. Your router design must provide the appropriate support for each type of IP traffic. Multicast routing is discussed later in this lesson.

Tip By default, IP routers don't forward IP broadcast traffic to reduce the traffic transmitted between network segments. In large IP networks, forwarding broadcast traffic can saturate routers, backbone segments, and WAN segments. Always specify that IP broadcast traffic isn't forwarded unless the design requirements or constraints mandate otherwise.

The majority of traffic exchanged in your design is unicast traffic. As a result, you must ensure that unicast traffic is exchanged as efficiently as possible. Each router in your design maintains a *unicast* routing table. The unicast routing table is a memory-based table that your routers use to determine the appropriate route path for unicast traffic.

The unicast routing table information is populated in your routers

- Manually by creating static routing table entries
- Automatically by
  - Autostatic entries
  - Dynamic routing entries
  - Entries for the subnets directly connected to the router's interfaces

---

Note Routing table entries are *automatically* created for network segments that directly connect to each interface in the router.

Making the Decision

Your IP routing design can include any combination of statically and dynamically managed routing table entries. Use a combination of static routing and dynamic routing to control the level of network utilization associated with routing table management.

Select the appropriate methods for managing routing table entries by determining

- **The network utilization level available for routing table maintenance** To optimize network utilization use
  - Dynamic routing between your private network segments within a location
  - Static routing between locations or between network segments where dynamic routing would saturate the network segment
- **The number of segments within a location that requires routing table updates** To minimize routing table management use
  - Static routing in locations containing a single network segment

- Dynamic routing in locations comprised of multiple network segments

- **Existing methods for managing routing tables**   Unless you're reconfiguring all existing routers, your method of managing routing tables must integrate with existing routers. Use the same routing table protocols as the existing routers.

Applying the Decision

Figure 4.9 illustrates the use of static and dynamic routing in the multiple location scenario. For each interface of each router, you must determine whether the interface will use static or dynamic routing.

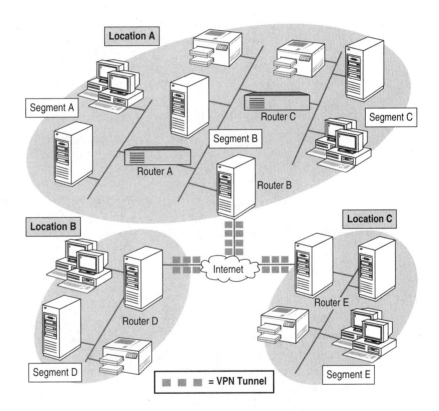

Figure 4.9   The appropriate use of static and dynamic routing in the multiple location scenario

For the purposes of this scenario, assume that

- The network segments (Segments A, B, C, D, and E) within each location are 100Mbps Ethernet

- Each location is directly connected to the Internet by using a T1 connection

- The network utilization required by the dynamic routing protocols is acceptable within each location

Table 4.5 lists each router interface, the method of managing the routing table for that interface, and the reason for selecting the method.

Table 4.5   Reasons for Selecting Each Method for Managing Routing Tables for Router Interfaces

For This Router Interface		Select	Reason
Router A	Segment A	Dynamic	The network capacity exists.
	Segment B	Dynamic	The network capacity exists.
Router B	Segment B	Dynamic	The network capacity exists.
	Internet	Static	The segment doesn't have the capacity for dynamic routing.
	VPN A	Static	Demand-dial interfaces require a static route entry.
	VPN B	Static	Demand-dial interfaces require a static route entry.
Router C	Segment B	Dynamic	The network capacity exists.
	Segment C	Dynamic	The network capacity exists.
Router D	Segment D	Static	Only one segment is within the location.
	Internet	Static	The segment doesn't have the capacity for dynamic routing.
	VPN A	Static	Demand-dial interfaces require a static route entry.
	VPN C	Static	Demand-dial interfaces require a static route entry.
Router E	Segment E	Static	Only one segment is within the location.
	Internet	Static	The segment doesn't have the capacity for dynamic routing.
	VPN B	Static	Demand-dial interfaces require a static route entry.
	VPN C	Static	Demand-dial interfaces require a static route entry.

Static Routing

Routers perform *static routing* when a static routing table entry determines route path. Static routing table entries are considered *static* because once the entries are placed in the routing table, the entries don't change.

You can't modify static routing table entries. Instead, you must delete them and then add new entries.

Making the Decision

Incorporate static routing in your design

- **To reduce network utilization due to routing table management**   Static routing table entries don't change after they're created. As a result, static routing reduces, or eliminates, network traffic associated with routing table maintenance.

- **To hide the structure of your private network from unauthorized users**   Because routing table updates aren't exchanged between routers, unauthorized users can't view network traffic and determine the network structure.

- **When the time required to update static routing table entries is acceptable**   Static routing requires a network administrator to delete and re-enter the static route entry when required. Ensure that the proper personnel resources exist to manage static routing.

- **When network route paths change infrequently**   A change in a route path requires an update in any corresponding static routing table entries. Frequent updates to these entries can become burdensome to networking personnel.

- **When the design includes a demand-dial interface**   A demand-dial interface requires at least one static routing table entry to specify how IP packets are forwarded through the interface. In most cases, the static routing table entry specifies the demand-dial interface as the *default gateway*.

- **When your design doesn't require redundant route paths**   Because static routing table entries aren't updated in the event of a connection or interface failure, the router doesn't forward packets through an alternate route path.

Applying the Decision

Figure 4.10 illustrates the use of static routing entries in the multiple locations connected by the Internet. Routers A and B contain routing table entries for Locations A and B respectively. Router A contains a static route entry that directs all traffic destined for Location B to Router B. Router B contains a corresponding static route entry that directs all traffic destined for Location A to Router A.

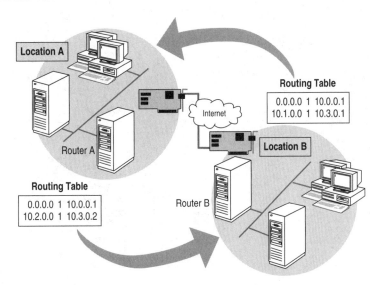

Figure 4.10   The appropriate use of static routing in multiple locations connected by the Internet

Default Route Entries

You can specify a *default route entry* for each router in your design. The default route entry is a special type of static route entry that specifies the route path for all destination networks unknown to the router.

Making the Decision

You can use the default route entry to

- Reduce the number of routing table entries
- Specify a single route path from one or more network segments

One of the disadvantages to default route entries is that the default route path is used for any destination not known to the router, even invalid destinations. For demand-dial connections that use default route entries, invalid destinations can cause the demand-dial connection to be initiated and incur unnecessary costs.

Applying the Decision

You can use a default route entry in routers with demand-dial interfaces. In Figure 4.9, you would specify a default route entry for Routers B, D, and E that directs all traffic destined outside the location to a router owned by the organization's Internet service provider (ISP).

Figure 4.11 illustrates the use of default route entries in the single location scenario. Router A contains routing table entries for Segments A, B, and C (10.1.0.0, 10.2.0.0, and 10.3.0.0 respectively). The default route entry, 0.0.0.0, directs all traffic destined for subnets other than Segments A, B, and C to the Internet (10.0.0.1).

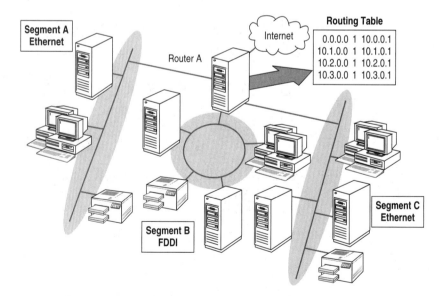

Figure 4.11   The appropriate use of default route entries in the single location scenario

Figure 4.12 shows an example of the routing table for Router A. The first entry is an example of a default route entry.

ATLANTA - IP Routing Table						
Destination	Network mask	Gateway	Interface	Metric	Protocol	
0.0.0.0	0.0.0.0	0.0.0.0	Local Area C...	1	Local	
10.1.0.0	255.255.0.0	10.1.0.1	Local Area C...	1	Local	
10.1.0.1	255.255.255.255	10.1.0.1	Local Area C...	1	Local	
10.2.0.0	255.255.0.0	10.2.0.1	Local Area C...	1	Local	
10.2.0.1	255.255.255.255	10.2.0.1	Local Area C...	1	Local	
10.3.0.0	255.255.0.0	10.3.0.1	Local Area C...	1	Local	
10.3.0.1	255.255.255.255	10.3.0.1	Local Area C...	1	Local	
127.0.0.0	255.0.0.0	127.0.0.1	Loopback	1	Local	
127.0.0.1	255.255.255.255	127.0.0.1	Loopback	1	Local	
255.255.255.255	255.255.255.255	10.3.0.1	Local Area C...	1	Local	
255.255.255.255	255.255.255.255	10.2.0.1	Local Area C...	1	Local	
255.255.255.255	255.255.255.255	10.1.0.1	Local Area C...	1	Local	

Figure 4.12   Example of the routing table for Router A in Figure 4.11

Note   The routing table entries for Segments A, B, and C aren't static route entries. Router A automatically creates the routing table entries because Router A is *directly* connected to each of the segments. As a result, the only static route entry that you create is the default route entry.

Autostatic Route Entries

Autostatic route entries allow you to combine the best features of dynamic and static routing. Autostatic routing is appropriate when you want to exchange dynamic routing entries from one location with another location at scheduled intervals.

Making the Decision

Dynamic routing protocols, such as Open Shortest Path First (OSPF) or Routing Information Protocol (RIP), exchange routing information regularly (for example, RIP announces routing changes every 30 seconds). As a result, dynamic routing protocols can saturate WAN links on congested backbone network segments.

Autostatic routing enables you to specify the time you want to exchange routing information. You can configure autostatic routing to update routing information at a time when the network is less congested or won't affect applications sensitive to response times.

Include autostatic routing in your design when you want to

- **Prevent the router from initiating a demand-dial connection for unreachable destinations**   Unlike default route entries, unreachable destinations don't cause the router to initiate the demand-dial connection. The router doesn't initiate the demand-dial connection because an explicit routing table entry doesn't exist for the destination. For unreachable destinations, the source computer receives an Internet Control Message Protocol (ICMP) message that indicates the destination network is unreachable.

- **Update routing information less frequently than dynamic routing protocols**   The only disadvantage to autostatic routing is that autostatic entries aren't updated between the update intervals, even if a network segment is added or removed. However, you can manually force autostatic updates to occur by using the Routing and Remote Access Console or the netsh command.

Note   You can use autostatic routing with RIP for IP, RIP for IPX, and Service Advertising Protocol (SAP) for IPX. OSPF isn't supported in autostatic routing.

Applying the Decision

Figure 4.13 illustrates how you can modify the multiple location scenario to utilize autostatic routing. For IP routing, autostatic routing works in conjunction with the RIP for IP dynamic routing protocol. Routers B, D, and E can exchange routing information at scheduled intervals.

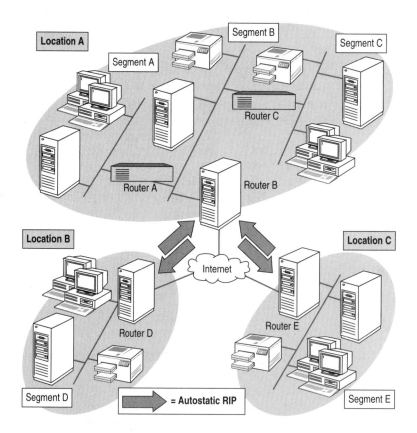

Figure 4.13   Example of autostatic RIP routing in the multiple location scenario

You must specify autostatic routing for each direction you want to exchange routing table updates. For example, in Figure 4.13, you must specify that Router B requests autostatic updates from Routers D and E. You must also specify that Routers D and E request autostatic updates from Router B.

Consider the following sequence for autostatic RIP routing updates when Router B requests updates from Router E at 3 A.M. every day.

1. At 3 A.M., Router B initiates the VPN connection with Router E (if not already established).
2. Router B deletes any entries in the local routing table that are autostatic RIP entries.
3. Router B requests routing information updates from Router E.
4. Router B disconnects the VPN connection with Router E (if required).
5. Thereafter, Router B initiates the VPN connection with Router E for any IP traffic destined for Location C.
6. The sequence starts again at 3 A.M. the following day.

RIP for IP Routing

RIP for IP is the most mature and well documented of the dynamic IP routing protocols. Every IP router, and almost every operating system, that you can include in your design supports some version of the RIP for IP routing protocol.

You can use Routing and Remote Access to support RIP versions 1 or 2 in your IP routing design. In addition, you can use RIP for IP to enable autostatic RIP routing, as described in the previous section.

Making the Decision

Incorporate the RIP for IP protocol in your design when

- **The existing routers in your design use RIP for IP**   You can reduce the cost associated with deploying your IP routing design by utilizing any existing routers. In addition, by using the existing RIP for IP infrastructure, you don't need to budget additional funds for training the network engineers and administrators.

- **The amount of time spent updating static routing table entries is unacceptable**   As the size of your network increases, the number of changes in the status of network segments changes accordingly. RIP for IP relieves network administrators and support engineers from manually modifying routing table entries.

- **The network route path changes frequently**   Any changes in a route path require a change in any corresponding routing table entry. Because RIP for IP automatically updates the routing table information, the route paths in your network remain current.

- **Your design includes a demand-dial interface and you want to use autostatic RIP routing**   You can use autostatic RIP routing for a demand-dial interface instead of a static, default route entry. Autostatic RIP routing requires that RIP for IP be enabled on the demand-dial interface. For more information on autostatic RIP routing and default route entries, see the previous sections.

- **The total diameter of the network (the number of routers that an IP packet must cross) is less than 15**   RIP for IP has a maximum limit of 15 *hops*. A hop occurs when an IP router forwards a packet. When the hop count of a packet reaches 16, the packet is discarded and an ICMP message is sent to the source computer indicating that the network is unreachable.

Note   RIP for IP routers set the route cost or metric of a router interface to 16 when the interface, or the associated network connection, fails.

- **Your design requires redundant route paths**   Dynamic routing table entries are updated in the event of a connection or interface failure. As a result, the router can forward packets through an alternate route path (if one exists).

You can include either RIP for IP version 1 or 2 in your routing design. RIP for IP version 2 is a superset of RIP for IP version 1. Include RIP for IP version 2 on all routers in your IP routing design that must support

- **Classless Interdomain Routing (CIDR)**   For more information on CIDR, see Chapter 2, "Networking Protocol Design," Lesson 2, "Essential TCP/IP Design Concepts."

- **Variable Length Subnet Masks (VLSM)**   For more information on VLSM, see Chapter 2, "Networking Protocol Design," Lesson 2, "Essential TCP/IP Design Concepts."

- **Multicast traffic to exchange routing table information**   You can reduce the network utilization associated with routing table updates by using multicast traffic. Multicast updates are required for autostatic RIP routing.

- **Mutual router authentication by exchanging a password**   You can define a password that the routers will use to identify one another. The RIP for IP version 2 password authentication takes place in addition to any VPN or demand-dial authentication that might exist.

Applying the Decision

Figure 4.14 illustrates how you can adjust the cost metrics on a RIP for IP router to designate a preference in route path. Router A is connected to Router B with a T1 connection and a dial-up connection. The cost metric on the dial-up connection is set higher to force traffic through the T1 connection. The dial-up connection is used only when the T1 connection fails (which sets the cost metric of the T1 connection to 16).

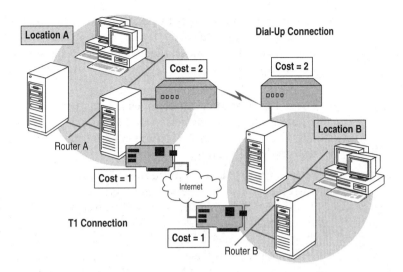

Figure 4.14 Example of assigning cost metrics to designate a preference in route path

---

Tip If you're using custom costs to indicate link speed, delay, or reliability factors, ensure that the hop count between any two endpoints on the internetwork doesn't exceed 15.

OSPF Routing

OSPF, a more recent dynamic routing protocol than RIP for IP, addresses many of the disadvantages of RIP for IP. You can use Routing and Remote Access to support OSPF and the OSPF related protocols, such as Border Gateway Protocol (BGP).

OSPF maintains a map of the network in a *link state database*. OSPF routers use the link state database instead of routing tables to determine the status of another router or network segment in the internetwork. OSPF routers recalculate route paths when any change in the link state database occurs, and propagate the changes throughout the network.

Making the Decision

Incorporate the OSPF routing protocol in your design when

- **The existing routers in your design use OSPF**   You can reduce the cost associated with deploying your IP routing design by utilizing existing OSPF routers. In addition, by using the existing OSPF infrastructure, you don't need to budget additional funds for training the network engineers and administrators.

- **The total diameter of the network (the number of routers that an IP packet must cross) is larger than 15 segments**   You must use OSPF for dynamic routing when the diameter of the network is larger than 15 network segments. RIP for IP, the other dynamic routing protocol, can't exceed a path of 15 network segments.

- **The amount of time spent updating static routing table entries is unacceptable**   As the size of your network increases, the number of changes in the status of network segments increases accordingly. OSPF eliminates manual updating of routing table entries by network administrators and support engineers.

- **The network route path changes frequently**   Any changes in a route path require a change in any corresponding routing table entry. Because OSPF automatically updates the routing table information, the route paths in your network remain current.

- **Your design requires redundant route paths**   Dynamic routing table entries are updated in the event of a connection or interface failure. As a result, the OSPF router can forward packets through an alternate route path (if one exists).

To minimize the performance impact of frequent updates to the link state table, you can organize your OSPF design into hierarchical levels. By using a *top down* approach, you can design the highest level of your OSPF design first and then proceed to lower levels in the design.

You can divide your OSPF design into

- **An OSPF Autonomous System**   All the OSPF routers in your design must belong to the same autonomous system to automatically exchange routing information. Network segments outside your OSPF autonomous system can be reached through external routes. OSPF external routes in your design can include

  - Other OSPF autonomous systems

  - RIP for IP networks

  - Static routes

  - Route paths added by Simple Network Management Protocol (SNMP)

Note   You connect your OSPF autonomous system to external routes by using autonomous system boundary routers (ASBRs).

- **One or more OSPF areas**   Your OSPF autonomous system is comprised of one or more OSPF areas. An OSPF area is a grouping of routers that connect to contiguous network segments. Your OSPF autonomous system must include an area known as a backbone area. A backbone area is a common area that connects all other areas within the autonomous system.

Note   You connect your OSPF areas together by using area border routers (ABRs).

- **One or more OSPF networks**   Your OSPF areas are comprised of one or more OSPF networks. An OSPF network is a network segment that resides within and is managed by an OSPF area.

Arrange the routers in your OSPF routing design hierarchically. OSPF aggregates routing information just like VLSM. When you arrange your OSPF routers hierarchically, you reduce the number of entries in the link state database.

Applying the Decision

Figure 4.15 shows how to use the OSPF routing protocol in the multiple location scenario. Locations A, B, and C belong to the same OSPF autonomous system. Locations A, B, and C are separate OSPF areas. Each network segment in each location is a separate OSPF network.

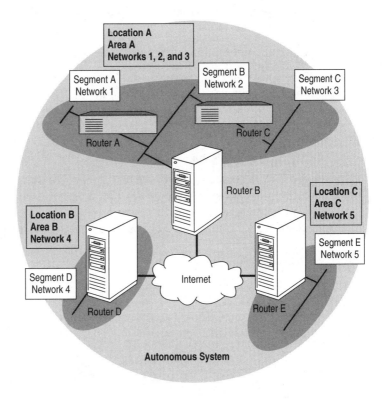

Figure 4.15   Using the OSPF dynamic routing protocol in the multiple location scenario

Routers B, D, and E are ABRs that connect Areas A, B, and C. Router B is also an autonomous system boundary router that connects the autonomous system to the Internet.

Multicast Routing

Multicasting technologies are on the forefront of the current trends in networking technologies. Many of the multimedia applications that your design must support use multicast transmissions between multimedia servers and clients.

Any routers in your design that include RIP for IP version 2 can support multicast traffic to exchange routing information. As a result, the designs you create must support these multimedia applications or RIP for IP version 2.

You can use the Internet Group Messaging Protocol (IGMP) in Routing and Remote Access as a multicast proxy. A multicast proxy performs a subset of the features of a multicast router.

Making the Decision

You must specify a *proxy mode* interface and a *router mode* interface for the multicast proxy. You can specify only one proxy mode interface but multiple router mode interfaces.

Incorporate multicast proxying in your design when

- You want to provide multicast traffic to multicast clients directly connected to the *same* network segment as the router
- The routers between the multicast proxy and the multicast source are full-featured multicast routers

Applying the Decision

Figure 4.16 illustrates the use of the IGMP multicast routing protocol to create a multicast proxy. Router B is a multicast proxy that forwards multicast traffic to the network segment in Location B. Router A is a full-featured multicast router that registers and forwards multicast requests to the multimedia server in Location A.

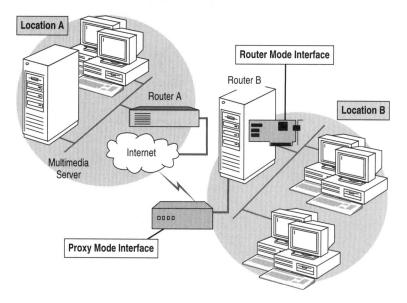

Figure 4.16   Using the IGMP multicast routing protocol to create a multicast proxy

Table 4.6 lists the type of multicast proxy interfaces and the functions provided by the multicast proxy.

Table 4.6   Types and Functions of Multicast Proxy Interfaces

These Interfaces	Perform These Functions
Router mode	■ Appears as a multicast router to the multicast clients at Location B ■ Listens for multicast registration requests and multicast traffic from the multicast clients
Proxy mode	■ Appears as a multicast client to Router A ■ Forwards multicast registration requests and multicast traffic from the multicast clients to Router A

Note You can't connect multicast routers or other multicast proxies beneath the network segment in Location B. In addition, Router A must be a full-featured multicast router.

DHCP Relay Agent

Most of the routing designs you create will include a DHCP configuration. Because DHCP uses broadcast traffic to communicate between DHCP clients and DHCP servers, the IP routers in your network may not forward the DHCP traffic.

You can include the DHCP Relay Agent in your routing design to forward DHCP traffic between routed network segments. The DHCP Relay Agent allows your routers to filter broadcast traffic while forwarding DHCP requests.

Making the Decision

There are different approaches you can use to forward DHCP traffic between DHCP clients and servers. These are

■ Enabling broadcast traffic forwarding on routers

■ Enabling DHCP/BOOTP (Boot Protocol) forwarding on routers

■ Enabling DHCP Relay Agent on routers

Table 4.7 lists the advantage and disadvantage of enabling broadcast traffic forwarding on routers to forward DHCP traffic between DHCP clients and servers.

Table 4.7   Advantage and Disadvantage of Enabling Broadcast Traffic Forwarding

Advantage	Disadvantage
All routers support the ability to enable the forwarding of broadcast traffic, which means any existing routers don't require replacement	All broadcast traffic, not just DHCP traffic, is forwarded between network segments, which means the broadcast traffic can saturate congested network segments or routers

Table 4.8 lists the advantages and disadvantages of enabling DHCP/BOOTP forwarding on routers to forward DHCP traffic between DHCP clients and servers.

Table 4.8   Advantages and Disadvantages of Enabling DHCP/BOOTP Forwarding

Advantages	Disadvantages
Existing, or new, routers can forward just DHCP/BOOTP traffic. Existing routers that support DHCP/BOOTP forwarding don't require replacement.	DHCP requests are still broadcast packets and propagate throughout the network. The broadcast traffic can saturate congested network segments or routers. Not only DHCP requests are forwarded, but BOOTP requests are also forwarded. An IP-based network device, such as a hub or router, may use BOOTP for IP configuration. Many of these devices continuously broadcast BOOTP requests until they are powered off or are manually configured.

Table 4.9 lists the advantages and disadvantages of enabling DHCP Relay Agent on routers to forward DHCP traffic between DHCP clients and servers.

Table 4.9   Advantages and Disadvantages of Enabling DHCP Relay Agent

Advantages	Disadvantages
DHCP Relay Agent converts DHCP traffic to unicast traffic. Routers that exist between the DHCP Relay Agent and the DHCP client or server can forward the unicast DHCP requests.	You might need to replace existing routers that are connected to network segments that contain DHCP clients or servers.

Applying the Decision

Figure 4.17 illustrates the use of a DHCP Relay Agent, on Router A, to forward DHCP traffic between Segments A, B, and C. The DHCP clients on Segments A and C can request DHCP configuration from the DHCP server on Segment B.

You add the DHCP Relay Agent to the router interfaces that connect to Segments A, B, and C. You don't add the DHCP Relay Agent to the Internet interface.

For more information on the DHCP Relay Agent, see Chapter 8, "DHCP in IP Configuration Designs."

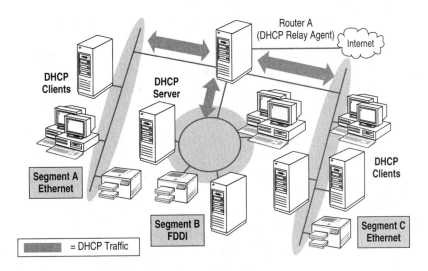

Figure 4.17   Using a DHCP Relay Agent to forward DHCP traffic between routed network segments

Activity 4.1: Evaluating an IP Routing Design

In this activity, you're presented with a scenario. To complete the exercise:

1. Evaluate the scenario and determine the design requirements

2. Answer questions regarding design recommendations

In Figure 4.18, you see a diagram of a regional library system. The regional library system has a main branch and smaller branches in five different townships. The library system reserves books and checks out books by using a manual process. However, the library system is deploying a Microsoft SQL–based application that will automate the book inventory, the book acquisition, and the financial information of the library system.

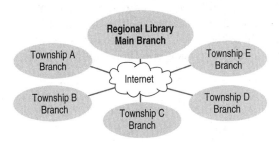

Figure 4.18   Diagram of a regional library system

The library application is a Web-based application that will allow library patrons to reserve and check out books over the Internet. The Web servers that will host the library's Web site are located in the main branch. Each of the remote branches will connect to the structured query language (SQL) server, located in the main branch, over the Internet to manage their own book inventory.

Each library branch must

- Support 20 computers that are used by the local branch personnel on a separate network segment

- Support up to 100 computers that are used by library patrons on a separate network segment

- Provide 75 Ethernet jacks for use by patrons that bring their own laptops on a separate network segment

- Facilitate three meeting rooms. Each meeting room must be able to support 36 computers for seminars and workshops held in the library branch. Each meeting room must be on a separate network segment

Answer the following questions concerning your design recommendations. You can find answers to the questions in the Appendix, "Questions and Answers."

1. As the director of information services for the library system, you're responsible for creating the networking services design. You have decided to connect each of the remote branches to the Internet by using a T1 connection. Because all remote branches will be accessing resources in the main branch, you have decided to install a T3 Internet connection at the main branch. What do you recommend as a routing solution between the remote branches and the main branch?

2. After performing pilot testing, you have determined that you want to connect each network segment to a backbone segment within each branch. The backbone segment will be connected to the Internet. You have determined that the number of computers on each network segment won't increase significantly over the life of the new deployment. How do you provide routing between the network segments in each branch and to the Internet?

3. You want to provide automatic IP address configuration for all desktop and laptop computers at each location by using DHCP. How can you modify your routing design to support DHCP configuration on all network segments within each branch?

4. The facilities and community relations director for the library system has funding to install a multimedia server at each branch. The multimedia server will be used to present streaming audio and video presentations within each branch. You want to reduce the amount of traffic used by the multimedia traffic. How can you modify your routing design to support the multimedia traffic while reducing the network utilization?

Lesson 3: Data Protection on Unsecured Segments

Many of the IP routing designs that you will create connect locations over public networks, such as the Internet. In this lesson, you learn how to protect any confidential data that is transmitted between routers from unauthorized users.

After this lesson, you will be able to

- Prevent unwanted IP traffic between network segments by using IP packet filtering
- Ensure that IP packets are sent only to known routers by using router authentication
- Prevent unauthorized access to confidential data by using IPSec or VPN technologies to encrypt the data

Estimated lesson time: 30 minutes

Filtering Unwanted IP Traffic

The requirements and constraints of your network will specify that certain types of traffic are unwanted or unauthorized. The unwanted traffic can originate within or outside your private network. Some examples of unwanted traffic include

- Unauthorized Internet-based users who attempt to access your private network resources
- Unauthorized private network-based users who attempt to access confidential network resources
- Unsupported applications within your organization, such as certain chat programs or games

Making the Decision

You can prevent unwanted IP traffic by using the IP filters in Routing and Remote Access by specifying a combination of IP filters on each router interface.

The IP filters in Routing and Remote Access are similar to the rules in a firewall. Just like firewall rules, you can filter inbound and outbound IP traffic between two or more network segments.

Tip You can use IP filters on internal routers to create protected network segments within your private network.

Table 4.10 lists the criteria used to create Routing and Remote Access IP filters and when you use those criteria.

Table 4.10   When to Use Specific Routing and Remote Access IP Filters

Use This Filter Criteria	When You Want to Restrict Traffic
Source or destination IP address range	Originating from or destined to a specific computer by specifying a single IP address Originating from or destined to an IP address range assigned to an organization or a network segment within an organization by specifying the IP address range
IP protocol number	To or from a specific application

You can combine any number of IP filters to control network traffic forwarded through one or more routers. However, you must recognize that these filters

- Restrict all traffic forwarded through these routers
- Are cumulative across multiple routers and multiple interfaces

Note   You can use IP filters to protect your network like a firewall when the security requirements of your design can be achieved with an IP filter.

Applying the Decision

Figure 4.19 illustrates the cumulative effects of multiple IP filters in your design. The IP filters affect all traffic between the source and destination hosts.

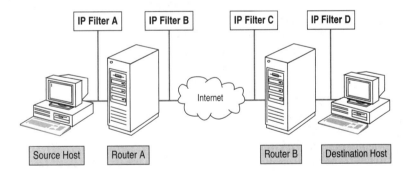

Figure 4.19   Illustration of the cumulative effects of multiple IP filters

The following sequence describes how the IP filters affect an IP packet sent from the source host to the destination host.

1. The source host sends the IP packet to Router A.

2. The router uses the criteria of IP Filter A to determine whether the IP packet is forwarded or discarded by Router A.

3. If the IP filter rejects the packet, the corresponding router discards the IP packet. The source host isn't notified that the packet is discarded.

4. Steps 1, 2, and 3 are repeated for IP filters B, C, and D until the IP packet reaches the destination host.

Figure 4.20 illustrates how to use IP router filters to limit traffic between your private network and the Internet. You can assign IP filters to the router interface that connects the private network to the Internet. You can use the IP filters to prevent unauthorized and unwanted access to Segments A, B, and C.

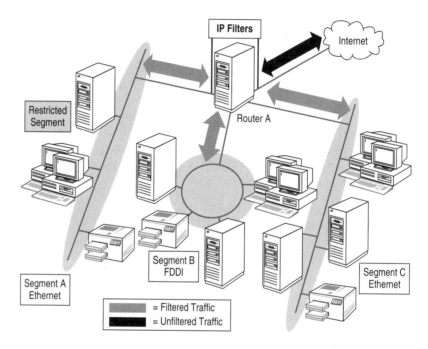

Figure 4.20   Example of how IP router filters can limit traffic between your private network and the Internet

In the scenario, Router A provides the same function as a firewall. The IP router filters protect the private network from unauthorized access, just as a firewall does.

In addition, an IP filter is specified on the router interface connected to Segment A. The IP filter can further restrict the traffic destined for Segment A. For example, you can specify that the IP filter reject any IP packets that originate outside the private network.

Router Identification

You can reduce unauthorized access to your private network by ensuring that your routers exchange confidential data only with known routers. You can identify routers by a variety of methods; however, the level of security varies with each authentication method.

Making the Decision

Table 4.11 contrasts and compares the methods that Routing and Remote Access can use to identify routers.

Table 4.11   Routing and Remote Access Router Identification Methods

Method	Uses	Select for Routers That Are
Routing protocol	Plain text password, peer security, and RIP neighbors	Internal routers within your private network
IPSec	Encrypted machine certificates	Internal routers within your private network
Demand-dial (including VPN)	Plain text, or encrypted, account name and password	Edge of network routers that connect network segments by dial-up modem, ISDN, or other technologies

You can use any combination of these methods to identify routers within your design. On routers that connect private network segments to public network segments, you may use a combination of identification for internal and edge of network routers.

Routing Protocol Methods for Router Identification

Each routing protocol in your routing design has methods that allow you to identify the routers within your design. Each of these methods is specific to the routing protocol.

You can use routing protocols to provide router identification in your design by using

- **RIP for IP version 2 or OSPF passwords**   You can identify routers by using RIP for IP version 2 or OSPF passwords. The following sequence describes how these passwords are used to identify routers.

  1. A router sends an advertisement packet with an attached password.

  2. Each receiving router checks the password in the advertisement packet.

  3. If the password of the router and the password in the advertisement packet match, the receiving router updates the routing table. Otherwise, the advertisement packet is discarded.

Note   RIP for IP version 2 and OSPF passwords are sent as plain text and are susceptible to viewing by protocol analyzers. You encrypt the passwords, and other data, exchanged between the routers by using IPSec.

- **RIP for IP peer security**   When you specify RIP for IP peer security on a router, the router accepts RIP announcements only from a list of designated routers. Any RIP announcements that are received from routers not in the peer list are discarded.

- **RIP for IP neighbors** By default, RIP for IP-based routers use broadcast, or multicast, packets to transmit RIP announcements. By specifying RIP for IP neighbors, the router sends RIP advertisements as unicast packets that are directed to *neighboring routers*. Neighboring routers are the routers directly accessible to the router that has RIP for IP neighbors enabled.

IPSec for Router Identification

You can use IPSec to provide router identification in your design. IPSec-based routers exchange *machine certificates* that identify the routers to one another. Machine certificates authenticate the computer, not the user running applications on the computer. You can use the IPSec Authentication Header (AH) or the Encapsulating Security Payload (ESP) protocols to provide router identification.

The IPSec machine certificates can include

- Kerberos version 5 tickets
- X509 certificates
- Preshared keys

For more information on IPSec, see Chapter 2, "Networking Protocol Design," Lesson 3, "TCP/IP Data Protection."

Demand-Dial for Router Identification

You must identify routers that communicate over demand-dial interfaces by using demand-dial authentication. You specify one or more user accounts within your design that the routers use to identify one another. The user accounts can be stored locally on the router or in Active Directory directory service.

Note VPN is a special case of a demand-dial interface. Use the same authentication protocols for VPN as you do any other demand-dial interface. However, when you use VPN with IPSec, you receive the best features of demand-dial and IPSec authentication. VPN and IPSec can potentially provide the highest security.

Demand-dial routers can use any of the authentication protocols available in Routing and Remote Access. With the exception of Microsoft Challenge Handshake Authentication Protocol version 2 (MS-CHAP v2), all authentication protocols provide one-way authentication.

One-way authentication means that the responding router can identify the originating router, but the originating router can't identify the responding router. MS-CHAP v2 provides two-way authentication that allows both the responding and originating routers to identify one another. As a result, MS-CHAP v2 is recommended for router-to-router demand-dial authentication.

For more information on the authentication protocols available in Routing and Remote Access and on VPN, see Chapter 2, "Networking Protocol Design," Lesson 3, "TCP/IP Data Protection."

Applying the Decision

Figure 4.21 illustrates a scenario that requires router identification. In the scenario, assume the following.

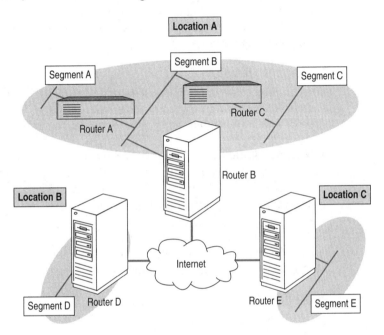

Figure 4.21 A scenario to determine how to perform router identification in your design

- Routers A and C use the RIP for IP dynamic routing protocol.
- A T1 link connects Routers B, D, and E to the Internet.
- Routers B, D, and E use autostatic RIP routing between locations.
- Layer 2 Tunneling Protocols (L2TP) with IPSec tunnels protect all data transmitted between Locations A, B, and C.

You can create a design that meets the scenario requirements and constraints by using

- RIP for IP version 2 passwords for Routers A, B, and C
- RIP for IP neighbors on all routers
- RIP for IP peers on all routers
- Demand-dial authentication for Routers B, D, and E
- IPSec machine certification authentication for Routers B, D, and E

As illustrated in the solution, higher security is required for the edge of network routers than the internal routers. Unless otherwise directed by the requirements and constraints of the organization, ensure that you focus on edge of network routers when adding router identification to your design.

Router-to-Router Data Protection

Many of your IP routing designs will send confidential data over public networks, such as the Internet. Unless otherwise specified by the requirements of the organization, your design must protect any confidential data transmitted over these public networks.

Making the Decision

You can protect the confidential data sent over public networks by using VPN tunnels or IPSec, as described in the previous section. VPN tunnels and IPSec support router authentication in addition to data encryption.

VPN Tunnels in Router-to-Router Data Protection

You can use either Point-to-Point Tunneling Protocol (PPTP) or L2TP/IPSec tunnels to encrypt confidential data between routers. Each tunneling protocol provides different data encryption algorithms.

Tip   VPN tunnels are the most appropriate for edge of network routers. To protect confidential data transmitted between internal routers, use IPSec or Microsoft Point-to-Point Encryption (MPPE) encryption.

Select the tunneling protocol for your design by determining

- The tunneling protocols supported by existing routers
- Authentication requirements for the tunnel
- Any governmental regulations that constrict the strength of data encryption

For more information on the encryption protocols available in Routing and Remote Access and on VPN, see Chapter 2, "Networking Protocol Design," Lesson 3, "TCP/IP Data Protection."

IPSec in Router-to-Router Data Protection

Use either IPSec transport mode or IPSec tunnel mode to encrypt the data transmitted between routers. As with VPN, IPSec provides both router identification and data encryption. IPSec can be used alone or in conjunction with L2TP.

Review the information in Table 4.12 to determine whether IPSec alone or IPSec with L2TP is more appropriate for your design requirements and constraints.

Tip   Because routers send data from point to point, you can use IPSec tunnel mode rather than transport mode. IPSec tunnel mode ensures that all data transmitted between the routers is protected.

Table 4.12   When to Use IPSec or IPSec with L2TP

Select	When
IPSec only	■ You want to encrypt data between internal routers ■ The overhead associated with L2TP tunneling is unnecessary ■ Machine authentication is sufficient to identify routers
L2TP with IPSec	■ You want to encrypt data between edge of network routers ■ You want the router interface to appear as a demand-dial interface ■ User and machine authentication are required to identify routers

You can use IPSec tunnel mode between the routers in your design. You must specify a separate IPSec tunnel between each combination of routers in your design. When you specify *only* IPSec tunnel mode on a router interface in your design, *all* traffic sent through the router interface must be destined to the other endpoint of the IPSec tunnel. IPSec discards any traffic not destined for the other endpoint of the tunnel.

For more information on the encryption protocols available in Routing and Remote Access and on VPN, see Chapter 2, "Networking Protocol Design," Lesson 3, "TCP/IP Data Protection."

Note   The Windows 2000 Resource Kit chapter on IPSec describes IPSec tunnel scenarios and configurations in more detail and should be understood before implementing IPSec tunnel mode.

Applying the Decision

Figure 4.22 illustrates a scenario where you must determine how to protect confidential data transmitted between routers. In the scenario, assume the following.

■ All routers support IPSec, L2TP, and PPTP.

■ A T1 link connects Routers B, D, and E to the Internet.

■ Any confidential data transmitted across Segment B, the organization's backbone, must be protected to enhance the security in Location A.

■ All data transmitted between Locations A, B, and C must be protected.

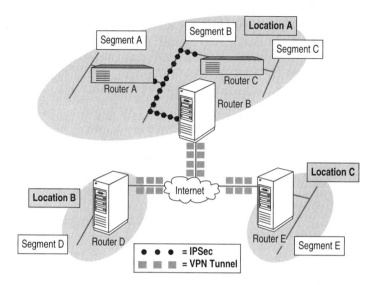

Figure 4.22   A scenario that illustrates how to protect confidential data transmitted between routers

You can create a design that meets the scenario requirements and constraints by using

- IPSec tunnel mode between Routers A, B, and C
- A VPN tunnel between Routers B, D, and E
- The strongest possible encryption and authentication between Routers B, D, and E
- Minimal encryption and authentication between Routers A, B, and C to reduce the consumption of memory and CPU resources

Lesson 4: IP Routing Design Optimization

After you establish essential routing and secure your design, you can optimize the design to ensure that the route paths are available at the highest possible data rates. In this lesson, you learn how to improve the availability and performance of your routing solution.

After this lesson, you will be able to

- Improve the availability in an IP routing design
- Improve the performance in an IP routing design

Estimated lesson time: 30 minutes

Improving IP Routing Availability and Performance

Many of the strategies used to improve IP routing availability also improve IP routing performance. Conversely, the strategies used to improve IP routing performance often also improve IP routing availability.

Making the Decision

You can improve IP routing availability and performance by

- **Configuring routers with the RIP for IP routing protocol to use RIP neighbors**   Because RIP advertisements are sent by unicast instead of broadcast or multicast, enabling RIP neighbors can enhance performance. Unicast traffic decreases the number of packets received by IP devices *other* than routers and eliminates or reduces broadcast traffic.

- **Replacing nonpersistent connections with persistent connections** Nonpersistent connections, such as dial-up connections, affect
    - Availability because the connection might receive a busy signal and not connect
    - Availability and performance because of the delay in establishing the connection

- **Adding additional connections**   Additional connections affect
    - Availability because additional connections act as redundant paths when one of the connections fails
    - Performance because additional connections increase bandwidth between routes when one of the route paths is saturated

- **Adding additional router interfaces**   Additional router interfaces affect
    - Availability because additional router interfaces provide redundancy when one of the interfaces fails
    - Performance because additional router interfaces provide increased bandwidth between route paths when one of the interfaces is congested

- **Adding additional routers**   Additional routers affect
  - Availability because additional routers provide redundancy when one of the routers fails
  - Performance because additional routers increase bandwidth between route paths when one of the routers is congested

Applying the Decision

Figure 4.23 illustrates an IP routing scenario prior to optimization for availability and performance. Router A connects Segments A, B, and C to one another and to the Internet.

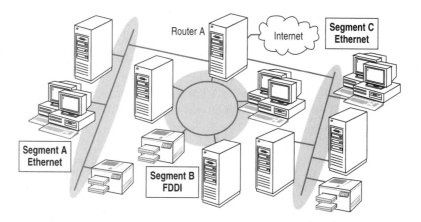

Figure 4.23   IP routing scenario prior to availability and performance optimization

In this IP routing scenario, assume the following.

- Users in the private network must be able to access the Internet at all times.
- The organization is deploying a multimedia application that requires higher data rates between Segments A, B, and C.
- Users require access to the multimedia application at all times.

Figure 4.24 illustrates the IP routing scenario after optimization for availability and performance. This solution meets the scenario requirements and constraints by

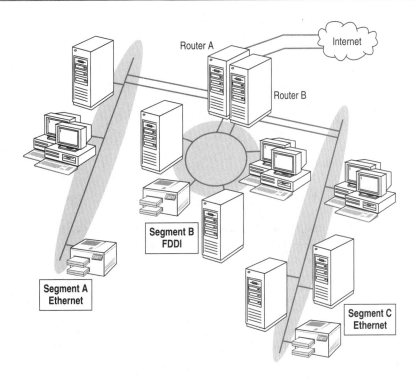

Figure 4.24   IP routing scenario after availability and performance optimization

- Adding Router B to serve as a redundant router for connections between Segments A, B, and C and the Internet
- Adding redundant connections to Segments A, B, and C, and to the Internet
- Minimizing encryption and authentication between Routers A, B, and C to reduce the consumption of memory and CPU resources

Activity 4.2: Completing an IP Routing Design

In this activity, you're presented with a scenario. To complete the exercise:

1. Evaluate the scenario and determine the design requirements

2. Answer questions regarding design recommendations

Figure 4.25 represents a diagram of a regional library system network. As the director of information services for the library system, you're in the process of revising your current network design to reflect the current security, availability and performance requirements of the regional library system.

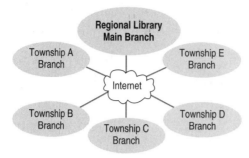

Figure 4.25   Diagram of a regional library system

The library system has deployed a Web-based application that allows library patrons to reserve, request, and check on the status of books. The Web-based application can be accessed by kiosks within each library or by the Internet.

Answer the following questions concerning your design recommendations. You can find answers to the questions in the Appendix, "Questions and Answers."

1. The board of directors for the library system is concerned about library patrons and Internet-based users accessing the new Web-based application and the structured query language (SQL) server database that acts as the repository for application's data. You also want to reduce the risk of unauthorized access to the library confidential data. How can you address the concerns of the board of directors?

2. The library personnel must be able to access the Web-based library application at all times. The facilities and community relations director requires that the meeting room computers access the Internet only during normal library branch hours. Internet-based library patrons must be able to reserve a book 24 hours a day, 7 days a week. How can you ensure that these design requirements and constraints are met?

3. The library system rents the meeting rooms to individuals and organizations. The proceeds from the meeting room rentals help fund future enhancements to the library system facilities and equipment. The facilities and community relations director wants to ensure that the people who rent the meeting rooms are satisfied with network response times. How can you optimize your design to ensure optimal response times?

Lab: Creating an IP Routing Design

After this lab, you will be able to
- Evaluate a scenario and determine the design requirements
- Create an IP routing design based on the design requirements

Estimated lab time: 45 minutes

In this lab, you're the director of information services for a university and are responsible for the creation of an IP routing design for the university. The university has 12 buildings arranged in a campus setting.

To complete this lab:

1. Examine the networking environment presented in the scenario, the network diagrams, the business requirements and constraints, and the technical requirements and constraints

2. Use the worksheet(s) for each location and router to assist you in creating your IP routing design (you can find completed sample design worksheets on the Supplemental Course Materials CD-ROM in the Completed Worksheets folder)

Note   For each location there are four worksheets, one worksheet for each router. If your design contains fewer than four routers, leave the remaining worksheets blank.

3. Create, eliminate, or replace existing networking devices and network segments when required.

4. Ensure that your design fulfills the business requirements and constraints and technical requirements and constraints of the scenario by
   - Assigning the appropriate specifications for each router interface
   - Including the appropriate unicast routing protocols on each router
   - Including the IGMP multicast proxy on appropriate routers
   - Including the DHCP Relay Agent on appropriate routers
   - Optimizing your design to provide the security, availability, performance, and affordability

Note   To reduce the length of time for this lab, create an IP routing design for only three of the university buildings.

Scenario

A science and engineering university is migrating its existing network to accommodate the increase in student population and faculty. The university has 12 buildings organized in a campus setting.

Building	Description	Building	Description
1	Administration Building	7	Field House/Gymnasium
2	Student Union and Campus Security	8	Performing Arts Center
3	Chemistry	9	Electrical Engineering
4	Mathematics and Computer Science	10	Civil Engineering
5	Physics	11	Fine Arts
6	Mechanical Engineering	12	Liberal Arts

Figure 4.26 is a map of the buildings in the university's campus. Point-to-point leased lines currently connect the buildings to one another. The university is migrating the existing point-to-point leased lines to a public ATM backbone. The new ATM backbone will provide higher speed data rates between the buildings in the campus. The university is connected to the Internet by three T3 leased lines in the Administration Building.

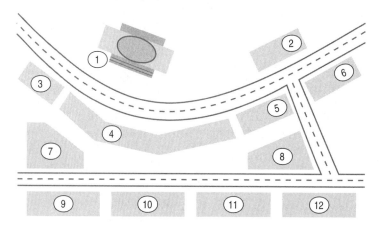

Figure 4.26   Map of the buildings in the university's campus

The network in each university building supports

- The administrative staff, faculty, and student work-study program participants who work in the individual university departments

- Interactive kiosks that students can use to access their own information, class schedules, professor office schedules, and other pertinent information

- 10BaseT Ethernet connectivity for students who use laptops
- Computer-based labs for use by the students to complete course assignments

Business Requirements and Constraints

The university has a number of requirements and constraints based on the business model of the university. As you create your IP routing design, ensure that your design meets the business requirements and stays within the business constraints.

To achieve the business requirements and constraints, your design must

- Prevent students from accessing resources and data that are for exclusive use by the faculty and administrative staff
- Provide Internet access to all faculty, administrative staff, and students
- Support Active Directory as the directory services for the university
- Provide an Internet presence for the university that is hosted on the Web servers in the Administration Building
- Ensure that connectivity between the university buildings is available 24 hours a day, 7 days a week
- Ensure that the interactive student kiosks are available during normal hours of operation for each respective building

Technical Requirements and Constraints

The existing physical network, hardware, and operating systems place certain technical requirements and constraints on your design. As you create your IP routing design, ensure that it meets the technical requirements and stays within the technical constraints.

In addition, the applications that run within the university require connectivity within each building, with other buildings, and with the Internet. These applications run on the computers used by the faculty, administrative staff, and student work-study program participants and on computers used in interactive kiosks.

To achieve the technical requirements and constraints, your design must

- Provide access to the Web servers located in the Administration Building to Internet-based users and users within the university's private network
- Isolate the university's private network from the Internet
- Isolate the network segments designated for use by the students from the network segments designated for use by the faculty, administrative staff, and student work-study program participants
- Protect all data transmitted over the public ATM network

- Reduce the utilization of the ATM network from 7 A.M. through 9 P.M.
- Utilize the existing TCP/IP address, 10.0.0.0/8, which is assigned to the university

---

Note   For the purposes of this lab, treat the private IP address range 10.0.0.0/8 as a public address.

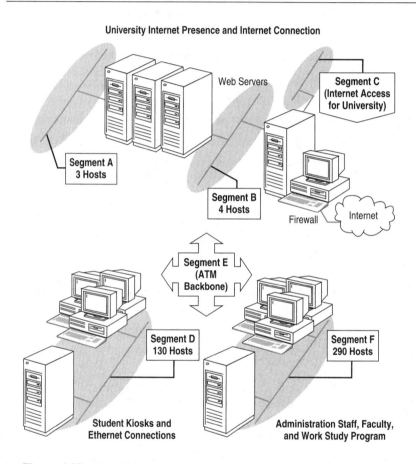

Figure 4.27   This is the existing network at the Administration building.

Design Worksheet – Figure 4.27
Administration Building – Router A

Router Specifications	Comments
Interface A connects to segment: _____	
Routing Protocol Support	
❑ Static Routes (*specify static route entries in Comments column*)	
❑ Auto-Static RIP for IP with updates scheduled at: _____	
❑ RIP for IP v1	
❑ RIP for IP v2 ❑ RIP for IP v2 password: _____	
❑ RIP for IP Peers (*specify peers in Comments column*)	
❑ RIP for IP Neighbors (*specify neighbors in Comments column*)	
❑ OSPF ❑ OSPF password: _____	
❑ IGMP ❑ Proxy Mode interface or ❑ Router Mode interface	
❑ DHCP Relay Agent – Forward DHCP traffic to DHCP server at: _____	
Security	
❑ VPN (*specify tunnel parameters in Comments column*)	
❑ IPSec (*specify IPSec parameters in Comments column*)	
❑ IP Routing Filters (*specify filter criteria in Comments column*)	
Interface B connects to segment: _____	
Routing Protocol Support	
❑ Static Routes (*specify static route entries in Comments column*)	
❑ Auto-Static RIP for IP with updates scheduled at: _____	
❑ RIP for IP v1	
❑ RIP for IP v2 ❑ RIP for IP v2 password: _____	
❑ RIP for IP Peers (*specify peers in Comments column*)	
❑ RIP for IP Neighbors (*specify neighbors in Comments column*)	
❑ OSPF ❑ OSPF password: _____	
❑ IGMP ❑ Proxy Mode interface or ❑ Router Mode interface	
❑ DHCP Relay Agent – Forward DHCP traffic to DHCP server at: _____	
Security	
❑ VPN (*specify tunnel parameters in Comments column*)	
❑ IPSec (*specify IPSec parameters in Comments column*)	
❑ IP Routing Filters (*specify filter criteria in Comments column*)	

Design Worksheet – Figure 4.27
Administration Building – Router B

Router Specifications	Comments
Interface A connects to segment: _____	
Routing Protocol Support	
❑ Static Routes (*specify static route entries in Comments column*)	
❑ Auto-Static RIP for IP with updates scheduled at: _____	
❑ RIP for IP v1	
❑ RIP for IP v2 ❑ RIP for IP v2 password: _____	
❑ RIP for IP Peers (*specify peers in Comments column*)	
❑ RIP for IP Neighbors (*specify neighbors in Comments column*)	
❑ OSPF ❑ OSPF password: _____	
❑ IGMP ❑ Proxy Mode interface or ❑ Router Mode interface	
❑ DHCP Relay Agent – Forward DHCP traffic to DHCP server at: _____	
Security	
❑ VPN (*specify tunnel parameters in Comments column*)	
❑ IPSec (*specify IPSec parameters in Comments column*)	
❑ IP Routing Filters (*specify filter criteria in Comments column*)	
Interface B connects to segment: _____	
Routing Protocol Support	
❑ Static Routes (*specify static route entries in Comments column*)	
❑ Auto-Static RIP for IP with updates scheduled at: _____	
❑ RIP for IP v1	
❑ RIP for IP v2 ❑ RIP for IP v2 password: _____	
❑ RIP for IP Peers (*specify peers in Comments column*)	
❑ RIP for IP Neighbors (*specify neighbors in Comments column*)	
❑ OSPF ❑ OSPF password: _____	
❑ IGMP ❑ Proxy Mode interface or ❑ Router Mode interface	
❑ DHCP Relay Agent – Forward DHCP traffic to DHCP server at: _____	
Security	
❑ VPN (*specify tunnel parameters in Comments column*)	
❑ IPSec (*specify IPSec parameters in Comments column*)	
❑ IP Routing Filters (*specify filter criteria in Comments column*)	

Design Worksheet – Figure 4.27
Administration Building – Router C

Router Specifications	Comments
Interface A connects to segment: _____	
Routing Protocol Support	
❑ Static Routes (*specify static route entries in Comments column*)	
❑ Auto-Static RIP for IP with updates scheduled at: _____	
❑ RIP for IP v1	
❑ RIP for IP v2 ❑ RIP for IP v2 password: _____	
❑ RIP for IP Peers (*specify peers in Comments column*)	
❑ RIP for IP Neighbors (*specify neighbors in Comments column*)	
❑ OSPF ❑ OSPF password: _____	
❑ IGMP ❑ Proxy Mode interface or ❑ Router Mode interface	
❑ DHCP Relay Agent – Forward DHCP traffic to DHCP server at: _____	
Security	
❑ VPN (*specify tunnel parameters in Comments column*)	
❑ IPSec (*specify IPSec parameters in Comments column*)	
❑ IP Routing Filters (*specify filter criteria in Comments column*)	
Interface B connects to segment: _____	
Routing Protocol Support	
❑ Static Routes (*specify static route entries in Comments column*)	
❑ Auto-Static RIP for IP with updates scheduled at: _____	
❑ RIP for IP v1	
❑ RIP for IP v2 ❑ RIP for IP v2 password: _____	
❑ RIP for IP Peers (*specify peers in Comments column*)	
❑ RIP for IP Neighbors (*specify neighbors in Comments column*)	
❑ OSPF ❑ OSPF password: _____	
❑ IGMP ❑ Proxy Mode interface or ❑ Router Mode interface	
❑ DHCP Relay Agent – Forward DHCP traffic to DHCP server at: _____	
Security	
❑ VPN (*specify tunnel parameters in Comments column*)	
❑ IPSec (*specify IPSec parameters in Comments column*)	
❑ IP Routing Filters (*specify filter criteria in Comments column*)	

Design Worksheet – Figure 4.27
Administration Building – Router D

Router Specifications	Comments
Interface A connects to segment: _____	
Routing Protocol Support	
❏ Static Routes (*specify static route entries in Comments column*)	
❏ Auto-Static RIP for IP with updates scheduled at: _____	
❏ RIP for IP v1	
❏ RIP for IP v2 ❏ RIP for IP v2 password: _____	
❏ RIP for IP Peers (*specify peers in Comments column*)	
❏ RIP for IP Neighbors (*specify neighbors in Comments column*)	
❏ OSPF ❏ OSPF password: _____	
❏ IGMP ❏ Proxy Mode interface or ❏ Router Mode interface	
❏ DHCP Relay Agent – Forward DHCP traffic to DHCP server at: _____	
Security	
❏ VPN (*specify tunnel parameters in Comments column*)	
❏ IPSec (*specify IPSec parameters in Comments column*)	
❏ IP Routing Filters (*specify filter criteria in Comments column*)	
Interface B connects to segment: _____	
Routing Protocol Support	
❏ Static Routes (*specify static route entries in Comments column*)	
❏ Auto-Static RIP for IP with updates scheduled at: _____	
❏ RIP for IP v1	
❏ RIP for IP v2 ❏ RIP for IP v2 password:_____	
❏ RIP for IP Peers (*specify peers in Comments column*)	
❏ RIP for IP Neighbors (*specify neighbors in Comments column*)	
❏ OSPF ❏ OSPF password: _____	
❏ IGMP ❏ Proxy Mode interface or ❏ Router Mode interface	
❏ DHCP Relay Agent – Forward DHCP traffic to DHCP server at: _____	
Security	
❏ VPN (*specify tunnel parameters in Comments column*)	
❏ IPSec (*specify IPSec parameters in Comments column*)	
❏ IP Routing Filters (*specify filter criteria in Comments column*)	

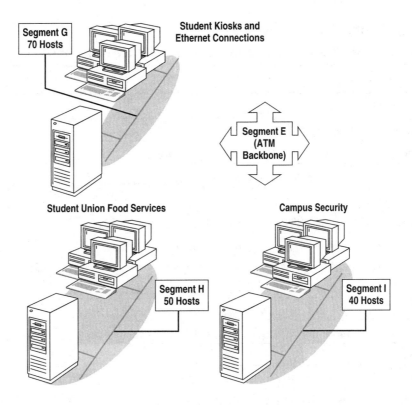

Figure 4.28 This is the existing network at the Student Union and Campus Security building.

Design Worksheet – Figure 4.28
Student Union and Campus Security Building – Router A

Router Specifications	Comments
Interface A connects to segment: _____	
Routing Protocol Support	
❑ Static Routes (*specify static route entries in Comments column*)	
❑ Auto-Static RIP for IP with updates scheduled at: _____	
❑ RIP for IP v1	
❑ RIP for IP v2 ❑ RIP for IP v2 password: _____	
❑ RIP for IP Peers (*specify peers in Comments column*)	
❑ RIP for IP Neighbors (*specify neighbors in Comments column*)	
❑ OSPF ❑ OSPF password: _____	
❑ IGMP ❑ Proxy Mode interface or ❑ Router Mode interface	
❑ DHCP Relay Agent – Forward DHCP traffic to DHCP server at: _____	
Security	
❑ VPN (*specify tunnel parameters in Comments column*)	
❑ IPSec (*specify IPSec parameters in Comments column*)	
❑ IP Routing Filters (*specify filter criteria in Comments column*)	
Interface B connects to segment: _____	
Routing Protocol Support	
❑ Static Routes (*specify static route entries in Comments column*)	
❑ Auto-Static RIP for IP with updates scheduled at:_____	
❑ RIP for IP v1	
❑ RIP for IP v2 ❑ RIP for IP v2 password:_____	
❑ RIP for IP Peers (*specify peers in Comments column*)	
❑ RIP for IP Neighbors (*specify neighbors in Comments column*)	
❑ OSPF ❑ OSPF password: _____	
❑ IGMP ❑ Proxy Mode interface or ❑ Router Mode interface	
❑ DHCP Relay Agent – Forward DHCP traffic to DHCP server at: _____	
Security	
❑ VPN (*specify tunnel parameters in Comments column*)	
❑ IPSec (*specify IPSec parameters in Comments column*)	
❑ IP Routing Filters (*specify filter criteria in Comments column*)	

Design Worksheet – Figure 4.28
Student Union and Campus Security Building – Router B

Router Specifications	Comments
Interface A connects to segment: _____	
Routing Protocol Support	
❑ Static Routes (*specify static route entries in Comments column*)	
❑ Auto-Static RIP for IP with updates scheduled at: _____	
❑ RIP for IP v1	
❑ RIP for IP v2 ❑ RIP for IP v2 password: _____	
❑ RIP for IP Peers (*specify peers in Comments column*)	
❑ RIP for IP Neighbors (*specify neighbors in Comments column*)	
❑ OSPF ❑ OSPF password: _____	
❑ IGMP ❑ Proxy Mode interface or ❑ Router Mode interface	
❑ DHCP Relay Agent – Forward DHCP traffic to DHCP server at: _____	
Security	
❑ VPN (*specify tunnel parameters in Comments column*)	
❑ IPSec (*specify IPSec parameters in Comments column*)	
❑ IP Routing Filters (*specify filter criteria in Comments column*)	
Interface B connects to segment: _____	
Routing Protocol Support	
❑ Static Routes (*specify static route entries in Comments column*)	
❑ Auto-Static RIP for IP with updates scheduled at:_____	
❑ RIP for IP v1	
❑ RIP for IP v2 ❑ RIP for IP v2 password: _____	
❑ RIP for IP Peers (*specify peers in Comments column*)	
❑ RIP for IP Neighbors (*specify neighbors in Comments column*)	
❑ OSPF ❑ OSPF password: _____	
❑ IGMP ❑ Proxy Mode interface or ❑ Router Mode interface	
❑ DHCP Relay Agent – Forward DHCP traffic to DHCP server at: _____	
Security	
❑ VPN (*specify tunnel parameters in Comments column*)	
❑ IPSec (*specify IPSec parameters in Comments column*)	
❑ IP Routing Filters (*specify filter criteria in Comments column*)	

Design Worksheet – Figure 4.28
Student Union and Campus Security Building – Router C

Router Specifications	Comments
Interface A connects to segment: _____	
Routing Protocol Support	
❑ Static Routes (*specify static route entries in Comments column*)	
❑ Auto-Static RIP for IP with updates scheduled at: _____	
❑ RIP for IP v1	
❑ RIP for IP v2 ❑ RIP for IP v2 password: _____	
❑ RIP for IP Peers (*specify peers in Comments column*)	
❑ RIP for IP Neighbors (*specify neighbors in Comments column*)	
❑ OSPF ❑ OSPF password: _____	
❑ IGMP ❑ Proxy Mode interface or ❑ Router Mode interface	
❑ DHCP Relay Agent – Forward DHCP traffic to DHCP server at: _____	
Security	
❑ VPN (*specify tunnel parameters in Comments column*)	
❑ IPSec (*specify IPSec parameters in Comments column*)	
❑ IP Routing Filters (*specify filter criteria in Comments column*)	
Interface B connects to segment: _____	
Routing Protocol Support	
❑ Static Routes (*specify static route entries in Comments column*)	
❑ Auto-Static RIP for IP with updates scheduled at: _____	
❑ RIP for IP v1	
❑ RIP for IP v2 ❑ RIP for IP v2 password: _____	
❑ RIP for IP Peers (*specify peers in Comments column*)	
❑ RIP for IP Neighbors (*specify neighbors in Comments column*)	
❑ OSPF ❑ OSPF password: _____	
❑ IGMP ❑ Proxy Mode interface or ❑ Router Mode interface	
❑ DHCP Relay Agent – Forward DHCP traffic to DHCP server at: _____	
Security	
❑ VPN (*specify tunnel parameters in Comments column*)	
❑ IPSec (*specify IPSec parameters in Comments column*)	
❑ IP Routing Filters (*specify filter criteria in Comments column*)	

Design Worksheet – Figure 4.28
Student Union and Campus Security Building – Router D

Router Specifications	Comments
Interface A connects to segment: _____	
Routing Protocol Support	
❏ Static Routes (*specify static route entries in Comments column*)	
❏ Auto-Static RIP for IP with updates scheduled at: _____	
❏ RIP for IP v1	
❏ RIP for IP v2 ❏ RIP for IP v2 password: _____	
❏ RIP for IP Peers (*specify peers in Comments column*)	
❏ RIP for IP Neighbors (*specify neighbors in Comments column*)	
❏ OSPF ❏ OSPF password: _____	
❏ IGMP ❏ Proxy Mode interface or ❏ Router Mode interface	
❏ DHCP Relay Agent – Forward DHCP traffic to DHCP server at: _____	
Security	
❏ VPN (*specify tunnel parameters in Comments column*)	
❏ IPSec (*specify IPSec parameters in Comments column*)	
❏ IP Routing Filters (*specify filter criteria in Comments column*)	
Interface B connects to segment: _____	
Routing Protocol Support	
❏ Static Routes (*specify static route entries in Comments column*)	
❏ Auto-Static RIP for IP with updates scheduled at: _____	
❏ RIP for IP v1	
❏ RIP for IP v2 ❏ RIP for IP v2 password: _____	
❏ RIP for IP Peers (*specify peers in Comments column*)	
❏ RIP for IP Neighbors (*specify neighbors in Comments column*)	
❏ OSPF ❏ OSPF password: _____	
❏ IGMP ❏ Proxy Mode interface or ❏ Router Mode interface	
❏ DHCP Relay Agent – Forward DHCP traffic to DHCP server at: _____	
Security	
❏ VPN (*specify tunnel parameters in Comments column*)	
❏ IPSec (*specify IPSec parameters in Comments column*)	
❏ IP Routing Filters (*specify filter criteria in Comments column*)	

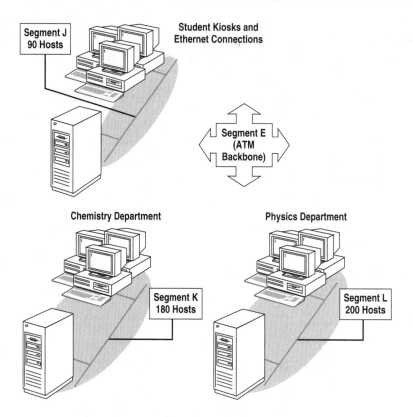

Figure 4.29   This is the existing network at the Chemistry and Physics buildings. For the purposes of this lab, assume that these buildings have the same network configuration.

Design Worksheet – Figure 4.29
Chemistry and Physics Buildings – Router A

Router Specifications	Comments
Interface A connects to segment: _____	
Routing Protocol Support	
❏ Static Routes (*specify static route entries in Comments column*)	
❏ Auto-Static RIP for IP with updates scheduled at: _____	
❏ RIP for IP v1	
❏ RIP for IP v2 ❏ RIP for IP v2 password: _____	
❏ RIP for IP Peers (*specify peers in Comments column*)	
❏ RIP for IP Neighbors (*specify neighbors in Comments column*)	
❏ OSPF ❏ OSPF password: _____	
❏ IGMP ❏ Proxy Mode interface or ❏ Router Mode interface	
❏ DHCP Relay Agent – Forward DHCP traffic to DHCP server at: _____	
Security	
❏ VPN (*specify tunnel parameters in Comments column*)	
❏ IPSec (*specify IPSec parameters in Comments column*)	
❏ IP Routing Filters (*specify filter criteria in Comments column*)	
Interface B connects to segment: _____	
Routing Protocol Support	
❏ Static Routes (*specify static route entries in Comments column*)	
❏ Auto-Static RIP for IP with updates scheduled at: _____	
❏ RIP for IP v1	
❏ RIP for IP v2 ❏ RIP for IP v2 password: _____	
❏ RIP for IP Peers (*specify peers in Comments column*)	
❏ RIP for IP Neighbors (*specify neighbors in Comments column*)	
❏ OSPF ❏ OSPF password: _____	
❏ IGMP ❏ Proxy Mode interface or ❏ Router Mode interface	
❏ DHCP Relay Agent – Forward DHCP traffic to DHCP server at: _____	
Security	
❏ VPN (*specify tunnel parameters in Comments column*)	
❏ IPSec (*specify IPSec parameters in Comments column*)	
❏ IP Routing Filters (*specify filter criteria in Comments column*)	

Design Worksheet – Figure 4.29
Chemistry and Physics Buildings – Router B

Router Specifications	Comments
Interface A connects to segment: _____	
Routing Protocol Support	
❏ Static Routes (*specify static route entries in Comments column*)	
❏ Auto-Static RIP for IP with updates scheduled at: _____	
❏ RIP for IP v1	
❏ RIP for IP v2 ❏ RIP for IP v2 password: _____	
❏ RIP for IP Peers (*specify peers in Comments column*)	
❏ RIP for IP Neighbors (*specify neighbors in Comments column*)	
❏ OSPF ❏ OSPF password: _____	
❏ IGMP ❏ Proxy Mode interface or ❏ Router Mode interface	
❏ DHCP Relay Agent – Forward DHCP traffic to DHCP server at: _____	
Security	
❏ VPN (*specify tunnel parameters in Comments column*)	
❏ IPSec (*specify IPSec parameters in Comments column*)	
❏ IP Routing Filters (*specify filter criteria in Comments column*)	
Interface B connects to segment: _____	
Routing Protocol Support	
❏ Static Routes (*specify static route entries in Comments column*)	
❏ Auto-Static RIP for IP with updates scheduled at: _____	
❏ RIP for IP v1	
❏ RIP for IP v2 ❏ RIP for IP v2 password: _____	
❏ RIP for IP Peers (*specify peers in Comments column*)	
❏ RIP for IP Neighbors (*specify neighbors in Comments column*)	
❏ OSPF ❏ OSPF password: _____	
❏ IGMP ❏ Proxy Mode interface or ❏ Router Mode interface	
❏ DHCP Relay Agent – Forward DHCP traffic to DHCP server at: _____	
Security	
❏ VPN (*specify tunnel parameters in Comments column*)	
❏ IPSec (*specify IPSec parameters in Comments column*)	
❏ IP Routing Filters (*specify filter criteria in Comments column*)	

Design Worksheet – Figure 4.29
Chemistry and Physics Buildings – Router C

Router Specifications	Comments
Interface A connects to segment: _____	
Routing Protocol Support	
❑ Static Routes (*specify static route entries in Comments column*)	
❑ Auto-Static RIP for IP with updates scheduled at: _____	
❑ RIP for IP v1	
❑ RIP for IP v2 ❑ RIP for IP v2 password: _____	
❑ RIP for IP Peers (*specify peers in Comments column*)	
❑ RIP for IP Neighbors (*specify neighbors in Comments column*)	
❑ OSPF ❑ OSPF password: _____	
❑ IGMP ❑ Proxy Mode interface or ❑ Router Mode interface	
❑ DHCP Relay Agent – Forward DHCP traffic to DHCP server at: _____	
Security	
❑ VPN (*specify tunnel parameters in Comments column*)	
❑ IPSec (*specify IPSec parameters in Comments column*)	
❑ IP Routing Filters (*specify filter criteria in Comments column*)	
Interface B connects to segment: _____	
Routing Protocol Support	
❑ Static Routes (*specify static route entries in Comments column*)	
❑ Auto-Static RIP for IP with updates scheduled at: _____	
❑ RIP for IP v1	
❑ RIP for IP v2 ❑ RIP for IP v2 password: _____	
❑ RIP for IP Peers (*specify peers in Comments column*)	
❑ RIP for IP Neighbors (*specify neighbors in Comments column*)	
❑ OSPF ❑ OSPF password: _____	
❑ IGMP ❑ Proxy Mode interface or ❑ Router Mode interface	
❑ DHCP Relay Agent – Forward DHCP traffic to DHCP server at: _____	
Security	
❑ VPN (*specify tunnel parameters in Comments column*)	
❑ IPSec (*specify IPSec parameters in Comments column*)	
❑ IP Routing Filters (*specify filter criteria in Comments column*)	

Design Worksheet – Figure 4.29
Chemistry and Physics Buildings – Router D

Router Specifications	Comments
Interface A connects to segment: _____	
Routing Protocol Support	
❑ Static Routes (*specify static route entries in Comments column*)	
❑ Auto-Static RIP for IP with updates scheduled at: _____	
❑ RIP for IP v1	
❑ RIP for IP v2 ❑ RIP for IP v2 password: _____	
❑ RIP for IP Peers (*specify peers in Comments column*)	
❑ RIP for IP Neighbors (*specify neighbors in Comments column*)	
❑ OSPF ❑ OSPF password: _____	
❑ IGMP ❑ Proxy Mode interface or ❑ Router Mode interface	
❑ DHCP Relay Agent – Forward DHCP traffic to DHCP server at: _____	
Security	
❑ VPN (*specify tunnel parameters in Comments column*)	
❑ IPSec (*specify IPSec parameters in Comments column*)	
❑ IP Routing Filters (*specify filter criteria in Comments column*)	
Interface B connects to segment: _____	
Routing Protocol Support	
❑ Static Routes (*specify static route entries in Comments column*)	
❑ Auto-Static RIP for IP with updates scheduled at: _____	
❑ RIP for IP v1	
❑ RIP for IP v2 ❑ RIP for IP v2 password: _____	
❑ RIP for IP Peers (*specify peers in Comments column*)	
❑ RIP for IP Neighbors (*specify neighbors in Comments column*)	
❑ OSPF ❑ OSPF password: _____	
❑ IGMP ❑ Proxy Mode interface or ❑ Router Mode interface	
❑ DHCP Relay Agent – Forward DHCP traffic to DHCP server at: _____	
Security	
❑ VPN (*specify tunnel parameters in Comments column*)	
❑ IPSec (*specify IPSec parameters in Comments column*)	
❑ IP Routing Filters (*specify filter criteria in Comments column*)	

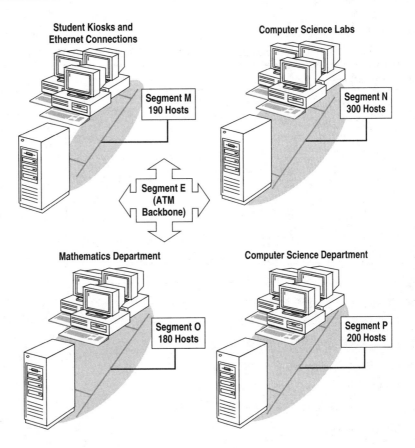

Figure 4.30 This is the existing network at the Mathematics and Computer Science building.

Design Worksheet – Figure 4.30
Mathematics and Computer Science Building – Router A

Router Specifications	Comments
Interface A connects to segment: _____	
Routing Protocol Support	
❑ Static Routes (*specify static route entries in Comments column*)	
❑ Auto-Static RIP for IP with updates scheduled at: _____	
❑ RIP for IP v1	
❑ RIP for IP v2 ❑ RIP for IP v2 password: _____	
❑ RIP for IP Peers (*specify peers in Comments column*)	
❑ RIP for IP Neighbors (*specify neighbors in Comments column*)	
❑ OSPF ❑ OSPF password: _____	
❑ IGMP ❑ Proxy Mode interface or ❑ Router Mode interface	
❑ DHCP Relay Agent – Forward DHCP traffic to DHCP server at: _____	
Security	
❑ VPN (*specify tunnel parameters in Comments column*)	
❑ IPSec (*specify IPSec parameters in Comments column*)	
❑ IP Routing Filters (*specify filter criteria in Comments column*)	
Interface B connects to segment: _____	
Routing Protocol Support	
❑ Static Routes (*specify static route entries in Comments column*)	
❑ Auto-Static RIP for IP with updates scheduled at: _____	
❑ RIP for IP v1	
❑ RIP for IP v2 ❑ RIP for IP v2 password: _____	
❑ RIP for IP Peers (*specify peers in Comments column*)	
❑ RIP for IP Neighbors (*specify neighbors in Comments column*)	
❑ OSPF ❑ OSPF password: _____	
❑ IGMP ❑ Proxy Mode interface or ❑ Router Mode interface	
❑ DHCP Relay Agent – Forward DHCP traffic to DHCP server at: _____	
Security	
❑ VPN (*specify tunnel parameters in Comments column*)	
❑ IPSec (*specify IPSec parameters in Comments column*)	
❑ IP Routing Filters (*specify filter criteria in Comments column*)	

Design Worksheet – Figure 4.30
Mathematics and Computer Science Building – Router B

Router Specifications	Comments
Interface A connects to segment: _____	
Routing Protocol Support	
❑ Static Routes (*specify static route entries in Comments column*)	
❑ Auto-Static RIP for IP with updates scheduled at: _____	
❑ RIP for IP v1	
❑ RIP for IP v2 ❑ RIP for IP v2 password: _____	
❑ RIP for IP Peers (*specify peers in Comments column*)	
❑ RIP for IP Neighbors (*specify neighbors in Comments column*)	
❑ OSPF ❑ OSPF password: _____	
❑ IGMP ❑ Proxy Mode interface or ❑ Router Mode interface	
❑ DHCP Relay Agent – Forward DHCP traffic to DHCP server at: _____	
Security	
❑ VPN (*specify tunnel parameters in Comments column*)	
❑ IPSec (*specify IPSec parameters in Comments column*)	
❑ IP Routing Filters (*specify filter criteria in Comments column*)	
Interface B connects to segment: _____	
Routing Protocol Support	
❑ Static Routes (*specify static route entries in Comments column*)	
❑ Auto-Static RIP for IP with updates scheduled at: _____	
❑ RIP for IP v1	
❑ RIP for IP v2 ❑ RIP for IP v2 password: _____	
❑ RIP for IP Peers (*specify peers in Comments column*)	
❑ RIP for IP Neighbors (*specify neighbors in Comments column*)	
❑ OSPF ❑ OSPF password: _____	
❑ IGMP ❑ Proxy Mode interface or ❑ Router Mode interface	
❑ DHCP Relay Agent – Forward DHCP traffic to DHCP server at: _____	
Security	
❑ VPN (*specify tunnel parameters in Comments column*)	
❑ IPSec (*specify IPSec parameters in Comments column*)	
❑ IP Routing Filters (*specify filter criteria in Comments column*)	

Design Worksheet – Figure 4.30
Mathematics and Computer Science Building – Router C

Router Specifications	Comments
Interface A connects to segment: _____	
Routing Protocol Support	
❑ Static Routes (*specify static route entries in Comments column*)	
❑ Auto-Static RIP for IP with updates scheduled at: _____	
❑ RIP for IP v1	
❑ RIP for IP v2 ❑ RIP for IP v2 password: _____	
❑ RIP for IP Peers (*specify peers in Comments column*)	
❑ RIP for IP Neighbors (*specify neighbors in Comments column*)	
❑ OSPF ❑ OSPF password: _____	
❑ IGMP ❑ Proxy Mode interface or ❑ Router Mode interface	
❑ DHCP Relay Agent – Forward DHCP traffic to DHCP server at: _____	
Security	
❑ VPN (*specify tunnel parameters in Comments column*)	
❑ IPSec (*specify IPSec parameters in Comments column*)	
❑ IP Routing Filters (*specify filter criteria in Comments column*)	
Interface B connects to segment: _____	
Routing Protocol Support	
❑ Static Routes (*specify static route entries in Comments column*)	
❑ Auto-Static RIP for IP with updates scheduled at: _____	
❑ RIP for IP v1	
❑ RIP for IP v2 ❑ RIP for IP v2 password: _____	
❑ RIP for IP Peers (*specify peers in Comments column*)`	
❑ RIP for IP Neighbors (*specify neighbors in Comments column*)	
❑ OSPF ❑ OSPF password: _____	
❑ IGMP ❑ Proxy Mode interface or ❑ Router Mode interface	
❑ DHCP Relay Agent – Forward DHCP traffic to DHCP server at: _____	
Security	
❑ VPN (*specify tunnel parameters in Comments column*)	
❑ IPSec (*specify IPSec parameters in Comments column*)	
❑ IP Routing Filters (*specify filter criteria in Comments column*)	

Design Worksheet – Figure 4.30
Mathematics and Computer Science Building – Router D

Router Specifications	Comments
Interface A connects to segment: _____	
Routing Protocol Support	
❑ Static Routes (*specify static route entries in Comments column*)	
❑ Auto-Static RIP for IP with updates scheduled at: _____	
❑ RIP for IP v1	
❑ RIP for IP v2 ❑ RIP for IP v2 password: _____	
❑ RIP for IP Peers (*specify peers in Comments column*)	
❑ RIP for IP Neighbors (*specify neighbors in Comments column*)	
❑ OSPF ❑ OSPF password: _____	
❑ IGMP ❑ Proxy Mode interface or ❑ Router Mode interface	
❑ DHCP Relay Agent – Forward DHCP traffic to DHCP server at: _____	
Security	
❑ VPN (*specify tunnel parameters in Comments column*)	
❑ IPSec (*specify IPSec parameters in Comments column*)	
❑ IP Routing Filters (*specify filter criteria in Comments column*)	
Interface B connects to segment: _____	
Routing Protocol Support	
❑ Static Routes (*specify static route entries in Comments column*)	
❑ Auto-Static RIP for IP with updates scheduled at: _____	
❑ RIP for IP v1	
❑ RIP for IP v2 ❑ RIP for IP v2 password: _____	
❑ RIP for IP Peers (*specify peers in Comments column*)	
❑ RIP for IP Neighbors (*specify neighbors in Comments column*)	
❑ OSPF ❑ OSPF password: _____	
❑ IGMP ❑ Proxy Mode interface or ❑ Router Mode interface	
❑ DHCP Relay Agent – Forward DHCP traffic to DHCP server at: _____	
Security	
❑ VPN (*specify tunnel parameters in Comments column*)	
❑ IPSec (*specify IPSec parameters in Comments column*)	
❑ IP Routing Filters (*specify filter criteria in Comments column*)	

Review

The following questions are intended to reinforce key information in this chapter. If you're unable to answer a question, review the lesson and then try to answer the question again. You can find answers to the questions in the Appendix, "Questions and Answers."

1. An organization has 35 locations throughout North and South America. The locations are connected over point-to-point communications links that include 56Kbps, T1, and T3 communications links. The organization wants to reduce the cost associated with these point-to-point communications links. The organization also wants to ensure that confidential data is protected in any new solution. As a consultant to the organization, what recommendations can you make?

2. An organization has a number of Web-based services and applications that are provided to its customers. A computer running Windows 2000 and Routing and Remote Access provides the connectivity to the servers that host these services and applications. The majority of the revenue for the organization is derived from the Web-based services and applications. The board of directors is concerned about the ability of the customers to access the Web-based services and applications at all times. What recommendations can you make to ensure that customers can access the Web-based services and applications?

3. You're creating a routing design for your network. Your organization has a number of locations. Each location has a number of networking segments. What information must you collect to create your routing design?

4. You're creating a routing design for an organization that has 10 locations throughout the world. The existing network design has evolved over the last eight years, and needs to be redesigned. The organization has a range of IP addresses allocated from an ISP by using CIDR. The operations staff of the organization's information services department wants to ensure that the new network is easy to manage. What routing protocols do you include in your design, and what are the reasons for selecting the respective routing protocols?

CHAPTER 5

Multiprotocol Routing Designs

About This Chapter

In addition to Transmission Control Protocol/Internet Protocol (TCP/IP), many of the networks that you'll design will include other network protocols. These networks can be comprised of many locations that will be connected over wide area networks (WANs). Each of these locations will contain one or more network segments. In some instances these WANs will communicate over the Internet. Your networking services designs must provide connectivity for these networks.

You can use Microsoft Windows 2000 to provide connectivity between Internetwork Packet Exchange (IPX)-based and AppleTalk-based network segments. As a result, you can provide multiprotocol routing designs that can connect network segments and locations. When sensitive information is transmitted between unsecured network segments, your design must protect the data's confidentiality.

This chapter answers questions such as:

- In what situations are the IPX and AppleTalk routing services provided by Windows 2000 appropriate for your design?
- Which routing protocols can minimize network route paths while reducing the network traffic required to manage IPX and AppleTalk routing tables?

- How can confidential data be transmitted securely between network segments and locations?

- How can you ensure that IPX and AppleTalk packets are always delivered when transmitted between network segments and locations?

- How can you optimize the aggregate data transfer rate between network segments and locations?

Before You Begin

Before you begin, you must have an overall understanding of

- Network technologies (including Ethernet, Token Ring, hubs, switches, and concentrators)

- The common transport protocol configuration for Internetwork Packet Exchange (IPX) and AppleTalk (such as IPX network number or IPX frame type)

- IPX routed networks (including network segments, routers, and IPX to IP gateways)

- AppleTalk routed networks (including network segments, network numbers, network address ranges, routers, and AppleTalk zones)

Lesson 1: Designs That Include Multiprotocol Routers

This lesson presents the requirements and constraints, both business and technical, that identify the multiprotocol routing services in Windows 2000 as a solution.

After this lesson, you will be able to

- Describe the role of IPX or AppleTalk routing in the Windows 2000 architecture
- Identify the business and technical requirements and constraints that must be collected to create an IPX or AppleTalk routing design
- Identify the IPX or AppleTalk routing design decisions
- Evaluate scenarios and determine when the IPX or AppleTalk routing services provided by Windows 2000 are an appropriate solution
- Evaluate scenarios and determine which capabilities and features of Windows 2000 IPX or AppleTalk routing services are appropriate

Estimated lesson time: 30 minutes

IPX and AppleTalk Routing in Windows 2000

Because Routing and Remote Access is an integral feature of Windows 2000, any computer running Microsoft Windows 2000 Server, Microsoft Windows 2000 Advanced Server, or Microsoft Windows 2000 Datacenter Server can provide IPX or AppleTalk routing for your network.

All multiprotocol devices in your network can participate in IPX or AppleTalk routing because each device maintains a routing table. Figure 5.1 illustrates the multiprotocol devices involved in multiprotocol routing.

Consider the following sequence.

1. Host A (the source host) wants to send an IPX (or AppleTalk) packet to Host B, C, or D (the destination host).
2. The source host determines the IPX (or AppleTalk) address of the destination host.
3. The source host examines its local routing table and determines that the destination host can be reached through Router A.
4. The source host sends the IPX (or AppleTalk) packet to Router A.
5. Router A examines its local routing table and determines that the destination host can be reached through Router B, C, or D.
6. Router A forwards the IPX (or AppleTalk) packet to the respective router (either Router B, C, or D).

7. Router B, C, or D examines its local routing table and determines that the respective destination host can be reached directly.

8. Router B, C, or D forwards the IPX (or AppleTalk) packet to the respective destination host.

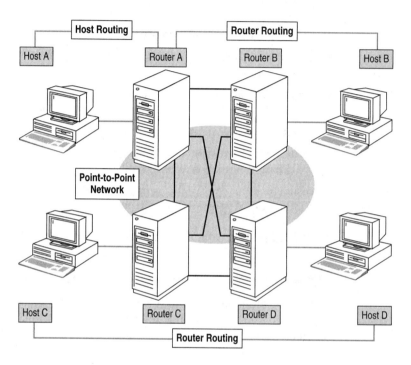

Figure 5.1   The role of various multiprotocol devices in multiprotocol routing

Each of the devices in the scenario participates in the routing between the source host and the destination host, which is very similar to Internet Protocol (IP) routing found in Chapter 4, "IP Routing Designs," Lesson 1, "Designs That Include IP Routers." The routing that occurs between the source host and Router A is known as *host routing*. The routing that occurs between Router A, Router B, and the destination host is known as *router routing*.

All IPX-based or AppleTalk-based devices must support host routing to send IPX or AppleTalk packets in a routed network. Microsoft Window 95, Microsoft Windows 98, Microsoft Windows NT 4.0, Windows 2000, UNIX, Macintosh, and other operating systems support host routing.

Hardware routers, hardware IP switches, and other hardware-based devices support router routing. The Routing and Remote Access feature in Windows 2000 provides software-based router routing.

In this chapter, you learn how to create multiprotocol router routing solutions with Windows 2000 for IPX-based and AppleTalk-based networks. To successfully create multiprotocol routing designs, you must be familiar with general routing theory and IPX, or AppleTalk, routing protocols.

Note   In this book, unless otherwise specified, routing always refers to the IPX and AppleTalk routing provided by Windows 2000. In this chapter, unless otherwise specified, routers are Windows 2000–based IPX or AppleTalk routers.

Multiprotocol Routing Design Requirements and Constraints

Before you create your routing design, you must gather the requirements and constraints, both business and technical, of the organization. As you create your design, you make design decisions based on the requirements and constraints you collect.

The list of the design requirements and constraints that you collect will include

- Characteristics of the data transmitted through the router, including
    - The amount of data transmitted through the router
    - The confidentiality of the data transmitted through the router
- Plans for future network growth
- Characteristics of existing routers including
    - Protocols to be routed
    - Router placement
    - WAN connections in use
    - Routing protocols in use
- Response times for applications that access resources through the router
- Acceptable percentage of time that users require access through the router

IP Routing Design Decisions

After you determine the business and technical requirements and constraints, apply the information you gathered to make routing design decisions.

To create your routing design, you must choose the

- Types of connections, persistent or nonpersistent, that each router must support
- Connection technologies, including T1, Public Switched Telephone Network (PSTN), Integrated Services Digital Network (ISDN), Digital Subscriber Line (DSL), or X.25, that each router must support

- Dynamic routing protocols or manual routing table entries that each router must support

- Multiple route paths and multiple routers to improve availability and performance

- Criteria that you'll adopt to filter packet traffic

- Authentication and encryption algorithms that will protect your confidential data

---

Note You can protect IPX traffic by encrypting data in virtual private network (VPN) tunnels. No data protection is available for AppleTalk traffic.

The lessons that follow in this chapter provide the information required for you to make specific IPX and AppleTalk routing design recommendations.

Edge of Network Scenario

The most common scenario for multiprotocol routing in Windows 2000 uses an *edge of network* design. An edge of network design connects your private network to a public network, such as point-to-point networks or the Internet.

Making the Decision

When you create designs that require edge of network routers, the routers can

- **Prevent unauthorized access to private network resources**   IPX filters and VPN technology prevent unauthorized access.

- **Provide connectivity across IP-based public networks, such as the Internet**   Routing and Remote Access supports the ability to transmit IPX traffic across IP-based networks, such as the Internet.

- **Protect confidential data transmitted over public networks, such as point-to-point networks or the Internet**   The VPN technologies in Routing and Remote Access protect confidential data by providing router identity, data integrity, and data encryption.

- **Connect to a variety of WAN technologies**   Routing and Remote Access can route data over any network interface supported by Windows 2000.

Applying the Decision

Figure 5.2 illustrates a design that connects multiple locations in your private network to a packet-switched public network. The edge of your private network is where you connect to the packet-switched public network, in this case at Routers A and B. All network segments behind Routers A and B (Segments A, B, and C) are considered part of your private network.

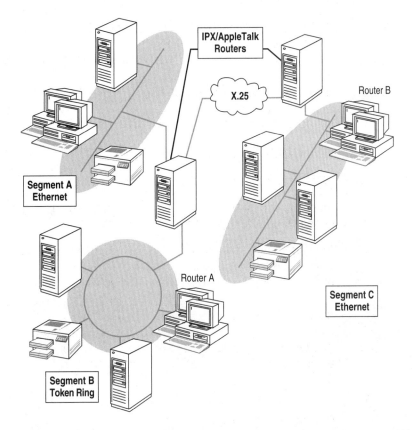

Figure 5.2   A scenario in which multiprotocol routers are used to connect multiple locations across a packet-switched public network

Router A is also an example of an *internal* router. Typically, internal routers require no features other than the ability to provide multiprotocol routing. Besides acting as an edge of network router, Router A connects network segments within the private network.

The added security and WAN connectivity options of edge of network routers increase the cost of the routers. As a result, you can use routers without the enhanced features of Routing and Remote Access for internal routers.

A firewall is optional in the design shown in Figure 5.2 when

- **The routers support point-to-point communications**   When you use the routers for point-to-point communications, such as connecting two or more locations, the endpoints are known. You can restrict the router so that the router communicates only with the known endpoints. In addition, you can encrypt the data transmitted between the known endpoints.

- **Router filters provide sufficient security**   You can restrict the traffic that Routing and Remote Access transmits and receives with IPX routing filters. IPX routing filters allow you to create filters that discard unauthorized traffic.

Note   IPX routing filters and data encryption are discussed further in Lesson 2 in this chapter.

IPX Tunneling Scenario

You can identify an IPX tunneling scenario when you connect multiple locations together over an IP public network, such as the Internet. You create your IPX tunneling design based on the assumption that the locations belong to the same organization or to trusted partner organizations.

You can connect remote locations by using point-to-point leased lines, the Internet, or other public networks. Any of these connectivity options require you to protect confidential data transmitted between locations.

Note   IPX tunneling doesn't provide Internet connectivity to the IPX-based computers within the private network. IPX tunneling transmits only IPX packets through VPN tunnels over the Internet. To provide Internet connectivity to IPX-based computers, you must use an IPX to IP gateway, such as Microsoft Proxy Server 2.0.

Making the Decision

When you create designs that connect IPX networks through IP networks, each router must

- **Meet all the requirements of an edge of network design**   All the Routing and Remote Access features that are used in an edge of network scenario are required in the IPX tunnel scenario.
- **Authenticate routers**   Routing and Remote Access can authenticate routers and VPN tunnels with
  - User account authentication that is managed by the organization (for additional security, you can authenticate user accounts in Active Directory directory service)
  - Machine certificates based on Kerberos V5 tickets, X509 certificates, or a preshared key

Applying the Decision

Figure 5.3 illustrates a scenario in which IPX traffic is transmitted between multiple locations over the Internet through an IP tunnel. At the edge of each location's network, you place a router (Routers B, D, and E) that connects the

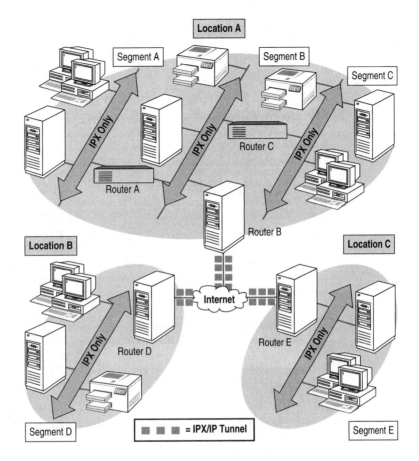

Figure 5.3   A scenario where you transmit IPX traffic between multiple locations
over the Internet through an IP tunnel

location to the Internet. The IPX traffic between locations is tunneled inside an
IP packet and then transmitted between the edge of network routers. Upon reach-
ing the other end of the tunnel, the IP header is removed from the packet and the
IPX packet is routed like a normal IPX packet.

As with any data transmitted across public networks, Routers B, D, and E are
responsible for the protection of any confidential data exchanged between locations, by providing router identity, data integrity, and data encryption. You can
use any of the IP data protection mechanisms discussed in Chapter 2, "Networking Protocol Design," Lesson 3, "TCP/IP Data Protection."

Lesson 2: IPX Routing Design Concepts

This lesson discusses the requirements, constraints, and design decisions that are used in creating an IPX routing design. Your design provides IPX routing when the routers can transmit IPX packets between different network segments, protect data transmitted over public networks, and achieve the availability and performance requirements of the organization.

After this lesson, you will be able to

- Determine the appropriate placement of routers in an IPX routing design
- Identify the appropriate design specifications for each router interface
- Select an appropriate internal IPX network number for each router
- Select the appropriate method for maintaining IPX router information
- Select the appropriate method for protecting IPX traffic
- Select the appropriate method for optimizing design to improve the availability and performance of IPX routing

Estimated lesson time: 45 minutes

Placing Routers in the Network Design

In Lesson 1 of this chapter and in Chapter 4, "IP Routing Designs," you examined scenarios that depicted the placement of routers within a network. The scenarios illustrated that you can place routers at the edge of your private network (edge of network routers) or within your private network (internal routers).

Making the Decision

You can approach the placement of IPX routers in your design as you do the placement of IP routers—the design decisions are the same. For more information on the placement of IP routers, and subsequently IPX routers, see Chapter 4, "IP Routing Designs," Lesson 2, "Essential IP Routing Design Concepts."

Applying the Decision

Figure 5.4 illustrates a scenario with IPX routers that tunnel IPX traffic through an IP tunnel across the Internet. The organization in the scenario is comprised of six locations. Each location is identical to the location illustrated in Figure 5.4. Router A is responsible for providing internal routing and edge of network routing.

For the purposes of this scenario, assume that

- The existing network segments are optimized to localize traffic within each network segment

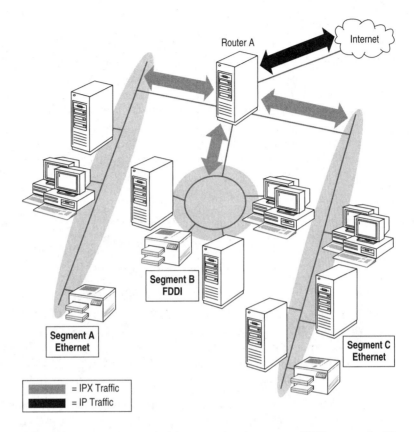

Figure 5.4   A scenario that illustrates the placement of IPX routers for IP tunneling

- The organization is concerned about the security of packets transmitted between locations
- Only IPX traffic is transmitted within each location
- The router is connected to the Internet by using ISDN

Table 5.1 lists the reasons for placing routers in your design and discusses the appropriateness of the reason in the scenario.

Table 5.1   Reasons to Place Routers in Your Design and Their Appropriateness

Place Routers in Your Design to	Internal Segments (Segments A, B, and C)	Edge of Network Segments (Internet)
Connect network segments with dissimilar local area network (LAN) or WAN technologies	**Appropriate** Segments A and C are Ethernet while Segment B is Fiber Distributed Data Interface (FDDI)	**Appropriate** The router is connected to the Internet by using ISDN

(continued)

Table 5.1   *(continued)*

Place Routers in Your Design to	Internal Segments (Segments A, B, and C)	Edge of Network Segments (Internet)
Reduce network traffic between network segments	**Appropriate** You want to reduce the traffic between Segments A, B, and C	**Appropriate** You want to reduce the traffic between locations
Prevent unauthorized network traffic between network segments by using IPX and IP filters	**Inappropriate** The organization isn't concerned about unauthorized traffic within each location	**Appropriate** The organization wants to block unauthorized traffic from the Internet
Prevent unauthorized access to confidential data transmitted over public networks by using encryption and authentication	**Inappropriate** The organization isn't concerned about unauthorized viewing of confidential data within each location	**Appropriate** The organization wants to prevent unauthorized viewing of confidential data transmitted between locations

The IPX routing provided by Routing and Remote Access can be used as an internal router or an edge of network router. Routing and Remote Access meets all the requirements for an edge of network router. As a result, you can use Routing and Remote Access to provide a cost-effective solution.

As you learned in Chapter 4, "IP Routing Designs," Lesson 2, "Essential IP Routing Design Concepts," Routing and Remote Access has features that exceed the requirements for internal routers. As a result, the cost associated with using Routing and Remote Access as an internal router might be too expensive. As a result, consider using lower cost hardware routers as internal routers.

Figure 5.5 illustrates a scenario with internal and edge of network IPX routers. Each location in the scenario is connected to the other locations through point-to-point connections. The requirements for the edge of network routers (Routers B, D, and E) in this scenario are the same as Router A in the scenario illustrated in Figure 5.4.

For the purposes of this scenario, assume that

- The existing network segments are optimized to localize traffic within each network segment
- The organization is concerned about the security of packets transmitted between locations
- Only IPX traffic is transmitted within each location
- The router is connected to the other locations by using point-to-point 56 Kbps leased lines

Table 5.2 lists the reasons for placing internal routers and edge of network routers in your design and discusses the appropriateness of the reason in the scenario.

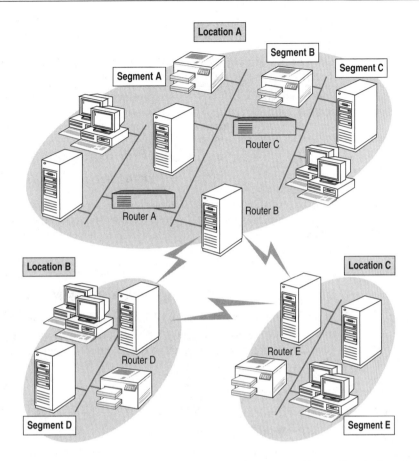

Figure 5.5   A scenario that illustrates the placement of internal and edge of network routers within your design

Table 5.2   Reasons for Placing Certain Routers in Your Design and Their Appropriateness

Place Routers in Your Design to	Internal Routers (Routers A and C)	Edge of Network Routers (Routers B, D, and E)
Connect network segments with dissimilar LAN or WAN technologies	**Inappropriate** The network segments (Segments A, B, and C) are not dissimilar technologies	**Appropriate** The router interfaces connected to the Internet are connecting dissimilar technologies
Reduce network traffic between network segments	**Appropriate** You want to reduce the traffic between Segments A, B, and C	**Appropriate** You want to reduce the traffic between locations

(continued)

Table 5.2   *(continued)*

Place Routers in Your Design to	Internal Routers (Routers A and C)	Edge of Network Routers (Routers B, D, and E)
Prevent unauthorized network traffic between network segments by using IP filters	**Inappropriate** The organization isn't concerned about unauthorized traffic within each location	**Appropriate** The organization wants to block unauthorized traffic from the Internet
Prevent unauthorized access to confidential data transmitted over public networks by using encryption and authentication	**Inappropriate** The organization isn't concerned about unauthorized viewing of confidential data within each location	**Appropriate** The organization wants to prevent unauthorized viewing of confidential data transmitted between locations

Integrating Routers into an Existing Network

Most routers in your designs will have at least two network interfaces. The router interfaces provide connectivity between the routers and the network segments in your design. For each interface in each router in your design, you must specify

- The IPX configuration information, including the IPX network number and IPX frame type

- The type of connection between the router interface and the network, such as persistent or nonpersistent

- The level of authentication, filtering, and encryption when transmitting IPX through an IP tunnel

Note   You can create a router that has a single network interface card with two IPX frame types bound to the same interface. Each IPX frame type requires a separate and unique IPX network number. With this arrangement, you can route IPX packets between the two IPX frame types on the same interface. Use this method to support multiple IPX frame types on one network segment.

Router Interface IPX Specifications

You must specify an IPX network number and IPX frame type for each router interface in your design.

Making the Decision

Select the IPX network number from the IPX network number(s) assigned to the network segment that the interface is directly connected to. The IPX frame type(s) that you assign to the router interface must match the IPX frame types transmitted on the network segment to which the interface is directly connected.

Note The network segments in your design may support more than one IPX frame type. For each IPX frame type on each network segment, you must provide IPX routing. To Routing and Remote Access, each IPX frame type appears as a logical network interface. For more information on IPX frame types, see Chapter 3, "Multiprotocol Network Design," Lesson 2, "IPX/SPX Design Concepts."

When the network segments in your design have more than one IPX frame type, IPX-based devices with different IPX frame types can't communicate directly to one another. Although the IPX-based devices are on the same network segment, you must provide IPX routing between the different IPX frame types. When you create IPX routing designs that include multiple IPX frame types

- **Reduce the number of IPX frame types in your design**   As you reduce the number of IPX frame types in your design, you reduce the amount of traffic that must be routed. In addition, when you reduce the number of IPX frame types, you reduce the possibility of configuration errors.

- **Provide routing between the IPX frame types in your design**   You must provide routing between computers with different IPX frame types, even if the computers are on the same network segment. Ensure that your design provides routes between different IPX frame types.

- **Assign an IPX network number to each IPX frame type on each network segment**   You must assign an IPX network number to each IPX frame type on each network segment so you can provide routing between the IPX frame types in your design.

Applying the Decision

Figure 5.6 illustrates a network with multiple IPX frame types. For each IPX frame type, you must provide IPX routing to other IPX frame types on the same network segment and on other network segments.

Table 5.3 lists each network segment, the frame type on each network segment, and an example of the network numbers that can be assigned.

Table 5.3   Example of Network Numbers That Can Be Assigned to Frame Types on Network Segments

Segment	Frame Type	Network Number
Segment A	EtherNet_802.2	0A08022
	EtherNet_802.3	0A08023
Segment B	Token_802.2	0B08022
	Token_SNAP	0B08000
Segment C	Ethernet_II	0C08002
	Ethernet_802.2	0C08022
X.25	N/A	0D00025

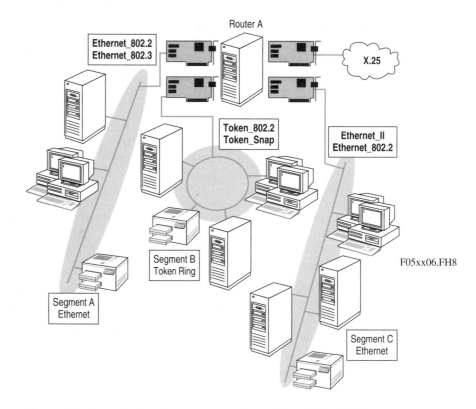

F05xx06.FH8

Figure 5.6   Scenario that illustrates a network with multiple IPX frame types

The IPX network numbers assigned in the previous example use a scheme that identifies the segment and frame type. For example, network number 0C08022 indicates that the IPX network number is assigned to IPX frame type Ethernet_802.2 on Segment C. In your designs, ensure that you create meaningful IPX network numbering schemes.

Router Interface Connection Specifications

You must specify the IPX router interface connection for each router interface in your design. You must also specify the technology and the persistence of each IPX router interface.

Making the Decision

The design decisions for IPX router interface connections are the same as the decisions for IP router interface connections. For more information on the placement of IP routers, and subsequently IPX routers, see Chapter 4, "IP Routing Designs," Lesson 2, "Essential IP Routing Design Concepts."

Applying the Decision

Figure 5.7 illustrates the router interface connections required to support IPX tunneling through the Internet. For each interface in each router, you must determine the router interface type.

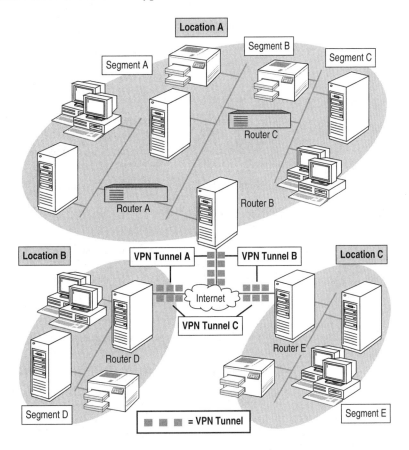

Figure 5.7   The router interface connections in routers that provide IPX tunneling

For the purposes of this scenario, assume that

- The network segments (Segments A, B, C, D, and E) within each location are 100Mbps Ethernet
- Each location is directly connected to the Internet by using a DSL connection
- Any confidential data transmitted between locations must be protected

Table 5.4 lists each router interface, the interface type and persistence, and reason for selecting the interface type and persistence.

Table 5.4   Reasons for Choosing Specific Router Interface Types and Persistences

For This Router and Interface		Select This Interface Type and Persistence	Reason
Router A	Segment A	LAN, persistent	Ethernet LAN connection
	Segment B	LAN, persistent	Ethernet LAN connection
Router B	Segment B	LAN, persistent	Ethernet LAN connection
	Internet	LAN, persistent	Dedicated DSL connection
	VPN Tunnel A	Demand-dial, nonpersistent	VPN tunnels require authentication
	VPN Tunnel B	Demand-dial, nonpersistent	VPN tunnels require authentication
Router C	Segment B	LAN, persistent	Ethernet LAN connection
	Segment C	LAN, persistent	Ethernet LAN connection
Router D	Segment D	LAN, persistent	Ethernet LAN connection
	Internet	LAN, persistent	Dedicated DSL connection
	VPN Tunnel A	Demand-dial, nonpersistent	VPN tunnels require authentication
	VPN Tunnel C	Demand-dial, nonpersistent	VPN tunnels require authentication
Router E	Segment E	LAN, persistent	Ethernet LAN connection
	Internet	LAN, persistent	Dedicated DSL connection
	VPN Tunnel B	Demand-dial, nonpersistent	VPN tunnels require authentication
	VPN Tunnel C	Demand-dial, nonpersistent	VPN tunnels require authentication

Router Security Options

You can assign a different level of security to each interface on each router and can customize the security of your design to meet the requirements of the organization.

Making the Decision

For each interface that transmits confidential data over public networks, your design must

■ Authenticate the routers that exchange the confidential data

- Encrypt the confidential data
- Prevent unauthorized access to private network resources

Note Because IPX has no inherent security, you can authenticate the routers and encrypt the confidential data only by tunneling IPX traffic through an IP-based VPN tunnel. You can then use any authentication or encryption mechanisms available to VPN tunnels.

Applying the Decision

The scenario in Figure 5.7 protects the confidential data transmitted between locations over the Internet by using VPN. The routers in Figure 5.7 prevent access to resources within each location by using IP and IPX router filters. For more information on securing router-to-router traffic see the section, "Protecting IPX Traffic," later in this lesson.

Internal IPX Network Numbers

Each Novell NetWare file or print server, Windows 2000 router, or any application server that supports IPX in your design must be assigned an internal IPX network number. Internal IPX network numbers are used by applications and services running on the computer to communicate with other IPX-based applications and services.

For example, a message server, such as Microsoft Exchange 2000 Server, can use IPX to communicate between the computer running Microsoft Exchange Server and messaging client computers. You must assign a unique internal IPX network number to the computer running Microsoft Exchange Server.

Making the Decision

Each internal IPX network number that you assign must be different from

- Internal IPX network numbers assigned to other IPX-based devices
- IPX network numbers assigned to network segments or IPX frame types

Applying the Decision

Figure 5.8 illustrates the proper assignment of internal IPX network numbers in a design. Each router, application server, file server, and print server is assigned a unique IPX network number.

For the purposes of this scenario, assume that

- Each location is directly connected to the other location by using a X.25 connection
- All Ethernet network segments support only the Ethernet_802.2 IPX frame type
- All Token Ring network segments support only the Token_SNAP IPX frame type

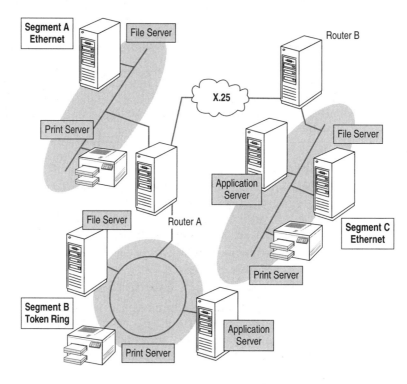

Figure 5.8   The proper assignment of internal IPX network numbers in a design

Table 5.5 illustrates an example of the IPX network numbers that must be assigned to each network segment and the internal IPX network numbers that must be assigned to IPX-based devices in the scenario.

Table 5.5   Network Numbers and Types and Where They Must Be Assigned To

Network Number	Type	Assigned To
0A08022	Network number	Segment A network interfaces
0A01001	Internal network number	File server on Segment A
0A02001	Internal network number	Print server on Segment A
0B09001	Network number	Segment B network interfaces
0B01001	Internal network number	File server on Segment B
0B02001	Internal network number	Print server on Segment B
0B03001	Internal network number	Application server on Segment B
0C08022	Network number	Segment C network interfaces
0C01001	Internal network number	File server on Segment C
0C02001	Internal network number	Print server on Segment C
0C03001	Internal network number	Application server on Segment C

Table 5.5 *(continued)*

Network Number	Type	Assigned To
1000001	Internal network number	Router A
1000002	Internal network number	Router B
2000000	Network number	X.25

The IPX network numbers and internal IPX network numbers assigned in the previous example use a scheme that identifies the

- Segment and frame type for IPX network numbers
- Segment and IPX-based computer type (such as router, application server, or file server) for internal IPX network numbers

For example, the internal IPX network number 0B02001 indicates that the internal IPX network number is assigned to the first print server (02 = print server, 001 = unique identifier for the network segment on Segment B). In your designs, ensure that you create meaningful internal IPX network numbering schemes.

For more information on creating meaningful IPX network numbering schemes, see the section, "Router Interface IPX Specifications," earlier in this lesson.

IPX Router Information Management

For each IPX router in your design, you must determine how the routers manage their IPX routing information. Your design must specify IPX routing information that enables the router to determine how

- IPX packets are forwarded between network segments by using manual routing table entries, Routing Information Protocol for IPX (RIPX), or autostatic RIPX
- IPX-based computers and routers notify other computers of available applications and services by using manual service entries, Service Advertising Protocol (SAP), or autostatic SAP

You can think of SAP as a yellow page listing in a phone book that lists the available services on the network, grouped by the types of services (such as file services, print services, and so on). RIPX can be thought of as directions to reach a service that you select from the yellow pages.

IPX Routing Table Management

Like IP routers, IPX routers determine how to route IPX packets with information stored in a memory-based routing table. You can manage the routing table information

- Manually by using static routing entries

- Automatically by using
  - The IPX dynamic routing protocol RIPX
  - Autostatic RIPX routing entries

Making the Decision

The design decisions for selecting the appropriate method of managing IPX routing table information are the same as the design decisions for IP routing table information. You can specify IPX static routing entries by using the same decision process as IP static routing entries. By using the same design decisions as RIP, you can determine how best to use RIPX. Autostatic RIPX routing requires the same decision process as autostatic RIP routing. For more information on managing IP routing table information, see Chapter 4, "IP Routing Designs," Lesson 2, "Essential IP Routing Concepts."

Table 5.6 lists the methods for managing routing table information and the advantages and disadvantages for each method.

Table 5.6   Advantages and Disadvantages of Methods for Managing Routing Table Information

Method	Advantages	Disadvantages
Static routing entries	▪ Reduces network traffic because no routing information is exchanged between routers ▪ Prevents unauthorized users from gaining information regarding the IPX network addressing scheme of your private network	▪ Requires administrator intervention as network segments are added or removed ▪ Increases the possibility of invalid routing table entries
RIPX	▪ Automatically updates routing information as network segments are added or removed ▪ Reduces the possibility of invalid routing table entries ▪ Routing information is updated on a periodic interval (30 seconds by default)	▪ Increases network traffic because routing information is exchanged between routers
Autostatic RIPX	▪ Automatically updates routing information as network segments are added or removed ▪ Reduces the possibility of invalid routing table entries	▪ Increases network traffic because routing information is exchanged between routers ▪ Routing information is updated only at scheduled intervals (typically hours in length)

When your designs include tunneling IPX through IP-based networks, you can use RIPX, autostatic RIPX, or static routing entries to establish route paths through the tunnel. Determine the method for managing routing information based on the amount of network traffic that the tunnel can support. When you want to reduce the network traffic in a tunnel, use static routing or autostatic RIPX instead of RIPX.

In your designs, manage routing table information

- Between locations by using static routing entries when RIPX or auto-static RIPX traffic impacts the network performance between the locations

- Between locations by using autostatic RIPX routing when updates to routing information can be scheduled at a time when autostatic RIPX traffic doesn't impact the network performance between the locations

- Within the same location by using RIPX or between locations when the RIPX traffic doesn't impact the network performance between the locations

---

Note   IPX-based networks are limited to a maximum diameter of 16 routers. Like RIP for IP, RIPX identifies an inactive interface by setting the routing cost metric to 17. Network segments, applications, or services that are 17 hops, or more, away are considered unreachable.

Applying the Decision

Figure 5.9 illustrates a scenario where the routing tables are managed by using static routing entries and RIPX. For each network segment and each IPX frame type, you must determine the method the router will use for managing the routing information for the respective network segment and IPX frame type.

For the purposes of this scenario, assume that

- The network segments (Segments A, B, C, D, and E) within each location are 100 Mbps Ethernet

- Each location is directly connected to the Internet by using a T1 connection

- The network utilization required by RIPX is acceptable within each location

- The network utilization for the Internet connections is very low during non-business hours

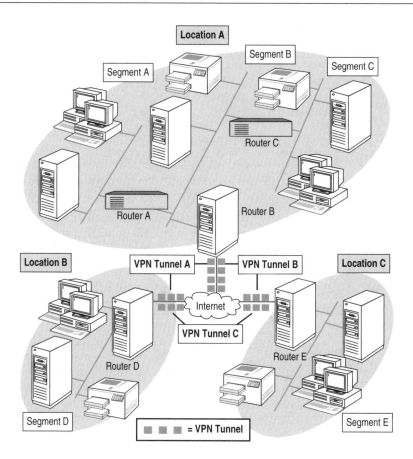

Figure 5.9   The appropriate management of routing tables by using static routing entries, Autostatic, and RIPX

Table 5.7 lists each router interface, the method of managing the routing table for that interface, and the reason for selecting the method.

Table 5.7   Reasons for Selecting Specific Methods of Managing Interface Routing Tables

For This Router Interface		Select	Reason
Router A	Segment A	RIPX	The network capacity exists.
	Segment B	RIPX	The network capacity exists.
Router B	Segment B	RIPX	The network capacity exists.
	Internet	Neither	The Internet connection is an IP-based connection. IPX routing isn't appropriate.
	VPN A	Autostatic RIPX	The network capacity exists during nonbusiness hours.
	VPN B	Autostatic RIPX	The network capacity exists during nonbusiness hours.

Table 5.7   *(continued)*

For This Router Interface		Select	Reason
Router C	Segment B	RIPX	The network capacity exists.
	Segment C	RIPX	The network capacity exists.
Router D	Segment D	Static	Only one segment exists within the location.
	Internet	Static	The Internet connection is an IP-based connection. IPX routing isn't appropriate.
	VPN A	Autostatic RIPX	The network capacity exists during nonbusiness hours.
	VPN C	Autostatic RIPX	The network capacity exists during nonbusiness hours.
Router E	Segment E	Static	Only one segment exists within the location.
	Internet	Static	The Internet connection is an IP-based connection. IPX routing isn't appropriate.
	VPN B	Autostatic RIPX	The network capacity exists during nonbusiness hours.
	VPN C	Autostatic RIPX	The network capacity exists during nonbusiness hours.

IPX Routing and Service Advertising

IP-based networks advertise applications, servers, or services by using Domain Name System (DNS) or Windows Internet Name Service (WINS). IPX-based computers advertise applications and services by using SAP.

Like RIPX, SAP-based computers determine the computers offering the services by examining information stored in a memory-based table. You can manage the available services information in this table

- Manually by using static services entries
- Automatically by using
    - SAP
    - Autostatic SAP

SAP advertisements are broadcast to the local IPX-based network segments. Routers connected to the network segments receive the SAP advertisements and forward them to other network segments and routers. The SAP advertisements continue to propagate throughout the entire network until all routers, file server, print servers, or other SAP-enabled devices receive the SAP advertisement.

The design decisions for selecting the appropriate method of managing SAP service advertisements are the same as the design decisions for IPX routing table information. You can specify SAP static entries by using the same decision process as IPX static routing entries. By using the same design decisions as RIPX, you can determine how best to use SAP. Autostatic SAP requires the same decision process as autostatic RIPX routing.

Making the Decision

The IPX routers in your design must forward, selectively filter, or discard SAP advertisement packets. Based on the business goals or technical goals of the organization, you must determine how to manage SAP traffic. You can specify how to manage SAP packets for each router interface in your design.

Table 5.8 lists the approaches to managing SAP traffic and the advantages and disadvantages for each approach.

Table 5.8   Advantages and Disadvantages of Specific Ways to Manage SAP Traffic

Approach	Advantages	Disadvantages
Static SAP entries	■ Reduces network traffic because no SAP advertisements are propagated ■ Prevents unauthorized users from gaining information about the applications and services on a specific network segment ■ Restricts access to specific services provided by specific computers	■ Users on other network segments are unaware of the services for which no static SAP entries are created
Disable SAP forwarding	■ Reduces network traffic because no SAP advertisements are propagated ■ Prevents unauthorized users from gaining information about the applications and services on a specific network segment	■ Users on other network segments are unaware of the services on the network segment connected to the router interface with SAP disabled
Filtered SAP forwarding	■ Reduces network traffic because not all SAP advertisements are propagated ■ Prevents unauthorized users from gaining information about certain applications and services on a specific network segment ■ Restricts access to specific services provided by specific computers	■ Increases network traffic because some SAP advertisements are forwarded ■ Users on other network segments are unaware of the services that are filtered by the router interface

Table 5.8 *(continued)*

Approach	Advantages	Disadvantages
Enable SAP forwarding	▪ Users on other network segments are advised of the services on the network segment connected to the router interface with SAP enabled	▪ Increases network traffic because all SAP advertisements are forwarded
Autostatic SAP	▪ Automatically updates SAP information as services are added or removed ▪ Reduces the possibility of invalid static SAP entries ▪ Reduces network traffic because all SAP advertisements are forwarded at nonpeak network intervals	▪ Service advertisement information is updated only at scheduled intervals (typically hours in length)

When your designs include SAP advertising across WAN network segments (or through IPX in IP tunnels), you can use SAP, autostatic SAP, or static SAP entries to advertise network services and resources. Determine the method for managing SAP advertisements based on the amount of network traffic that the WAN network segment or tunnel supports. When you want to reduce the network traffic, select static SAP entries or autostatic SAP instead of SAP.

Applying the Decision

Figure 5.10 illustrates a scenario where the service advertisements are managed by using static SAP entries, autostatic SAP, and SAP. For each network segment and each IPX frame type, you must determine the method the router will use for managing the service advertisement information for the respective network segment and IPX frame type.

For the purposes of this scenario, assume that

- Segments A and C are 100 Mbps Ethernet
- Segment B is 16 Mbps Token Ring
- Each location is directly connected to each other by using an X.25 connection
- The network utilization required by SAP is acceptable within each location
- The network utilization for the X.25 connections is very low during nonbusiness hours

Table 5.9 lists each router interface, the method of managing the routing table for that interface, and reason for selecting the method.

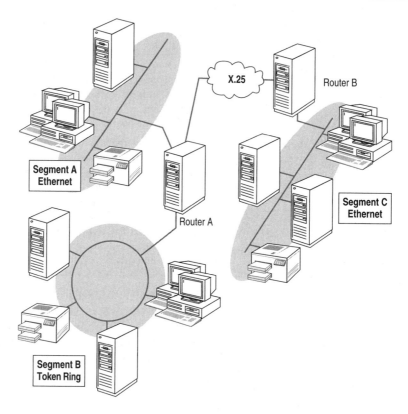

Figure 5.10   The appropriate management of service advertisements by using static SAP entries, autostatic SAP entries, and SAP

Table 5.9   Reasons for Choosing Specific Methods for Managing Interface Routing Tables

For This Router Interface		Select	Reason
Router A	Segment A	SAP	The network capacity exists.
	Segment B	SAP	The network capacity exists.
	X.25	Autostatic SAP	The network capacity exists.
Router B	Segment C	SAP	The network capacity exists.
	X.25	Autostatic SAP	The Internet connection is an IP-based connection. IPX routing isn't appropriate.

IPX Routing and NetBIOS

IPX-based networks provide support for NetBIOS over IPX. The NetBIOS support in IPX allows NetBIOS-based applications to run on IPX-based networks. Because NetBIOS is a broadcast-oriented application programming interface (API), many of the IPX packets that contain NetBIOS data are IPX broadcast packets.

Note   Microsoft Windows–based networks rely on NetBIOS for many network services (such as file and print services). When your designs include IPX as the primary transport, you must include NetBIOS to provide these networking services to client computers.

Making the Decision

You can select any combination of the following approaches to manage the NetBIOS over IPX traffic in your design.

- **Forward all NetBIOS over IPX traffic**   Select this approach when you want to allow access to all NetBIOS-based resources on a network segment. All NetBIOS over IPX traffic will be propagated to other network segments.

  Note   By default, Routing and Remote Access forwards all NetBIOS over IPX traffic.

- **Filter specific NetBIOS over IPX traffic**   Select this approach when you want to allow access to specific NetBIOS-based resources on a network segment. Because you filter some of the NetBIOS over IPX traffic, you reduce network traffic.

- **Create static NetBIOS name entries**   Select this approach when a network segment contains a small number of fixed NetBIOS-based resources. Because the NetBIOS names are statically created, you reduce network traffic.

- **Disable NetBIOS over IPX traffic**   Select this approach when a network segment contains no NetBIOS-based resources or you're specifying the resources by using static NetBIOS name entries. Disabling all NetBIOS over IPX traffic allows you to eliminate the NetBIOS over IPX traffic.

Applying the Decision

Figure 5.11 illustrates a scenario where NetBIOS over IPX traffic is managed by using static NetBIOS name entries, NetBIOS over IPX filters, and forwarding of NetBIOS over IPX traffic. For each network segment, you must determine the method the router will use for managing NetBIOS over IPX traffic.

For the purposes of this scenario, assume that

- Segments A and C are 100 Mbps Ethernet
- Segment B is 16 Mbps Token Ring
- The location is directly connected to other locations by using an X.25 connection
- Users *outside* Segment C are prevented from communicating with the restricted server on Segment C by using NetBIOS over IPX

- The network utilization required by NetBIOS over IPX is acceptable within each location

- The network utilization required by NetBIOS over IPX is unacceptable across the X.25 connection

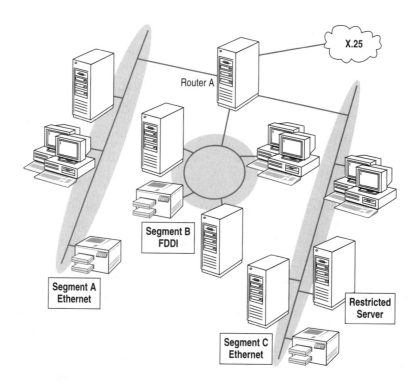

Figure 5.11   Managing NetBIOS over IPX traffic by using static NetBIOS name entries, NetBIOS over IPX filters, and NetBIOS over IPX forwarding

Table 5.10 lists each router interface, the method of managing the NetBIOS over IPX traffic for that interface, and the reason for selecting the method.

Table 5.10   Reasons for Selecting Specific Methods for Managing NetBIOS over IPX Traffic for Router Interfaces

For This Segment	Select	Reason
Segment A	Forward all traffic	Allows all NetBIOS over IPX traffic to be exchanged with the computers on Segment A
Segment B	Forward all traffic	Allows all NetBIOS over IPX traffic to be exchanged with the computers on Segment B
Segment C	Filter all traffic	Prevents access to the restricted server on Segment C by users on other network segments
X.25	Static NetBIOS names	Reduces the network traffic over the X.25 network

Protecting IPX Traffic

Many of the networking services designs that you create will require you to transmit confidential data by using IPX over public networks. Based on the security requirements of the organization, your design must protect the confidentiality of the data.

In addition, your design must protect private network resources from being accessed by unauthorized users. These unauthorized users might attempt to access the private network resources through WAN or remote access connections through your router design.

Making the Decision

You can protect the IPX traffic in your network by using

- **IPX over IP tunnels to authenticate routers and encrypt data**   You can protect the data in the IPX over IP tunnels by using any of the authentication and encryption methods available to IP. For more information on protecting IP traffic, see Chapter 4, "IP Routing Designs," Lesson 3, "Data Protection on Unsecured Segments."

- **RIPX or SAP ability to advertise only or listen only to RIPX and SAP traffic**   By default, the router interface advertises and accepts advertisements for RIPX and SAP traffic. You can specify that the router interface will advertise only, listen only, or both. You can also specify the routers' interaction with RIPX and SAP advertisements for RIPX and SAP individually. By specifying that a router advertise only, you can ensure that other routers can't modify the routing information. By specifying that a router listen only, you can prevent other routers from obtaining routing information from the router.

- **IPX, RIPX, and SAP filters to prevent private network access from unknown users or networks**   You can prevent private network access from unknown users or networks by using

  - **IPX filters** You can use IPX filters to restrict inbound or outbound traffic through a router interface. You can specify multiple IPX filters on a router interface to customize the security you want based on the requirements of the organization. You can specify the criteria for your IPX filters based on

    - A single IPX network number or a range of IPX network numbers

    - A single IPX node or a range of IPX nodes

    - A single IPX socket number or a range of IPX socket numbers

    - The IPX packet type

  - **RIPX filters** You can use RIPX filters to restrict inbound or outbound RIPX advertisements through a router interface. Like IPX filters, you can specify multiple RIPX filters on a router interface. You can specify the criteria for your RIPX filters based on a single IPX network number or a range of IPX network numbers.

- **SAP filters** You can use SAP filters to restrict inbound or outbound service advertisements through a router interface. As with IPX filters and RIPX filters, you can specify multiple SAP filters on a router interface. You can specify the criteria for your SAP filters based on

  - A single SAP service type or all service types
  - A single service name (typically the name of the server hosting the service) or all service names

Applying the Decision

Figure 5.12 illustrates a scenario where you must provide the appropriate protection of IPX traffic. For each network segment and each IPX frame type, you must determine the method the router will use for protecting IPX traffic.

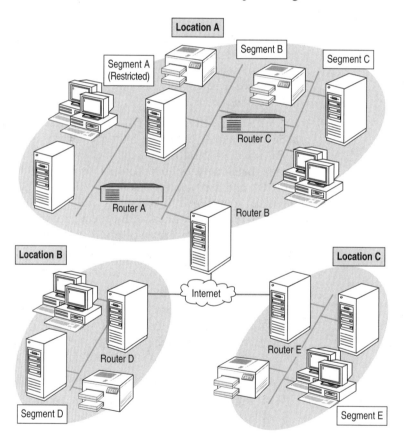

Figure 5.12   Scenario that illustrates the appropriate protection of IPX traffic

For the purposes of this scenario, assume that

- All segments are 100 Mbps Ethernet
- Each location is directly connected to the Internet by using a T1 connection

- Any data transmitted over the Internet must be protected from unauthorized users
- Only the user in Location A can access the computers on Segment A
- RIPX and SAP advertisements are sent through all segments, including the Internet

Table 5.11 lists each router interface, the method of managing the routing table for that interface, and the reason for selecting the method.

Table 5.11   Reasons for Choosing Specific Methods of Managing Interface Routing Tables

For This Router Interface		Select	Reason
Router A	Segment A	None	IPX filters on Segment B interface will prevent unauthorized traffic.
	Segment B	Inbound IPX filters	Configures the IPX filters to allow only IPX packets originating from Location A to access Segment A.
Router B	Segment B	None	No security is required.
	Internet	Appropriate IP data protection	Because the Internet connection is an IP-based connection, you select IP-based mechanisms (such as IP filters) for providing data protection.
	Tunnel (Location A to B)	VPN, IPX filters, RIPX filters, and SAP filters	Authenticates routers, encrypts data, and prevents any IPX, RIPX, or SAP traffic from unknown routers or computers.
	Tunnel (Location A to C).	VPN, IPX filters, RIPX filters, and SAP filters	Authenticates routers, encrypts data, and prevents any IPX, RIPX, or SAP traffic from unknown routers or computers.
Router C	Segment B	None	No security is required.
	Segment C	None	No security is required.
Router D	Segment D	None	No security is required.
	Internet	Appropriate IP data protection	Because the Internet connection is an IP-based connection, you select IP-based mechanisms (such as IP filters) for providing data protection.
	Tunnel (Location B to A)	VPN, IPX filters, RIPX filters, and SAP filters	Authenticates routers, encrypts data, and prevents any IPX, RIPX, or SAP traffic from unknown routers or computers.
	Tunnel (Location B to C)	VPN, IPX filters, RIPX filters, and SAP filters	Authenticates routers, encrypts data, and prevents any IPX, RIPX, or SAP traffic from unknown routers or computers.

Table 5.11   *(continued)*

For This Router Interface		Select	Reason
Router E	Segment E	Static	Only one segment exists within the location.
	Internet	Appropriate IP data protection	Because the Internet connection is an IP-based connection, you select IP-based mechanisms (such as IP filters) for providing data protection.
	Tunnel (Location C to A)	VPN, IPX filters, RIPX filters, and SAP filters	Authenticates routers, encrypts data, and prevents any IPX, RIPX, or SAP traffic from unknown routers or computers.
	Tunnel (Location C to B)	VPN, IPX filters, RIPX filters, and SAP filters	Authenticates routers, encrypts data, and prevents any IPX, RIPX, or SAP traffic from unknown routers or computers.

Optimizing IPX Routing

After you have considered the essential and security requirements of your IPX router design, you need to optimize your IPX routing design for availability and performance. You base the optimization of your IPX routing design on the organization's requirements.

Making the Decision

You can approach the optimization of IPX router design as you do the optimization of IP router design—the design decisions for both are the same. For more information on the optimization of IP routers, and subsequently IPX routers, see Chapter 4, "IP Routing Designs," Lesson 4, "IP Routing Design Optimization."

Applying the Decision

Figure 5.13 illustrates a scenario with a single IPX router prior to optimization for performance and availability. Any failure on the part of Router A results in a loss of communications between all network segments. In addition, if Router A becomes saturated, the performance of network traffic routed between segments is reduced.

Figure 5.14 illustrates the same IPX-based network after optimization for performance and availability. The redundant router (Router B) and the redundant connections to each network segment improve the availability of your design.

The additional router and network connections also allow traffic to be load-balanced across the two routers. By load-balancing the network traffic across the two routers, your design maximizes the network performance of any network traffic forwarded by the routers.

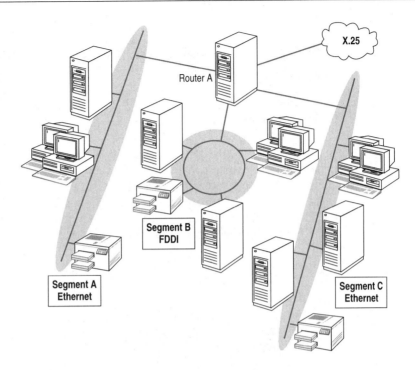

Figure 5.13   Diagram of IPX network prior to optimization

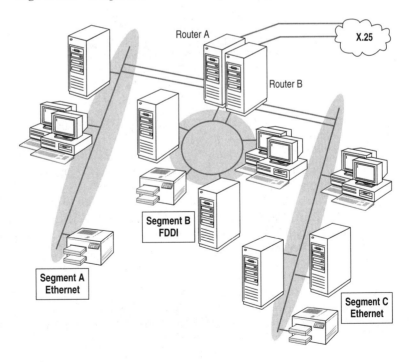

Figure 5.14   Diagram of IPX network after optimization

Activity 5.1: Evaluating an IPX Routing Design

In this activity, you're presented with a scenario. To complete the activity:

1. Evaluate the scenario and determine the design requirements
2. Answer questions and make design recommendations

In Figure 5.15, you see a map for a chain of vacation resorts. The marketing department of the resort chain provides inbound and outbound telesales for a chain of vacation resorts. The marketing representatives for a property are located at each resort property. Besides providing inbound and outbound telesales, each representative provides tours of the resort property to prospective customers. The central office for the resort chain is in Mexico City.

Figure 5.15   Map of the vacation resort marketing company

The marketing department currently runs reservation and billing software that requires NetWare file and print servers. The resorts are connected to one another by using 33.6 Kpbs dial-up modems. The majority of the traffic between locations is e-mail messages and customer referrals for other locations. All business transactions are uploaded to the central office in Mexico City nightly.

The resort chain wants to migrate the connections between locations to X.25 to reduce the long distance telephone charges. Long term, they want to centralize the reservation and billing software in the central office in Mexico City.

Answer the following questions concerning your design recommendations. You can find answers to the questions in the Appendix, "Questions and Answers."

1. As an outside consultant hired to help the resort chain migrate to the X.25 network, you're responsible for creating the networking services design. The management of the vacation resort wants to ensure that the migration to X.25 won't disrupt the normal operation of business. What do you recommend as an IPX routing solution for the resort chain?

2. After subsequent meetings, the management of the vacation resort wants you to ensure that unauthorized users aren't able to view any data transmitted over the X.25 network. The management wants you to provide the strongest possible security. How do you protect the data transmitted over the X.25 network between each of the resort properties and the central office?

3. In another meeting, the management of the resort property chain wants to ensure that communications between resort properties and between the resort properties and the central office are always available during normal business hours. How can you ensure that these business requirements are met?

4. The director of information services for the vacation resort chain reviews the results of pilot tests that have been run. The response time for some applications is less than the minimum response times in the vacation resort chain's requirements. After further investigation, the pilot test team discovers the reduction in response time is due to network traffic congestion on the edge of network router at some of the locations. What recommendations can you make to reduce the network traffic congestion?

Lesson 3: AppleTalk Routing Design Concepts

This lesson discusses the requirements, constraints, and design decisions that are used in creating an AppleTalk routing design. Your design provides AppleTalk routing when the routers can transmit AppleTalk packets between different network segments and achieve the availability and performance requirements of the organization.

After this lesson, you will be able to

- Determine the appropriate placement of routers in an AppleTalk routing design
- Identify the appropriate design specifications for each router interface
- Select the appropriate AppleTalk network number or range of AppleTalk network numbers for each network segment
- Select an appropriate AppleTalk seed router for each network segment
- Select the appropriate method for optimizing design to improve the availability and performance of AppleTalk routing

Estimated lesson time: 45 minutes

Placing Routers in the Network Design

In Lesson 1 of this chapter and in Chapter 4, "IP Routing Designs," you examined scenarios that depicted the placement of routers within a network. The scenarios illustrated that you can place routers at the edge of your private network (edge of network routers) or within your private network (internal routers).

Making the Decision

You can approach the placement of AppleTalk routers in your design as you do the placement of IP routers—the design decisions for both are the same. For more information on the placement of IP routers, and subsequently AppleTalk routers, see Chapter 4, "IP Routing Designs," Lesson 2, "Essential IP Routing Design Concepts."

Applying the Decision

Figure 5.16 illustrates the placement of AppleTalk routers in a network. Router A connects Segments A and B (LocalTalk and TokenTalk respectively) to the X.25 network. Router B connects Segment C to the X.25 network. You place the routers in your design to connect network segments within a location and to connect segments between locations.

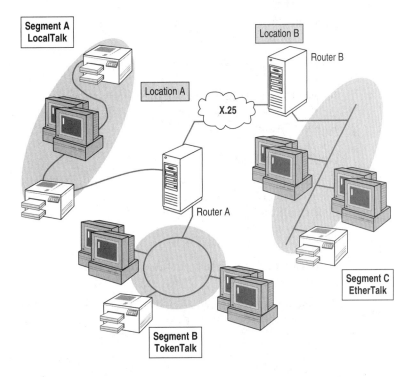

Figure 5.16   A scenario that illustrates the placement of AppleTalk routers in a network

Router Interface Specifications

As with other routers, such as IP or IPX routers, the AppleTalk routers in your designs will have at least two network interfaces. The router interfaces provide connectivity between the routers and the network segments in your design.

For each interface in each router in your design, you must specify

- The type of connection between the router interface and the network, such as persistent or nonpersistent (discussed in this section)
- The AppleTalk configuration information, including an AppleTalk network number or an AppleTalk network numbers range (discussed in a later section in this lesson titled, "Determining AppleTalk Network Numbers")
- If the router will act as a seed router for the network segment (discussed in a later section in this lesson titled, "Selecting AppleTalk Seed Routers")

Making the Decision

The design decisions for determining the type of connection between the AppleTalk router interface and the network segment are the same as the design decisions for IP router interfaces. You must specify the technology and the persistence of each router interface.

You can apply the same principles to AppleTalk router interfaces that you use for IP router interfaces. For more information on determining the type of connection between IP router interface and the network segments, and subsequently AppleTalk routers, see Chapter 4, "IP Routing Designs," Lesson 2, "Essential IP Routing Design Concepts."

Applying the Decision

Figure 5.17 illustrates a network with a variety of router interface connections. For each interface in each router, you must determine the technology and the persistence of each router interface.

For the purposes of this scenario, assume that

- Each location is directly connected to each other by using an ISDN connection

- The organization wants to reduce the charges associated with the ISDN connection, which charges by each minute the connection is active

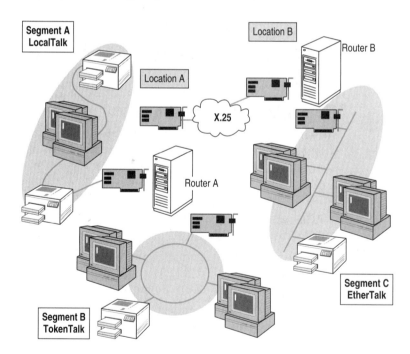

Figure 5.17   A scenario that illustrates the router interface connections for AppleTalk routers in a network

Table 5.12 lists each router interface, the interface type and persistence, and the reason for selecting the interface type and persistence.

Table 5.12   Reasons for Choosing Specific Interface Types and Persistences

For This Router and Interface		Select This Interface Type and Persistence	Reason
Router A	Segment A	LAN, persistent	Ethernet LAN connection
	Segment B	LAN, persistent	Ethernet LAN connection
	X.25	Demand-dial, nonpersistent	Organization wants to reduce the cost associated with the ISDN connection
Router B	Segment C	LAN, persistent	Ethernet LAN connection
	Internet	LAN, persistent	Dedicated T1 connection

Determining AppleTalk Network Numbers

Select the AppleTalk network number or range of AppleTalk network numbers from the network number(s) assigned to the network segment that the interface is directly connected to.

Making the Decision

You must assign at least one AppleTalk network number to each network segment. You must assign

- At least one network number to each physical network segment in your network
- Additional network numbers for all 253 devices

For EtherTalk or TokenTalk network segments, you must assign a unique AppleTalk network number for every 253 computers on the same network segment. LocalTalk network segments require only a single network number because the maximum number of computers on a LocalTalk network segment is fewer than 253. For more information about AppleTalk network numbers, see Chapter 3, "Multiprotocol Network Design," Lesson 3, "AppleTalk Design Concepts."

Applying the Decision

Figure 5.18 illustrates the proper assignment of AppleTalk network numbers in your design. For each network segment, you must determine the proper number of unique AppleTalk network numbers to assign.

Table 5.13 lists each network segment, the AppleTalk network number(s) assigned to each network segment, and reason for assigning the network number(s) to the network segment.

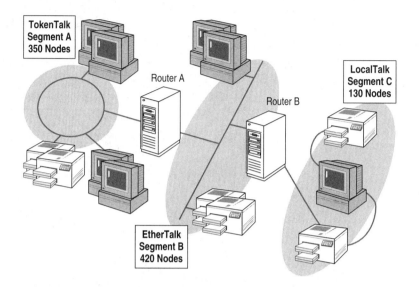

Figure 5.18   A scenario that illustrates the proper assignment of AppleTalk network numbers

Table 5.13   Reasons for Assigning Specific Network Numbers to Network Segments

Segment	Assign	Reason
Segment A	10101 – 10102	You must assign a range of two network numbers to accommodate the 350 nodes.
Segment B	20201 – 20202	You must assign a range of two network numbers to accommodate the 420 nodes.
Segment C	30301	You need to assign only a single network number to LocalTalk network segments.

Create meaningful network numbers when you specify them in your design. In the scenario, the network number 20201 can be used to identify the network segment (the first digit, 2), the type of network segment (Ethernet = 02), and the network number range for the network segment (01). Creating meaningful network numbering schemes will assist the support personnel when locating a network segment or network device while troubleshooting network-related issues.

Selecting AppleTalk Seed Routers

Each network segment in your AppleTalk router design must be assigned at least one *seed router*. A seed router is the authoritative source for the network numbers and AppleTalk zones that exist on a network segment. Other routers and devices on the same network segment derive the segment's *seed information* from the seed router. The seed information provided by the seed router consists of the network number(s) and zone(s) that exist on a network segment.

Making the Decision

As previously discussed, you must designate at least one seed router for each network segment. You can, however, designate more than one seed router for each network segment. When you designate more than one seed router on a network segment, the first seed router you start on the segment becomes the seed router for that network segment. Other seed routers, and nonseed routers, that start later use the seed information established by the first seed router.

When determining the number of seed routers in your design, consider the following:

- **Designate at least one seed router for each network segment**   To communicate with other routed network segments, you must assign a seed router to the network segment. Network segments without seed routers are unable to communicate with other network segments.

- **Designate additional seed routers for each network segment in the event of a failure of the primary seed router**   In the event the primary seed router fails, designate additional seed routers to ensure the continuation of AppleTalk routing. Remaining seed routers will continue to provide seed information for the network segment.

- **Ensure that all seed routers on the same network segment provide the same network number configuration**   When you specify more than one seed router on a network segment, the first seed router started establishes the seed information for the network segment. If the network support staff starts other seed routers with different seed information first, the network segment will be seeded with incorrect seed information.

Applying the Decision

Figure 5.19 illustrates the proper designation of AppleTalk seed routers in your design. For each network segment, you must designate the appropriate number of seed routers.

For the purposes of this scenario, assume that

- All segments are 100 Mbps Ethernet
- Each location is directly connected to one another by using a X.25 connection

Table 5.14 lists each network segment, the router(s) that will be designated as a seed router for that segment, and the reason for designating the router(s) as a seed router.

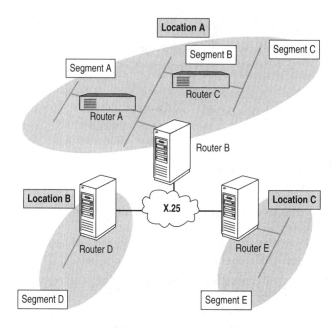

Figure 5.19   A scenario that illustrates the proper designation of AppleTalk
seed routers

Table 5.14   Reasons for Designating Specific Seed Routers

Segment	Designate	Reason
Segment A	Router A	Router A is the only router connected to Segment A.
Segment B	Router A, B, and C	All the routers are directly connected to Segment B. All routers are designated to provide redundant seed routing.
Segment C	Router C	Router C is the only router connected to Segment C.
Segment D	Router D	Router D is the only router connected to Segment D.
Segment E	Router E	Router E is the only router connected to Segment E.
X.25	Router B, D, and E	All the routers are directly connected to the X.25 network. All routers are designated to provide redundant seed routing.

Optimizing AppleTalk Routing

After you have considered the essential requirements of your AppleTalk router
design, you need to optimize your AppleTalk routing design for availability and
performance. As with other router designs, base the optimization of your
AppleTalk routing design on the organization's requirements.

Tip   The AppleTalk routing provided by Windows 2000 doesn't support the protection of confidential data transmitted over private and public networks. You can select third-party AppleTalk routers to provide router-to-router data encryption.

Making the Decision

Approach the optimization of AppleTalk router design as you do the optimization of IP router design—the design decisions for both are the same. For more information on the optimization of IP routers, and subsequently AppleTalk routers, see Chapter 4, "IP Routing Designs," Lesson 4, "IP Routing Design Optimization."

Applying the Decision

Figure 5.20 illustrates an AppleTalk router design prior to optimization for availability and performance. Any failure on the part of Router A or Router B results in a loss of communications between some of the local network segments and between locations. In addition, if either router becomes saturated, the performance of network traffic routed between segments directly connected to the saturated router is reduced.

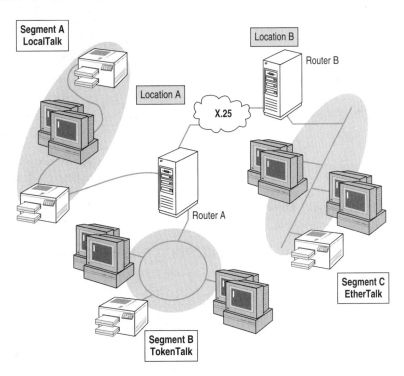

Figure 5.20   A scenario that illustrates an AppleTalk router design prior to optimization

Figure 5.21 illustrates the same AppleTalk-based network after optimization for performance and availability. The redundant routers (Routers C and D) and the redundant connections to each network segment improve the availability of your design.

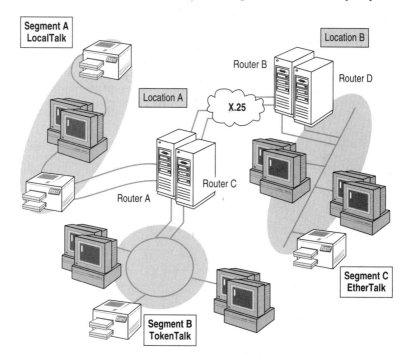

Figure 5.21   A scenario that illustrates an AppleTalk router design after optimization

The additional routers and network connections also allow traffic to be load-balanced across the two routers. By load-balancing the network traffic across the two routers, your design maximizes the network performance of any network traffic forwarded by the routers.

Activity 5.2: Evaluating an AppleTalk Routing Design

In this activity, you're presented with a scenario. To complete the activity:

1. Evaluate the scenario and determine the design requirements
2. Answer questions and make design recommendations

In Figure 5.22, you see a map for a chain of vacation resorts that was discussed earlier in this lesson. Since the initial deployment a year ago, the vacation resort chain has decided to produce all its marketing literature in-house To produce the marketing literature in house, the chain purchased 200 Macintosh computers that are evenly distributed across the resort properties.

Figure 5.22   Map of the vacation resort marketing company

Answer the following questions concerning your design recommendations. You can find answers to the questions in the Appendix, "Questions and Answers."

1. The chain of vacation resorts has retained you as a consultant to update the existing design that you created to integrate the Macintosh computers into the existing network. The management of the vacation resort wants to ensure that the integration of the Macintosh computers into the existing network won't disrupt the normal operation of business. What do you recommend as an AppleTalk routing solution for the resort chain?

2. Just as with IPX, the management of the resort property is concerned about the confidentiality of any data transmitted by using AppleTalk over the X.25 network. How do you protect the data transmitted over the X.25 network between each of the resort properties and the central office?

3. In another meeting, the management of the resort property chain wants to ensure that communications between resort properties and between the resort properties and the central office are always available during normal business hours. In addition, the director of information services wants to ensure that the routers and network segments won't become saturated. How can you ensure that these business and technical requirements are met?

Lab: Creating a Multiprotocol Routing Design

After this lab, you will be able to

- Evaluate a scenario and determine the design requirements
- Create multiprotocol routing designs based on the design requirements

Estimated lab time: 45 minutes

In this lab, you're a consultant to an entertainment company and are responsible for creating a multiprotocol routing design for the company. The company has various locations and business interests throughout the world.

To complete this lab:

1. Examine the networking environment presented in the scenario, the network diagrams, the business requirements and constraints, and the technical requirements and constraints

2. Use the worksheet(s) for each location and router to assist you in creating your multiprotocol routing design (you can find completed sample design worksheets on the Supplemental Course Materials CD-ROM in the Completed Worksheets folder)

Note   For each location there are four worksheets, one worksheet for each router. If your design contains fewer than four routers, leave the remaining worksheets blank.

---

3. Create, eliminate, or replace existing networking devices and network segments when required

4. Ensure that your design fulfills the business requirements and constraints and technical requirements and constraints of the scenario by

- Assigning the appropriate specifications for each router interface
- Including the appropriate routing protocols on each router
- Optimizing your design to provide the security, availability, performance, and affordability

---

Note   To reduce the length of time for this lab, create a multiprotocol routing design for only four of the entertainment company's locations.

Scenario

An entertainment company, headquartered in New York, owns a number of cable TV networks, theme parks, and production studios. The entertainment company acquired most of the cable TV networks, theme parks, and production studios. As the parent company acquired each separate business unit, the existing information services staff and networks were left in place.

Initially, the individual business units required little or no connectivity with one another. However, the business model changed within the parent company, and connectivity between the business units is critical.

Figure 5.23 is a map of the locations where the entertainment company has offices. A variety of technologies currently connect the locations to one another. The company is migrating the existing assortment of technologies that connect the locations to asynchronous transfer mode (ATM)-based, high-speed leased lines. The new ATM-based leased lines provide higher speed data rates between the locations. The company maintains an Internet connection with T3 leased lines in the New York headquarters. Figure 5.24 shows the existing network at the New York corporate headquarters.

Table 5.15 lists each location where the entertainment company has offices and the types of business units at each location. Figure 5.25 shows the existing network at each of the news studios, Figure 5.26 shows the existing network at each of the production studios, and Figure 5.27 shows the existing network at each of the theme parks.

Table 5.15   Locations and Types of Business Units

Location	Description of the Business Units at the Location
New York	*Corporate headquarters.* The administration and management of the entertainment company is located here. *News studio.* One of the cable network news companies has studios here. The video broadcasts are taped or televised live from here. *Production studio.* A number of the cable network channels and other portions of the entertainment company share a common production studio for producing video and multimedia productions.
Los Angeles	*News studio.* One of the cable network news companies has studios here. The video broadcasts are taped or televised live from here. *Production studio.* A number of the cable network channels and other portions of the entertainment company share a common production studio for producing video and multimedia productions. *Theme park.* A theme park focusing on characters and movies owned by the entertainment company is located here.
Miami	*Production studio.* A number of the cable network channels and other portions of the entertainment company share a common production studio for producing video and multimedia productions. *Theme park.* A theme park focusing on characters and movies owned by the entertainment company is located here.

(continued)

Table 5.15   *(continued)*

Location	Description of the Business Units at the Location
London	*News studio.* One of the cable network news companies has studios here. The video broadcasts are taped or televised live from here. *Production studio.* A number of the cable network channels and other portions of the entertainment company share a common production studio for producing video and multimedia productions.
Paris	*Production studio.* A number of the cable network channels and other portions of the entertainment company share a common production studio for producing video and multimedia productions.
Frankfurt	*News studio.* One of the cable network news companies has studios here. The video broadcasts are taped or televised live from here.
Rome	*News studio.* One of the cable network news companies has studios here. The video broadcasts are taped or televised live from here. *Production studio.* A number of the cable network channels and other portions of the entertainment company share a common production studio for producing video and multimedia productions.
Hong Kong	*News studio.* One of the cable network news companies has studios here. The video broadcasts are taped or televised live from here. *Production studio.* A number of the cable network channels and other portions of the entertainment company share a common production studio for producing video and multimedia productions.
Sydney	*News studio.* One of the cable network news companies has studios here. The video broadcasts are taped or televised live from here. *Production studio.* A number of the cable network channels and other portions of the entertainment company share a common production studio for producing video and multimedia productions.

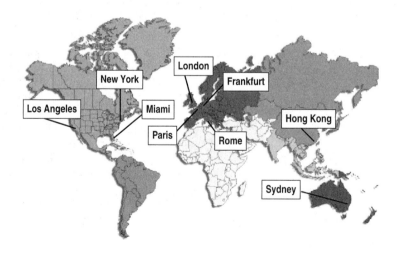

Figure 5.23   Map of the locations in the entertainment company

Table 5.16 lists each type of business owned by the entertainment company and a description of the support required by each business type.

Table 5.16   Types of Businesses and Support Required

Business Type	Must Support
News studios	▪ The employees and accounting functions for the news studio that utilize IPX-based file and print servers ▪ Macintosh-based graphics and video editing computers used to produce the news programs ▪ IPX-based teleprompters used by the news reporters, and other personnel who appear in front of the camera, to read their scripts
Production studios	▪ The employees and accounting functions for the production studio that utilize IPX-based file and print servers ▪ Macintosh-based graphics and video editing computers used to produce the video and multimedia content
Theme park	▪ The employees and accounting functions for the theme park that utilize IPX-based file and print servers ▪ Automated rides and attractions within the park that utilize IPX-based process control equipment ▪ Macintosh-based kiosks that park visitors can use to find attractions and leave messages for other members in their group

Business Requirements and Constraints

The entertainment company has a number of requirements and constraints based on the business model of the entertainment company. As you create your multiprotocol routing design, ensure that your design meets the business requirements and stays within the business constraints.

To achieve the business requirements and constraints, your design must

- Prevent visitors at the theme parks from accessing resources and data that are for exclusive use by the entertainment company employees

- Ensure that connectivity between the locations is available 24 hours a day, 7 days a week

- Ensure that the interactive theme park kiosks are available during normal hours of operation for each respective theme park

Technical Requirements and Constraints

The existing physical network, hardware, and operating systems place certain technical requirements and constraints on your design. As you create your multiprotocol routing design, ensure that your design meets the technical requirements and stays within the technical constraints.

In addition, the applications that run within the entertainment company require connectivity within each location, with other locations, and with the Internet. These applications run on the computers used by the employees and on computers used in interactive kiosks.

To achieve the technical requirements and constraints, your design must

- Isolate the network segments designated for use by the theme park visitors from the network segments designated for use by the employees
- Provide connectivity between the network segments that support Macintosh computers within a location and between locations
- Support the Ethernet_8022 and Token_Ring IPX frame types (the only IPX frame types in the organization)
- Organize AppleTalk zones by business functions
- Provide connectivity between the network segments that support IPX-based computers within a location and between locations
- Provide connectivity between IPX-based network segments and the IPX-to-IP gateway in the headquarters in New York
- When possible, protect data transmitted over the ATM network
- Reduce the utilization of the ATM network from 7 A.M. through 9 P.M. in the respective time zones
- Integrate with any existing IP-routed network segments

Note   For the purposes of this lab, assume that all IP-routed network segments are properly configured. Focus only on providing IPX and AppleTalk connectivity between network segments.

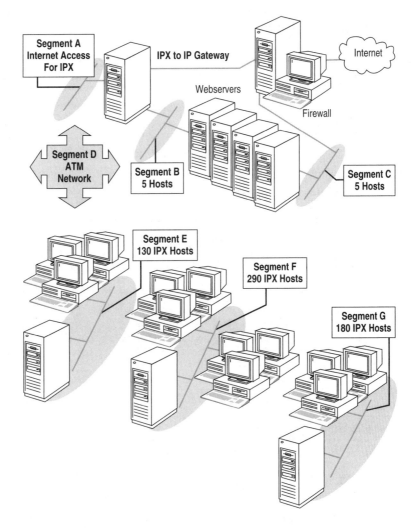

Figure 5.24   This is the existing network at the corporate headquarters building in New York.

Design Worksheet – Figure 5.24
Corporate Headquarters – Router A

Router Specifications	Comments
Internal IPX network number: _____	
Interface A connects to segment: _____	
❑ IPX Protocol Support Interface IPX network number: _____	
❑ Static Routes (*specify static route entries in Comments column*)	
❑ RIPX ❑ RIPX Filters (*specify filter criteria in Comments column*)	
❑ RIPX ❑ SAP Filters (*specify filter criteria in Comments column*)	
❑ Auto-Static RIPX with updates scheduled at: _____	
❑ Auto-Static SAP with updates scheduled at: _____	
❑ IPX Routing Filters (*specify filter criteria in Comments column*)	
❑ IPX over IP tunnel	
❑ Authentication (*specify authentication method in Comments column*)	
❑ Encryption (*specify encryption method in Comments column*)	
❑ AppleTalk Protocol Support ❑ Seed router for the network segment	
Zones: _____	
Network number (or range): _____	
Interface B connects to segment: _____	
❑ IPX Protocol Support Interface IPX network number: _____	
❑ Static Routes (*specify static route entries in Comments column*)	
❑ RIPX ❑ RIPX Filters (*specify filter criteria in Comments column*)	
❑ SAP ❑ SAP Filters (*specify filter criteria in Comments column*)	
❑ Auto-Static RIPX with updates scheduled at: _____	
❑ Auto-Static SAP with updates scheduled at: _____	
❑ IPX Routing Filters (*specify filter criteria in Comments column*)	
❑ IPX over IP tunnel	
❑ Authentication (*specify authentication method in Comments column*)	
❑ Encryption (*specify encryption method in Comments column*)	
❑ AppleTalk Protocol Support ❑ Seed router for the network segment	
Zones: _____	
Network number (or range): _____	

Design Worksheet – Figure 5.24
Corporate Headquarters – Router B

Router Specifications	Comments
Internal IPX network number: _____	
Interface A connects to segment: _____	
❑ IPX Protocol Support Interface IPX network number: _____	
❑ Static Routes (*specify static route entries in Comments column*)	
❑ RIPX ❑ RIPX Filters (*specify filter criteria in Comments column*)	
❑ SAP ❑ SAP Filters (*specify filter criteria in Comments column*)	
❑ Auto-Static RIPX with updates scheduled at: _____	
❑ Auto-Static SAP with updates scheduled at: _____	
❑ IPX Routing Filters (*specify filter criteria in Comments column*)	
❑ IPX over IP tunnel	
❑ Authentication (*specify authentication method in Comments column*)	
❑ Encryption (*specify encryption method in Comments column*)	
❑ AppleTalk Protocol Support ❑ Seed router for the network segment	
Zones: _____	
Network number (or range): _____	
Interface B connects to segment: _____	
❑ IPX Protocol Support Interface IPX network number: _____	
❑ Static Routes (*specify static route entries in Comments column*)	
❑ RIPX ❑ RIPX Filters (*specify filter criteria in Comments column*)	
❑ SAP ❑ SAP Filters (*specify filter criteria in Comments column*)	
❑ Auto-Static RIPX with updates scheduled at: _____	
❑ Auto-Static SAP with updates scheduled at: _____	
❑ IPX Routing Filters (*specify filter criteria in Comments column*)	
❑ IPX over IP tunnel	
❑ Authentication (*specify authentication method in Comments column*)	
❑ Encryption (*specify encryption method in Comments column*)	
❑ AppleTalk Protocol Support ❑ Seed router for the network segment	
Zones: _____	
Network number (or range): _____	

Design Worksheet – Figure 5.24
Corporate Headquarters – Router C

Router Specifications	Comments
Internal IPX network number: _____	
Interface A connects to segment: _____	
❑ IPX Protocol Support Interface IPX network number: _____	
❑ Static Routes (*specify static route entries in Comments column*)	
❑ RIPX ❑ RIPX Filters (*specify filter criteria in Comments column*)	
❑ SAP ❑ SAP Filters (*specify filter criteria in Comments column*)	
❑ Auto-Static RIPX with updates scheduled at: _____	
❑ Auto-Static SAP with updates scheduled at: _____	
❑ IPX Routing Filters (*specify filter criteria in Comments column*).	
❑ IPX over IP tunnel	
❑ Authentication (*specify authentication method in Comments column*)	
❑ Encryption (*specify encryption method in Comments column*)	
❑ AppleTalk Protocol Support ❑ Seed router for the network segment	
Zones: _____	
Network number (or range): _____	
Interface B connects to segment: _____	
❑ IPX Protocol Support Interface IPX network number: _____	
❑ Static Routes (*specify static route entries in Comments column*)	
❑ RIPX ❑ RIPX Filters (*specify filter criteria in Comments column*)	
❑ SAP ❑ SAP Filters (*specify filter criteria in Comments column*)	
❑ Auto-Static RIPX with updates scheduled at: _____	
❑ Auto-Static SAP with updates scheduled at: _____	
❑ IPX Routing Filters (*specify filter criteria in Comments column*)	
❑ IPX over IP tunnel	
❑ Authentication (*specify authentication method in Comments column*)	
❑ Encryption (*specify encryption method in Comments column*)	
❑ AppleTalk Protocol Support ❑ Seed router for the network segment	
Zones: _____	
Network number (or range): _____	

Design Worksheet – Figure 5.24
Corporate Headquarters – Router D

Router Specifications	Comments
Internal IPX network number: _____	
Interface A connects to segment: _____	
❑ IPX Protocol Support Interface IPX network number: _____	
❑ Static Routes (*specify static route entries in Comments column*)	
❑ RIPX ❑ RIPX Filters (*specify filter criteria in Comments column*)	
❑ SAP ❑ SAP Filters (*specify filter criteria in Comments column*)	
❑ Auto-Static RIPX with updates scheduled at: _____	
❑ Auto-Static SAP with updates scheduled at: _____	
❑ IPX Routing Filters (*specify filter criteria in Comments column*)	
❑ IPX over IP tunnel	
❑ Authentication (*specify authentication method in Comments column*)	
❑ Encryption (*specify encryption method in Comments column*)	
❑ AppleTalk Protocol Support ❑ Seed router for the network segment	
Zones: _____	
Network number (or range): _____	
Interface B connects to segment: _____	
❑ IPX Protocol Support Interface IPX network number: _____	
❑ Static Routes (*specify static route entries in Comments column*)	
❑ RIPX ❑ RIPX Filters (*specify filter criteria in Comments column*)	
❑ SAP ❑ SAP Filters (*specify filter criteria in Comments column*)	
❑ Auto-Static RIPX with updates scheduled at: _____	
❑ Auto-Static SAP with updates scheduled at: _____	
❑ IPX Routing Filters (*specify filter criteria in Comments column*)	
❑ IPX over IP tunnel	
❑ Authentication (*specify authentication method in Comments column*)	
❑ Encryption (*specify encryption method in Comments column*)	
❑ AppleTalk Protocol Support ❑ Seed router for the network segment	
Zones: _____	
Network number (or range): _____	

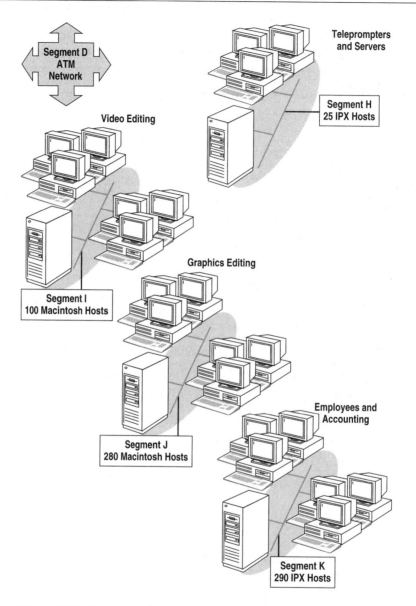

Figure 5.25   This is the existing network at one of the news studios. For the
purposes of this lab, assume that these buildings have the same
network configuration.

Design Worksheet – Figure 5.25
News Studio – Router A

Router Specifications	Comments
Internal IPX network number: _____	
Interface A connects to segment: _____	
❑ IPX Protocol Support Interface IPX network number: _____	
❑ Static Routes (*specify static route entries in Comments column*)	
❑ RIPX ❑ RIPX Filters (*specify filter criteria in Comments column*)	
❑ SAP ❑ SAP Filters (*specify filter criteria in Comments column*)	
❑ Auto-Static RIPX with updates scheduled at: _____	
❑ Auto-Static SAP with updates scheduled at: _____	
❑ IPX Routing Filters (*specify filter criteria in Comments column*)	
❑ IPX over IP tunnel	
❑ Authentication (*specify authentication method in Comments column*)	
❑ Encryption (*specify encryption method in Comments column*)	
❑ AppleTalk Protocol Support ❑ Seed router for the network segment	
Zones: _____	
Network number (or range): _____	
Interface B connects to segment: _____	
❑ IPX Protocol Support Interface IPX network number: _____	
❑ Static Routes (*specify static route entries in Comments column*)	
❑ RIPX ❑ RIPX Filters (*specify filter criteria in Comments column*)	
❑ SAP ❑ SAP Filters (*specify filter criteria in Comments column*)	
❑ Auto-Static RIPX with updates scheduled at: _____	
❑ Auto-Static SAP with updates scheduled at: _____	
❑ IPX Routing Filters (*specify filter criteria in Comments column*)	
❑ IPX over IP tunnel	
❑ Authentication (*specify authentication method in Comments column*)	
❑ Encryption (*specify encryption method in Comments column*)	
❑ AppleTalk Protocol Support ❑ Seed router for the network segment	
Zones: _____	
Network number (or range): _____	

Design Worksheet – Figure 5.25
News Studio – Router B

Router Specifications	Comments
Internal IPX network number: _____	
Interface A connects to segment: _____	
❏ IPX Protocol Support Interface IPX network number: _____	
❏ Static Routes (*specify static route entries in Comments column*)	
❏ RIPX ❏ RIPX Filters (*specify filter criteria in Comments column*)	
❏ SAP ❏ SAP Filters (*specify filter criteria in Comments column*)	
❏ Auto-Static RIPX with updates scheduled at: _____	
❏ Auto-Static SAP with updates scheduled at: _____	
❏ IPX Routing Filters (*specify filter criteria in Comments column*)	
❏ IPX over IP tunnel	
❏ Authentication (*specify authentication method in Comments column*)	
❏ Encryption (*specify encryption method in Comments column*)	
❏ AppleTalk Protocol Support ❏ Seed router for the network segment	
Zones: _____	
Network number (or range): _____	
Interface B connects to segment: _____	
❏ IPX Protocol Support Interface IPX network number: _____	
❏ Static Routes (*specify static route entries in Comments column*)	
❏ RIPX ❏ RIPX Filters (*specify filter criteria in Comments column*)	
❏ SAP ❏ SAP Filters (*specify filter criteria in Comments column*)	
❏ Auto-Static RIPX with updates scheduled at: _____	
❏ Auto-Static SAP with updates scheduled at: _____	
❏ IPX Routing Filters (*specify filter criteria in Comments column*)	
❏ IPX over IP tunnel	
❏ Authentication (*specify authentication method in Comments column*)	
❏ Encryption (*specify encryption method in Comments column*)	
❏ AppleTalk Protocol Support ❏ Seed router for the network segment	
Zones: _____	
Network number (or range): _____	

Design Worksheet – Figure 5.25
News Studio – Router C

Router Specifications	Comments
Internal IPX network number: _____	
Interface A connects to segment: _____	
❑ IPX Protocol Support Interface IPX network number: _____	
❑ Static Routes (*specify static route entries in Comments column*)	
❑ RIPX ❑ RIPX Filters (*specify filter criteria in Comments column*)	
❑ SAP ❑ SAP Filters (*specify filter criteria in Comments column*)	
❑ Auto-Static RIPX with updates scheduled at: _____	
❑ Auto-Static SAP with updates scheduled at: _____	
❑ IPX Routing Filters (*specify filter criteria in Comments column*)	
❑ IPX over IP tunnel	
❑ Authentication (*specify authentication method in Comments column*)	
❑ Encryption (*specify encryption method in Comments column*)	
❑ AppleTalk Protocol Support ❑ Seed router for the network segment	
Zones: _____	
Network number (or range): _____	
Interface B connects to segment: _____	
❑ IPX Protocol Support Interface IPX network number: _____	
❑ Static Routes (*specify static route entries in Comments column*)	
❑ RIPX ❑ RIPX Filters (*specify filter criteria in Comments column*)	
❑ SAP ❑ SAP Filters (*specify filter criteria in Comments column*)	
❑ Auto-Static RIPX with updates scheduled at: _____	
❑ Auto-Static SAP with updates scheduled at: _____	
❑ IPX Routing Filters (*specify filter criteria in Comments column*)	
❑ IPX over IP tunnel	
❑ Authentication (*specify authentication method in Comments column*)	
❑ Encryption (*specify encryption method in Comments column*)	
❑ AppleTalk Protocol Support ❑ Seed router for the network segment	
Zones: _____	
Network number (or range): _____	

Design Worksheet – Figure 5.25
News Studio – Router D

Router Specifications	Comments
Internal IPX network number: _____	
Interface A connects to segment: _____	
❏ IPX Protocol Support Interface IPX network number: _____	
❏ Static Routes (*specify static route entries in Comments column*)	
❏ RIPX ❏ RIPX Filters (*specify filter criteria in Comments column*)	
❏ SAP ❏ SAP Filters (*specify filter criteria in Comments column*)	
❏ Auto-Static RIPX with updates scheduled at: _____	
❏ Auto-Static SAP with updates scheduled at: _____	
❏ IPX Routing Filters (*specify filter criteria in Comments column*)	
❏ IPX over IP tunnel	
❏ Authentication (*specify authentication method in Comments column*)	
❏ Encryption (*specify encryption method in Comments column*)	
❏ AppleTalk Protocol Support ❏ Seed router for the network segment	
Zones: _____	
Network number (or range): _____	
Interface B connects to segment: _____	
❏ IPX Protocol Support Interface IPX network number: _____	
❏ Static Routes (*specify static route entries in Comments column*)	
❏ RIPX ❏ RIPX Filters (*specify filter criteria in Comments column*)	
❏ SAP ❏ SAP Filters (*specify filter criteria in Comments column*)	
❏ Auto-Static RIPX with updates scheduled at: _____	
❏ Auto-Static SAP with updates scheduled at: _____	
❏ IPX Routing Filters (*specify filter criteria in Comments column*)	
❏ IPX over IP tunnel	
❏ Authentication (*specify authentication method in Comments column*)	
❏ Encryption (*specify encryption method in Comments column*)	
❏ AppleTalk Protocol Support ❏ Seed router for the network segment	
Zones: _____	
Network number (or range): _____	

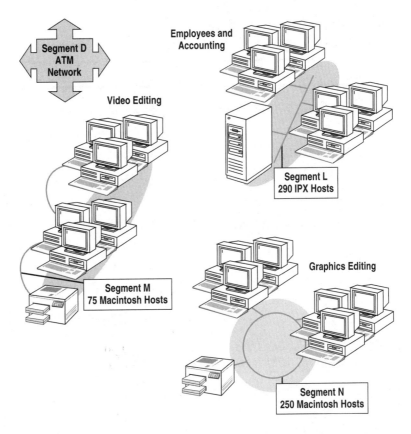

Figure 5.26   This is the existing network at one of the production studios. For the purposes of this lab, assume that these buildings have the same network configuration.

Design Worksheet – Figure 5.26
Production Studio – Router A

Router Specifications	Comments
Internal IPX network number: _____	
Interface A connects to segment: _____	
❑ IPX Protocol Support Interface IPX network number: _____	
❑ Static Routes (*specify static route entries in Comments column*)	
❑ RIPX ❑ RIPX Filters (*specify filter criteria in Comments column*)	
❑ SAP ❑ SAP Filters (*specify filter criteria in Comments column*)	
❑ Auto-Static RIPX with updates scheduled at: _____	
❑ Auto-Static SAP with updates scheduled at: _____	
❑ IPX Routing Filters (*specify filter criteria in Comments column*)	
❑ IPX over IP tunnel	
❑ Authentication (*specify authentication method in Comments column*)	
❑ Encryption (*specify encryption method in Comments column*)	
❑ AppleTalk Protocol Support ❑ Seed router for the network segment	
Zones: _____	
Network number (or range): _____	
Interface B connects to segment: _____	
❑ IPX Protocol Support Interface IPX network number: _____	
❑ Static Routes (*specify static route entries in Comments column*)	
❑ RIPX ❑ RIPX Filters (*specify filter criteria in Comments column*)	
❑ SAP ❑ SAP Filters (*specify filter criteria in Comments column*)	
❑ Auto-Static RIPX with updates scheduled at: _____	
❑ Auto-Static SAP with updates scheduled at: _____	
❑ IPX Routing Filters (*specify filter criteria in Comments column*)	
❑ IPX over IP tunnel	
❑ Authentication (*specify authentication method in Comments column*)	
❑ Encryption (*specify encryption method in Comments column*)	
❑ AppleTalk Protocol Support ❑ Seed router for the network segment	
Zones: _____	
Network number (or range): _____	

Design Worksheet – Figure 5.26
Production Studio – Router B

Router Specifications	Comments
Internal IPX network number: _____	
Interface A connects to segment: _____	
❏ IPX Protocol Support Interface IPX network number: _____	
❏ Static Routes (*specify static route entries in Comments column*)	
❏ RIPX ❏ RIPX Filters (*specify filter criteria in Comments column*)	
❏ SAP ❏ SAP Filters (*specify filter criteria in Comments column*)	
❏ Auto-Static RIPX with updates scheduled at: _____	
❏ Auto-Static SAP with updates scheduled at: _____	
❏ IPX Routing Filters (*specify filter criteria in Comments column*)	
❏ IPX over IP tunnel	
❏ Authentication (*specify authentication method in Comments column*)	
❏ Encryption (*specify encryption method in Comments column*)	
❏ AppleTalk Protocol Support ❏ Seed router for the network segment	
Zones: _____	
Network number (or range): _____	
Interface B connects to segment: _____	
❏ IPX Protocol Support Interface IPX network number: _____	
❏ Static Routes (*specify static route entries in Comments column*)	
❏ RIPX ❏ RIPX Filters (*specify filter criteria in Comments column*)	
❏ SAP ❏ SAP Filters (*specify filter criteria in Comments column*)	
❏ Auto-Static RIPX with updates scheduled at: _____	
❏ Auto-Static SAP with updates scheduled at: _____	
❏ IPX Routing Filters (*specify filter criteria in Comments column*)	
❏ IPX over IP tunnel	
❏ Authentication (*specify authentication method in Comments column*)	
❏ Encryption (*specify encryption method in Comments column*)	
❏ AppleTalk Protocol Support ❏ Seed router for the network segment	
Zones: _____	
Network number (or range): _____	

Design Worksheet – Figure 5.26
Production Studio – Router C

Router Specifications	Comments
Internal IPX network number: _____	
Interface A connects to segment: _____	
❏ IPX Protocol Support Interface IPX network number: _____	
❏ Static Routes (*specify static route entries in Comments column*)	
❏ RIPX ❏ RIPX Filters (*specify filter criteria in Comments column*)	
❏ SAP ❏ SAP Filters (*specify filter criteria in Comments column*)	
❏ Auto-Static RIPX with updates scheduled at: _____	
❏ Auto-Static SAP with updates scheduled at: _____	
❏ IPX Routing Filters (*specify filter criteria in Comments column*)	
❏ IPX over IP tunnel	
❏ Authentication (*specify authentication method in Comments column*)	
❏ Encryption (*specify encryption method in Comments column*)	
❏ AppleTalk Protocol Support ❏ Seed router for the network segment	
Zones: _____	
Network number (or range): _____	
Interface B connects to segment: _____	
❏ IPX Protocol Support Interface IPX network number: _____	
❏ Static Routes (*specify static route entries in Comments column*)	
❏ RIPX ❏ RIPX Filters (*specify filter criteria in Comments column*)	
❏ SAP ❏ SAP Filters (*specify filter criteria in Comments column*)	
❏ Auto-Static RIPX with updates scheduled at: _____	
❏ Auto-Static SAP with updates scheduled at: _____	
❏ IPX Routing Filters (*specify filter criteria in Comments column*)	
❏ IPX over IP tunnel	
❏ Authentication (*specify authentication method in Comments column*)	
❏ Encryption (*specify encryption method in Comments column*)	
❏ AppleTalk Protocol Support ❏ Seed router for the network segment	
Zones: _____	
Network number (or range): _____	

Design Worksheet – Figure 5.26
Production Studio – Router D

Router Specifications	Comments
Internal IPX network number: _____	
Interface A connects to segment: _____	
❏ IPX Protocol Support Interface IPX network number: _____	
❏ Static Routes (*specify static route entries in Comments column*)	
❏ RIPX ❏ RIPX Filters (*specify filter criteria in Comments column*)	
❏ SAP ❏ SAP Filters (*specify filter criteria in Comments column*)	
❏ Auto-Static RIPX with updates scheduled at: _____	
❏ Auto-Static SAP with updates scheduled at: _____	
❏ IPX Routing Filters (*specify filter criteria in Comments column*)	
❏ IPX over IP tunnel	
❏ Authentication (*specify authentication method in Comments column*)	
❏ Encryption (*specify encryption method in Comments column*)	
❏ AppleTalk Protocol Support ❏ Seed router for the network segment	
Zones: _____	
Network number (or range): _____	
Interface B connects to segment: _____	
❏ IPX Protocol Support Interface IPX network number: _____	
❏ Static Routes (*specify static route entries in Comments column*)	
❏ RIPX ❏ RIPX Filters (*specify filter criteria in Comments column*)	
❏ SAP ❏ SAP Filters (*specify filter criteria in Comments column*)	
❏ Auto-Static RIPX with updates scheduled at: _____	
❏ Auto-Static SAP with updates scheduled at: _____	
❏ IPX Routing Filters (*specify filter criteria in Comments column*)	
❏ IPX over IP tunnel	
❏ Authentication (*specify authentication method in Comments column*)	
❏ Encryption (*specify encryption method in Comments column*)	
❏ AppleTalk Protocol Support ❏ Seed router for the network segment	
Zones: _____	
Network number (or range): _____	

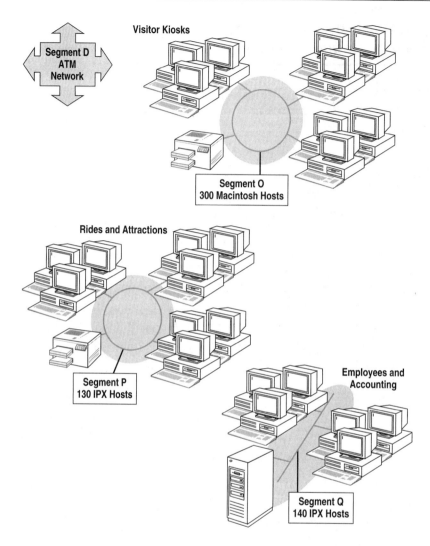

Figure 5.27   This is the existing network at one of the theme parks. For the purposes of this lab, assume that these buildings have the same network configuration.

Design Worksheet – Figure 5.27
Theme Park – Router A

Router Specifications	Comments
Internal IPX network number: _____	
Interface A connects to segment:_____	
❑ IPX Protocol Support Interface IPX network number: _____	
❑ Static Routes (*specify static route entries in Comments column*)	
❑ RIPX ❑ RIPX Filters (*specify filter criteria in Comments column*)	
❑ SAP ❑ SAP Filters (*specify filter criteria in Comments column*)	
❑ Auto-Static RIPX with updates scheduled at: _____	
❑ Auto-Static SAP with updates scheduled at: _____	
❑ IPX Routing Filters (*specify filter criteria in Comments column*)	
❑ IPX over IP tunnel	
❑ Authentication (*specify authentication method in Comments column*)	
❑ Encryption (*specify encryption method in Comments column*)	
❑ AppleTalk Protocol Support ❑ Seed router for the network segment	
Zones: _____	
Network number (or range): _____	
Interface B connects to segment: _____	
❑ IPX Protocol Support Interface IPX network number: _____	
❑ Static Routes (*specify static route entries in Comments column*)	
❑ RIPX ❑ RIPX Filters (*specify filter criteria in Comments column*)	
❑ SAP ❑ SAP Filters (*specify filter criteria in Comments column*)	
❑ Auto-Static RIPX with updates scheduled at: _____	
❑ Auto-Static SAP with updates scheduled at: _____	
❑ IPX Routing Filters (*specify filter criteria in Comments column*)	
❑ IPX over IP tunnel	
❑ Authentication (*specify authentication method in Comments column*)	
❑ Encryption (*specify encryption method in Comments column*)	
❑ AppleTalk Protocol Support ❑ Seed router for the network segment	
Zones: _____	
Network number (or range): _____	

Design Worksheet – Figure 5.27
Theme Park – Router B

Router Specifications	Comments
Internal IPX network number: _____	
Interface A connects to segment: _____	
❑ IPX Protocol Support Interface IPX network number: _____	
❑ Static Routes (*specify static route entries in Comments column*)	
❑ RIPX ❑ RIPX Filters (*specify filter criteria in Comments column*)	
❑ SAP ❑ SAP Filters (*specify filter criteria in Comments column*)	
❑ Auto-Static RIPX with updates scheduled at: _____	
❑ Auto-Static SAP with updates scheduled at: _____	
❑ IPX Routing Filters (*specify filter criteria in Comments column*)	
❑ IPX over IP tunnel	
❑ Authentication (*specify authentication method in Comments column*)	
❑ Encryption (*specify encryption method in Comments column*)	
❑ AppleTalk Protocol Support ❑ Seed router for the network segment	
Zones: _____	
Network number (or range): _____	
Interface B connects to segment: _____	
❑ IPX Protocol Support Interface IPX network number: _____	
❑ Static Routes (*specify static route entries in Comments column*)	
❑ RIPX ❑ RIPX Filters (*specify filter criteria in Comments column*)	
❑ SAP ❑ SAP Filters (*specify filter criteria in Comments column*)	
❑ Auto-Static RIPX with updates scheduled at: _____	
❑ Auto-Static SAP with updates scheduled at: _____	
❑ IPX Routing Filters (*specify filter criteria in Comments column*)	
❑ IPX over IP tunnel	
❑ Authentication (*specify authentication method in Comments column*)	
❑ Encryption (*specify encryption method in Comments column*)	
❑ AppleTalk Protocol Support ❑ Seed router for the network segment	
Zones: _____	
Network number (or range): _____	

Design Worksheet – Figure 5.27
Theme Park – Router C

Router Specifications	Comments
Internal IPX network number: _____	
Interface A connects to segment: _____	
❑ IPX Protocol Support Interface IPX network number: _____	
❑ Static Routes (*specify static route entries in Comments column*)	
❑ RIPX ❑ RIPX Filters (*specify filter criteria in Comments column*)	
❑ SAP ❑ SAP Filters (*specify filter criteria in Comments column*)	
❑ Auto-Static RIPX with updates scheduled at: _____	
❑ Auto-Static SAP with updates scheduled at: _____	
❑ IPX Routing Filters (*specify filter criteria in Comments column*)	
❑ IPX over IP tunnel	
❑ Authentication (*specify authentication method in Comments column*)	
❑ Encryption (*specify encryption method in Comments column*)	
❑ AppleTalk Protocol Support ❑ Seed router for the network segment	
Zones: _____	
Network number (or range): _____	
Interface B connects to segment: _____	
❑ IPX Protocol Support Interface IPX network number: _____	
❑ Static Routes (*specify static route entries in Comments column*)	
❑ RIPX ❑ RIPX Filters (*specify filter criteria in Comments column*)	
❑ SAP ❑ SAP Filters (*specify filter criteria in Comments column*)	
❑ Auto-Static RIPX with updates scheduled at: _____	
❑ Auto-Static SAP with updates scheduled at: _____	
❑ IPX Routing Filters (*specify filter criteria in Comments column*)	
❑ IPX over IP tunnel	
❑ Authentication (*specify authentication method in Comments column*)	
❑ Encryption (*specify encryption method in Comments column*)	
❑ AppleTalk Protocol Support ❑ Seed router for the network segment	
Zones: _____	
Network number (or range): _____	

Design Worksheet – Figure 5.27
Theme Park – Router D

Router Specifications	Comments
Internal IPX network number: _____	
Interface A connects to segment: _____	
❏ IPX Protocol Support Interface IPX network number: _____	
❏ Static Routes (*specify static route entries in Comments column*)	
❏ RIPX ❏ RIPX Filters (*specify filter criteria in Comments column*)	
❏ SAP ❏ SAP Filters (*specify filter criteria in Comments column*)	
❏ Auto-Static RIPX with updates scheduled at: _____	
❏ Auto-Static SAP with updates scheduled at: _____	
❏ IPX Routing Filters (*specify filter criteria in Comments column*)	
❏ IPX over IP tunnel	
❏ Authentication (*specify authentication method in Comments column*)	
❏ Encryption (*specify encryption method in Comments column*)	
❏ AppleTalk Protocol Support ❏ Seed router for the network segment	
Zones: _____	
Network number (or range): _____	
Interface B connects to segment: _____	
❏ IPX Protocol Support Interface IPX network number: _____	
❏ Static Routes (*specify static route entries in Comments column*)	
❏ RIPX ❏ RIPX Filters (*specify filter criteria in Comments column*)	
❏ SAP ❏ SAP Filters (*specify filter criteria in Comments column*)	
❏ Auto-Static RIPX with updates scheduled at: _____	
❏ Auto-Static SAP with updates scheduled at: _____	
❏ IPX Routing Filters (*specify filter criteria in Comments column*)	
❏ IPX over IP tunnel	
❏ Authentication (*specify authentication method in Comments column*)	
❏ Encryption (*specify encryption method in Comments column*)	
❏ AppleTalk Protocol Support ❏ Seed router for the network segment	
Zones: _____	
Network number (or range): _____	

Review

The following questions are intended to reinforce key information in this chapter. If you're unable to answer a question, review the lesson and then try to answer the question again. You can find answers to the questions in the Appendix, "Questions and Answers."

1. You're creating an IPX routing design for an organization with 15 locations in Europe. The locations are connected over point-to-point communications links that include dial-up modems and ISDN communications links. The organization wants to reduce the cost associated with these point-to-point communications links. What recommendations can you make to the organization?

2. Your services as a consultant have been retained by an organization to resolve connectivity outages it is experiencing. The organization is comprised of a number of locations. During normal business hours, the connectivity between these locations must be maintained. What recommendations can you make to ensure that the connectivity between these locations isn't interrupted during normal business hours?

3. You're creating an AppleTalk routing design for your network. The network is comprised of a number of locations. Each location contains numerous EtherTalk, TokenTalk and LocalTalk network segments. The AppleTalk network numbers and zones have been assigned to each network segment. What must you do to complete the AppleTalk routing design?

Proxy Server in Internet and Intranet Designs

About This Chapter

With the explosive expansion of the Internet, most of the networks you'll design will include Internet connectivity. These networks won't only require connectivity to the Internet, but also isolation from unauthorized Internet-based users. The majority of your designs will also share the Internet connection with potentially thousands of users who access common Internet sites and files. Some of these networks might be based on Internetwork Packet Exchange (IPX), but require Internet connectivity. Many networks providing Internet connectivity for the first time use private Internet Protocol (IP) addressing schemes. Your networking services designs must provide connectivity for these networks.

You can use Microsoft Proxy Server 2.0 to provide Internet connectivity for IP and IPX-based networks. Proxy Server can keep locally cached copies of commonly accessed Internet sites and files to improve Internet performance. Proxy Server also provides network address translation to facilitate private IP addressing schemes. You can secure the Internet connection by using Proxy Server to restrict the Internet sites that users can access and to prevent unauthorized access by Internet users.

This chapter answers questions such as:

- In what situations are the Internet connectivity services provided by Proxy Server appropriate for your design?
- Which client computer operating systems and software can connect to the Internet through Proxy Server?
- How can you restrict private network users' access to Internet Hypertext Transfer Protocol (HTTP) and File Transfer Protocol (FTP) sites?
- How can you restrict Internet users' access to private network resources?
- How can you ensure that Internet connectivity is always available to private network users and Internet users?
- How can you improve the performance of accessing private network resources or Internet resources?

Before You Begin

Before you begin, you must have an overall understanding of

- Network technologies (including Ethernet, Token Ring, hubs, switches, and concentrators)
- Common transport protocol configuration for Internet Protocol (IP) (such as IP address, subnet mask, or default gateway for IP)
- IP routed networks (including subnets, network segments, routers, and IP switches)
- IPX routed networks (including network segments, routers, and IPX to IP gateways)
- Proxy server technologies (including Web content caching, protocol filtering, or domain filtering)
- Network address translation between public and private IP addressing schemes

Lesson 1: Designs That Include Proxy Server

This lesson presents the requirements and constraints, both business and technical, that identify the Internet connectivity services in Microsoft Proxy Server 2.0 as a solution.

After this lesson, you will be able to

- Describe the relationship between Proxy Server and Microsoft Windows 2000
- Identify the business and technical requirements and constraints that must be collected to create a Proxy Server design
- Identify the Proxy Server design decisions
- Evaluate scenarios and determine when the Internet connectivity services provided by Proxy Server are an appropriate solution
- Evaluate scenarios and determine which capabilities and features of Proxy Server are appropriate

Estimated lesson time: 30 minutes

Microsoft Proxy Server 2.0 and Windows 2000

Unlike the other networking services discussed in this book, Proxy Server 2.0 is a product you buy separately from Windows 2000 but which runs on Windows 2000. From the Windows 2000 perspective, Proxy Server is a group of services that runs on Windows 2000.

Proxy Server uses IP in Windows 2000 to communicate with the private network and with the Internet (see Figure 6.1). In addition, Proxy Server can assign permissions to Active Directory–based users and groups. Also, Proxy Server uses NT file system (NTFS) partitions to store locally cached Web objects, such as Hypertext Markup Language (HTML) pages or File Transfer Protocol (FTP) files.

Note   To prevent compromising the security provided by Proxy Server, don't enable Routing and Remote Access on the same computer as Proxy Server. If the same computer is providing IP routing and Proxy Server services, you can't guarantee that proper Proxy Server security will be maintained in your designs.

In this chapter, you learn how to create Internet connectivity solutions with Proxy Server and Windows 2000.

To successfully create Proxy Server designs, you must be familiar with

- General IP routing theory (and IPX routing theory when appropriate)
- Firewalls and the creation of firewall rules
- File types and protocols for use in Web-based applications

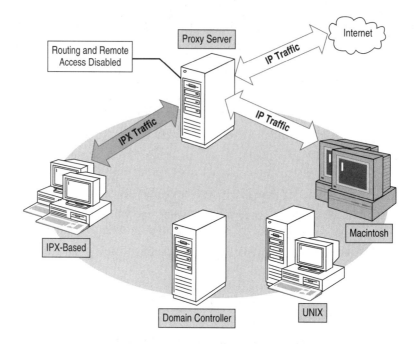

Figure 6.1   The interaction between Microsoft Proxy Server 2.0 and Windows 2000

Note   In this book, unless otherwise specified, Proxy Server (note caps) always refers to the Microsoft Proxy Server 2.0 product, and proxy server always refers to a computer running the Microsoft Proxy Server 2.0 product.

Proxy Server Design Requirements and Constraints

Before you create your Proxy Server design, you must gather the requirements and constraints, both business and technical, of the organization. As you create your design, you make design decisions based on the requirements and constraints that you collect.

The list of the design requirements and constraints that you collect includes

- Characteristics of the data transmitted through the proxy server, including
    - The amount of data transmitted through the proxy server
    - The confidentiality of the data transmitted through the proxy server
- Resources in the private network that must be accessed by Internet-based users
- Plans for future network growth
- Characteristics of existing proxy server including
    - Protocols in use in the private network
    - Proxy server placement

- Wide area network (WAN) connections in use
- Response times for applications that access resources through the proxy server(s)

- Acceptable percentage of time that users require access through the proxy server(s)

Proxy Server Design Decisions

After you determine the business and technical requirements and constraints, apply the information you gathered to make Proxy Server design decisions.

To create your Proxy Server design, you must choose the

- Types of connections, persistent or nonpersistent, that each proxy server must support
- Types of Proxy Server clients that must be supported by each proxy server
- Connection technologies, including T1, Public Switched Telephone Network (PSTN), Integrated Services Digital Network (ISDN), Digital Subscriber Line (DSL), or X.25, that each proxy server must support
- Dynamic routing protocols or manual routing table entries that each router must support
- Multiple connections and multiple proxy servers to improve availability and performance
- Criteria that you will adopt to filter traffic

The lessons that follow in this chapter provide the information required for you to make specific Proxy Server design recommendations.

Internet Connectivity Designs

The most common solution that you'll provide in your designs is found in *Internet connectivity* designs. In Internet connectivity designs, you connect private networks to the Internet. Your primary concern in Internet connectivity designs is to provide Internet access for private network users and to give private network resources access to Internet users.

Typically, in Internet connectivity designs, the proxy server takes the place of a firewall. As a result, security is one of your primary concerns in Internet connectivity designs.

Making the Decision

When you create designs that require Internet connectivity, the proxy servers can

- **Prevent unauthorized access to private network resources**   Proxy Server filters prevent unauthorized access to private network resources.

- **Restrict access to Internet resources**   Proxy Server filters and user authentication allow only authorized users with appropriate permissions to access Internet resources.

- **Provide network address translation for private IP addressing schemes** Proxy Server automatically provides network address translation between the private network and the Internet. As a result, Proxy Server supports public and private IP addressing schemes.

- **Improve Internet access performance**   Proxy Server can cache Web content locally to reduce the network traffic across the Internet connection.

- **Connect to a variety of WAN technologies**   Proxy Server can provide Internet connectivity over any network interface supported by Windows 2000.

Note   To provide the security features in the previous list, you must specify at least two network interfaces in the proxy server. One network interface connects to the private network and the other interface connects to the Internet.

Applying the Decision

Figure 6.2 illustrates a design where Proxy Server A provides Internet connectivity. Proxy Server A is placed where your private network connects to the Internet. Because Proxy Server A is also performing the function of a firewall in this design, all Internet traffic must pass through the proxy server to enforce network security.

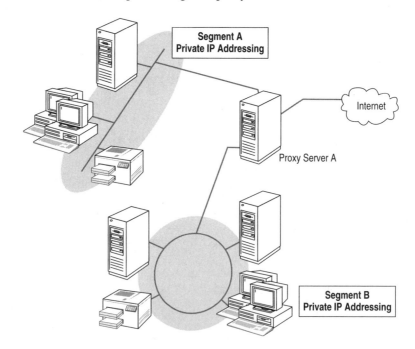

Figure 6.2   Scenario that uses Proxy Server for Internet connectivity

Note For designs that require stronger security, place a firewall between the proxy server and the Internet.

Because Segments A and B require private IP addressing schemes, Proxy Server A provides network address translation. You must assign a private IP address from the IP address range on Segments A and B respectively. You must assign a public IP address to the Internet interface connection in Proxy Server A. For more information on private IP addressing schemes, see Chapter 2, "Networking Protocol Design," Lesson 2, "Essential TCP/IP Design Concepts."

Note Network address translation is automatically performed in Proxy Server. No design specifications are required and no design decisions need to be made.

Web Content Caching Designs

In many of your designs, the organization might have existing firewalls that provide security between the private network and the Internet. However, the organization might want to improve Internet access performance by caching commonly used Web content locally on the private network. You create *Web content caching* designs to provide these performance enhancements in your design.

The following sequence describes how Web content caching occurs.

1. A client computer on the private network requests content from a Uniform Resource Locater (URL) on the Internet.

2. The client computer's URL request is forwarded to the proxy server.

3. The proxy server examines the local cache to determine whether the URL content is already cached. If the URL content is already in cache, the proxy server returns the content to the client computer.

4. If the content is not in cache, the proxy server requests the URL content from the Internet server.

5. The Internet server returns the URL content to the proxy server.

6. The proxy server places the URL content in local cache and returns the content to the client computer.

In these designs, the organization isn't concerned with the proxy server providing security—only improvements in Internet access performance.

Making the Decision

When you create designs that cache Web content for performance enhancement, each proxy server must

- **Manage at least one NTFS partition** Proxy Server stores Web content only on NTFS partitions. The NTFS partition must be sufficient to store the Web content that users commonly access.

- **Include at least one network adapter to the network**   Because security isn't a concern in this design, you don't need to provide more than one network adapter. However, two network adapters allow you to reduce network segment congestion by segregating private network traffic with Internet traffic.

- **Connect to a variety of WAN technologies**   Proxy Server can provide Internet connectivity over any network interface supported by Windows 2000.

Applying the Decision

Figure 6.3 illustrates a scenario in which Proxy Server provides caching of Internet-based Web content. All HTTP and FTP traffic is directed through the proxy server. All other types of IP traffic are forwarded to Router C. The firewall provides the security for the Internet connection.

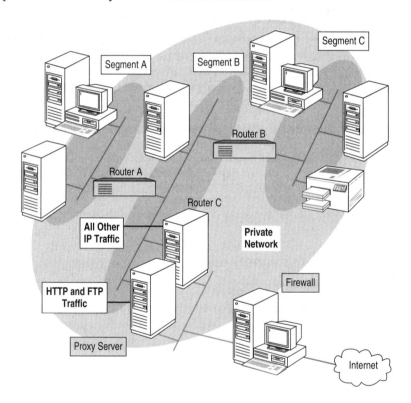

Figure 6.3   Scenario that uses Proxy Server for Web content caching

IPX to IP Gateway Designs

Although not as common as the previous designs, the *IPX to IP gateway* designs allow you to provide Internet connectivity (or simple IP connectivity) to IPX-based private networks. Many organizations might have existing IPX networks, but are unwilling or unable to migrate to IP in the immediate future. Proxy Server provides you with a tool to use as either a long-term or short-term solution.

The following sequence describes how the IPX to IP gateway feature of Proxy Server operates.

1. A client computer on the private network requests content from a URL on the Internet.
2. The client computer's URL request is forwarded to the proxy server by using IPX.
3. The proxy server receives the client computer's request, removes the URL request from the IPX packet, and places the URL request into an IP packet.
4. The proxy server forwards the repackaged URL request to the Internet server.
5. The Internet server returns the Web content to the proxy server.
6. The proxy server receives the Internet server response, removes the response from the IP packet, and places the response into an IPX packet.
7. The proxy server forwards the URL response to the client computer.

Making the Decision

When you create designs that connect IPX networks through IP networks, each proxy server must

- **Meet all the requirements as specified in the Internet connectivity design** You can use Proxy Server to provide only IPX to IP gateway services. However, you can also provide the security as described previously in the Internet connectivity designs. In instances where you are only providing IPX to IP gateway services, only one network interface is required. When you are also providing Internet connectivity security, two network interfaces are required.

- **Communicate with the appropriate network segments by using IPX and IP** Because the proxy server is providing gateway services between IPX and IP, it must have both protocols specified and proper configuration information included. For more information on IP specifications, see Chapter 2, "Networking Protocol Design," Lesson 2, "Essential TCP/IP Design Concepts." For more information on IPX protocol design specifications, see Chapter 3, "Multiprotocol Network Design," Lesson 2, "IPX Design Concepts."

Note IPX to IP gateways require the installation of the Proxy Server client software on all IPX-based computers to access Proxy Server.

Applying the Decision

Figure 6.4 illustrates a scenario in which Proxy Server is used as an IPX to IP gateway. The IPX-based private network forwards all Internet URL requests to

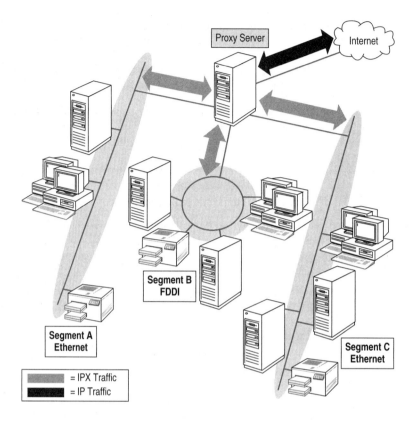

Figure 6.4   Scenario that uses Proxy Server as an IPX to IP gateway

the proxy server. The proxy server receives the URL requests and forwards them on the IP network segments.

In addition, because there is no firewall between the proxy server and the Internet, the proxy server is responsible for all private network security. However, if the organization has a firewall, you place the proxy server between the firewall and the private network.

Note   Because the IPX to IP gateway is the least common design, this chapter focuses on Internet connectivity and Web content caching designs.

Lesson 2: Essential Proxy Server Design Concepts

This lesson discusses the requirements, constraints, and design decisions used in creating a Proxy Server design. This lesson also discusses the design concepts common to all proxy server designs. Lessons 3 and 4 in this chapter discuss how to achieve the security, availability, and performance requirements of the organization.

After this lesson, you will be able to

- Determine the appropriate placement of proxy servers in your design
- Identify the appropriate design specifications for each proxy server interface
- Select the appropriate information to be placed in the local address table (LAT) for each proxy server and proxy server clients
- Select the appropriate method for connecting the client computer to the proxy servers

Estimated lesson time: 30 minutes

Placing Proxy Servers in the Network Design

You place the proxy servers in your network design based on the requirements of your organization. In Lesson 1 of this chapter, you examined scenarios that depicted the placement of proxy servers within a network. You can place the proxy servers in your design between the private network and the Internet (for Internet connectivity) or with the private network (for Web content caching).

Making the Decision

Depending on the reasons for including Proxy Server in your design, you can determine where to place proxy servers in your network design. Table 6.1 lists the reasons for including proxy servers in your design and where you place the proxy servers.

Table 6.1   Where to Place Proxy Servers Based on Why They Are Needed

If Your Design Includes Proxy Server(s) to Provide	Place the Proxy Server(s)
Internet connectivity	Between your private network and the Internet
Web content caching	Local to the users who are requesting the Web content
Both Internet connectivity and Web content caching	Between your private network and the Internet and local to the users who are requesting the Web content

In many of your Proxy Server designs, the proxy server is placed in parallel with IP routers. The benefit of placing a proxy server in parallel with routers is that the network traffic is load-balanced. You can forward all HTTP and FTP traffic through the proxy server and all other IP traffic through the router.

Applying the Decision

Figure 6.5 illustrates the proper placement of proxy servers in a network. In the scenario, you include Proxy Server for Internet connectivity and for Web content caching.

For the purposes of this scenario, assume that

- Only IP traffic is transmitted within the private network
- The organization wants to restrict access to Internet resources
- The organization wants to prevent unauthorized access to private network resources
- The organization is connected to the Internet by using ISDN

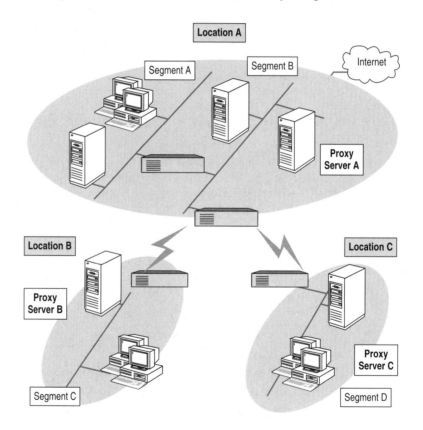

Figure 6.5   Diagram that illustrates the proper placement of proxy servers in a network

Table 6.2 lists each proxy server and the reason for placing the proxy servers your design.

Table 6.2   Reason for Placing Proxy Servers in Your Design

This Proxy Server Is Placed	To Provide
Proxy Server A	Internet connectivity for the organization
Proxy Server B	Web content caching for Location B
Proxy Server C	Web content caching for Location C

You must specify two network interface adapters for Proxy Server A in your design to provide isolation between the private network and the Internet. You need specify only one network interface adapter for Proxy Servers B and C in your design to provide Web content caching.

Figure 6.6 illustrates the proper placement of proxy servers when IP routers exist in the design. In the scenario, you include Proxy Server in a design where Proxy Server and an IP router connect the private network to the Internet.

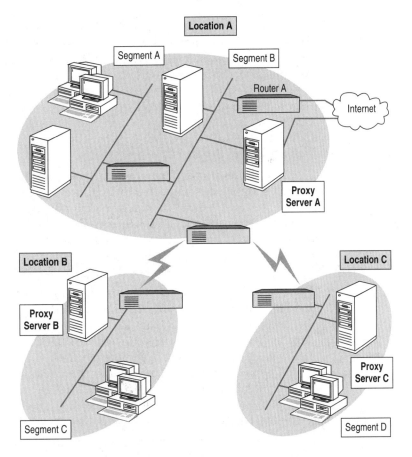

Figure 6.6   Diagram that illustrates the proper placement of proxy servers in relation to IP routers

When you integrate a Proxy Server and an IP router in an Internet connectivity design

- Specify IP filters on Router A to prevent HTTP and FTP traffic from being forwarded by Router A
- Forward all HTTP and FTP traffic through Proxy Server A
- Forward all other traffic through Router A

Determining Proxy Server Interface Specifications

Every proxy server in your design must have at least one network interface. Proxy servers with a single network interface can provide Web content caching and IPX to IP gateway services. To provide Internet connectivity, you must specify two or more network interfaces for the proxy server.

Making the Decision

For each interface in each proxy server in your design, you must specify

- **The type of connection between the router interface and the network, such as persistent or nonpersistent**   The decision-making process for the type of connection that you must specify for the proxy server interface is the same as the process for IP and IPX router interface connections. For more information on determining the type of network interface connection, see Chapter 4, "IP Routing Designs," Lesson 2, "Essential IP Routing Design Concepts" and Chapter 5, "Multiprotocol Routing Designs," Lesson 2, "IPX Routing Design Concepts."
- **The IP configuration information, including the IP address and IP subnet mask, for interfaces connected to IP network segments**   The decision-making process for the IP configuration information that you must specify for the proxy server interface is the same as the process for IP router interface connections. For more information on determining the IP configuration information for proxy server interface connections, see Chapter 4, "IP Routing Designs," Lesson 2, "Essential IP Routing Design Concepts."
- **The IPX configuration information, including the IPX network number and IPX frame type, for interfaces connected to IPX network segments**   The decision-making process for the IPX configuration information that you must specify for the proxy server interface is the same as the process for IPX router interface connections. For more information on determining the IPX configuration information for proxy server interface connections, see Chapter 5, "Multiprotocol Routing Designs," Lesson 2, "IPX Routing Design Concepts."

Applying the Decision

Figure 6.7 illustrates the proper configuration of proxy server network interfaces. In the scenario, you include Proxy Server for Internet connectivity and for Web content caching.

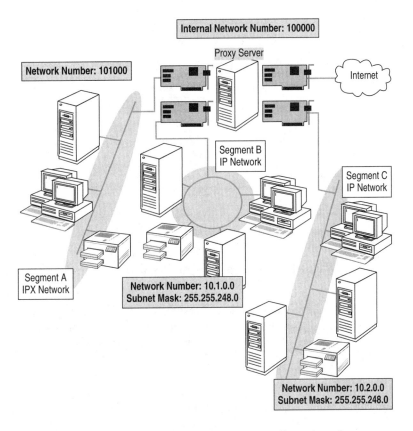

Figure 6.7   Diagram that illustrates the proper configuration of proxy server network interfaces

For the purposes of this scenario, assume that

- Only IPX traffic is transmitted on Segment A and only the Ethernet_8022 IPX frame type is in use
- Only IP traffic is transmitted on Segments B and C
- The organization wants to restrict access to Internet resources
- The IP address range of 172.16.3.0/24 is allocated from an Internet service provider (ISP) for use by the organization

Note   Although normally a private IP address, for the purposes of this scenario, treat 172.16.3.0/24 as a public IP address range.

- The organization wants to prevent unauthorized access to private network resources
- The organization is connected to the Internet by using DSL

Table 6.3 lists each network segment and the proxy server interface specifications you must include in your design.

Table 6.3   Network Segment and Proxy Server Interface Specifications

Network Segment	Proxy Server Interface Specifications
Segment A	Specify Ethernet_8022 as the IPX frame type and 101000 as the IPX network number
Segment B	Specify IP address from network 10.1.0.0 with a subnet mask of 255.255.248.0
Segment C	Specify IP address from network 10.1.0.0 with a subnet mask of 255.255.248.0
Internet	Specify IP address from network 172.16.3.0 with a subnet mask of 255.255.255.0

Specifying the Proxy Server LAT Information

The proxy servers or proxy server clients in your design must determine whether a destination IP address resides within the private network. The proxy server and proxy server clients determine whether the destination resides within or outside the private network by using the LAT information.

Making the Decision

For the proxy servers in your design to properly forward URL requests, the LAT must contain a list of all the IP address ranges within the private network.

You can place the entries in the LAT by using the Proxy Server setup program

- **Automatically**   The Proxy Server setup program can automatically populate the LAT information by examining the local Windows 2000 IP configuration. The setup program can derive LAT information from

  - The Windows 2000 IP routing information

  - The IP configuration of local network interface adapters

- **Manually**   You must specify an entry in the LAT information for each IP network number that exists within your private network. The LAT information can be manually entered through the setup program.

Proxy Server clients automatically download a copy of the LAT when they install the Proxy Server client software. In addition, updates to the LAT are automatically sent to computers that have the Proxy Server client software installed.

Note   Automatic installation and management of LAT information on client computers is available only when the client computer installs the Proxy Server client software. Automatic installation and management of LAT doesn't occur with other methods of communicating with the proxy server, such as SOCKS client or Microsoft Internet Explorer 5.0 proxy server detection.

Applying the Decision

Figure 6.8 illustrates the proper entries that must exist in the LAT of a proxy server. In the scenario, you include a LAT entry for each IP address number assigned to the private network. For the proxy server, and the clients, to properly determine whether the destination IP address is within the private network or on the Internet, you must include 10.1.0.0, 192.168.0.0, and 172.24.0.0 in the LAT.

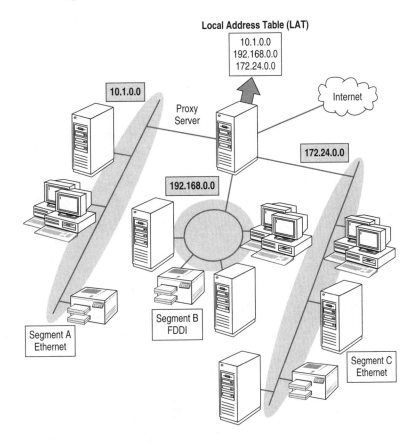

Figure 6.8   Diagram that illustrates the proper entries for the LAT in a proxy server

Selecting the Proxy Server Client Support

Proxy Server supports many different client computer operating systems. You must determine the client computer operating support that you must include in your design.

Making the Decision

Table 6.4 lists the Proxy Server support you can provide for client operating systems and why you include that support in your design.

Table 6.4   Why You Include Specific Proxy Server Support

Include	When You Want To
Windows Proxy Server client	Support any Windows operating system that includes Windows Sockets Enable clients to use the LAT to determine destination IP addresses within or outside the private network Redirect all IP traffic through Proxy Server Support IPX to IP gateways
Microsoft Internet Explorer 5.0	Support any operating system that includes Internet Explorer 5.0 Manage Proxy Server client configuration through the Internet Explorer Administrator Kit (IEAK) Redirect only HTTP and FTP traffic through Proxy Server
SOCKS	Support UNIX, Macintosh, or other operating systems that utilize the SOCKS standard Redirect all IPs supported by SOCKS applications
Default gateway	Support any operating system by configuring the default gateway setting so that all nonlocal traffic is redirected to the proxy server Redirect all IPs

Note When you have the option of including more than one type of Proxy Server client software, select the Windows Proxy Server client first. The Windows Proxy Server client provides the highest integration with Proxy Server. Select other client software support based on the requirements of the operating system.

Applying the Decision

Figure 6.9 illustrates a network that includes a variety of Proxy Server clients. Table 6.5 lists the client operating systems in the scenario and the Proxy Server client support to include in your design.

Table 6.5   Operating Systems and Proxy Server Client Support

Operating System	Proxy Server Client Support
Windows 2000	Select Proxy Server client software, Internet Explorer 5.0, or default gateway support
Microsoft Windows Me	Select Proxy Server client software, Internet Explorer 5.0, or default gateway support
Macintosh	Select SOCKS, Internet Explorer 5.0, or default gateway support
UNIX	Select SOCKS, Internet Explorer 5.0, or default gateway support (not all versions of UNIX support Internet Explorer 5.0)

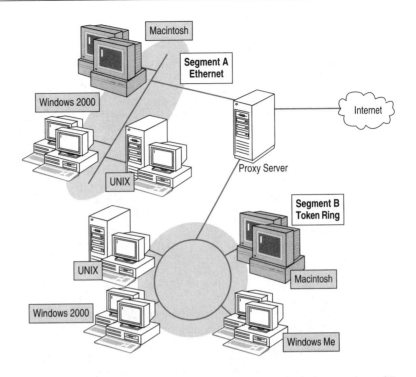

Figure 6.9   Diagram that illustrates a network that includes a variety of Proxy
Server clients

Activity 6.1: Evaluating a Proxy Server Design

In this activity, you're presented with a scenario. To complete the activity:

1. Evaluate the scenario and determine the design requirements

2. Answer questions and make design recommendations

In Figure 6.10, you see a map for an international shipping company that provides commercial shipment of materials and good internationally. The shipping
company has a Web site that allows customers to place shipment requests, check
pricing, and check shipment status. An Application Service Provider (ASP) hosts
the shipping company's Web site.

The customer service representatives for the company update the status of each
shipment as the shipments move through the various stages of shipment and customs clearance. The customer service representatives for a geographic region are
located at each office.

Each office is connected to the Internet by using a combination of 56 Kpbs,
ISDN, DSL, T1, and T3 connections.

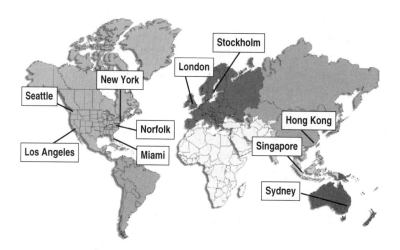

Figure 6.10   Map of an international shipping company

Answer the following questions concerning your design recommendations. You can find answers to the questions in the Appendix, "Questions and Answers."

1. Currently, an IP router provides the Internet connectivity at each location. The organization wants to investigate other technologies that might improve the Internet connectivity services provided. As the director of information services for the shipping company, you're responsible for the networking services design. What recommendations can you make?

2. A variety of operating systems, including Windows 95, Windows 2000, Macintosh, and UNIX, are used within each office in the shipping company. A version of Internet Explorer 5.0 exists for each operating system. Currently, the shipping company is only concerned about HTTP and FTP traffic to the company's Web site. What client computer configurations are appropriate and why would you recommend the solution?

3. You find out in a later meeting that a number of the private networks in the offices are IPX-based. Currently, the customer representatives connect to the Internet by using dial-up modems connected to their computers. What recommendations can you make?

Lesson 3: Data Protection in Proxy Server Designs

This lesson discusses how to create designs that protect the confidential data in an organization by using Proxy Server. This lesson focuses on protecting Proxy Server inbound and outbound data traffic.

After this lesson, you will be able to

- Identify the methods available in Proxy Server to protect inbound and outbound network traffic

- Select the appropriate methods for protecting private network resources from inbound Internet traffic by using Proxy Server

- Select the appropriate methods for restricting user access to Internet resources from outbound traffic by using Proxy Server

Estimated lesson time: 30 minutes

Identifying Proxy Server Data Protection Methods

When you include Proxy Server in your design to provide Internet connectivity, you must protect private network resources from Internet users. In addition, the security requirements of the organization might require your design to restrict private network users' access to Internet resources.

In this lesson, the direction of traffic is relative to the organization's private network. To protect private network resources from Internet users, you must restrict Proxy Server *inbound* traffic. To restrict private network users' access to Internet resources, you must restrict Proxy Server *outbound* traffic.

Note In designs where you include Proxy Server to provide only Web content caching, you must provide private network security by including a firewall or other security device. As a result, you don't need to include Proxy Server security in designs where Web content caching is the only reason for including Proxy Server.

Making the Decision

To determine the security requirements for your design, you must evaluate the data protection the organization requires. Most of your Proxy Server security designs will require you to protect the private network resources. A subset of your Proxy Server security designs will require you to restrict the private network users' access to Internet resources.

Note For any proxy server to provide security, the proxy server must contain at least two network interface adapters to isolate the private network from the Internet.

Table 6.6 lists the Proxy Server data protection methods, the direction of traffic they protect, and the type of data protection provided.

Table 6.6   Data Protection Methods, Traffic They Protect, and Type of Protection

Method	Direction	Data Protection Provided
Packet filters	Inbound and outbound	Restricts any inbound or outbound traffic based on the criteria you specify for all types of IP traffic
Web publishing	Inbound	Restricts inbound traffic based on the URL requested by Internet users
Domain filters	Outbound	Restricts outbound traffic based on a single IP address, a range of IP addresses, or a fully qualified domain name (FQDN)
User authentication	Outbound	Restricts outbound traffic only to authenticated users

Your Proxy Server designs can use any combination of these data protection methods, based on the security requirements of the organization.

Note   Each of the Proxy Server data protection methods are discussed further in later sections of this lesson.

Applying the Decision

Figure 6.11 illustrates a network that includes Proxy Server security. For each proxy server in the design, you must determine the Proxy Server security you have to include in your design.

For the purposes of this scenario, assume that the business and technical requirements of the organization are that

- Only authenticated users can access the Internet
- Private network users can access only the following Internet FQDNs
    - www.contoso.msft
    - www.salesco.msft
    - www.freeinfo.msft
- Internet users can access the Web servers that host the organization's Internet presence within the private network
- Any inbound or outbound Internet Relay Chat (IRC) traffic must be prevented
- The ISDN connection to the Internet must be supported

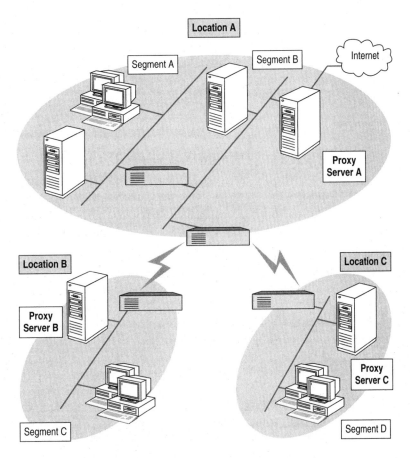

Figure 6.11   Diagram that illustrates a network that includes Proxy Server security

Table 6.7 lists each proxy server in the design, the Proxy Server security method that you'll include, and the reasons you must include the Proxy Server security method in your design.

Table 6.7   Reasons You Must Include Specific Proxy Server Security Methods

For This Server	Select	To
Proxy Server A	Packet filters	Prevent the IRC traffic from inbound or outbound transmission
	Web publishing	Allow the private network Web server to be accessed from the Internet
	Domain filters	Restrict private network users access to only www.contoso.msft, www.salesco.msft, and www.freeinfo.msft
	User account authentication	Allow only authenticated users to access the Internet through Proxy Server A

(continued)

Table 6.7   *(continued)*

For This Server	Select	To
Proxy Server B	No security	Proxy Server B only provides Web content caching and provides no Internet connectivity
Proxy Server C	No security	Proxy Server C only provides Web content caching and provides no Internet connectivity

Protecting Private Network Resources

In your Proxy Server designs that provide Internet connectivity, protecting the private network resources is the highest priority in the solution. As previously mentioned, when you include Proxy Server in your design to provide Web content caching, a firewall or other device typically provides security.

You can protect the private network resources by restricting Proxy Server inbound traffic. Based on the security requirements of the organization, you must select the appropriate Proxy Server security method for restricting inbound traffic.

Making the Decision

You can restrict inbound Proxy Server traffic by using Proxy Server packet filters and the Web Publishing feature. You can elect to include Proxy Server packet filters, Web Publishing, or both in your designs.

Packet Filters

You can include Proxy Server packet filters to restrict traffic based on the IP header information. You can build the criteria for the packet filters based on any combination of IP header information.

Table 6.8 lists the criteria you can include in your packet filter specifications, and the reason for specifying the criteria in your packet filter specifications.

Table 6.8   Reasons for Specifying Certain Criteria in Your Packet Filter Specifications

Include	In Your Packet Filter Criteria to Specify
Direction	The direction of the IP traffic *relative to the Proxy Server network interface*. To provide the maximum protection of private network resources, restrict the inbound traffic on the Proxy Server interface(s) connected to the Internet. By restricting the inbound traffic on the interface(s) connected to the Internet, you prevent the Proxy Server from even receiving the IP packet.
Protocol ID	The IP ID for the inbound traffic. You can specify the protocol ID to restrict traffic based on applications or specific services. For example, you can restrict application specific traffic that uses Transmission Control Protocol (TCP) to transmit data.

Table 6.8 *(continued)*

Include	In Your Packet Filter Criteria to Specify
Local port	The TCP or User Datagram Protocol (UDP) port number within the private network. For inbound traffic, the local port number refers to the destination port number. You can specify an individual port number or a range of port numbers. For example, you can restrict application traffic that uses a specific TCP or UDP port number.
Remote port	The TCP or UDP port number on the Internet. For inbound traffic, the local port number refers to the source port number. You can specify an individual port number or a range of port numbers. For example, you can restrict application traffic that uses a specific TCP or UDP port number.
Local host IP address	The IP address of a computer on the private network; typically, the IP address of the Proxy Server interface connected to the Internet. You can specify any IP address within the private network. For example, you can restrict traffic to a Web server within the private network by specifying the IP address of the Web server.
Remote host IP address	The IP address of a computer on the Internet. You can specify any IP address that exists on the Internet. For example, you can allow traffic *only* from a range of IP addresses that belongs to remote users or business partners.

Web Publishing

By default, Proxy Server discards all inbound URL requests to access Web and FTP servers in the private network. You can include the Web Publishing feature of Proxy Server to provide Internet users with access to Web and FTP servers in the private network.

You can specify the URLs you want to redirect to Web and FTP servers within the private network. For each URL you want to redirect, you can specify a separate entry in the Web Publishing list. You can specify any combination of URL entries in the Web Publishing list.

For inbound URLs requests that aren't specified in the Web Publishing list, Proxy Server can respond by

- Discarding the requests
- Redirecting the requests to the default Web site installed on the same computer as Proxy Server
- Redirecting the requests to any Web site within the private network

Applying the Decision

Figure 6.12 illustrates the appropriate Proxy Server security methods for protecting private network resources. The Proxy Server protects the private network resources that reside on Servers A through F.

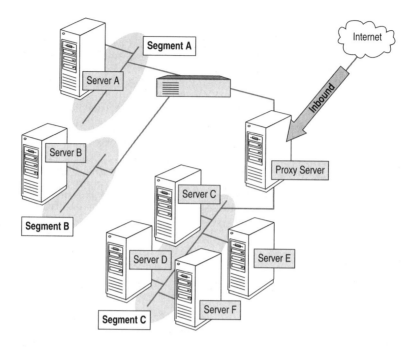

Figure 6.12   Scenario to illustrate the appropriate Proxy Server methods for protecting private network resources

For the purposes of this scenario, assume that the business and technical requirements of the organization include

- Providing Internet user access to Servers C, D, E, and F.
- Preventing Internet user access to Servers A and B.
- Allowing only HTTP and FTP packets to be sent between Servers C, D, E, and F and Internet users.
- That the organization's FQDN is contoso.msft and each server will be relative to the contoso.msft domain name. For example, the FQDN for Server C is serverc.contoso.msft.

Table 6.9 lists the Proxy Server security methods appropriate for the design, and the reason you include the method in the design.

Table 6.9   Appropriate Security Methods and Reasons to Include Them

Include	To Protect Private Network Resource By
Packet filters	Preventing access to any network resources on Segments A and B Ensuring that only HTTP and FTP IP traffic can be sent to Segment C
Web Publishing	Only providing access to Servers C, D, E, and F by creating a Web Publishing entry for each server

Note The Proxy Server in the previous scenario provides security similar to a firewall. The combination of Proxy Server packet filters and Web Publishing entries are analogous to firewall rules.

The Proxy Server solution depicted in the previous scenario creates a *screened subnet* (otherwise known as a DMZ). You create a screened subnet when you restrict traffic between the screened subnet and other subnets.

Restricting Access to Internet Resources

In your Proxy Server designs that provide Internet connectivity, your next priority in the solution is to restrict private network user access to Internet resources. You restrict private network user access to Internet resources by restricting Proxy Server outbound traffic. Based on the security requirements of the organization, you must select the appropriate Proxy Server security method for restricting outbound traffic.

Making the Decision

You can restrict outbound Proxy Server traffic by using Proxy Server packet filters, domain filters, and user account authentication. You can include any combination of these Proxy Server security methods to restrict outbound traffic.

Packet Filters

As mentioned in the previous section, you can include Proxy Server packet filters to restrict traffic based on the IP header information. You can build the criteria for the packet filters based on any combination of IP header information.

Restricting outbound traffic is the same as restricting inbound traffic, except for the *Direction* criteria of the packet filter. To restrict access to Internet, specify outbound in the Direction criteria for the packet filters. For more information on Proxy Server packet filters, see the previous section, "Protecting Private Network Resources."

Domain Filters

You can include Proxy Server domain filters to restrict Internet access to specific IP addresses or FQDNs. You can filter requests for Internet resources based on an IP address, a range of IP addresses, or a FQDN. You can build the criteria for the domain filters based on any one of these methods.

You can specify a list of Internet sites in your domain filters. Your domain filters can respond to requests to these Internet sites by

- Rejecting all packets to these Internet sites and forwarding all other packets
- Forwarding all packets to these Internet sites and rejecting all other packets

Table 6.10 lists the criteria you can include in your domain filter specifications, and the reason for selecting the criteria in your domain filter specifications.

Table 6.10   Reasons for Choosing Specific Criteria for Your Domain Filter Specifications

Include	In Your Domain Filter Criteria to Specify
IP address	A single computer, or cluster IP address. You can restrict all traffic between the private network and this IP address.
IP address range	More than one computer. You can restrict all traffic between the private network and any IP address in this range.
FQDN	All or a portion of the Internet resources supported by an organization.

For example, if you specify an FQDN such as contoso.msft in your domain filter, you can either reject all IP packets destined for contoso.msft, or forward all packets destined for contoso.msft.

User Authentication

You can include Proxy Server user authentication to provide Internet access to authenticated users on the private network. You can assign Proxy Server access to

- Any user or group in Active Directory directory services
- Any local user or group in a member server

The user or groups are simply permitted access, enabling or disabling the user's or groups' ability to transmit data through Proxy Server. When you enable a group to access Proxy Server, all users (or groups) that belong to the group are permitted to access Proxy Server.

For example, if you grant Proxy Server access to the group Everyone, all users are able to transmit data through the Proxy Server. However, granting the group Everyone access to Proxy Server doesn't circumvent Proxy Server packet filters or domain filters.

Tip   Granting Proxy Server access to the group Everyone grants access to all users, including anonymous users. If the Guest account is enabled, anonymous users are able to transmit data through Proxy Server.

Applying the Decision

Figure 6.13 illustrates the appropriate Proxy Server security methods for restricting access to Internet resources. The Proxy Server restricts the Internet access for private network users.

For the purposes of this scenario, assume that the business and technical requirements of the organization include

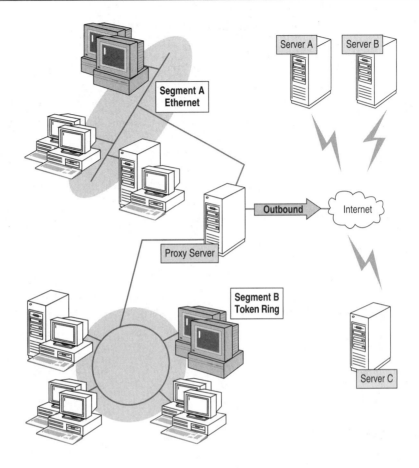

Figure 6.13   Scenario to illustrate the appropriate Proxy Server methods for restricting access to Internet resources

- Providing Internet access to only authenticated users—no anonymous access
- Preventing private network user access to Server B
- Allowing only HTTP and FTP packets to be sent between Servers A and C and private network users
- That the FQDN for Server A is www.contoso.msft
- That the FQDN for Server B is www.salesco.msft
- That the FQDN for Server C is www.freeinfo.msft

Table 6.11 lists the Proxy Server security methods appropriate for the design, and the reason you include the method in the design.

Table 6.11   Reasons You Include Specific Proxy Server Security Methods

Include	To Restrict Access to Internet Resources By
Packet filters	Ensuring that only HTTP and FTP IP traffic can be sent to Servers A and C
Domain filters	Preventing any access to www.salesco.msft
User authentication	Allowing only authenticated users to transmit data through the Proxy Server

Lesson 4: Proxy Server Design Optimization

This lesson discusses how to optimize Proxy Server designs to improve the availability and performance characteristics in your design. This lesson focuses on the strategies that increase the percentage of time users can access the Proxy Server and that increase the data transmission rate through the Proxy Server.

After this lesson, you will be able to

- Identify the methods available to increase the availability and performance characteristics of a Proxy Server design
- Select the appropriate methods for increasing the availability and performance design characteristics for traffic when private network users access Internet resources
- Select the appropriate methods for increasing the availability and performance design characteristics for traffic when Internet users access private network resources

Estimated lesson time: 45 minutes

Identifying Proxy Server Optimization Techniques

Once you have established the essential aspects and security aspects of your Proxy Server design, you can optimize the design for availability and performance. The business requirements of the organization might require your design to ensure access to Internet and private network resources. In addition, the business requirements might include application response times that must be maintained.

As with security, the direction of traffic determines which Proxy Server optimization methods are appropriate. You can optimize the Proxy Server design to improve the availability and performance of inbound or outbound traffic.

Making the Decision

To determine the availability and performance requirements for your design, you must evaluate the application response times, the aggregate Internet data transmission rate, and the percentage of time that traffic must pass through the Proxy Server.

Table 6.12 lists the Proxy Server optimization methods, the direction of traffic to be optimized, and the type of optimization provided.

Table 6.12   Optimization Records, Direction, and Optimization Provided

Method	Direction	Optimization Provided
Web content cache	Outbound	Improves only performance by making copies of Web content locally available to private network users

(continued)

Table 6.12   *(continued)*

Method	Direction	Optimization Provided
Proxy array	Outbound	Distributes outbound traffic and Web content cache across multiple proxy servers to improve performance and availability
Network Load Balancing	Inbound	Distributes inbound traffic across multiple proxy servers to improve performance and availability
Round Robin DNS	Inbound	Distributes inbound traffic across multiple proxy servers to improve performance and availability

Your Proxy Server designs can use any combination of these optimization methods, based on the availability and performance requirements of the organization. Each of the Proxy Server optimization methods is discussed further in later sections of this lesson.

Note   You can also include hardware solutions in your Proxy Server design to improve performance and availability. This lesson discusses only the software solutions provided by Proxy Server and Windows 2000.

Applying the Decision

Figure 6.14 illustrates the appropriate methods for optimizing Proxy Server availability and performance. For the purposes of this scenario, assume that the business and technical requirements of the organization include

- Private network users must always be able to access Internet resources
- Private network users require the highest possible performance while accessing Internet resources
- Internet users must be prevented from accessing private network resources

Table 6.13 lists the Proxy Server optimization methods appropriate for the design, and the reason you include the method in the design.

Table 6.13   Reasons to Include Specific Optimization Methods

Include	To Optimize the Proxy Server Design By
Web content cache	Locally caching Web content at each location to improve performance. Proxy Array A, Proxy Array B, and Proxy Server C include Web content caching to improve performance within each location.
Proxy arrays	Distributing Proxy Server cached Web content and traffic across multiple proxy servers to improve availability and performance. Proxy Arrays A and B are proxy arrays that improve availability and performance for Internet access.

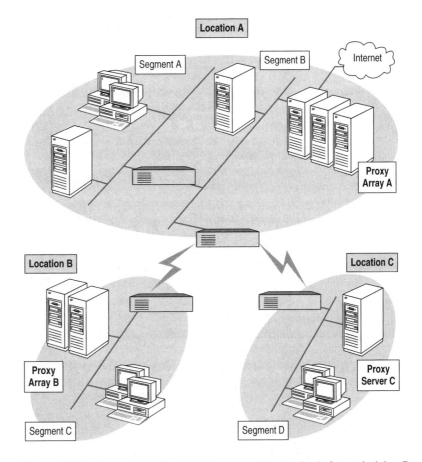

Figure 6.14   Scenario to illustrate the appropriate methods for optimizing Proxy
Server availability and performance

Note   Because no private network resources are accessed from the Internet, Network Load Balancing and round robin DNS aren't required.

Figure 6.15 presents another scenario that illustrates the appropriate methods for optimizing Proxy Server availability and performance. For the purposes of this scenario, assume that the business and technical requirements of the organization include

- Private network users must always be able to access Internet resources
- Private network users require the highest possible performance while accessing Internet resources
- Internet users must always be able to access private network resources

Table 6.14 lists the Proxy Server optimization methods appropriate for the design, and the reason you include the method in the design.

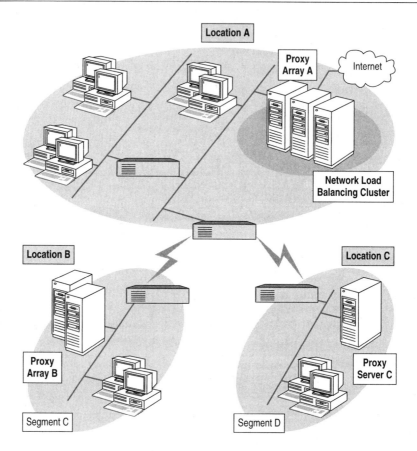

Figure 6.15   Another scenario to illustrate the appropriate methods for optimizing Proxy Server availability and performance

Table 6.14   Reasons to Include Specific Optimization Methods

Include	To Optimize the Proxy Server Design By
Web content cache	Locally caching Web content to improve performance. Proxy Array A includes Web content caching to improve performance.
Proxy arrays	Distributing Proxy Server cached Web content and traffic across multiple proxy servers to improve availability and performance. Proxy Array A improves availability and performance for Internet access.
Network Load Balancing	Distributing incoming Proxy Server traffic across the proxy servers that belong to Proxy Array A. The servers in the proxy array also belong to the same Network Load Balancing cluster. The Network Load Balancing service on each proxy server *dynamically* distributes inbound traffic across the proxy servers in the proxy array.

Note   You can also use round robin DNS instead of Network Load Balancing. However, unlike Network Load Balancing, round robin DNS *statically* distributes inbound traffic.

Optimizing Internet Access

In Proxy Server designs that provide Internet access, the business and technical requirements of the organization might require you to achieve a certain percentage of uptime or certain application response times. You can optimize the availability and performance aspects of your Proxy Server design for Internet access by improving the availability and performance characteristics of outbound requests and inbound responses. Based on the requirements of the organization, you must select the appropriate Proxy Server optimization methods for Internet access.

Making the Decision

You can optimize Internet access in your Proxy Server design by using Web content caching and proxy arrays. In your Proxy Server solutions, you can include any combination of Web content caching or proxy arrays to optimize Internet access traffic. In addition, you can organize proxy servers and proxy arrays hierarchically to improve performance.

Web Content Caching

You can include Proxy Server Web content caching to improve the response times when accessing Web pages that are cached on *local* proxy servers. The proxy servers store commonly accessed Internet Web content on drives attached to the proxy server.

Figure 6.16 illustrates a proxy server with Web content caching enabled. The proxy server stores the cached Web content on the local NTFS partition.

When the proxy server receives requests for Web content, the proxy server checks to see whether the Web content is in the local cache. If the Web content is cached locally, the proxy server retrieves the Web content from cache and responds to the client computer. If the Web content is not found in the local cache, the proxy server retrieves the Web content from the Internet, stores the Web content in local cache, and then responds to the client computer.

Note   Proxy Server Web content cache must be stored on an NTFS partition.

Proxy Server supports the following Web content caching methods:

- **Active caching**   Active caching is the default when you include Web content caching in your design. Active caching *proactively* retrieves updates to cached Web content when the processor utilization of the proxy server is low. Active caching retrieves the updates to cached Web objects during low processor utilization so client computer response times aren't affected.

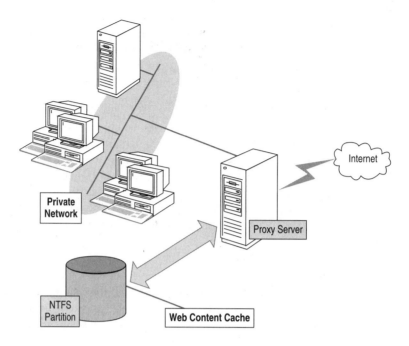

Figure 6.16   Proxy server with Web content caching enabled

Active caching determines when to check for updated Web content by aging criteria you can specify in your design. You can specify criteria based on

- HTML header information
- URL of the content
- Date and time of cached Web content files
- **Passive caching**   Passive caching can be specified when you include Web content caching in your design. Passive caching retrieves updates to cached Web content when client computers request the content.

When the request for cached Web content is received by the proxy server, the proxy server checks the source of the Web content to see whether the content has changed. If the source of the Web content has changed, the proxy server retrieves the updates to the cached Web objects immediately and returns the updated content to the client computer.

Like active caching, passive caching determines when to check for updated Web content by using aging criteria you can specify in your design. However, the Web content is updated only when client computers request the Web content.

Note   Active caching updates Web content during low processor utilization *and* when requested (just like passive caching).

Table 6.15 lists the Proxy Server caching methods and the advantages and the disadvantages of including that method in your design.

Table 6.15   Advantages and Disadvantages of Caching Methods

Caching Method	Advantages	Disadvantages
Active caching	Reduces processor overhead and Internet traffic during peak periods of usage	Creates activity when client computers aren't accessing the Internet. Might increase costs if the organization is charged while the Internet connection is active because active caching automatically initiates the connection when users aren't accessing the Internet
Passive caching	Eliminates activity when client computers aren't accessing the Internet. Reduces costs if the organization is charged while the Internet connection is active because passive caching initiates the connection when users *are* accessing the Internet	Can increase processor overhead and Internet traffic during peak periods of usage because Web content updates are performed immediately, regardless of current processor overhead or Internet traffic

Proxy Arrays

A proxy array is an extension of Web content caching. In Web content caching, Web content is stored on a single proxy server. In a proxy array, the Web content is stored across all proxy servers that belong to the proxy array.

Figure 6.17 illustrates a proxy array with Web content caching distributed across multiple proxy servers. The cached Web content and network traffic is evenly distributed across the proxy servers in the proxy array. Because the Web content is distributed across all proxy servers in the proxy array

- Network traffic, disk access, and processor utilization is load-balanced across all the proxy servers in the array to improve performance

- When any proxy server in the array fails, the remaining proxy servers continue to provide connectivity and increase availability

You can create a proxy array in your design by assigning the same proxy array name to one or more proxy servers. In addition, you can dynamically add and remove proxy servers to the proxy array without affecting existing proxy servers in the proxy array.

There is no special Proxy Server client configuration required to use a proxy array. Client computer requests forwarded to any proxy server in the proxy array are automatically forwarded to the appropriate proxy server in the proxy array.

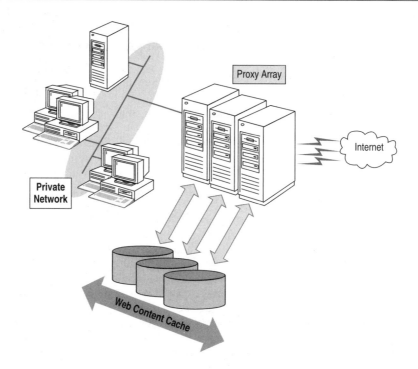

Figure 6.17   Proxy array with Web content cache distributed across multiple proxy servers

---

Tip   You can create a proxy array with one proxy server for future expansion. By creating a proxy array with one proxy server, you make the task of adding additional servers require less time and reconfiguration.

To evenly distribute the proxy server traffic across all the proxy servers in the proxy array, the proxy servers must have comparable hardware specifications (such as memory, processor, and disk storage). For example, if one of the proxy servers in the proxy array has significantly less disk storage, the proxy server isn't able to manage the same amount of cached Web content as the other proxy servers in the proxy array.

Hierarchical Proxy Servers and Proxy Arrays

You can specify a combination of proxy servers and proxy arrays in a hierarchy to improve Internet access performance within the private network.

Figure 6.18 illustrates a hierarchical arrangement of proxy servers and proxy arrays. The proxy array at the top of the hierarchy, Proxy Array A, provides Internet access and connectivity for the private network.

Proxy Array A receives requests from other proxy servers or proxy arrays in the private network and retrieves content from the Internet. Proxy Server B and Proxy Array C forward requests to Proxy Array A.

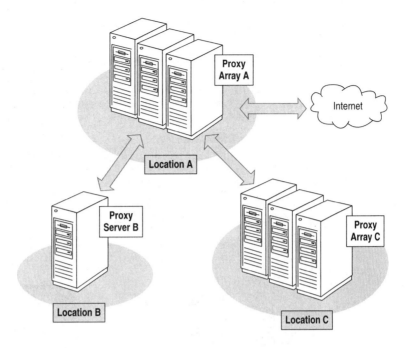

Figure 6.18   Hierarchical arrangement of proxy servers and proxy arrays

You can specify that the proxy server, or proxy array, upstream connection is

- **An Internet connection**   The proxy server or array configured with an upstream Internet connection forwards all requests directly to the Internet site. Configure the proxy server or proxy array at the top of your hierarchy with an upstream Internet connection.
- **An upstream proxy server or proxy array**   The proxy server configured for an upstream proxy server forwards all requests directly to the upstream proxy server or proxy array. Configure the proxy server, or proxy array, at the top of your hierarchy with an upstream proxy server connection.

Applying the Decision

Figure 6.19 illustrates the appropriate methods for optimizing Internet access availability and performance. For the purposes of this scenario, assume that the business and technical requirements of the organization include

- Private network users must always be able to access Internet resources
- Private network users require the highest possible performance while accessing Internet resources

Table 6.16 lists the Proxy Server optimization methods appropriate for the design, and the reason you include the method in the design.

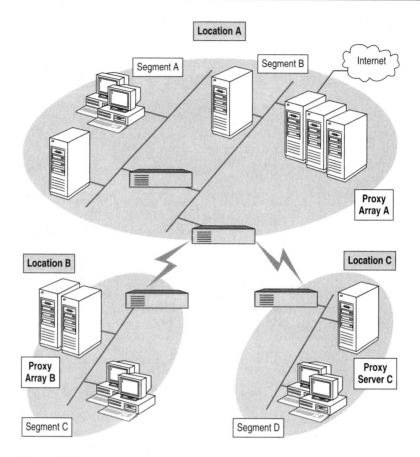

Figure 6.19   Scenario to illustrate the appropriate methods for optimizing Internet access availability and performance

Table 6.16   Reasons to Include Specific Optimization Methods

Include	To Optimize Internet Access in the Design By
Web content cache	Specifying active caching on Proxy Array A, Proxy Array B, and Proxy Server C to improve performance. Specifying an upstream Internet connection for Proxy Array A to reduce Internet traffic and improve performance. Specifying an upstream proxy server connection for Proxy Array B and Proxy Server C. Specify Proxy Array B and Proxy Server C to forward all requests to Proxy Array A to reduce Internet traffic and improve performance.
Proxy arrays	Specifying that all proxy servers in Proxy Arrays A and B share the same proxy array name to distribute network traffic and Web content. The distribution of network traffic and Web content improves availability and performance.

Optimizing Private Network Resource Access

In Proxy Server designs that allow access to private network resources, the business and technical requirements of the organization might require you to achieve a certain percentage of uptime and certain response times to Internet user requests. Based on the requirements of the organization, you must select the appropriate Proxy Server optimization methods for private network resource access.

Making the Decision

You can optimize private network resource access traffic in your Proxy Server design by using Network Load Balancing and round robin DNS. In your Proxy Server solutions, you can include either Network Load Balancing or round robin DNS to optimize private network resource traffic.

Table 6.17 lists the Proxy Server optimization methods for private network access and the advantages and disadvantages of including these methods in your design.

Table 6.17   Advantages and Disadvantages of Optimization Methods for Private Network Access

Method	Advantages	Disadvantages
Network Load Balancing	Dynamically provides load balancing across all the proxy servers in the Network Load Balancing cluster Allows dynamic addition or removal of proxy servers in the cluster Automatically reconfigures the cluster if a proxy server fails Improves availability and performance because the load balancing and the addition or removal of proxy servers is dynamic	Requires extra processor and memory resources to run the Network Load Balancing service Doesn't work with proxy servers running on other operating systems, such as UNIX or Macintosh computers
Round robin DNS	Works on all operating system platforms Statically provides load balancing across all the proxy servers listed in round robin DNS Improves performance for private network access by load balancing network traffic across multiple proxy servers	Doesn't automatically remove failed proxy servers, so client computers might experience time-out or other error messages Proxy servers must be manually added or removed from the DNS entries Doesn't improve the availability of the Proxy Server solution

Network Load Balancing Service

The Network Load Balancing service is included in Microsoft Windows 2000 Advanced Server and Microsoft Windows 2000 Datacenter Server. Microsoft Windows 2000 Server and Microsoft Windows 2000 Professional don't include the Network Load Balancing service.

The Network Load Balancing service must be included on all Proxy Servers that you want to include in the cluster. In addition, you must specify an IP address for use by the cluster. Any Proxy Server traffic forwarded to the cluster IP address is load-balanced automatically across all proxy servers in the cluster.

If any server of the cluster fails, the cluster automatically redistributes the network traffic to the remaining servers in the cluster. Also, if you add a new server to the cluster, the network traffic is automatically rebalanced across the cluster to include the new server.

Note There's no requirement that the proxy servers in the cluster belong to the same proxy array. However, to reduce costs, most designs use the same proxy servers for both Internet access traffic and private network access traffic.

In Figure 6.20, you can see that an IP address is assigned to Proxy Servers A, B, and C. In addition, the Network Load Balancing cluster is also assigned an IP address. The private network access traffic is sent to the cluster IP address, not the individual proxy server IP addresses.

For more information on the Network Load Balancing service, see the Windows 2000 help files.

Round Robin DNS

You can also use round robin DNS entries to distribute private network traffic across multiple proxy servers. The proxy servers can belong to the same proxy array or be individual proxy servers.

You create round robin DNS entries by specifying the same FQDN with different IP addresses. Consider a DNS database that contains the following round robin DNS entries for four proxy servers that provide private network access:

```
www.contoso.msft    172.168.1.101

www.contoso.msft    172.168.1.102

www.contoso.msft    172.168.1.103

www.contoso.msft    172.168.1.104
```

The following sequence describes how the DNS server responds to DNS queries for www.contoso.msft.

1. The first query returns the first IP address (172.168.1.101).

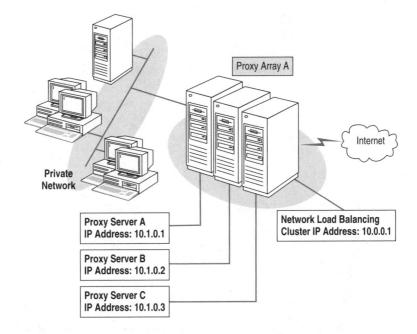

Figure 6.20   Network Load Balancing service and proxy servers

2. Subsequent queries return the next IP address in the list (172.168.1.102 and 172.168.1.103, and 172.168.1.104).

3. Once the last round robin entry is returned (172.168.1.104), the DNS server starts at the top of the list again (172.168.1.101).

The round robin DNS entries are returned regardless of the proxy server's functional status. If a proxy server fails, the DNS entry is returned for the failed proxy server. As a result, round robin DNS entries assist in improving performance, but not availability.

In Figure 6.21, you can see that a round robin DNS entry is created for each proxy server. As DNS queries for contoso.msft are received, the DNS server alternates responses between 10.1.0.1 and 10.1.0.2.

For more information on round robin DNS entries, see the Windows 2000 help files.

Applying the Decision

Figure 6.22 illustrates the appropriate methods for optimizing private network availability and performance. For the purposes of this scenario, assume that the business and technical requirements of the organization include

- Internet users must always be able to *transparently* access private network resources through the proxy servers

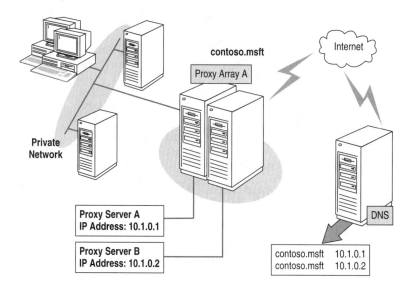

Figure 6.21   Round robin DNS and proxy arrays

- The highest possible performance must be provided for Internet users who access the Web servers in the private network

- All proxy servers in the design are running Microsoft Proxy Server 2.0 and Windows 2000

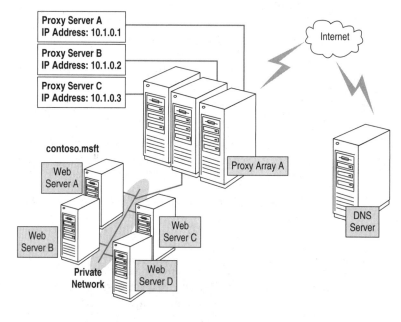

Figure 6.22   Scenario to illustrate the appropriate methods for optimizing private network availability and performance

For the organization's requirements, Network Load Balancing is appropriate for the solution. The availability requirements of the organization mandate Network Load Balancing to provide improvement in availability. Because round robin DNS provides improvements in performance but not availability, round robin DNS isn't an appropriate solution.

Activity 6.2: Completing a Proxy Server Design

In this activity, you're presented with a scenario. To complete the activity:

1. Evaluate the scenario and determine the design requirements

2. Answer questions and make design recommendations

In Figure 6.23, you see a map for an international shipping company that was discussed in an earlier lesson. The design process is proceeding and you are now creating the security and optimization specifications for the design.

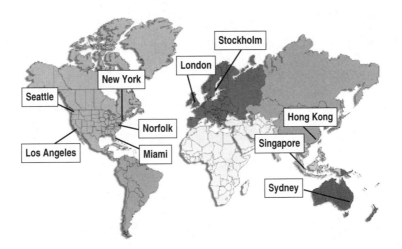

Figure 6.23   Map of an international shipping company

Answer the following questions concerning your design recommendations. You can find answers to the questions in the Appendix, "Questions and Answers."

1. The management of the shipping company wants to restrict the customer representatives so they can access only the company's Web site. The chief information office of the company (CIO) wants to ensure that only HTTP and FTP traffic is sent to the company's Web site. The ASP that hosts the Web site might change—however, the impact on changing ASPs must be minimal in your design. Also, only authenticated users should be able to access the proxy server. As the director of information services, what Proxy Server solution do you recommend to management?

2. Within each regional office, the marketing and sales team wants to host its own Web site that provides information and contact numbers for the customers of the region. Although the board of directors strongly supports the initiative, the CIO is concerned about protecting private network resources. How do you protect private network resources while providing access to a Web server within each office?

3. After a few months of operation, certain offices are experiencing performance problems. Also, offices in remote countries are experiencing outages due to hardware and telecommunications failure. How can you improve the performance and increase the availability for these offices?

Lab: Creating a Proxy Server Design

After this lab, you will be able to
- Evaluate a scenario and determine the design requirements
- Create multiprotocol routing designs based on the design requirements

Estimated lab time: 45 minutes

In this lab, you're the director of information services for a domestic extended stay hotel chain and are responsible for the creation of a Proxy Server design. The hotel chain has 15 locations throughout the United States.

To complete this lab

1. Examine the networking environment presented in the scenario, the network diagrams, the business requirements and constraints, and the technical requirements and constraints

2. Use the worksheet(s) for each location and proxy server to assist you in creating your Proxy Server design (you can find completed sample design worksheets on the Supplemental Course Materials CD-ROM in the Completed Worksheets folder)

Note   For each location there are four worksheets, one worksheet for each router. If your design contains fewer than four routers, leave the remaining worksheets blank.

---

3. Create, eliminate, or replace existing networking devices and network segments when required.

4. Ensure that your design fulfills the business requirements and constraints and technical requirements and constraints of the scenario by
   - Assigning the appropriate specifications for each proxy server interface
   - Specifying the appropriate client software
   - Optimizing your design to provide the security, availability, performance, and affordability

---

Note   To reduce the length of time for this lab, create a multiprotocol routing design for the hotel chain corporate office and only one of the hotels.

Scenario

A chain of suite hotels (shown in Figure 6.24) that caters to extended-stay business travelers, headquartered in Atlanta, owns 15 locations throughout the United States. The headquarters for the hotel chain (shown in Figure 6.25) are located in the hotel property in Atlanta. The hotel chain provides full business services to each guest's suite, including fax machines, photocopiers, and fax modem telephone connections.

Each hotel location (shown in Figure 6.26) is managed as a separate business unit, but currently ships monthly financial information to the headquarters in Atlanta. The hotel chain has purchased a hotel reservation and accounting system that will allow each location to upload financial and room availability to headquarters. The newly purchased software is a Web-based application that will run on Web and database servers hosted by an ASP.

Currently, the hotel chain is installing T3 connections to the Internet at each location. The guest services personnel at each hotel will access the Web-based reservation and accounting system through the T3 connection. In addition, the hotel chain wants to provide high-speed Internet access to the hotel's guests.

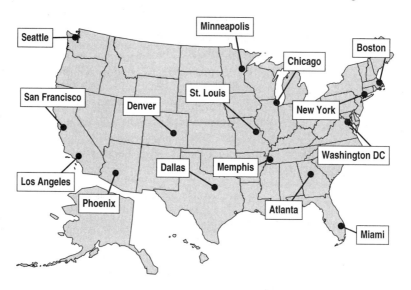

Figure 6.24   Map of the locations in the hotel chain

Business Requirements and Constraints

The hotel chain has a number of requirements and constraints based on its business model. As you create your Proxy Server design, ensure that your design meets the business requirements and stays within the business constraints.

To achieve the business requirements and constraints, your design must

- Prevent hotel guests and Internet users from accessing the hotel chain's private networks

- Allow hotel guests and Internet users to access hotel guest's computers

- Prevent guest services representatives at the front desk from accessing any Web site other than the Web-based reservation and accounting system

- Ensure that connectivity between each hotel and the Internet is available 24 hours a day, 7 days a week

Technical Requirements and Constraints

The existing physical network, hardware, and operating systems place certain technical requirements and constraints on your design. As you create your Proxy Server design, ensure that your design meets the technical requirements and stays within the technical constraints.

In addition, the Web-based application managed by the ASP requires connectivity with each hotel and with the Internet. These Web-based reservation and accounting applications are accessed on the computers used by the guest services representatives and by Internet users that want to make reservations.

To achieve the technical requirements and constraints, your design must

- Isolate the network segments designated for use by the guest services representatives from the Internet and the network segments designated for use by the hotel guests

- Support the private IP addressing scheme, 172.16.0.0/12, assigned within each hotel

- Utilize the assigned public IP addressing scheme, 10.133.25.0/24, allocated from an Internet registry

---

Note   Although 10.133.25.0/24 is a private IP address range, assume the IP address range is a public IP address range for the purposes of this lab.

- Integrate with any existing IP routed network segments

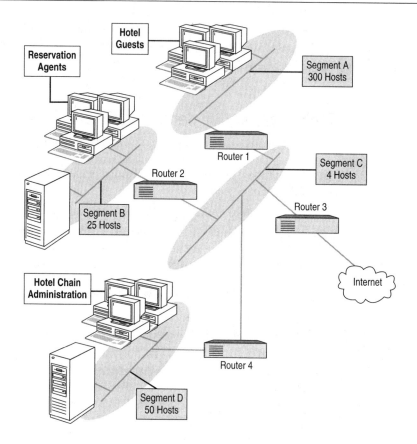

Figure 6.25   This is the existing network at the hotel chain headquarters in Atlanta.

Design Worksheet – Figure 6.25
Hotel Chain Headquarters – Proxy Server A

Proxy Server Specifications	Comments
Interface A connects to segment: _____ IP address: _____	
Interface B connects to segment: _____ IP address: _____	
❑ Upstream connection to Internet ❑ Upstream connection to proxy server/array	
Desktop Client Software	
❑ Proxy Server client software ❑ SOCKS ❑ Internet Explorer 5.0 ❑ Default gateway	
Proxy Server Security	
❑ Packet filter (specify packet filter criteria in Comments column) ❑ Domain filter (specify domain filter criteria in Comments column) ❑ User authentication (*specify users to be authorized in Comments column*) ❑ Web publishing (*specify URLs to be published in Comments column*)	
Proxy Server Availability and Performance	

❑ Active caching   ❑ Passive caching
❑ Member of proxy array   Proxy array name: _____
❑ Network Load Balancing cluster
  Cluster name: _____
  Cluster IP address: _____
❑ Round robin DNS
  ❑ Proxy server FQDN: _____
  ❑ Proxy server IP address: _____	

Design Worksheet – Figure 6.25
Hotel Chain Headquarters – Proxy Server B

Proxy Server Specifications	Comments
Interface A connects to segment: _____ IP address: _____	
Interface B connects to segment: _____ IP address: _____	
❑ Upstream connection to Internet ❑ Upstream connection to proxy server/array	
Desktop Client Software	
❑ Proxy Server client software ❑ SOCKS	
❑ Internet Explorer 5.0 ❑ Default gateway	
Proxy Server Security	
❑ Packet filter (specify packet filter criteria in Comments column)	
❑ Domain filter (specify domain filter criteria in Comments column)	
❑ User authentication (*specify users to be authorized in Comments column*)	
❑ Web publishing (*specify URLs to be published in Comments column*)	
Proxy Server Availability and Performance	
❑ Active caching ❑ Passive caching	
❑ Member of proxy array Proxy array name: _____	
❑ Network Load Balancing cluster	
Cluster name: _____	
Cluster IP address: _____	
❑ Round robin DNS	
❑ Proxy server FQDN: _____	
❑ Proxy server IP address: _____	

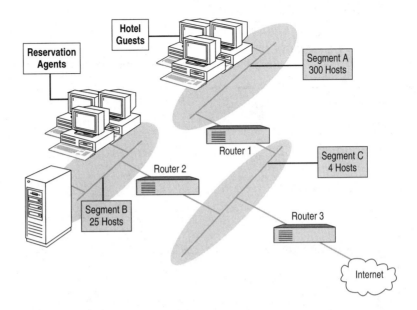

Figure 6.26 This is the existing network at one of the hotels. For the purposes of this lab, assume that the hotels have the same network configuration.

Design Worksheet – Figure 6.26
Hotel – Proxy Server A

Proxy Server Specifications	Comments
Interface A connects to segment: _____ IP address: _____	
Interface B connects to segment: _____ IP address: _____	
❑ Upstream connection to Internet ❑ Upstream connection to proxy server/array	
Desktop Client Software	
❑ Proxy Server client software ❑ SOCKS ❑ Internet Explorer 5.0 ❑ Default gateway	
Proxy Server Security	
❑ Packet filter (specify packet filter criteria in Comments column)	
❑ Domain filter (specify domain filter criteria in Comments column)	
❑ User authentication (*specify users to be authorized in Comments column*)	
❑ Web publishing (*specify URLs to be published in Comments column*)	
Proxy Server Availability and Performance	
❑ Active caching ❑ Passive caching	
❑ Member of proxy array Proxy array name: _____	
❑ Network Load Balancing cluster Cluster name: _____ Cluster IP address: _____	
❑ Round robin DNS ❑ Proxy server FQDN: _____ ❑ Proxy server IP address: _____	

Design Worksheet – Figure 6.26
Hotel – Proxy Server B

Proxy Server Specifications	Comments
Interface A connects to segment: _____ IP address: _____	
Interface B connects to segment: _____ IP address: _____	
❏ Upstream connection to Internet ❏ Upstream connection to proxy server/array	
Desktop Client Software	
❏ Proxy Server client software ❏ SOCKS ❏ Internet Explorer 5.0 ❏ Default gateway	
Proxy Server Security	
❏ Packet filter (specify packet filter criteria in Comments column)	
❏ Domain filter (specify domain filter criteria in Comments column)	
❏ User authentication (*specify users to be authorized in Comments column*)	
❏ Web publishing (*specify URLs to be published in Comments column*)	
Proxy Server Availability and Performance	
❏ Active caching ❏ Passive caching	
❏ Member of proxy array Proxy array name: _____	

❏ Network Load Balancing cluster
 	
   Cluster name: _____
 	
   Cluster IP address: _____	

❏ Round robin DNS
   ❏ Proxy server FQDN: _____
   ❏ Proxy server IP address: _____	

Review

The following questions are intended to reinforce key information in this chapter. If you're unable to answer a question, review the lesson and then try to answer the question again. You can find answers to the questions in the Appendix, "Questions and Answers."

1. An organization with 35 locations throughout the world has retained your services as a consultant to create a Proxy Server design. Each of the locations is connected to a central office by using point-to-point communications links. The organization's Internet connection is comprised of multiple T3 connections. The organization wants to provide Internet access to the private network users. Also, the organization has Web servers located in the private network that must be accessed by Internet users. The client computers in the network run Windows 95, Windows 98, Windows Me, and Windows 2000. What recommendations can you make to the organization?

2. As the director of information services for an international organization, you're responsible for evaluating your organization's Proxy Server design. The management of the organization is concerned about the unauthorized use of the organization's high-speed Internet connection and the accessing of unauthorized Internet sites. What recommendations can you make to ensure that the security requirements of the organization are achieved?

3. You're optimizing an existing Proxy Server design. The network users report that response time for Internet access is slow. What changes to the design can you recommend to improve Internet access response time?

C H A P T E R 7

NAT in Internet and Intranet Designs

About This Chapter

Regardless of the size of the private network, Internet connectivity is an important part of any networking services design you create. In fact, the workforce for many large organizations may be based in small offices or home offices (SOHOs).

In addition, many organizations can't justify the expenditure for a firewall or proxy server solution. Typically, these organizations aren't as security-conscious as organizations that require a firewall or proxy server solution.

You can use the NAT protocol in Routing and Remote Access to provide Internet connectivity for SOHOs or large organizations comprised of numerous SOHOs. The NAT protocol in Routing and Remote Access (referred to as NAT for the remainder of this chapter) provides basic Internet connectivity. You can secure private network resources by using the security features in NAT. NAT also replaces the need for Dynamic Host Configuration Protocol (DHCP) servers in your design because NAT supports DHCP-compatible Internet Protocol (IP) configuration. NAT also allows all Domain Name System (DNS) queries to be forwarded to any DNS server specified in NAT, eliminating the requirement for a DNS server in the private network.

This chapter answers questions such as:

- In what situations are the Internet connectivity services provided by NAT appropriate for your design?
- Which client computer operating systems and software can connect to the Internet through NAT?
- Which application programming interfaces (APIs) and protocols can communicate through NAT?
- How can you restrict Internet users' access to private network resources?
- How can you ensure that Internet connectivity is always available to private network users and Internet users?
- How can you improve the performance of accessing private network resources or Internet resources?

Before You Begin

Before you begin, you must have an overall understanding of

- Network technologies (including Ethernet, Token Ring, hubs, switches, and concentrators)
- Common transport protocol configuration for Internet Protocol (IP) (such as IP address, subnet mask, or default gateway for IP)
- IP routed networks (including subnets, network segments, routers, and IP switches)
- Router security technologies (including protocol filtering)
- Network address translation between public and private IP addressing schemes

Lesson 1: Designs That Include NAT

This lesson presents the requirements and constraints, both business and technical, that identify the Internet connectivity services in NAT as a solution.

After this lesson, you will be able to

- Describe the relationship between NAT and Microsoft Windows 2000
- Identify the business and technical requirements and constraints that must be collected to create a NAT design
- Identify the NAT design decisions
- Evaluate scenarios and determine which capabilities and features of NAT are appropriate in Internet connectivity solutions

Estimated lesson time: 30 minutes

NAT and Windows 2000

There are two methods of connecting a small office or home office to the Internet—*routed* connections and *translated* connections. Routed connections require that public IP addressing schemes be used in the private network. The IP routing in Routing and Remote Access provides support for routed connections. For more information on IP routing solutions, see Chapter 4, "IP Routing Designs."

Translated connections allow the private network to use a private IP addressing scheme. The NAT protocol in Routing and Remote Access provides support for translated connections. Because NAT is a protocol available in Routing and Remote Access, it is a standard feature of Microsoft Windows 2000 Server, Microsoft Windows 2000 Advanced Server, and Microsoft Windows 2000 Datacenter Server. NAT isn't available in Microsoft Windows 2000 Professional.

From the Windows 2000 perspective, NAT and Routing and Remote Access are services that run on Windows 2000. NAT uses IP in Windows 2000 to communicate with the private network and with the Internet. NAT uses the IP routing filters in Routing and Remote Access to restrict network traffic. Figure 7.1 shows the interaction between NAT and Windows 2000.

Tip   Don't enable IP routing on the same computer running NAT.

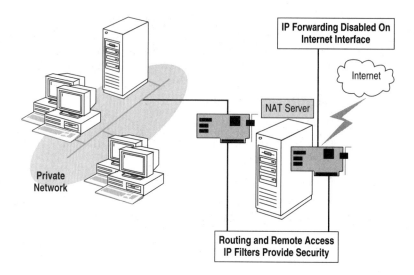

Figure 7.1   The interaction between NAT and Windows 2000

In this chapter, you learn how to create Internet connectivity solutions with NAT and Windows 2000. To successfully create NAT designs, you must be familiar with

- General IP and IP routing theory
- Firewalls and the creation of firewall rules
- File types and protocols for use in Web-based and IP-based applications

All versions of Windows 2000 include Internet Connection Sharing, a product similar to NAT. Table 7.1 summarizes the features and capabilities of NAT and Internet Connection Sharing.

Table 7.1   Comparison of NAT and Internet Connection Sharing

NAT	Internet Connection Sharing
Provides many configurable options	Has only single check box configuration
Supports multiple public IP addresses to improve performance and facilitate private network resource access	Supports single public IP address
Allows selection of the private IP address range for the private network	Private IP address range is fixed for the private network
Supports multiple interfaces connected to the private network	Supports a single interface connected to the private network

For more information on Internet Connection Sharing, see the Windows 2000 help files.

NAT Design Requirements and Constraints

Before you create your NAT design, you must gather the requirements and constraints, both business and technical, of the organization. As you create your design, you make design decisions based on the requirements and constraints you collect.

The list of the design requirements and constraints you collect will include

- Characteristics of the data transmitted through the NAT server, including
  - The amoun t of data transmitted through the NAT server
  - The confidentiality of the data transmitted through the NAT server
- Resources in the private network that must be accessed by Internet-based users
- Plans for future network growth
- Characteristics of existing routers including
  - Protocols in use in the private network
  - Router placement
  - Wide area network (WAN) connections in use
- Response times for applications that access resources through the Internet connection
- Acceptable percentage of time that users require access through the Internet connection

To perform network address translation, NAT modifies the content of the IP header, Transmission Control Protocol (TCP) header, User Datagram Protocol (UDP) header, and data portion of IP packets. To modify the content of IP packets, NAT must understand the structure and content of the IP packet.

Unfortunately, NAT can't perform network address translation on certain protocols. The following protocols aren't supported by NAT:

- Component Object Model (COM) or Distributed Component Object Model (DCOM)
- Microsoft Remote Procedure Call (RPC)
- Kerberos Version 5
- Internet Protocol Security (IPSec) packets that provide IP header encryption by using the Authentication Header (AH) protocol
- Simple Network Management Protocol (SNMP)
- Lightweight Directory Access Protocol (LDAP)

Note   When your design must support protocols not supported by NAT, use Microsoft Proxy Server 2.0 proxy server solutions or Routing and Remote Access routing solutions.

NAT Design Decisions

After you determine the business and technical requirements and constraints, apply the information you gathered to make NAT design decisions. To create your NAT design, you must choose the

- Type of connections, persistent or nonpersistent, that each proxy server must support
- Type of client computers that must be supported by the NAT server
- Connection technologies, including T1, Public Switched Telephone Network (PSTN), Integrated Services Digital Network (ISDN), Digital Subscriber Line (DSL), or X.25, that each proxy server must support
- Private network IP addressing scheme and the number of public IP addresses to obtain
- Criteria that you'll adopt to filter traffic
- Method of providing access to private network resources
- Number of connections to improve availability and performance

The lessons that follow in this chapter provide the information required for you to make specific NAT design recommendations.

Standalone SOHO Internet Connectivity Designs

Most of the SOHO Internet connectivity designs that you create will be for standalone networks. You'll create these designs for small organizations or individuals. Your primary concern in the standalone SOHO Internet connectivity design is to provide Internet connectivity for private network users.

In standalone SOHO Internet designs, the NAT server takes the place of the firewall, router, or proxy server. The NAT server can provide comparable security to an IP router with IP filters.

Making the Decision

When you create designs that require standalone SOHO Internet connectivity, NAT can

- **Provide automatic IP configuration to computers on private network segments**   NAT provides automatic IP configuration to any Dynamic Host Configuration Protocol (DHCP) client.

- **Restrict access to Internet resources or restrict the type of IP traffic**
  NAT, by using Routing and Remote Access IP filters, can restrict access to Internet resources and restrict the types of IP traffic sent through the NAT server.

- **Provide network address translation for private IP addressing schemes**
  NAT automatically provides network address translation between the private network and the Internet. As a result, NAT supports public and private IP addressing schemes.

- **Share Internet connection with multiple users at a minimal incremental cost**   NAT is a standard feature of Windows 2000 Server, Windows 2000 Advanced Server, and Windows 2000 Datacenter Server. Unlike Microsoft Proxy Server 2.0 or firewall Internet connectivity designs, there's no additional software to purchase in a NAT solution.

- **Connect to a variety of WAN technologies**   NAT can provide Internet connectivity over any network interface supported by Windows 2000.

Applying the Decision

Figure 7.2 illustrates a design where NAT Server A provides standalone SOHO Internet connectivity. NAT Server A is placed where your private network connects to the Internet. Because NAT Server A is the only device connected to the Internet, all the protection of the private network is provided by NAT Server A.

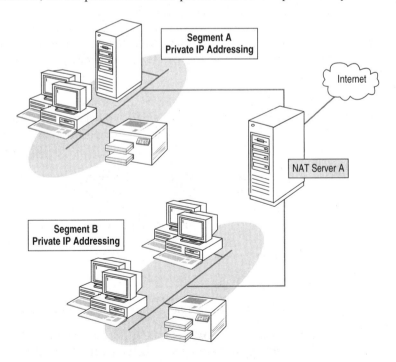

Figure 7.2   Scenario that uses NAT for standalone SOHO Internet connectivity

Note   For designs that require stronger security, you can include a firewall or a proxy server in your design instead of NAT.

Because Segments A and B require private IP addressing schemes, NAT Server A provides network address translation. You must assign a private IP address from the IP address range on Segments A and B respectively. You must assign a public IP address to the Internet interface connection in NAT Server A. For more information on private IP addressing schemes, see Chapter 2, "Networking Protocol Design," Lesson 2, "Essential TCP/IP Design Concepts."

To protect private network resources, you must disable IP routing on the NAT server interface that connects to the Internet. However, you must enable IP routing on the NAT server interfaces that connect to Segments A and B. Otherwise, no IP traffic is forwarded between Segments A and B.

Branch Office Connectivity Designs

Many large organizations have a significant percentage of their workforce that works from SOHOs. Some of the designs that you create will require employees who work from SOHOs to connect to the organizations' corporate network. Protecting the SOHO's private network resources and the organizations' corporate network is your primary design consideration in branch office connectivity designs.

Computers in the SOHO's private network can access the organization's corporate network through the NAT server by using virtual private network (VPN) tunnels. You can enforce any data protection requirements of the organization by requiring VPN tunnels for remote access connectivity to the organization's corporate network.

Because NAT provides network address translation, the NAT server modifies IP headers, TCP headers, UDP headers, and data in IP packets sent through the NAT server. As a result, some applications and networking services don't run properly through a NAT.

You can work around application and networking services problems by using VPNs. Because the IP information inside the VPN tunnel (the IP information corresponds to the organization's corporate network IP addressing scheme), no address translation is performed on the tunneled IP packet. For more information on VPN tunnels, see Chapter 2, "Networking Protocol Design," Lesson 3, "TCP/IP Data Protection."

Making the Decision

When you create designs that require branch office connectivity, NAT must

- **Provide all the requirements of the standalone SOHO Internet connectivity solution**   Any branch office connectivity solution must achieve the busi-

ness and technical requirements of a standalone SOHO Internet connectivity
solution.

- **Provide secured connectivity between the branch office and the organization's corporate network**   You must protect any data transmitted between computers within the branch office and the organization's corporate network. You can protect the data by using VPN tunnels to provide authentication and data encryption.

Applying the Decision

Figure 7.3 illustrates a scenario in which NAT provides connectivity between a branch office of an organization and the organization's corporate network. The client computers in the branch office connect to the organization's corporate network through VPN Server A in the corporate network. The VPN tunnel between the client computers and VPN Server A protects any confidential data transmitted over the Internet.

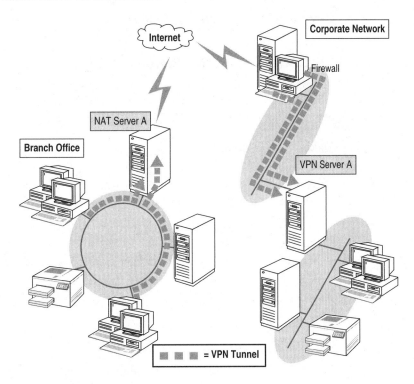

Figure 7.3   Scenario that uses NAT for branch office connectivity

You can enforce the strength of security for the VPN tunnels by specifying the authentication and encryption methods for VPN Server A. Setting the strength of security on the VPN server allows the organization to control the security for access to the corporate network.

Lesson 2: Essential NAT Design Concepts

This lesson discusses the requirements, constraints, and design decisions that are used in establishing the essential specifications in a NAT server design. This lesson discusses the design concepts common to all NAT designs. Lessons 3 and 4 in this chapter discuss how to achieve the security, availability, and performance requirements of the organization.

After this lesson, you will be able to

- Determine the placement of a NAT server in your network design
- Identify the appropriate design specifications for each NAT server interface
- Determine when to include the NAT automatic IP address assignment feature in your design
- Determine when to include the NAT DNS name resolution feature in your design

Estimated lesson time: 30 minutes

Placing NAT in the Network Design

You place the NAT server in your network design to isolate the SOHO or branch office from the Internet. In Lesson 1 of this chapter, you examined scenarios that depicted the placement of NAT servers within a network.

Making the Decision

You always place the NAT servers in your design between the SOHO's or branch office's private network segment(s) and the Internet. When you place your NAT server in your design, you must ensure that

- All SOHO or branch office private network segments are isolated from the Internet
- IP forwarding (IP routing) is enabled on all NAT server interfaces connected to SOHO or branch office private network segments
- IP forwarding (IP routing) is disabled on the NAT server interface connected to the Internet

Applying the Decision

Figure 7.4 illustrates the proper placement of NAT servers in a network. In the scenario, you include NAT for Internet connectivity only. NAT Server A connects to all the SOHO network segments that use private IP addressing schemes. In addition, NAT Server A connects to the Internet.

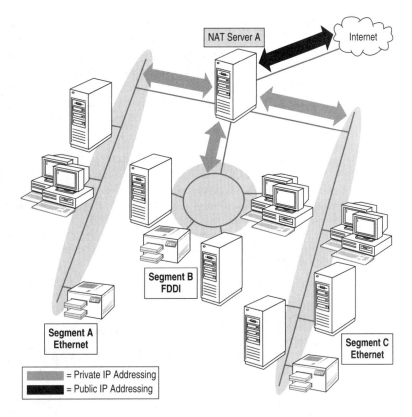

Figure 7.4   Diagram that illustrates the proper placement of NAT servers in a
network

Determining NAT Server Interface Specifications

Every NAT server in your design must have at least two network interfaces. You
can specify only one NAT server interface to the Internet. You can specify one or
more NAT server interfaces to the SOHO or branch office network.

Making the Decision

For each interface in each NAT server in your design, you must specify

- **The type of connection between the NAT interface and the network, such
  as persistent or nonpersistent**   The decision-making process for the type of
  connection you must specify for the NAT server interface is the same as the
  process for IP router interface connections. For more information on determining the type of network interface connection, see Chapter 4, "IP Routing
  Designs," Lesson 2, "Essential IP Routing Design Concepts."

■ **The IP configuration information, including the IP address and IP subnet mask, for interfaces connected to IP network segments** The decision-making process for the IP configuration information you must specify for the NAT server interface is the same as the process for IP router interface connections. For more information on determining the IP configuration information for IP router interface connections, and subsequently NAT server interface connections, see Chapter 4, "IP Routing Designs," Lesson 2.

Tip By default, NAT selects the IP address 192.168.0.1 for the interface that connects to the SOHO or branch office network segment. When your design has more than one NAT server interface connected to the SOHO or branch office network segments, assign the first IP address from the IP address range for the corresponding network segment.

Applying the Decision

Figure 7.5 illustrates the proper configuration of NAT server network interfaces. For the purposes of this scenario, assume that

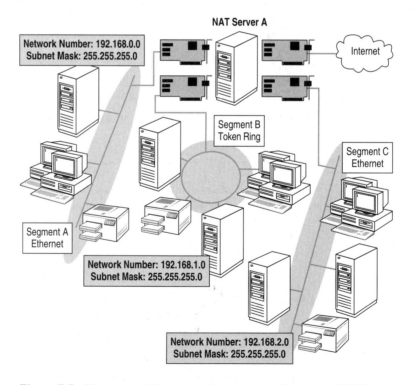

Figure 7.5 Diagram that illustrates the proper configuration of NAT server network interfaces

- The IP address of 172.16.3.101/24 is allocated from an Internet service provider (ISP) for use by the organization
- The organization is connected to the Internet by using DSL

Note Although normally a private IP address, for the purposes of this scenario, treat 172.16.3.101/24 as a public IP address.

Table 7.2 lists each network segment and the NAT server interface specifications you must include in your design.

Table 7.2   Network Segment and NAT Server Interface Specifications

Network Segment	NAT Server Interface Specifications
Segment A	Ethernet interface with an IP address of 192.168.0.1 and a subnet mask of 255.255.255.0
Segment B	Token Ring interface with an IP address of 192.168.1.1 and a subnet mask of 255.255.255.0
Segment C	Ethernet interface with an IP address of 192.168.2.1 and a subnet mask of 255.255.255.0
Internet	DSL interface with an IP address of 172.16.3.101 and a subnet mask of 255.255.255.0.

Providing Automatic IP Address Assignment

You must determine how the IP information of client computers is configured in your design. You can configure the IP configuration of client computers either manually or automatically.

Making the Decision

Table 7.3 lists the IP configuration methods and the advantages and disadvantages of each method.

Table 7.3   Advantages and Disadvantages of IP Configuration Methods

Method	Advantages	Disadvantages
NAT automatic IP address assignment feature	Reduces configuration errors Little or no time spent in configuration Requires no additional purchases Supports multiple network segments	Available only to DHCP client computers
Manual configuration	Can be used for any IP clients clients	Time consuming Prone to configuration errors

(continued)

Table 7.3   *(continued)*

Method	Advantages	Disadvantages
Automatic Private IP Assignment (APIPA)	Reduces configuration errors Little or no time spent in configuration Requires no additional purchases	Available only to Windows 98, Windows Me, and Windows 2000 client computers Supports only a single segment SOHO or branch office networks
DHCP server	Reduces configuration errors Little or no time spent in configuration Supports multiple network segments	Available only to DHCP client computers Requires additional computers to function as DHCP servers

Applying the Decision

Figure 7.6 illustrates the appropriate use of automatic IP address assignment in NAT. NAT Server A is responsible for the IP configuration of Segments A and B.

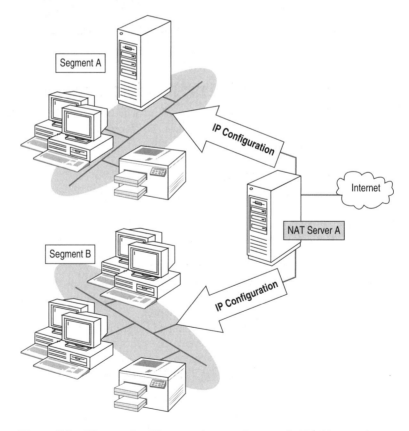

Figure 7.6   Diagram that illustrates the use of automatic IP address assignment in NAT

You must specify a unique IP address range for Segments A and B and specify that the respective interfaces in NAT Server A assign IP addresses from each range.

Providing DNS Name Resolution

The client computers in your NAT design need to access Internet resources by using fully qualified domain names (FQDNs). These FQDNs must be resolved to IP addresses by DNS servers. You must determine how DNS name resolution will be performed for the client computers in your design.

Making the Decision

You can specify the DNS server that client computers use to resolve FQDNs

- **Manually by configuration of each client computer**   Select this method when you want to specify different DNS name resolution methods for various client computers.
- **Automatically by specifying the DNS server NAT**   Select this method when you want to automatically specify the same DNS name resolution method for all client computers.

Applying the Decision

Figure 7.7 illustrates the appropriate use of automatic DNS server assignment in NAT. NAT Server A is responsible for configuring the DNS server IP addresses for the client computers on Segments A, B, and C. NAT Server A configures all client computers in the SOHO or branch office to resolve FQDNs by using DNS Server A.

Activity 7.1: Evaluating a NAT Design

In this activity, you're presented with a scenario. To complete the activity:

1. Evaluate the scenario and determine the design requirements

2. Answer questions and make design recommendations

In Figure 7.8, you see a map of the regional offices for an electronics field service firm. The firm provides a warranty and postwarranty for computers and computer peripherals for a number of computer manufacturers. The field engineers of the firm operate from SOHOs.

The field service firm requires the field engineers to maintain a SOHO network. Each field engineer's SOHO network must contain at least one model of each computer serviced by the engineer. The engineer uses the computers to provide self-training in the repair and maintenance of the computers. In the event of a critical account failure, the computers can also serve as a replacement computer for customers.

The field engineers run Web-based applications to report the status of service calls, manage parts inventories, and collect field service history. Web servers at the field service firm's home office host the Web-based application.

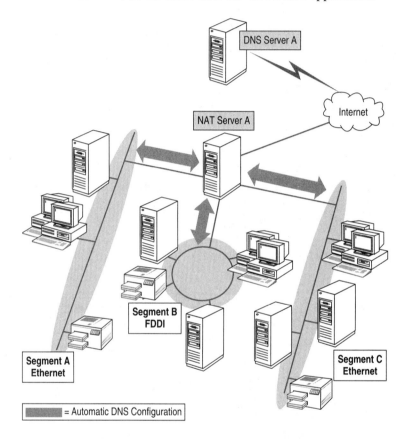

Figure 7.7   Diagram that illustrates the use of automatic DNS server assignment in NAT

Answer the following questions concerning your design recommendations. You can find answers to the questions in the Appendix, "Questions and Answers."

1. Currently the field engineers connect to the Internet to run the Web-based applications by using dial-up modems. The field service firm wants to

Figure 7.8   Map of an electronics field service firm

upgrade the Internet connection for the field engineers for future applications and expansion. Also, the field server firm wants the field engineers to gain experience in Internet connectivity solutions. As a consultant to the field service firm, what recommendations can you make?

2. A variety of operating systems, including Windows 95, Windows 98, Windows Me, Windows 2000, and UNIX, must be supported by the field engineer's SOHO network. The field engineers change operating systems on the computers in the SOHO to gain experience in installation and support issues. How can you reduce the amount of time spent configuring the operating systems after installation?

3. The director of customer services is evaluating new customer account management software specifically written for the electronics field service industry. The customer account management software is written as a multitier, client server application. The field engineers will run the client portion of the application on the SOHO network. What must you consider when selecting the new application?

Lesson 3: Data Protection in NAT Designs

This lesson discusses how to create designs that protect the confidential data in an organization by using NAT. This lesson focuses on protecting NAT inbound and outbound data traffic.

After this lesson, you will be able to

- Select the appropriate method for protecting SOHO network resources by using NAT
- Select the appropriate method for restricting user access to Internet resources by using NAT
- Select the appropriate method of protecting corporate network resources by using NAT and VPN

Estimated lesson time: 30 minutes

Protecting SOHO Network Resources

In your NAT designs, protecting the SOHO network resources is the highest priority in the solution. Typically, there's no firewall or other Internet security device in your design, because of cost considerations. As a result, the NAT server is solely responsible for protecting SOHO network resources.

You can protect the SOHO network resources by restricting the inbound traffic on the NAT server. Based on the security requirements of the organization, you must select the appropriate NAT security method for restricting inbound traffic.

Making the Decision

You can restrict inbound NAT traffic by using Routing and Remote Access IP packet filters, NAT address mapping, and NAT address pools. You can elect to include Routing and Remote Access IP packet filters along with either NAT address mapping or NAT address pools. You can't include NAT address mapping and NAT address pools in the same design.

Routing and Remote Access IP Packet Filters

You can include Routing and Remote Access IP packet filters to restrict traffic based on the IP header information. You can build the criteria for the packet filters based on any combination of IP header information.

The design decisions for Routing and Remote Access IP packet filters in a NAT design are identical to an IP routing design. For more information on Routing and Remote Access IP packet filters, and their subsequent use in NAT designs, see Chapter 4, "IP Routing Designs," Lesson 3, "Data Protection on Unsecured Segments."

By default, NAT discards all inbound traffic requests for SOHO network resources. If you want to provide access to SOHO network resources, additional specifications are necessary.

NAT Address Mapping

You can include the NAT address mapping feature of NAT to provide Internet users with access to resources in the SOHO network. You include NAT address mapping when you're assigned a single public IP address for use in the NAT design.

The NAT server maps requests for the public IP address with a specific TCP or UDP port number to a resource within the SOHO network. You can specify a NAT address map entry for each SOHO resource you want Internet users to access.

The number of SOHO resources you can expose to Internet users is constrained by the number of TCP or UDP port numbers. Because NAT address mapping works with a single public IP address, you must provide access to multiple resources by using additional port numbers.

NAT Address Pools

You can include the NAT address pool feature of NAT to provide Internet users with access to resources in the SOHO network. You include NAT address pools when you're assigned multiple public IP addresses for use in the NAT design.

The NAT server maps requests for one of the public IP addresses with a specific TCP or UDP port number to resources within the SOHO network. You can determine the combination of public IP address and TCP or UDP port number for each SOHO resource you want Internet users to access.

The number of SOHO resources you can expose to Internet users is constrained by the number of public IP addresses in the NAT address pool and the number of TCP or UDP port numbers. Because NAT address pools work with multiple public IP addresses, you can provide access to multiple resources by using any combination of public IP addresses and additional port numbers.

Applying the Decision

Figure 7.9 illustrates the appropriate NAT security methods for protecting SOHO resources. NAT Server A protects the SOHO resources that reside on Web Servers A, B, and C.

For the purposes of this scenario, assume that the business and technical requirements of the organization include

- Providing Internet user access to Web Servers A and C

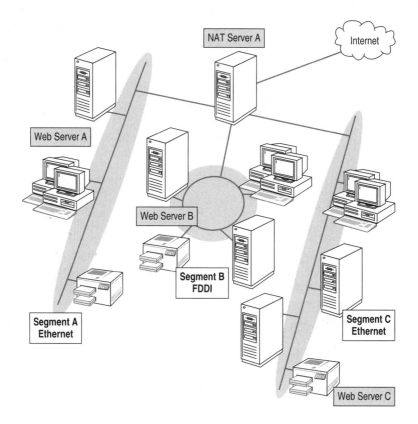

Figure 7.9 Scenario to illustrate the appropriate NAT methods for protecting SOHO resources

- Preventing Internet user access to Web Server B
- Allowing only Hypertext Transfer Protocol (HTTP) and File Transfer Protocol (FTP) packets to be sent between Web Servers A and C and Internet users
- Utilizing the IP address of 10.53.73.179/24 that was allocated from an ISP for use by the organization

---

Note Although normally a private IP address, for the purposes of this scenario, treat 10.53.73.179/24 as a public IP address range.

- Using ISDN to connect the organization to the Internet

Table 7.4 lists the Proxy Server security methods appropriate for the design, and the reason you include the method in the design.

Table 7.4   Reasons to Include Specific Proxy Server Security Methods

Include	To Protect Private Network Resource By
Packet filters	Ensuring that only HTTP and FTP IP traffic is exchanged between Internet users and Web Servers A and C.
NAT address mapping	Mapping from the single assigned public IP address to Web Servers A and C. Only providing access to Web Servers A and C by creating an address mapping entry for each server. Because no address mapping entry exists for Web Server B, Web Server B is inaccessible from the Internet.

Restricting Access to Internet Resources

In your NAT designs, your next priority in the solution is to restrict SOHO network user access to Internet resources, which you do by restricting NAT server outbound traffic. Based on the security requirements of the organization, you must select the appropriate NAT security method for restricting outbound traffic.

Making the Decision

The only NAT security method available for restricting outbound Proxy Server traffic is Routing and Remote Access IP packet filters. You can build the criteria for the packet filters based on any combination of IP header information.

You can grant SOHO network user access to individual Internet resources or to a group of Internet resources. Or you can prevent SOHO network users from accessing individual Internet resources or a group of Internet resources.

The design decisions for Routing and Remote Access IP packet filters in a NAT design are identical to an IP routing design. For more information on Routing and Remote Access IP packet filters, and their subsequent use in NAT designs, see Chapter 4, "IP Routing Designs," Lesson 3, "Data Protection on Unsecured Segments."

Applying the Decision

Figure 7.10 illustrates the appropriate NAT security methods for restricting access to Internet resources. NAT Server A restricts the Internet access for SOHO network users.

For the purposes of this scenario, assume that the business and technical requirements of the organization include

- Providing Internet access to SOHO network users

- Preventing access to any Internet resources except for *www.contoso.msft*

- Allowing only HTTP and FTP packets to be sent between *www.contoso.msft* and SOHO network users

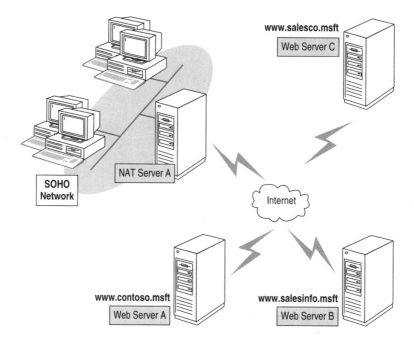

Figure 7.10   Scenario to illustrate the appropriate NAT methods for restricting access to Internet resources

You can achieve the requirements of the design by creating a Routing and Remote Access IP filter on NAT Server A's Internet interface. The Routing and Remote Access IP filters restrict SOHO network user access to only *www.contoso.msft*. In addition, only HTTP and FTP traffic is allowed between the SOHO network users and *www.contoso.msft*.

Protecting Corporate Network Resources

Lesson 1 in this chapter discussed a scenario where branch offices incorporate NAT to provide Internet connectivity. To connect to the corporate network, computers on the branch office private network use VPN.

For more information on VPNs and protecting IP traffic, see Chapter 2, "Networking Protocol Design," Lesson 3, "TCP/IP Data Protection," and Chapter 12, "VPN in Remote Access Designs," Lesson 3, "Data Protection in VPN Remote Access Designs."

Making the Decision

When your NAT solution requires connectivity to corporate networks, you must use VPN to protect confidential data transmitted over the Internet. You can protect the confidential data by using any authentication and encryption method available.

You can use any of the following VPN solutions to protect confidential data between the SOHO network and the corporate network:

- Point-to-Point Tunneling Protocol (PPTP) and Microsoft Point-to-Point Encryption (MPPE)
- Layer 2 Tunneling Protocol (L2TP) and IPSec using the Encapsulating Security Payload (ESP) protocol

---

Note You can't use L2TP and the IPSec AH protocol with NAT, because AH encrypts the IP header information.

Applying the Decision

Figure 7.11 illustrates the appropriate method for protecting corporate network connectivity. NAT Server A protects the branch office network resources from Internet access.

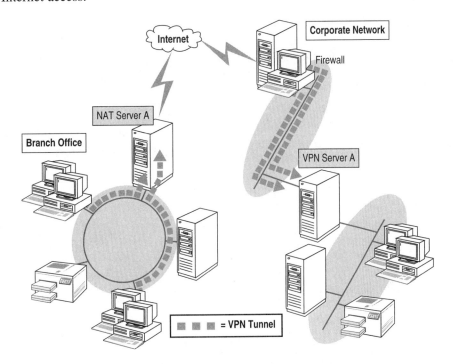

Figure 7.11   Scenario to illustrate the appropriate method for protecting corporate network connectivity

For the purposes of this scenario, assume that the business and technical requirements of the organization include

- Providing Internet access to branch office network users
- Providing corporate network access to branch office network users

You can achieve the requirements of the design by establishing VPN connections between the computers in the branch office and the VPN server in the corporate network.

NAT Server A provides Internet access to the branch office network users. VPN Server A provides VPN remote access connectivity for the branch office network users.

Lesson 4: NAT Design Optimization

This lesson discusses how to optimize NAT designs to improve the availability and performance characteristics in your design. This lesson focuses on the strategies that increase the percentage of time that users can access the Internet through the NAT server and that increase the data transmission rate through the NAT server.

After this lesson, you will be able to

- Select the appropriate method for improving the availability characteristics in your NAT design
- Select the appropriate methods for increasing the performance characteristics in your NAT design

Estimated lesson time: 20 minutes

NAT Optimization Techniques

Once you have established the essential aspects and security aspects of your NAT design, you can optimize the design for availability and performance. The business requirements of the organization might require your design to ensure access to Internet and private network resources. In addition, the business requirements might include application response times that must be maintained.

Making the Decision

One of the primary constraints of NAT is that NAT has no methods for improving availability or performance. When your designs require higher availability or performance, include Microsoft Proxy Server 2.0 proxy servers or Routing and Remote Access-based routing solutions. You can, however, optimize the hardware and Windows 2000 configuration to improve Internet connectivity performance and availability.

You can optimize the NAT server hardware and Windows 2000 configuration by selecting one or more of the following optimization methods:

- **Dedicating a computer to running NAT**   By dedicating a computer to running NAT, you improve availability by preventing other applications or services from becoming unstable and requiring the NAT server to be restarted.

  In addition, by preventing other applications or services from running on the same computer as NAT, you ensure that all the system resources are dedicated to NAT and that NAT provides optimal performance.

- **Select a different Internet connection technology**   By selecting a persistent Internet connection, you ensure that the NAT server is always able to connect to the Internet. Dial-up connections, for example, might receive busy signals and not be able to provide Internet connectivity.

By selecting a higher data rate Internet connection, you improve the performance of all traffic sent through the Internet connection.

Note Because NAT isn't a cluster-aware application, you can't improve the availability or performance of NAT by using Windows 2000 server clusters or Network Load Balancing clusters.

Applying the Decision

Figure 7.12 illustrates a NAT design prior to optimization for NAT availability and performance. For the purposes of this scenario, assume that the business and technical requirements of the organization include

- Reducing the delays in accessing Internet resources for SOHO network users
- Improving the performance when accessing Internet resources for SOHO network users
- Providing Microsoft file and print services by NAT Server A

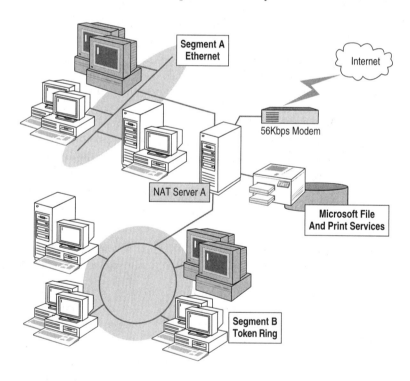

Figure 7.12 Scenario to illustrate a NAT design prior to optimization for availability and performance

Figure 7.13 illustrates a NAT design after optimization for NAT availability and performance. The design is optimized by

- Upgrading the Internet connection to an ISDN connection to improve performance and to reduce the delay in establishing the Internet connection
- Migrating the Microsoft file and print services to another Windows 2000 computer on Segment B

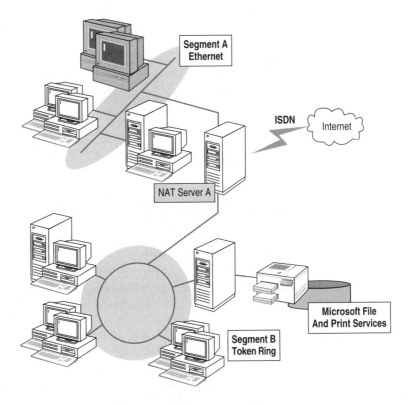

Figure 7.13   Scenario to illustrate a NAT design after optimization for availability and performance

Activity 7.2: Completing a NAT Design

In this activity, you're presented with a scenario. To complete the activity:

1. Evaluate the scenario and determine the design requirements
2. Answer questions and make design recommendations

In Figure 7.14, you see a map of the regional offices for an electronics field service firm that was discussed in an earlier lesson. The design process is proceeding and you're now creating the security and optimization specifications for the design.

Figure 7.14   Map of an electronics field service firm

Answer the following questions concerning your design recommendations. You can find answers to the questions in the Appendix, "Questions and Answers."

1. The management of the field service firm wants the regional offices to transfer customer information between the servers at each regional office and computers within the field engineer's SOHO network. The data will be summarized in data files that will be exchanged by using FTP. As a consultant to the firm, what NAT solution do you recommend to management?

2. The management of the field engineering firm wants to ensure that only the regional office has access to the computer in the field engineer's SOHO network. In addition, because FTP transmits data in clear text, the organization wants to protect the confidential customer information transmitted over the Internet. How can you ensure that these security requirements are met?

3. After a few months of operation, certain field engineer SOHOs are experiencing performance problems. How can you improve the performance for these offices?

Lab: Creating a NAT Design

After this lab, you will be able to

- Evaluate a scenario and determine the design requirements
- Create a NAT design based on the design requirements

Estimated lab time: 45 minutes

In this lab, you're a consultant to a chain of retail stores and are responsible for the creation of a NAT design for the retail chain. The retail chain has 3,200 locations throughout the United States.

To complete this lab:

1. Examine the networking environment presented in the scenario, the network diagrams, the business requirements and constraints, and the technical requirements and constraints

2. Use the worksheet for each location to assist you in creating your NAT design (you can find completed sample design worksheets on the Supplemental Course Materials CD-ROM in the Completed Worksheets folder)

3. Create, eliminate, or replace existing networking devices and network segments when required

4. Ensure that your design fulfills the business requirements and constraints and technical requirements and constraints of the scenario by

   - Assigning the appropriate specifications for each NAT interface
   - Specifying the appropriate client IP configuration method
   - Optimizing your design to provide the security, availability, performance, and affordability

Scenario

A chain of retail stores (shown in Figure 7.15) that caters to wireless telephone, paging, and other telecommunications services owns 3,200 locations throughout the United States. The retail stores provide both sales and postsales customer support for the company's customers.

Each store transmits nightly financial information and orders for new inventory to the headquarters. The headquarters of the retail stores (shown in Figure 7.16) receives the orders, fills the orders, ships the product, and updates the order status. The store (shown in Figure 7.17) can check customer information and order status on a multitiered application that runs on Web and database servers located at the headquarters.

Within each store, the following computers are attached to the local network:

- Three point-of-sale computers that can invoice customers and check the status of customer accounts
- Two information kiosks that customers can use to find information about the services provided by the company and to inquire about their account
- Two computers used by the manager and assistant manager for reviewing financial information, inventory status, and e-mail communication

In addition, the manager and assistant manager must establish connectivity with the retail store chain's corporate network to access reports, marketing information, employee benefits, and other human resource information.

Currently, the retail stores connect to the headquarters by using dial-up modems. The headquarters of the retail store chain is installing multiple T1 connections to the Internet. Each retail store is installing an ISDN or DSL connection to the Internet.

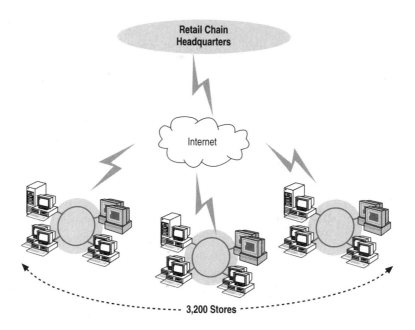

Figure 7.15   Diagram of the retail store chain

Business Requirements and Constraints

The retail store chain has a number of requirements and constraints based on the business model of the retail store chain. As you create your NAT design, ensure that your design meets the business requirements and stays within the business constraints.

To achieve the business requirements and constraints, your design must

- Prevent Internet users from accessing the retail store's private network
- Prevent the point-of-sale computers from accessing the Internet
- Prevent the kiosk computers from accessing any Web site other than the retail store chain's Web site
- Reduce the support required at each retail store by automating any configuration possible
- Protect any confidential data transmitted between the retail stores and the retail store chain's corporate network at headquarters

Technical Requirements and Constraints

The existing physical network, hardware, and operating systems place certain technical requirements and constraints on your design. As you create your NAT design, ensure that it meets the technical requirements and stays within the technical constraints.

In addition, the Web-based application that allows the retail store to check customer information and order status requires connectivity with each store and with the Internet. These Web-based applications are accessed on the manager's computer, the assistant manager's computer, and the kiosk computers.

To achieve the technical requirements and constraints, your design must

- Isolate the retail store's network segments from the Internet
- Support the private IP addressing scheme, 192.168.0.0/24, assigned within each store
- Resolve FQDNs by using the DNS server provided by the ISP that provides the Internet connectivity for each store
- Utilize the assigned public IP addressing scheme, 10.133.25.0/24, allocated from an Internet registry

Note Although 10.133.25.0/24 is a private IP address range, assume the IP address range is a public IP address range for the purposes of this lab.

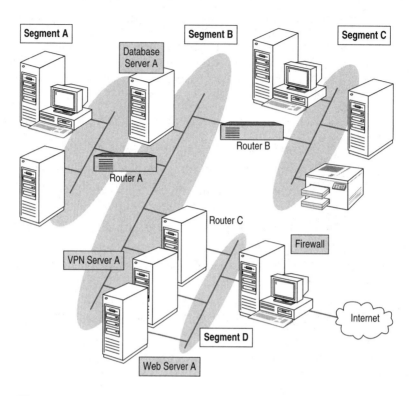

Figure 7.16   This is the existing network at the retail store chain headquarters.

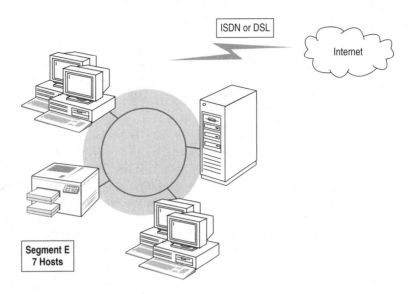

Figure 7.17   This is the existing network at one of the retail stores. For the purposes of this lab, assume that the stores have the same network configuration.

Design Worksheet – Figure 7.17
Retail Store – NAT Server A

NAT Server Specifications	Comments
Interface A connects to segment: _____ IP address: _____	
Interface B connects to segment: _____ IP address: _____	
Desktop Client IP Configuration	
❑ NAT automatic IP assignment ❑ Manual ❑ Automatic Private IP Address (APIPA) ❑ DHCP Server	
❑ DNS automatic assignment (specify DNS server in Comments column)	
NAT Server Security	
❑ IP packet filter (specify packet filter criteria in Comments column)	
❑ IP address mapping (specify address map entries in Comments column)	
❑ IP address pool (*specify address pool mappings in Comments column*)	
❑ VPN connectivity (*specify VPN tunnel specification in Comments column*)	

Review

The following questions are intended to reinforce key information in this chapter. If you're unable to answer a question, review the lesson and then try to answer the question again. You can find answers to the questions in the Appendix, "Questions and Answers."

1. An insurance company has agents who work from their homes. Currently, the agents connect to the insurance company's corporate network by establishing a dial-up Internet connection and then establishing a VPN tunnel. The insurance firm is in the process of upgrading the applications and services available to the agents. The applications and services will require the agents to upgrade their Internet connection to a high-speed connection such as ISDN or DSL. Many of the agents want to use the new high-speed Internet connection with other computers in their SOHO. As an independent consultant, what recommendations can you make to the organization?

2. You're evaluating an existing NAT design for a franchised restaurant chain. Each of the restaurants has a database server located within the local restaurant. Nightly updates to financial and sales information are uploaded to regional franchise offices. However, the regional managers are unable to query the database server in any of the restaurants. What recommendations can you make that allow the managers to access information on the database servers?

3. You're optimizing an existing NAT design. The network users report that response time for Internet access is slow. What changes to the design can you recommend to improve Internet access response time?

C H A P T E R 8

DHCP in IP Configuration Designs

About This Chapter

Most of the networking services designs that you create will incorporate Internet Protocol (IP). Each of these IP-based networks requires the IP information for each computer to be configured. As the number of computers in these networks increases, the probability of IP configuration errors increases and the amount of time spent configuring the IP information increases. Regardless of the size of the network, determining how IP configuration occurs is a critical part of any networking services design that you create.

You can use the Dynamic Host Configuration Protocol (DHCP) services in Microsoft Windows 2000 to provide automatic IP configuration for client computers in your design. The DHCP services in Windows 2000 can automatically manage the IP configuration of client computers to reduce the errors associated with IP configuration. Because DHCP performs IP configuration automatically, the amount of time spent in IP configuration and management is reduced or eliminated.

This chapter answers questions such as:

- In what situations are the IP configuration services provided by DHCP appropriate for your design?
- Which client computer operating systems and software can be configured by DHCP?
- How can you protect the DHCP configuration to ensure that clients are configured properly?
- How can you ensure that DHCP IP configuration is always available to private network users?
- How can you improve the performance of configuring client computers during peak periods?

Before You Begin

Before you begin, you must have an overall understanding of

- Network technologies (including Ethernet, Token Ring, hubs, switches, and concentrators)
- Common transport protocol configuration for IP (such as IP address, subnet mask, or default gateway for IP)
- IP routed networks (including subnets, network segments, routers, and IP switches)
- Dial-up telephony and connectivity technologies used by Internet service providers (ISPs)
- Automated IP configuration, including DHCP or Automatic Private IP Addressing (APIPA)

Lesson 1: Designs That Include DHCP

This lesson presents the requirements and constraints, both business and technical, that identify the IP configuration services in DHCP as a solution.

After this lesson, you will be able to

- Describe the relationship between DHCP and Windows 2000
- Identify the business and technical requirements and constraints that must be collected to create a DHCP design
- Identify the DHCP design decisions
- Evaluate scenarios and determine which capabilities and features of DHCP are appropriate in IP configuration solutions

Estimated lesson time: 30 minutes

DHCP and Windows 2000

You can configure IP settings for the computers in your network manually or automatically. Automatic IP configuration is an essential part of any networking services design that you create.

The amount of resources required to support your design, once your design is implemented, significantly affects the success or failure of your design. By reducing the possibility of IP configuration errors and by reducing the amount of time spent administering IP configuration, automatic IP configuration can contribute considerably to the success of your design.

DHCP is an industry standard protocol that provides automatic IP configuration. DHCP makes extensive use of IP broadcasts to provide automatic IP configuration. By default, IP routers don't forward IP broadcasts. As a result, you must consider the existing IP routing design to complete your DHCP design.

The DHCP services in Windows 2000 can be divided into the following:

- **DHCP Client**   You can configure the IP stack for all versions of Windows by using DHCP. The DHCP Client is an integral part of the IP implemented in Windows 2000. The DHCP Client receives IP configuration information from DHCP servers and updates the local IP configuration.

  Note   Microsoft Windows 95, Microsoft Windows 98, Microsoft Windows Me, Microsoft Windows NT 4.0, UNIX, and other operating systems include DHCP clients as well.

- **DHCP Server**   The DHCP Server service in Windows 2000 can provide IP configuration to DHCP clients in your design. From the Windows 2000 perspective, DHCP Server is a service that runs on Windows 2000. The DHCP Server service utilizes the IP and file services of Windows 2000.

The DHCP Server service communicates with DHCP clients, other DHCP servers, Active Directory domain controllers, and DHCP Relay Agents by using the IP stack in Windows 2000. You must specify a fixed IP address for all network interfaces that communicate with the DHCP Server service.

The DHCP Server service in Windows 2000 manages a database stored locally on the DHCP. The DHCP database contains the status of the IP address ranges managed by the DHCP server.

The DHCP Server service is available in Microsoft Windows 2000 Server, Microsoft Windows 2000 Advanced Server, and Microsoft Windows 2000 Datacenter Server. The DHCP Relay Agent isn't available in Microsoft Windows 2000 Professional.

- **DHCP Relay Agent**   The DHCP Relay Agent is a protocol you can include in Routing and Remote Access. The DHCP Relay Agent in Routing and Remote Access forwards DHCP between IP routed network segments. It also receives the DHCP broadcast traffic and forwards the DHCP requests as a unicast IP packet directed to the DHCP server. In addition, the DHCP Relay Agent eliminates DHCP broadcast traffic between network segments.

  Just like the DHCP Server service, the DHCP Relay Agent requires you to assign a fixed IP address to the network interfaces in the computer running it.

  Because the DHCP Relay Agent is available in Routing and Remote Access, it's a standard feature of Windows 2000 Server, Windows 2000 Advanced Server, and Windows 2000 Datacenter Server. The DHCP Relay Agent isn't available in Windows 2000 Professional.

Tip   Don't install the DHCP Server and the DHCP Relay Agent on the same computer.

In this chapter, you learn how to create Internet connectivity solutions with DHCP and Windows 2000. Figure 8.1 illustrates the interaction between DHCP and the other networking services in Windows 2000.

To successfully create DHCP designs, you must be familiar with

- General IP configuration and IP routing theory
- General DHCP theory

DHCP Design Requirements and Constraints

Before you create your DHCP design, you must gather the requirements and constraints, both business and technical, of the organization. As you create your design, you make design decisions based on the requirements and constraints you collect.

The list of the design requirements and constraints that you collect includes

- The amount of data transmitted between the existing network segments containing the DHCP clients and the DHCP server

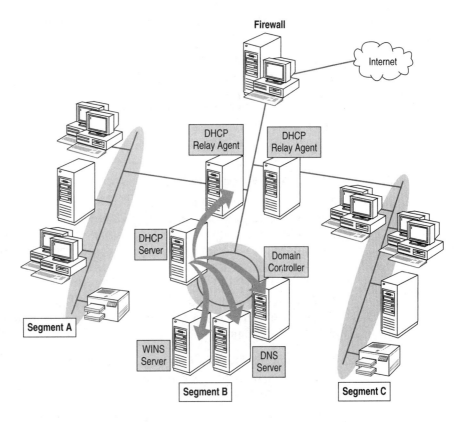

Figure 8.1   The interaction between DHCP and Windows 2000

- Number of locations and network segments that require automatic IP configuration
- Plans for future network growth
- Characteristics of existing routers including
  - Router broadcast traffic forwarding
  - Router placement
  - Wide area network (WAN) connections in use

DHCP Design Decisions

After you determine the business and technical requirements and constraints, apply the information you gathered to make DHCP design decisions.

To create your DHCP design, you must choose the

- Type of client computers that must be supported by the DHCP servers
- Method of providing IP configuration for each network segment

- Placement of DHCP servers and DHCP Relay Agents in your design
- Method of ensuring that DHCP automatic IP configuration is always available to DHCP clients
- Method of optimizing the network traffic between DHCP clients and DHCP servers

The lessons that follow in this chapter provide the information required for you to make specific DHCP design recommendations.

IP Configuration Designs

Most of the IP configuration designs that you create will be for routed networks. You will create these designs for various sized organizations. Your primary concern in IP configuration designs is to ensure that the IP parameters on each computer in the organization's private network are properly configured.

Making the Decision

In IP configuration designs, you must decide the method that you will use to configure IP for each computer. You can select any of the following methods to provide IP configuration:

- **Manual configuration**   You must use manual configuration for file servers, print servers, routers, gateways, or other IP devices that provide resources and services to client computers.

  For computers that don't manage network resources, such as desktop computers, use automatic IP configuration to reduce IP configuration error and the amount of time spent administering IP configuration.

  Note   All IP configuration designs include a certain amount of manual IP configuration.

- **DHCP services provided by third-party operating systems**   Most modern operating systems, such as Novell NetWare or UNIX operating systems, provide a DHCP server implementation. You can use the DHCP services provided by these operating systems to automatically configure client computers. If the organization is standardized on these network operating systems, you can include the respective DHCP server implementation.

  However, these operating systems don't include the following features provided by the DHCP services in Windows 2000:

  - Integration with Active Directory directory services
  - Prevention of unauthorized DHCP servers in the organization's private network
  - Integration with high availability solutions, such as Microsoft Windows Clustering solutions

- **DHCP services provided by Windows 2000**   The DHCP services provided by Windows 2000 are tightly integrated with Windows 2000 and other Microsoft operating systems (such as Windows 95, Windows 98, Windows Me, Microsoft Windows CE, or Windows NT 4.0). However, the DHCP services provided by Windows 2000 can provide IP configuration for other operating systems as well.

Include the DHCP services provided by Windows 2000 in your design when

- The organization is standardizing on Windows 2000

- The client computer operating systems include Windows 95, Windows 98, Windows Me, or Windows NT 4.0

- You want to prevent DHCP configuration errors from unauthorized DHCP servers

- You want to standardize the management of your network by using Active Directory directory service

- You want to provide highly available IP configurations by using DHCP and Windows clustering

---

Note   The remainder of this chapter focuses on providing IP configuration solutions by using DHCP.

In addition, the DHCP Server service in Windows 2000 is tightly integrated with the Domain Name System (DNS) and Routing and Remote Access services in Windows 2000. The DHCP Server service can automatically update DNS entries, for the DNS in Windows 2000, to include IP addresses assigned to computers by the DHCP server. For more information on DHCP and DNS integration, see Chapter 9, "DNS in Name Resolution Designs."

Routing and Remote Access can dynamically allocate IP addresses from DHCP servers to remote access users. The IP addresses allocated by Routing and Remote Access are assigned to remote access clients as they connect. After a remote access client disconnects, its assigned IP address is *immediately* available for other remote access clients. For more information on DHCP and Routing and Remote Access integration, see Chapter 11, "Dial-Up Connectivity in Remote Access Designs," and Chapter 12, "VPN Connectivity in Remote Access Designs."

Applying the Decision

Figure 8.2 illustrates a design where DHCP Server A provides IP configuration for the organization's private network. DHCP Server A is placed centrally in the private network.

For the purposes of this scenario, assume that

- The IP address of 10.0.0.0/8 is allocated from an Internet service provider (ISP) for use by the organization

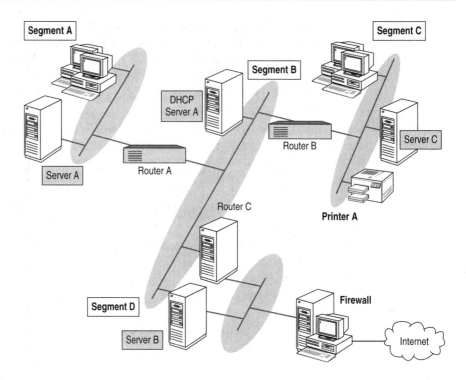

Figure 8.2   Scenario that uses DHCP for automatic IP configuration

---

Note   Although normally a private IP address, for the purposes of this scenario, treat 10.0.0.0/8 as a public IP address.

- Routers A and B forward DHCP broadcasts between Segments A, B, and C
- The organization has decided to standardize Active Directory as their directory service
- Approximately 400 client computers exist on Segments A and C

Table 8.1 lists each network device, the IP configuration method used, and the reason for selecting the method.

Table 8.1   **Reasons for Choosing Specific IP Configuration Methods
for Network Devices**

Device	Method	NAT Server Interface Specifications
Server A	Manual	Server A provides resources to the network and requires a fixed IP address.
Server B	Manual	Server C provides resources to the network and requires a fixed IP address.
Server C	Manual	Server C provides resources to the network and requires a fixed IP address.
Firewall	Manual	Firewall provides connectivity between the private network segments and the Internet, and requires a fixed IP address.
Router A	Manual	Router A provides routing between network segments and requires a fixed IP address.
Router B	Manual	Router B provides routing between network segments and requires a fixed IP address.
Router C	Manual	Router C provides routing between network segments and requires a fixed IP address.
Printer A	Manual	Printer C provides printer resources for the network and requires a fixed IP address.
Clients on Segment A	Windows 2000 DHPC	Windows 2000 DHCP services can provide IP configuration for the client computers to reduce IP configuration errors and to reduce the time spent in IP management.
Clients on Segment C	Windows 2000 DHPC	Windows 2000 DHCP services can provide IP configuration for the client computers to reduce IP configuration errors and to reduce the time spent in IP management.

Lesson 2: Essential DHCP Design Concepts

This lesson discusses the requirements, constraints, and design decisions used in establishing the essential specifications in a DHCP design. This lesson will covers the design concepts common to all DHCP designs.

After this lesson, you will be able to

- Determine the network segments in your design that require automatic IP configuration by using DHCP

- Select the appropriate method for providing automatic IP configuration for each network segment by using DHCP

- Determine the appropriate DHCP Scopes and DHCP Scope options in your designs

Estimated lesson time: 30 minutes

Determining Which Segments Require Automatic IP Configuration

You must determine which network segments in your design require automatic IP configuration. Typically, any network segments containing desktop computers should be configured automatically by using DHCP.

Making the Decision

Provide automatic IP configuration for all network segments except

- **Network segments that contain only computers that manage network resources**   Computers that manage network resources, such as file servers, print servers, database servers, or Web servers, require fixed IP addressing. Because no automatic IP addressing is used, you don't need to provide DHCP services to these network segments.

- **Backbone segments that contain only routers that connect other network segments to the backbone**   Routers require fixed IP addressing for all router interfaces. On network segments that contain only routers, you don't need to provide DHCP services.

- **WAN segments**   You want to eliminate all unnecessary traffic on WAN segments to conserve the WAN segment capacity for required traffic. As a result, assign fixed IP addresses to all devices that connect to WAN segments.

- **Screened subnet segments**   Screened subnet segments (otherwise known as DMZs) are secured network segments. Screened subnets contain resources accessible only by certain users. Most of these screened subnets exist between an organization's private network and the Internet. The resources in these screened subnets are accessed by unauthorized users. For security reasons, don't place DHCP servers in these screened subnets or respond to DHCP requests from Internet users.

Applying the Decision

The scenario in Figure 8.3 illustrates the appropriate selection of network segments that can use automatic IP configuration by using DHCP. For the purposes of this scenario, assume that

- Segment B contains only servers that manage network resources
- The firewall provides Internet users with access only to the private network resources on Segment B
- Segments A and C each contain 15 file servers, 10 print servers, and 280 desktop client computers

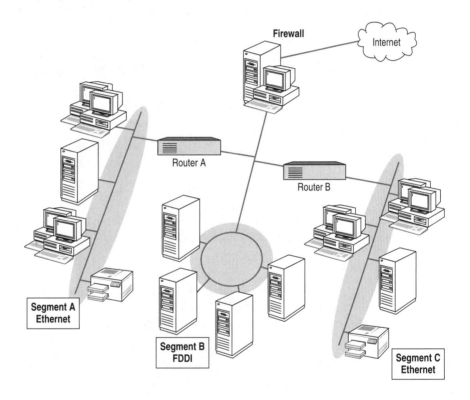

Figure 8.3   Scenario that illustrates the appropriate selection of network segments that can use automatic IP configuration by using DHCP

Table 8.2 lists each network segment, the IP configuration method to use, and the reason for including that method in your design.

Table 8.2   Reasons for Choosing Specific IP Configurations for Network Segments

Segment	Method	Reason
Segment A	Automatic IP configuration	Desktop client computers exist on the network segment.
Segment B	Manual IP configuration	Only computers that manage network resources exist on the network segment. In addition, the network segment is a secured, screened subnet.
Segment C	Automatic IP configuration	Desktop client computers exist on the network segment.
Internet	Manual IP configuration	Only fixed IP addresses are assigned to the firewall network interfaces.

Determining the DHCP Automatic IP Configuration Method

After you have determined which network segments require automatic IP configuration, you must determine the automatic IP configuration method for each network segment. For each network segment, you can select the method to provide automatic IP configuration by using DHCP.

As mentioned in the previous section, provide DHCP services only within

- **The organization's private network**   The DHCP servers within your design must provide automatic IP configuration only for network segments in the organization's private network (or remote connections established with virtual private networking (VPN)).

- **Each location in the organization's private network**   The DHCP servers within your design should provide automatic IP configuration only for network segments within the same geographic location as the DHCP server. Don't provide DHCP services over WAN segments to ensure that the capacity of the WAN segments is available for data.

You can ensure that automatic IP configuration is provided to the appropriate network segments by

- Directly connecting a DHCP server to the segments
- Directly connecting a DHCP Relay Agent to the segments
- Enabling DHCP/BOOTP forwarding on the routers that connect to the segments

Each of the network segments in your design must select one of the previous methods to provide automatic IP configuration.

DHCP Servers

You must include DHCP servers in each of your networking services designs that include automatic IP configuration. These DHCP servers manage the IP address ranges to be automatically assigned to your network.

Making the Decision

Include at least one DHCP server at each geographic location in your networking services design. Within a location, minimize the number of DHCP servers to reduce the number of DHCP servers that must be administered.

A single DHCP server can service more than 15,000 client computers. As a result, a single DHPC server per location is sufficient for most locations. Include additional DHCP servers in your design to provide enhanced availability or performance in your design. For more information on enhancing DHCP availability and performance, see Lesson 4, "Optimizing DHCP Designs," later in this chapter.

You can include multiple network interface adapters in the computer running the DHCP Server service to provide DHCP services to more than one network segment. When you add multiple network interface adapters to the computer running the DHCP Server service, you create a *multihomed* DHCP server.

Applying the Decision

Figure 8.4 illustrates the proper placement of DHCP servers in a network. For the purposes of this scenario, assume that

- Segment B contains only Routers A, B, and C
- Segments A and C each contain 15 file servers, 10 print servers, and 280 desktop client computers
- Segments D and E each contain 20 file servers, 15 print servers, and 320 desktop client computers

Table 8.3 lists each DHCP server placed in the organization and the reason for including that DHCP server in your design.

Table 8.3   Reasons for Including Specific DHCP Servers in Designs

DHCP Server	Reason for Including DHCP Server
DHCP Server A	Segments A and C require automatic IP configuration. Segment B is centrally located between Segment A and C. Location A requires a minimum of one DHCP server.
DHCP Server B	Segment D requires automatic IP configuration. Location B requires a minimum of one DHCP server.
DHCP Server C	Segment E requires automatic IP configuration. Location C requires a minimum of one DHCP server.

DHCP Relay Agents

You include DHCP Relay Agents in your networking services designs where network segments aren't directly connected to DHCP servers. These DHCP Relay Agents forward DHCP traffic between the network segment and the segment that contains the DHCP server(s).

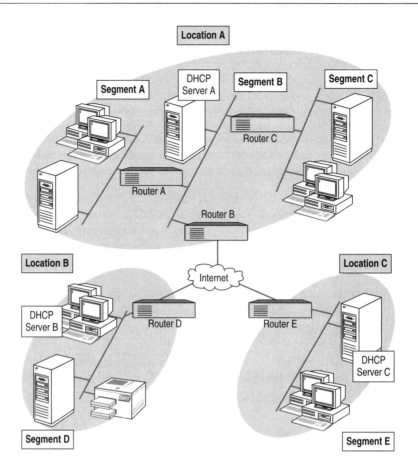

Figure 8.4 Diagram that illustrates the proper placement of DHCP servers in a network

Making the Decision

Include a DHCP Relay Agent on network segments not directly connected to a DHCP server. The DHCP client requests received by the DHCP Relay Agent are broadcast packets. The DHCP Relay Agent receives the requests and forwards them to a DHCP server that you specify as unicast packets. Unicast traffic ensures that the DHCP client requests are forwarded through intermediary routers or other network devices.

A DHCP Relay Agent can service thousands of client computers. In addition, you can include multiple network interface adapters in the computer running the DHCP Relay Agent to service more than one network segment. When you add multiple network interface adapters to the computer running the DHCP Relay Agent, you create a *multihomed* DHCP Relay Agent.

The primary advantage of a DHCP Relay Agent over enabling DHCP/BOOTP forwarding on routers is that the DHCP Relay agent converts the DHCP requests from broadcast to unicast. A router with DHCP/BOOTP forwarding enabled forwards only the broadcast packet, requiring that DHCP/BOOTP forwarding be enabled on all routers between the DHCP clients and the DHCP server.

Tip You can replace existing IP routers in your design with Routing and Remote Access-based routers. Because the DHCP Relay Agent is an integral part of Routing and Remote Access, you can ensure that each network segment has access to a DHCP Relay Agent.

Applying the Decision

Figure 8.5 illustrates the proper placement of DHCP Relay Agents in a network. For the purposes of this scenario, assume that

- The organization wants to reduce any broadcast traffic in the network
- Routers A and C are Routing and Remote Access-based routers

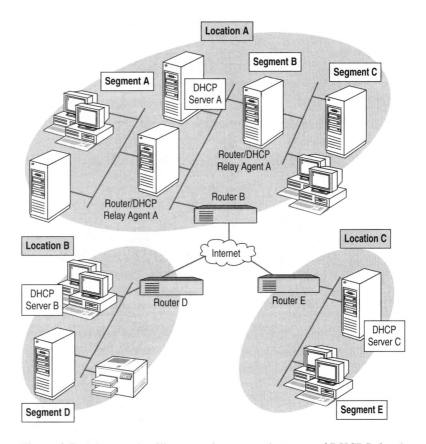

Figure 8.5 Diagram that illustrates the proper placement of DHCP Relay Agents in a network

- Segment B contains only Routers A, B, and C

- Segments A and C each contain 15 file servers, 10 print servers, and 280 desktop client computers

- Segments D and E each contain 20 file servers, 15 print servers, and 320 desktop client computers

- DHCP Server A manages the IP address ranges automatically assigned to Segments A and C

- DHCP Server B manages the IP address ranges automatically assigned to Segment D

- DHCP Server C manages the IP address ranges automatically assigned to Segment E

Table 8.4 lists each DHCP Relay Agent placed in the organization and the reason for including that DHCP Relay Agent in your design.

Table 8.4   Reasons for Including Specific DHCP Relay Agents in the Design

DHCP Relay Agent	Reason for Including DHCP Relay Agent
DHCP Relay Agent A	Segment A isn't directly connected to DHCP Server A
DHCP Relay Agent B	Segment C isn't directly connected to DHCP Server B

DHCP/BOOTP Forwarding on Routers

Many hardware or third-party routers include the ability to forward DHCP/BOOTP traffic. You can enable DHCP/BOOTP forwarding for routers that are connected to network segments that are not directly connected to the DHCP server (instead of including DHCP Relay Agents to forward DHCP/BOOTP traffic).

Making the Decision

You can enable DHCP/BOOTP forwarding for routers on network segments that aren't directly connected to a DHCP server. The DHCP client requests are broadcast on the local network segment. The routers with DHCP/BOOTP forwarding enabled receive the DHCP broadcast traffic and forward the DHCP packets to other network segments.

Routers with more than two network interfaces and with DHCP/BOOTP forwarding enabled can provide DHCP services to more than one network segment. For more information on IP routing, see Chapter 4, "IP Routing Designs."

The DHCP Relay Agents are required because the organization requires the elimination of all broadcast traffic between all network segments. DHCP/BOOTP forwarding on routers forwards only the DHCP broadcast traffic.

Applying the Decision

Figure 8.6 illustrates the proper enabling of DHCP/BOOTP forwarding on IP routers in a network. For the purposes of this scenario, assume that

- Routers A and C are third-party routers that support DHCP/BOOTP forwarding
- Segment B contains only Routers A, B, and C
- Segments A and C each contain 15 file servers, 10 print servers, and 280 desktop client computers
- Segments D and E each contain 20 file servers, 15 print servers, and 320 desktop client computers
- DHCP Server A manages the IP address ranges automatically assigned to Segments A and C
- DHCP Server B manages the IP address ranges automatically assigned to Segment D
- DHCP Server C manages the IP address ranges automatically assigned to Segment E

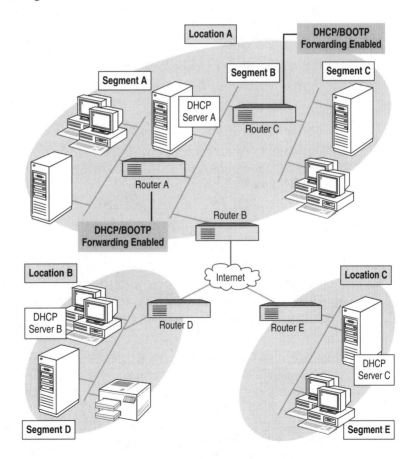

Figure 8.6 Diagram that illustrates the proper enabling of DHCP/BOOTP forwarding on IP routers in a network

Segments A and C are the only network segments not directly connected to a DHCP server. DHCP/BOOTP forwarding is enabled on Routers A and C to provide automatic IP configuration to Segments A and C.

DHCP Relay Agents aren't used because the existing routers support DHCP/BOOTP forwarding and the organization doesn't require the elimination of broadcast traffic *within* a location.

The primary advantage of enabling DHCP/BOOTP forwarding on routers over a DHCP Relay Agent is when the router previously exists. When the routers previously exist, no additional hardware or software purchases are necessary.

Determining DHCP Scopes and DHCP Scope Options

After you ensure that all DHCP clients can be serviced by DHCP servers, you must determine the DHPC scopes and DHCP scope options to include in your design. *DHCP scopes* are defined by specifying a range of IP addresses to be managed by the DHCP server. *DHCP scope options* are assigned to a DHCP scope to provide IP configuration options specific to a specific IP address range.

DHCP scope options can specify IP configuration information for DHCP clients such as

- Default gateway
- Domain Name System (DNS) server(s)
- Windows Internet Name Service (WINS) server(s)

DHCP Scopes

A DHCP scope defines a range of IP addresses to be managed by a DHCP server. There is a one-to-one relationship between the IP address ranges that you assign to DHCP-managed network segments and a corresponding DHCP scope.

Making the Decision

You must create a DHCP scope for each IP address range you want to automatically configure by using DHCP. To determine the number of DHCP scopes to include in your design, count the number of IP address ranges you want to be managed by DHCP.

The DHCP Server in Windows 2000 includes a new administrative feature called *superscopes*. A superscope is a grouping of two or more DHCP scopes. You create superscopes when you want to support two IP address ranges on the same physical network segment. When you support two or more IP address ranges on the same physical network segment, you create a *multinet*. Include superscopes in your design when the requirements of the organization include

- Supporting network segments serviced by DHCP Relay Agents or routers with DHCP/BOOTP forwarding.

- Providing additional IP address ranges for network segments that have depleted the existing available IP address ranges. You can provide the additional IP address ranges for future expansion.

- Collapsing multiple IP subnets into a single subnet without redesigning IP addressing scheme and subnet masks.

Another portion of the DHCP scope that you must specify in your design is the DHCP IP address *lease length*. The lease length determines when an IP address assigned to a computer, that has been subsequently removed from the network segment, is available for use by other computers on the network segment.

Increasing the DHCP lease length results in IP addresses being held longer after the computer is removed from the network segment, but creates less DHCP traffic because the existing computers contact the DHCP server less frequently. Decreasing the DHCP lease length results in IP addresses being returned sooner, but creates more DHCP traffic.

For network segments where computers are moved between network segments frequently, you can specify a shorter lease length to ensure that the network segments don't deplete the available DHCP addresses. When computers are seldom moved from one network segment to another network segment, you can lengthen the lease to reduce network traffic.

Applying the Decision

Figure 8.7 illustrates the proper assignment of DHCP scopes and superscopes in a network. For the purposes of this scenario, assume that

- Segment B contains only servers, routers, and DHCP Server A

- Segments A and C each contain 15 file servers, 10 print servers, and 280 desktop client computers

- DHCP Server A manages the IP address ranges automatically assigned to for all network segments

Table 8.5 lists the network segments in the scenario, the DHCP scopes that you include, and the reason for including the DHCP scopes in your design.

Table 8.5   Reasons for Including Specific DHCP Scopes in Designs

Segment	Scope	Reason
Segment A	Create scope called SegmentA that includes the IP address range of 10.1.1.1 – 10.1.1.254	You must create a scope to manage the IP address range (10.1.1.1 – 10.1.1.254) assigned to Segment A. The scope name must be a meaningful name (SegmentA describes the segment where the address range exists).

(continued)

Table 8.5 *(continued)*

Segment	Scope	Reason
Segment B	No scope is required	No DHCP configurable devices exist on this network segment.
Segment C	Create scope called SegmentC that includes the IP address range of 10.1.2.1 – 10.1.2.254	You must create a scope to manage the IP address range (10.1.2.1 – 10.1.2.254) assigned to Segment C. The scope name must be a meaningful name (SegmentC describes the segment where the address range exists).
Internet	No scope is required	No DHCP configurable devices exist on this network segment.

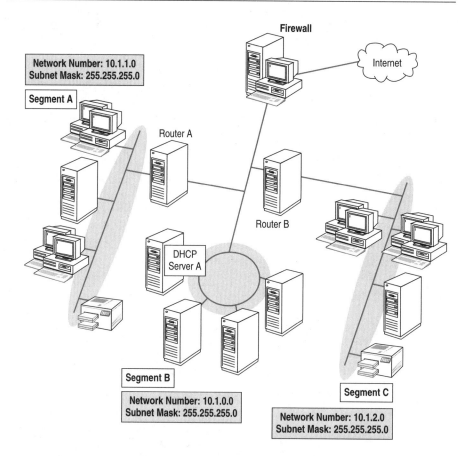

Figure 8.7   Diagram that illustrates the assignment of DHCP scopes and superscopes in a network

Because fault tolerance isn't part of the organization's requirements, additional DHCP servers aren't included. If you include an additional DHCP server for fault tolerance, you need to include a superscope to distribute the scope's IP address range across the DHCP servers. For more information on fault-tolerant DHCP solutions that utilize superscopes, see Lesson 4, "DHCP Design Optimization," later in this chapter.

DHCP Scope IP Address Exclusion

After you determine the appropriate DHCP scope or superscopes that you must include in your design, you have to determine the IP address to be excluded from the IP address range defined by the DHCP scope. You must exclude any IP addresses that you manually assign to network devices from the IP address range defined by the DHCP scope.

Making the Decision

You must exclude any manually assigned IP addresses within the DHCP scope's IP address range. Examples of devices assigned manual IP addresses include

- IP routers
- Firewalls
- File, print, and application servers
- Gateways
- Any operating system or device that can't be configured by DHCP

For each device that you manually assign an IP address within a DHCP scope IP address range, you must exclude the corresponding manually assigned IP address. Many organizations that you create solutions for will have established IP addressing standards for fixed IP addresses. These organizations reserve IP addresses in the range for routers, file servers, print servers, and other devices. In addition to existing devices, ensure that you exclude any IP address ranges designated for use by manually assigned IP addresses.

Applying the Decision

Figure 8.8 illustrates the devices that must be excluded from DHCP scopes. For the purposes of this scenario, assume that

- Scope named SegmentA manages the IP address range 10.1.1.1 – 10.1.1.254 assigned to Segment A
- Scope named SegmentC manages the IP address range 10.1.2.1 – 10.1.2.254 assigned to Segment C
- The organization has reserved the IP address range 10.1.x.1 – 10.1.x.10 for IP routers on the network segment (where x is the third octet of the subnet)
- The organization has reserved the IP address range 10.1.x.201 – 10.1.x.224 for servers on the network segment (where x is the third octet of the subnet)

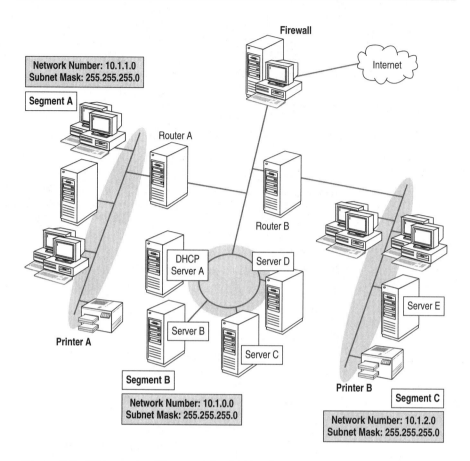

Figure 8.8 Diagram that illustrates the devices that must be excluded from DHCP scopes

- The organization has reserved the IP address range 10.1.*x*.225 – 10.1.*x*.254 for printers on the network segment (where *x* is the third octet of the subnet)

Table 8.6 lists the DHCP scopes, the IP address ranges to be excluded from the scope, and the reason for excluding the IP address ranges from the DHCP scopes in your design.

Table 8.6   Reasons for Excluding Specific IP Address Ranges from DHCP Scopes

DHCP Scope	Excluded IP Addresses	Reason
SegmentA	10.1.1.1 – 10.1.1.10	IP address range is reserved for IP routers
	10.1.1.201 – 10.1.1.254	IP address range is reserved for network server and printers

Table 8.6 *(continued)*

DHCP Scope	Excluded IP Addresses	Reason
SegmentC	10.1.1.1 – 10.1.1.10	IP address range is reserved for IP routers
	10.1.1.201 – 10.1.1.254	IP address range is reserved for network server and printers

DHCP Scope Options

After you determine the DHCP scopes, or superscopes, that must exist in your design and the IP addresses that must be excluded from the scope, you have to determine the appropriate DHPC scope options to include in your design. A DHCP scope option is a specific client IP configuration parameter such as

- Routers

- DNS servers

- DNS domain name

- WINS node type

- WINS servers

Making the Decision

You can define the DHCP scope options that can be assigned by the DHCP administrator. You can also create, modify, or remove the DHCP scope options that the DHCP administrator can assign. The DHCP administrator can assign only the DHCP scope options that you specify.

You can assign DHCP scope options to affect different groupings, or levels, of DHCP clients serviced by the DHCP server. For example, you can assign DHCP options that affect all scopes managed by the server or for individual client computers.

Table 8.7 lists the levels to which you can assign DHCP scope options and the reason to assign the scope options to that level.

Table 8.7   Reasons to Assign Specific Scope Options to Levels

Assign Options At	Reason
Server options	Defines scope options that affect all scopes managed by the DHCP server. Be cautious about assigning DHCP options at this level because they affect all DHCP clients serviced by this server.
Scope options	Defines scope options that affect all DHCP clients that fall within the IP address range (network segment) defined by the DHCP scope.

(continued)

Table 8.7   *(continued)*

Assign Options At	Reason
Class options	Defines scope options for a specific category of DHCP clients. You can define custom classes to group DHCP clients based on specific needs. For example, you can create a custom class for Windows 2000–based DHCP computers. You can assign Windows 2000–specific DHCP options to the custom class you created.
Client options	Defines scope options for individual client computers. For example, you might need to assign a specific WINS node type for only one computer in the organization.

Applying the Decision

Figure 8.9 illustrates the appropriate assignment of DHCP scope options.

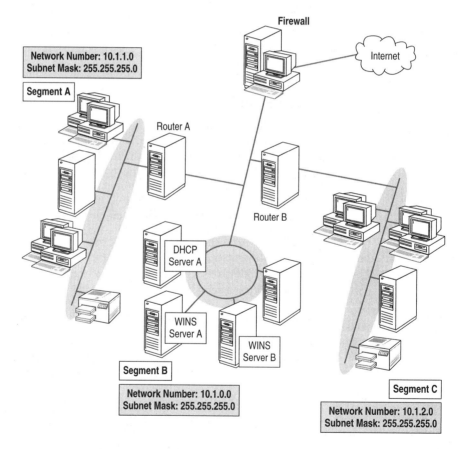

Figure 8.9   Diagram that illustrates the appropriate assignment of DHCP scope options

For the purposes of this scenario, assume that

- Scope named ScopeA manages the IP address range 10.1.1.1 – 10.1.1.254 assigned to Segment A

- Scope named ScopeC manages the IP address range 10.1.2.1 – 10.1.2.254 assigned to Segment C

- Segments A and C have a mixture of Windows 95, Windows 98, Windows Me, Microsoft Windows NT Workstation, and Windows 2000 Professional

- The desktop computers on Segments A and C must be configured with Routers A and B as their respective default gateway

- The desktop computers on Segments A and C must be configured with WINS Server A and B as their WINS servers

- Disable the NetBIOS over TCP/IP (NetBT) option that is available only on Windows 2000 DHCP clients

Table 8.8 lists the DHCP scopes options that you will include in your design, the level that the DHCP scope options are assigned, and the reason for including the scope options at the corresponding level in your design.

Table 8.8   Reasons for Including Specific DHCP Scope Options at Specific Levels

Scope Option	Level	Reason
Router A is default gateway for scope ScopeA	Scope	Router A is the only router accessible to Segment A. All the client computers within ScopeA should have Router A as the default router.
Router B is default gateway for ScopeC	Scope	Router B is the only router accessible to Segment C. All the client computers within ScopeC should have Router B as the default router.
WINS Server A and B are the WINS servers for all client computers	Server	All client computers on Segments A and C require the same WINS server settings. Setting this option in the server options ensures that all clients serviced by DHCP Server A are configured accordingly.
Disable NetBT	Class	Only computers running Windows 2000 can use this option. Create a class that includes only computers running Windows 2000 and specify this option on the class.

Activity 8.1: Evaluating a DHCP Design

In this activity, you are presented with a scenario. To complete the activity:

1. Evaluate the scenario and determine the design requirements

2. Answer the questions and make design recommendations

In Figure 8.10, you see a diagram of a regional library system with a main branch and five smaller branches in different townships. The library system currently reserves and checks out books manually. However, the library system is deploying a Microsoft SQL–based application that will automate book inventory, book acquisition, and financial records for the entire library system.

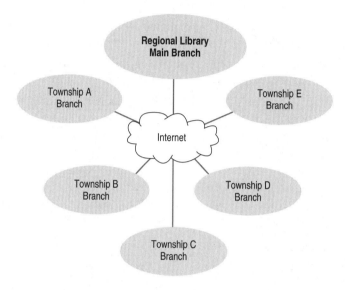

Figure 8.10   Diagram of a regional library system

The library management application is a Web-based application that allows library patrons to reserve and check out books over the Internet. The library's main branch will house the Web servers that host the public Web site. To manage its own book inventory, each remote branch will connect to the SQL server, also located in the main branch, over the Internet.

Each library branch network must

- Support 20 computers on a separate network segment used by the local branch personnel

- Support up to 100 computers on a separate network segment used by library patrons

- Provide 75 Ethernet jacks on a separate network segment for patrons who bring their own laptops

- Support three meeting rooms, each of which must provide 36 computers for seminars and workshops held in the library branch and which must be on a separate network segment

Answer the following questions concerning your design recommendations. Answers to the questions can be found in the Appendix, "Questions and Answers."

1. The library wants to ensure that local administration of the network is minimized. In addition, the director of technology for the library wants to make certain that IP configuration errors are minimized as well. As a consultant to the library, what recommendations can you make?

2. The director of technology for the library wants to reduce any costs possible in the design and isn't concerned about broadcast traffic within a location. How can you minimize the costs associated with the DHCP design?

3. The library has deployed Microsoft Internet Explorer 5.0 on all computers running Windows 2000. All other desktop computers are running older versions of Internet Explorer, but will be upgraded to Internet Explorer 5.0 as Windows 2000 is deployed to the respective computers. You want to enable the Internet Explorer 5.0 configuration option to automatically detect proxy server settings. How can you ensure that only Windows 2000 computers receive the Internet Explorer 5.0 configuration options?

Lesson 3: Configuration Protection in DHCP Designs

This lesson discusses how to create designs that protect the integrity of the automatic IP configuration by using DHCP. This lesson focuses on preventing unauthorized DHCP servers and unauthorized configuration changes to your DHCP servers.

After this lesson, you will be able to

- Prevent IP configuration errors caused by unauthorized DHCP servers
- Prevent unauthorized users from modifying the configuration of the DHCP servers in your design

Estimated lesson time: 30 minutes

Preventing Unauthorized DHCP Servers

Ensuring the integrity of the automatic IP configuration is the highest priority in your DHCP designs. Any unauthorized DHCP servers started on your network automatically provide IP configuration to DHCP clients. If these unauthorized DHCP servers are started, the DHCP clients are configured with incorrect IP information and the DHCP clients aren't able to communicate with the network.

In Figure 8.11 you see an example of how a single DHCP server, or the first DHCP server, starts when Active Directory is included in your design.

The DHCP Server service performs the following start-up sequence.

1. The DHCP Server service sends out a DHCPINFORM request to the local subnet to locate the Active Directory root domain from other existing DHCP servers (none will exist or reply).

2. Because no replies were received, the DHCP Server service queries Active Directory to verify that the DHCP server is authorized.

3. If the DHCP server is authorized, the DHCP Server service starts and begins to provide DHCP configuration for DHCP clients.

4. If the DHCP server is unauthorized, the DHCP Server service writes an event in the Windows 2000 Event Log and stops.

In Figure 8.12, you see an example of how subsequent DHCP servers start when other authorized DHCP servers have already started. In this example, DHCP/BOOTP forwarding is enabled on Router A and B.

When subsequent DHCP servers start, the following sequence occurs.

1. The DHCP Server service sends out a DHCPINFORM request to the local subnet to locate the Active Directory root domain from other existing DHCP servers.

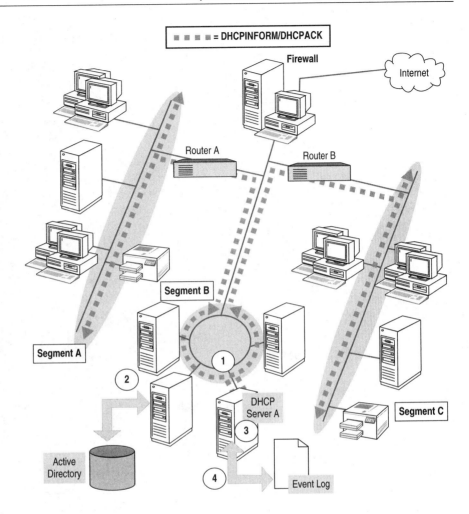

Figure 8.11   Example of how a single DHCP server, or the first DHCP server, starts when Active Directory is included in your design

2. The existing DHCP server(s) replies with a DHCPACK to acknowledge the request, and also returns the root domain information (multiple root domains may be returned by multiple DHCP servers).

3. The list of root domains and the list of all active DHCP servers are created.

4. If the DHCP Server service is installed on a domain controller or member server, the DHCP Server service queries Active Directory, relative to the root domain specified for that computer, to verify that the DHCP server is authorized.

5. If the DHCP Server service is installed on a standalone computer, DHCP Server service queries Active Directory, with each of the root domains returned in step 3, to verify that the DHCP server is authorized in one of the lists.

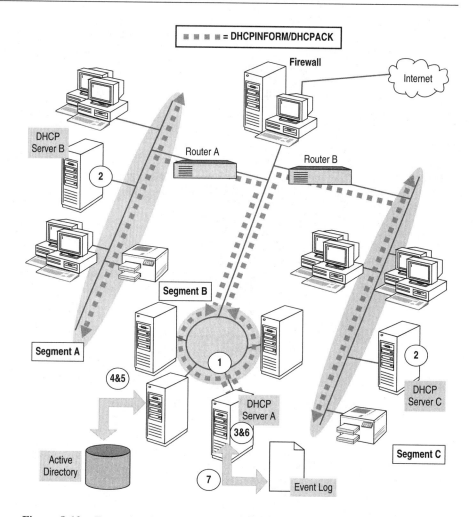

Figure 8.12   Example of how subsequent DHCP servers start when other authorized
DHCP servers have already started

6. If the DHCP server is authorized, the DHCP Server service starts and begins
to provide DHCP configuration for DHCP clients.

7. If the DHCP server is unauthorized, the DHCP Server service writes an event
in the Windows 2000 Event Log and stops.

Making the Decision

You prevent unauthorized Windows 2000–based DHCP servers in your designs
by authorizing Windows 2000–based DHCP servers in Active Directory directory
service. When DHCP is installed on a domain controller, member server, or
standalone server, the DHCP Server service in Windows 2000 automatically queries
Active Directory to determine whether the DHCP server is authorized to start.

To include unauthorized DHCP server detection and prevention in your design you must

- **Specify that one or more DHCP Server services be installed on a domain controller or member server**   You specify more than one DHPC Server to be installed on a domain controller or member server to provide fault tolerance in the event one of the computers that is a DHCP server and a domain controller fails.

- **Specify the list of DHCP servers that you want to authorize in Active Directory**   Ensure that you specify all DHCP servers that you include in your design. Only DHCP servers in the authorization list will start.

- **Specify DHPC Relay Agents or enable DHCP/BOOTP forwarding on routers**   The DHCPINFORM and DHCPACK packets are sent as broadcasts. You must ensure that the DHCPINFORM and DHCPACK packets are received by and can be replied to from all network segments.

Note   DHCP servers on operating systems other than Windows 2000 can't be prevented from starting. Only the DHCP Server service in Windows 2000 automatically checks to ensure that the DHCP server is authorized.

Applying the Decision

Figure 8.13 illustrates the appropriate method for preventing unauthorized DHCP servers. For the purposes of this scenario, assume that the business and technical requirements of the organization include

- Unauthorized Windows 2000–based DHCP servers must be prevented from connecting to any network segments in the organization's private network

- DHCP Servers A, B, and C must provide automatic IP configuration for Segments A, B, and C respectively

- Routers A and B are Routing and Remote Access-based routers that have the DHCP Relay Agent enabled and configured

Table 8.9 lists the DHCP servers in the scenario and the specifications that prevent unauthorized DHCP servers in your design.

Table 8.9   Specifications That Prevent Unauthorized DHCP Servers in Your Design

DHCP Server	Prevents Unauthorized DHCP Servers By
DHCP Server A	Ensuring that DHCP Server A is a domain controller or member server Authorizing DHCP Server A in Active Directory
DHCP Server B	Ensuring that DHCP Server B is a domain controller or member server Authorizing DHCP Server B in Active Directory
DHCP Server C	Ensuring that DHCP Server C is a domain controller or member server Authorizing DHCP Server C in Active Directory

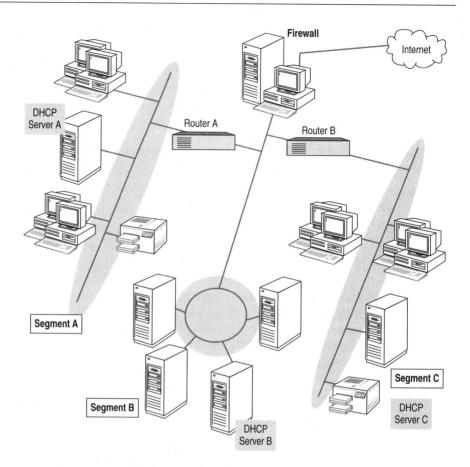

Figure 8.13   Scenario to illustrate the appropriate method for preventing unauthorized DHCP servers

Preventing Unauthorized Users

To ensure the integrity of the DHCP database, you must prevent unauthorized users from directly accessing the DHCP server. You prevent unauthorized users by restricting DHCP administrators and isolating the DHCP server from public networks.

Making the Decision

You can prevent unauthorized users from compromising the integrity of the DHCP database by

- **Restricting the number of users granted permission to manage DHCP servers within the organization**   Grant only authorized network administrators the permission to manage DHCP servers. Create a Windows 2000 group and assign the group permissions to manage DHCP servers in the organization. Include the authorized network in the Windows 2000 group you created.

■ **Isolating the DHCP server from public network access**   Ensure that DHCP servers don't exist on network segments accessible from public networks, such as the Internet. Ensure that only computers within the organization's private network can directly communicate with the DHCP servers.

Applying the Decision

Figure 8.14 illustrates the proper methods for preventing unauthorized user access to DHCP servers. The firewalls at Locations A, B, and C prevent unauthorized users from accessing the DHCP servers in each respective location.

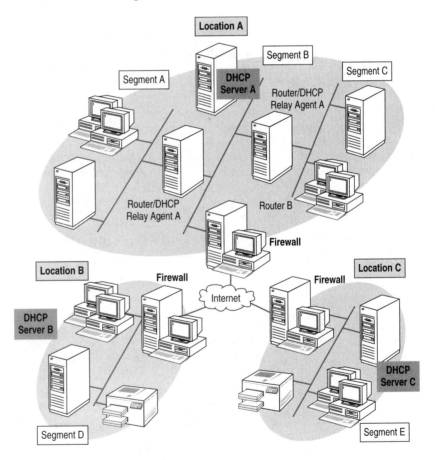

Figure 8.14   A scenario that illustrates the proper methods for preventing unauthorized user access to DHCP servers

The organization must allow only authorized network administrators to manage the DHCP servers. If each location is managed separately, only authorized administrators within each location should be allowed to manage the DHCP servers within the corresponding location.

Lesson 4: DHCP Design Optimization

This lesson discusses how to optimize DHCP designs to improve the availability and performance characteristics in your design. This lesson focuses on the strategies that increase the percentage of time that computers can be configured by DHCP and that decrease any latency in IP configuration by using DHCP.

After this lesson, you will be able to

- Select the appropriate method for enhancing the availability characteristics in your DHCP design
- Select the appropriate methods for improving the performance characteristics in your DHCP design

Estimated lesson time: 20 minutes

Enhancing DHCP Availability

Once you have established the essential aspects and security aspects of your DHCP design, you can optimize the design for availability. The business requirements of the organization might require your design to ensure DHCP configuration at all times. Regardless of a single point of failure, your design must provide redundancy for each DHCP server.

You can improve the availability of your DHCP designs by

- Using Windows Clustering server clusters
- Distributing a DHCP scope across multiple DHCP servers
- Dedicating a computer to running DHCP

Making the Decision

Windows Clustering Server Clusters

The DHCP Server service in Windows 2000 is a *cluster-aware* application. Cluster-aware applications can interact with Windows Clustering *server clusters.* You can create server clusters by sharing a common *cluster drive* between two computers. The cluster drive is attached to a Small Computer System Interface (SCSI) bus common to both computers, also known as *cluster nodes*, in the cluster.

Figure 8.15 illustrates the components in a Windows Clustering server cluster. The DHCP Server service actually runs on only one of the cluster nodes at a time. The DHCP database is stored on the shared cluster drive. The cluster node currently running the DHCP Server services is known as the *active node* for DHCP.

If the DHCP active node fails, the remaining cluster node automatically starts the DHCP Server service. Because the DHCP database is stored on the shared cluster drive, the redundant DHCP Server service has the current DHCP reservation information from the failed cluster node.

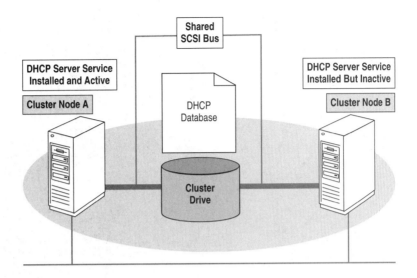

Figure 8.15   Components in a Windows Clustering server cluster

The primary advantages to DHCP on server clusters are

- The redundant cluster node automatically starts and no action is required on the part of the network administrators.

- The DHCP database information is stored on the cluster drive and is available to either cluster node. As a result, DHCP clients are unaware of the failure.

For more information on Window Clustering server clusters, see the Windows 2000 help files.

Multiple DHCP Servers with Distributed Scopes

You can distribute the IP address range managed by a DHCP scope across two DHCP servers. A portion of the IP address range is managed by a DHCP scope on each server. If one DHCP server fails, the remaining DHCP server can provide IP configuration for the network segment with the remaining portion of the IP address range.

For example, a network segment is assigned the IP address range 172.16.0.1 – 172.16.0.254. You create a scope on both servers that contains the entire IP address range (172.16.0.1 – 172.16.0.254). On one of the DHCP servers, exclude the I address range 172.16.0.129 – 172.16.0.254 from the scope. On the other DHCP server, exclude the IP address range 172.16.0.1 – 172.16.0.128 from the scope.

Figure 8.16 illustrates how distributed DHCP scopes can provide enhanced availability. The DHCP scope 172.16.0.1 – 172.16.0.254 is distributed between DHCP Servers A and B. DHCP Server A has excluded the IP address range 172.16.0.129 – 172.16.0.254. DHCP Server B has excluded the IP address range 172.16.0.1 – 172.16.0.128.

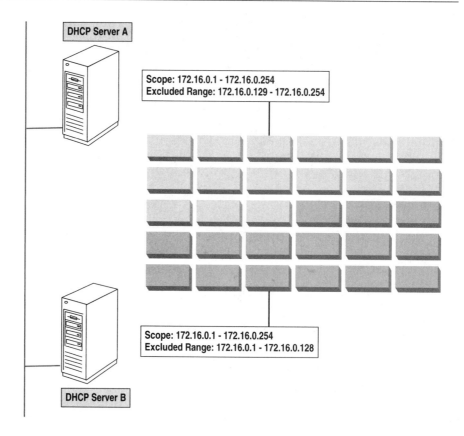

Figure 8.16 Example of how distributed DHCP scopes provide enhanced availability

The primary advantage of distributing DHCP scopes across multiple DHCP servers in comparison to server clusters is that no additional hardware and software resources are required. If one of the DHCP servers fails, the portion of the scope's IP address range managed by the server isn't available to the network. However, the remaining portion of the scope's IP address range is available.

Dedicating a Computer to DHCP

By dedicating a computer to running DHCP, you improve availability by preventing other applications or services from becoming unstable and requiring the DHCP server to be restarted.

Applying the Decision

Figure 8.17 illustrates the proper methods for enhancing the availability of a DHCP design.

For the purposes of this scenario, assume that the business and technical requirements of the organization include

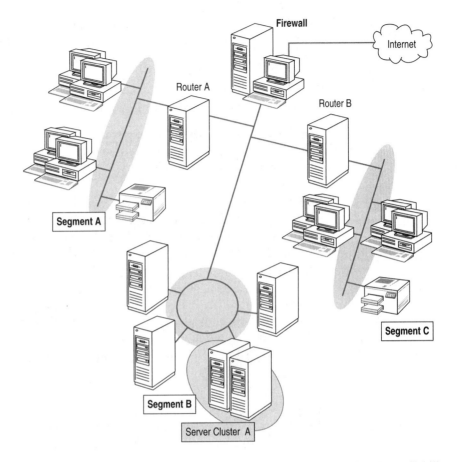

Figure 8.17   Scenario to illustrate the proper methods for enhancing the availability
of a DHCP design

- Any failure of a DHCP server is automatically corrected
- DHCP clients perceive no changes in the DHCP server configuration
- Routers A and B are Routing and Remote Access routers that have the DHCP
  Relay Agent enabled

To provide the proper solution, Windows Clustering server clusters must be used
to achieve the business and technical requirements of the organization. Server
Cluster A has the DHCP Server service installed on both cluster nodes, but only
active on one cluster node. Server Cluster A provides DHCP automatic IP configuration for Segments A and C.

Improving DHCP Performance

Once you have established the essential aspects, the security aspects, and availability
aspects of your DHCP design, you can optimize the design for performance.

The business requirements may include that DHCP configuration must occur within a given period of time, based on the number of simultaneous DHCP requests.

Making the Decision

You can improve the performance of DHCP configuration by

- **Load balancing the DHCP configuration across multiple DHCP servers**
  When the existing DHCP servers are saturated and you can't upgrade the hardware to improve performance, you can add additional DHCP servers to your design.

  Evenly distribute the DHCP scopes across the multiple DHCP servers, ensuring that each DHCP server manages approximately the same number of DHCP scopes. You can distribute the DHCP configuration traffic across the additional servers to reduce the latency in DHCP configuration.

- **Modifying the lease length**   DHCP clients must renew their DHCP lease based on the lease length specified in the DHCP scope. If you extend the length of time until the DHCP lease expires, the DHCP clients contact the DHCP servers less frequently and reduce the configuration traffic sent to the DHCP servers over a period of time.

  Conversely, if you shorten the length of time until the DHCP lease expires, the DHCP clients contact the DHCP servers more frequently and increase the configuration traffic sent to the DHCP servers over a period of time.

- **Dedicating a computer to DHCP**   By dedicating a computer to running DHCP, you improve the performance because you prevent other applications or services from consuming system resources.

Applying the Decision

Figure 8.18 illustrates a DHCP design prior to optimization for performance. For the purposes of this scenario, assume that the business and technical requirements of the organization include the following.

- The existing DHCP scope lease length is set to expire at three days.
- The existing computer running the DHCP Server service can't be further upgraded.
- A DHCP scope exists for the IP address range assigned to Segment A and Segment B.
- Routers A and B are Routing and Remote Access routers that have the DHCP Relay Agent enabled.

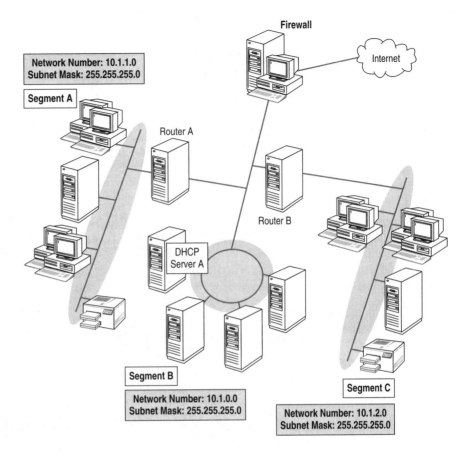

Figure 8.18 Scenario to illustrate a DHCP design prior to optimization for performance

Figure 8.19 illustrates a DHCP design after optimization for performance. The following performance optimization changes were made to the design.

- DHCP Server B is installed to load balance the DHCP traffic between DHCP Servers A and B.
- DHCP Server A manages the scope that corresponds to Segment A.
- DHCP Server B manages the scope that corresponds to Segment C.
- The DHCP lease length was increased to 14 days.

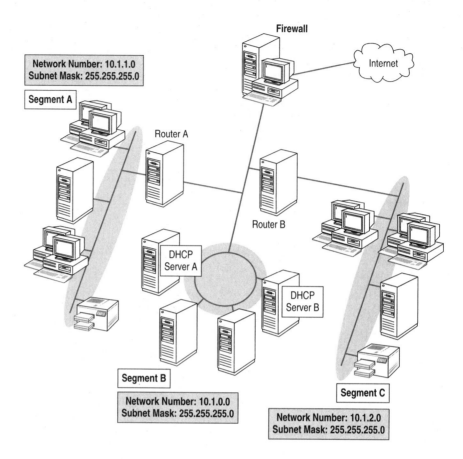

Figure 8.19   Scenario to illustrate a DHCP design after optimization for performance

Activity 8.2: Completing a DHCP Design

In this activity, you are presented with a scenario. To complete the activity:

1. Evaluate the scenario and determine the design requirements
2. Answer the questions and make design recommendations

Figure 8.20 represents a diagram of a regional library system network. As the director of information services for the library system, you're in the process of revising your current network design to reflect the current security, availability, and performance requirements of the regional library system.

The library system has deployed a Web-based application that allows library patrons to reserve, request, and check on the status of books. The Web-based application can be accessed by kiosks within each library or by the Internet.

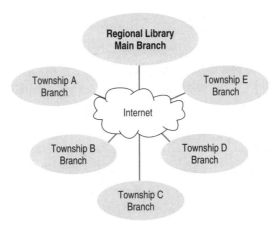

Figure 8.20   Diagram of a regional library system

Answer the following questions concerning your design recommendations.
Answers to the questions can be found in the Appendix, "Questions and Answers."

1. The library system is concerned about Internet users gaining access to the servers and resources in each library. What specifications can you include in your design to prevent Internet users from accessing DHCP servers?

2. DHCP servers running on Windows NT 4.0 Server currently manage the IP configuration for each library. You want to ensure that unauthorized DHCP servers aren't started within each library's private network. How do you ensure that these security requirements are met?

3. Each library has a local network administrator responsible for the operations within the respective library. In addition, the library system has three network administrators responsible for the operations of all the libraries. You want to ensure that only the local network administrator and the library system's network administrators can manage the DHCP servers in the design. How can you ensure that these requirements are achieved?

4. The existing design includes a single DHCP server within each library. At peak periods of activity, the DHCP server within many of the libraries becomes saturated with DHCP client requests. You want to ensure that if the DHCP server fails, DHCP automatic IP configuration occurs transparently to the users. In addition, you want to minimize any latency the DHCP client computers experience during DHCP automatic IP configuration. How can you ensure that these requirements are achieved?

Lab: Creating a DHCP Design

After this lab, you will be able to
- Evaluate a scenario and determine the design requirements
- Create a DHCP design based on the design requirements

Estimated lab time: 45 minutes

In this lab, you're the director of information services for a cruise line and are responsible for creating a DHCP design. The cruise line has a central reservation location, 18 seaport facilities, and 15 cruise liners.

To complete this lab:

1. Examine the networking environment presented in the scenario, the network diagrams, the business requirements, the business constraints, and the technical requirements and constraints

2. Use the worksheet for each location to create your DHCP design (you can find completed sample design worksheets on the Supplemental Course Materials CD-ROM in the Completed Worksheets folder)

3. Create, eliminate, or replace existing networking devices and network segments when required

4. Ensure that your design fulfills the business requirements and constraints and technical requirements and constraints of the scenario by
   - Determining the network segments that require DHCP automatic configuration
   - Determining the DHCP scopes and scope options that are required
   - Optimizing your design to provide security, availability, performance, and affordability

Note   To reduce the length of time spent on this lab, create a DHCP design for the reservation location, one of the seaports, and one of the cruise liners.

Scenario

A cruise ship line is migrating its network to Windows 2000. The cruise line has a central reservation center where reservation agents take reservations for cruises. The cruise line maintains a fleet of 15 luxury cruise ships and operates out of 18 seaports where the vessels dock and customers board.

Figure 8.21 provides a high-level overview of the cruise ship line's network. Each seaport facility (shown in Figure 8.23) is connected to the Internet by a T1 line. The company's reservation center (shown in Figure 8.22) is located in Miami and is connected to the Internet by a T3 line.

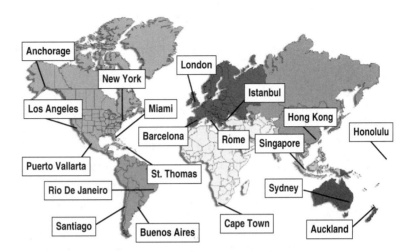

Figure 8.21   Overview network diagram of the cruise ship line

In addition to reservations made at the cruise ship line's reservation center, each seaport facility can also take reservations. Each seaport facility connects to the reservation center over the Internet.

Each cruise ship (shown in Figure 8.24) has a primary microwave connection to the Internet. In addition, each cruise ship has a satellite connection that acts as a redundant Internet connection in the event the microwave connection fails. Because of the costs associated with the satellite connection, the satellite connection is for cruise ship personnel's use exclusively. Passengers may access the Internet through the microwave connection to the Internet at business centers located on each cruise ship.

The cruise ships receive passenger manifests, baggage, and e-mail messages from the reservation center. In addition, each cruise ship maintains a maintenance and inventory system that the ship personnel use to manage the maintenance and parts inventory for the cruise ship. The restaurants and food services on the cruise ships also maintain an inventory of food and beverage items they require. The food services group orders the necessary items at its next port before the cruise ship docks.

Business Requirements and Constraints

The cruise ship line has a number of requirements and constraints based on the business model of the company. As you create your DHCP design, ensure that it meets the business requirements and stays within the business constraints. To achieve the business requirements and constraints, your design must

- Utilize the existing hardware and operating systems in each seaport facility and cruise liner; these facilities include

  - Baggage check-in and reservation kiosks at each seaport

- Reservation and baggage computers for use by cruise line personnel at each seaport
- Business centers on cruise liners for use by passengers
- Ship operations computers for use by ship personnel

- Provide automatic IP configuration for all desktop operating systems and kiosks that include Windows 2000 Professional, Windows NT 4 Workstation, Windows 98, and Windows Me
- Support Active Directory as the directory services for the cruise line
- Provide an Internet presence hosted on Web servers in the reservation center
- Ensure that DHCP automatic IP configuration is available 24 hours a day, 7 days a week
- Ensure that any DHCP server failures are transparent to DHPC clients
- Ensure that the baggage check-in and reservation kiosks are available during normal hours of operation

Technical Requirements and Constraints

The applications that run on each seaport and cruise ship network require internal connectivity as well as connectivity with other seaport facilities and cruise ships, and with the reservation center. These applications run on computers used by the reservation agents, baggage handlers, and cruise ship personnel, and on computers used in the reservation and baggage kiosks.

The existing physical network, hardware, and operating systems place certain technical requirements and constraints on your design. As you create your TCP/IP network design, ensure that your design meets the technical requirements and stays within the technical constraints. To achieve the technical requirements and constraints, your design must

- Ensure that IP addresses previously assigned to computers no longer connected to a network segment are removed after 45 days
- Provide automatic IP configuration for each network segment that contains desktop computers or kiosks
- Automatically set the default gateway to the router connected to each network segment that contains desktop computers or kiosks
- Automatically set the DNS entries to use the DNS server within each private network
- Utilize 10.0.0.0/8 to assign private IP addresses

Note For the purposes of this lab, treat the private IP address range 10.0.0.0/8 as a public address.

- Reserve 10.x.y.1 – 10.x.y.10 for IP routers, and 10.x.y.200 – 10.x.y.254 for file and print servers on each network segment
- All IP routers in the design are Routing and Remote Access-based routers
- Eliminate any broadcast traffic between network segments

Table 8.10 lists each network segment and the IP address range assigned to the network segment.

Table 8.10   IP Address Ranges Assigned to Network Segments

Segment	IP Address Range
Segment A	10.0.1.1 – 10.0.1.254 (10.0.1.0/24)
Segment B	10.0.2.1 – 10.0.2.254 (10.0.2.0/24)
Segment C	10.0.3.1 – 10.0.3.254 (10.0.3.0/24)
Segment D	10.0.4.1 – 10.0.4.254 (10.0.4.0/24)
Segment E	10.0.5.1 – 10.0.5.254 (10.0.5.0/24)
Segment F	10.0.6.1 – 10.0.6.254 (10.0.6.0/24)
Segment G	10.0.7.1 – 10.0.7.254 (10.0.7.0/24)
Segment H	10.0.8.1 – 10.0.8.254 (10.0.8.0/24)
Segment I	10.0.9.1 – 10.0.9.254 (10.0.9.0/24)
Segment J	10.0.10.1 – 10.0.10.254 (10.0.10.0/24)
Segment K	10.0.11.1 – 10.0.11.254 (10.0.11.0/24)
Segment L	10.0.12.1 – 10.0.12.254 (10.0.12.0/24)

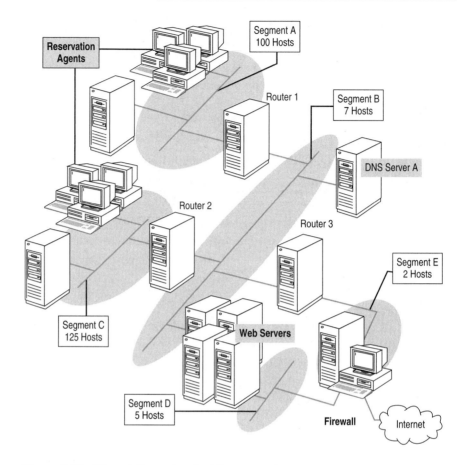

Figure 8.22   The existing network at the reservation center

Design Worksheet – Figure 8.22
Reservation Center – DHCP Servers A and B

DHCP Server A Specifications				Comments
DHCP server connects to segment: _____				
Scopes managed by the DHCP server				
Scope name	IP address range	IP address exclusion range	Lease length	
DHCP scope options				
❏ Server options (specify options in Comments column)				
❏ Scope options (specify options in Comments column)				
❏ Class options (specify options in Comments column)				
❏ Client options (specify options in Comments column)				
❏ Install on cluster node Cluster name: _____				
DHCP Server B Specifications				**Comments**
DHCP server connects to segment: _____				
Scopes managed by the DHCP server				
Scope name	IP address range	IP address exclusion range	Lease length	
DHCP scope options				
❏ Server options (specify options in Comments column)				
❏ Scope options (specify options in Comments column)				
❏ Class options (specify options in Comments column)				
❏ Client options (specify options in Comments column)				
❏ Install on cluster node Cluster name: _____				

Design Worksheet – Figure 8.22
Reservation Center – DHCP Servers C and D

DHCP Server C Specifications				Comments
DHCP server connects to segment: _____				
Scopes managed by the DHCP server				
Scope name	IP address range	IP address exclusion range	Lease length	
DHCP scope options				
❏ Server options (specify options in Comments column)				
❏ Scope options (specify options in Comments column)				
❏ Class options (specify options in Comments column)				
❏ Client options (specify options in Comments column)				
❏ Install on cluster node Cluster name: _____				
DHCP Server D Specifications				**Comments**
DHCP server connects to segment: _____				
Scopes managed by the DHCP server				
Scope name	IP address range	IP address exclusion range	Lease length	
DHCP scope options				
❏ Server options (specify options in Comments column)				
❏ Scope options (specify options in Comments column)				
❏ Class options (specify options in Comments column)				
❏ Client options (specify options in Comments column)				
❏ Install on cluster node Cluster name: _____				

Design Worksheet – Figure 8.22
Reservation Center – Router/DHCP Relay Agents

Router name	Router specifications	Comments
Router 1	❑ Enable DHCP/BOOTP forwarding ❑ Enable DHCP Relay Agent (specify DHCP server name to forward DHCP traffic to in the *Comments* column).	
Router 1	❑ Enable DHCP/BOOTP forwarding ❑ Enable DHCP Relay Agent (specify DHCP server name to forward DHCP traffic to in the *Comments* column).	
	❑ Enable DHCP/BOOTP forwarding ❑ Enable DHCP Relay Agent (specify DHCP server name to forward DHCP traffic to in the *Comments* column).	
	❑ Enable DHCP/BOOTP forwarding ❑ Enable DHCP Relay Agent (specify DHCP server name to forward DHCP traffic to in the *Comments* column).	

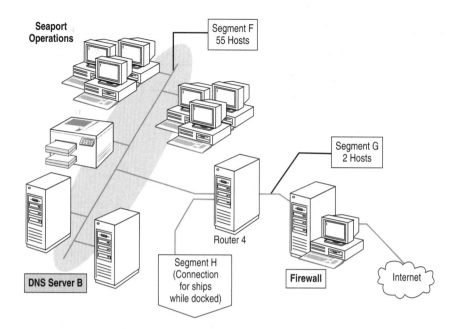

Figure 8.23   The existing network at seaports. For the purposes of this lab, assume that all these seaports have the same network configuration.

Design Worksheet – Figure 8.23
Seaport – DHCP Servers A and B

DHCP Server A Specifications				Comments
DHCP server connects to segment: _____				
Scopes managed by the DHCP server				
Scope name	IP address range	IP address exclusion range	Lease length	
DHCP scope options				
❏ Server options (specify options in Comments column)				
❏ Scope options (specify options in Comments column)				
❏ Class options (specify options in Comments column)				
❏ Client options (specify options in Comments column)				
❏ Install on cluster node Cluster name: _____				
DHCP Server B Specifications				**Comments**
DHCP server connects to segment: _____				
Scopes managed by the DHCP server				
Scope name	IP address range	IP address exclusion range	Lease length	
DHCP scope options				
❏ Server options (specify options in Comments column)				
❏ Scope options (specify options in Comments column)				
❏ Class options (specify options in Comments column)				
❏ Client options (specify options in Comments column)				
❏ Install on cluster node Cluster name: _____				

Design Worksheet – Figure 8.23
Seaport – DHCP Servers C and D

DHCP Server C Specifications				Comments
DHCP server connects to segment: _____				
Scopes managed by the DHCP server				
Scope name	IP address range	IP address exclusion range	Lease length	
DHCP scope options				
❑ Server options (specify options in Comments column)				
❑ Scope options (specify options in Comments column)				
❑ Class options (specify options in Comments column)				
❑ Client options (specify options in Comments column)				
❑ Install on cluster node Cluster name: _____				

DHCP Server D Specifications				Comments
DHCP server connects to segment: _____				
Scopes managed by the DHCP server				
Scope name	IP address range	IP address exclusion range	Lease length	
DHCP scope options				
❑ Server options (specify options in Comments column)				
❑ Scope options (specify options in Comments column)				
❑ Class options (specify options in Comments column)				
❑ Client options (specify options in Comments column)				
❑ Install on cluster node Cluster name: _____				

Design Worksheet – Figure 8.23
Seaport – Router/DHCP Relay Agents

Router name	Router specifications	Comments
	❑ Enable DHCP/BOOTP forwarding ❑ Enable DHCP Relay Agent (specify DHCP server name to forward DHCP traffic to in the *Comments* column).	
	❑ Enable DHCP/BOOTP forwarding ❑ Enable DHCP Relay Agent (specify DHCP server name to forward DHCP traffic to in the *Comments* column).	
	❑ Enable DHCP/BOOTP forwarding ❑ Enable DHCP Relay Agent (specify DHCP server name to forward DHCP traffic to in the *Comments* column).	
	❑ Enable DHCP/BOOTP forwarding ❑ Enable DHCP Relay Agent (specify DHCP server name to forward DHCP traffic to in the *Comments* column).	

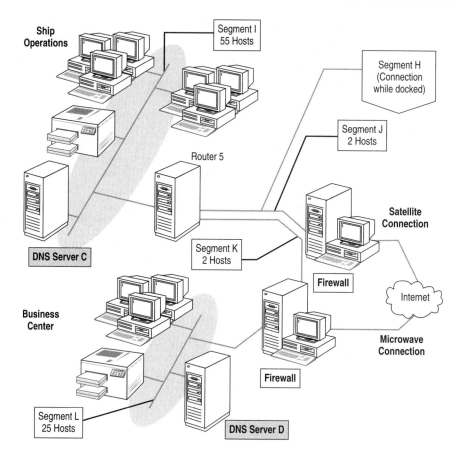

Figure 8.24   The existing network on a cruise ship. For the purposes of this lab, assume that all cruise ships have the same network configuration.

Design Worksheet – Figure 8.24
Cruise Ship – DHCP Servers A and B

DHCP Server A Specifications				Comments
DHCP server connects to segment: _____				
Scopes managed by the DHCP server				
Scope name	IP address range	IP address exclusion range	Lease length	
DHCP scope options				
❏ Server options (specify options in Comments column)				
❏ Scope options (specify options in Comments column)				
❏ Class options (specify options in Comments column)				
❏ Client options (specify options in Comments column)				
❏ Install on cluster node Cluster name: _____				

DHCP Server B Specifications				Comments
DHCP server connects to segment: _____				
Scopes managed by the DHCP server				
Scope name	IP address range	IP address exclusion range	Lease length	
DHCP scope options				
❏ Server options (specify options in Comments column)				
❏ Scope options (specify options in Comments column)				
❏ Class options (specify options in Comments column)				
❏ Client options (specify options in Comments column)				
❏ Install on cluster node Cluster name: _____				

Design Worksheet – Figure 8.24
Cruise Ship – DHCP Servers C and D

DHCP Server C Specifications				**Comments**
DHCP server connects to segment: _____				
Scopes managed by the DHCP server				
Scope name	**IP address range**	**IP address exclusion range**	**Lease length**	
DHCP scope options				
❑ Server options (specify options in Comments column)				
❑ Scope options (specify options in Comments column)				
❑ Class options (specify options in Comments column)				
❑ Client options (specify options in Comments column)				
❑ Install on cluster node Cluster name: _____				
DHCP Server D Specifications				**Comments**
DHCP server connects to segment: _____				
Scopes managed by the DHCP server				
Scope name	**IP address range**	**IP address exclusion range**	**Lease length**	
DHCP scope options				
❑ Server options (specify options in Comments column)				
❑ Scope options (specify options in Comments column)				
❑ Class options (specify options in Comments column)				
❑ Client options (specify options in Comments column)				
❑ Install on cluster node Cluster name: _____				

Design Worksheet – Figure 8.24
Cruise Ship – Router/DHCP Relay Agents

Router name	Router specifications	Comments
	❑ Enable DHCP/BOOTP forwarding ❑ Enable DHCP Relay Agent (specify DHCP server name to forward DHCP traffic to in the *Comments* column).	
	❑ Enable DHCP/BOOTP forwarding ❑ Enable DHCP Relay Agent (specify DHCP server name to forward DHCP traffic to in the *Comments* column).	
	❑ Enable DHCP/BOOTP forwarding ❑ Enable DHCP Relay Agent (specify DHCP server name to forward DHCP traffic to in the *Comments* column).	
	❑ Enable DHCP/BOOTP forwarding ❑ Enable DHCP Relay Agent (specify DHCP server name to forward DHCP traffic to in the *Comments* column).	

Review

The following questions are intended to reinforce key information in this chapter. If you're unable to answer a question, review the lesson and then try to answer the question again. Answers to the questions can be found in the Appendix, "Questions and Answers."

1. An organization currently administers the IP network configuration manually. The organization is comprised of 35 locations and each location has an average of 20 routed network segments. Each location contains a 100Mbps backbone segment that connects the other network segments to one another. The organization supports a variety of desktop operating systems. As an independent consultant, what recommendations can you make to the organization?

2. You're evaluating an existing DHCP design for a pharmaceutical company that has 230 research and development facilities throughout the world. The organization wants to ensure that all computers, those with manually assigned IP addresses and those with automatically assigned IP addresses, are listed in the organization's DNS servers. What recommendations can you make to the company?

3. You're evaluating an existing DHCP design for an international accounting firm that has locations throughout the world. The accounting firm is concerned about the ability of the Windows 2000–based DHCP servers to provide IP configuration at all times, regardless of a single point of failure. What changes to the design can you recommend to ensure that DHCP clients always receive the IP configuration *transparently*?

4. During the first 30 minutes of the business day, the users on your network notice a perceptible delay in DHCP configuration. You examine the network segment and router utilization and determine that the network segments and routers aren't the source of the DHCP configuration latency. You determine that the disk subsystem for the DHCP servers is unable to fulfill all the concurrent DHCP configuration requests. What changes to your DHCP design can you recommend to resolve these performance issues?

C H A P T E R   9

DNS in Name Resolution Designs

About This Chapter

The majority of the networking services designs that you create will utilize Internet Protocol (IP) to access resources within the organization and resources on the Internet. These resources can be accessed by the IP address assigned to the resource. Although accessing these resources by IP address is technically possible, many users are unable to cope with the complexities of accessing resources by IP address.

Most of the designs that you create will provide the facility to associate a meaningful name to the resources within the organization and on the Internet. Your design must translate these meaningful resource names to IP addresses. Also, most of your designs will require you to perform the reverse operation (translate an IP address into a meaningful resource name).

Your designs will often include migrating networks from Microsoft Windows NT 4.0 to Microsoft Windows 2000. The majority of Windows NT 4.0–based networks run on the Transmission Control Protocol/Internet Protocol (TCP/IP) and rely heavily on Windows Internet Name Service (WINS) for accessing resources within the organization. Your design must be capable of integrating WINS–based name resolution into your name resolution design.

You can use the Domain Name System (DNS) services in Windows 2000 to translate or *resolve* these meaningful resource names to IP addresses and to translate an IP address to a meaningful resource name. The DNS services in Windows 2000 can automatically register the organization's computers in DNS, reducing the amount of time required to administer DNS.

You can integrate WINS-based computers into a DNS-based network by using the integration between the DNS services and WINS services in Windows 2000. Windows 2000 allows users on your network to transparently resolve names by using DNS or WINS.

This chapter answers questions such as:

- In what situations are the name resolution services provided by DNS appropriate for your design?
- What must you include in your DNS design to support Active Directory?
- How can you integrate DNS in Windows 2000 with other DNS servers?
- What must you include in your design to integrate DNS with WINS?
- How can you ensure the integrity of the DNS database?
- What can you include in your design to ensure that DNS name resolution is always available to network users?
- How can you improve the performance of DNS name resolution during peak periods of activity?

Before You Begin

Before you begin, you must have an overall understanding of

- Network technologies (including Ethernet, Token Ring, hubs, switches, and concentrators)
- Common transport protocol configuration for IP (such as IP address, subnet mask, or default gateway for IP)
- IP routed networks (including subnets, network segments, routers, and IP switches)
- DNS usage in a network (including DNS namespace conventions, resource-record types, and name resolution)
- Integration between DNS and WINS (when both DNS and WINS are included in the same name resolution design)
- Integration between DNS and Dynamic Host Configuration Protocol (DHCP) (when both DNS and DHCP are included in the same name resolution design)

Lesson 1: Designs That Include DNS

This lesson presents the requirements and constraints, both business and technical, that identify the name resolution services in DNS as a solution.

After this lesson, you will be able to

- Identify the situation in which DNS is the appropriate choice for name resolution
- Describe the relationship between DNS and Windows 2000
- Identify the business and technical requirements and constraints that must be collected to create a DNS design
- Identify the DNS design decisions
- Evaluate scenarios and determine which capabilities and features of DNS are appropriate in name resolution solutions

Estimated lesson time: 30 minutes

DNS and Name Resolution in Networking Services Designs

In the "About This Chapter" section, the primary requirement for including DNS in your design was presented—name resolution. However, there are solutions other than DNS that you can include in your design to provide name resolution.

In addition to DNS, you can provide name resolution by using

- A HOSTS file on the local computer
- A LMHOSTS file on the local computer or on shared computers
- WINS

Table 9.1 lists each of the methods of DNS and the advantages and disadvantages of including that method in your design.

Table 9.1   Advantages and Disadvantages of DNS Methods

Method	Advantages	Disadvantages
HOSTS	Available on all network operating systems Independent of other computers because the HOSTS file is stored locally	Requires administration on every computer Integrity of the HOSTS file can be compromised because users can modify the file
LMHOSTS	Provides enhanced support above HOSTS file for WINS (NetBIOS) names Can reference a centralized copy of a LMHOSTS file to reduce administration	Available only on Microsoft operating systems Requires administration on every computer Integrity of the LMHOSTS file can be compromised because users can modify the file

(continued)

Table 9.1   *(continued)*

Method	Advantages	Disadvantages
WINS	Supports automatic registration of client computers Centralized name resolution database to reduce administration and configuration errors	Designed for name resolution for NetBIOS names [fully qualified domain names (FQDNs) aren't fully supported]
DNS	Only name resolution method that supports Active Directory directory service Centralized name resolution to reduce administration and configuration errors Provides full support for FQDNs Can provide name resolution for NetBIOS names in addition to FQDNs	Name registration may not be automatic (requires dynamically updateable DNS servers) Not all versions on other operating systems support Active Directory Complexity associated with configuring DNS might be daunting for some administrators or organizations

Although other methods are available, DNS is the only method that provides all of the following:

- Centralized administration
- Support for Active Directory
- Support for FQDN name resolution
- Support for NetBIOS name resolution

This chapter focuses on designs that include DNS for FQDN name resolution. For more information on NetBIOS name resolution and WINS, see Chapter 10, "WINS in Name Resolution Designs."

DNS and Windows 2000

DNS is an industry standard protocol that provides *forward name resolution* and *reverse name resolution*. In forward name resolution, a DNS server receives FQDNs from DNS clients and returns corresponding IP addresses. In reverse name resolution, a DNS server receives IP addresses and returns corresponding FQDNs.

The DNS services in Windows 2000 can be divided into

- **DNS Client**   You can configure the IP stack for all versions of Windows to resolve FQDNs by using DNS. The DNS Client is an integral part of the IP implemented in Windows 2000. The DNS Client receives requests for FQDN name resolution from applications running on the same computer and forwards the requests to DNS servers.

> **Note** Microsoft Windows 95, Microsoft Windows 98, Microsoft Windows Me, Microsoft Windows NT 4.0, UNIX, Macintosh, and other operating systems include DNS clients as well.

- **DNS Server** The DNS Server service in Windows 2000 can provide forward and reverse name resolution to DNS clients in your design. From the Windows 2000 perspective, DNS Server is a service that runs on Windows 2000. The DNS Server service utilizes IP and the file services of Windows 2000.

  The DNS Server service communicates with DNS clients, other DNS servers, Active Directory domain controllers, WINS servers, and Dynamic Host Configuration Protocol (DHCP) servers by using the IP stack in Windows 2000. You must specify a fixed IP address for all network interfaces on the DNS server that communicate with the DNS Server service.

  The DNS Server service in Windows 2000 manages a database stored locally on the DNS server. The DNS database contains the DNS records for forward and reverse name resolution that are resolved by the DNS server.

  The DNS Server service is available in Microsoft Windows 2000 Server, Microsoft Windows 2000 Advanced Server, and Microsoft Windows 2000 Datacenter Server. The DNS Server service isn't available in Microsoft Windows 2000 Professional.

In this chapter, you learn how to create name resolution designs with DNS and Windows 2000. Figure 9.1 illustrates the interaction between DHCP and the other networking services in Windows 2000.

To successfully create DNS designs, you must be familiar with

- General IP and IP routing theory
- General DNS and Berkeley Internet Name Domain (BIND) server theory
- Common DNS resource records types and formats
- General domain namespace design theory

> **Note** A full discussion of domain namespace design is beyond the scope of this chapter. Domain namespace design is only discussed as how domain namespace design affects DNS networking services designs.

DNS Design Requirements and Constraints

Before you create your DNS design, you must gather the requirements and constraints, both business and technical, of the organization. As you create your design, you make design decisions based on the requirements and constraints you collect.

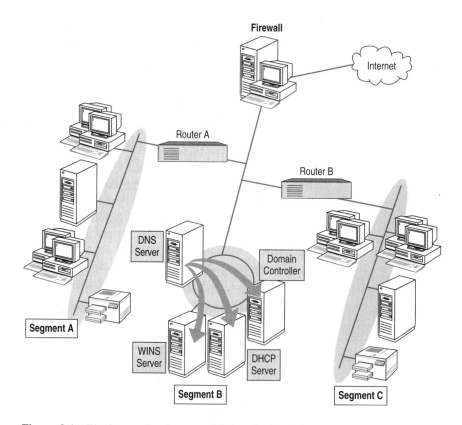

Figure 9.1   The interaction between DNS and other Windows 2000 networking services

The list of the design requirements and constraints that you collect will include

- The amount of data transmitted between the existing network segments containing the DNS clients and the DNS server
- Number of locations and network segments that require name resolution
- Wide area network (WAN) connections in use
- Plans for network growth
- Current domain namespace design for the organization
- Characteristics of existing DNS servers including
  - Number of DNS resource records in existing DNS databases
  - DNS server placement
  - Operating systems running current DNS servers
  - Versions of DNS servers running on other operating systems

DNS Design Decisions

After you determine the business and technical requirements and constraints, apply the information you gathered to make DNS design decisions.

To create your DNS design, you must choose the

- Methods for integrating DNS into the existing network based on the
    - Existing domain namespace design
    - Operating systems and the DNS or BIND versions of any existing DNS servers
    - Placement of existing DNS servers
    - Existing WINS servers
    - Type of DNS zones required in the design
- Method of ensuring that DNS name resolution is always available to DNS clients
- Method of optimizing the network traffic between DNS clients and DNS servers

The lessons that follow in this chapter provide the information required for you to make specific DNS design recommendations.

DNS and Active Directory Designs

Most of the DNS solutions that you create must support Active Directory directory service. When the organization's requirements include Active Directory, you must include DNS in your design. Your primary concern in Active Directory is ensuring that domain controllers, member servers, and client computers can resolve IP addresses for Active Directory objects stored in DNS.

Making the Decision

In DNS and Active Directory designs, you must decide the DNS features utilized by Active Directory. Some of the DNS features must be included in your design because Active Directory requires them. Other features aren't required, but can reduce the complexity and administration associated with your design.

Table 9.2 lists the DNS features to include, whether the feature is required, and the versions of DNS that support the feature.

Table 9.2   DNS Features That Support Active Directory

Feature	Required	DNS Versions
Support for SRV (service) resource records	Required	BIND 4.9.6 and later versions DNS in Windows 2000

(continued)

Table 9.2   *(continued)*

Feature	Required	DNS Versions
Dynamically updated zones	Optional	BIND 8.1.2 and later versions DNS in Windows 2000
Incremental zone updates	Optional	BIND 8.2.1 and later versions DNS in Windows 2000

Tip   Although BIND 4.9.6 and later versions can support Active Directory, BIND version 8.2.2 is recommended because it's the latest version and supports all the enhanced DNS features.

In addition to the features provided by BIND DNS servers, the DNS services in Windows 2000 provide these additional features:

- **Store DNS zone databases in Active Directory**   When you include Active Directory directory service in your design, you can store the zone database resource records in Active Directory. To store zone database resource records in Active Directory, you must specify the zone an Active Directory integrated zone.

- **Replicate DNS zone databases between DNS servers by using Active Directory replication**   Any Active Directory integrated zones in your design can be replicated by using traditional DNS zone replication or by using Active Directory. Because the zone database is stored in Active Directory, the zone database is replicated along with the other data stored in Active Directory.

- **Automatic management of DNS resource records for computers running Windows 2000 or for computers configured by using DHCP**   You can specify that any computer running Windows 2000 or any computer configured by the DHCP Server service in Windows 2000 dynamically update corresponding resource records in DNS. When the DNS zone is an Active Directory integrated zone, you can restrict the computers, groups, or users that can modify the DNS zone information.

  DNS and DHCP integration are discussed further in Lesson 2, "Essential DNS Design Concepts," and Lesson 3, "Name Resolution Protection in DNS Designs," later in this chapter. For more information on DHCP, see Chapter 8, "DHCP in IP Configuration Designs."

- **Integration with WINS servers**   You can forward unresolved DNS queries to WINS servers in the organization. The WINS servers search the WINS database to resolve host names. In addition, you can forward unresolved WINS queries to DNS servers. The DNS servers search the specified domain namespace to resolve NetBIOS names.

DNS and WINS integration are discussed further in Lesson 2, "Essential DNS Design Concepts," later in this chapter. For more information on WINS, see Chapter 10, "WINS in Name Resolution Designs."

Applying the Decision

Figure 9.2 illustrates a scenario where Active Directory is the primary reason for including DNS. DNS Server A provides name configuration for Active Directory domain controllers, member servers, and client computers. DNS Server A is placed centrally in the private network to provide equal access to all domain controllers, member servers, and client computers.

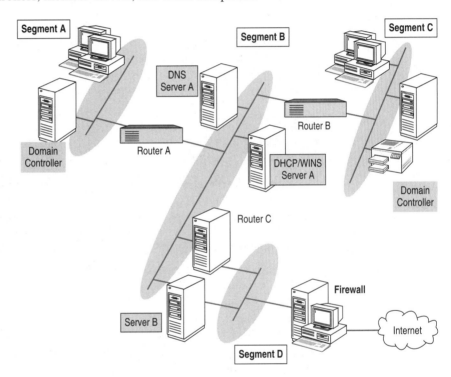

Figure 9.2   Scenario that includes DNS to support Active Directory

For the purposes of this scenario, assume that

- Approximately 400 client computers exist on Segments A and C

- The organization has decided to standardize Active Directory as its directory service

- The organization wants to reduce the administration by automatically registering client computers in DNS

- DHCP servers in the organization configure all client computers

- Any unresolved DNS queries must be forwarded to the organization's WINS servers

The DNS in Windows 2000 is the only solution that meets the requirements of the organization. As a result, HOSTS files, LMHOSTS files, WINS, or other implementations of DNS aren't appropriate solutions.

Traditional DNS Designs

There might be instances when you require DNS services, but Active Directory isn't one of the requirements of the organization. Traditional DNS designs require only a subset of the features in designs that include Active Directory.

Your traditional DNS designs interact with DNS servers on the Internet and within the organization's private network. In these situations, your primary concern in these designs is providing Request for Comments (RFC)-compliant interoperability with other DNS servers.

Making the Decision

You can achieve interoperability with other DNS servers by ensuring that your DNS server design supports

- **A common character set**   The character set approved for Internet host names is restricted to the US-ASCII-based characters. These restrictions limit names that include upper- and lowercase letters (A-Z, a-z), numbers (0-9), and hyphens (-). These restrictions were included in RFC 1035 as part of the core specifications for DNS.

  The DNS server in Windows 2000 supports all the requirements for RFC 1035. In addition, the DNS server in Windows 2000 supports Unicode transformation format-8 (UTF-8). UTF-8 supports extended ASCII to incorporate other languages. In addition UTF-8 can incorporate names that use characters beyond the RFC 1035 restrictions.

  To support interoperability with other DNS servers, you must specify that all DNS servers adhere to the specifications of RFC 1035.

- **The same DNS zone transfer method**   DNS servers can exchange updates to resource records in DNS zones by performing *incremental zone transfers* or *full zone transfers*. Incremental zone transfers send only the resource records that change. Full zone transfers send the entire contents of the zone.

  Complete zone transfers are supported by all versions of DNS. Incremental zone transfers are supported only on DNS servers that are compliant with RFC 1995, such as BIND versions 8.2.1 and later. To ensure proper interoperability, all DNS servers must use either incremental zone transfers or full zone transfers.

- **The same compression method in DNS zone transfers**   DNS servers can perform incremental DNS zone transfers by using a *slow transfer method* or *fast transfer method*. The slow transfer method transfers a single resource record in an uncompressed format. The fast transfer method transfers multiple resource records at a time in a compressed format.

  The DNS services in Windows 2000 transfer resource records by using the fast transfer method as the default. When your designs include DNS servers running BIND versions 4.9.4 or earlier, you must specify that all DNS servers support the slow transfer method.

- **The appropriate DNS resource record types**   Different implementations of DNS servers can support different DNS resource record types. Most DNS servers reject any DNS resource records that aren't supported by the DNS server.

  For example, assume that a DNS server doesn't support service (SRV) resources records. If another DNS server transfers SRV resource records to the DNS server, the DNS server rejects the SRV resource records.

  You must ensure that all the DNS servers in the design support the DNS resource records in use by the organization.

- **Dynamic DNS zone update protocol**   If the organization requires dynamic updates to DNS, you must ensure that all DNS servers in your design support dynamic updates. The DNS services in Windows 2000 support dynamic updates compatible with RFC 2136. DNS servers running BIND versions 8.1.2 or later are compatible with RFC 2136 and support dynamic updates.

Applying the Decision

Figure 9.3 illustrates a design where the DNS services in Windows 2000 are incorporated with BIND DNS servers. For the purposes of this scenario, assume that

- DNS Servers A and B in the organization are running Windows 2000

- DNS Servers C, D, and E in the organization are BIND version 4.9.4

- DNS Server A replicates zone information to DNS Server C and E

- DNS Server D replicates zone information to DNS Server B

To provide interoperability between the DNS servers running on Windows 2000 and the BIND DNS servers, you must ensure that your design includes

- Only standard ASCII characters for host names as specified in RFC 1035

- Full zone transfers between DNS servers

- Slow zone transfers between DNS servers

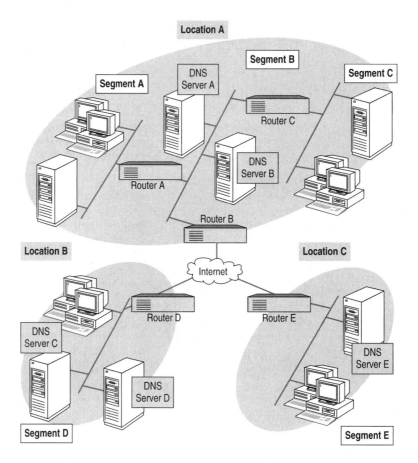

Figure 9.3 Scenario that incorporates DNS services in Windows 2000 with BIND DNS servers

Lesson 2: Essential DNS Design Concepts

This lesson discusses the requirements, constraints, and design decisions used in establishing the essential specifications in a DNS design. This lesson discusses the design concepts common to all DNS designs.

After this lesson, you will be able to

- Determine how the organization's domain namespace affects your design
- Select the appropriate zone types to include in your design
- Determine the placement of DNS servers in your design
- Select the appropriate method for integrating DNS with other versions of DNS
- Select the appropriate method for integrating DNS name resolution and WINS name resolution

Estimated lesson time: 45 minutes

Determining Domain Namespace Influences on DNS

You must determine the structure of the organization's domain namespace to create your DNS design. The domain namespace is represented in your design by the DNS resource records managed by the DNS servers.

The organization's domain namespace affects the type of zones you can include in your design. In addition, the placement of DNS servers in your design is partially based on the organization's domain namespace.

Making the Decision

To determine how the organization's domain namespace affects a DNS design, you must evaluate the relationships between

- The organization's domain namespace and Internet naming conventions
- The external and internal namespaces of the organization
- Active Directory and the organization's domain namespace
- The organization's namespace and subdomains that exist within the namespace
- The domain namespace and DNS zones

Domain Namespaces and Internet Naming Conventions

The majority of the designs you create will include domain namespaces accessed by Internet users. Domain namespaces you expose to the Internet must adhere to specific naming conventions. All domain namespace designs you encounter are based, at least in part, on these Internet naming conventions.

The DNS domain namespace is based on the concept of a hierarchical tree structure of named domains. Each level in the tree structure of your domain namespace is either a *branch level* or a *leaf level* of the tree. The branch level domain names in your design contain other domain names (branch levels) or multiple DNS resource records (leaf levels). The leaf level domain names in your design are resource records that represent a specific resource.

The structure of any domain name is interpreted from right to left. The rightmost portion of any domain name is the highest portion in the domain name's hierarchical structure. The leftmost portion of any domain name is the lowest portion in the domain name's hierarchical structure.

Table 9.3 lists the types of domain names found in a domain namespace and a description of each type.

Table 9.3   Descriptions of Domain Namespaces

Domain Name Type	Description
Domain root	The highest portion of the domain namespace tree. The domain root is an unnamed portion of a domain name space that is designated by a trailing period ".". You must include the domain root to specify a FQDN.
Top-level domain	Two or three letter names that designate the country, region, or type of organization using the name. You must obtain top-level domain names from Internet governing originations (currently managed by Network Solutions, Inc.).
Second-level domain	Variable length domain names that designate the organization or individual for use on the Internet. You must obtain second-level domain names from Internet governing originations (currently managed by Network Solutions, Inc.).
Subdomains	Additional variable length domain names that designate an organization's internal structure (for example geographic or departmental). You can specify any number and levels of subdomains within your domain namespace design.
Host or resource name	Name of computers or groups of computers (such as clusters) within the organization. You can specify any number of resource names within your design.

Figure 9.4 illustrates an example of a domain namespace structure. In the example, you can see the following name structure:

- msft is the top-level domain name
- contoso is the second-level domain name
- asia is a subdomain name
- sales is a subdomain name
- ServerA is a host or resource name

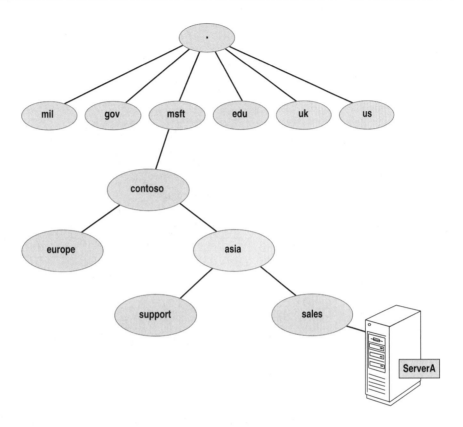

Figure 9.4   Example of a domain namespace structure

You can access ServerA from the Internet by specifying the FQDN for ServerA: *ServerA.sales.asia.contoso.msft.* (note the trailing period to specify the root).

Note   Although *msft* isn't an appropriate top-level domain, for the purposes of the example, assume that msft is a valid top-level domain name.

External and Internal Domain Namespaces

You can specify an organization's domain namespace as an *external* domain namespace, an *internal* domain namespace, or a combination of both. An external namespace is visible to Internet users and computers. An external namespace is the domain namespace that you're probably the most familiar with. All Internet domain names that you access are found in external namespaces. An internal domain namespace is visible only to the users and computers within the organization.

Figure 9.5 illustrates an example of an organization that has a combination of external and internal domain namespaces. In the example, Server-A resides in an external namespace (*external.contoso.msft.*) accessible by Internet users or

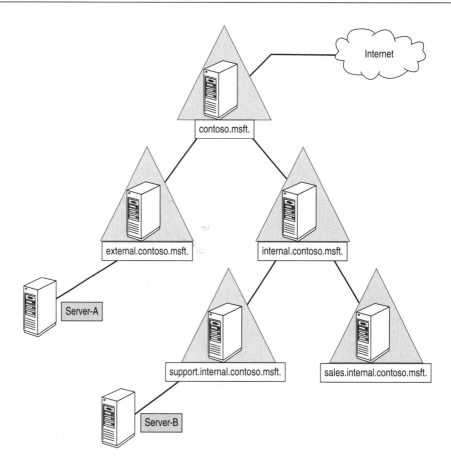

Figure 9.5   Example where an organization has a combination of external and internal domain namespaces

private network users. Server-B resides in an internal namespace (*support.internal.contoso.msft.*) accessible by only private network users.

An organization's internal domain namespace root can be a part of the same namespace root as the organization's external domain namespace root or a completely separate namespace. Ensure that your design's internal domain namespace root is different from *external* domain namespace roots for *other* organizations.

Figure 9.6 illustrates an example of an organization that has separate external and internal domain namespaces. In the example, *contoso.msft.* is the external namespace and Server-A resides in the external namespace. The internal namespace, *contoso-i.msft.*, contains the domain names for all the organization's resources that are accessed only by private network users. Server-B resides in the internal namespace and can be accessed only by private network users.

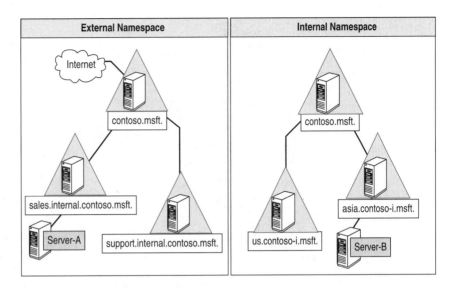

Figure 9.6   Example where an organization has separate external and internal
domain namespaces

In the example in Figure 9.6, the organization requires two domain namespace
roots (*contoso.msft.* and *contoso-i.msft.*). In the example in Figure 9.5, the external
and internal namespace share the same domain namespace root (*contoso.msft.*).

Although other organizations are unaware of your internal domain namespace
root, private network users access the internal domain namespace root to access
resources within the private network. If your *internal* domain namespace root is
identical to *another* organization's external domain namespace, the private network users aren't able to access resources in the *other* organization.

Figure 9.7 illustrates an example where an organization's internal domain
namespace is identical to another organization's external domain namespace.
When clients in Organization A attempt to access external domain names in Organization B (*salesco.msft.*), the DNS servers in Organization A attempt to resolve DNS
requests for *salesco.msft.* by using the internal DNS namespace servers. The DNS
requests aren't forwarded to the DNS servers in Organization B.

Domain Namespace and Subdomains

After you establish your external and internal namespaces, you must determine
the subdomains that exist in the namespace design. You can include subdomains
in your design to organize resources within an organization by departmental,
geographic, or other specifications.

You can include subdomains in the organization's external or internal namespace.
You can create any number of levels in your DNS tree structure by nesting
subdomains.

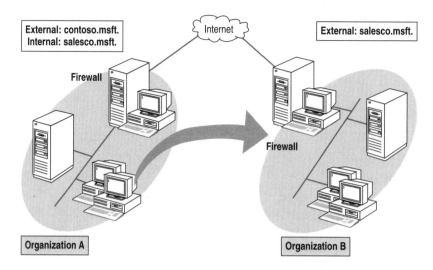

Figure 9.7   Example where an organization's internal domain namespace is identical to another organization's external domain namespace

Figure 9.8 illustrates an example where an organization's domain namespace includes subdomains. The organization has one namespace (*contoso.msft.*) that is subdivided by subdomains (*asia.contoso.msft.* and *europe.contoso.msft.*). The subdomain *europe.contoso.msft.* is further subdivided by subdomains (*support.europe.contoso.msft.* and *sales.europe.contoso.msft.*).

You can use subdomains to separate the external and internal namespaces when your namespace design contains a single domain namespace root. The examples in Figure 9.5, *external.contoso.msft.* and *internal.contoso.msft.*, are subdomains that divide the organization's internal and external namespace.

Domain Namespace and Active Directory

In the designs you create, you must determine how Active Directory is integrated into the organization's domain namespace. Active Directory domains correspond to DNS domain or subdomain names in your DNS designs.

In the DNS designs you create, ensure that the domains, and subdomains, used by Active Directory reside in the internal namespace. For more information on internal and external namespaces, see the previous section, "External and Internal Domain Namespaces."

For each domain in your Active Directory design, you must

- Include a DNS domain or subdomain in your DNS design
- Enable dynamically updated DNS zones when you want Active Directory to automatically create the domains or subdomains (when the DNS servers support dynamically updated DNS zones)

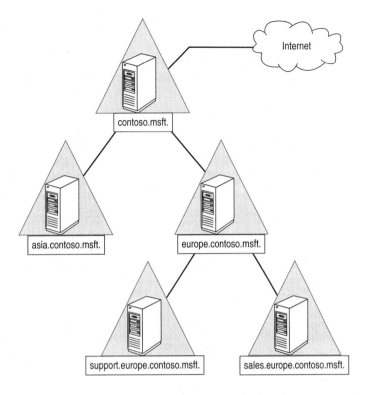

Figure 9.8 Example where an organization's domain namespace includes subdomains

- Manually create DNS domains or subdomains (when the DNS servers don't support dynamically updated DNS zones)

Domain Namespace and DNS Zones

After you analyze the organization's domain namespace, you must convert the domain namespace to DNS zones.

You can convert the domain namespace to DNS zones by

- **Including all domains, subdomains, and resource records in a single DNS zone** You place the entire domain namespace in a single DNS zone when the

  - Size of the organization's domain namespace is relatively small (to reduce the amount of zone replication between DNS servers)

  - Administration of the DNS servers is centrally performed (only one DNS zone to be administered)

  - Entire namespace is entirely an internal or external namespace

  - Entire namespace is entirely dynamically updated or manually updated

- **Specifying multiple DNS zones for corresponding domains and subdomains**   You can specify multiple DNS zones for corresponding domains and subdomains when the

  - Size of the organization's domain namespace is large and you want to reduce the number of resource records in a DNS zone (to reduce the amount of zone replication between DNS servers)
  - Administration of the DNS servers must be decentralized (each geographic region, department, or other subdomains must be individually administered)
  - Domain namespace includes the internal or external namespace (so you can segregate the internal namespace from the external namespace)
  - Domain namespace includes dynamically updated zones and manually updated zones

For each resource you want to advertise in DNS, create a corresponding DNS resource record. Resource records can include individual computers or cluster IP addresses.

Applying the Decision

Figure 9.9 depicts a scenario where the domain namespace must be converted to DNS zones. For the purposes of this scenario, assume that

- The *activedir* subdomain contains the organization's Active Directory domain information
- The *europe*, *asia*, and *africa* subdomains must be individually administered
- The *headq* and *admin* subdomains must be individually administered
- *msft* is a top-level domain name

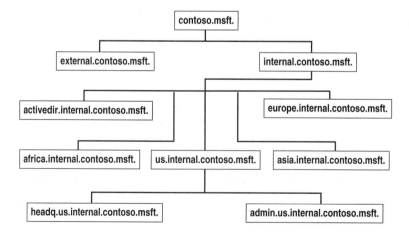

Figure 9.9   Scenario that illustrates the appropriate decisions in converting a domain namespace to DNS zones

Table 9.4 lists the DNS zones that can be created to achieve the organization's requirements and reason for including the DNS zones in your design.

Table 9.4   Reasons for Including DNS Zones in Your Design

DNS Zone	Reason for Including Zone
contoso.msft.	Organization's root domain that contains the external and internal namespace subdomains.
external.contoso.msft.	Subdomain that contains all resource records for resources accessed by Internet users.
internal.contoso.msft.	Subdomain that contains the subdomains for the organization's internal namespace.
activedir.internal.contoso.msft.	Subdomain that contains all the subdomains and resource records for Active Directory. In most designs, this zone is dynamically updated.
europe.internal.contoso.msft.	Subdomain that contains all resource records for the Europe geographic region that is administered by administrators in the same region.
africa.internal.contoso.msft.	Subdomain that contains all resource records for the Africa geographic region that is administered by administrators in the same region.
us.internal.contoso.msft.	Subdomain that contains all the subdomains for the United States geographic region that is administered by the administrators in the same region.
asia.internal.contoso.msft.	Subdomain that contains all resource records for the Asia geographic region that is administered by administrators in the same region.
headq.us.internal.contoso.msft.	Subdomain that contains all resource records for the United States geographic region and headquarters department that is administered by administrators in the same region and department.
admin.us.internal.contoso.msft.	Subdomain that contains all resource records for the United States geographic region and administration department that is administered by administrators in the same region and department.

Selecting the Zone Types

After you have evaluated the organization's domain namespace and converted the domain namespace to zones, you must determine the zone types to include in your design. Each DNS server in your design can manage one or more zones. Each zone you include on a DNS server can be a different zone type.

Making the Decision

Your design can include any combination of the following zone types:

- Active Directory integrated zones
- Traditional DNS zones

You can base your DNS design on Active Directory integrated or traditional DNS zones. DNS zone designs based on Active Directory integrated zones require that Active Directory be a part of your design. You can use traditional DNS zones with or without Active Directory.

Active Directory integrated zones are all the same in features and functions. Traditional DNS zones are either standard primary zones or standard secondary zones. Each traditional DNS zone type has unique features and functions.

The most important decision in your DNS design is the type of zone that will be *predominant* in your design. Your DNS design can be comprised of

- Only traditional DNS zones
- Only Active Directory integrated zones
- A combination of Active Directory integrated and traditional DNS zones

Traditional DNS Zones

Traditional DNS zones are identical to the DNS zones in BIND DNS servers. Traditional DNS zones

- **Store zone information in operating system files**   The zone information (resource records) is stored in separate files (one for each respective zone) by the operating system. The DNS service in Windows 2000 scans these files to resolve queries within the zone.

- **Store a *single*, read-write copy of the zone information in *primary* zones**   Traditional DNS zones can include only *one* read-write copy of the zone information, and the primary zone contains the *only* read-write copy of the zone information. The primary zone can be copied to secondary zones by using full or incremental zone transfers.

   You include primary zones in your design when you must provide read-write copies of the zone information to

   - Administer the domain namespace
   - Dynamically update the zone information
   - Create subdomains within the namespace and decrease the number of resource records within a domain

- **Store *multiple* read-only copies of the zone information in *secondary* zones**   Traditional DNS zones can include any number of read-only copies of the zone information. The secondary zone contains these read-only copies of the zone information. A secondary zone must be replicated from an existing primary zone. A secondary zone can't contain zone information from more than one primary zone.

  You include secondary zones in your design when you need to provide additional read-only copies of the zone information

  - To unsecured portions of the network

  - For DNS servers at remote locations to reduce WAN network traffic

  - For redundancy if the primary DNS zone becomes unavailable

  - For load balancing between DNS servers

- **Replicate zone information between DNS servers by using the same zone transfer methods available to BIND DNS servers**   You can replicate from primary zones to secondary zones by using full or incremental zone transfers.

You include traditional DNS zones as the predominant zone type in your design when

- **Interoperability with BIND DNS servers is desired**   You can transfer zone information between BIND DNS servers and the DNS services in Windows 2000. The DNS services in Windows 2000 can support standard primary zones or standard secondary zones in relation to BIND DNS servers.

- **The organization is unwilling or unable to include Active Directory in the design**   When requirements of the organization preclude Active Directory, you must include traditional DNS zones in your design.

- **Existing network support staff is familiar with BIND DNS servers**   When the existing staff is experienced in the support and administration of BIND DNS servers, you can include traditional DNS zones to reduce the training and learning curve when deploying the DNS services in Windows 2000.

- ***Secured* dynamic zone updates aren't a requirement in the design**   Primary DNS zones can't provide secured dynamic zone updates. Only Active Directory integrated zones can provide secured dynamic zone updates.

- **Read-only copies of the zone information must be placed on unsecured network segments**   When you must place a DNS server on unsecured network segments, you want to ensure that unauthorized users can't change the DNS zone information. You can include secondary DNS zones to ensure the integrity of the DNS zone information.

Active Directory Integrated Zone Designs

Active Directory integrated zones are unique to the DNS services in Windows 2000. Active Directory integrated zones

- **Store zone information in Active Directory**   The zone information (resource records) is stored in Active Directory. The DNS service scans Active Directory to resolve the DNS queries. The DNS service in Windows 2000 creates a separate organizational unit (OU) for each zone.

- **Store a *multimaster*, read-write copy of the zone information**   All copies of the Active Directory integrated zones are read-write copies of the zone information. You can modify any copy of an Active Directory integrated zone. Modifications to the Active Directory integrated zone are automatically replicated to other copies of the Active Directory integrated zone.

You include Active Directory integrated zones as your predominant zone type in your design when

- **Dynamically updated DNS zones are included in the design**   Because Active Directory integrated zones are multimaster copies of the zone information, you can perform dynamic updates to *any* copy of the zone. Traditional DNS zones only support a *single* read-write copy of a zone.

- ***Secured* dynamic zone updates are a requirement in the design**   Only Active Directory integrated zones can provide secured dynamic zone updates.

- **You want to reduce the administration associated with DNS replication**   Because Active Directory integrated zones store the zone information in Active Directory, zone information is replicated just like any other Active Directory data.

Traditional and Active Directory Integrated Zones

You can incorporate traditional and Active Directory integrated zones in the same design. You can substitute Active Directory integrated zones for any standard primary zones in your DNS design. Active Directory integrated zones can replicate zone information to secondary zones by using traditional DNS zone replication.

Applying the Decision

In Figure 9.10, a scenario illustrates the appropriate DNS zones in the design. For the purposes of this scenario, assume that

- The organization is standardizing Active Directory as its directory service

- Each geographic region must be individually administered

- All zones must be dynamically updated

You can include Active Directory integrated zones or traditional DNS zones to create a solution. All DNS zones must be either Active Directory integrated zones or standard primary zones because all zones must be dynamically updated.

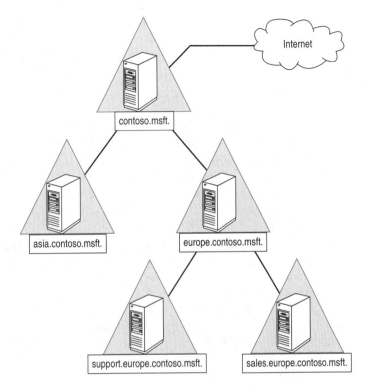

Figure 9.10   Scenario that illustrates the appropriate selection of DNS zones in the
design

Determining the Placement of DNS Servers

You must determine where to place the DNS servers in your design so you can
specify the appropriate number of DNS servers. Your design must include
enough DNS servers to support the DNS zones, and ultimately the domain
namespace, in your design.

Making the Decision

You must include DNS servers at each location within the organization to

- **Reduce WAN network traffic**   When your design includes multiple locations, include a DNS server at each location to reduce network traffic over
  WAN network segments that connect the locations. By including a DNS
  server at each location, you allow DNS queries to be resolved locally.

- **Provide support for Active Directory domain controllers**   Active Directory domain controllers make extensive use of DNS to resolve names for
  Active Directory objects. Include a DNS server in each location that you
  place an Active Directory domain controller.

- **Administer DNS at each location**   Any locations that must be locally administered must include a local DNS server. The local DNS servers must manage the portion of the domain namespace that contains local subdomains and resource records.

- **Improve DNS query response times**   By including a DNS server in each location, you allow DNS clients to resolve names locally. The local DNS server must contain the portion of the domain namespace commonly queried by the local DNS clients to improve query response times.

- **Provide load balancing between multiple DNS servers within the location** You can place additional DNS servers at each location to distribute DNS query traffic across the multiple DNS servers and improve performance. For more information on improving DNS performance with multiple DNS servers, see Lesson 4, "DNS Design Optimization," later in this chapter.

- **Provide redundancy with multiple DNS servers in the event of a DNS server failure**   You can place additional DNS servers at each location to provide fault-tolerance for existing DNS servers within the location. For more information on enhancing DNS availability with multiple DNS servers, see Lesson 4, "DNS Design Optimization," later in this chapter.

Applying the Decision

In Figure 9.11, a scenario illustrates the appropriate placement of DNS servers in the DNS design. For the purposes of this scenario, assume that

- Performance or availability issues aren't to be considered

- The organization wants to reduce the network traffic between locations

- DNS domains and resource records that correspond to each location must be individually administered

- Active Directory domain controllers are placed at each location

You must place at least one DNS server at each location to meet the requirements of the organization. Additional DNS servers aren't required currently because performance and availability issues aren't currently considered.

Integrating DNS with Other Versions of DNS

Many of the DNS designs that you create will require you to integrate the DNS services in Windows 2000 with other versions of DNS. The most common versions of DNS that you will encounter include BIND-based and Windows NT 4.0–based DNS servers.

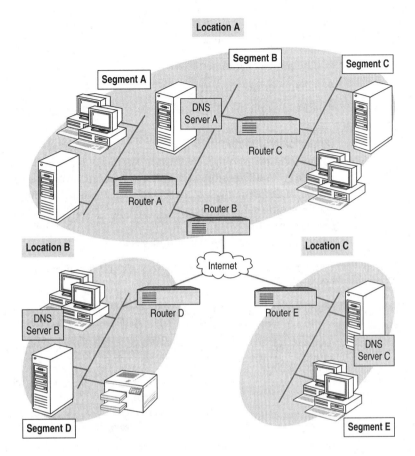

Figure 9.11   Scenario that illustrates the appropriate placement of DNS servers

Making the Decision

BIND DNS servers and the DNS services in Windows NT 4.0 support only traditional DNS zone types (standard primary and standard secondary zones). The design decisions for BIND-based and Windows NT 4.0–based DNS servers are the same as Window 2000–based DNS servers with traditional DNS zones.

Although Window 2000–based, BIND-based, and Windows NT 4.0–based DNS servers all support traditional DNS zones, the types of DNS resource records supported by each version of DNS server are different. In addition, not all versions of BIND-based and Windows NT 4.0–based DNS servers support dynamically updated DNS zones.

In your DNS design, you must examine each of the following integration features for all DNS servers in your design:

- Dynamically updated DNS zones
- Character set support
- RFC compliant and non-RFC compliant resource records

Dynamically Updated DNS Zones

Many solutions require *dynamically updated* DNS zones (especially those that include Active Directory) to reduce the administration of resource records in the zones. In dynamically updated DNS zones, desktop computers or automatic IP configuration servers, such as DHCP servers, automatically add and remove resource records from DNS zones. As a result, the DNS zones require little administration by network administrators.

Table 9.5 lists the type of DNS servers and the support for dynamically updated DNS zones.

Table 9.5   Dynamically Updated DNS Zone Support Based on the Type of DNS Server

DNS Servers	Dynamically Updated DNS Zone Support
Windows 2000	All zone types, Active Directory integrated and traditional DNS zones, support dynamic updates. Active Directory integrated zones are required to support *secured* dynamic updates. For more information on secured dynamically updated zones, see Lesson 3, "Name Resolution Protection in DNS Designs," later in this chapter.
BIND	Requires BIND 8.1.2 and later versions to support dynamically updated DNS zones.
Windows NT 4.0	Dynamically updated DNS zones aren't supported.

Character Set Supported in Zones

The DNS servers that manage the same zone must support the same character set. When you're including interoperability with other DNS servers in your design, include character sets as specified in RFC 1035. RFC 1035 is one of the core specifications for DNS on the Internet. All versions of DNS servers support the character sets as specified in RFC 1035.

The RFC 1035 specifications specify that characters you include in DNS zones include

- Only US-ASCII characters
- Uppercase and lowercase letters (A-Z, a-z)
- Numbers (0-9)
- Hyphens (-)

To provide compatibility with BIND-based and Windows NT 4.0–based DNS servers, ensure that all domain names within your domain namespace adhere to the specifications in RFC 1035. The names you must consider include

- Computer names
- Domain names
- NetBIOS names

Windows 2000 supports UTF-8 compatible characters in DNS zones. UTF-8 is a 16-bit Unicode character that supports extended ASCII characters and multiple languages. Include UTF-8 characters in your design only when all DNS servers are running Windows 2000.

Resource Records Supported in Zones

The DNS servers that manage the same zone must support the same types of resource records. The majority of DNS resource records, such as host address (A) and canonical name (CNAME) resource records, are common to all versions of DNS and are RFC compliant.

By default, most DNS servers ignore invalid resource records that are in the zone database. In addition, when most DNS servers receive invalid resource records during zone transfers, the DNS server can

- Ignore the invalid resource records
- Terminate the zone transfer when any invalid resource records are encountered

When Active Directory or WINS interoperability are included in your DNS design, your DNS zones include SRV, WINS forward lookup (WINS) resource records, or WINS reverse lookup (WINS-R) resource records. SRV records are required when Active Directory is included in your design.

WINS and WINS-R resource records are required when you want to integrate WINS and DNS in your design. For more information on WINS and DNS integration, see the following section, "Integrating DNS and WINS."

Table 9.6 lists the types of DNS resource records you may need to include in your design and the versions of DNS that support the resource record types.

Table 9.6   Resource Record Type Support in Operating Systems

Resource Records	Supported By
SRV	Windows 2000, Windows NT 4.0 with Service Pack 4 or later, and BIND 4.9.6 and later versions
WINS and WINS-R	Windows 2000 and Windows NT 4.0

Applying the Decision

In Figure 9.12, a scenario illustrates the integration of Windows 2000 and other DNS servers. For the purposes of this scenario, assume that

- Active Directory support is a requirement
- Future expansion might include DNS servers running on operating systems other than Windows 2000
- Secured dynamic updates must be performed on all DNS zones
- Names can also be resolved by using WINS servers

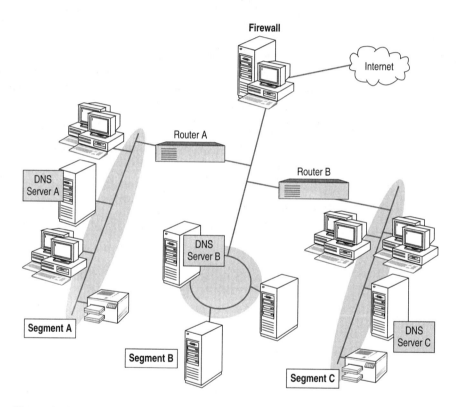

Figure 9.12   Scenario that illustrates the integration of Windows 2000 and other DNS servers

To fulfill the requirements of the organization, Active Directory integrated zones must be used for all zones on DNS Servers A, B, and C. Active Directory integrated zones are required because secured dynamic updates must be performed on all DNS severs.

Integrating DNS and WINS

Many of the organizations for which you create designs will have existing networks based on Windows NT 4.0. Windows NT 4.0 depends on NetBIOS names to locate network resources. As a result, the majority of organizations based on Windows NT 4.0 include WINS to register and resolve NetBIOS names.

In contrast, networks based on Windows 2000, especially network designs that include Active Directory, depend on domain names to locate network resources. As discussed previously in this chapter, networks based on Windows 2000 include DNS to register and resolve domain names.

You can resolve domain names in WINS by integrating the DNS service and WINS Server service in Windows 2000. You can integrate DNS and WINS as part of your migration strategy or as part of your permanent solution.

Making the Decision

Networks based on Windows NT 4.0 contain all the existing computer names and domain names in the WINS databases managed by the WINS servers. You can integrate the WINS NetBIOS names into DNS by specifying

- **A subdomain in your namespace for WINS resolution**   You must specify a subdomain within your namespace that acts as a container for the NetBIOS names that are resolved by WINS. When your domain namespace design includes external and internal namespaces, create the subdomain for WINS in the internal namespace.

  To reduce WAN traffic, create a subdomain for each location in your design. Ensure that the subdomain includes the WINS servers in the corresponding location.

- **The order in which names are resolved**   You must specify the order for name resolution in your design. You can resolve names from DNS and then WINS or from WINS and then DNS.

- **The WINS servers to integrate with DNS**   You must specify the IP address for the WINS servers that provide WINS name resolution for your design. To improve the availability in your name resolution design, reference more than one WINS server in your design.

Note   You can integrate WINS servers running on Windows 2000 or Windows NT 4.0 in your DNS design.

Applying the Decision

In Figure 9.13, a scenario illustrates the proper integration of DNS and WINS. For the purposes of this scenario, assume that

- The existing WINS servers are running Windows NT 4.0
- The WINS databases' content on WINS Servers A, B, and C is identical
- The organization has an external namespace (*external.contoso.msft.*) and internal namespace (*internal.contoso.msft.*)

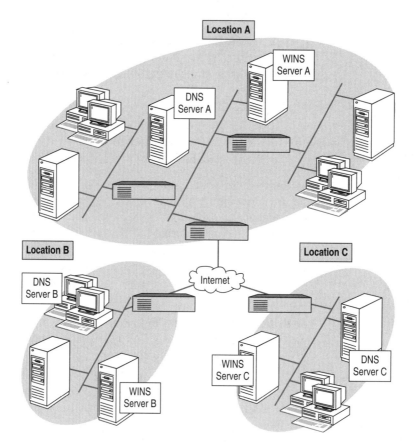

Figure 9.13   Scenario that illustrates the integration of DNS and WINS

You can integrate WINS into your DNS design by specifying

- Subdomains named wins.location-a.internal.contoso.msft., wins.location-b.internal.contoso.msft., and wins.location-c.internal.contoso.msft.
- Specify WINS Servers A, B, and C for each of the corresponding subdomains

Activity 9.1: Evaluating a DNS Design

In this activity, you're presented with a scenario. To complete the activity:

1. Evaluate the scenario and determine the design requirements
2. Answer questions and make design recommendations

In Figure 9.14, you see a map that illustrates the location of research facilities in a biotech consortium. The biotech consortium is comprised of eight biotech research firms working on a joint project to develop enhanced DNA sequencing equipment. Within *each* biotech research firm, a research facility is dedicated for use by the consortium.

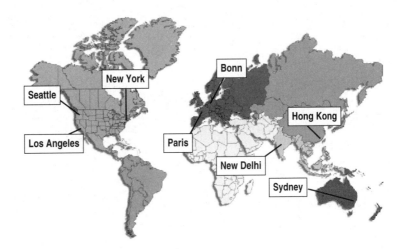

Figure 9.14 Map that illustrates the location of research facilities in a biotech consortium

The consortium is deploying Windows 2000 and Active Directory for use within the research facilities dedicated for use by the consortium. Scientists working within the research facilities must be able to access resources in other research facilities.

Each research facility's private network must

- Be administered by network support engineers within the biotech firm where the research facility is located
- Provide a unique domain namespace for the consortium

Answer the following questions concerning your design recommendations. Answers to the questions can be found in the Appendix, "Questions and Answers."

1. The consortium wants to allow the biotech firm's network support engineers to select the type of DNS servers in their own locations. As a consultant to the consortium, what recommendations can you make?

2. The director of information services for the consortium wants to reduce the administration for DNS zones. The director of technology is also concerned about the security of any automated updates to DNS zones. How can you minimize the DNS administration while ensuring integrity of DNS zones?

3. While collecting requirements from the biotech firms, you discover that many of the biotech firms have existing WINS servers. The biotech firms want to incorporate these WINS servers in their DNS designs (separate from the consortium's DNS design). What recommendations can you make to the biotech firms?

Lesson 3: Name Resolution Protection in DNS Designs

This lesson discusses how to create designs that protect the integrity of the name resolution by using DNS. This lesson focuses on preventing unauthorized updates to the DNS zones.

After this lesson, you will be able to

- Prevent unauthorized dynamic updates to DNS zones
- Prevent unauthorized administration of or access to DNS servers

Estimated lesson time: 30 minutes

Preventing Unauthorized Dynamic Updates to DNS Zones

When your designs include dynamically updated DNS zones, you can prevent unauthorized users or computers from dynamically updating the DNS zones. You can dynamically update DNS zones by using client operating systems (such as Windows 2000) or IP configuration servers (such as the DHCP Server in Windows 2000).

Making the Decision

You must determine how dynamic zone updates are performed and how to secure the updates to the zone in your design.

Performing Dynamic Zone Updates

You can dynamically update the host (A) and pointer (PTR) resource records in DNS by using

- **DHCP Server in Windows 2000**   Any IP configuration leased from a DHCP server in Windows 2000 can automatically update a DNS zone. You specify the DNS zone(s) that you want the DHCP server to update. On the corresponding DNS server, you specify that the DHCP server is the only computer authorized to update the records.

  Allowing DHCP to dynamically update DNS zones

  - Allows updates to DNS zone information for *any* DHCP client
  - Reduces the administration required because the DHCP server updates DNS for many clients

- **Windows 2000 DNS Client**   You can specify that the DNS Client in Windows 2000 automatically update DNS zone information. You specify the DNS zone(s) you want the DHCP server to update. On the corresponding DNS server, you specify that the computer running the DNS Client is the only computer authorized to update the records.

Allowing the DNS Client to dynamically update DNS zones

- Requires the DNS Client in Windows 2000

- Increases administration because each DNS Client must be configured to perform dynamic updates (however, they can be configured by using DHCP)

Securing Dynamic Zone Updates

To provide secured dynamic zone updates in your design, you must

- **Specify Active Directory integrated zones for each dynamically updated zone**   You can provide secured dynamic zone updates only by using Active Directory integrated zones. Standard primary zones can't provide secured dynamic zone updates.

- **Specify the permissions to update the dynamically updated zones in Active Directory**   DNS zone updates are made to the DNS zone container in Active Directory. You must specify the computer, group, or user account that is authorized to perform dynamic updates. You can assign the permissions to the entire DNS zone or to individual resource records.

For zones that are dynamically updated by DHCP servers, you must grant the DHCP servers permissions to

- Dynamically update corresponding zones

- Modify all the resource records in the zone

For zones that are dynamically updated by DNS Clients, you must grant each DNS client permission to

- Dynamically update corresponding zones

- Modify only the corresponding resource records in the zone

Applying the Decision

Figure 9.15 illustrates the appropriate method for securing dynamically updated zones. For the purposes of this scenario, assume that the business and technical requirements of the organization include

- Unauthorized updates to any dynamically updated DNS zones in the design must be prevented

- DHCP Server A provides automatic IP configuration for Segments A, B, and C

- Routers A and B are Routing and Remote Access-based routers that have the DHCP Relay Agent enabled and configured

- Client computers on Segments A, B, and C are running Windows 95, Windows 98, Windows Me, Windows NT 4.0, and Windows 2000

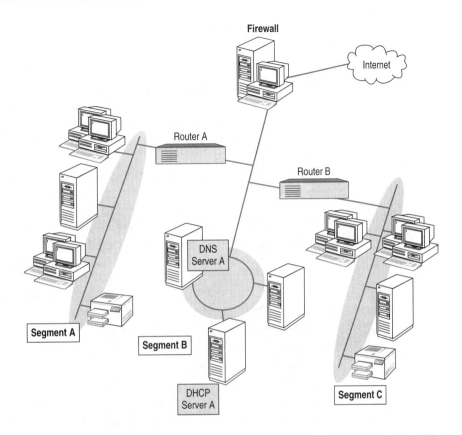

Figure 9.15 Scenario to illustrate the appropriate method for securing dynamically updated zones

To ensure that you achieve the requirements of the design, you must specify that

- All zones on DNS Server A are Active Directory integrated zones
- DHCP Server A dynamically updates DNS zones
- Only DHCP Server A has the permission to update the *entire* DNS zone(s)

DHCP updates to the DNS zones are required because the client computers run operating systems other than Windows 2000. Only the DNS Client in Windows 2000 can dynamically update DNS zones.

Preventing Unauthorized Access to DNS Servers

To ensure the integrity of the DNS zones, you must prevent unauthorized users from directly accessing the DNS server. You can include various methods of preventing unauthorized access to DNS servers based on the zone types (such as Active Directory integrated or standard primary zones).

Making the Decision

You can prevent unauthorized users from compromising the integrity of the DNS zones by

- **Restricting DNS administrators**   Grant only authorized network administrators the permission to manage DNS servers. Create a Windows 2000 group and assign the group permissions to manage DNS servers in the organization. Include the authorized network users in the Windows 2000 group that you created.

- **Isolating read-write copies of DNS zones from public networks, such as the Internet**   Ensure that unauthorized or anonymous users can access *only* standard secondary zones. Because secondary zones are read-only, the unauthorized or anonymous users can't modify the contents of the DNS zone.

- **Isolating zones that manage internal namespaces from public networks, such as the Internet**   Ensure that unauthorized or anonymous users can access *only* the external portions of the organization's namespace. Ensure that *all* the computers, or clusters, in the external namespace meet one of the following criteria:

  - Can be accessed by unauthorized or anonymous users

  - Provide sufficient security to protect confidential data from unauthorized or anonymous users

- **Requiring only Active Directory integrated zones**   Within the private network, Active Directory integrated zones provide enhanced security because users don't have direct access to the zone information. Include Active Directory integrated zones to protect the integrity of the zones within your private network.

Applying the Decision

Figure 9.16 illustrates the proper methods for preventing unauthorized user access to DNS servers. For the purposes of this scenario, assume that the business and technical requirements of the organization include

- Active Directory must be supported within the organization

- Unauthorized access to DNS servers that manage the organization's internal namespace must be prevented

- DNS Servers A, B, and C manage the DNS zones that contain the organization's internal namespace

- DNS Server D manages the DNS zone that contains the organization's external namespace

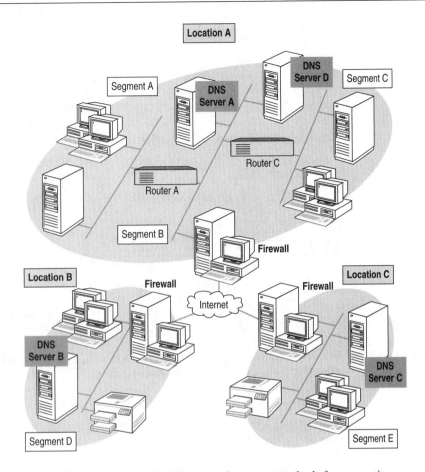

Figure 9.16 A scenario that illustrates the proper methods for preventing unauthorized user access to DNS servers

To ensure that you achieve the requirements of the design, you must specify that

- All zones on DNS Server D are standard secondary zones
- All zones on DNS Servers A, B, and C are Active Directory integrated zones
- Firewalls prevent unauthorized access to DNS Servers A, B, and C
- The firewall at Location A allows unauthorized or anonymous access to DNS Server D
- All resource records in the zones managed by DNS Server D point to servers that should be accessed by Internet users

Lesson 4: DNS Design Optimization

This lesson discusses how to optimize DNS designs to improve the availability and performance characteristics in your design. This lesson focuses on the strategies that increase the percentage of time that computers can resolve DNS queries and that decrease any latency in resolving DNS queries.

After this lesson, you will be able to

- Select the appropriate method for enhancing the availability characteristics in your DNS design
- Select the appropriate methods for improving the performance characteristics in your DNS design

Estimated lesson time: 20 minutes

Enhancing DNS Availability

Once you have established the essential aspects and security aspects of your DNS design, you can optimize the design for availability. The business requirements of the organization may require your design to ensure DNS query resolution at all times, and as such, require you to provide redundancy for the DNS servers in your design, regardless of a single point of failure.

Making the Decision

You can improve the availability of your DNS designs by

- Replicating DNS zones across multiple DNS servers
- Using Microsoft Windows Clustering server clusters
- Dedicating a computer to running DNS

Multiple DNS Servers with Replicated Zones

You can distribute DNS query traffic for a DNS zone across two DNS servers. You can replicate the zones between the two DNS servers to ensure that both servers return the same responses to DNS queries. If one DNS server fails, the remaining DNS server can provide DNS name resolution.

You must specify that the DNS clients in the design include both DNS servers in the list of DNS servers to use for name resolution. If you specify only one of the DNS servers in the DNS clients, the DNS clients are unaware of the remaining DNS server.

You can replicate zone information between

- **Two Active Directory integrated zones**   You can replicate zone information between any two DNS servers that support Active Directory integrated zones. Querying either DNS server returns the same DNS query results.

- **Standard primary and secondary zones**   You can replicate zone information between a DNS server that supports a standard primary zone and a DNS server that supports a standard secondary zone. Querying either DNS server returns the same DNS query results.

  If the DNS server that supports the standard primary zone fails, no updates can be made to the zone (including dynamic zone updates). To ensure that zone updates can always be performed, select Active Directory integrated zones or Windows Clustering server clusters instead.

The primary advantage of multiple DNS servers with replicated zones in comparison to server clusters is that no additional hardware and software resources are required. The disadvantage of multiple DNS servers with replicated zones is that there is no automatic *failover*. If the failed DNS server is configured in the DNS clients to be queried first, the DNS clients experience a delay in DNS query resolution. The delay in query resolution results from the DNS client waiting for a response from the first (and now failed) DNS server, before timing out and proceeding to the next DNS server in the list.

Figure 9.17 illustrates how multiple DNS servers with replicated zones provide enhanced availability. For the purposes of this scenario, assume that the business and technical requirements of the organization include

- Active Directory must be supported within the organization
- Dynamic updates must always be performed, regardless of the failure of any DNS server
- DNS Servers A and B manage the same DNS zones that contain the organization's namespace

To ensure that you achieve the requirements of the design, you must specify that

- All zones are Active Directory integrated zones
- All zones are replicated between DNS Servers A and B
- DNS clients and all network segments are configured to use both DNS Servers A and B to perform name resolution

Active Directory integrated zones are required because the organization requires dynamic updates to be performed, regardless of which DNS server fails.

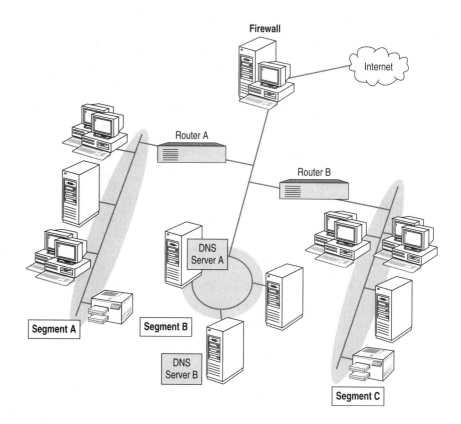

Figure 9.17   Example of how multiple DNS servers with replicated zones provide enhanced availability

Windows Clustering Server Clusters

For DNS servers that use standard DNS zones, you can utilize Windows Clustering server clusters to provide enhanced availability. The DNS Server service in Windows 2000 is a *cluster-unaware* application. *Cluster-aware* applications can interact with Windows Clustering server clusters by using Windows Clustering application programming interfaces (APIs). Cluster-unaware applications can run on Windows Clustering server clusters, but can't communicate with the cluster by using Windows Clustering APIs.

Note   Active Directory integrated zones store the zone resource records in Active Directory. As a result, you cannot use Windows Clustering server clusters to improve the availability of DNS servers that manage Active Directory integrated zones.

You can store the DNS zones on a common *cluster drive* between two computers. The cluster drive is attached to a SCSI bus common to both computers, also known as *cluster nodes*, in the cluster.

Figure 9.18 illustrates the components in a Windows Clustering server cluster. The DNS Server service actually runs on only one of the cluster nodes at a time. The DNS zones are stored on the shared cluster drive. The cluster node currently running the DNS Server services is known as the *active node* for DNS.

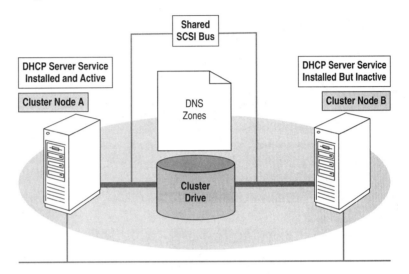

Figure 9.18   Components in a Windows Clustering server cluster

If the DNS active node fails, the remaining cluster node automatically starts the DNS Server service. Because the DNS zones are stored on the shared cluster drive, the redundant DNS Server service has the current DNS zone contents from the failed cluster node.

The primary advantages to DNS on server clusters are

- The redundant cluster node automatically starts and no action is required on the part of the network administrators

- The DNS zones are stored on the cluster drive and are available to either cluster node. As a result, DNS clients will be unaware of the failure

For more information on Window Clustering server clusters, see the Windows 2000 help files on how to support cluster-unaware applications.

Dedicating a Computer to DNS

By dedicating a computer to running DNS, you improve availability by preventing other applications or services from becoming unstable and requiring the DNS server to be restarted.

Applying the Decision

Figure 9.19 illustrates the proper methods for enhancing the availability of a DNS design.

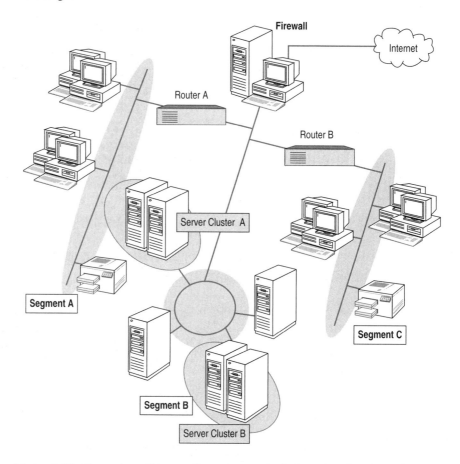

Figure 9.19   Scenario to illustrate the proper methods for enhancing the availability of a DNS design

For the purposes of this scenario, assume that the business and technical requirements of the organization include

- Any failure of a DNS server is automatically corrected
- DNS clients perceive no changes in the DNS server configuration

- Secured dynamic updates must be performed at all times
- Server Cluster A supports the internal namespace of the organization
- Server Cluster B supports the external namespace of the organization

To provide the proper solution, Windows Clustering server clusters must be used to achieve the business and technical requirements of the organization. Server Clusters A and B have the DNS Server service installed on both cluster nodes, but active on only one cluster node. Server Cluster A provides DNS name resolution for all network segments within the private network. Server Cluster B provides DNS name resolution for all network segments within the private network and the Internet.

Improving DNS Performance

Once you have established the essential aspects, the security aspects, and availability aspects of your DNS design, you can optimize the design for performance. The business requirements may include that DNS name resolution must occur within a given period of time, based on the number of simultaneous DNS queries.

Making the Decision

You can improve the performance of your DNS designs by

- Reducing DNS query resolution latency
- Reducing or rescheduling DNS zone replication traffic
- Dedicating a computer to running DNS

Reducing DNS Query Resolution Latency

You can reduce the length of time to perform DNS queries by

- **Placing DNS servers at remote locations**   You can reduce the WAN traffic between locations by placing DNS servers at remote locations. By providing local name resolution, the DNS server improves DNS query response times within the remote location.

- **Load balancing DNS queries across multiple DNS servers**   When the existing DNS servers are saturated and you can't upgrade the hardware to improve performance, you can add additional DNS servers to your design.

    Evenly distribute the DNS clients across the multiple DNS servers, ensuring that each DNS server responds to approximately the same number of DNS queries over a period of time. You must configure the DNS clients in your network to utilize different servers as their primary DNS server to distribute DNS queries across the multiple DNS servers. You can utilize DHCP to reduce the administration in configuring the DNS clients to distribute DNS queries between the multiple DNS servers.

- **Dividing domains into subdomains**   As the number of resource records in a zone becomes larger, the DNS server requires a longer period of time to find a resource record in the zone. To improve query resolution time, you can

  - Specify two or more subdomains beneath the current domain

  - Divide the existing resource records evenly between the new subdomains

  - Specify that the original domain forward appropriate DNS queries to the new subdomains

  When you create subdomains in the manner previously described, you create *delegated domains*. Delegated domains contain a subset of the parent domain. The parent domain *delegates* the responsibility for query resolution to these subdomains.

  Because the delegated domains contain a subset of the resource records in the original domain, the DNS server spends less time searching the zone, and subsequently resolves DNS queries faster.

- **Including caching-only DNS servers**   Caching-only DNS servers don't store DNS zone information in file or Active Directory, but rather cache responses to DNS queries in local memory. Because the caching-only DNS server locally caches responses to DNS queries, you can reduce traffic to other DNS servers in the network.

  The advantages of caching-only DNS servers include

  - Responses to DNS queries are cached locally

  - Zone transfers aren't required

  You can include caching-only DNS servers in your design to provide local caching of DNS queries at remote locations without performing zone transfers. However, caching-only DNS servers require another DNS server to forward DNS queries to and receive DNS query replies from.

  Placing caching-only DNS servers at remote locations is recommended when the

  - Network connections between locations are reliable

  - Caching-only DNS servers forward queries to reliable DNS servers

  Placing a DNS server at remote locations with an Active Directory integrated or traditional DNS zone is recommended when

  - Network connections between locations are unreliable

  - DNS servers at other locations are unreliable

  - Network traffic generated by zone replication is acceptable

Reducing or Rescheduling DNS Zone Replication Traffic

You can reduce network capacity utilized by DNS zone replication traffic by

- **Placing caching-only DNS servers at remote locations**   Because caching-only DNS servers don't store a complete copy of the zone locally, zone replication isn't necessary.

- **Performing incremental zone transfers**   You can perform incremental zone transfers to reduce the network traffic in comparison to full zone transfers. Incremental zone transfers utilize less network traffic because only updates to the zone resource records are transmitted. Full zone transfers resend all zone resource records.

- **Performing fast zone transfers**   DNS servers running Windows 2000 support fast zone transfers. Fast zone transfers send multiple zone resource records updates at a time and compress the zone updates. The combination of sending multiple zone resource records at a time and the compression of zone updates results in a reduction in network utilization.

You can also prevent zone replication traffic from overutilizing network capacity by performing zone updates during nonpeak periods of network activity. Although rescheduling zone replication doesn't reduce the network traffic, the impact on the network capacity is averted during peak periods of operation.

Dedicating a Computer to DNS

By dedicating a computer to running DNS, you improve the performance because you prevent other applications or services from consuming system resources.

Applying the Decision

Figure 9.20 illustrates a DNS design prior to optimization for performance. For the purposes of this scenario, assume that the business and technical requirements of the organization include

- Active Directory must be supported as the directory service

- DNS Server A manages the internal namespace for the organization

- DNS Server B manages the external namespace for the organization

- Locations B and C must be able to provide DNS name resolution if the Internet connection is lost or the DNS servers at Location A fail

- Network utilization between locations is currently 14 percent of capacity with no significant increases over the last 12 months

- Organization's e-commerce Web site is expected to expand more than 300 percent over the next 12 months

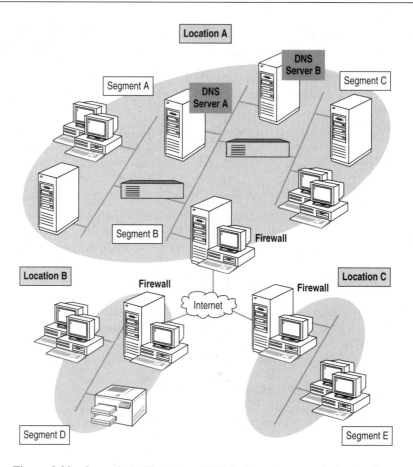

Figure 9.20   Scenario to illustrate a DNS design prior to optimization for performance

Figure 9.21 illustrates a DNS design after optimization for performance. The following performance optimization changes were made to the design.

- DNS Server C is installed to provide local DNS name resolution at Location B.

- DNS Server D is installed to provide local DNS name resolution at Location C.

- DNS Server E is installed to distribute DNS queries between DNS Servers B and E because of the increase in the e-commerce Web site.

Activity 9.2: Completing a DNS Design

In this activity, you're presented with a scenario. To complete the activity:

1. Evaluate the scenario and determine the design requirements

2. Answer questions and make design recommendations

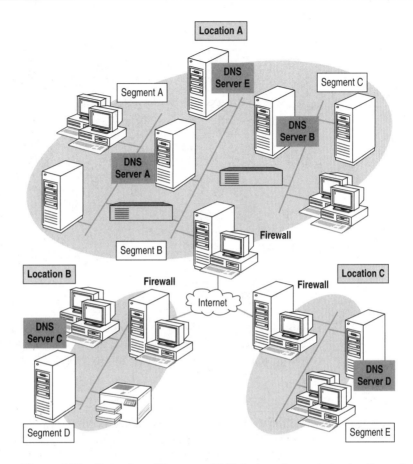

Figure 9.21   Scenario to illustrate a DNS design after optimization for performance

In Figure 9.22, you see a map that illustrates the location of research facilities in a biotech consortium. As the consultant retained to create the original DNS design, you're in the process of revising the design to incorporate technical changes and differences in business practices. You're revising the design to reflect the current security, availability, and performance requirements of the biotech consortium.

Answer the following questions concerning your design recommendations. Answers to the questions can be found in the Appendix, "Questions and Answers."

1. The biotech consortium is concerned about Internet users gaining access to the servers and resources in each research facility. What specifications can you include in your design to prevent Internet users from modifying the contents of consortium's DNS zones?

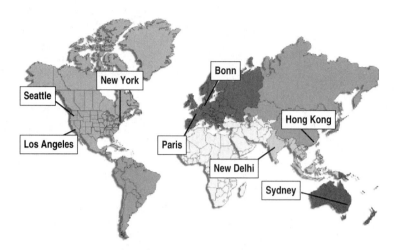

Figure 9.22 Map that illustrates the location of research facilities in a biotech
consortium

2. Six months after the initial deployment of your DNS design, some of the
research facilities are experiencing delays in domain name resolution. What
recommendations can you make to improve the DNS query response times?

3. The director of research for the biotech consortium obtained a Web-based
groupware application that allows research scientists to collaborate on their
research. Because the research scientists are located throughout the world, the
servers that host the groupware application must be accessible at all times.
How can you ensure that these requirements are achieved?

Lab: Creating a DNS Design

After this lab, you will be able to

- Evaluate a scenario and determine the design requirements
- Create a DNS based on the design requirements

Estimated lab time: 45 minutes

In this lab, you're the director of information services for a university and are responsible for creating a DNS design for the university. The university has 12 buildings arranged in a campus setting.

To complete this lab:

1. Examine the networking environment presented in the scenario, the network diagrams, the business requirements and constraints, and the technical requirements and constraints

2. Use the worksheet(s) for each location and router to assist you in creating your DNS design (you can find completed sample design worksheets on the Supplemental Course Materials CD-ROM in the Completed Worksheets folder)

   Note For each location there are four worksheets, one worksheet for each DNS server. If your design contains fewer than four DNS servers, leave the remaining worksheets blank.

3. Create, eliminate, or replace existing networking devices and network segments when required

4. Ensure that your design fulfills the business requirements and constraints and technical requirements and constraints of the scenario by

   - Determining the number of DNS servers to include in each building
   - Including the appropriate zones that each DNS server will manage
   - Including dynamic updates, or secured dynamic updates, for the appropriate zones
   - Including the appropriate WINS lookups for appropriate zones
   - Including the appropriate zone replication method for each zone
   - Optimizing your design to provide security, availability, performance, and affordability

   Note To reduce the length of time for this lab, create a DNS design for only three of the university buildings.

Scenario

A science and engineering university is migrating its existing DNS design to accommodate the increase in student population and faculty. The university has 12 buildings organized in a campus setting.

Figure 9.23 is a map of the buildings in the university's campus. Point-to-point leased lines currently connect the buildings to one another. The university is migrating the existing point-to-point leased lines to a public ATM backbone. The new ATM backbone will provide higher speed data rates between the buildings in the campus. The university is connected to the Internet by three T3 leased lines in the Administration Building.

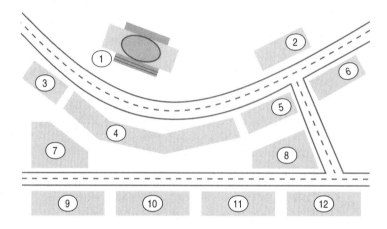

Figure 9.23   Map of the buildings in the university's campus

Building	Description	Building	Description
1	Administration Building	2	Student Union and Campus Security
3	Chemistry	4	Mathematics and Computer Science
5	Physics	6	Mechanical Engineering
7	Field House/Gymnasium	8	Performing Arts Center
9	Electrical Engineering	10	Civil Engineering
11	Fine Arts	12	Liberal Arts

The network in each university building supports

- The administrative staff, faculty, and student work-study program participants who work in the individual university departments
- Interactive kiosks that students can use to access their own information, class schedules, professor office schedules, and other pertinent information

- 10BaseT Ethernet connectivity for students who use laptops
- Computer-based labs for use by the students to complete course assignments

The following table lists each building on the university's campus and the corresponding figure that illustrates the existing network in that building.

Building	Figure
Administration Building	Figure 9.25
Student Union and Campus Security	Figure 9.26
Chemistry and Physics	Figure 9.27
Mathematics and Computer Science	Figure 9.28

Business Requirements and Constraints

The university has a number of requirements and constraints based on the business model of the university. As you create your DNS design, ensure that your design meets the business requirements and stays within the business constraints.

To achieve the business requirements and constraints, your design must

- Prevent students from accessing resources and data that are for exclusive use by the faculty and administrative staff
- Prevent Internet users from accessing resources and data that are for exclusive use by the faculty and administrative staff
- Provide Internet access to all faculty, administrative staff, and students
- Support Active Directory as the directory service for the university
- Provide an Internet presence for the university that is hosted on the Web servers in the Administration Building
- Ensure that the Internet presence for the university is available 24 hours a day, 7 days a week
- Ensure that the interactive student kiosks are available during normal hours of operation for each respective building

Technical Requirements and Constraints

The existing physical network, hardware, and operating systems place certain technical requirements and constraints on your design. As you create your DNS design, ensure that your design meets the technical requirements and stays within the technical constraints.

In addition, the applications that run within the university require connectivity within each building, with other buildings, and with the Internet. These applications run on the computers used by the faculty, administrative staff, and student work-study program participants and on computers used in interactive kiosks. These applications require DNS domain name resolution to function properly.

To achieve the technical requirements and constraints, your design must

- Utilize the university's existing domain namespace
- Isolate the university's internal namespace from Internet access
- Isolate the internal namespaces that are designated for use by the students from the network segments designated for use by the faculty, administrative staff, and student work-study program participants
- Integrate with the existing DHCP servers in the design that provide IP configuration for desktop and laptop computers
- Integrate with the existing WINS servers in the design that provide NetBIOS name resolution
- Reduce the administration associated with DNS while ensuring that DNS zone integrity is maintained
- Ensure that in the future BIND version 8.2.1 DNS servers can be integrated into the design (although none are to be included in your initial design)

The university's domain namespace, shown in Figure 9.24, can be described as follows.

- *activedir.contoso-u.msft.* is the domain that contains the Active Directory domain namespace. All subdomains and resource records required by Active Directory are contained beneath this domain. The domain must be available to each network segment if ATM backbone fails.

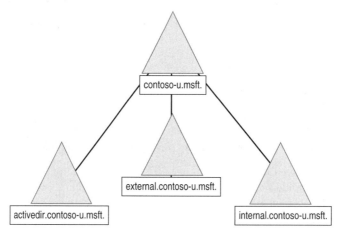

Figure 9.24   Diagram of the university's existing domain namespace

- *external.contoso-u.msft.* is the domain that contains the resource records for all the resources accessed by Internet users. Network administrators located on Segment F administer the domain. The domain must be accessible to Internet users that access the Web servers on Segment B (Internet users can only access Segment B).

- *internal.contoso-u.msft.* is the domain that contains the resource records for all the resources and computers that aren't defined by Active Directory (such as computers running UNIX or Macintosh operating systems). Network administrators located on Segment F administer the domain. The domain must be available to each network segment if the ATM backbone fails.

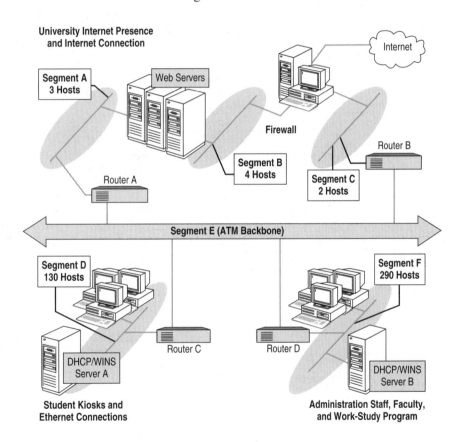

Figure 9.25   Existing network at the Administration building

Design Worksheet – Figure 9.25
Administration Building – DNS Server A

DNS Server A Specifications	Comments
DNS server connects to segment: _____	
❑ Install on cluster node Cluster name: _____	
Zone A Domain name: _____	
❑ Active Directory integrated	
❑ Standard Primary (specify DNS servers to replicate to in Comments column)	
❑ Standard Secondary (specify DNS servers to replicate from in Comments column)	
❑ Incremental zone transfers and or fast zone transfers	
❑ Dynamic updates ❑ Secured (specify permissions in Comments column)	
❑ Update with DHCP Server DHCP server: _____	
❑ Update with DNS Client	
❑ WINS lookup WINS server: _____	
Character set ❑ ASCII ❑ UTF-8	
Zone B Domain name: _____	
❑ Active Directory integrated	
❑ Standard Primary (specify DNS servers to replicate to in Comments column)	
❑ Standard Secondary (specify DNS servers to replicate from in Comments column)	
❑ Incremental zone transfers and or fast zone transfers	
❑ Dynamic updates ❑ Secured (specify permissions in Comments column)	
❑ Update with DHCP Server DHCP server: _____	
❑ Update with DNS Client	
❑ WINS lookup WINS server: _____	
Character set ❑ ASCII ❑ UTF-8	
Zone C Domain name: _____	
❑ Active Directory integrated	
❑ Standard Primary (specify DNS servers to replicate to in Comments column)	
❑ Standard Secondary (specify DNS servers to replicate from in Comments column)	
❑ Incremental zone transfers and or fast zone transfers	
❑ Dynamic updates ❑ Secured (specify permissions in Comments column)	
❑ Update with DHCP Server DHCP server: _____	
❑ Update with DNS Client	
❑ WINS lookup WINS server: _____	
Character set ❑ ASCII ❑ UTF-8	

Design Worksheet – Figure 9.25
Administration Building – DNS Server B

DNS Server B Specifications	Comments
DNS server connects to segment: _____	
❑ Install on cluster node Cluster name: _____	
Zone A Domain name: _____	
❑ Active Directory integrated	
❑ Standard Primary (specify DNS servers to replicate to in Comments column)	
❑ Standard Secondary (specify DNS servers to replicate from in Comments column)	
❑ Incremental zone transfers and or fast zone transfers	
❑ Dynamic updates ❑ Secured (specify permissions in Comments column)	
❑ Update with DHCP Server DHCP server: _____	
❑ Update with DNS Client	
❑ WINS lookup WINS server: _____	
Character set ❑ ASCII ❑ UTF-8	
Zone B Domain name: _____	
❑ Active Directory integrated	
❑ Standard Primary (specify DNS servers to replicate to in Comments column)	
❑ Standard Secondary (specify DNS servers to replicate from in Comments column)	
❑ Incremental zone transfers and or fast zone transfers	
❑ Dynamic updates ❑ Secured (specify permissions in Comments column)	
❑ Update with DHCP Server DHCP server: _____	
❑ Update with DNS Client	
❑ WINS lookup WINS server: _____	
Character set ❑ ASCII ❑ UTF-8	
Zone C Domain name: _____	
❑ Active Directory integrated	
❑ Standard Primary (specify DNS servers to replicate to in Comments column)	
❑ Standard Secondary (specify DNS servers to replicate from in Comments column)	
❑ Incremental zone transfers and or fast zone transfers	
❑ Dynamic updates ❑ Secured (specify permissions in Comments column)	
❑ Update with DHCP Server DHCP server: _____	
❑ Update with DNS Client	
❑ WINS lookup WINS server: _____	
Character set ❑ ASCII ❑ UTF-8	

Design Worksheet – Figure 9.25
Administration Building – DNS Server C

DNS Server C Specifications	Comments
DNS server connects to segment: _____	
❑ Install on cluster node Cluster name: _____	
Zone A Domain name: _____	
❑ Active Directory integrated	
❑ Standard Primary (specify DNS servers to replicate to in Comments column)	
❑ Standard Secondary (specify DNS servers to replicate from in Comments column)	
❑ Incremental zone transfers and or fast zone transfers	
❑ Dynamic updates ❑ Secured (specify permissions in Comments column)	
❑ Update with DHCP Server DHCP server: _____	
❑ Update with DNS Client	
❑ WINS lookup WINS server: _____	
Character set ❑ ASCII ❑ UTF-8	
Zone B Domain name: _____	
❑ Active Directory integrated	
❑ Standard Primary (specify DNS servers to replicate to in Comments column)	
❑ Standard Secondary (specify DNS servers to replicate from in Comments column)	
❑ Incremental zone transfers and or fast zone transfers	
❑ Dynamic updates ❑ Secured (specify permissions in Comments column)	
❑ Update with DHCP Server DHCP server: _____	
❑ Update with DNS Client	
❑ WINS lookup WINS server: _____	
Character set ❑ ASCII ❑ UTF-8	
Zone C Domain name: _____	
❑ Active Directory integrated	
❑ Standard Primary (specify DNS servers to replicate to in Comments column)	
❑ Standard Secondary (specify DNS servers to replicate from in Comments column)	
❑ Incremental zone transfers and or fast zone transfers	
❑ Dynamic updates ❑ Secured (specify permissions in Comments column)	
❑ Update with DHCP Server DHCP server: _____	
❑ Update with DNS Client	
❑ WINS lookup WINS server: _____	
Character set ❑ ASCII ❑ UTF-8	

Design Worksheet – Figure 9.25
Administration Building – DNS Server D

DNS Server D Specifications	Comments
DNS server connects to segment: _____	
❏ Install on cluster node Cluster name: _____	
Zone A Domain name: _____	
❏ Active Directory integrated (specify replica zones in Comments column)	
❏ Standard Primary (specify DNS servers to replicate to in Comments column)	
❏ Standard Secondary (specify DNS servers to replicate from in Comments column)	
❏ Incremental zone transfers and or fast zone transfers	
❏ Dynamic updates ❏ Secured (specify permissions in Comments column)	
❏ Update with DHCP Server DHCP server: _____	
❏ Update with DNS Client	
❏ WINS lookup WINS server: _____	
Character set ❏ ASCII ❏ UTF-8	
Zone B Domain name: _____	
❏ Active Directory integrated	
❏ Standard Primary (specify DNS servers to replicate to in Comments column)	
❏ Standard Secondary (specify DNS servers to replicate from in Comments column)	
❏ Incremental zone transfers and or fast zone transfers	
❏ Dynamic updates ❏ Secured (specify permissions in Comments column)	
❏ Update with DHCP Server DHCP server: _____	
❏ Update with DNS Client	
❏ WINS lookup WINS server: _____	
Character set ❏ ASCII ❏ UTF-8	
Zone C Domain name: _____	
❏ Active Directory integrated	
❏ Standard Primary (specify DNS servers to replicate to in Comments column)	
❏ Standard Secondary (specify DNS servers to replicate from in Comments column)	
❏ Incremental zone transfers and or fast zone transfers	
❏ Dynamic updates ❏ Secured (specify permissions in Comments column)	
❏ Update with DHCP Server DHCP server: _____	
❏ Update with DNS Client	
❏ WINS lookup WINS server: _____	
Character set ❏ ASCII ❏ UTF-8	

Design Worksheet – Figure 9.25
Administration Building – DNS Clients

Segment	DNS Client Specifications	Comments
	❑ Enable dynamic DNS zone updates DNS Server List 1: _____ 2: _____ 3: _____ 4: _____	
	❑ Enable dynamic DNS zone updates DNS Server List 1: _____ 2: _____ 3: _____ 4: _____	
	❑ Enable dynamic DNS zone updates DNS Server List 1: _____ 2: _____ 3: _____ 4: _____	
	❑ Enable dynamic DNS zone updates DNS Server List 1: _____ 2: _____ 3: _____ 4: _____	

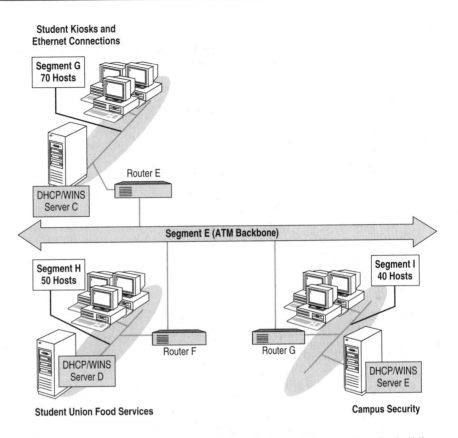

Student Kiosks and Ethernet Connections

Segment G
70 Hosts

Router E

DHCP/WINS
Server C

Segment E (ATM Backbone)

Segment H
50 Hosts

Router F

DHCP/WINS
Server D

Segment I
40 Hosts

Router G

DHCP/WINS
Server E

Student Union Food Services

Campus Security

Figure 9.26 Existing network at the Student Union and Campus Security building

Design Worksheet – Figure 9.26
Student Union and Campus Security Building – DNS Server A

DNS Server A Specifications	Comments
DNS server connects to segment: _____	
❏ Install on cluster node Cluster name: _____	
Zone A Domain name: _____	
❏ Active Directory integrated	
❏ Standard Primary (specify DNS servers to replicate to in Comments column)	
❏ Standard Secondary (specify DNS servers to replicate from in Comments column)	
❏ Incremental zone transfers and or fast zone transfers	
❏ Dynamic updates ❏ Secured (specify permissions in Comments column)	
❏ Update with DHCP Server DHCP server: _____	
❏ Update with DNS Client	
❏ WINS lookup WINS server: _____	
Character set ❏ ASCII ❏ UTF-8	
Zone B Domain name: _____	
❏ Active Directory integrated	
❏ Standard Primary (specify DNS servers to replicate to in Comments column)	
❏ Standard Secondary (specify DNS servers to replicate from in Comments column)	
❏ Incremental zone transfers and or fast zone transfers	
❏ Dynamic updates ❏ Secured (specify permissions in Comments column)	
❏ Update with DHCP Server DHCP server: _____	
❏ Update with DNS Client	
❏ WINS lookup WINS server: _____	
Character set ❏ ASCII ❏ UTF-8	
Zone C Domain name: _____	
❏ Active Directory integrated	
❏ Standard Primary (specify DNS servers to replicate to in Comments column)	
❏ Standard Secondary (specify DNS servers to replicate from in Comments column)	
❏ Incremental zone transfers and or fast zone transfers	
❏ Dynamic updates ❏ Secured (specify permissions in Comments column)	
❏ Update with DHCP Server DHCP server: _____	
❏ Update with DNS Client	
❏ WINS lookup WINS server: _____	
Character set ❏ ASCII ❏ UTF-8	

Design Worksheet – Figure 9.26
Student Union and Campus Security Building – DNS Server B

DNS Server B Specifications	Comments
DNS server connects to segment: _____	
❑ Install on cluster node Cluster name: _____	
Zone A Domain name: _____	
❑ Active Directory integrated	
❑ Standard Primary (specify DNS servers to replicate to in Comments column)	
❑ Standard Secondary (specify DNS servers to replicate from in Comments column)	
❑ Incremental zone transfers and or fast zone transfers	
❑ Dynamic updates ❑ Secured (specify permissions in Comments column)	
❑ Update with DHCP Server DHCP server: _____	
❑ Update with DNS Client	
❑ WINS lookup WINS server: _____	
Character set ❑ ASCII ❑ UTF-8	
Zone B Domain name: _____	
❑ Active Directory integrated	
❑ Standard Primary (specify DNS servers to replicate to in Comments column)	
❑ Standard Secondary (specify DNS servers to replicate from in Comments column)	
❑ Incremental zone transfers and or fast zone transfers	
❑ Dynamic updates ❑ Secured (specify permissions in Comments column)	
❑ Update with DHCP Server DHCP server: _____	
❑ Update with DNS Client	
❑ WINS lookup WINS server: _____	
Character set ❑ ASCII ❑ UTF-8	
Zone C Domain name: _____	
❑ Active Directory integrated	
❑ Standard Primary (specify DNS servers to replicate to in Comments column)	
❑ Standard Secondary (specify DNS servers to replicate from in Comments column)	
❑ Incremental zone transfers and or fast zone transfers	
❑ Dynamic updates ❑ Secured (specify permissions in Comments column)	
❑ Update with DHCP Server DHCP server: _____	
❑ Update with DNS Client	
❑ WINS lookup WINS server: _____	
Character set ❑ ASCII ❑ UTF-8	

Design Worksheet – Figure 9.26
Student Union and Campus Security Building – DNS Server C

DNS Server C Specifications	Comments
DNS server connects to segment: _____	
❑ Install on cluster node Cluster name: _____	
Zone A Domain name: _____	
❑ Active Directory integrated	
❑ Standard Primary (specify DNS servers to replicate to in Comments column)	
❑ Standard Secondary (specify DNS servers to replicate from in Comments column)	
❑ Incremental zone transfers and or fast zone transfers	
❑ Dynamic updates ❑ Secured (specify permissions in Comments column)	
❑ Update with DHCP Server DHCP server: _____	
❑ Update with DNS Client	
❑ WINS lookup WINS server: _____	
Character set ❑ ASCII ❑ UTF-8	
Zone B Domain name: _____	
❑ Active Directory integrated	
❑ Standard Primary (specify DNS servers to replicate to in Comments column)	
❑ Standard Secondary (specify DNS servers to replicate from in Comments column)	
❑ Incremental zone transfers and or fast zone transfers	
❑ Dynamic updates ❑ Secured (specify permissions in Comments column)	
❑ Update with DHCP Server DHCP server: _____	
❑ Update with DNS Client	
❑ WINS lookup WINS server: _____	
Character set ❑ ASCII ❑ UTF-8	
Zone C Domain name: _____	
❑ Active Directory integrated	
❑ Standard Primary (specify DNS servers to replicate to in Comments column)	
❑ Standard Secondary (specify DNS servers to replicate from in Comments column)	
❑ Incremental zone transfers and or fast zone transfers	
❑ Dynamic updates ❑ Secured (specify permissions in Comments column)	
❑ Update with DHCP Server DHCP server: _____	
❑ Update with DNS Client	
❑ WINS lookup WINS server: _____	
Character set ❑ ASCII ❑ UTF-8	

Design Worksheet – Figure 9.26
Student Union and Campus Security Building – DNS Server D

DNS Server D Specifications	Comments
DNS server connects to segment: _____	
❑ Install on cluster node Cluster name: _____	
Zone A Domain name: _____	
❑ Active Directory integrated (specify replica zones in Comments column)	
❑ Standard Primary (specify DNS servers to replicate to in Comments column)	
❑ Standard Secondary (specify DNS servers to replicate from in Comments column)	
❑ Incremental zone transfers and or fast zone transfers	
❑ Dynamic updates ❑ Secured (specify permissions in Comments column)	
❑ Update with DHCP Server DHCP server: _____	
❑ Update with DNS Client	
❑ WINS lookup WINS server: _____	
Character set ❑ ASCII ❑ UTF-8	
Zone B Domain name: _____	
❑ Active Directory integrated	
❑ Standard Primary (specify DNS servers to replicate to in Comments column)	
❑ Standard Secondary (specify DNS servers to replicate from in Comments column)	
❑ Incremental zone transfers and or fast zone transfers	
❑ Dynamic updates ❑ Secured (specify permissions in Comments column)	
❑ Update with DHCP Server DHCP server: _____	
❑ Update with DNS Client	
❑ WINS lookup WINS server: _____	
Character set ❑ ASCII ❑ UTF-8	
Zone C Domain name: _____	
❑ Active Directory integrated	
❑ Standard Primary (specify DNS servers to replicate to in Comments column)	
❑ Standard Secondary (specify DNS servers to replicate from in Comments column)	
❑ Incremental zone transfers and or fast zone transfers	
❑ Dynamic updates ❑ Secured (specify permissions in Comments column)	
❑ Update with DHCP Server DHCP server: _____	
❑ Update with DNS Client	
❑ WINS lookup WINS server: _____	
Character set ❑ ASCII ❑ UTF-8	

Design Worksheet – Figure 9.26
Student Union and Campus Security Building – DNS Clients

Segment	DNS Client Specifications	Comments
	❑ Enable dynamic DNS zone updates DNS Server List 1: _____ 2: _____ 3: _____ 4: _____	
	❑ Enable dynamic DNS zone updates DNS Server List 1: _____ 2: _____ 3: _____ 4: _____	
	❑ Enable dynamic DNS zone updates DNS Server List 1: _____ 2: _____ 3: _____ 4: _____	
	❑ Enable dynamic DNS zone updates DNS Server List 1: _____ 2: _____ 3: _____ 4: _____	

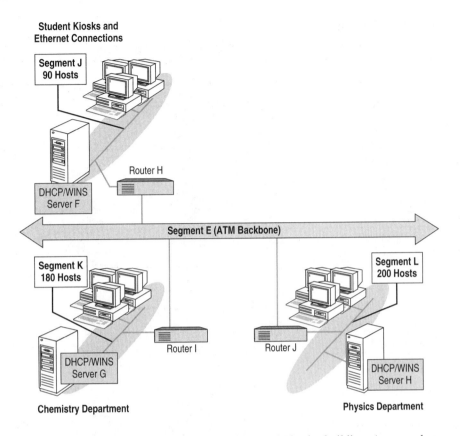

Figure 9.27   Existing network at the Chemistry and Physics buildings (assume that these buildings have the same network configuration)

Design Worksheet – Figure 9.27
Chemistry and Physics Buildings – DNS Server A

DNS Server A Specifications	Comments
DNS server connects to segment: _____	
❑ Install on cluster node Cluster name: _____	
Zone A Domain name: _____	
❑ Active Directory integrated	
❑ Standard Primary (specify DNS servers to replicate to in Comments column)	
❑ Standard Secondary (specify DNS servers to replicate from in Comments column)	
❑ Incremental zone transfers and or fast zone transfers	
❑ Dynamic updates ❑ Secured (specify permissions in Comments column)	
❑ Update with DHCP Server DHCP server: _____	
❑ Update with DNS Client	
❑ WINS lookup WINS server: _____	
Character set ❑ ASCII ❑ UTF-8	
Zone B Domain name: _____	
❑ Active Directory integrated	
❑ Standard Primary (specify DNS servers to replicate to in Comments column)	
❑ Standard Secondary (specify DNS servers to replicate from in Comments column)	
❑ Incremental zone transfers and or fast zone transfers	
❑ Dynamic updates ❑ Secured (specify permissions in Comments column)	
❑ Update with DHCP Server DHCP server: _____	
❑ Update with DNS Client	
❑ WINS lookup WINS server: _____	
Character set ❑ ASCII ❑ UTF-8	
Zone C Domain name: _____	
❑ Active Directory integrated	
❑ Standard Primary (specify DNS servers to replicate to in Comments column)	
❑ Standard Secondary (specify DNS servers to replicate from in Comments column)	
❑ Incremental zone transfers and or fast zone transfers	
❑ Dynamic updates ❑ Secured (specify permissions in Comments column)	
❑ Update with DHCP Server DHCP server: _____	
❑ Update with DNS Client	
❑ WINS lookup WINS server: _____	
Character set ❑ ASCII ❑ UTF-8	

Design Worksheet – Figure 9.27
Chemistry and Physics Buildings – DNS Server B

DNS Server B Specifications	Comments
DNS server connects to segment: _____	
❑ Install on cluster node Cluster name: _____	
Zone A Domain name: _____	
❑ Active Directory integrated	
❑ Standard Primary (specify DNS servers to replicate to in Comments column)	
❑ Standard Secondary (specify DNS servers to replicate from in Comments column)	
❑ Incremental zone transfers and or fast zone transfers	
❑ Dynamic updates ❑ Secured (specify permissions in Comments column)	
❑ Update with DHCP Server DHCP server: _____	
❑ Update with DNS Client	
❑ WINS lookup WINS server: _____	
Character set ❑ ASCII ❑ UTF-8	
Zone B Domain name: _____	
❑ Active Directory integrated	
❑ Standard Primary (specify DNS servers to replicate to in Comments column)	
❑ Standard Secondary (specify DNS servers to replicate from in Comments column)	
❑ Incremental zone transfers and or fast zone transfers	
❑ Dynamic updates ❑ Secured (specify permissions in Comments column)	
❑ Update with DHCP Server DHCP server: _____	
❑ Update with DNS Client	
❑ WINS lookup WINS server: _____	
Character set ❑ ASCII ❑ UTF-8	
Zone C Domain name: _____	
❑ Active Directory integrated	
❑ Standard Primary (specify DNS servers to replicate to in Comments column)	
❑ Standard Secondary (specify DNS servers to replicate from in Comments column)	
❑ Incremental zone transfers and or fast zone transfers	
❑ Dynamic updates ❑ Secured (specify permissions in Comments column)	
❑ Update with DHCP Server DHCP server: _____	
❑ Update with DNS Client	
❑ WINS lookup WINS server: _____	
Character set ❑ ASCII ❑ UTF-8	

Design Worksheet – Figure 9.27
Chemistry and Physics Buildings – DNS Server C

DNS Server C Specifications	Comments
DNS server connects to segment: _____	
❏ Install on cluster node Cluster name: _____	
Zone A Domain name: _____	
❏ Active Directory integrated	
❏ Standard Primary (specify DNS servers to replicate to in Comments column)	
❏ Standard Secondary (specify DNS servers to replicate from in Comments column)	
❏ Incremental zone transfers and or fast zone transfers	
❏ Dynamic updates ❏ Secured (specify permissions in Comments column)	
❏ Update with DHCP Server DHCP server: _____	
❏ Update with DNS Client	
❏ WINS lookup WINS server: _____	
Character set ❏ ASCII ❏ UTF-8	
Zone B Domain name: _____	
❏ Active Directory integrated	
❏ Standard Primary (specify DNS servers to replicate to in Comments column)	
❏ Standard Secondary (specify DNS servers to replicate from in Comments column)	
❏ Incremental zone transfers and or fast zone transfers	
❏ Dynamic updates ❏ Secured (specify permissions in Comments column)	
❏ Update with DHCP Server DHCP server: _____	
❏ Update with DNS Client	
❏ WINS lookup WINS server: _____	
Character set ❏ ASCII ❏ UTF-8	
Zone C Domain name: _____	
❏ Active Directory integrated	
❏ Standard Primary (specify DNS servers to replicate to in Comments column)	
❏ Standard Secondary (specify DNS servers to replicate from in Comments column)	
❏ Incremental zone transfers and or fast zone transfers	
❏ Dynamic updates ❏ Secured (specify permissions in Comments column)	
❏ Update with DHCP Server DHCP server: _____	
❏ Update with DNS Client	
❏ WINS lookup WINS server: _____	
Character set ❏ ASCII ❏ UTF-8	

Design Worksheet – Figure 9.27
Chemistry and Physics Buildings – DNS Server D

DNS Server D Specifications	Comments
DNS server connects to segment: _____	
❑ Install on cluster node Cluster name: _____	
Zone A Domain name: _____	
❑ Active Directory integrated (specify replica zones in Comments column)	
❑ Standard Primary (specify DNS servers to replicate to in Comments column)	
❑ Standard Secondary (specify DNS servers to replicate from in Comments column)	
❑ Incremental zone transfers and or fast zone transfers	
❑ Dynamic updates ❑ Secured (specify permissions in Comments column)	
❑ Update with DHCP Server DHCP server: _____	
❑ Update with DNS Client	
❑ WINS lookup WINS server: _____	
Character set ❑ ASCII ❑ UTF-8	
Zone B Domain name: _____	
❑ Active Directory integrated	
❑ Standard Primary (specify DNS servers to replicate to in Comments column)	
❑ Standard Secondary (specify DNS servers to replicate from in Comments column)	
❑ Incremental zone transfers and or fast zone transfers	
❑ Dynamic updates ❑ Secured (specify permissions in Comments column)	
❑ Update with DHCP Server DHCP server: _____	
❑ Update with DNS Client	
❑ WINS lookup WINS server: _____	
Character set ❑ ASCII ❑ UTF-8	
Zone C Domain name: _____	
❑ Active Directory integrated	
❑ Standard Primary (specify DNS servers to replicate to in Comments column)	
❑ Standard Secondary (specify DNS servers to replicate from in Comments column)	
❑ Incremental zone transfers and or fast zone transfers	
❑ Dynamic updates ❑ Secured (specify permissions in Comments column)	
❑ Update with DHCP Server DHCP server: _____	
❑ Update with DNS Client	
❑ WINS lookup WINS server: _____	
Character set ❑ ASCII ❑ UTF-8	

Design Worksheet – Figure 9.27
Chemistry and Physics Buildings – DNS Clients

Segment	DNS Client Specifications	Comments
	❑ Enable dynamic DNS zone updates DNS Server List 1: _____ 2: _____ 3: _____ 4: _____	
	❑ Enable dynamic DNS zone updates DNS Server List 1: _____ 2: _____ 3: _____ 4: _____	
	❑ Enable dynamic DNS zone updates DNS Server List 1: _____ 2: _____ 3: _____ 4: _____	
	❑ Enable dynamic DNS zone updates DNS Server List 1: _____ 2: _____ 3: _____ 4: _____	

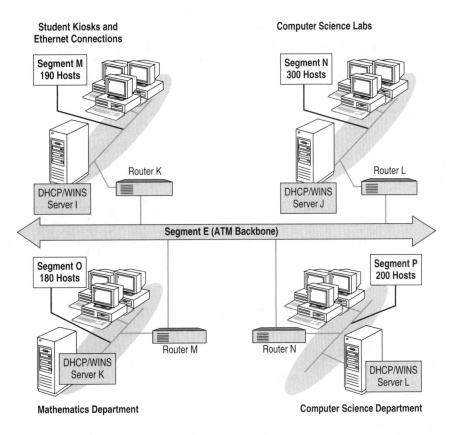

Figure 9.28   Existing network at the Mathematics and Computer Science building

Design Worksheet – Figure 9.28
Mathematics and Computer Science Building – DNS Server A

DNS Server A Specifications	Comments
DNS server connects to segment: _____	
❑ Install on cluster node Cluster name: _____	
Zone A Domain name: _____	
❑ Active Directory integrated	
❑ Standard Primary (specify DNS servers to replicate to in Comments column)	
❑ Standard Secondary (specify DNS servers to replicate from in Comments column)	
❑ Incremental zone transfers and or fast zone transfers	
❑ Dynamic updates ❑ Secured (specify permissions in Comments column)	
❑ Update with DHCP Server DHCP server: _____	
❑ Update with DNS Client	
❑ WINS lookup WINS server: _____	
Character set ❑ ASCII ❑ UTF-8	
Zone B Domain name: _____	
❑ Active Directory integrated	
❑ Standard Primary (specify DNS servers to replicate to in Comments column)	
❑ Standard Secondary (specify DNS servers to replicate from in Comments column)	
❑ Incremental zone transfers and or fast zone transfers	
❑ Dynamic updates ❑ Secured (specify permissions in Comments column)	
❑ Update with DHCP Server DHCP server: _____	
❑ Update with DNS Client	
❑ WINS lookup WINS server: _____	
Character set ❑ ASCII ❑ UTF-8	
Zone C Domain name: _____	
❑ Active Directory integrated	
❑ Standard Primary (specify DNS servers to replicate to in Comments column)	
❑ Standard Secondary (specify DNS servers to replicate from in Comments column)	
❑ Incremental zone transfers and or fast zone transfers	
❑ Dynamic updates ❑ Secured (specify permissions in Comments column)	
❑ Update with DHCP Server DHCP server: _____	
❑ Update with DNS Client	
❑ WINS lookup WINS server: _____	
Character set ❑ ASCII ❑ UTF-8	

Design Worksheet – Figure 9.28
Mathematics and Computer Science Building – DNS Server B

DNS Server B Specifications	Comments
DNS server connects to segment: _____	
❑ Install on cluster node Cluster name: _____	
Zone A Domain name: _____	
❑ Active Directory integrated	
❑ Standard Primary (specify DNS servers to replicate to in Comments column)	
❑ Standard Secondary (specify DNS servers to replicate from in Comments column)	
❑ Incremental zone transfers and or fast zone transfers	
❑ Dynamic updates ❑ Secured (specify permissions in Comments column)	
❑ Update with DHCP Server DHCP server: _____	
❑ Update with DNS Client	
❑ WINS lookup WINS server: _____	
Character set ❑ ASCII ❑ UTF-8	
Zone B Domain name: _____	
❑ Active Directory integrated	
❑ Standard Primary (specify DNS servers to replicate to in Comments column)	
❑ Standard Secondary (specify DNS servers to replicate from in Comments column)	
❑ Incremental zone transfers and or fast zone transfers	
❑ Dynamic updates ❑ Secured (specify permissions in Comments column)	
❑ Update with DHCP Server DHCP server: _____	
❑ Update with DNS Client	
❑ WINS lookup WINS server: _____	
Character set ❑ ASCII ❑ UTF-8	
Zone C Domain name: _____	
❑ Active Directory integrated	
❑ Standard Primary (specify DNS servers to replicate to in Comments column)	
❑ Standard Secondary (specify DNS servers to replicate from in Comments column)	
❑ Incremental zone transfers and or fast zone transfers	
❑ Dynamic updates ❑ Secured (specify permissions in Comments column)	
❑ Update with DHCP Server DHCP server: _____	
❑ Update with DNS Client	
❑ WINS lookup WINS server: _____	
Character set ❑ ASCII ❑ UTF-8	

Design Worksheet – Figure 9.28
Mathematics and Computer Science Building – DNS Server C

DNS Server C Specifications	Comments
DNS server connects to segment: _____	
❑ Install on cluster node Cluster name: _____	
Zone A Domain name: _____	
❑ Active Directory integrated	
❑ Standard Primary (specify DNS servers to replicate to in Comments column)	
❑ Standard Secondary (specify DNS servers to replicate from in Comments column)	
❑ Incremental zone transfers and or fast zone transfers	
❑ Dynamic updates ❑ Secured (specify permissions in Comments column)	
❑ Update with DHCP Server DHCP server: _____	
❑ Update with DNS Client	
❑ WINS lookup WINS server: _____	
Character set ❑ ASCII ❑ UTF-8	
Zone B Domain name: _____	
❑ Active Directory integrated	
❑ Standard Primary (specify DNS servers to replicate to in Comments column)	
❑ Standard Secondary (specify DNS servers to replicate from in Comments column)	
❑ Incremental zone transfers and or fast zone transfers	
❑ Dynamic updates ❑ Secured (specify permissions in Comments column)	
❑ Update with DHCP Server DHCP server: _____	
❑ Update with DNS Client	
❑ WINS lookup WINS server: _____	
Character set ❑ ASCII ❑ UTF-8	
Zone C Domain name: _____	
❑ Active Directory integrated	
❑ Standard Primary (specify DNS servers to replicate to in Comments column)	
❑ Standard Secondary (specify DNS servers to replicate from in Comments column)	
❑ Incremental zone transfers and or fast zone transfers	
❑ Dynamic updates ❑ Secured (specify permissions in Comments column)	
❑ Update with DHCP Server DHCP server: _____	
❑ Update with DNS Client	
❑ WINS lookup WINS server: _____	
Character set ❑ ASCII ❑ UTF-8	

Design Worksheet – Figure 9.28
Mathematics and Computer Science Building – DNS Server D

DNS Server D Specifications	Comments
DNS server connects to segment: _____	
❑ Install on cluster node Cluster name: _____	
Zone A Domain name: _____	
❑ Active Directory integrated	
❑ Standard Primary (specify DNS servers to replicate to in Comments column)	
❑ Standard Secondary (specify DNS servers to replicate from in Comments column)	
❑ Incremental zone transfers and or fast zone transfers	
❑ Dynamic updates ❑ Secured (specify permissions in Comments column)	
❑ Update with DHCP Server DHCP server: _____	
❑ Update with DNS Client	
❑ WINS lookup WINS server: _____	
Character set ❑ ASCII ❑ UTF-8	
Zone B Domain name: _____	
❑ Active Directory integrated	
❑ Standard Primary (specify DNS servers to replicate to in Comments column)	
❑ Standard Secondary (specify DNS servers to replicate from in Comments column)	
❑ Incremental zone transfers and or fast zone transfers	
❑ Dynamic updates ❑ Secured (specify permissions in Comments column)	
❑ Update with DHCP Server DHCP server: _____	
❑ Update with DNS Client	
❑ WINS lookup WINS server: _____	
Character set ❑ ASCII ❑ UTF-8	
Zone C Domain name: _____	
❑ Active Directory integrated	
❑ Standard Primary (specify DNS servers to replicate to in Comments column)	
❑ Standard Secondary (specify DNS servers to replicate from in Comments column)	
❑ Incremental zone transfers and or fast zone transfers	
❑ Dynamic updates ❑ Secured (specify permissions in Comments column)	
❑ Update with DHCP Server DHCP server:_____	
❑ Update with DNS Client	
❑ WINS lookup WINS server: _____	
Character set ❑ ASCII ❑ UTF-8	

Design Worksheet – Figure 9.28
Mathematics and Computer Science Building – DNS Clients

Segment	DNS Client Specifications	Comments
	❑ Enable dynamic DNS zone updates DNS Server List 1: _____ 2: _____ 3: _____ 4: _____	
	❑ Enable dynamic DNS zone updates DNS Server List 1: _____ 2: _____ 3: _____ 4: _____	
	❑ Enable dynamic DNS zone updates DNS Server List 1: _____ 2: _____ 3: _____ 4: _____	
	❑ Enable dynamic DNS zone updates DNS Server List 1: _____ 2: _____ 3: _____ 4: _____	

Review

The following questions are intended to reinforce key information in this chapter. If you're unable to answer a question, review the lesson and then try to answer the question again. Answers to the questions can be found in the Appendix, "Questions and Answers."

1. An organization is creating a design in preparation for the deployment of Windows 2000 and Active Directory. The organization has an existing DNS infrastructure based on BIND version 8.2.1 DNS servers. What additional information must you collect to determine the requirements and constraints for a DNS design?

2. You're creating a DNS design for an organization that has existing BIND DNS servers. The organization is deploying Active Directory and requires the DNS design to support the Active Directory deployment. The organization has an existing external and internal namespace and wants to reduce the administration of DNS by automatically populating the DNS zone resource records. However, the organization wants to protect the integrity of the DNS resource records. What recommendations can you make to the organization?

3. You're evaluating an existing DNS design for an Internet-based auction firm that has a significant e-commerce Web presence. The auction firm sells collectibles, memorabilia, celebrity estate items, and other rare goods. The director of information services for the auction firm is concerned about the ability of the Windows 2000–based DNS servers to provide name resolution at all times, regardless of a single point of failure. What changes to the design can you recommend to ensure that customers always *transparently* resolve domain names and subsequently access the e-commerce Web site?

4. An aerospace engineering firm that designs and builds satellite launch vehicles has retained your services to evaluate the existing DNS design. The firm started three years ago as a small entrepreneurial firm. In the last three years, the number of users, and corresponding computers, in the firm has tripled each year. Users are noticing a delay when initially accessing resources and accessing Active Directory. You determine that the DNS query response times are the root cause for the delays users are experiencing. After examining the network segment and router utilization, you determine that the network segments and routers aren't the source of the DNS query latency. What changes to the DNS design can you recommend to resolve these performance issues?

C H A P T E R   1 0

WINS in Name Resolution Designs

About This Chapter

The majority of the networking services designs you create will utilize the Internet Protocol (IP) to access resources within the organization. These resources can be accessed by the IP address assigned to the resource. Although accessing these resources by IP address is technically possible, many users are unable to cope with the complexities of accessing resources by IP address.

Most of the designs you create must allow users to associate a meaningful name to the resources within the organization. Your design must translate these meaningful resource names to IP addresses. Also, most of your designs will require you to perform the reverse operation (translate an IP address into a meaningful resource name).

Your designs will often include migrating networks from Microsoft Windows NT 4.0 to Microsoft Windows 2000. The majority of Windows NT 4.0–based networks run on the Transmission Control Protocol/Internet Protocol (TCP/IP) and rely heavily on Network Basic Input Output System (NetBIOS) names and Windows Internet Name Service (WINS) for accessing resources within the organization. Your design must be capable of integrating WINS-based NetBIOS name resolution into your name resolution design.

You can use the WINS services in Windows 2000 to translate or *resolve* these meaningful resource names to IP addresses and to translate an IP address to a meaningful resource name. The WINS services in Windows 2000 can automatically register the organization's computers in WINS, reducing the amount of time required to administer WINS.

You can integrate computers that use Domain Name System (DNS) for name resolution into a WINS-based network by using the integration between the WINS services and DNS services in Windows 2000. Windows 2000 allows users on your network to transparently resolve NetBIOS names by using WINS or DNS.

This chapter answers questions such as:

- In what situations is the name resolution service provided by WINS appropriate for your design?
- How can you integrate WINS in Windows 2000 with other WINS servers?
- What must you include in your design to integrate WINS with DNS?
- How can you ensure the integrity of the WINS database?
- What can you include in your design to ensure that WINS NetBIOS name resolution is always available to network users?
- How can you improve the performance of WINS NetBIOS name resolution during peak periods of activity?

Before You Begin

Before you begin, you must have an overall understanding of

- Network technologies (including Ethernet, Token Ring, hubs, switches, and concentrators)
- The common TCP/IP configuration parameters (such as IP address, subnet mask, or default gateway)
- Routed networks (including subnets, network segments, routers, and IP switches)
- NetBIOS usage in a network (including NetBIOS naming conventions, name types, name registration, name resolution, and name release)

Lesson 1: Designs That Include WINS

This lesson presents the requirements and constraints, both business and technical, that identify the name resolution services in WINS as a solution.

After this lesson, you will be able to

- Identify the situation in which WINS is the appropriate choice for name resolution
- Describe the relationship between WINS and Windows 2000
- Identify the business and technical requirements and constraints that must be collected to create a WINS design
- Identify the WINS design decisions
- Evaluate scenarios and determine which capabilities and features of WINS are appropriate in name resolution solutions

Estimated lesson time: 30 minutes

WINS and Name Resolution in Networking Services Designs

In "About This Chapter," the primary requirement for including WINS in your design was presented—NetBIOS over TCP/IP (NetBT) name resolution. However, there are solutions other than WINS you can include in your design to provide NetBIOS name resolution.

In addition to WINS, you can provide NetBIOS name resolution by using

- A HOSTS file on the local computer
- A LMHOSTS file on the local computer, or on shared computers
- Domain Name System (DNS)

Although other methods are available, WINS is the only method that provides

- Centralized administration
- Support for NetBIOS name types (such as NetBIOS groups)
- Support for NetBIOS name registration and resolution

Table 10.1 lists each of the methods of NetBIOS name resolution and the advantages and disadvantages of including that method in your design.

Table 10.1   Advantages and Disadvantages of NetBIOS Name Resolution Methods

Method	Advantages	Disadvantages
HOSTS	Available on all network operating systems. Independent of other computers because the HOSTS file is stored locally.	DNS zones don't contain extended information to support NetBIOS name types (such as NetBIOS groups).
LMHOSTS	Provides enhanced support above the HOSTS file for NetBIOS names. Can reference a centralized copy of a LMHOSTS file to reduce administration.	Available only on Microsoft operating systems. Requires administration on every computer. Integrity of the LMHOSTS file can be compromised because users can modify the file.
B-Node Broadcasts	Supports automatic NetBIOS name registration of client computers. Supported by all Windows operating systems and other operating systems.	Designed for name resolution on local subnet. IP routed networks typically don't forward IP broadcasts.
WINS	Supports automatic NetBIOS name registration of client computers. Supported by all Windows operating systems. Centralized name resolution database to reduce administration and configuration errors.	Designed for name resolution for NetBIOS names [fully qualified domain names (FQDNs) aren't fully supported].
DNS	Only name resolution method that supports Active Directory. Centralized name resolution to reduce administration and configuration errors. Can provide name resolution for NetBIOS names in addition to FQDNs.	NetBIOS name registration isn't automatic with DNS servers. DNS zones don't contain extended information to support NetBIOS name types (such as NetBIOS groups).

This chapter focuses on designs that include WINS for NetBIOS name resolution. For more information on domain name resolution and DNS, see Chapter 9, "DNS in Name Resolution Designs."

WINS and Windows 2000

WINS is an industry standard protocol that provides NetBIOS name *registration*, *resolution*, and *release*. In NetBIOS name registration, a WINS server receives

NetBIOS name registration requests from WINS clients and places the NetBIOS name in the WINS database. In NetBIOS name resolution, a WINS server receives a NetBIOS name and returns the corresponding IP addresses. In NetBIOS name release, the WINS client notifies the WINS server that the computer is shutting down.

The WINS services in Windows 2000 can be divided into the following:

- **WINS Client**   You can configure the IP stack for all versions of Microsoft Windows to resolve NetBIOS names by using WINS. The WINS Client is an integral part of the IP implemented in Windows 2000. The WINS Client receives requests for NetBIOS name resolution from applications running on the same computer and forwards the requests to WINS servers.

  You can specify that WINS clients resolve NetBIOS names by specifying different NetBT node types. Each NetBT node type allows Windows 2000 clients to resolve NetBIOS names by using different methods.

  Table 10.2 lists each NetBT node type and how the WINS Client resolves NetBIOS names for the corresponding node type.

Table 10.2   NetBT Node Type Name Resolution

Node Type	Resolves NetBIOS Names By
B-node	Sending IP broadcasts on the local network segment. B-node broadcasts aren't typically forwarded across IP routed network segments unless the routers are specifically configured to route broadcast packets.
P-node	Sending IP unicast traffic to a NetBIOS names server (such as a WINS servers). Because p-node performs NetBIOS name resolution by using unicast traffic, p-node is appropriate for IP routed network segments.
M-node	Attempting to use b-node to resolve NetBIOS names first. If b-node is unable to resolve the NetBIOS name, the WINS Client attempts to use p-node to resolve NetBIOS names.
H-node	Attempting to use p-node to resolve NetBIOS names first. If p-node is unable to resolve the NetBIOS name, the WINS Client attempts to use b-node to resolve NetBIOS names.

Note   Microsoft Windows 95, Microsoft Windows 98, Microsoft Windows Me, Microsoft Windows NT 4.0, and other operating systems include WINS clients as well.

- **WINS Proxies**   The WINS Client can also provide WINS NetBIOS name registration and resolution to non-WINS clients. The WINS proxy is an integral part of the WINS Client, and subsequently, the IP implemented in

Windows 2000. The WINS Client receives requests for NetBIOS name registration or resolution from non-WINS clients running on the same network segment and forwards the requests to WINS servers.

- **WINS Server**   The WINS Server service in Windows 2000 can provide NetBIOS registration, resolution, and release to WINS clients in your design. From the Windows 2000 perspective, WINS Server is a service that runs on Windows 2000. The WINS Server service utilizes the IP and file services of Windows 2000.

   The WINS Server service communicates with WINS clients, other WINS servers, DNS servers, and Dynamic Host Configuration Protocol (DHCP) servers by using the IP stack in Windows 2000. You must specify a fixed IP address for all network interfaces on the WINS server that communicate with the WINS Server service.

   The WINS Server service in Windows 2000 manages a database stored locally on the WINS server. The WINS database contains the WINS records for name resolution that are resolved by the WINS server.

   The WINS Server service is available in Microsoft Windows 2000 Server, Microsoft Windows 2000 Advanced Server, and Microsoft Windows 2000 Datacenter Server. The WINS Server service isn't available in Windows Microsoft 2000 Professional.

The NetBT portion of the IP in Windows 2000 is the WINS Client. Figure 10.1 illustrates the relationship between the NetBT and the IP in Windows 2000.

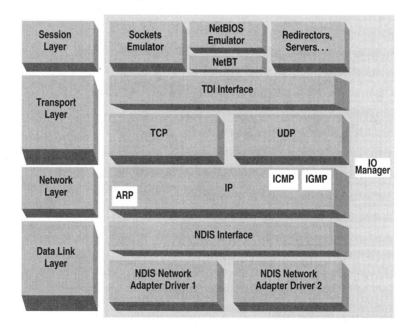

Figure 10.1   The relationship between NetBT and the IP in Windows 2000

In this chapter, you learn how to create name resolution designs with WINS and Windows 2000.

To successfully create WINS designs, you must be familiar with

- The common TCP/IP configuration parameters (such as IP address, subnet mask, or default gateway)

- IP routed networks (including subnets, network segments, routers, and IP switches)

- NetBIOS usage in a network (including NetBIOS naming conventions, name registration, name resolution, and name release)

- NetBIOS name resolution methods (IP packet broadcasts, LMHOSTS file, HOSTS file, and WINS name servers)

- Methods of providing name resolution by using DNS (in designs where WINS and DNS are integrated)

- Common NetBIOS name types and their usage in WINS resolution

WINS Design Requirements and Constraints

Before you create your WINS design, you must gather the requirements and constraints, both business and technical, of the organization. As you create your design, you make design decisions based on the requirements and constraints you collect.

The list of the design requirements and constraints you collect will include

- The amount of data transmitted between the existing network segments containing the WINS clients and the WINS server

- Number of locations and network segments that require NetBIOS name resolution

- Wide area network (WAN) connections in use

- Plans for future network growth

  - Number of NetBIOS-based computers resource records in existing network databases

  - WINS server placement

  - Operating systems that are running NetBIOS

WINS Design Decisions

After you determine the business and technical requirements and constraints, apply the information you gathered to make WINS design decisions.

To create your WINS design, you must choose the

- Methods for integrating WINS into the existing network based on the
  - Existing desktop operating systems
  - Existing WINS servers
  - Existing routed network segments
- Method of ensuring that NetBIOS name resolution is always available to DNS clients
- Method of optimizing the network traffic between NetBIOS clients and NetBIOS servers

The lessons that follow in this chapter provide the information required for you to make specific WINS design recommendations.

WINS and Microsoft Network Designs

The WINS solutions you create must provide support for accessing Microsoft network resources. When the organization's requirements include Microsoft networking and routed IP networks, you must include WINS in your design. Your primary concern in WINS is ensuring that domain controllers, member servers, application servers, and client computers can resolve IP addresses for NetBIOS names stored in WINS.

All versions of Microsoft networking prior to Windows 2000 require NetBIOS to communicate. As a result, the file sharing, print sharing, administrative utilities, client/server applications, and the network operating system as a whole rely on NetBIOS.

Making the Decision

In WINS and Microsoft networking designs, you must determine whether WINS is required to support the networking protocols, the applications, and the operating systems in use. You must examine the requirements of the organization and determine whether WINS is required.

You must include WINS in your Windows 2000 design when any combination of the following is true.

- **Users running Microsoft operating systems prior to Windows 2000, such as Windows 95, Windows 98, Windows Me, and Windows NT 4.0, require authentication in Active Directory directory service.**   All Microsoft operating systems prior to Windows 2000 use the LAN Manager authentication method. LAN Manager authentication relies on the NetBIOS protocol.
- **NetBIOS name support is required on IP-routed network segments.**   You can use b-node broadcasts to resolve NetBIOS names on nonrouted network

segments. However, b-node broadcasts aren't forwarded through IP-routed network segments because b-node broadcasts utilize IP broadcasts.

WINS uses directed (or unicast) IP packets to resolve NetBIOS names. When your designs include IP-routed networks, include WINS to provide NetBIOS name resolution.

- **Client/server applications running on the network require NetBIOS for communications.**   Many client/server applications require NetBIOS to communicate between the client computers and the application servers. Some peer-to-peer application programming interfaces (APIs), such as named pipes, depend on NetBIOS to communicate.

   When your designs include client/server applications that require NetBIOS on IP-routed networks, include WINS to provide NetBIOS name resolution.

- **File services or print services are provided by Microsoft operating systems prior to Windows 2000 (such as Microsoft Windows NT 4.0 Server or Advanced Server).**   All file services or print services provided by Microsoft operating systems prior to Windows 2000 require NetBIOS.

   When your designs include file services or print services provided by Microsoft operating systems prior to Windows 2000, include WINS in your design.

Applying the Decision

Figure 10.2 illustrates a scenario where NetBIOS name resolution in an IP-routed network is the primary reason for including WINS. WINS Server A provides NetBIOS name resolution for file and print servers running Windows NT 4.0, member servers running Windows NT 4.0, and client computers that are running Microsoft operating systems prior to Windows 2000. WINS Server A is placed centrally in the private network to provide equal access to all domain controllers, member servers, and client computers.

For the purposes of this scenario, assume that

- Approximately 400 client computers exist on Segments A and C

- Client computers on Segments A and C are running Windows 98, Windows Me, Windows NT 4.0 Workstation, and Windows 2000 Professional

- The organization has decided to standardize Active Directory as its directory service

- The organization wants to reduce the administration by automatically registering client computers in WINS

- DHCP servers in the organization configure all client computers

- Any unresolved WINS queries must be forwarded to the organization's DNS servers

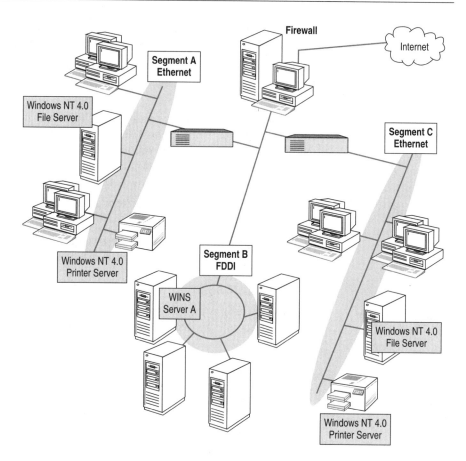

Figure 10.2   Scenario that includes WINS to provide NetBIOS name resolution in an IP-routed network

The WINS services in Windows 2000 are the only solution that meets the requirements of the organization. As a result, HOSTS files, LMHOSTS files, DNS, or b-node broadcasts aren't appropriate solutions.

Windows 2000 Without NetBT and WINS

As discussed in the previous section, all Microsoft Windows operating systems prior to Windows 2000 require NetBIOS, and subsequently NetBT and WINS. Beginning with Windows 2000, you can provide file services, print services, application services, and authentication without NetBIOS.

Making the Decision

To remove NetBT from all Windows 2000 computers, and subsequently eliminate the requirement for WINS in your networking services designs, you must ensure that *all*

- Computers in the network, which access file and print services provided by Windows 2000, are also running Windows 2000

- Applications running on the network don't require NetBIOS for communications

- Users in the network are authenticated by using Windows 2000 and Active Directory

You must specify that all computers running Windows 2000 in your design disable NetBT in the IP. By disabling NetBT, you ensure that all NetBT traffic is eliminated from your design. As a result, WINS is superfluous and any existing WINS servers in the network can be redeployed for other purposes.

Applying the Decision

Figure 10.3 illustrates a scenario where NetBIOS, NetBT, and WINS are eliminated in the design. For the purposes of this scenario, assume that

- Approximately 400 client computers exist on Segments A and C

- Client computers on Segments A and C are running Windows 2000 Professional

- All file servers, print servers, and application servers in the organization are running Windows 2000

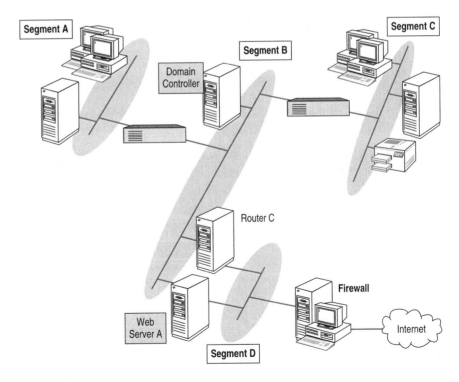

Figure 10.3   Scenario where NetBIOS, NetBT, and WINS are eliminated in the design

- The organization has decided to standardize Active Directory as its directory service

- All applications are certified to communicate by using Windows Sockets or Microsoft Remote Procedure Call (RPC)

Because the organization is running Windows 2000 for Microsoft file and print services exclusively, is authenticating users in Active Directory, and is using Windows Sockets or Microsoft RPC, NetBIOS name resolution (and subsequently WINS) isn't required.

Lesson 2: Essential WINS Design Concepts

This lesson discusses the requirements, constraints, and design decisions that are used in establishing the essential specifications in a WINS design. This lesson discusses the design concepts common to all WINS designs.

After this lesson, you will be able to

- Determine the network segments that require NetBIOS name resolution
- Determine the network segments that require WINS client proxy support
- Select the appropriate WINS client options to include in your design
- Determine the appropriate placement of WINS servers in your design
- Select the appropriate methods for replicating WINS updates between WINS servers

Estimated lesson time: 30 minutes

Determining Which Segments Require NetBIOS Name Resolution

You must determine which network segments in your design require NetBIOS name resolution. Any network segments containing computers that use NetBIOS to communicate require NetBIOS name resolution.

Making the Decision

Provide NetBIOS name resolution for all network segments that include the following:

- **File servers, print servers, or application servers that communicate by using NetBIOS** As mentioned in Lesson 1, Microsoft networking file and print services running on computers prior to Windows 2000 require NetBIOS. In addition, many application servers communicate with client computers by using NetBIOS. You must provide NetBIOS name resolution for the network segments that include these file, print, and application servers.

- **Desktop computers that access file servers, print servers, or application servers that communicate by using NetBIOS** The client computers that access the NetBIOS-based file servers, print servers, and application servers require NetBIOS. You must provide NetBIOS name resolution for the network segments that include these client computers.

  Internet users typically access resources within your design by using client/server protocols and peer-to-peer protocols other than NetBIOS. Unless otherwise specified by the organization, don't provide NetBIOS name resolution for Internet users.

Applying the Decision

Figure 10.4 displays a scenario that illustrates the appropriate selection of network segments that require NetBIOS name resolution as provided by WINS. For the purposes of this scenario, assume that

- Segment B contains only Web servers, DNS servers, and other servers that communicate by using Windows Sockets

- Segments A and C each contain 15 file servers and 10 print servers that are running Windows 2000

- Segments A and C each contain 190 desktop computers running Windows 95, Windows 98, Windows Me, Windows NT 4.0 Workstation, and Windows 2000 Professional

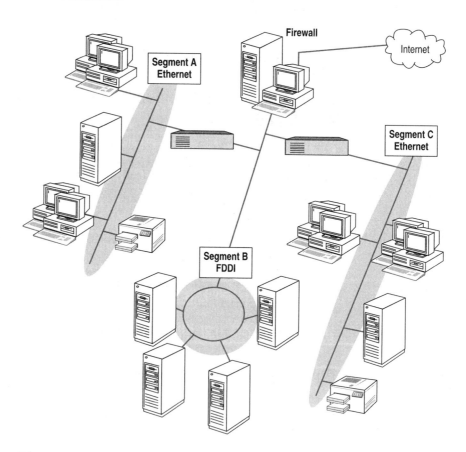

Figure 10.4   Scenario that illustrates the appropriate selection of network segments that require NetBIOS name resolution

Table 10.3 lists each network segment, the NetBIOS name resolution support required, and the reason for including that support in your design.

Table 10.3   Reasons for Including Specific NetBIOS Name Resolution Support

Segment	NetBIOS Name Resolution	Reason
Segment A	Required	Desktop computers run operating systems that require NetBIOS for file and print services on the network segment
Segment B	Not required	No computers on the network segment require NetBIOS
Segment C	Automatic IP configuration	Desktop computers run operating systems that require NetBIOS for file and print services on the network segment
Internet	Not required	No computers on the network segment require NetBIOS

Selecting WINS Client Proxy Support

After you have determined which network segments require NetBIOS name resolution, you must determine the network segments that require WINS client proxy support. For each network segment that includes WINS clients, you must determine when to include *WINS proxies*.

A WINS proxy is a component of the WINS client that allows *non-WINS clients* to resolve NetBIOS names by using WINS servers. Non-WINS clients include operating systems such as IBM OS/2, UNIX, and Microsoft MS-DOS LAN Manager clients.

Figure 10.5 illustrates the interaction among non-WINS clients, WINS clients, and WINS servers. The following sequence describes how non-WINS clients can resolve NetBIOS names by using WINS through WINS Client proxies.

1. Non-WINS clients on the network segment use b-node broadcasts to resolve NetBIOS names.

2. The WINS client(s) on the network segment receives the b-node broadcasts and forwards the non-WINS client's requests to the WINS server.

3. The WINS server resolves the WINS lookup and returns the IP address to the WINS client.

4. The WINS client receives the response from the WINS server and returns the response to the non-WINS client as a b-node broadcast reply.

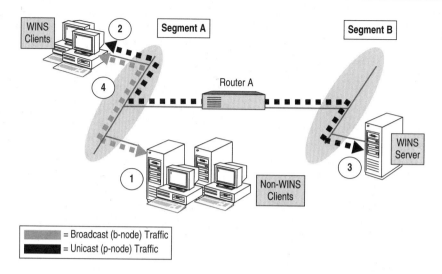

Figure 10.5   Illustration of the interaction among non-WINS clients, WINS clients, and WINS servers

Making the Decision

Any network segment that requires NetBIOS name resolution can include

- **Only WINS clients**   On network segments that include only WINS clients, WINS proxies aren't required. Because all client computers are WINS clients, they are capable of communicating directly with the WINS servers.

- **All non-WINS clients**   On network segments that include only non-WINS clients, WINS proxies are required. You must include at least one WINS client to provide communications with the WINS server on behalf of the non-WINS clients.

  Include more than one WINS client on each network segment to ensure that non-WINS clients can resolve NetBIOS names if a WINS client on the network segment fails.

- **Mixture of WINS and non-WINS clients**   On network segments that include WINS and non-WINS clients, WINS proxies are required. Specify at least one of the WINS clients as a WINS proxy for the non-WINS clients. Specify additional WINS clients as WINS proxies if a WINS client fails.

Applying the Decision

Figure 10.6 illustrates when to include WINS proxies on network segments to provide NetBIOS name resolution to non-WINS clients. For the purposes of this scenario, assume that

- Segment B contains only the WINS server (WINS Server A) and routers

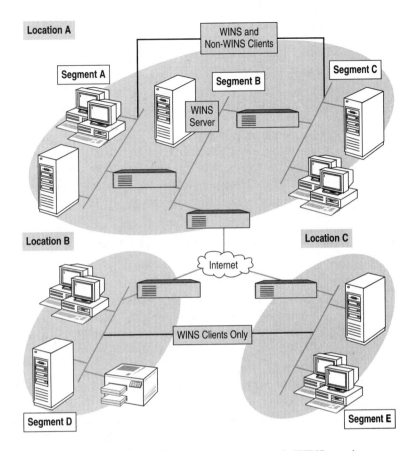

Figure 10.6 Scenario that illustrates when to include WINS proxies

- Segments A and C each contain 15 file servers, 10 print servers, and 280 desktop client computers
- Segments A and C contain WINS clients and non-WINS clients
- Segments D and E each contain 20 file servers, 15 print servers, and 320 desktop client computers
- Segments D and E contain only WINS clients

For the scenario depicted in Figure 10.6, WINS proxies are required only for Segments A and C. All other segments either contain only WINS clients or contain no client computers.

Selecting WINS Client Options

After you determine the network segments that require WINS Client and WINS proxy support, you must determine the WINS Client options to include in your design. WINS Client options determine how the WINS Client resolves NetBIOS names.

Making the Decision

You can include any of the following WINS Client options in your design to specify how the WINS Client resolves NetBIOS names.

- **Sequence of WINS servers**   You can specify one or more WINS servers that the WINS client can utilize for NetBIOS name registration and to resolve NetBIOS names. When you specify more than one WINS server, the WINS client attempts to contact the WINS servers in sequence.

  The WINS client starts with the first WINS server in the list and continues until

  - A WINS server in the list is contacted

  - The WINS client exhausts the list of WINS servers and is unable to contact a WINS server

  You can change the sequence of WINS servers to provide load balancing of WINS queries between multiple WINS servers. For more information on load balancing WINS queries across multiple WINS servers, see Lesson 4, "WINS Design Optimization," later in this chapter.

- **WINS node type**   As discussed in Lesson 1, you can select the NetBT WINS node type for each WINS client. The WINS node type can be specified as b-node, p-node, h-node, and m-node. By default, when you enable WINS on a WINS client, the node type is set to h-node. You can override the default setting to ensure that either the local network segment or the WINS servers are used to resolve NetBIOS names first.

  Select m-node when the majority of the NetBIOS names that must be resolved are on the local network segment. M-node attempts to resolve the NetBIOS names on the local network segment first (by using b-node) and then contacts WINS servers (by using p-node) when the NetBIOS names can't be resolved on the local network segment.

  Select h-node when the majority of NetBIOS names that must be resolved are located on other network segments. H-node attempts to resolve the NetBIOS names on other network segments first (by using p-node) and then attempts to resolve the NetBIOS names on the local network segment (by using b-node).

- **LMHOSTS lookup**   You can enable the WINS client to utilize the LMHOSTS file to resolve NetBIOS names. Include LMHOSTS lookup when you want to create manual entries for NetBIOS resources that aren't registered and that you don't want to manually enter in WINS.

  Typically LMHOSTS lookup isn't included in a WINS design.

- **HOSTS lookup**   The WINS client always utilizes the HOSTS file to resolve NetBIOS names. When the b-node and p-node NetBIOS name resolution is unable to resolve the NetBIOS name, the WINS client attempts to resolve the NetBIOS name by using the HOSTS file.

The primary difference between utilizing the LMHOSTS file and the HOSTS file is that you can enable or disable the LMHOSTS file. The WINS client always utilizes the HOSTS file. Also, the HOSTS file doesn't contain the extended NetBIOS information (such as NetBIOS groups).

- **DNS lookup**   You can also specify that the WINS client utilize DNS to resolve NetBIOS names. If p-node and b-node are unable to resolve the NetBIOS name, the WINS client can forward the query to the DNS servers specified by the DNS client configuration.

You can specify that DNS lookup for NetBIOS names is enabled or disabled on each WINS client.

Applying the Decision

Figure 10.7 illustrates the appropriate selection of WINS Client options. For the purposes of this scenario, assume that

- Segment B contains only Routers A, B, and C; WINS Server A; and DNS Server A

- Segments A and C each contain 15 file servers, 10 print servers, and 280 desktop client computers that are a mixture of WINS and non-WINS clients

- Segments D and E each contain 20 file servers, 15 print servers, and 320 desktop client computers that are WINS clients

- The DNS servers contain no entries that can assist in resolving NetBIOS names

- The WINS clients primarily access resources located on the same network segment

For the scenario depicted in Figure 10.7, specify the following:

- WINS node type is set to m-node
- DNS lookup is disabled
- LMHOSTS lookup is disabled
- No local HOSTS file exists

Determining WINS Server Placement

You must determine where to place WINS servers in your design to ensure that WINS clients can resolve NetBIOS names. You can specify one or more WINS servers in your NetBIOS name resolution design.

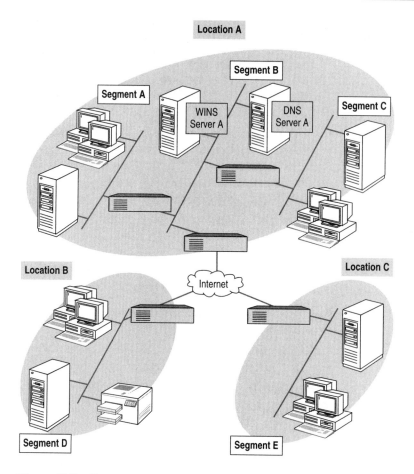

Figure 10.7   Scenario that illustrates the appropriate selection of WINS Client
options

Making the Decision

A single WINS server is capable of supporting up to 10,000 WINS client computers. You can include multiple WINS servers in your design to support more
WINS clients than can be supported by a single WINS server.

As you place WINS servers within your design, you can include

- **At least one WINS server within each location to reduce or eliminate
  WINS traffic between locations**   Place at least one WINS server within a
  location to ensure that WINS queries are resolved while reducing or eliminating WINS traffic between locations. Depending on the requirements of the
  organizations, you might need to add additional WINS servers to enhance the
  performance or availability of your WINS design. For more information on
  WINS improving performance or availability, see Lesson 4, "WINS
  Design Optimization."

- **Additional WINS servers to reduce or eliminate WINS traffic between network segments within the location**   Within a location, you can include additional servers to reduce network traffic on congested network segments, such as backbone network segments. You can place WINS servers on local network segments to ensure that WINS queries are resolved on the local network segment.

Applying the Decision

Figure 10.8 illustrates where to place WINS servers in your design. For the purposes of this scenario, assume that

- All locations contain WINS clients
- You must reduce network traffic between locations

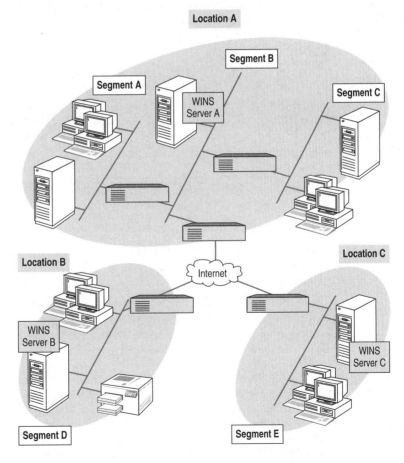

Figure 10.8   Scenario that illustrates where to place WINS servers

- Location A contains 380 WINS client computers
- Location B contains 220 WINS client computers
- Location C contains 170 WINS client computers

For the scenario depicted in Figure 10.8, you can place a WINS server at each location. WINS Servers A, B, and C provide NetBIOS name resolution for each respective location.

Selecting WINS Replication Methods

When your WINS design includes more than one WINS server, you must replicate the WINS database on each WINS server to the other WINS servers in the organization. Unless each WINS server contains a complete listing of all WINS clients (and manually entered WINS entries), the WINS servers can't properly resolve all NetBIOS names.

Making the Decision

When you create the WINS replication portion of your WINS design, you ensure that all WINS servers participate in replication. Your primary concern in creating your WINS replication specifications is the maximum *convergence time* for all the WINS servers in your design. The convergence time is the length of time required for a change in the WINS database at one WINS server to be replicated and appear at other WINS servers in the network.

You can control the convergence time in your design by

- Modifying the WINS replication topology
- Calculating the maximum convergence time
- Specifying replication partner type

WINS Replication Topology

The WINS replication topology of your design defines the logical replication connections between all WINS servers. Although you can create any type of replication topology, the *hub-and-spoke* replication topology model is the most effective in reducing the WINS convergence time in your design.

In the hub-and-spoke model, a centralized WINS server (that acts as the hub) replicates to all other WINS servers (that act as the spokes). The convergence time is minimized because WINS updates must be replicated only by a maximum of two WINS servers.

In Figure 10.9, WINS Server A is the hub that provides replication between all other WINS servers. For example, assume that WINS Server B receives a new NetBIOS name registration from a WINS client. The following sequence describes how the convergence process occurs.

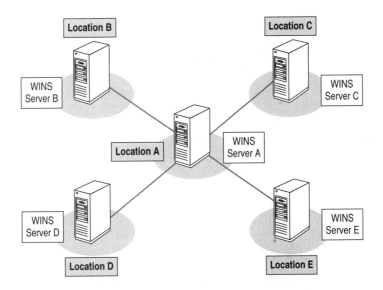

Figure 10.9   Illustration of the hub-and-spoke replication topology model

1. WINS Server B receives the new NetBIOS name registration.

2. WINS Server B replicates the new NetBIOS name registration to WINS Server A.

3. WINS Server A replicates the new NetBIOS name registration to WINS Servers C, D, and E.

In some instances, the organization might have multiple locations that each contain multiple WINS servers. You can extend the hub-and-spoke replication model to incorporate larger designs. You can specify multiple hub WINS servers in your design (typically designated within a location or a region).

The WINS servers within the location or region are the spokes to their *local* hub WINS server. You must specify a hub WINS server for the entire organization, and then specify that the local WINS servers are spokes to the hub WINS server for the entire organization.

In Figure 10.10, the organization has multiple locations and multiple WINS servers at each location. WINS Server A is the hub WINS server for the entire organization. WINS Servers D and G are hub WINS servers for their respective locations. WINS Servers D and G are spokes to WINS Server A.

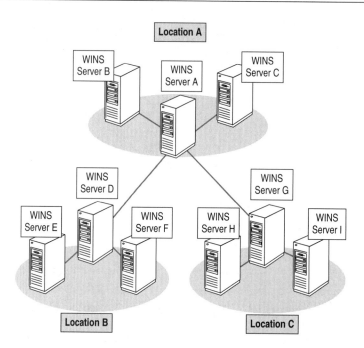

Figure 10.10   Illustration of the hub-and-spoke replication topology mode with multiple hub WINS servers

WINS Maximum Convergence Time

After you specify the replication topology, you know the placement of the WINS servers and the type of connections that support the replication topology. To calculate the maximum convergence time, you must determine the acceptable length of time between when a NetBIOS name is registered on any WINS server and when WINS clients can resolve the NetBIOS name from any WINS server.

You can determine the maximum convergence time by

- **Examining how frequently users access resources in other locations** When your design includes WINS servers that replicate over WAN (or low-speed) connections, you usually sacrifice convergence time for network utilization. WINS servers that replicate over LAN (or high-speed) connections aren't usually constrained by the network utilization.

- **Determining how frequently resources are added or removed from the network**   WINS entries are updated each time a resource is added or removed. When your design includes resources that are added and removed frequently, your design must be capable of replicating a larger volume of WINS updates. When the resources in your design are static, your design can replicate a smaller volume of WINS updates.

You must examine *both* the frequency which users access resources in other locations and the amount of WINS updates to determine your minimal convergence time. For example, when an organization moves or updates any servers accessed by users once every 12 hours, your WINS convergence time must be less than 12 hours. Conversely, when an organization is concerned about conserving WAN network segment utilization, you can increase the convergence time to create less WAN network traffic.

You calculate the convergence time by

- **Determining the replication schedule in hours between all WINS servers** In designs where you adopt the hub-and-spoke topology design, you must determine the replication schedule between the *hub* WINS server and each individual *spoke* WINS server. For other topology designs, you must determine the replication schedule between all possible replication paths.

  Always assume that the WINS update occurred *immediately after* the last WINS replication. For example, a new WINS entry is added, but the WINS server just finished a replication interval. The new WINS entry isn't replicated until the next interval.

- **Adding the *cumulative* hours together between all WINS servers** After you determine the replication schedule, you calculate how many hours the replication will take between all possible combinations of WINS server replication. You must examine each possible replication path to determine the number of hours required to replicate WINS updates between any two WINS servers. You must account for the replication time required for any *intermediary* WINS servers in your design (such as the *hub* WINS server between two *spoke* WINS servers).

- **Identifying the longest replication time required between any two WINS servers** The longest replication time required between any two WINS servers is the convergence time for your WINS design.

Figure 10.11 illustrates the appropriate calculation of WINS convergence time. Assume that a new WINS entry is added to WINS Server E. By examining the topology of the WINS design, you can see that WINS Server H or I will receive the new WINS entry last.

Note For the purposes of the scenario, assume that only pull partner replication is being used. For more information on pull partner, push partner, and push/pull partner replication, see the following section, "WINS Replication Partner Type."

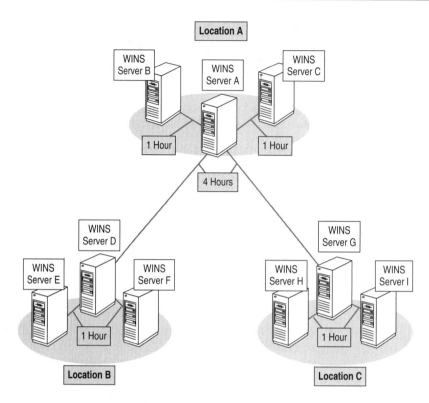

Figure 10.11   Scenario that illustrates the appropriate calculation of WINS convergence time

Table 10.4 lists each step in the replication process, the length of time required for each step, and the cumulative time.

Table 10.4   Steps in the Replication Process

Replication Process	Time Required	Cumulative Time
New WINS entry is added to WINS Server E	0	0
The new WINS entry is replicated to WINS Server D	1	1
The new WINS entry is replicated to WINS Server A	4	5
The new WINS entry is replicated to WINS Server G	4	9
The new WINS entry is replicated to WINS Server I	1	10

In the scenario presented in Figure 10.11, the maximum convergence time is 10 hours.

WINS Replication Partner Type

After you specify the replication topology and calculate the maximum convergence time, you must specify the WINS replication partner type to control the convergence time in your design. You can specify that each WINS server in your design replicate to other WINS servers by using

- **Pull partner replication**   A pull partner is a WINS server that requests (or pulls) updates from other WINS servers in the design on a scheduled interval. You specify pull partner replication for WINS servers when the network segments between the WINS servers have limited data rates or network traffic capacity (such as WAN network segments). Specify pull partner replication for WINS servers in separate locations.

  The advantage to pull partner replication is that you can adjust the replication to reduce network utilization. The disadvantage to pull partner replication is that more convergence time is required.

- **Push partner replication**   A push partner is a WINS server that notifies (or pushes) other WINS servers that the WINS server has updates ready for replication. You specify push partner replication for WINS servers when the network segments between the WINS servers have high-speed data rates or high network traffic capacity (such as LAN network segments). Specify push partner replication for WINS servers within the same location.

  The advantage to push partner replication is that you minimize the convergence time. The disadvantage to push partner replication is that updates are replicated immediately and you can't adjust the replication to reduce network utilization.

- **Push/pull partner replication**   A push/pull partner is a WINS server that notifies other WINS servers of updates and requests updates from other WINS servers. You specify push/pull partner replication for WINS servers when the network segments between the WINS servers have high-speed data rates or high network traffic capacity (such as LAN network segments). Specify push/pull partner replication for WINS servers within the same location.

  Push/pull replication has the same advantages and disadvantages as push replication.

Applying the Decision

Figure 10.12 illustrates the appropriate WINS replication topology and replication partner type. For the purposes of this scenario, assume that

- All locations contain WINS clients
- You must reduce network traffic between locations
- The network segments within locations have sufficient capacity for WINS replication traffic

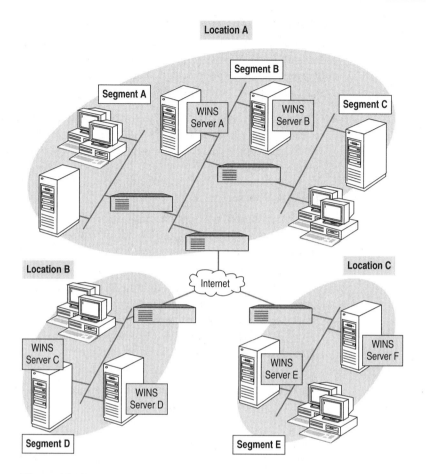

Figure 10.12   Scenario that illustrates the appropriate WINS replication topology and replication partner type

For the scenario depicted in Figure 10.11, specify push/pull partner replication within each location and pull partner replication between locations. Table 10.5 lists each WINS server in the design and the replication partners and replication partner type with the corresponding WINS server.

Table 10.5   WINS Server Replication Partner and Type

WINS Server	Replication Partner and Replication Partner Type
WINS Server A	WINS Server B with push/pull replication because WINS Server B is within the same location WINS Server C with pull replication because WINS Server C is in a different location WINS Server E with pull replication because WINS Server E is in a different location WINS Server A is a hub WINS server

Table 10.5   *(continued)*

WINS Server	Replication Partner and Replication Partner Type
WINS Server B	WINS Server B with push/pull replication because WINS Server A is within the same location WINS Server B is a spoke WINS server
WINS Server C	WINS Server D with push/pull replication because WINS Server D is within the same location WINS Server A with pull replication because WINS Server A is in a different location WINS Server C is a hub WINS server to WINS Server D and a spoke WINS server to WINS Server A
WINS Server D	WINS Server D with push/pull replication because WINS Server C is within the same location WINS Server D is a spoke WINS server
WINS Server E	WINS Server F with push/pull replication because WINS Server F is within the same location WINS Server A with pull replication because WINS Server A is in a different location WINS Server E is a hub WINS server to WINS Server F and a spoke WINS server to WINS Server A
WINS Server F	WINS Server E with push/pull replication because WINS Server E is within the same location WINS Server F is a spoke WINS server

Activity 10.1: Evaluating a WINS Design

In this activity, you're presented with a scenario. To complete the activity:

1. Evaluate the scenario and determine the design requirements

2. Answer questions and make design recommendations

In Figure 10.13, you see a map for a chain of vacation resorts. The marketing department of the resort chain provides inbound and outbound telesales for a chain of vacation resorts. The marketing representatives for a property are located at each resort property. Besides providing inbound and outbound telesales, each representative provides tours of the resort property to prospective customers. The central office for the resort chain is in Mexico City.

The marketing department currently runs reservation and billing software that requires file and print servers. The resorts are connected to one another by using an X.25 network. The majority of the traffic between locations is e-mail messages and customer referrals for other locations. All business transactions are uploaded to the central office in Mexico City nightly.

Answer the following questions concerning your design recommendations. You can find answers to the questions in the Appendix, "Questions and Answers."

Figure 10.13   Map of the vacation resort marketing company

1. You're an outside consultant retained to create the networking services design for the resort chain. Each resort property has fewer than 3,500 computers within the location. The client computers at each resort property run various versions of Windows operating systems that include Windows 95, Windows 98, Windows Me, Windows NT 4.0 Workstation, and Windows 2000 Professional. What do you recommend as a WINS solution for the resort chain?

2. While collecting the requirements and constraints for your design, you discover that a number of the computers at each location are non-WINS clients. How can you provide NetBIOS name resolution to these non-WINS clients?

3. The file and print resources accessed by the reservation and billing system at each resort property are located on network segments other than the WINS clients. The DNS zones at each resort property contain only external resource names. The director of information services for the resort chain wants to ensure that management of the name resolution is performed centrally. How can you ensure that these requirements are met?

Lesson 3: Name Resolution Protection in WINS Designs

This lesson discusses how to create designs that protect the integrity of the WINS NetBIOS name resolution. This lesson focuses on preventing unauthorized configuration changes to your WINS servers.

After this lesson, you will be able to

- Prevent unauthorized private network users from modifying the configuration of the WINS servers
- Prevent Internet users from modifying the configuration of the WINS servers

Estimated lesson time: 15 minutes

Preventing Unauthorized User Access

Ensuring the integrity of the WINS database is the highest security priority in your WINS designs. Ensure that your design prevents any unauthorized private network user access to the WINS servers.

Making the Decision

You can prevent unauthorized users from compromising the integrity of the WINS database by

- **Restricting the number of users who are granted permission to manage WINS servers within the organization**   Grant only authorized network administrators the permission to manage WINS servers. Create a Windows 2000 group and assign the group permissions to manage WINS servers in the organization. Include the authorized network in the Windows 2000 group you created.

- **Isolating the WINS server from public network access**   Ensure that WINS servers don't exist on network segments that are accessible from public networks, such as the Internet. Ensure that only computers within the organization's private network can directly communicate with the WINS servers.

Applying the Decision

Figure 10.14 illustrates the proper methods for preventing unauthorized user access to WINS servers. The firewalls at Locations A, B, and C prevent unauthorized users from accessing the WINS servers in each respective location.

The organization must allow only authorized network administrators to manage the WINS servers. If each location is managed separately, only authorized administrators within each location should be allowed to manage the WINS servers within the corresponding location.

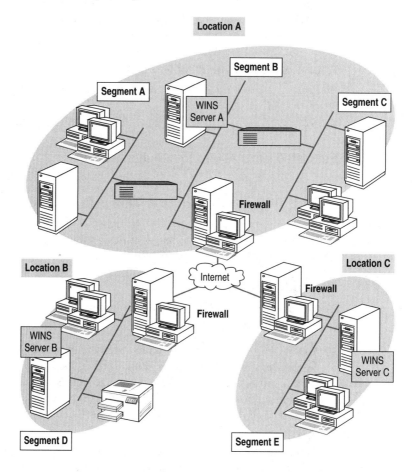

Figure 10.14   A scenario that illustrates the proper methods for preventing unauthorized user access to WINS servers

Lesson 4: WINS Design Optimization

This lesson discusses how to optimize WINS designs to improve the availability and performance characteristics in your design. This lesson focuses on the strategies that increase the percentage of time that computers can resolve NetBIOS names by using WINS, decrease any latency in NetBIOS name resolution, and reduce the network utilization created by WINS replication.

After this lesson, you will be able to

- Select the appropriate method for enhancing the availability characteristics in your WINS design
- Select the appropriate methods for improving the performance characteristics in your WINS design

Estimated lesson time: 20 minutes

Enhancing WINS Availability

Once you have established the essential aspects and security aspects of your WINS design, you can optimize the design for availability. The business requirements of the organization may require your design to ensure WINS configuration at all times. Regardless of a single point of failure, your design must provide redundancy for each WINS server.

You can improve the availability of your WINS designs by

- Including Windows Clustering server clusters
- Including multiple WINS servers with replicated WINS databases
- Dedicating a computer to running WINS

Making the Decision

Windows Clustering Server Clusters

The WINS Server service in Windows 2000 is a *cluster-aware* application. Cluster-aware applications can interact with Windows Clustering *server clusters*. You can create server clusters by sharing a common *cluster drive* between two computers. The cluster drive is attached to a Small Computer System Interface (SCSI) bus common to both computers, also known as *cluster nodes*, in the cluster.

Figure 10.15 illustrates the components in a Windows Clustering server cluster. The WINS Server service actually only runs on one of the cluster nodes at a time. The WINS database is stored on the shared cluster drive. The cluster node currently running the WINS Server services is known as the *active node* for WINS.

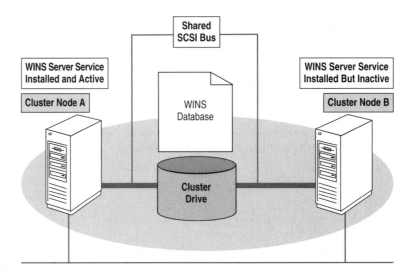

Figure 10.15   Components in a Windows Clustering server cluster

If the WINS active node fails, the remaining cluster node automatically starts the WINS Server service. Because the WINS database is stored on the shared cluster drive, the redundant WINS Server service has the current WINS NetBIOS name database from the failed cluster node.

The primary advantages to WINS on server clusters are

- The redundant cluster node automatically starts and no action is required on the part of the network administrators
- The WINS database is stored on the cluster drive and is available to either cluster node. As a result, WINS clients will be unaware of the failure

For more information on Window Clustering server clusters, see the Windows 2000 help files.

Multiple WINS Servers with Replicated WINS Databases

You can replicate the WINS database entries between two or more WINS servers. Each WINS server manages a portion of the WINS clients registered in the WINS database. If one WINS server fails, the remaining WINS server can provide NetBIOS name resolution for the WINS clients.

Figure 10.16 illustrates how multiple WINS servers with replicated WINS entries provide enhanced availability. For the purposes of this scenario, assume that the business and technical requirements of the organization include

- NetBIOS name registration and resolution must always be performed, regardless of the failure of any WINS server
- Existing computer hardware can't be upgraded

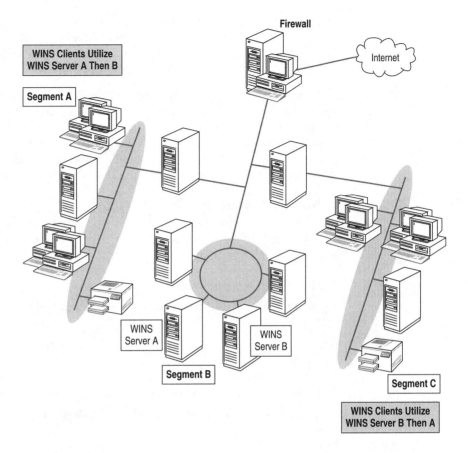

Figure 10.16 Example of how multiple WINS servers with replicated WINS entries provide enhanced availability

To ensure that you achieve the requirements of the design, you must specify that

- All WINS entries are replicated between WINS Servers A and B
- WINS clients on all network segments are configured to use both WINS Servers A and B to perform name resolution

In addition, you can improve performance by specifying a different sequence of WINS servers for the WINS clients to provide load balancing between the WINS servers. In Figure 10.15, the WINS clients on Segment A are configured to query WINS Server A first, and then WINS Server B. The WINS clients on Segment C are configured to query WINS Server B first, and then WINS Server A. For more information on improving WINS performance, see the section, "Improving WINS Performance," later in this lesson.

The primary advantage of multiple WINS servers with replicated WINS entries in comparison to server clusters is that no additional hardware and software resources are required. The disadvantage of multiple WINS servers with replicated WINS entries is that there is no automatic *failover*.

If the failed WINS server is configured in the WINS clients to be queried first, the WINS clients experience a delay in NetBIOS name resolution. The delay in NetBIOS name resolution results from the WINS client waiting for a response from the first (and now failed) WINS server, before timing out and proceeding to the next WINS server in the list. Also, any WINS entries that aren't replicated from the failed WINS server will be missing from the remaining WINS server.

Dedicating a Computer to WINS

By dedicating a computer to running WINS, you improve availability by preventing other applications or services from becoming unstable and requiring the WINS server to be restarted.

Applying the Decision

Figure 10.17 illustrates the proper methods for enhancing the availability of a WINS design.

For the purposes of this scenario, assume that the business and technical requirements of the organization include

- Ensuring that any failure of a WINS server is automatically corrected
- Ensuring that WINS clients perceive no changes in the WINS server configuration

To provide the proper solution, Windows Clustering server clusters must be used to achieve the business and technical requirements of the organization. Server Clusters A, B, and C have the WINS Server service installed on both cluster nodes, but only active on one cluster node. Server Clusters A, B, and C provide WINS NetBIOS name resolution for all network segments within each respective location.

Improving WINS Performance

Once you have established the essential aspects, the security aspects, and availability aspects of your WINS design, you can optimize the design for performance. The business requirements may include that WINS name resolution must occur within a given period of time, based on the number of simultaneous WINS requests. Or the business requirements may include that WINS replication traffic can utilize only a specific portion of WAN network segments.

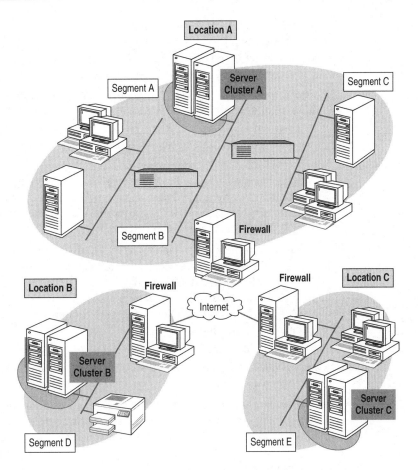

Figure 10.17   Scenario to illustrate the proper methods for enhancing the availability of a WINS design

Making the Decision

You can improve WINS performance by reducing the WINS query resolution time. You can reduce WAN segment utilization by reducing WINS replication traffic.

Reducing WINS Query Resolution Time

You can reduce the WINS query resolution time by

- **Load balancing WINS NetBIOS name resolution across multiple WINS servers**   When the existing WINS servers are saturated and you can't upgrade the hardware to improve performance, you can add additional WINS servers to your design.

Evenly distribute the WINS clients across the multiple WINS servers, ensuring that each WINS server manages approximately the same number of WINS clients. You can distribute the WINS traffic across the additional servers to reduce the latency in WINS-based NetBIOS name resolution.

- **Burst handling**   WINS clients must register their NetBIOS names with the corresponding WINS servers. When a high volume of WINS clients attempt to simultaneously register their NetBIOS names, the WINS servers can become saturated and be unable to register names within the response time requirements of the organization.

  You can enable burst handling of NetBIOS name registration on WINS servers to improve the NetBIOS name registration response times. Below a specified volume of simultaneous WINS registration requests, the WINS server performs WINS registration as normal.

  Once the volume of simultaneous WINS registration requests exceeds a specified volume, the WINS server positively acknowledges the NetBIOS registration request with a varied Time to Live (TTL). The WINS clients must reattempt to register the NetBIOS names after the TTL has expired. Because the TTL is varied across the WINS clients, the WINS clients reattempt the registration over a period of time.

  Specify a burst-handling threshold low enough so the WINS servers utilize burst handling before the hardware resources of the computer running WINS are exhausted and WINS registration performance degrades.

- **Dedicating a computer to WINS**   By dedicating a computer to running WINS, you improve the performance because you prevent other applications or services from consuming system resources.

Reducing WINS Replication Traffic

You can reduce the WINS replication traffic by

- **Specifying pull partner replication**   You can specify the replication partnership between any two WINS servers. Specify pull partner replication between WINS servers to reduce the replication traffic. Pull partner replication utilizes WAN network segments more efficiently because updates to the WINS database are collected and retrieved at regular intervals, rather than as the updates occur.

- **Changing the pull partner replication interval**   Pull partners request updates from the partner WINS servers on specified intervals. You can change the interval used by pull partners to request WINS updates from the corresponding pull partner to change the network utilization. As you change the pull partner replication interval, you also change the length of time required for the WINS servers to synchronize (also known as the *convergence time*).

  Increase the pull partner replication interval to send more WINS updates during one pull partner replication. Decrease the pull partner interval to reduce the convergence time.

  For more information on pull partner replication and convergence time, see Lesson 2, "Essential WINS Design Concepts," in this chapter and the Windows help files.

- **Specify WINS persistent connections**   For WINS servers prior to Windows 2000, new WINS server connections must be established each time replication is performed. Typically, the WINS service in Windows 2000 disconnects from replication partners each time replication completes.

  You can reduce the network traffic associated with WINS replication by enabling *WINS persistent connections*. WINS persistent connections allow the WINS server to retain open connections with replication partners. Because connections between the WINS replication are already established, the network traffic associated with establishing the connection is eliminated.

Applying the Decision

Figure 10.18 illustrates a WINS design prior to optimization for performance. For the purposes of this scenario, assume that the business and technical requirements of the organization include

- The existing computers running WINS can simultaneously register the NetBIOS names for 200 computers

- The existing computers running WINS can't be further upgraded

- The current number of WINS clients can require up to 400 simultaneous NetBIOS name registrations

- Segments A and C each contain 350 client computers, 25 file servers, and 15 print servers

- Segment B contains 15 devices, including WINS Server A

- Segments D and E each contain 175 client computers, 15 file servers, and 10 print servers including WINS Servers B and C

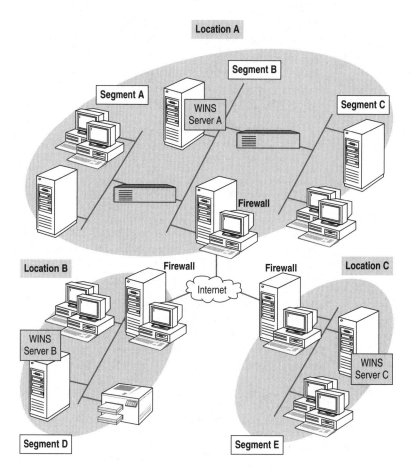

Figure 10.18   Scenario to illustrate a WINS design prior to optimization for performance

Figure 10.19 illustrates a WINS design after optimization for performance. The following performance optimization changes were made to the design.

- WINS Server D is installed to load balance the WINS traffic between WINS Server A and D.
  - WINS Server A manages the WINS clients on Segment A.
  - WINS Server D manages the WINS clients on Segment C.
- WINS Server E is installed to load balance the WINS traffic between WINS Servers B and E.
  - WINS Server B manages the one half of the WINS clients on Segment D.
  - WINS Server E manages the one half of the WINS clients on Segment D.

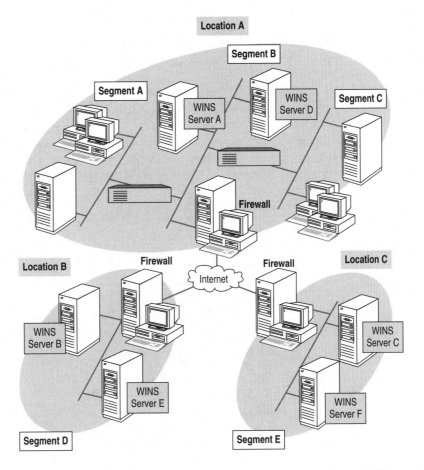

Figure 10.19   Scenario to illustrate a WINS design after optimization for performance

- WINS Server F is installed to load balance the WINS traffic between WINS Servers C and F.

    - WINS Server C manages the one half of the WINS clients on Segment E.

    - WINS Server F manages the one half of the WINS clients on Segment E.

- Burst-handling thresholds are set to 200 on all WINS servers.

- WINS pull replication partners are specified between the WINS servers in different locations.

- WINS push/pull replication partners are specified between the WINS servers within the same location.

Activity 10.2: Evaluating a WINS Design

In this activity, you are presented with a scenario. To complete the activity:

1. Evaluate the scenario and determine the design requirements

2. Answer questions and make design recommendations

In Figure 10.20, you see a map for a chain of vacation resorts that was discussed earlier in this lesson. Since the initial deployment a year ago, the vacation resort chain has extended the hours for making reservations to 24 hours per day. To facilitate the new reservation hours, the resort chain has doubled the marketing and sales representatives at each location.

Figure 10.20   Map of the vacation resort marketing company

Answer the following questions concerning your design recommendations. You can find answers to the questions in the Appendix, "Questions and Answers."

1. The marketing and sales representatives report that the length of time to start the computers has increased proportionally to the number of users added. You examine the network traffic and router statistics and determine that the increased time in starting the computers isn't related to network segment or router saturation. By examining the network traffic for a sampling of the computers exhibiting the performance problems, you determine the WINS servers are one of the primary reasons for the increased time in starting the computers. When you examine the WINS servers, you determine that during peak

periods of activity, the WINS servers have as many as 1,000 NetBIOS registrations in the queue. What recommendations can you make to the vacation resort chain?

2. Each resort property is concerned about security from within the resort property and from the public X.25 network that connects the resort properties. How do you protect WINS servers from access by unauthorized users through the X.25 network and within each resort property?

3. In another meeting, the management of the resort property chain wants to ensure that the marketing and sales representatives can access resources within the resort at all times (to accommodate the new hours of operation). How can you ensure that these business and technical requirements are met?

4. The resort property chain's director of information services has reviewed the current utilization of the X.25 network that connects the locations. During peak periods of activity, the X.25 connections in many locations are at maximum utilization. The director of information services wants to eliminate traffic to ensure that the X.25 network segments don't become saturated. What modification can you make to your WINS design to ensure that these business and technical requirements are met?

Lab: Creating a WINS Design

After this lab, you will be able to

- Evaluate a scenario and determine the design requirements
- Create a multiprotocol network design based on the design requirements

Estimated lab time: 45 minutes

In this lab, you're a consultant hired to create a WINS design for a museum. The museum has a central administrative office and five separate museums in a campus setting.

To complete this lab:

1. Examine the networking environment presented in the scenario, the network diagrams, the business requirements and constraints, and the technical requirements and constraints

2. Use the worksheet for each location to assist you in creating your WINS design (you can find completed sample design worksheets on the Supplemental Course Materials CD-ROM in the Completed Worksheets folder)

3. Create, eliminate, or replace existing networking devices and network segments when required

4. Ensure that your design fulfills the business requirements and constraints and technical requirements and constraints of the scenario by

   - Appropriately placing the WINS servers within each museum
   - Including the appropriate WINS client support on each network segment
   - Including the appropriate WINS client options on each network segment
   - Optimizing your design to provide the security, availability, performance, and affordability

Note   To reduce the length of time for this lab, create a WINS design for the central office and two of the museums only.

Scenario

A foundation that manages a group of museums is restructuring its network in preparation for deploying Windows 2000. The foundation has a central office (shown in Figure 10.22) where the administration and management of the museums occur. The foundation manages a Museum of Natural History (shown in Figure 10.23), an American History Museum (shown in Figure 10.23), an Aerospace Museum (shown in Figure 10.23), a Museum of Art (shown in Figure 10.24), and a Museum of Modern Art (shown in Figure 10.24).

Figure 10.21 illustrates the high-level overview of the foundation's network. The museums are connected to the foundation's central office through a 100Mbps Ethernet fiber-optic network. The foundation is connected to the Internet by a T1 line at the central office.

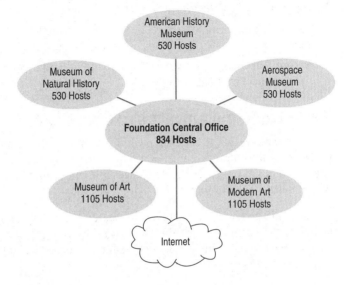

Figure 10.21   Overview network diagram of the foundation that manages the museums

In addition to the funding received through the foundation, each museum receives individual grants and funding. As a result, each museum has different hardware and operating system platforms.

The network in each museum supports

- The museum curators and docents who work in the individual museums
- Interactive displays and kiosks that museum visitors use while visiting the museum

Business Requirements and Constraints

The foundation has a number of requirements and constraints based on the business model of the foundation. As you create your multiprotocol design, ensure that it meets the business requirements and stays within the business constraints.

To achieve the business requirements and constraints, your design must

- Utilize the existing hardware and operating systems in each museum
    - The interactive displays, exhibits, and kiosks at the Museum of Art and the Museum of Modern Art are UNIX-based computers that were provided by a corporate grant

- The file and print servers used by the museum curators and docents at the Museum of Natural History, the American History Museum, and the Aerospace Museum are Windows NT 4.0 servers that were donated to the museums

- Support Active Directory as the directory service for the foundation

- Ensure that the computers used by the museum curators and docents can access museum resources 24 hours a day, 7 days a week

- Ensure that the interactive displays, exhibits, and kiosks are available during normal museum hours of operation

Technical Requirements and Constraints

The applications that run within each museum require connectivity within each museum, with other museums, and with the foundation's central office. These applications run on the computers used by the museum curators and docents and on computers used in interactive exhibits or kiosks.

The existing physical network, hardware, and operating systems place certain technical requirements and constraints on your design. As you create your WINS design, ensure that it meets the technical requirements and stays within the technical constraints.

To achieve the technical requirements and constraints, your design must

- Support the file and print servers running Windows NT 4.0

- Support the UNIX-based computers that access file and print services by using a NetBIOS-based Common Internet File System (CIFS) protocol client

- Ensure that NetBIOS name resolution is attempted first by using the WINS servers and then by using broadcasts on the local network segment

- Prevent any Internet users from accessing any WINS servers

- Support 200 simultaneous WINS NetBIOS name registrations

- Ensure that network traffic on Segment F (Museum Backbone) is minimized

- Ensure that the convergence time for the WINS databases is less than 12 hours

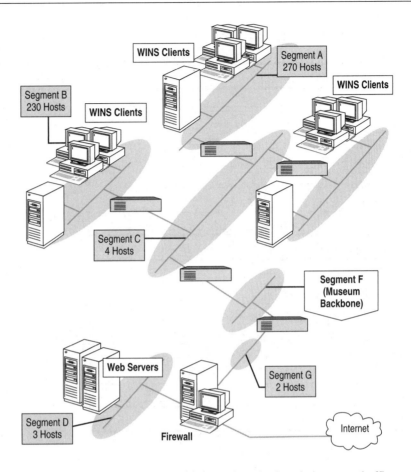

Figure 10.22   This is the existing network at the foundation central office.

Design Worksheet – Figure 10.22
Foundation Central Office – WINS Servers

WINS Server A Specifications	Comments
WINS server connects to segment: _____	
❑ Burst handling Burst-queue threshold size: _____	
❑ Push/Pull partner replication (specify replication partners in Comments column) Replication interval every: _____ hours.	
❑ Pull partner replication (specify replication partners in Comments column) Replication interval every: _____ hours.	
❑ Install on cluster node Cluster name: _____	
WINS Server B Specifications	
WINS server connects to segment: _____	
❑ Burst handling Burst-queue threshold size: _____	
❑ Push/Pull partner replication (specify replication partners in Comments column) Replication interval every: _____ hours.	
❑ Pull partner replication (specify replication partners in Comments column) Replication interval every: _____ hours.	
❑ Install on cluster node Cluster name: _____	
WINS Server C Specifications	
WINS server connects to segment: _____	
❑ Burst handling Burst-queue threshold size: _____	
❑ Push/Pull partner replication (specify replication partners in Comments column) Replication interval every: _____ hours.	
❑ Pull partner replication (specify replication partners in Comments column) Replication interval every: _____ hours.	
❑ Install on cluster node Cluster name: _____	
WINS Server D Specifications	
WINS server connects to segment: _____	
❑ Burst handling Burst-queue threshold size: _____	
❑ Push/Pull partner replication (specify replication partners in Comments column) Replication interval every: _____ hours.	
❑ Pull partner replication (specify replication partners in Comments column) Replication interval every: _____ hours.	
❑ Install on cluster node Cluster name: _____	

Design Worksheet – Figure 10.22
Foundation Central Office – WINS Clients

Segment	WINS Client Specifications	Comments
	WINS Server List 1: _____ 2: _____ 3: _____ 4: WINS node type ❑ b-node ❑ p-node ❑ h-node ❑ m-node ❑ Enable WINS proxies ❑ Enable Lmhosts lookup ❑ Enable DNS lookup	
	WINS Server List 1: _____ 2: _____ 3: _____ 4: WINS node type ❑ b-node ❑ p-node ❑ h-node ❑ m-node ❑ Enable WINS proxies ❑ Enable Lmhosts lookup ❑ Enable DNS lookup	
	WINS Server List 1: _____ 2: _____ 3: _____ 4: WINS node type ❑ b-node ❑ p-node ❑ h-node ❑ m-node ❑ Enable WINS proxies ❑ Enable Lmhosts lookup ❑ Enable DNS lookup	
	WINS Server List 1: _____ 2: _____ 3: _____ 4: WINS node type ❑ b-node ❑ p-node ❑ h-node ❑ m-node ❑ Enable WINS proxies ❑ Enable Lmhosts lookup ❑ Enable DNS lookup	

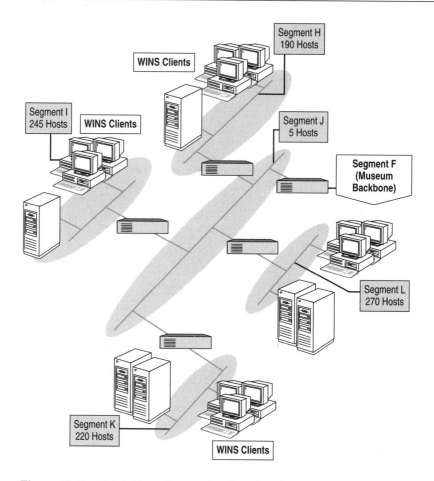

Figure 10.23 This is the existing network at the Museum of Natural History, the American History Museum, and the Aerospace Museum. For the purposes of this lab, assume that all these museums have the same network configuration.

Design Worksheet – Figure 10.23
Museum of Natural History, American History Museum, and Aerospace Museum – WINS Servers

WINS Server A Specifications	Comments
WINS server connects to segment: _____	
❑ Burst handling Burst-queue threshold size: _____	
❑ Push/Pull partner replication (specify replication partners in Comments column) Replication interval every: _____ hours.	
❑ Pull partner replication (specify replication partners in Comments column) Replication interval every: _____ hours.	
❑ Install on cluster node Cluster name: _____	
WINS Server B Specifications	
WINS server connects to segment: _____	
❑ Burst handling Burst-queue threshold size: _____	
❑ Push/Pull partner replication (specify replication partners in Comments column) Replication interval every: _____ hours.	
❑ Pull partner replication (specify replication partners in Comments column) Replication interval every: _____ hours.	
❑ Install on cluster node Cluster name: _____	
WINS Server C Specifications	
WINS server connects to segment: _____	
❑ Burst handling Burst-queue threshold size: _____	
❑ Push/Pull partner replication (specify replication partners in Comments column) Replication interval every: _____ hours.	
❑ Pull partner replication (specify replication partners in Comments column) Replication interval every: _____ hours.	
❑ Install on cluster node Cluster name: _____	
WINS Server D Specifications	
WINS server connects to segment: _____	
❑ Burst handling Burst-queue threshold size: _____	
❑ Push/Pull partner replication (specify replication partners in Comments column) Replication interval every: _____ hours.	
❑ Pull partner replication (specify replication partners in Comments column) Replication interval every: _____ hours.	
❑ Install on cluster node Cluster name: _____	

Design Worksheet – Figure 10.23
Museum of Natural History, American History Museum, and Aerospace Museum – WINS Clients

Segment	WINS Client Specifications	Comments
	WINS Server List 1: _____ 2: _____ 3: _____ 4:	
	WINS node type ☐ b-node ☐ p-node ☐ h-node ☐ m-node	
	☐ Enable WINS proxies	
	☐ Enable Lmhosts lookup ☐ Enable DNS lookup	
	WINS Server List 1: _____ 2: _____ 3: _____ 4:	
	WINS node type ☐ b-node ☐ p-node ☐ h-node ☐ m-node	
	☐ Enable WINS proxies	
	☐ Enable Lmhosts lookup ☐ Enable DNS lookup	
	WINS Server List 1: _____ 2: _____ 3: _____ 4:	
	WINS node type ☐ b-node ☐ p-node ☐ h-node ☐ m-node	
	☐ Enable WINS proxies	
	☐ Enable Lmhosts lookup ☐ Enable DNS lookup	
	WINS Server List 1: _____ 2: _____ 3: _____ 4:	
	WINS node type ☐ b-node ☐ p-node ☐ h-node ☐ m-node	
	☐ Enable WINS proxies	
	☐ Enable Lmhosts lookup ☐ Enable DNS lookup	

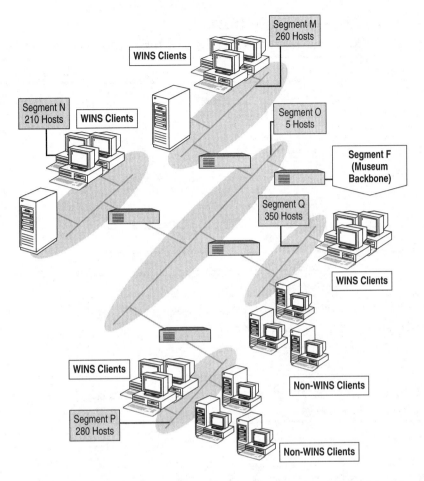

Figure 10.24   This is the existing network at the Museum of Art and the Museum of
Modern Art. For the purposes of this lab, assume that all these
museums have the same network configuration.

Design Worksheet – Figure 10.24
Museum of Art and the Museum of Modern Art– WINS Servers

WINS Server A Specifications	Comments
WINS server connects to segment: _____	
❑ Burst handling Burst-queue threshold size: _____	
❑ Push/Pull partner replication (specify replication partners in Comments column) Replication interval every: _____ hours.	
❑ Pull partner replication (specify replication partners in Comments column) Replication interval every: _____hours.	
❑ Install on cluster node Cluster name: _____	
WINS Server B Specifications	
WINS server connects to segment: _____	
❑ Burst handling Burst-queue threshold size: _____	
❑ Push/Pull partner replication (specify replication partners in Comments column) Replication interval every: _____ hours.	
❑ Pull partner replication (specify replication partners in Comments column) Replication interval every: _____ hours.	
❑ Install on cluster node Cluster name: _____	
WINS Server C Specifications	
WINS server connects to segment: _____	
❑ Burst handling Burst-queue threshold size: _____	
❑ Push/Pull partner replication (specify replication partners in Comments column) Replication interval every: _____ hours.	
❑ Pull partner replication (specify replication partners in Comments column) Replication interval every: _____ hours.	
❑ Install on cluster node Cluster name: _____	
WINS Server D Specifications	
WINS server connects to segment: _____	
❑ Burst handling Burst-queue threshold size: _____	
❑ Push/Pull partner replication (specify replication partners in Comments column) Replication interval every: _____ hours.	
❑ Pull partner replication (specify replication partners in Comments column) Replication interval every: _____ hours.	
❑ Install on cluster node Cluster name: _____	

Design Worksheet – Figure 10.24
Museum of Art and the Museum of Modern Art– WINS Clients

Segment	WINS Client Specifications	Comments
	WINS Server List 1: _____ 2: _____ 3: _____ 4: _____ WINS node type ❑ b-node ❑ p-node ❑ h-node ❑ m-node ❑ Enable WINS proxies ❑ Enable Lmhosts lookup ❑ Enable DNS lookup	
	WINS Server List 1: _____ 2: _____ 3: _____ 4: _____ WINS node type ❑ b-node ❑ p-node ❑ h-node ❑ m-node ❑ Enable WINS proxies ❑ Enable Lmhosts lookup ❑ Enable DNS lookup	
	WINS Server List 1: _____ 2: _____ 3: _____ 4: _____ WINS node type ❑ b-node ❑ p-node ❑ h-node ❑ m-node ❑ Enable WINS proxies ❑ Enable Lmhosts lookup ❑ Enable DNS lookup	
	WINS Server List 1: _____ 2: _____ 3: _____ 4: _____ WINS node type ❑ b-node ❑ p-node ❑ h-node ❑ m-node ❑ Enable WINS proxies ❑ Enable Lmhosts lookup ❑ Enable DNS lookup	

Review

The following questions are intended to reinforce key information in this chapter. If you're unable to answer a question, review the lesson and then try to answer the question again. Answers to the questions can be found in the Appendix, "Questions and Answers."

1. An organization is comprised of 130 locations and each location has an average of 35 routed network segments. Each location contains a 100Mbps backbone segment that connects the other network segments to one another. The organization supports a variety of desktop operating systems. As an independent consultant to the organization, you're retained to create a WINS design. What recommendations can you make to the organization?

2. You're evaluating an existing WINS design for an international legal firm. The legal firm has 190 locations throughout the world. The desktop and laptop client computers in the legal firm run various network operating systems, including Windows 98, Windows Me, Windows NT 4.0, and Windows 2000. The legal firm wants to ensure that all networking services, including WINS, are protected from unauthorized users. Because the legal firm has locations worldwide, the users must be able to resolve NetBIOS names at all times. What recommendations can you make to the legal firm?

3. You're evaluating an existing WINS design for an organization. The organization has 25 locations throughout Europe. Each location contains approximately 275 desktop computers, 15 file servers, and 25 print servers. Currently, the organization's WINS servers are running Windows NT 4.0 Server. The WAN network segments that connect the locations are saturated during peak periods of activity. What changes to the WINS design can you recommend to reduce the utilization of the WAN network segments during these peak periods of activity?

4. An organization is deploying Windows 2000 exclusively for all computers in the network. The existing network is running Windows 95, Windows 98, Windows NT, and other operating systems. The existing networking services are running on Windows NT 4.0 Server. The information services manager of the organization wants to eliminate NetBIOS traffic to reduce network traffic and remove the requirement for WINS servers. What must be done so you can achieve these business and technical requirements in your design?

CHAPTER 11

Dial-Up Connectivity in Remote Access Designs

About This Chapter

Remote access to the private network is an important and common component to networking services designs. Today, many users work from small home offices or while traveling. These users must access private network resources as though they are directly connected to the private network.

Some organizations require remote access that can *only* be used by the organization's remote users. These organizations are unwilling to share remote access communications with other organizations (such as connectivity over the Internet). These organizations use *dial-up remote access* to maintain control of the security and costs associated with remote access. By owning the remote access servers, modems, and phone lines, the organization can control all aspects of their remote access design.

Some organizations provide remote access for other organizations' usage, such as Internet service providers (ISPs) that provide dial-up remote access for their customers. The ISP is responsible for maintaining the remote access servers, modems, and phone lines associated with the remote access solution.

The ISP's customers typically access their private networks by using virtual private networking (VPN) connections. From the ISP's perspective, the ISP is providing dial-up remote access. From the ISP customer's perspective, the ISP customer is providing VPN remote access.

All organizations that provide dial-up remote access must authenticate users, encrypt confidential data, and restrict access to private network resources. The remote access users must be able to transparently access the private network resources.

You can provide dial-up remote access by using the Routing and Remote Access feature in Microsoft Windows 2000. Routing and Remote Access can authenticate remote access users in Active Directory, Microsoft Windows NT 4 domains, or any Remote Authentication Dial-In User Service (RADIUS) server, such as Internet Authentication Server (IAS), found in Windows 2000.

Your designs must protect confidential data by encrypting the traffic between the remote access users and the remote access servers. Routing and Remote Access can encrypt data over dial-up connects by using Microsoft Point-to-Point Encryption (MPPE) or Internet Protocol Security (IPSec). Finally, Routing and Remote Access can restrict the private network segments that can be accessed by remote access users.

This chapter answers questions such as:

- In what situations are the dial-up remote access services provided by Routing and Remote Access appropriate for your design?
- How can you integrate Routing and Remote Access in your network?
- What must you include in your design to integrate Routing and Remote Access with other Windows 2000 networking services?
- How can you ensure the confidentiality of data between remote access clients and remote access servers?
- What can you include in your design to ensure that dial-up remote access is always available to remote access users?
- How can you improve the performance of dial-up remote access solutions during peak periods of activity?

Before You Begin

Before you begin, you must have an overall understanding of

- Network technologies (including Ethernet, Token Ring, hubs, switches, and concentrators)

- The common transport protocol configuration for Internet Protocol (IP), Internetwork Packet Exchange (IPX), and AppleTalk (such as IP address, subnet mask, or default gateway for IP)

- IP, IPX, and AppleTalk routed networks (including subnets, network segments, routers, and IP switches)

- Dial-up telephony and other connectivity technologies

Lesson 1: Designs That Include Dial-Up Remote Access

This lesson presents the requirements and constraints, both business and technical, that identify the dial-up remote access services in Routing and Remote Access as a solution.

After this lesson, you will be able to

- Identify the situation in which Routing and Remote Access is the appropriate choice for dial-up remote access

- Describe the relationship between Routing and Remote Access and Windows 2000

- Identify the business and technical requirements and constraints that must be collected to create a dial-up remote access design

- Identify the dial-up remote access design decisions

- Evaluate scenarios and determine which capabilities and features of Routing and Remote Access are appropriate in dial-up remote access solutions

Estimated lesson time: 30 minutes

Routing and Remote Access in Dial-Up Remote Access Designs

You can include Routing and Remote Access in remote access designs to provide dial-up remote access, provide VPN remote access, or function as a RADIUS client. To create successful remote access solutions, you must determine whether the solution requires dial-up remote access, VPN remote access, or a RADIUS client.

In addition to dial-up remote access connectivity, you can provide remote access by using

- VPN remote access connectivity
- Outsourced remote access connectivity by using RADIUS

Although other remote access methods are available, dial-up remote access is the only method that allows the organization to control *all* aspects of the dial-up portion of remote access connectivity. Only dial-up remote access connectivity solutions allow the organization to control the

- Remote access servers
- Dial-up modems types and data rates
- Access phone numbers and associated charges
- User accounts authorized for remote access
- Private network resources that remote users can access

Dial-up remote access solutions utilize Point-to-Point Protocol (PPP) to connect remote clients to the remote access server. PPP is an industry standard collection of protocols that defines how to authenticate remote users and transmit IP, IPX, AppleTalk, and Network Basic Enhanced User Interface (NetBEUI) traffic. Multiple vendors and operating systems support PPP.

VPN and RADIUS solutions utilize PPP to provide dial-up connectivity, exactly like the dial-up remote access solution. In addition, VPN and RADIUS solutions require Point-to-Point Tunneling Protocol (PPTP) or Layer 2 Tunneling Protocol (L2TP) to provide virtual connections to the organization's private network resources.

The addition of PPTP and L2TP increases the amount of traffic required to send the equivalent amount of information by using PPP. As a result, when using comparable hardware, dial-up remote access solutions (using PPP only) provide better performance.

Figure 11.1 compares the differences between a PPP and a PPTP packet. The PPTP packet is a superset of the PPP packet. The additional information [the additional IP header and Generic Routing Encapsulation (GRE) header] increases the amount of traffic required to send the same amount of data (in the PPP payload).

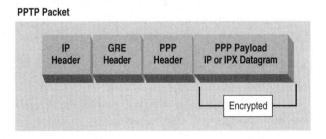

Figure 11.1   Comparison of a PPP and a PPTP packet

In addition, other protocols (such as AppleTalk and NetBEUI) don't support PPTP or L2TP. Only IP and IPX can be transmitted through PPTP and L2TP tunnels. Because dial-up remote access solutions utilize PPP (and PPP supports

IP, IPX, AppleTalk, and NetBEUI), you can provide solutions for remote users running AppleTalk and NetBEUI protocols.

This chapter discusses dial-up remote access solutions provided by Routing and Remote Access. For more information on VPN remote access solutions by using Routing and Remote Access, see Chapter 12, "VPN Connectivity in Remote Access Designs." For more information on RADIUS client solutions by using Routing and Remote Access, see Chapter 13, "RADIUS in Remote Access Designs."

Routing and Remote Access and Windows 2000

Routing and Remote Access is the Windows 2000 feature that provides remote access solutions and routing solutions. As discussed in the previous section, you can create a variety of remote access solutions by using Routing and Remote Access. Routing and Remote Access also is appropriate for any multiprotocol routing solution, including IP, IPX, and AppleTalk protocols.

For more information on IP routing solutions provided by Routing and Remote Access, see Chapter 4, "IP Routing Designs." For more information on multiprotocol routing solutions provided by Routing and Remote Access, see Chapter 5, "Multiprotocol Routing Designs."

The remote access services in Windows 2000 can be divided into the following:

- **Remote access client**   Windows 2000 and all other Windows operating systems, including Microsoft Windows 95, Microsoft Windows 98, Microsoft Windows Me, and Windows NT 4, include a remote access client. In Windows 2000, the *dial-up networking client* feature is the remote access client. The name of the remote access client, dial-up networking client, is misleading because the client provides dial-up and VPN remote access connectivity.

- **Remote access server**   Routing and Remote Access in Windows 2000 can provide remote access connectivity in your design. From the Windows 2000 perspective, Routing and Remote Access is a service that runs on Windows 2000. Routing and Remote Access utilizes the IP, IPX, AppleTalk, and NetBEUI protocols of Windows 2000. In addition, you can authenticate remote users by using local user accounts or user accounts in Active Directory directory service.

  The remote access server is essentially a specialized router that routes IP, IPX, or AppleTalk traffic between the remote access clients and network segments in the private network. All the design decisions that apply to IP, IPX, or AppleTalk routers must be included in your dial-up remote access design. For more information on IP routing, see Chapter 4, "IP Routing Designs." For more information on IPX or AppleTalk routing, see Chapter 5, "Multiprotocol Routing Designs."

Routing and Remote Access can dynamically assign IP addresses allocated from Dynamic Host Configuration Protocol (DHCP) servers. You must specify a fixed IP address for the network interfaces on the Routing and Remote Access server that communicate with the private network. Routing and Remote Access utilizes the protocols provided by Windows 2000 to communicate with the private network and remote access clients.

Routing and Remote Access is available in Microsoft Windows 2000 Server, Microsoft Windows 2000 Advanced Server, and Microsoft Windows 2000 Datacenter Server. Routing and Remote Access isn't available in Microsoft Windows 2000 Professional.

Figure 11.2 illustrates the relationship between remote access clients and remote access servers in dial-up remote access designs. The dial-up network client in Windows 2000 is the remote access client that connects to the remote access servers running Routing and Remote Access on Windows 2000.

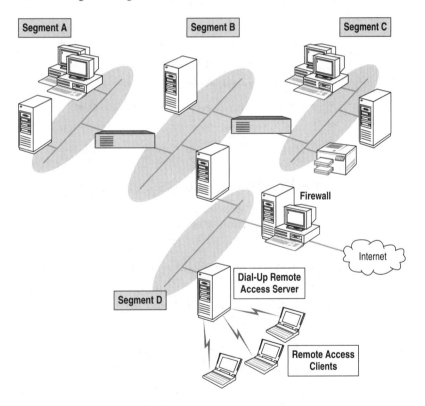

Figure 11.2   The relationship between remote access clients and remote access servers in dial-up remote access designs

In this chapter, you learn how to create dial-up remote access designs with Routing and Remote Access and Windows 2000. To successfully create dial-up remote access designs, you must be familiar with

- General local area network (LAN) protocol and LAN routing theory for IP, IPX, or AppleTalk
- Telephony and other connectivity technologies

Dial-Up Remote Access Design Requirements and Constraints

Before you create your dial-up remote access design, you must gather the requirements and constraints, both business and technical, of the organization. As you create your design, you make design decisions based on the requirements and constraints you collect.

The list of the design requirements and constraints that you'll collect includes the following:

- The amount of data transmitted between the remote access clients and the remote access servers
- Number of locations that require dial-up remote access
- Existing modems and phone lines
- Plans for network growth
- Number of simultaneous remote access clients
- Operating systems that the remote access clients are running
- Protocols utilized by the remote access clients

Dial-Up Remote Access Design Decisions

After you determine the business and technical requirements and constraints, apply the information you gathered to make dial-up remote access design decisions. To create your dial-up remote access design, you must choose the

- Methods for integrating dial-up remote access into the existing network based on the
    - Remote access client operating systems
    - Existing remote access servers
    - Existing phone lines and modems
- Hardware requirements for the dial-up remote access servers, including
    - Number of communications ports, modems, and phone lines required to support the maximum number of simultaneous remote access users
    - Data rate of the modems
    - Phone numbers, such as local, long distance, or toll-free phone numbers, to be called by the remote access users

- Methods for protecting confidential data exchanged by the remote access clients that include

  - Authenticating remote access users

  - Encrypting confidential data

  - Enhancing user authentication by using features such as caller-ID and callback

- Method of ensuring that dial-up remote access is always available to remote access clients

- Method of optimizing the network traffic between remote access clients and remote access servers

The lessons that follow in this chapter provide the information required for you to make specific dial-up remote access design recommendations.

Dial-Up Remote Access Designs

Your dial-up remote access solutions must provide remote users with access to private network resources. When the organization wants to control all aspects of the remote access design, you must include *dial-up* remote access in your design.

In *VPN* remote access solutions, some portion of the remote access connectivity is provided by other organizations, such as an ISP. Because the ISP owns the phone lines, modems, and dial-up remote access servers, the organization providing VPN access loses some control over the design (such as modem data rates, available phone numbers, physical security of the remote access servers, or other specifications).

You can include Routing and Remote Access in your designs to provide dial-up remote access solutions. The remote users can access the private network by using Transmission Control Protocol/Internet Protocol (TCP/IP), IPX, or AppleTalk protocols.

Making the Decision

In remote access designs, you must determine whether dial-up remote access is the appropriate solution by examining the requirements and constraints of the organization.

As previously mentioned, the primary advantage to including dial-up remote access is that the organization can control all aspects of the remote access design. Most of the issues associated with selecting dial-up remote access are related to security. Some organizations are unable or unwilling to utilize public network connectivity and require exclusive connectivity for security reasons.

The primary disadvantage to dial-up remote access is cost of ownership. The cost of ownership associated with dial-up remote access solutions includes

- **Number of simultaneous remote users**   As the number of simultaneous remote users increases, the complexity of supporting the remote users increases. A larger number of remote users requires more remote access servers, modems, and phone lines.

- **Geographic dispersal of remote access users**   When your design must include more than one location where you must provide remote access, the complexity of the design increases. As the number of locations where remote access must be provided increases, the number of remote access servers, modems, phone lines, and support personnel increases.

- **Monthly costs associated with the phone lines**   For each phone line you include in your design, the monthly costs associated with phone lines increases incrementally. Depending on interstate or intrastate tariffs, the costs associated with the phone lines might increase in larger increments.

- **Initial investment in modems and phone line installation**   The initial investment in the modems (or other communications hardware) and the installation charges for phone lines are another cost that must be amortized throughout the life cycle of the dial-up remote access design. Typically, the cost associated with the initial investment is far less than the total amount the organization will invest over the life cycle of the dial-up remote access design.

- **Ongoing support for remote access servers, phone lines, modems, and help desk support for remote users**   Proportional to the other costs, the cost for ongoing support is the largest financial investment the organization makes over the life cycle of the dial-up remote access design. These support costs include network support engineers, testing equipment, training, and help desk personnel to support and manage the remote access design.

You can reduce the costs associated with remote access by *outsourcing* a portion of the remote access design. Outsourcing portions of the remote access design requires that the organization is willing to relinquish some of the control over the design to another organization, such as an ISP. Regardless of the agreement between the organizations, outsourcing reduces the control that either organization has on the total solution.

For example, an organization can significantly reduce costs by outsourcing its international dial-up connectivity to an ISP. The ISP provides dial-up connectivity for the organization's remote users. The ISP incurs the costs associated with the dial-up remote access connectivity. Because the ISP can amortize the costs associated with the initial investment and ongoing costs associated with the dial-up network solution across multiple organizations, the cost to the organization is significantly less.

Note   Even when dial-up remote access outsourcing is selected, the organization is required to include VPN remote access to provide remote access to private network resources.

When the organization is willing to relinquish control of portions of the remote access solution to other organization, consider a VPN or RADIUS remote access solution. For more information on VPN remote access solutions by using Routing and Remote Access, see Chapter 12, "VPN Connectivity in Remote Access Designs." For more information on RADIUS client solutions by using Routing and Remote Access, see Chapter 13, "RADIUS in Remote Access Designs."

Applying the Decision

Figure 11.3 illustrates a scenario where Routing and Remote Access provides a dial-up remote access solution. The organization requires that all aspects of the design must be under the direct control of the organization. Due to security reasons, the organization is unwilling to outsource any portion of the remote access solution.

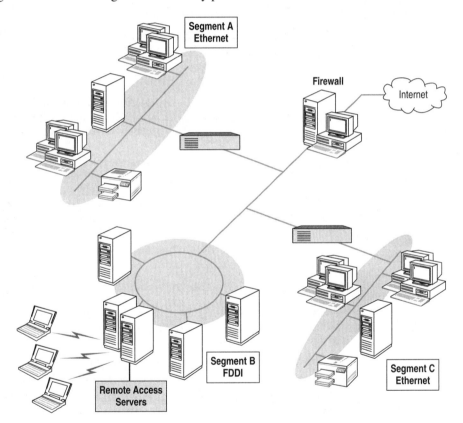

Figure 11.3   Scenario that includes Routing and Remote Access to provide dial-up remote access solutions

The dial-up remote access services provided by Routing and Remote Access in Windows 2000 are the only solution that meets the requirements of the organization. As a result, VPN remote access or outsourced RADIUS solutions aren't appropriate solutions.

Lesson 2: Essential Dial-Up Remote Access Design Concepts

This lesson discusses the requirements, constraints, and design decisions that are used in establishing the essential specifications in a dial-up remote access design. This lesson also discusses the design concepts common to all dial-up remote access designs.

After this lesson, you will be able to

- Determine the number of dial-up remote access servers to include in your design
- Determine the appropriate placement of dial-up remote access servers in your design
- Select the remote access client support

Estimated lesson time: 30 minutes

Determining the Placement of Remote Access Servers

You must determine the number of dial-up remote access servers required in your design. You can specify one or more dial-up remote access servers in your remote access design.

Making the Decision

A single dial-up remote access server can potentially support hundreds of remote access client computers. You can include multiple remote access servers in your design to support more remote access clients than can be supported by a single remote access server. To decide how many remote access servers to include in your design, you must know the

- Maximum number of simultaneous remote users that must access resources *at each location* within the organization
- Amount of data to be transmitted *over a period of time* (or sustained data rate) between the remote users and the remote access servers

After you know the maximum number of simultaneous users and the sustained data rate, you can determine the number of remote access servers you must include by conducting a pilot test. In the pilot test, you determine the number of remote users that can be supported by the remote access servers and ensure that each remote access connection is transmitting data at the sustained data rate.

Upon completion of the pilot tests, you know the maximum number of users that your remote access servers can support at the sustained data rate. To determine the number of remote access servers to include in your design, divide the maximum number of users required by the number of users that each remote access server can support. Round your calculation up to the next nearest whole number to finalize the number of remote access servers required in your design.

Applying the Decision

An organization wants to provide dial-up remote access to remote users. You must calculate the number of remote access servers required in your design. For the purposes of this scenario, assume that

- The organization has 2,500 users that require remote access
- Up to 750 remote users may simultaneously access the remote access servers
- Acceptable application response times require a sustained data rate of 22.3Kbps or higher for each remote access client
- Each remote user connects to the dial-up remote access server by using a modem capable of at least 28.8Kbps
- Pilot tests confirm that the approved remote access servers can support 60 remote users with a sustained data rate of 28.8Kbps

Table 11.1 shows the calculations used in determining the number of remote access servers required in the design.

Table 11.1   Calculations for the Number of Remote Access Servers Required

Perform These Calculations		Using
A	Maximum number of simultaneous remote users	700
B	Number of remote users that each remote access server can support	60
C	Number of remote access servers required ($C=A/B$)	11.3
D	Round up to the nearest even number of remote access servers	12

Determining the Placement of Remote Access Servers

You must determine where to place the dial-up remote access servers in your design so remote access clients can access private network resources. You place the dial-up remote access servers to centralize administration, reduce costs, and reduce the network traffic between locations.

Making the Decision

You can place remote access servers within your design such that

- All the remote access servers are in a single location in the organization
- The remote access servers are distributed across multiple locations

You must place dial-up remote access servers to ensure that remote access clients can access private network resources while reducing or eliminating remote access traffic between locations. Depending on the requirements of the organizations, you might need to add additional remote access servers to enhance the performance or availability of your dial-up remote access design. For more information on remote access servers improving performance or availability, see Lesson 4, "Dial-up Remote Access Design Optimization."

All Remote Access Servers in a Single Location

When all the remote access servers are in a single location, you must provide enough communications ports, modems, and phone lines to support the maximum number of simultaneous remote access users for the entire organization.

The advantage of placing all the remote access servers in a single location is that you

- **Centralize the administration and support of the remote access servers** Centralized administration and support ensures that consistency in configuration, such as the same security configuration, exists on all the remote access servers.

- **Potentially reduce the costs associated with administration and support** Because all the remote access servers are in one location, the administration and support costs are amortized across *all* the remote access servers.

The disadvantage of placing all the remote access servers in a single location is that you

- **Potentially increase network traffic on wide area network (WAN) segments** When an organization is comprised of multiple locations, the remote access users might want to access resources in locations *other* than the location where the remote access servers are placed. Accessing resources in locations other than where the remote access servers are placed forces traffic across the WAN segments that connect the locations.

- **Potentially increase telephone access charges** When the remote users are geographically distributed, placing all the remote access servers in a central location can increase the telephone access charges because the remote user might be required to call long distance. Typically, the organization is responsible for any long distance charges that the remote users incur.

- **Potentially lose all remote access connectivity** When *all* the remote access servers are placed in a central location, users will be unable to gain remote access if a catastrophic event (such as an earthquake, hurricane, or tornado) interrupts service at that location. When organizations have network resources in multiple geographic locations, consider placing remote access servers at each location to provide redundancy in the event of a disaster.

Note   For organizations that have network resources in a single geographic location, consider providing offsite connectivity in the event of a disaster.

Remote Access Servers Distributed Across Multiple Locations

When the remote access servers are distributed across multiple locations, you must provide enough communications ports, modems, and phone lines to support the maximum number of simultaneous remote access users that connect at each location.

The advantage of placing the remote access in multiple locations is that you potentially reduce the

- **Network traffic between locations within the organization**   When the remote users predominantly access resources within the same location as the dial-up remote access server, network traffic between locations is reduced or eliminated. Reducing the network traffic between locations can reduce WAN utilization and improve data transfer rates for other applications.

- **Telephone access charges**   When the dial-up remote access servers are placed in the appropriate locations, remote users call local telephone numbers. Because the remote users call local telephone numbers, no long distance telephone charges are incurred.

- **Potential for loss of remote access due to a catastrophic event**   When the remote access servers are distributed across multiple locations, users can access the network remotely even when a catastrophic event interrupts services at one geographic location.

The disadvantage of placing the remote access in multiple locations is that you potentially

- **Decentralize the administration and support of the remote access servers** Because the dial-up remote access servers are in multiple locations, administration and support must be provided at each location that contains remote access servers.

- **Increase the costs associated with administration and support**   Because the remote access servers are in multiple locations, the administration and support costs are amortized across *fewer* remote access servers. As a result, the average cost to administer and support the dial-up remote access servers is increased.

Applying the Decision

Figure 11.4 illustrates where to place dial-up remote access servers in your design. For the purposes of this scenario, assume that

- The highest priority is the reduction of costs associated with dial-up remote access

- The reduction of network traffic between locations is the second highest priority

- Location A has 130 users who work remotely

- Location B has 85 users who work remotely

- Location C has 70 users who work remotely

- Three-quarters of the remote users must be supported simultaneously

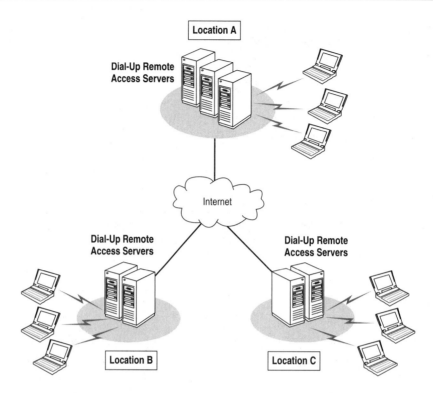

Figure 11.4 Scenario that illustrates where to place dial-up remote access servers in your design

For the scenario depicted in Figure 11.4, you place dial-up remote access servers at each location. The remote users connect to the dial-up remote access servers in their respective location.

Selecting the Remote Access Client Support

You must determine the remote access client support to incorporate into your dial-up remote access design. You must evaluate the applications run by the remote access clients and the resources accessed by the remote access clients.

Making the Decision

For each remote access client that connects to the dial-up remote access servers, you must determine the

- Number and type of communications ports to include
- Transport protocols required
- Method of assigning network addressing

Determining the Communications Ports to Include

You must determine the number and type of communications ports to include in your design to support the remote access clients. You must include a communications port for each simultaneous remote access client.

Each communications port must be capable of supporting the sustained data rate required by the remote access client. Most multiport communications adapters support a maximum sustained data rate for all ports. Ensure that the multiport communications adapter is capable of supporting the sustained data rate required by the remote access client.

Selecting the Transport Protocols

You can determine the transport protocols to include in your dial-up remote access design by examining the

- **Operating system running on the remote access client** The operating system running on the remote access client may require a specific transport protocol; for example, a Macintosh remote access client may support only the AppleTalk protocol. As a result, you need to include the AppleTalk protocol in your dial-up remote access design.

- **Applications running on the remote access clients** Many of the applications may require specific transport protocols to run properly; for example, File Transport Protocol (FTP) requires TCP/IP to operate properly. As a result, you need to include TCP/IP in your dial-up remote access design.

- **Network management tools running on the remote access clients** Many network management tools require specific transport protocols to run properly; for example, management tools for NetWare servers may require IPX to operate properly. In this instance, you need to include IPX in your dial-up remote access design.

- **Resource servers accessed by the remote access clients** The resource servers accessed by the remote access client's network may require a specific transport protocol to be accessed; for example, NetWare servers may require IPX to access private network resources. To access these NetWare servers, you need to include IPX in your dial-up remote access design.

Determining the Method of Assigning Network Addressing

Each remote access client must be assigned a network address from the address range assigned to the organization's private network. When the remote access client connects to the dial-up remote access server, a valid private network address (either IP, IPX, or AppleTalk address) must be assigned to the remote access client.

You can assign network addresses to remote access clients by

- **Manually specifying a range of addresses to be assigned to remote access clients** You can allocate ranges of network addresses from the private network-addressing scheme that can be assigned to remote access clients. You can allocate IP network address ranges, IPX network numbers, and AppleTalk network numbers that can be assigned to remote access clients.

You must assign a unique network address range to each dial-up remote access server. The network address range assigned to each dial-up remote access server must be unique within the private network and across all the dial-up remote access servers.

- **Automatically assigning IP addresses allocated from DHCP servers** Routing and Remote Access can allocate a range of IP addresses from a DHCP server. Routing and Remote Access initially allocates 10 IP addresses to be assigned to remote access clients by the remote access server. Routing and Remote Access continues to allocate IP addresses in groups of 10 until all simultaneous remote access users are assigned to all remote access clients.

  By default, remote access clients receive only an IP address and subnet mask. However, when you install a DHCP Relay Agent on the remote access server, the remote access clients can receive all IP configuration provided by DHCP.

Applying the Decision

In Figure 11.5, the scenario illustrates the appropriate selection of remote access client support to include in your design. For the purposes of this scenario, assume that

- All the remote access clients access FTP and Web servers in the organization's private network
- Some of the remote access clients require access to AppleShare servers running the Macintosh operating system
- Some of the remote access clients require access to NetWare 4.2 file servers that use only the IPX protocol
- Up to 300 remote users must be able to simultaneously access the private network
- DHCP must be used to assign all IP addresses and provide *total* IP configuration

To fulfill the requirements and constraints of the organization, you must include

- The TCP/IP protocol on all remote access clients to support access to the FTP and Web servers
- AppleTalk on the remote access clients that access AppleShare servers
- IPX on the remote access clients that access the Netware 4.2 file servers
- Manual network address ranges allocated for the IPX and AppleTalk protocols
- DHCP configuration for IP
- DHCP Relay Agent installed on each remote access server
- Up to 300 remote access communications ports to support the maximum number of simultaneous remote access clients

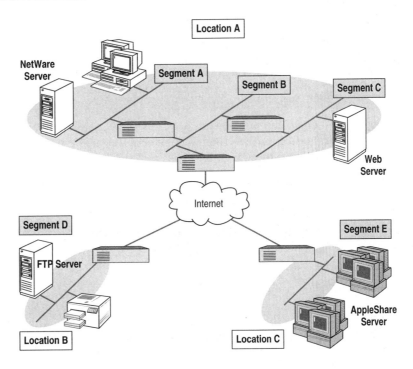

Figure 11.5   Scenario that illustrates the appropriate selection of remote access
client support to include in your design

Activity 11.1: Evaluating a Dial-Up Remote Access Design

In this activity, you're presented with a scenario. To complete the activity:

1. Evaluate the scenario and determine the design requirements
2. Answer questions and make design recommendations

Figure 11.6 illustrates a scenario for a structural engineering consulting firm. The
engineering firm's central office is in Winnipeg, with branch offices in
Vancouver, Toronto, and Montreal. Servers in the central office host the company
Web site. The Web site describes the services provided by the firm and provides a
list of projects managed by the firm.

Currently, the firm is running Windows 2000 Professional and Windows 2000 Server
on desktop and server computers respectively. The firm has selected Active Directory
to provide directory services. The field engineers for the firm run a variety of operating systems, including Windows 98, Microsoft Windows NT 4.0 Workstation,
Windows 2000 Professional, and Macintosh operating systems.

The Winnipeg office has 120 administrative and support personnel. The
Vancouver, Toronto, and Montreal offices each have 70 administrative and

support personnel. The Winnipeg, Vancouver, Toronto, and Montreal offices each support 500 engineers who work in the field.

The Winnipeg, Vancouver, Toronto, and Montreal offices all have file and print servers running Windows 2000. Also, all the file and print servers run File and Print Services for Macintosh to support Macintosh computers.

The engineering firm has acquired another structural engineering firm. The central office for the acquired engineering firm is in Calgary, with branch offices in Edmonton and Halifax.

The Calgary office has 65 administrative and support personnel. The Edmonton and Halifax offices each have 7 administrative and support personnel. The Calgary, Edmonton, and Halifax offices each support 300 engineers who work in the field. None of the new offices are connected to one another. The Calgary, Edmonton, and Halifax offices all have NetWare 4.2 file and print servers.

Figure 11.6   Structural engineering consulting firm scenario

Answer the following questions concerning your design recommendations. You can find answers to the questions in the Appendix, "Questions and Answers."

1. As a consultant to the engineering firm, you're responsible for creating the dial-up remote access design. The field engineers work within the same city as the office where they report. The firm wants to ensure that long-term costs for the dial-up remote access solution are minimized. What recommendations can you make to the structural engineering firm?

2. After conducting pilot tests on the computer platform selected to be remote access servers, you determine that each remote access server can support 90 simultaneous remote users at the minimum sustained data rate that provides acceptable application response time. Three-quarters of the remote users for each location must be able to simultaneously access the private network. How many remote access servers are required to fulfill the requirements of the organization?

3. You're preparing the specifications for each remote access server. The vendor that supplies the remote access servers wants to know how many multiport communications adapters to include in each server. Each multiport communications adapter supports 32 communications ports. What specifications do you provide to the remote access server vendor?

4. You're finalizing the specifications for the dial-up remote access design and are allocating network addresses from the firm's IP, IPX, and AppleTalk network addresses. The network administrators want to minimize the administration of addresses assigned to remote access clients. The firm utilizes DHCP to provide automatic IP address configuration for computers within each office. How do you assign network addresses to the remote access clients?

Lesson 3: Data Protection in Dial-Up Remote Access Designs

This lesson discusses how to create designs that protect confidential data in dial-up remote access designs. This lesson focuses on preventing unauthorized access to private network resources and protecting confidential data transmitted by remote users in your dial-up remote access design.

After this lesson, you will be able to

- Prevent unauthorized access to private network resources
- Protect confidential data transmitted between remote users and the dial-up remote access servers

Estimated lesson time: 30 minutes

Preventing Access to Private Network Resources

When your design includes dial-up remote access servers, the probability increases that private network resources can be accessed by unauthorized users. You must ensure that including dial-up remote access servers in your design doesn't compromise the organization's security.

Making the Decision

You can prevent unauthorized private network access through dial-up remote access servers by

- Restricting remote user access to only the resources on the dial-up remote access servers
- Restricting the traffic transmitted through the dial-up remote access servers
- Placing dial-up remote access servers on screened subnets or demilitarized zones (DMZs)

Restricting Access to Resources on the Dial-Up Remote Access Server

Routing and Remote Access allows you to restrict the resources that remote users can access to only the resources on the dial-up remote access server or to all the resources on the entire network. For *each protocol* on the remote access server, you can enable or disable access to

- Only the resources on the dial-up remote access servers
- Resources located anywhere in the private network

For example, you might want to allow remote users to access only a Web and FTP site. You can install the Web and FTP site on the dial-up remote access server and then disable access to other resources on the private network.

Restricting Traffic Transmitted Through the Dial-Up Remote Access Server

You can restrict the traffic transmitted through the dial-up remote access server by using packet filters. You can filter IP, IPX, and AppleTalk packets by specifying Routing and Remote Access packet filters.

You can specify any combination of packet filters to restrict access to

- Individual resources or servers
- Network segments
- Types of traffic, such as Hypertext Transfer Protocol (HTTP) or FTP traffic

For more information on Routing and Remote Access packet filters for IP, see Chapter 4, "IP Routing Designs," Lesson 3, "Data Protection on Unsecured Segments." For more information on Routing and Remote Access packet filters for IPX, see Chapter 5, "Multiprotocol Routing Designs," Lesson 2, "IPX Routing Design Concepts." For more information on Routing and Remote Access packet filters for AppleTalk, see Chapter 5, "Multiprotocol Routing Designs," Lesson 3, "AppleTalk Routing Design Concepts."

Placing Dial-Up Remote Access Servers on Screened Subnets

Always place dial-up remote access servers on screened subnets to restrict the resources that remote users can access and the network traffic to and from remote users. Placing proxy servers, firewalls, or routers with packet filters between the remote access servers and the private network creates screened subnets.

When you connect dial-up remote access servers directly to private networks, you risk unauthorized access to the private network. The only scenario where you connect dial-up remote access servers directly to private networks is when the private network contains only a single, nonrouted network segment.

Applying the Decision

Figure 11.7 illustrates the proper methods for preventing access to private network resources. For the purposes of this scenario, assume that the following apply:

- The remote access clients require the IP and IPX protocols.
- You must restrict remote access network traffic to HTTP and FTP traffic.
- You must allow IPX traffic to access only an IPX-based network segment that includes NetWare 4.2 file and print servers.
- Firewalls prevent unauthorized access to private network segments.

To fulfill the requirements and constraints of the organization, you must specify that

- The dial-up remote access server is on Segment D (between Firewall A and the router).
- Routing and Remote Access IP filters allow *only* HTTP and FTP traffic.
- Routing and Remote Access IPX filters allow traffic between the remote access clients and the network segment that contains NetWare 4.2 file and print servers.

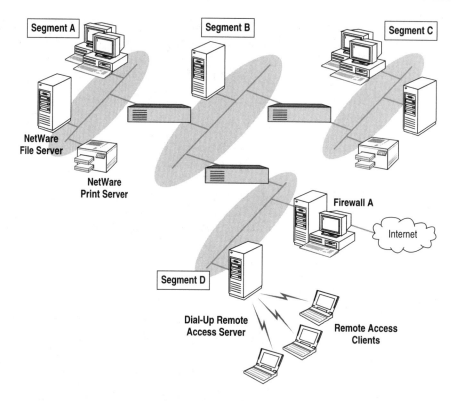

Figure 11.7   A scenario that illustrates the proper methods for preventing access to private network resources

Protecting Confidential Remote Access Data

When your design includes dial-up remote access servers, remote users will access confidential data. You must ensure that the confidentiality of the data is protected at all times.

Making the Decision

You can protect confidential data transmitted between remote users and the dial-up remote access server by

- Authenticating remote users
- Encrypting confidential data
- Enforcing remote access policies

Authenticating Remote Users

To ensure that only authorized remote users can access private network resources, your dial-up remote access design must authenticate the remote users (also known as *identity checking*). You can authenticate remote users by verifying their logon credentials, including user name, password, and domain (or realm). You can verify the remote user's credentials by using

- Local accounts, stored on the dial-up remote access server
- Active Directory accounts, stored on domain controllers

To protect the remote user's credentials (especially the user name and password), you can encrypt the credentials exchanged between the remote access client and the remote access server. You can select from a variety of authentication protocols to authenticate the remote users. You must select the appropriate authentication protocol based on the

- Authentication protocols available on the remote access client
- Strength of encryption you require to protect the remote user's credentials

The authentication protocols you can include in your dial-up remote access design are the same as VPN authentication protocols. You can select the appropriate dial-up remote access server authentication protocols by using the same design decisions for VPN authentication protocols. For more information on determining the appropriate VPN authentication protocols, and subsequently dial-up remote access server authentication protocols, see the section, "VPN Authentication Protocols," in Chapter 2, "Networking Protocol Design," Lesson 3, "TCP/IP Data Protection."

Encrypting Confidential Data

To ensure that confidential data is protected, your dial-up remote access design must encrypt any confidential data transmitted between the dial-up remote access servers and the remote access client. You can encrypt the confidential data by using

- Microsoft Point-to-Point Encryption (MPPE) protocol
- Internet Protocol Security (IPSec)

You must select the appropriate authentication protocol based on the

- Encryption protocols available on the remote access client
- Strength of encryption you require to protect the confidential data

The encryption protocols you can include in your dial-up remote access design are the same as VPN encryption protocols. You can select the appropriate dial-up remote access server encryption protocols by using the same design decisions for VPN encryption protocols. For more information on determining the appropriate VPN encryption protocols, and subsequently dial-up remote access server encryption protocols, see the section, "VPN Encryption Protocols," in Chapter 2, "Networking Protocol Design," Lesson 3, "TCP/IP Data Protection."

Note IPSec data encryption is currently available only on remote access clients running Windows 2000.

Enforcing Remote Access Policies

You can enforce the security requirements for remote access clients by using *remote access policies*. Remote access policies are named rules that consist of

- **Conditions**   Remote access policy conditions are one or more remote access attributes that are compared to the settings of the connection attempt. When your remote access policy contains multiple conditions, all the conditions must be met for the connection attempt to match the remote access policy.

- **Remote access permission**   When all the conditions of your remote access policy are met, the remote access permission is assigned to the remote user. You can either grant or deny remote access to the remote access client that meets the conditions of the remote access policy.

    In addition to the remote access permissions included in the remote access policy, you must grant or deny remote access for each user account. The user-based remote access permission overrides the policy-based remote access permission. However, you can specify that *only* the policy-based remote access permission determines whether the user is granted access.

Note   By default, all users are denied remote access.

- **Profile**   After remote access is granted to the remote user, the remote access server negotiates remote access settings found in the *remote access policy profile*. A remote access policy profile is a set of properties applied to a connection when the connection is authorized. Remote access clients that are to comply with the remote access settings specified in the remote access policy profile are rejected and disconnected.

Table 11.2 lists the groups of properties that can be included in a remote access policy profile and some examples of the properties included in the group.

Table 11.2   Property Profile Groups

Policy Profile Group	Includes
Dial-in constraints	Idle disconnect time, maximum session length, day and time limits, dial-in number, and dial-in media type (such as modem or ISDN)
IP	Requiring specific IP address and packet filters
Multilink	Maximum number of ports to use in multilink connection and Bandwidth Allocation Protocol (BAP) policies
Authentication	Authentication protocol that must be used by remote access client
Encryption	Encryption protocol that must be used by the remote access client
Advanced	RADIUS specific attributes

For more information on remote access policy profiles and remote access policy profile properties, see the Windows 2000 help files.

You can use remote access policies to enforce the security requirements of the design by forcing the remote access client to adhere to the remote access policies. Remote access clients that don't adhere to the remote access policies are automatically disconnected.

For example, you can enforce the use of Microsoft Challenge Handshake Authentication Protocol version 2 (MS-CHAP v2) as the authentication protocol and 128-bit MPPE as the encryption protocol by using remote access policies. Any remote access clients unable to support MS-CHAP v2 and 128-bit MPPE are disconnected from the remote access server.

Applying the Decision

Figure 11.8 illustrates the appropriate methods for protecting confidential data transmitted between remote users and dial-up remote access servers. For the purposes of this scenario, assume that

- All remote users must be authenticated
- Remote users must use the MS-CHAP or MS-CHAP v2 authentication protocol
- Remote users within the United States must encrypt confidential data by using 128-bit MPPE
- Remote users outside the United States must encrypt confidential data by using 40-bit MPPE

To fulfill the requirements and constraints of the organization, you must specify that all

- Remote access servers and remote access users within the United States must support 128-bit MPPE
- Remote access servers and remote access users outside the United States must support 40-bit MPPE
- MS-CHAP or MS-CHAP v2 authenticates remote users
- Remote access servers include remote access policies that deny remote access to remote access clients unable to meet the security requirements of the organization

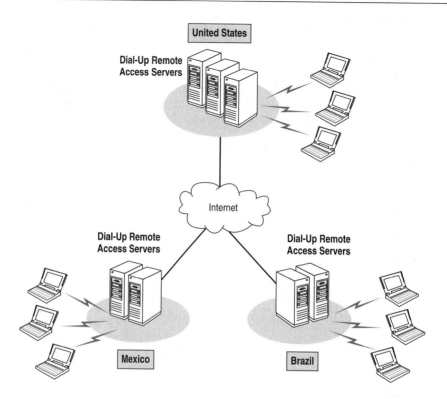

Figure 11.8 A scenario that illustrates the appropriate methods for protecting confidential data transmitted between remote users and dial-up remote access servers

Lesson 4: Dial-Up Remote Access Design Optimization

This lesson discusses how to optimize dial-up remote access designs to improve the availability and performance characteristics in your design. This lesson focuses on the strategies that increase the percentage of time that remote users can access the private network resources and that increase the data transfer rates between the remote access clients and the private network resources.

After this lesson, you will be able to

- Select the appropriate method for enhancing the availability characteristics in your dial-up remote access design
- Select the appropriate methods for improving the performance characteristics in your dial-up remote access design

Estimated lesson time: 30 minutes

Enhancing Dial-Up Remote Access Availability

Once you have established the essential aspects and security aspects of your dial-up remote access design, you can optimize the design for availability. The business requirements of the organization may require your design to ensure dial-up remote access at all times. Regardless of a single point of failure, your design must provide redundancy for each dial-up remote access server.

Making the Decision

You can improve the availability of your dial-up remote access designs by

- Including multiple dial-up remote access servers with backup phone numbers
- Dedicating a computer to running Routing and Remote Access

Multiple Dial-Up Remote Access Servers with Backup Phone Numbers

You can include multiple dial-up remote access servers in your design to provide redundancy and backup. You need to include a redundant dial-up remote access server for each existing dial-up remote access server in your design.

However, because the remote access clients are connected to a specific *phone number bank* and modem attached to a specific remote access server, the connection is lost when a failure occurs. To reestablish the remote access connection, the remote access client must dial a backup phone number bank that corresponds to a different phone number bank and modem attached to a different remote access server.

A phone number bank is a group of telephone numbers that reside within the same *hunt group*. The local telephone provider can create a hunt group by designating a primary phone number that the users call. When the first number in the hunt group is busy, the telephone provider automatically forwards another incoming call to the next telephone numbers in the hunt group.

The telephone provider continues to forward incoming calls to subsequent telephone numbers in the hunt group. As a result, the remote users need to enter only one telephone number to access potentially hundreds of phone number and modem combinations. For more information on telephone hunt groups, contact your local telephone provider.

Tip   Designate a phone number bank for each remote access server to allow you to direct remote users to a specific remote access server.

The specifications for the dial-up remote access servers that provide redundancy must be *identical*. You must ensure that the same data rates, authentication protocols, encryption protocols, and remote access policies exist on *all* servers.

Tip   You can use Microsoft Connection Manager to automate the connection process for primary and backup phone numbers on the remote access clients. For more information on Connection Manager, see the Windows 2000 help files.

Dedicating a Computer to Routing and Remote Access

By dedicating a computer to running Routing and Remote Access, you improve availability by preventing other applications or services from becoming unstable and requiring the dial-up remote access server to be restarted.

Applying the Decision

Figure 11.9 illustrates the proper methods for enhancing the availability of a dial-up remote access solution.

For the purposes of this scenario, assume that the business and technical requirements of the organization include

- Ensuring that any failure of a dial-up remote access server, modem, or phone line doesn't prevent remote access

- Ensuring that remote access clients are required to reconnect if a remote access server, modem, or phone line fails

To provide the proper solution, multiple dial-up remote access servers must be included to achieve the business and technical requirements of the organization. Remote Access Servers A and B have the same specifications. Remote access clients include a primary and backup phone number bank that connects to Remote Access Servers A and B respectively. If Remote Access Server A (the primary server) fails, remote users connected to it must reconnect by using the phone number bank associated with Remote Access Server B (the backup server).

In addition, you can improve the performance of your remote access design by distributing the remote access clients between Remote Access Servers A and B.

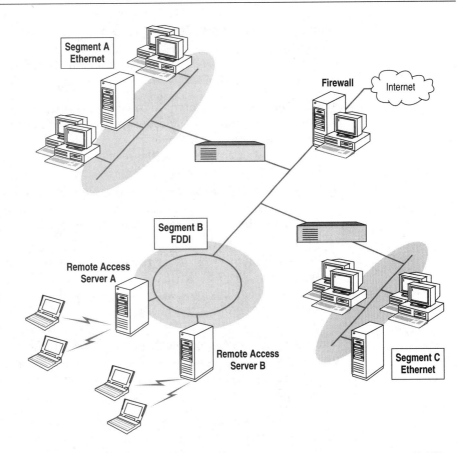

Figure 11.9   Scenario to illustrate the proper methods for enhancing the availability of a dial-up remote access solution

Improving Dial-Up Remote Access Performance

Once you have established the essential aspects, security aspects, and availability aspects of your dial-up remote access design, you can optimize the design for performance. The business requirements may include that dial-up remote access servers must support a sustained data rate, based on the number of simultaneous remote users.

Making the Decision

You can improve dial-up remote access performance by

- Upgrading remote access server hardware
- Distributing remote access clients across multiple remote access servers
- Dedicating a computer to running Routing and Remote Access

Upgrading Remote Access Server Hardware

When you can upgrade the hardware in the existing dial-up remote access servers, you can improve the performance of your dial-up remote access design. You can upgrade the existing

- **Communications adapters to intelligent communications adapters**
  When the existing communications adapters aren't intelligent, you can upgrade to intelligent communications adapters. Intelligent communications adapters utilize processors on the adapter to offload the processor(s) in the dial-up remote access server.

- **Modem to increase the data rate or hardware compression**   Increasing the potential maximum data rate of the modems in your design increases the data rate of the remote access clients and subsequently improves the performance of your design.

- **Processor, memory, or other resources on the computer running Routing and Remote Access**   When any of the system resources of the computer running Routing and Remote Access are exhausted, you can upgrade the system resource to improve performance.

Distributing Remote Access Clients Across Multiple Remote Access Servers

When the existing dial-up remote access servers are saturated and you can't upgrade the hardware to improve performance, you can add additional dial-up remote access servers to your design.

Evenly distribute the remote access clients across the multiple dial-up remote access servers, ensuring that each dial-up remote access server manages approximately the same number of remote access clients. You can distribute the remote access traffic across the additional dial-up remote access servers to reduce the network traffic that must be forwarded through an individual dial-up remote access server.

You distribute the remote access clients by assigning the appropriate phone numbers bank to the remote access clients. For each remote access server in your design, include a unique phone number bank to allow you to direct remote access clients to a specific remote access server.

Dedicating a Computer to Routing and Remote Access

By dedicating a computer to running Routing and Remote Access, you improve the performance because you prevent other applications or services from consuming system resources.

Applying the Decision

Figure 11.10 illustrates a dial-up remote access design prior to optimization for performance. For the purposes of this scenario, assume that the business and technical requirements of the organization include that the existing

- Computers running Routing and Remote Access can't be further upgraded

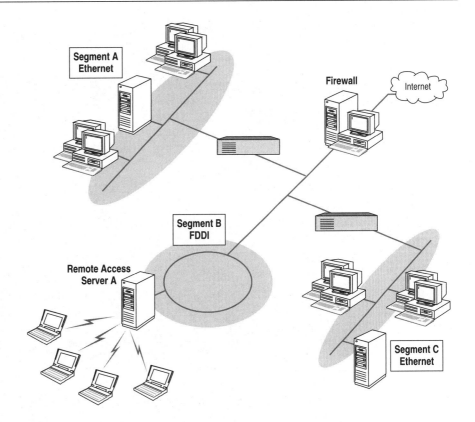

Figure 11.10   Scenario to illustrate a dial-up remote access design prior to optimization for performance

- Modems support the maximum data rate possible
- Communications adapters don't utilize processors

Figure 11.11 illustrates a dial-up remote access design after optimization for performance. The following performance optimization changes were made to the design.

- Remote Access Server B is installed to distribute the remote access traffic between Remote Access Server A and B.
- Remote access clients are evenly distributed between Remote Access Servers A and B.
- Intelligent communications adapters are installed in all dial-up remote access servers.

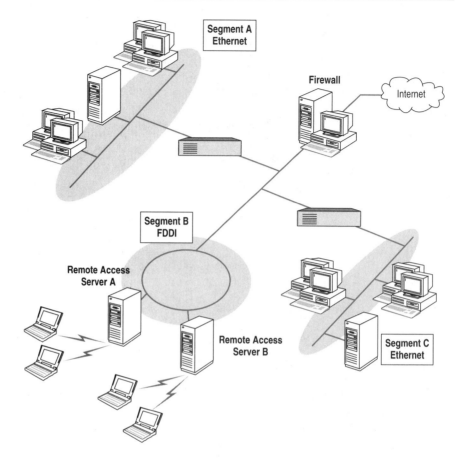

Figure 11.11   Scenario to illustrate a dial-up remote access design after optimization for performance

Activity 11.2: Completing a Dial-Up Remote Access Design

In this activity, you're presented with a scenario. To complete the activity:

1. Evaluate the scenario and determine the design requirements

2. Answer questions and make design recommendations

Figure 11.12 illustrates a scenario for the structural engineering consulting firm presented earlier in this chapter. You're in the process of refining your design that provides dial-up remote access for the consulting firm.

Answer the following questions concerning your design recommendations. You can find answers to the questions in the Appendix, "Questions and Answers."

Figure 11.12 Structural engineering consulting firm's additional locations

1. The consulting firm is concerned about the security associated with the new dial-up remote access design. What can you include in your design to ensure that private network resources and confidential data are protected?

2. The consulting firm wants to provide a dial-up remote access server that customers can access anonymously. Your design must allow the customers to access only the resources on the dial-up remote access server, while protecting the consulting firm's private network resources. How can you provide access to the dial-up remote access server while protecting private network resources?

3. Construction on many of the projects managed by the consulting firm continues 24 hours per day, 7 days per week. A team of field engineers assigned to these projects is always onsite while construction occurs. The field engineers require remote access while onsite. What can you include in your design to ensure that the field engineers can always access the consulting firm's private network?

4. A few months after deployment, the field engineers report that application response times through the remote access servers have decreased dramatically since the initial deployment. Upon investigation, you discover that the average data rate for each remote access connection has decreased accordingly. How can you modify your design to improve the application response times through the remote access servers?

Lab: Creating a Dial-Up Remote Access Design

After this lab, you will be able to
- Evaluate a scenario and determine the design requirements
- Create a dial-up remote access design based on the design requirements

Estimated lab time: 45 minutes

In this lab, you're a consultant to an entertainment company and are responsible for creating a dial-up remote access design for it. The company has various locations and business interests throughout the world.

To complete this lab:

1. Examine the networking environment presented in the scenario, the network diagrams, the business requirements and constraints, and the technical requirements and constraints

2. Use the worksheet(s) for each location and remote access server to assist you in creating your dial-up remote access design (you can find completed sample design worksheets on the Supplemental Course Materials CD-ROM in the Completed Worksheets folder)

   Note   For each location, there are four worksheets, one worksheet for each dial-up remote access server. If your design contains fewer than four dial-up remote access servers, leave the remaining worksheets blank.

3. Create, eliminate, or replace existing networking devices and network segments when required

4. Ensure that your design fulfills the business requirements and constraints and technical requirements and constraints of the scenario by

   - Assigning the appropriate number of dial-up remote access servers

   - Including the appropriate protocols on each dial-up remote access server

   - Optimizing your design to provide security, availability, performance, and affordability

   Note   To reduce the length of time for this lab, create a dial-up remote access design for only four of the entertainment company's locations.

Scenario

An entertainment company, headquartered in New York, owns a number of cable TV networks, theme parks, and production studios. The company acquired most of these separate business units and, as it did so, left the existing information services staff and networks in place.

Initially, the individual business units required little or no remote access connectivity. However, the business model changed within the parent company, and remote access connectivity is now critical.

Figure 11.13 is a map of the locations where the entertainment company has offices. A variety of technologies currently connect the locations to one another. The company is migrating the existing assortment of technologies that connect the locations to asynchronous transfer mode (ATM)–based, high-speed leased lines. The new ATM-based leased lines will provide higher speed data rates between the locations. The company maintains an Internet connection with T3 leased lines in the New York headquarters.

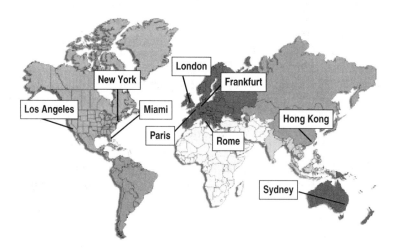

Figure 11.13   Map of the locations in the entertainment company

Table 11.3 lists each location where the entertainment company has offices and the types of business units at each location.

Table 11.3   Location and Description of Company's Business Units

Location	Description of the Business Units at the Location
New York (Figure 11.18)	*Corporate headquarters*. The administration and management of the entertainment company is located here. *News studio*. One of the cable network news companies has studios here. The video broadcasts are taped or televised live from here. *Production studio*. A number of the cable network channels and other portions of the entertainment company share a common production studio for producing video and multimedia productions.

Table 11.3 *(continued)*

Location	Description of the Business Units at the Location
Los Angeles (Figure 11.20)	*News studio.* One of the cable network news companies has studios here. The video broadcasts are taped or televised live from here. *Production studio.* A number of the cable network channels and other portions of the entertainment company share a common production studio for producing video and multimedia productions. *Theme park.* A theme park focusing on characters and movies owned by the entertainment company.
Miami	*Production studio.* A number of the cable network channels and other portions of the entertainment company share a common production studio for producing video and multimedia productions. *Theme park.* A theme park focusing on characters and movies owned by the entertainment company.
London (Figure 11.19)	*News studio.* One of the cable network news companies has studios here. The video broadcasts are taped or televised live from here. *Production studio.* A number of the cable network channels and other portions of the entertainment company share a common production studio for producing video and multimedia productions.
Paris	*Production studio.* A number of the cable network channels and other portions of the entertainment company share a common production studio for producing video and multimedia productions.
Frankfurt	*News studio.* One of the cable network news companies has studios here. The video broadcasts are taped or televised live from here.
Rome	*News studio.* One of the cable network news companies has studios here. The video broadcasts are taped or televised live from here. *Production studio.* A number of the cable network channels and other portions of the entertainment company share a common production studio for producing video and multimedia productions.
Hong Kong (Figure 11.21)	*News studio.* One of the cable network news companies has studios here. The video broadcasts are taped or televised live from here. *Production studio.* A number of the cable network channels and other portions of the entertainment company share a common production studio for producing video and multimedia productions.

(continued)

Table 11.3   *(continued)*

Location	Description of the Business Units at the Location
Sydney	*News studio.* One of the cable network news companies has studios here. The video broadcasts are taped or televised live from here. *Production studio.* A number of the cable network channels and other portions of the entertainment company share a common production studio for producing video and multimedia productions.

Note   In this lab, no solutions are required for the Miami, Paris, Frankfurt, and Sydney locations. As a result, the corresponding network diagrams are omitted.

Table 11.4 lists each type of business owned by the entertainment company and a description of the support required by each business type.

Table 11.4   Business Types Owned by the Company and Support Required

Business Type	Must Support Remote Access For
News studios (Figure 11.15)	▪ The employees and accounting functions for the news studios that utilize IPX-based file and print servers ▪ Macintosh-based graphics and video editing computers used to produce the news programs ▪ IPX-based teleprompters used by the news reporters, and other personnel who appear in front of the camera, to read their scripts ▪ File and print services on computers running Windows 2000
Production studios (Figure 11.16)	▪ The employees and accounting functions for the production studio that utilize IPX-based file and print servers ▪ Macintosh-based graphics and video editing computers used to produce the video and multimedia content ▪ File and print services on computers running Windows 2000
Theme park (Figure 11.17)	▪ The employees and accounting functions for the theme park that utilize IPX-based file and print servers ▪ Automated rides and attractions within the park that utilize IPX-based process control equipment ▪ Macintosh-based kiosks that park visitors can use to find attractions and leave messages for other members in their group ▪ File and print services on computers running Windows 2000

Business Requirements and Constraints

The entertainment company has a number of requirements and constraints based on the business model of the entertainment company. As you create your dial-up remote access design, ensure that your design meets the business requirements and stays within the business constraints.

To achieve the business requirements and constraints, your design must

- Prevent unauthorized users from remotely accessing resources within each location
- Require that all data exchanged with remote users be encrypted
- Ensure that remote connectivity to the locations is available 24 hours a day, 7 days a week
- Ensure that all employees can access their respective resources within the private network

Technical Requirements and Constraints

The existing physical network, hardware, and operating systems place certain technical requirements and constraints on your design. As you create your dial-up remote access design, ensure that your design meets the technical requirements and stays within the technical constraints.

In addition, the applications that run within the entertainment company require connectivity within each location, with other locations, and with the Internet. These applications run on the computers used by the employees and on computers used in interactive kiosks.

To achieve the technical requirements and constraints, your design must

- Protect the private network within each location from unauthorized remote access
- Provide connectivity between remote users and the private network resources by using the appropriate protocols
- Protect confidential data accessed by remote users by using the strongest possible authentication and encryption protocols
- Include a dial-up remote access server for every 128 users so the desired performance, determined in pilot testing, is ensured
- Assign a bank of phone numbers, by name that you designate, to each corresponding dial-up remote access server
- Support Active Directory as the directory service for the entertainment company

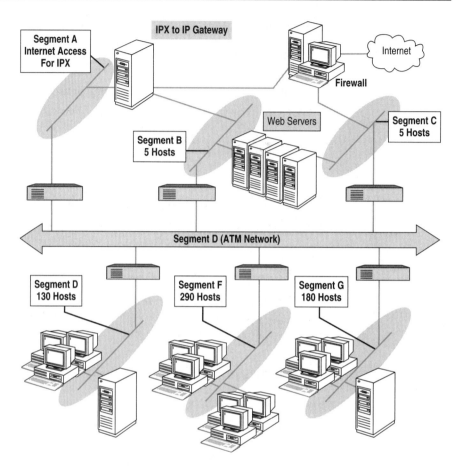

Figure 11.14   The existing network at the corporate headquarters building in New York

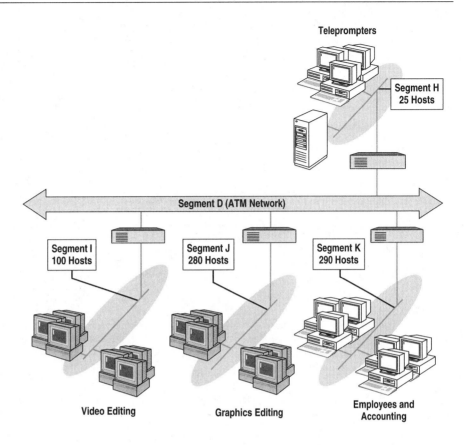

Figure 11.15   The existing network at one of the news studios. For the purposes of this lab, assume that all news studios have the same network configuration.

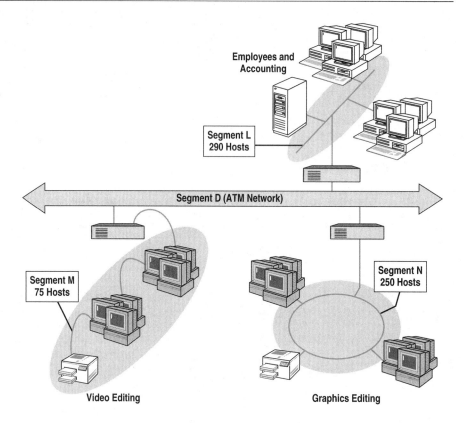

Figure 11.16   The existing network at one of the production studios. For the purposes of this lab, assume that all production studios have the same network configuration.

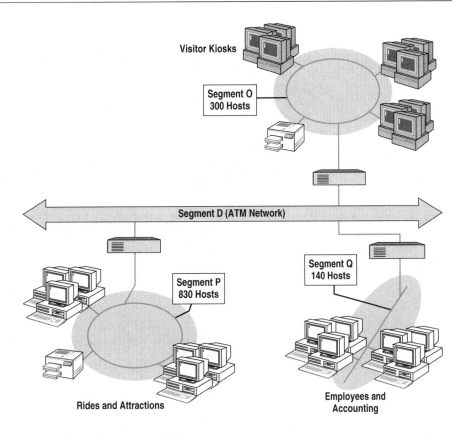

Figure 11.17   The existing network at one of the theme parks. For the purposes of
this lab, assume that all theme parks have the same network
configuration.

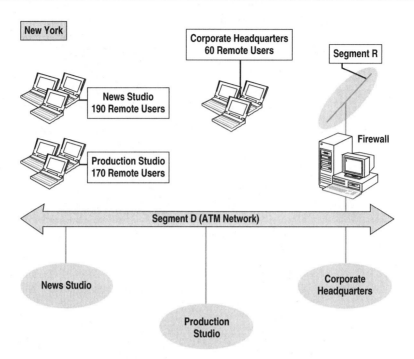

Figure 11.18   The existing network at New York

Design Worksheet – Figure 11.18
New York – Dial-Up Remote Access Server A

Dial-Up Remote Access Server Specifications	Comments
Dial-up remote access server connects to segment: _____	
Phone bank that connects to dial-up remote access server: _____	
Protocol Support	
❑ IP (Select the appropriate IP address assignment and configuration options) ❑ Manually assigned ❑ DHCP assigned ❑ Include DHCP Relay Agent	
❑ IPX	
❑ AppleTalk	
Security	
Authentication protocols (Select one or more authentication protocols) ❑ MS-CHAP ❑ MS-CHAP v2 ❑ CHAP ❑ PAP ❑ SPAP	
Encryption protocols (Select the appropriate data encryption protocols)	
❑ MPPE (Select the strength of MPPE encryption) ❑ 40-bit ❑ 128-bit	
❑ IPSec (Select the IPSec protection to utilize)	

Mode	Authentication	Identity	Protection	Encryption
❑ Transport	❑ Kerberos	❑ MD5	❑ Identity (AH)	Not required
❑ Tunnel	❑ X509 ❑ Preshared key	❑ SHA	❑ Identity and encryption (ESP)	❑ DES ❑ 56-bit DES ❑ 3DES

	Comments
❑ Remote access policies (Specify the remote access policy in the Comments column)	
Protocol packet filters	
❑ IP (Specify IP packet filter criteria in Comments column)	
❑ IPX (Specify IPX packet filter criteria in Comments column)	
❑ AppleTalk (Specify AppleTalk packet filter criteria in Comments column)	
Remote access to network resources	
❑ Dial-up remote access server only	
❑ Entire network	

Design Worksheet – Figure 11.18
New York – Dial-Up Remote Access Server B

Dial-Up Remote Access Server Specifications	Comments
Dial-up remote access server connects to segment: _____	
Phone bank that connects to dial-up remote access server: _____	
Protocol Support	
❏ IP (Select the appropriate IP address assignment and configuration options)	
❏ Manually assigned ❏ DHCP assigned ❏ Include DHCP Relay Agent	
❏ IPX	
❏ AppleTalk	
Security	
Authentication protocols (Select one or more authentication protocols)	
❏ MS-CHAP ❏ MS-CHAP v2 ❏ CHAP ❏ PAP ❏ SPAP	
Encryption protocols (Select the appropriate data encryption protocols)	
❏ MPPE (Select the strength of MPPE encryption)	
❏ 40-bit ❏ 128-bit	
❏ IPSec (Select the IPSec protection to utilize)	

	Mode	Authentication	Identity	Protection	Encryption
	❏ Transport	❏ Kerberos	❏ MD5	❏ Identity (AH)	Not required
	❏ Tunnel	❏ X509	❏ SHA	❏ Identity and encryption (ESP)	❏ DES
		❏ Preshared key			❏ 56-bit DES
					❏ 3DES

	Comments
❏ Remote access policies (Specify the remote access policy in the Comments column)	
Protocol packet filters	
❏ IP (Specify IP packet filter criteria in Comments column)	
❏ IPX (Specify IPX packet filter criteria in Comments column)	
❏ AppleTalk (Specify AppleTalk packet filter criteria in Comments column)	
Remote access to network resources	
❏ Dial-up remote access server only	
❏ Entire network	

Design Worksheet – Figure 11.18
New York – Dial-Up Remote Access Server C

Dial-Up Remote Access Server Specifications	Comments
Dial-up remote access server connects to segment: _____	
Phone bank that connects to dial-up remote access server: _____	
Protocol Support	
❑ IP (Select the appropriate IP address assignment and configuration options) ❑ Manually assigned ❑ DHCP assigned ❑ Include DHCP Relay Agent	
❑ IPX	
❑ AppleTalk	
Security	
Authentication protocols (Select one or more authentication protocols) ❑ MS-CHAP ❑ MS-CHAP v2 ❑ CHAP ❑ PAP ❑ SPAP	
Encryption protocols (Select the appropriate data encryption protocols)	
❑ MPPE (Select the strength of MPPE encryption) ❑ 40-bit ❑ 128-bit	
❑ IPSec (Select the IPSec protection to utilize)	

Mode	Authentication	Identity	Protection	Encryption
❑ Transport	❑ Kerberos	❑ MD5	❑ Identity (AH)	Not required
❑ Tunnel	❑ X509	❑ SHA	❑ Identity and encryption (ESP)	❑ DES
	❑ Preshared key			❑ 56-bit DES
				❑ 3DES

❑ Remote access policies (Specify the remote access policy in the Comments column)	
Protocol packet filters	
❑ IP (Specify IP packet filter criteria in Comments column)	
❑ IPX (Specify IPX packet filter criteria in Comments column)	
❑ AppleTalk (Specify AppleTalk packet filter criteria in Comments column)	
Remote access to network resources	
❑ Dial-up remote access server only	
❑ Entire network	

Design Worksheet – Figure 11.18
New York – Dial-Up Remote Access Server D

Dial-Up Remote Access Server Specifications	Comments
Dial-up remote access server connects to segment: _____	
Phone bank that connects to dial-up remote access server: _____	
Protocol Support	
☐ IP (Select the appropriate IP address assignment and configuration options) ☐ Manually assigned ☐ DHCP assigned ☐ Include DHCP Relay Agent	
☐ IPX	
☐ AppleTalk	
Security	
Authentication protocols (Select one or more authentication protocols)	
☐ MS-CHAP ☐ MS-CHAP v2 ☐ CHAP ☐ PAP ☐ SPAP	
Encryption protocols (Select the appropriate data encryption protocols)	
☐ MPPE (Select the strength of MPPE encryption)	
☐ 40-bit ☐ 128-bit	
☐ IPSec (Select the IPSec protection to utilize)	

Mode	Authentication	Identity	Protection	Encryption
☐ Transport	☐ Kerberos	☐ MD5	☐ Identity (AH)	Not required
☐ Tunnel	☐ X509 ☐ Preshared key	☐ SHA	☐ Identity and encryption (ESP)	☐ DES ☐ 56-bit DES ☐ 3DES

☐ Remote access policies (Specify the remote access policy in the Comments column)	
Protocol packet filters	
☐ IP (Specify IP packet filter criteria in Comments column)	
☐ IPX (Specify IPX packet filter criteria in Comments column)	
☐ AppleTalk (Specify AppleTalk packet filter criteria in Comments column)	
Remote access to network resources	
☐ Dial-up remote access server only	
☐ Entire network	

Design Worksheet — Figure 11.18
New York — Remote Access Clients

Remote Clients	Remote Access Client Specifications	Comments
	Primary phone number bank: _____ Backup phone number bank: _____	
	Primary phone number bank: _____ Backup phone number bank: _____	
	Primary phone number bank: _____ Backup phone number bank: _____	
	Primary phone number bank: _____ Backup phone number bank: _____	

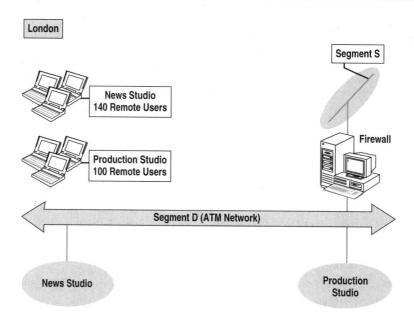

Figure 11.19   The existing network at London

Design Worksheet – Figure 11.19
London – Dial-Up Remote Access Server A

Dial-Up Remote Access Server Specifications	Comments
Dial-up remote access server connects to segment: _____	
Phone bank that connects to dial-up remote access server: _____	
Protocol Support	
❑ IP (Select the appropriate IP address assignment and configuration options) ❑ Manually assigned ❑ DHCP assigned ❑ Include DHCP Relay Agent	
❑ IPX	
❑ AppleTalk	
Security	
Authentication protocols (Select one or more authentication protocols) ❑ MS-CHAP ❑ MS-CHAP v2 ❑ CHAP ❑ PAP ❑ SPAP	
Encryption protocols (Select the appropriate data encryption protocols)	
❑ MPPE (Select the strength of MPPE encryption) ❑ 40-bit ❑ 128-bit	
❑ IPSec (Select the IPSec protection to utilize)	

Mode	Authentication	Identity	Protection	Encryption
❑ Transport	❑ Kerberos	❑ MD5	❑ Identity (AH)	Not required
❑ Tunnel	❑ X509 ❑ Preshared key	❑ SHA	❑ Identity and encryption (ESP)	❑ DES ❑ 56-bit DES ❑ 3DES

❑ Remote access policies (Specify the remote access policy in the Comments column)	
Protocol packet filters	
❑ IP (Specify IP packet filter criteria in Comments column)	
❑ IPX (Specify IPX packet filter criteria in Comments column)	
❑ AppleTalk (Specify AppleTalk packet filter criteria in Comments column)	
Remote access to network resources	
❑ Dial-up remote access server only	
❑ Entire network	

Design Worksheet – Figure 11.19
London – Dial-Up Remote Access Server B

Dial-Up Remote Access Server Specifications	Comments
Dial-up remote access server connects to segment: _____	
Phone bank that connects to dial-up remote access server: _____	
Protocol Support	
❏ IP (Select the appropriate IP address assignment and configuration options)	
❏ Manually assigned ❏ DHCP assigned ❏ Include DHCP Relay Agent	
❏ IPX	
❏ AppleTalk	
Security	
Authentication protocols (Select one or more authentication protocols)	
❏ MS-CHAP ❏ MS-CHAP v2 ❏ CHAP ❏ PAP ❏ SPAP	
Encryption protocols (Select the appropriate data encryption protocols)	
❏ MPPE (Select the strength of MPPE encryption)	
❏ 40-bit ❏ 128-bit	
❏ IPSec (Select the IPSec protection to utilize)	

Mode	Authentication	Identity	Protection	Encryption
❏ Transport	❏ Kerberos	❏ MD5	❏ Identity (AH)	Not required
❏ Tunnel	❏ X509	❏ SHA	❏ Identity and encryption (ESP)	❏ DES
	❏ Preshared key			❏ 56-bit DES
				❏ 3DES

❏ Remote access policies (Specify the remote access policy in the Comments column)	
Protocol packet filters	
❏ IP (Specify IP packet filter criteria in Comments column)	
❏ IPX (Specify IPX packet filter criteria in Comments column)	
❏ AppleTalk (Specify AppleTalk packet filter criteria in Comments column)	
Remote access to network resources	
❏ Dial-up remote access server only	
❏ Entire network	

Design Worksheet – Figure 11.19
London – Dial-Up Remote Access Server C

Dial-Up Remote Access Server Specifications	Comments
Dial-Up Remote Access Server Specifications	
Dial-up remote access server connects to segment: _____	
Phone bank that connects to dial-up remote access server: _____	
Protocol Support	
❏ IP (Select the appropriate IP address assignment and configuration options) ❏ Manually assigned ❏ DHCP assigned ❏ Include DHCP Relay Agent	
❏ IPX	
❏ AppleTalk	
Security	
Authentication protocols (Select one or more authentication protocols) ❏ MS-CHAP ❏ MS-CHAP v2 ❏ CHAP ❏ PAP ❏ SPAP	
Encryption protocols (Select the appropriate data encryption protocols)	
❏ MPPE (Select the strength of MPPE encryption) ❏ 40-bit ❏ 128-bit	
❏ IPSec (Select the IPSec protection to utilize)	

Mode	Authentication	Identity	Protection	Encryption
❏ Transport	❏ Kerberos	❏ MD5	❏ Identity (AH)	Not required
❏ Tunnel	❏ X509 ❏ Preshared key	❏ SHA	❏ Identity and encryption (ESP)	❏ DES ❏ 56-bit DES ❏ 3DES

	Comments
❏ Remote access policies (Specify the remote access policy in the Comments column)	
Protocol packet filters	
❏ IP (Specify IP packet filter criteria in Comments column)	
❏ IPX (Specify IPX packet filter criteria in Comments column)	
❏ AppleTalk (Specify AppleTalk packet filter criteria in Comments column)	
Remote access to network resources	
❏ Dial-up remote access server only	
❏ Entire network	

Design Worksheet – Figure 11.19
London – Dial-Up Remote Access Server D

Dial-Up Remote Access Server Specifications	Comments
Dial-up remote access server connects to segment: _____	
Phone bank that connects to dial-up remote access server: _____	
Protocol Support	
❑ IP (Select the appropriate IP address assignment and configuration options) ❑ Manually assigned ❑ DHCP assigned ❑ Include DHCP Relay Agent	
❑ IPX	
❑ AppleTalk	
Security	
Authentication protocols (Select one or more authentication protocols) ❑ MS-CHAP ❑ MS-CHAP v2 ❑ CHAP ❑ PAP ❑ SPAP	
Encryption protocols (Select the appropriate data encryption protocols)	
❑ MPPE (Select the strength of MPPE encryption) ❑ 40-bit ❑ 128-bit	
❑ IPSec (Select the IPSec protection to utilize)	

Mode	Authentication	Identity	Protection	Encryption
❑ Transport	❑ Kerberos	❑ MD5	❑ Identity (AH)	Not required
❑ Tunnel	❑ X509 ❑ Preshared key	❑ SHA	❑ Identity and encryption (ESP)	❑ DES ❑ 56-bit DES ❑ 3DES

❑ Remote access policies (Specify the remote access policy in the Comments column)	
Protocol packet filters	
❑ IP (Specify IP packet filter criteria in Comments column)	
❑ IPX (Specify IPX packet filter criteria in Comments column)	
❑ AppleTalk (Specify AppleTalk packet filter criteria in Comments column)	
Remote access to network resources	
❑ Dial-up remote access server only	
❑ Entire network	

Design Worksheet – Figure 11.19
London – Remote Access Clients

Remote Clients	Remote Access Client Specifications	Comments
	Primary phone number bank: _____ Backup phone number bank: _____	
	Primary phone number bank: _____ Backup phone number bank: _____	
	Primary phone number bank: _____ Backup phone number bank: _____	
	Primary phone number bank: _____ Backup phone number bank: _____	

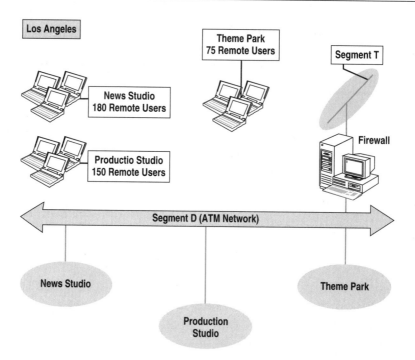

Figure 11.20 The existing network at Los Angeles

Design Worksheet – Figure 11.20
Los Angeles – Dial-Up Remote Access Server A

Dial-Up Remote Access Server Specifications	Comments
Dial-up remote access server connects to segment: _____	
Phone bank that connects to dial-up remote access server: _____	
Protocol Support	
❑ IP (Select the appropriate IP address assignment and configuration options) ❑ Manually assigned ❑ DHCP assigned ❑ Include DHCP Relay Agent	
❑ IPX	
❑ AppleTalk	
Security	
Authentication protocols (Select one or more authentication protocols) ❑ MS-CHAP ❑ MS-CHAP v2 ❑ CHAP ❑ PAP ❑ SPAP	
Encryption protocols (Select the appropriate data encryption protocols)	
❑ MPPE (Select the strength of MPPE encryption) ❑ 40-bit ❑ 128-bit	
❑ IPSec (Select the IPSec protection to utilize)	

Mode	Authentication	Identity	Protection	Encryption
❑ Transport	❑ Kerberos	❑ MD5	❑ Identity (AH)	Not required
❑ Tunnel	❑ X509 ❑ Preshared key	❑ SHA	❑ Identity and encryption (ESP)	❑ DES ❑ 56-bit DES ❑ 3DES

Dial-Up Remote Access Server Specifications (continued)	Comments
❑ Remote access policies (Specify the remote access policy in the Comments column)	
Protocol packet filters	
❑ IP (Specify IP packet filter criteria in Comments column)	
❑ IPX (Specify IPX packet filter criteria in Comments column)	
❑ AppleTalk (Specify AppleTalk packet filter criteria in Comments column)	
Remote access to network resources	
❑ Dial-up remote access server only	
❑ Entire network	

Design Worksheet – Figure 11.20
Los Angeles – Dial-Up Remote Access Server B

Dial-Up Remote Access Server Specifications	Comments
Dial-up remote access server connects to segment: _____	
Phone bank that connects to dial-up remote access server: _____	
Protocol Support	
❑ IP (Select the appropriate IP address assignment and configuration options) ❑ Manually assigned ❑DHCP assigned ❑ Include DHCP Relay Agent	
❑ IPX	
❑ AppleTalk	
Security	
Authentication protocols (Select one or more authentication protocols) ❑ MS-CHAP ❑ MS-CHAP v2 ❑ CHAP ❑ PAP ❑SPAP	
Encryption protocols (Select the appropriate data encryption protocols)	
❑ MPPE (Select the strength of MPPE encryption) ❑ 40-bit ❑128-bit	
❑ IPSec (Select the IPSec protection to utilize)	

Mode	Authentication	Identity	Protection	Encryption
❑ Transport	❑ Kerberos	❑ MD5	❑ Identity (AH)	Not required
❑ Tunnel	❑ X509 ❑ Preshared key	❑ SHA	❑ Identity and encryption (ESP)	❑ DES ❑ 56-bit DES ❑ 3DES

❑ Remote access policies (Specify the remote access policy in the Comments column)	
Protocol packet filters	
❑ IP (Specify IP packet filter criteria in Comments column)	
❑ IPX (Specify IPX packet filter criteria in Comments column)	
❑ AppleTalk (Specify AppleTalk packet filter criteria in Comments column)	
Remote access to network resources	
❑ Dial-up remote access server only	
❑ Entire network	

Design Worksheet – Figure 11.20
Los Angeles – Dial-Up Remote Access Server C

Dial-Up Remote Access Server Specifications	Comments
Dial-up remote access server connects to segment: _____	
Phone bank that connects to dial-up remote access server: _____	
Protocol Support	
❑ IP (Select the appropriate IP address assignment and configuration options) ❑ Manually assigned ❑ DHCP assigned ❑ Include DHCP Relay Agent	
❑ IPX	
❑ AppleTalk	
Security	
Authentication protocols (Select one or more authentication protocols) ❑ MS-CHAP ❑ MS-CHAP v2 ❑ CHAP ❑ PAP ❑ SPAP	
Encryption protocols (Select the appropriate data encryption protocols)	
❑ MPPE (Select the strength of MPPE encryption) ❑ 40-bit ❑ 128-bit	
❑ IPSec (Select the IPSec protection to utilize)	

Mode	Authentication	Identity	Protection	Encryption
❑ Transport	❑ Kerberos	❑ MD5	❑ Identity (AH)	Not required
❑ Tunnel	❑ X509	❑ SHA	❑ Identity and encryption (ESP)	❑ DES
	❑ Preshared key			❑ 56-bit DES
				❑ 3DES

❑ Remote access policies (Specify the remote access policy in the Comments column)	
Protocol packet filters	
❑ IP (Specify IP packet filter criteria in Comments column)	
❑ IPX (Specify IPX packet filter criteria in Comments column)	
❑ AppleTalk (Specify AppleTalk packet filter criteria in Comments column)	
Remote access to network resources	
❑ Dial-up remote access server only	
❑ Entire network	

Design Worksheet – Figure 11.20
Los Angeles – Dial-Up Remote Access Server D

Dial-Up Remote Access Server Specifications	Comments
Dial-up remote access server connects to segment: _____	
Phone bank that connects to dial-up remote access server: _____	
Protocol Support	
❏ IP (Select the appropriate IP address assignment and configuration options)	
❏ Manually assigned ❏ DHCP assigned ❏ Include DHCP Relay Agent	
❏ IPX	
❏ AppleTalk	
Security	
Authentication protocols (Select one or more authentication protocols)	
❏ MS-CHAP ❏ MS-CHAP v2 ❏ CHAP ❏ PAP ❏ SPAP	
Encryption protocols (Select the appropriate data encryption protocols)	
❏ MPPE (Select the strength of MPPE encryption)	
❏ 40-bit ❏ 128-bit	
❏ IPSec (Select the IPSec protection to utilize)	

Mode	Authentication	Identity	Protection	Encryption
❏ Transport	❏ Kerberos	❏ MD5	❏ Identity (AH)	Not required
❏ Tunnel	❏ X509	❏ SHA	❏ Identity and encryption (ESP)	❏ DES
	❏ Preshared key			❏ 56-bit DES
				❏ 3DES

❏ Remote access policies (Specify the remote access policy in the Comments column)	
Protocol packet filters	
❏ IP (Specify IP packet filter criteria in Comments column)	
❏ IPX (Specify IPX packet filter criteria in Comments column)	
❏ AppleTalk (Specify AppleTalk packet filter criteria in Comments column)	
Remote access to network resources	
❏ Dial-up remote access server only	
❏ Entire network	

Design Worksheet – Figure 11.20
Los Angeles – Remote Access Clients

Remote Clients	Remote Access Client Specifications	Comments
	Primary phone number bank: _____ Backup phone number bank: _____	
	Primary phone number bank: _____ Backup phone number bank: _____	
	Primary phone number bank: _____ Backup phone number bank: _____	
	Primary phone number bank: _____ Backup phone number bank: _____	

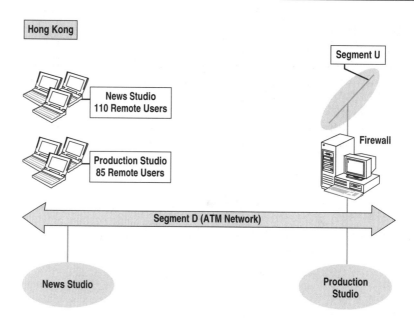

Figure 11.21   The existing network at Hong Kong

Design Worksheet – Figure 11.21
Hong Kong – Dial-Up Remote Access Server A

Dial-Up Remote Access Server Specifications	Comments
Dial-up remote access server connects to segment: _____	
Phone bank that connects to dial-up remote access server: _____	
Protocol Support	
❑ IP (Select the appropriate IP address assignment and configuration options) ❑ Manually assigned ❑ DHCP assigned ❑ Include DHCP Relay Agent	
❑ IPX	
❑ AppleTalk	
Security	
Authentication protocols (Select one or more authentication protocols) ❑ MS-CHAP ❑ MS-CHAP v2 ❑ CHAP ❑ PAP ❑ SPAP	
Encryption protocols (Select the appropriate data encryption protocols)	
❑ MPPE (Select the strength of MPPE encryption) ❑ 40-bit ❑128-bit	
❑ IPSec (Select the IPSec protection to utilize)	

Mode	Authentication	Identity	Protection	Encryption
❑ Transport	❑ Kerberos	❑ MD5	❑ Identity (AH)	Not required
❑ Tunnel	❑ X509 ❑ Preshared key	❑ SHA	❑ Identity and encryption (ESP)	❑ DES ❑ 56-bit DES ❑ 3DES

❑ Remote access policies (Specify the remote access policy in the Comments column)	
Protocol packet filters	
❑ IP (Specify IP packet filter criteria in Comments column)	
❑ IPX (Specify IPX packet filter criteria in Comments column)	
❑ AppleTalk (Specify AppleTalk packet filter criteria in Comments column)	
Remote access to network resources	
❑ Dial-up remote access server only	
❑ Entire network	

Design Worksheet – Figure 11.21
Hong Kong – Dial-Up Remote Access Server B

Dial-Up Remote Access Server Specifications	Comments
Dial-up remote access server connects to segment: _____	
Phone bank that connects to dial-up remote access server: _____	
Protocol Support	
❑ IP (Select the appropriate IP address assignment and configuration options)	
❑ Manually assigned ❑ DHCP assigned ❑ Include DHCP Relay Agent	
❑ IPX	
❑ AppleTalk	
Security	
Authentication protocols (Select one or more authentication protocols)	
❑ MS-CHAP ❑ MS-CHAP v2 ❑ CHAP ❑ PAP ❑ SPAP	
Encryption protocols (Select the appropriate data encryption protocols)	
❑ MPPE (Select the strength of MPPE encryption)	
❑ 40-bit ❑ 128-bit	
❑ IPSec (Select the IPSec protection to utilize)	

Mode	Authentication	Identity	Protection	Encryption
❑ Transport	❑ Kerberos	❑ MD5	❑ Identity (AH)	Not required
❑ Tunnel	❑ X509	❑ SHA	❑ Identity and encryption (ESP)	❑ DES
	❑ Preshared key			❑ 56-bit DES
				❑ 3DES

❑ Remote access policies (Specify the remote access policy in the Comments column)	
Protocol packet filters	
❑ IP (Specify IP packet filter criteria in Comments column)	
❑ IPX (Specify IPX packet filter criteria in Comments column)	
❑ AppleTalk (Specify AppleTalk packet filter criteria in Comments column)	
Remote access to network resources	
❑ Dial-up remote access server only	
❑ Entire network	

Design Worksheet – Figure 11.21
Hong Kong – Dial-Up Remote Access Server C

Dial-Up Remote Access Server Specifications	Comments
Dial-up remote access server connects to segment: _____	
Phone bank that connects to dial-up remote access server: _____	
Protocol Support	
❑ IP (Select the appropriate IP address assignment and configuration options)	
❑ Manually assigned ❑ DHCP assigned ❑ Include DHCP Relay Agent	
❑ IPX	
❑ AppleTalk	
Security	
Authentication protocols (Select one or more authentication protocols)	
❑ MS-CHAP ❑ MS-CHAP v2 ❑ CHAP ❑ PAP ❑ SPAP	
Encryption protocols (Select the appropriate data encryption protocols)	
❑ MPPE (Select the strength of MPPE encryption)	
❑ 40-bit ❑ 128-bit	
❑ IPSec (Select the IPSec protection to utilize)	

Mode	Authentication	Identity	Protection	Encryption
❑ Transport	❑ Kerberos	❑ MD5	❑ Identity (AH)	Not required
❑ Tunnel	❑ X509	❑ SHA	❑ Identity and encryption (ESP)	❑ DES
	❑ Preshared key			❑ 56-bit DES
				❑ 3DES

	Comments
❑ Remote access policies (Specify the remote access policy in the Comments column)	
Protocol packet filters	
❑ IP (Specify IP packet filter criteria in Comments column)	
❑ IPX (Specify IPX packet filter criteria in Comments column)	
❑ AppleTalk (Specify AppleTalk packet filter criteria in Comments column)	
Remote access to network resources	
❑ Dial-up remote access server only	
❑ Entire network	

Design Worksheet – Figure 11.21
Hong Kong – Dial-Up Remote Access Server D

Dial-Up Remote Access Server Specifications	Comments
Dial-up remote access server connects to segment: _____	
Phone bank that connects to dial-up remote access server: _____	
Protocol Support	
❑ IP (Select the appropriate IP address assignment and configuration options)	
❑ Manually assigned ❑ DHCP assigned ❑ Include DHCP Relay Agent	
❑ IPX	
❑ AppleTalk	
Security	
Authentication protocols (Select one or more authentication protocols)	
❑ MS-CHAP ❑ MS-CHAP v2 ❑ CHAP ❑ PAP ❑ SPAP	
Encryption protocols (Select the appropriate data encryption protocols)	
❑ MPPE (Select the strength of MPPE encryption)	
❑ 40-bit ❑ 128-bit	
❑ IPSec (Select the IPSec protection to utilize)	

	Mode	Authentication	Identity	Protection	Encryption
	❑ Transport	❑ Kerberos	❑ MD5	❑ Identity (AH)	Not required
	❑ Tunnel	❑ X509	❑ SHA	❑ Identity and encryption (ESP)	❑ DES
		❑ Preshared key			❑ 56-bit DES
					❑ 3DES

Dial-Up Remote Access Server Specifications (cont.)	Comments
❑ Remote access policies (Specify the remote access policy in the Comments column)	
Protocol packet filters	
❑ IP (Specify IP packet filter criteria in Comments column)	
❑ IPX (Specify IPX packet filter criteria in Comments column)	
❑ AppleTalk (Specify AppleTalk packet filter criteria in Comments column)	
Remote access to network resources	
❑ Dial-up remote access server only	
❑ Entire network	

Design Worksheet – Figure 11.21
Hong Kong – Remote Access Clients

Remote Clients	Remote Access Client Specifications	Comments
	Primary phone number bank: _____ Backup phone number bank: _____	
	Primary phone number bank: _____ Backup phone number bank: _____	
	Primary phone number bank: _____ Backup phone number bank: _____	
	Primary phone number bank: _____ Backup phone number bank: _____	

Review

The following questions are intended to reinforce key information in this chapter. If you're unable to answer a question, review the lesson and then try to answer the question again. You can find answers to the questions in the Appendix, "Questions and Answers."

1. An organization is considering remote access solutions to provide remote access to users that work from home. The users are distributed across a number of geographic locations, but all report to a local office. The director of information services is considering dial-up remote access solutions and VPN remote access solutions. As a consultant to the organization, what information do you need to obtain to assist the organization in determining the most appropriate solution?

2. You're preparing a list of recommendations that you must present to the board of directors for a large international trading company. The trading company has retained your services to evaluate its current dial-up remote access solution. During your investigation and evaluation of the current dial-up remote access solution, you determine that remote users often experience poor phone line quality. The poor phone line quality results in the users connecting at slower data rates and frequently disconnecting. Other than the poor phone line quality, the current remote access solution is meeting the trading company's requirements and constraints. What recommendations can you make to the trading company to resolve the slow data rates and frequent disconnections?

3. An organization has retained you as a consultant to create a dial-up remote access solution. The organization has a number of remote users that connect to the private network resources by using a variety of operating systems, including Windows 95, Windows 98, Windows NT 4 Workstation, Windows 2000 Professional, and Macintosh operating systems. Within the organization, the remote users must access resources on servers running Windows 2000, NetWare 4.2, and Macintosh operating systems. What do you include in your design to create a dial-up remote access solution for the organization?

4. One year after the initial deployment of the dial-up remote access design that you created for your organization, remote users are reporting slow application response times. You were informed of the performance problems during a meeting with the chief information officer (CIO) of your organization. The CIO is concerned about the slow application response times and wants to know what strategy you'll use to resolve the application response issues. What strategies can you use to determine the source of the application response time problems and resolve the issue?

C H A P T E R   1 2

VPN Connectivity in Remote Access Designs

About This Chapter

The users in many organizations work from small offices or home offices (SOHOs) or travel extensively. These users must access their organization's private network resources while not directly connected to the organization's private network. For these organizations, remote access to the private network is an important and common component to their networking services designs.

Today, many users have dial-up connectivity to the Internet. Organizations want to leverage these existing dial-up connections to provide access to private network resources. In addition, many organizations want to outsource the dial-up remote access because this reduces the costs associated with the initial investment and ongoing support in the remote access solution.

These organizations provide *virtual private network (VPN) remote access* to maintain control of the security and reduce the costs associated with remote access. Because the organization no longer directly owns and manages the dial-up remote access servers, it can utilize VPN remote access to enforce security between the remote access clients and remote access servers within the organization's private network. VPN remote access ensures that the organization can enforce all security aspects of its remote access design.

All organizations that provide VPN remote access connectivity must authenticate users, encrypt confidential data, and restrict access to private network resources. The remote access users must be able to transparently access the private network resources.

You can provide VPN remote access by using the Routing and Remote Access feature in Microsoft Windows 2000. Routing and Remote Access can authenticate remote access users in Active Directory directory service, Microsoft Windows NT 4 domains, or any Remote Authentication Dial-In User Service (RADIUS) server, such as Internet Authentication Server (IAS), found in Windows 2000.

Your designs must protect confidential data by encrypting the traffic between the remote access users and the VPN remote access servers. Routing and Remote Access can encrypt data over VPN connections by using Microsoft Point-to-Point Encryption (MPPE) or Internet Protocol Security (IPSec). Finally, Routing and Remote Access can restrict the private network segments that can be accessed by remote access users.

This chapter answers questions such as:

- In what situations are the VPN remote access services provided by Routing and Remote Access appropriate for your design?

- How can you integrate Routing and Remote Access in your network?

- How can you ensure the confidentiality of data between remote access clients and remote access servers?

- What can you include in your design to ensure that VPN remote access is always available to remote access users?

- How can you improve the performance of VPN remote access solutions during peak periods of activity?

Before You Begin

Before you begin, you must have an overall understanding of

- The common transport protocol configuration for Internet Protocol (IP) and Internetwork Packet Exchange (IPX) (such as the IP address, subnet mask, or default gateway for IP)

- IP and IPX routed networks (including subnets, network segments, routers, and IP switches)

- Dial-up telephony technologies used by Internet service providers (ISPs) or other dial-up outsourcing (wholesale dial-up) organizations

- Tunneling protocols (including how packets are encapsulated in tunnels and how tunnels are established)

Lesson 1: Designs That Include VPN Remote Access

This lesson presents the requirements and constraints, both business and technical, that identify the VPN remote access services in Routing and Remote Access as a solution.

After this lesson, you will be able to

- Identify the situation in which Routing and Remote Access is the appropriate choice for VPN remote access
- Describe the relationship between Routing and Remote Access and Windows 2000
- Identify the business and technical requirements and constraints that must be collected to create a VPN remote access design
- Identify the VPN remote access design decisions
- Evaluate scenarios and determine which capabilities and features of Routing and Remote Access are appropriate in VPN remote access solutions

Estimated lesson time: 30 minutes

Routing and Remote Access in VPN Remote Access Designs

You can include Routing and Remote Access in remote access designs to provide dial-up remote access, to provide VPN remote access, or to function as a RADIUS client. To create successful remote access solutions, you must determine whether the solution requires dial-up remote access, VPN remote access, or a RADIUS client.

In addition to VPN remote access connectivity, you can provide remote access by using

- Dial-up remote access connectivity
- Outsourced remote access connectivity by using RADIUS

Although other remote access methods are available, VPN remote access is the only method that allows the organization to control *all* security aspects of remote access connectivity while being independent of the dial-up remote access solution provided by third-party organizations. Only VPN remote access connectivity solutions allow the organization to be independent of the dial-up remote access solution while controlling the

- User accounts authorized for remote access
- Strength of security for protecting confidential data
- Private network resources that remote users can access

VPN remote access solutions utilize enhanced versions of the Point-to-Point Protocol (PPP), Point-to-Point Tunneling Protocol (PPTP), and Layer 2 Tunneling Protocol (L2TP), to connect remote clients to the remote access server. PPTP and L2TP are industry standard collections of protocols that define how to authenticate remote users, protect confidential data, and transmit IP and IPX traffic. Multiple vendors and operating systems support PPTP and L2TP.

VPN and RADIUS solutions utilize PPP to provide dial-up connectivity, exactly like the dial-up remote access solution. In addition, VPN and RADIUS solutions require PPTP or L2TP to provide virtual connections to the organization's private network resources.

The addition of PPTP and L2TP increases the amount of traffic required to send the equivalent amount of information by using PPP. As a result, when using comparable hardware, dial-up remote access solutions (using PPP only) provide better performance than VPN and RADIUS solutions.

However, VPN and RADIUS solutions allow the organization to outsource the dial-up remote access and reduce the overall costs for implementing and supporting remote access solutions. When organizations want to reduce the costs in their remote access solution and are willing to allow third-party organizations to manage and control dial-up remote access, VPN and RADIUS remote access solutions are appropriate solutions.

The primary difference between a VPN remote access solution and a RADIUS remote access solution is the level of integration with the dial-up remote access servers. In a VPN remote access solution, no service agreement exists with the third-party organization that provides dial-up remote access. Remote users must first be authenticated by the third-party organization (to provide dial-up connectivity) and then be authenticated by the organization's VPN remote access servers (to provide connectivity to the organization's private network). In a VPN remote access solution, you can't provide additional security measures, such as password requirements, caller-ID, or callback for remote users.

In a RADIUS solution, a service agreement exists with the third-party organization that provides dial-up remote access. Remote users are authenticated by the third-party organization by using the user account and password assigned to them by their organization. No additional remote user credentials are required. In a RADIUS solution, you can provide additional security measures, such as password requirements, caller-ID, or callback for remote users. Figure 12.1 and Figure 12.2 illustrate the differences between VPN and RADIUS remote access solutions.

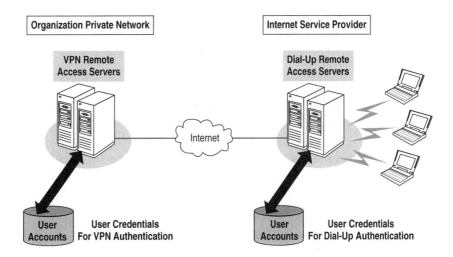

Figure 12.1   VPN remote access solutions

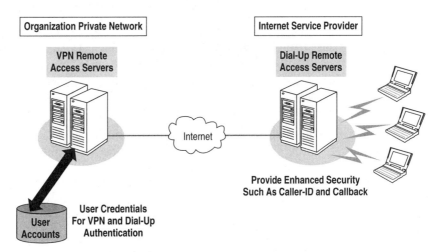

Figure 12.2   RADIUS remote access solutions

Only IP and IPX protocols can be transmitted through PPTP and L2TP tunnels. As a result, you must limit your design to include remote users who run only IP and IPX protocols. You can't include other protocols, such as AppleTalk and Network Basic Enhanced User Interface (NetBEUI), in your VPN remote access design.

This chapter discusses VPN remote access solutions provided by Routing and Remote Access. For more information on dial-up remote access solutions by using Routing and Remote Access, see Chapter 11, "Dial-Up Connectivity in Remote Access Designs." For more information on RADIUS client solutions by using Routing and Remote Access, see Chapter 13, "RADIUS in Remote Access Designs."

Routing and Remote Access and Windows 2000

Routing and Remote Access is the Windows 2000 feature that provides remote access solutions and routing solutions. As discussed in the previous section, you can create a variety of remote access solutions by using Routing and Remote Access. Routing and Remote Access also is appropriate for any multiprotocol routing solution, including IP, IPX, and AppleTalk protocols.

For more information on IP routing solutions provided by Routing and Remote Access, see Chapter 4, "IP Routing Designs." For more information on multiprotocol routing solutions provided by Routing and Remote Access, see Chapter 5, "Multiprotocol Routing Designs."

The remote access services in Windows 2000 can be divided into the following:

- **Remote access client**   Windows 2000 and all other Windows operating systems, including Microsoft Windows 95, Microsoft Windows 98, Microsoft Windows Me, and Windows NT 4, include a remote access client. In Windows 2000, the dial-up networking client feature is the remote access client. The name of the remote access client, dial-up networking client, is misleading because the client provides dial-up and VPN remote access connectivity.

- **Remote access server**   Routing and Remote Access in Windows 2000 can provide remote access connectivity in your design. From the Windows 2000 perspective, Routing and Remote Access is a service that runs on Windows 2000. Routing and Remote Access utilizes the IP and IPX protocols of Windows 2000. In addition, you can authenticate remote users by using local user accounts or user accounts in Active Directory.

  The remote access server is essentially a specialized router that routes IP, or tunneled IPX, traffic between the remote access clients and network segments in the private network. All the design decisions that apply to IP and IPX routers must be included in your VPN remote access design. For more information on IP routing, see Chapter 4, "IP Routing Designs." For more information on IPX routing, see Chapter 5, "Multiprotocol Routing Designs."

  Routing and Remote Access can dynamically assign VPN IP addresses allocated from Dynamic Host Configuration Protocol (DHCP) servers. You must specify a fixed IP address for the network interfaces on the Routing and Remote Access server that communicate with the private network. Routing and Remote Access utilizes the protocols provided by Windows 2000 to communicate with the private network and remote access clients.

Routing and Remote Access is available in Windows 2000 Server, Microsoft Windows 2000 Advanced Server, and Microsoft Windows 2000 Datacenter Server. Routing and Remote Access is not available in Microsoft Windows 2000 Professional.

Figure 12.3 illustrates the relationship between remote access clients and remote access servers in VPN remote access designs. The VPN network client in Windows 2000 is the remote access client that connects to the remote access servers running Routing and Remote Access on Windows 2000.

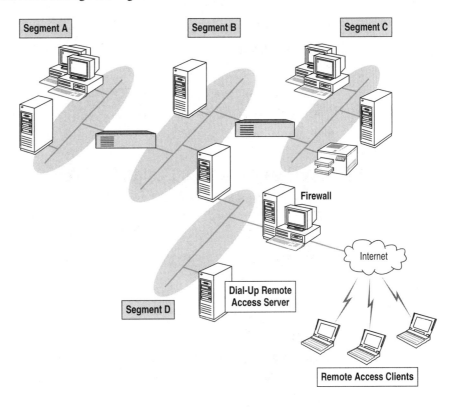

Figure 12.3   The relationship between remote access clients and remote access servers in VPN remote access designs

In this chapter, you learn how to create VPN remote access designs with Routing and Remote Access and Windows 2000. To successfully create dial-up remote access designs, you must be familiar with

- General local area network (LAN) protocol and LAN routing theory for IP or IPX
- General tunneling protocol theory

VPN Remote Access Design Requirements and Constraints

Before you create your VPN remote access design, you must gather the requirements and constraints, both business and technical, of the organization. As you create your design, you make design decisions based on the requirements and constraints that you collect.

The list of the design requirements and constraints that you collect includes

- The amount of data transmitted between the remote access clients and the remote access servers
- Number of locations that require VPN remote access
- Existing Internet connections
- Plans for network growth
- Number of simultaneous remote access clients
- Operating systems that the remote access clients are running
- Protocols utilized by the remote access clients

VPN Remote Access Design Decisions

After you determine the business and technical requirements and constraints, apply the information you gathered to make VPN remote access design decisions. To create your VPN remote access design, you must choose the

- Methods for integrating VPN remote access into the existing network based on the
  - Remote access client operating systems
  - Existing remote access servers
  - Existing Internet connectivity
- Hardware requirements for the VPN remote access servers, including the
  - Number of PPTP or L2TP ports required to support the maximum number of simultaneous remote access users
  - Data transmission rates of the remote access server's Internet connection
- Methods for protecting confidential data exchanged by the remote access clients that include
  - Authenticating remote access users
  - Encrypting confidential data

- Method of ensuring that VPN remote access is always available to remote access clients

- Method of optimizing the network traffic between remote access clients and remote access servers

The lessons that follow in this chapter provide the information required for you to make specific VPN remote access design recommendations.

VPN Remote Access Designs

Your VPN remote access solutions must provide remote users with access to private network resources. When the organization is willing to relinquish the dial-up remote access portion of the remote access design to a third-party organization, you can include VPN remote access in your design.

In VPN remote access solutions, some portion of the remote access connectivity is provided by other organizations, such as an Internet service provider (ISP). Because the ISP owns the phone lines, modems, and dial-up remote access servers, the organization providing VPN access loses some control over the design (such as modem data rates, available phone numbers, physical security of the remote access servers, or other specifications). However, by using VPN remote access solutions, the organization reduces the implementation and support costs associated with the remote access solution.

You can include Routing and Remote Access in your designs to provide VPN remote access solutions. The remote users can access the private network by using Transmission Control Protocol/Internet Protocol (TCP/IP) or IPX.

Making the Decision

In remote access designs, you must determine whether VPN remote access is the appropriate solution. You must examine the requirements and constraints of the organization and then determine whether VPN remote access is the appropriate solution.

As previously mentioned, the primary advantage to including VPN remote access is that the organization reduces the costs associated with providing dial-up remote access.

The primary disadvantage to VPN remote access is the lack of security that can be enforced on the dial-up remote access connections. As previously mentioned, the types of security that are relinquished with VPN remote access solutions include

- Caller-ID detection

- Remote user callback

- Authentication protocol used to authenticate the dial-up remote access connection
- Password security features including password length, password aging, password strength, and other password attributes

For example, an organization can significantly reduce costs by outsourcing its international dial-up connectivity to an ISP. The ISP provides dial-up connectivity for the organization's remote users. The ISP incurs the costs associated with the dial-up remote access connectivity. Because the ISP can amortize the costs associated with the initial investment and ongoing costs associated with the dial-up network solution across multiple organizations, the cost to the organization is significantly less.

When the organization is unwilling to relinquish control of portions of the remote access solution to other organizations, consider a dial-up remote access solution. For more information on dial-up remote access solutions by using Routing and Remote Access, see Chapter 11, "Dial-Up Connectivity in Remote Access Designs."

When the organization is willing to relinquish control of portions of the remote access solution to another organization, but wants to control more of the security of the dial-up remote access portion of the remote access design, consider including a RADIUS dial-up remote access solution. For more information on RADIUS client solutions by using Routing and Remote Access, see Chapter 13, "RADIUS in Remote Access Designs."

Applying the Decision

Figure 12.4 illustrates a scenario where Routing and Remote Access provides a VPN remote access solution. The organization wants to reduce the costs associated with its remote access solution. The security requirements of the organization allow it to outsource the dial-up remote access portion of the remote access solution.

The VPN remote access services provided by Routing and Remote Access in Windows 2000 is the only solution that meets the requirements of the organization. As a result, dial-up remote access or outsourced RADIUS solutions aren't appropriate solutions.

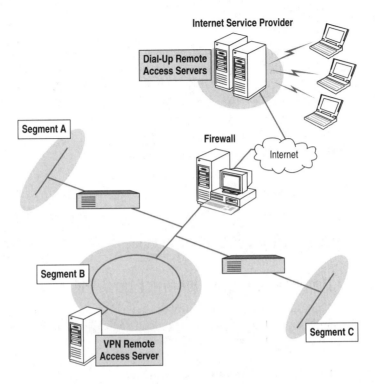

Figure 12.4   Scenario that includes Routing and Remote Access to provide VPN
remote access solutions

Lesson 2: Essential VPN Remote Access Design Concepts

This lesson discusses the requirements, constraints, and design decisions that are used in establishing the essential specifications in a VPN remote access design. This lesson covers the design concepts common to all VPN remote access designs.

After this lesson, you will be able to

- Determine the number of VPN remote access servers to include in your design
- Determine the appropriate placement of VPN remote access servers in your design
- Select the remote access client support

Estimated lesson time: 30 minutes

Determining the Placement of VPN Remote Access Servers

You must determine the number of VPN remote access servers required in your VPN remote access design. You can specify one or more VPN remote access servers in your design.

Making the Decision

A single VPN remote access server can potentially support hundreds of remote access client computers. You can include multiple VPN remote access servers in your design to support more remote access clients than can be supported by a single remote access server.

To decide how many VPN remote access servers to include in your design, you must know the

- Maximum number of simultaneous remote users that must access resources *at each location* within the organization
- Amount of data to be transmitted *over a period of time* (or sustained data rate) between the remote users and the remote access servers

After you know the maximum number of simultaneous users and the sustained data rate, you can determine the number of remote access servers that you must include by conducting a pilot test. In the pilot test, you determine the number of remote users that can be supported by the remote access servers. You must ensure that each remote access connection during the pilot test is transmitting data at the sustained data rate.

Upon completion of the pilot tests, you know the maximum number of users that your remote access servers can support at the sustained data rate. To determine the number of remote access servers to include in your design, divide the maximum number of users required by the number of users that each remote access server can support. Round your calculation up to the next nearest whole number to finalize the number of remote access servers required in your design.

Applying the Decision

An organization wants to provide dial-up remote access to remote users. You must calculate the number of VPN remote access servers required in your design. For the purposes of this scenario, assume that

- The organization has 1,000 users who require remote access
- Up to 600 remote users may simultaneously access the remote access servers
- Acceptable application response times require a sustained data rate of 33.6Kbps or higher for each remote access client
- Each remote user connects to the VPN remote access server through a dial-up modem (or other connection type) capable of at least 56Kbps
- Pilot tests confirm that the approved remote access servers can support 140 remote users with a sustained data rate of 56Kbps

Table 12.1 shows the calculations used in determining the number of remote access servers required in the design.

Table 12.1   Calculations for the Number of VPN Remote Access Servers Required

Perform These Calculations		Using
A	Maximum number of simultaneous remote users	600
B	Number of remote users that each remote access server can support	140
C	Number of remote access servers required (C=A/B)	4.29
D	Round up to the nearest even number of VPN remote access servers	5

Determining the Placement of Remote Access Servers

You must determine where to place the VPN remote access servers in your design so that remote access clients can access private network resources. You place the VPN remote access servers to centralize administration, reduce costs, and reduce the network traffic between locations.

Making the Decision

You can place remote access servers within your design such that

- All the remote access servers are in a single location in the organization
- The remote access servers are distributed across multiple locations
- The remote access servers are located near the resources accessed by the remote users

You must place VPN remote access servers to ensure that remote access clients can access private network resources while reducing or eliminating remote access traffic between locations. Depending on the requirements of the organizations, you might need to add additional remote access servers to enhance the performance or availability of your VPN remote access design. For more information on VPN remote access servers' improving performance or availability, see Lesson 4, "VPN Remote Access Design Optimization."

All Remote Access Servers in a Single Location

When all the remote access servers are in a single location, you must provide enough PPTP or L2TP virtual ports to support the maximum number of simultaneous remote access users for the entire organization.

The advantage of placing all the remote access in a single location is that you

- **Centralize the administration and support of the remote access servers** Centralized administration and support ensures that consistency in configuration, such as the same security configuration, exists on all the remote access servers.

- **Potentially reduce the costs associated with administration and support** Because all the remote access servers are in one location, the administration and support costs are amortized across *all* the remote access servers.

The disadvantages of placing all the remote access in a single location is that you potentially

- **Increase network traffic on wide area network (WAN) segments** When an organization is comprised of multiple locations, the remote access users might want to access resources in locations *other* than the location where the remote access servers are placed. Accessing resources in locations other than where the remote access servers are placed forces traffic across the WAN segments that connect the locations.

- **Lose all remote access connectivity** When *all* the remote access servers are placed in a central location, users will be unable to gain remote access if a catastrophic event (earthquake, hurricane, tornado, etc.) interrupts service at that location. When organizations have network resources in multiple geographic locations, consider placing remote access servers at each location to provide redundancy in the event of a disaster.

Note For organizations that have network resources in a single geographic location, consider providing off-site connectivity in the event of a disaster.

Remote Access Servers Distributed Across Multiple Locations

When the remote access servers are distributed across multiple locations, you must provide enough PPTP or L2TP virtual ports to support the maximum number of simultaneous remote access users that connect at each location.

The advantages of placing the remote access in multiple locations is that you potentially reduce the

- **Network traffic between locations within the organization**   When the remote users predominantly access resources within the same location as the VPN remote access server, network traffic between locations is reduced or eliminated. Reducing the network traffic between locations can reduce WAN utilization and improve data transfer rates for other applications.

- **Loss of remote access due to a catastrophic event**   When the remote access servers are distributed across multiple locations, users can access the network remotely even when a catastrophic event interrupts services at one geographic location.

The disadvantages of placing the VPN remote access servers in multiple locations is that you potentially

- **Decentralize the administration and support of the remote access servers**   Because the VPN remote access servers are in multiple locations, each location typically requires separate administration and support personnel.

- **Increase the costs associated with administration and support**   Because all the remote access servers are in multiple locations, the administration and support costs for each location is amortized across *fewer* remote access servers. As a result, the average cost to administer and support the VPN remote access servers is increased.

Remote Access Servers Placed Near the Resources Accessed by Remote Users

You can place the remote access servers in your design on network segments adjacent to the resources predominantly accessed by the remote users. Placing the remote access servers on network segments adjacent to the resources reduces the number of network segments and routers that must be traversed within the organization's private network and improves the performance of remote access clients.

When you want to improve the performance of the remote access clients, you must do one of the following:

- Place the remote access servers near the resources that the remote users access

- Move the servers hosting the resources closer to the remote access servers

Applying the Decision

Figure 12.5 illustrates where to place VPN remote access servers in your design. For the purposes of this scenario, assume that the following apply.

- The highest priority is the reduction of costs associated with VPN remote access.
- The reduction of network traffic between locations is the second highest priority.
- Location A has 200 users who work remotely.
- Location B has 120 users who work remotely.
- Location C has 100 users who work remotely.
- Three-quarters of the remote users must be supported simultaneously.
- Remote users frequently access resources in all locations.

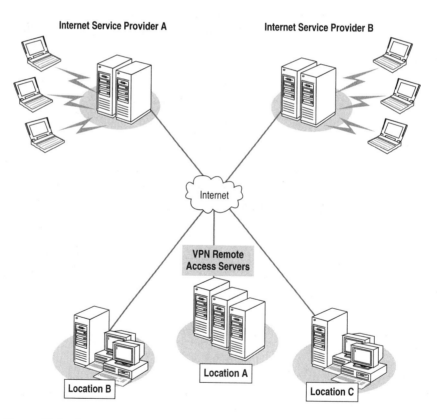

Figure 12.5   Scenario that illustrates where to place VPN remote access servers in your design

For the scenario depicted in Figure 12.5, you place VPN remote access servers at Location A to centralize the administration and support of the VPN remote access solution. Centralizing the administration and support of the VPN remote access solution reduces the costs associated with the deployment and ongoing support.

Selecting the Remote Access Client Support

You must determine the remote access client support to incorporate into your VPN remote access design. You must evaluate the applications run by the remote access clients and the resources accessed by the remote access clients.

Making the Decision

For each remote access client that connects to the VPN remote access servers, you must determine the

- Number and type of virtual ports to include
- Transport protocols required
- Method of assigning network addressing

Determining the Virtual Ports to Include

You must determine the number and type of virtual ports to include in your design to support the remote access clients. You must include a virtual port for each simultaneous remote access client.

You can include either PPTP or L2TP port types in your design. L2TP is currently supported only on remote access clients running Windows 2000. As a result, you must include PPTP in your design to support remote access clients running Windows 2000 and other operating systems (such as Windows 95, Windows 98, Windows Me, and Windows NT 4).

You must include enough virtual ports to support the remote access clients that require respective tunneling protocol type (either PPTP or L2TP). Ensure that you specify enough of each respective virtual port for the maximum number of simultaneous remote access clients. Ensure that the VPN remote access server is capable of supporting the required data rate when the maximum number of simultaneous remote access clients is connected.

Selecting the Transport Protocols

You can determine the transport protocols to include in your dial-up remote access design by examining the

- **Operating system running on the remote access client**   The operating system running on the remote access client may require a specific transport protocol. For example, a remote access client running Client Services for

NetWare in Windows 2000 requires the IPX protocol. Because IPX is tunneled in IP packets, the remote access client also requires IP. As a result, you need to include the IP and IPX protocols in your VPN remote access design.

- **Applications running on the remote access clients**   Many of the applications may require specific transport protocols to run properly. For example, File Transport Protocol (FTP) requires TCP/IP to operate properly. As a result, you need to include TCP/IP in your VPN remote access design.

- **Network management tools running on the remote access clients**   Many network management tools require specific transport protocols to run properly. For example, management tools for NetWare servers may require IPX to operate properly. In this instance, you need to include IPX and IP in your VPN remote access design.

- **Resource servers accessed by the remote access clients**   The resource servers accessed by the remote access clients network may require a specific transport protocol to be accessed. For example, NetWare servers may require IPX to access private network resources. To access these NetWare servers, you need to include IPX and IP in your VPN remote access design.

Determining the Method of Assigning Network Addressing

Each remote access client must be assigned a network address from the address range assigned to the organization's private network. When the remote access client connects to the VPN remote access server, a valid private network address (either IP or IPX address) must be assigned to the client.

You can assign network addresses to remote access clients by

- **Manually specifying a range of addresses to be assigned to remote access clients**   You can allocate ranges of both IP and IPX network addresses from the private network's IP and IPX addressing scheme that can be assigned to remote access clients.

  You must assign a unique network address range to each VPN remote access server. The network address range assigned to each VPN remote access server must be unique within the private network and across all the VPN remote access servers.

- **Automatically assigning an IP address allocated from DHCP servers**   Routing and Remote Access can allocate a range of IP addresses from a DHCP server. Routing and Remote Access initially allocates 10 IP addresses to be assigned to remote access clients by the remote access server. Routing and Remote Access continues to allocate IP addresses in groups of 10 until all simultaneous remote access users are assigned to all remote access clients.

  By default, remote access clients receive only an IP address and subnet mask. However, when you install a DHCP Relay Agent on the remote access server, the remote access clients can receive all IP configuration provided by DHCP.

Applying the Decision

In Figure 12.6, a scenario illustrates the appropriate selection of remote access client support to include in your design. For the purposes of this scenario, assume that

- All the remote access clients access FTP and Web servers in the organization's private network.

- Each virtual remote access port must support computers running Windows 2000 and other operating systems.

- Some of the remote access clients require access to NetWare 4.2 file servers that use only the IPX protocol.

- Up to 300 remote users must be able to simultaneously access the private network.

- DHCP must be used to assign all IP addresses and provide *total* IP configuration.

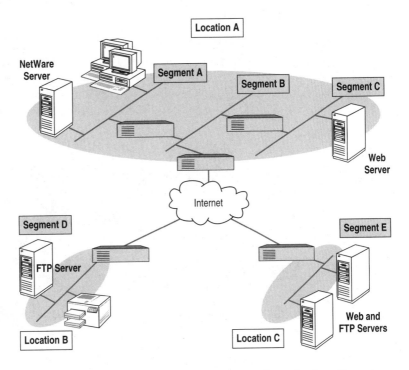

Figure 12.6 Scenario that illustrates the appropriate selection of remote access client support to include in your design

To fulfill the requirements and constraints of the organization, you must include

- TCP/IP on all remote access clients to support access to the FTP and Web servers

- IPX and TCP/IP on the remote access clients that access the NetWare 4.2 file servers
- Manual network address ranges allocated for the IPX protocol
- DHCP configuration for IP
- DHCP Relay Agent installed on each remote access server
- Up to 300 PPTP virtual ports to support the maximum number of simultaneous remote access clients

Activity 12.1: Evaluating a VPN Remote Access Design

In this activity, you're presented with a scenario. To complete the activity

1. Evaluate the scenario and determine the design requirements
2. Answer questions and make design recommendations

In Figure 12.7, you see a map for an international shipping company. The company provides commercial shipment of materials and goods internationally. The shipping company has a Web site that allows customers to place shipment requests, check pricing, and check shipment status. Computers running Internet Information Services 5.0 (IIS 5.0) host the shipping company's Web site.

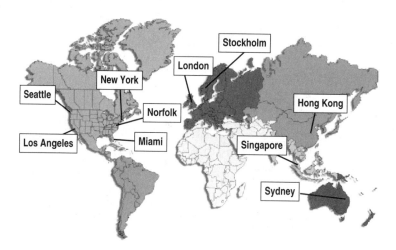

Figure 12.7   Map of an international shipping company

The customer service representatives for the shipping company update the status of each shipment as the shipments move through the various stages of shipment and customs clearance. The customer service representatives for a geographic region are located at each office.

Each office is connected to the Internet by using a combination of 56Kbps, Integrated Services Digital Network (ISDN), Digital Subscriber Line (DSL), T1, and T3 connections.

Answer the following questions concerning your design recommendations. You can find answers to the questions in the Appendix, "Questions and Answers."

1. The shipping company's director of marketing and customer service has decided that the majority of the customer service representatives will work remotely at the shipping customer's location to provide better service. The customer service representatives must connect to the shipping company's private network to access the Web applications and resources. As the director of information services for the shipping company, you're responsible for the networking services design. What recommendations can you make?

2. The board of directors for the shipping company is reviewing the proposal you submitted for the VPN remote access design. One of the board members is also on the board of directors for another company. The other company selected dial-up remote access servers for its remote access solutions and the board member wants to know why you're recommending a VPN remote access design for this company. How do you respond?

3. The shipping company's director of marketing and customer service reports that the customer service representatives are confused by the credentials required to initiate dial-up connectivity and the credentials required to initiate the VPN connection. The director of marketing and customer service wants to know whether there is any way to consolidate the credentials so the customer service representatives are required to remember only one set of credentials. What recommendations can you make?

Lesson 3: Data Protection in VPN Remote Access Designs

This lesson discusses how to create designs that protect confidential data in VPN remote access designs. This lesson focuses on preventing unauthorized access to private network resources and protecting confidential data transmitted by remote users in your VPN remote access design.

After this lesson, you will be able to

- Prevent unauthorized access to private network resources
- Protect confidential data transmitted between remote users and the VPN remote access servers

Estimated lesson time: 30 minutes

Preventing Access to Private Network Resources

When your design includes VPN remote access servers, the probability increases that private network resources can be accessed by unauthorized users. You must ensure that including VPN remote access servers in your design doesn't compromise the organization's security.

Making the Decision

You can prevent unauthorized private network access through VPN remote access servers by

- Restricting remote user access to only the resources on the VPN remote access servers
- Restricting the traffic transmitted through the VPN remote access servers
- Placing VPN remote access servers properly in relation to screened subnets or demilitarized zones (DMZs)

Restricting Access to Resources on the VPN Remote Access Server

Routing and Remote Access allows you to restrict the resources that remote users can access to only the resources on the VPN remote access server or to all the resources on the entire network. For *each protocol* on the remote access server, you can enable or disable access to

- Only the resources on the VPN remote access servers
- Resources located anywhere in the private network

For example, you might want to allow remote users to access only a Web and FTP site. You can install the Web and FTP site on the VPN remote access server and then disable access to other resources on the private network.

Restricting Traffic Transmitted Through the VPN Remote Access Server

You can restrict the traffic transmitted through the VPN remote access server by using packet filters. You can filter IP and IPX packets by specifying Routing and Remote Access packet filters.

You can specify any combination of packet filters to restrict access to

- Individual resources or servers
- Network segments
- Types of traffic, such as Hypertext Transfer Protocol (HTTP) or FTP traffic

For more information on Routing and Remote Access packet filters for IP, see Chapter 4, "IP Routing Designs," Lesson 3, "Data Protection on Unsecured Segments." For more information on Routing and Remote Access packet filters for IPX, see Chapter 5, "Multiprotocol Routing Designs," Lesson 2, "IPX Routing Design Concepts."

Placing VPN Remote Access Servers in Relation to Screened Subnets

As previously mentioned, you must place the VPN remote access servers in your design to protect private network resources. You can place VPN remote access servers

- Outside the private network
- On screened subnets
- Within the private network

Figure 12.8 illustrates the various options for placing VPN remote access servers outside the private network. When you place VPN remote access servers outside the private network, protect data even further by establishing a VPN tunnel between the remote access server (VPN Server A) and a router within the private network (Router C).

The advantage of placing the VPN remote access server outside the private network is that you can potentially reduce the complexity of firewall rules. The disadvantage of placing the VPN remote access server outside the private network is that you expose the VPN remote access server to direct access to unauthorized users.

Ensure that the computer(s) providing VPN remote access outside the private network are running only the essential networking services. Run only services, or applications, and place data on the server that can be accessed by unauthorized users.

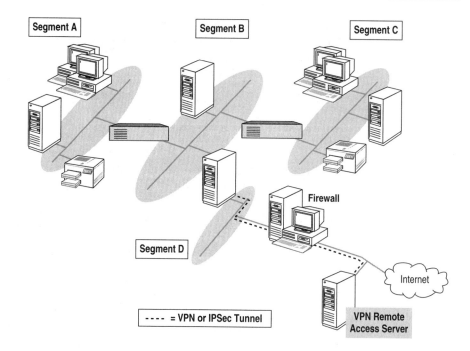

Figure 12.8 Example of placing VPN remote access servers outside the private network

Figure 12.9 illustrates the various options for placing VPN remote access servers on screened subnets. Just as with placing VPN remote access servers outside the private network, protect data even further by establishing a VPN tunnel between the remote access server (VPN Server A) and a router within the private network (Router A).

The advantages of placing the VPN remote access server on screened subnets are that you can

- Potentially reduce the complexity of firewall rules that protect the private network resources (Firewall B in Figure 12.9)
- Provide improved protection in comparison to placing the VPN remote access server outside the private network

The disadvantage of placing VPN remote access servers on screened subnets is that you increase the complexity of the firewall rules that protect the VPN server (Firewall A in Figure 12.9).

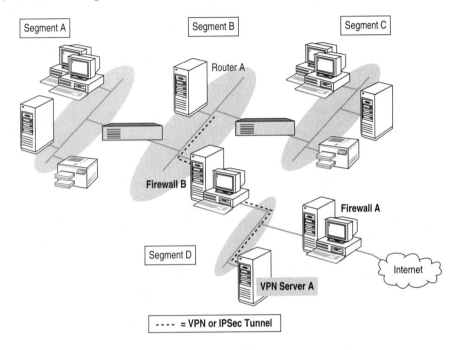

Figure 12.9   Example of placing VPN remote access servers on screened subnets

Figure 12.10 illustrates the various options for placing VPN remote access servers within the private network. Because the VPN remote access servers are placed inside the private network, no VPN tunnels are necessary to protect data transmitted between the remote access server (VPN Server A) and the private network.

The advantage of placing the VPN remote access server within the private network is that you can provide improved protection of the VPN remote access server in comparison to placing the VPN remote access server outside the private network or on screened subnets. The disadvantage of placing VPN remote access servers on screened subnets is that you increase the complexity of the firewall rules that protect the VPN server (Firewall A in Figure 12.11).

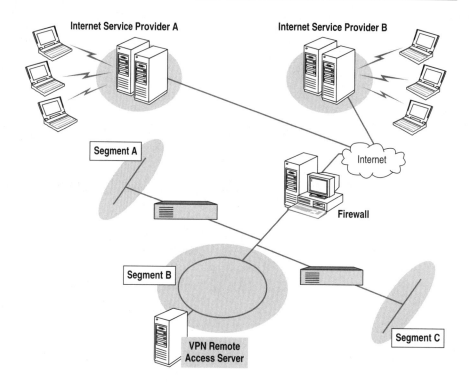

Figure 12.10 Example of placing VPN remote access servers within the private
network

Applying the Decision

Figure 12.11 illustrates the proper methods for preventing access to private network resources. For the purposes of this scenario, assume that

- The remote access clients require the IP and IPX protocols.
- You must restrict remote access network traffic to HTTP and FTP traffic.
- You must allow IPX traffic to access only an IPX-based network segment that
  includes NetWare 4.2 file and print servers.
- Firewalls prevent unauthorized access to private network segments.

To fulfill the requirements and constraints of the organization, you must specify

- That the VPN remote access server be placed on the network segment
  between Firewalls A and B
- Routing and Remote Access IP filters allow *only* HTTP and FTP traffic
- Routing and Remote Access IPX filters allow traffic between the remote
  access clients and the network segment that contains NetWare 4.2 file and
  print servers

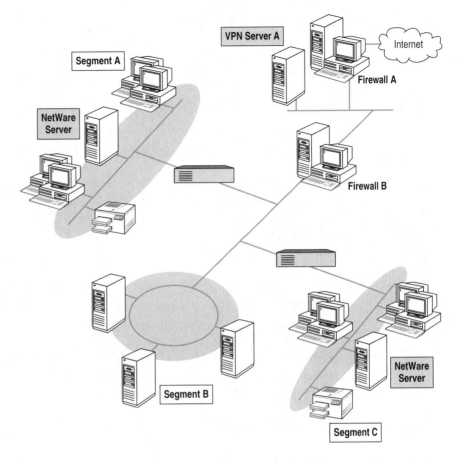

Figure 12.11   A scenario that illustrates the proper methods for preventing access to private network resources

Protecting Confidential Remote Access Data

When your design includes VPN remote access servers, remote users will access confidential data. You must ensure that the confidentiality of the data is protected at all times.

Making the Decision

You can protect confidential data transmitted between remote users and the VPN remote access server by

- Authenticating remote users
- Encrypting confidential data
- Enforcing remote access policies

Authenticating Remote Users

To ensure that only authorized remote users can access private network resources, your dial-up remote access design must authenticate the remote users (also known as *identity checking*). You can authenticate remote users by verifying their logon credentials, including user name, password, and domain (or realm). You can verify the remote user's credentials by using

- Local accounts, stored on the VPN remote access server
- Active Directory accounts, stored on domain controllers

To protect the remote user's credentials (especially the user name and password), you can encrypt the credentials exchanged between the remote access client and the remote access server. You can select from a variety of authentication protocols to authenticate the remote users.

You must select the appropriate authentication protocol based on the

- Authentication protocols available on the remote access client
- Strength of encryption that you require to protect the remote user's credentials
- Type of VPN tunnels (PPTP or L2TP) included in your design

For more information on determining the appropriate VPN authentication protocols, see the section, "VPN Authentication Protocols," in Chapter 2, "Networking Protocol Design," Lesson 3, "TCP/IP Data Protection."

Encrypting Confidential Data

To ensure that confidential data is protected, your VPN remote access design must encrypt any confidential data transmitted between the VPN remote access servers and the remote access client. You can encrypt the confidential data by using

- Microsoft Point-to-Point Encryption (MPPE) protocol
- Internet Protocol Security (IPSec)

You must select the appropriate authentication protocol based on the

- Encryption protocols available on the remote access client
- Strength of encryption that you require to protect the confidential data
- Type of VPN tunnels (PPTP or L2TP) included in your design

For more information on determining the appropriate VPN encryption protocols, see the section, "VPN Encryption Protocols," in Chapter 2, "Networking Protocol Design," Lesson 3, "TCP/IP Data Protection."

Note   IPSec data encryption is currently available only on remote access clients running Windows 2000.

Enforcing Remote Access Policies

You can enforce the security requirements for remote access clients by using remote access policies. Remote access policies are named rules that consist of

- Conditions
- Remote access permission
- Profiles

You can use remote access polices to enforce the security requirements of the design by forcing the remote access client to adhere to the remote access policies. Remote access clients that don't adhere to the remote access policies are automatically disconnected.

For more information on determining the appropriate remote access policies, see the section, "Enforcing Remote Access Policies," in Chapter 11, "Dial-Up Connectivity in Remote Access Designs," Lesson 3, "Data Protection in Dial-Up Remote Access Designs."

Applying the Decision

Figure 12.12 illustrates the appropriate methods for protecting confidential data transmitted between remote users and VPN remote access servers. For the purposes of this scenario, assume that

- All remote users must be authenticated
- Remote users can connect to the organization's private network from anywhere in the world
- Remote access clients are running a variety of operating systems including Windows 95, Windows 98, Windows Me, Windows NT, Windows 2000, UNIX, and Macintosh operating systems
- All remote users must encrypt all data transmitted between the remote access clients and the private network or be denied access to the private network

To fulfill the requirements and constraints of the organization, you must specify that all

- Remote access servers and remote access users within North America must support 128-bit MPPE
- Remote access servers and remote access users outside North America must support 40-bit MPPE

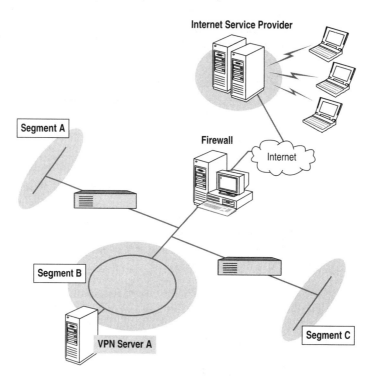

Figure 12.12 A scenario that illustrates the appropriate methods for protecting
confidential data transmitted between remote users and VPN remote
access servers

- Microsoft Challenge Handshake Authentication Protocol (MS-CHAP) or
  MS-CHAP v2 authenticates remote users.
- Remote access servers include remote access policies that deny remote access to
  remote users unable to meet the organization's security requirements.

Lesson 4: VPN Remote Access Design Optimization

This lesson discusses how to optimize VPN remote access designs to improve the availability and performance characteristics in your design. This lesson focuses on the strategies that increase the percentage of time that remote users can access the private network resources and that increase the data transfer rates between the remote access clients and the private network resources.

After this lesson, you will be able to

- Select the appropriate method for enhancing the availability characteristics in your VPN remote access design
- Select the appropriate methods for improving the performance characteristics in your VPN remote access design

Estimated lesson time: 45 minutes

Enhancing VPN Remote Access Availability

Once you have established the essential aspects and security aspects of your VPN remote access design, you can optimize the design for availability. The business requirements of the organization may require your design to ensure VPN remote access at all times. Regardless of a single point of failure, your design must provide redundancy for each VPN remote access server.

Making the Decision

You can improve the availability of your VPN remote access designs by

- Including multiple VPN remote access servers
- Including multiple Internet connections
- Dedicating a computer to running Routing and Remote Access

Multiple VPN Remote Access Servers

You can include multiple VPN remote access servers in your design to provide redundancy and backup. You need to include a redundant VPN remote access server for each existing VPN remote access server in your design.

You can distribute remote access clients across the multiple VPN remote access servers' traffic in your design by using Network Load Balancing and round robin Domain Name System (DNS). Network Load Balancing and round robin DNS have specific advantages and disadvantages.

However, because the remote access clients are connected to a specific remote access server, the connection is lost when a failure occurs. To reestablish the remote access connection, the remote access client must reestablish the VPN connection.

Table 12.2 lists the methods of improving VPN remote access, and the advantages and the disadvantages of including these methods in your design.

Table 12.2   Advantages and Disadvantages of Methods of Improving VPN Remote Access Availability

Method	Advantages	Disadvantages
Network Load Balancing	Allows dynamic addition or removal of VPN remote access servers in the cluster Automatically reconfigures the cluster if a VPN remote access server fails Provides improved availability because the addition or removal of VPN remote access servers is dynamic	Requires extra processor and memory resources to run the Network Load Balancing service Doesn't work with VPN remote access servers running on other operating systems, such as UNIX or Macintosh computers
Round robin DNS	Works on all operating system platforms	Doesn't automatically remove failed VPN remote access servers, so client computers might experience time-out or other error messages VPN remote access servers must be manually added or removed from the DNS entries

The specifications for the VPN remote access servers that provide redundancy must be *identical*. You must ensure that the same data rates, authentication protocols, encryption protocols, and remote access policies exists on *all* servers.

Providing Multiple Internet Connections

You can improve VPN remote access server availability by providing multiple connections to the Internet. Because remote users access the VPN remote access servers through Internet connections, you can improve the availability in your VPN remote access design by providing redundant Internet connections.

Dedicating a Computer to Routing and Remote Access

By dedicating a computer to running Routing and Remote Access, you improve availability by preventing other applications or services from becoming unstable and requiring the VPN remote access server to be restarted.

Applying the Decision

Figure 12.13 illustrates the proper methods for enhancing the availability of a VPN remote access solution.

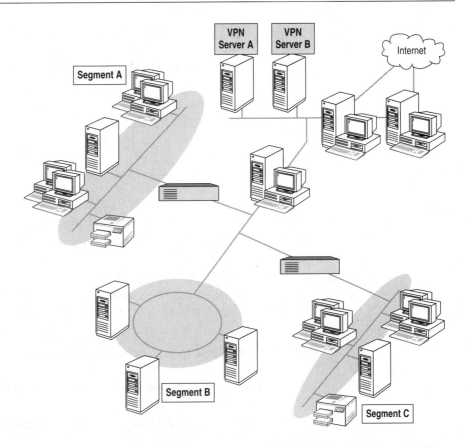

Figure 12.13   Scenario to illustrate the proper methods for enhancing the availability of a VPN remote access solution

For the purposes of this scenario, assume that the business and technical requirements of the organization include

- Any failure of a VPN remote access server or Internet connection doesn't prevent remote access

- Remote access clients are automatically reconnected if a VPN remote access server or Internet connection fails

- Remote access clients are prevented from accessing failed VPN remote access servers

To provide the appropriate solution, multiple VPN remote access servers and Internet connections must be included to achieve the business and technical requirements of the organization. VPN Servers A and B have the same specifications and belong to the same Network Load Balancing cluster.

Improving VPN Remote Access Performance

Once you have established the essential aspects, the security aspects, and availability aspects of your VPN remote access design, you can optimize the design for performance. The business requirements may include that VPN remote access servers must support a sustained data rate, based on the number of simultaneous remote users.

Making the Decision

You can improve VPN remote access performance by

- Upgrading VPN remote access server hardware
- Distributing remote access clients across multiple VPN remote access servers
- Dedicating a computer to running Routing and Remote Access

Upgrading Remote Access Server Hardware

When you can upgrade the hardware in the existing VPN remote access servers, you can improve the performance of your VPN remote access design. You can upgrade the existing

- **Internet connection(s) to increase the data rate**   Increasing the potential maximum data rate of the Internet connection(s) in your design increases the aggregate data rate of the remote access servers and subsequently improves the performance of your design.

- **Processor, memory, or other resources on the computer running Routing and Remote Access**   When any of the system resources of the computer running Routing and Remote Access are exhausted, you can upgrade the system resource to improve performance.

Distributing Remote Access Clients across Multiple Remote Access Servers

When the existing VPN remote access servers are saturated and you can't upgrade the hardware to improve performance, you can add additional VPN remote access servers to your design.

You can distribute remote users, and subsequently remote access traffic, in your VPN remote access design by using Network Load Balancing and round robin DNS. In your VPN remote access solutions, you can include either Network Load Balancing or round robin DNS to optimize remote access traffic.

Table 12.3 lists the method for distributing remote access clients across multiple VPN remote access servers and the advantages and the disadvantages of including these methods in your design.

**Table 12.3   Advantages and Disadvantages of Methods for Distributing Remote
Access Clients across Multiple Remote Access Servers**

Method	Advantages	Disadvantages
Network Load Balancing	Dynamically provides load balancing across all the VPN remote access servers in the Network Load Balancing cluster Improves performance because the load balancing is dynamic and the addition or removal of proxy servers is performed dynamically	Requires extra processor and memory resources to run the Network Load Balancing service Doesn't work with VPN remote access servers running on other operating systems, such as UNIX or Macintosh computers
Round robin DNS	Works on all operating system platforms Statically provides load balancing across all the VPN remote access servers listed in DNS Improves performance for private network access by load balancing network traffic across multiple VPN remote access servers	Doesn't automatically remove failed VPN remote access servers, so client computers might experience time-out or other error messages VPN remote access servers must be manually added or removed from the DNS entries

For more information on Network Load Balancing and round robin DNS entries,
see the section, "Optimizing Private Network Resource Access" in Chapter 6,
"Proxy Server in Internet and Intranet Designs," Lesson 4, "Proxy Server Design
Optimization."

Dedicating a Computer to Routing and Remote Access

By dedicating a computer to running Routing and Remote Access, you improve
the performance because you prevent other applications or services from consuming system resources.

Applying the Decision

Figure 12.14 illustrates a VPN remote access design prior to optimization for
performance. For the purposes of this scenario, assume that the business and
technical requirements of the organization include that the existing

- Computers running Routing and Remote Access can't be further upgraded

- Internet connections are ISDN connections

Figure 12.15 illustrates a VPN remote access design after optimization for
performance.

The following performance optimization changes were made to the design:

- VPN Server B is installed to distribute the remote access traffic between
  Remote Access Servers A and B.

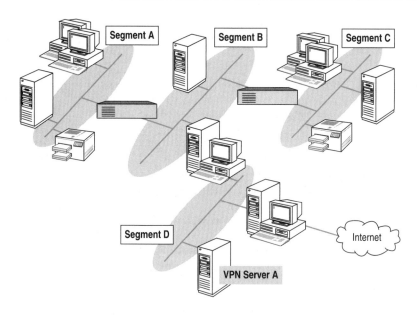

Figure 12.14   Scenario to illustrate a VPN remote access design prior to optimization for performance

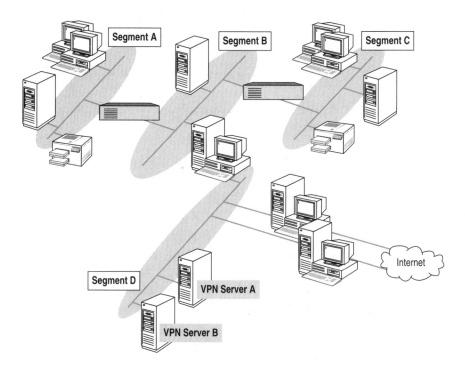

Figure 12.15   Scenario to illustrate a VPN remote access design after optimization for performance

- VPN Servers A and B belong to the same Network Load Balancing cluster.

- Internet connections are upgraded to T3 connections.

- Additional Internet connections are added to increase the aggregate Internet connection data rates.

Activity 12.2: Completing a VPN Remote Access Design

In this activity, you're presented with a scenario. To complete the activity

1. Evaluate the scenario and determine the design requirements.

2. Answer questions and make design recommendations.

In Figure 12.16, you see a map for an international shipping company that was discussed in an earlier lesson. The design process is proceeding and you're now creating the security and optimization specifications for the design.

Figure 12.16 Map of an international shipping company

Answer the following questions concerning your design recommendations. You can find answers to the questions in the Appendix, "Questions and Answers."

1. The management of the shipping company wants to restrict the customer representatives so they can only access the company's Web site remotely. The chief information office of the company (CIO) wants to ensure that only HTTP and FTP traffic are sent to the company's Web site. Also, only authenticated users should be granted remote access. As the director of information services, what VPN remote access solution do you recommend to management?

2. The remote users run a variety of operating systems, including Windows 98, Windows NT 4 Workstation, and Windows 2000 Professional. All remote access traffic must be encrypted by using the strongest possible encryption protocol. How do you protect private network resources while providing access to the Web servers?

3. After a few months of operation, remote users are experiencing performance problems. The existing Internet connections are T1 connections. Also, some remote users are experiencing outages due to hardware and Internet connection failure. How can you improve the performance and increase the availability for these offices?

Lab: Creating a VPN Remote Access Design

After this lab, you will be able to

- Evaluate a scenario and determine the design requirements
- Create VPN remote access design based on the design requirements

Estimated lab time: 45 minutes

In this lab, you're a consultant to a chain of retail stores and are responsible for the creation of a VPN remote access design for it. The retail chain has 3,200 locations throughout the United States.

To complete this lab:

1. Examine the networking environment presented in the scenario, the network diagrams, the business requirements and constraints, and the technical requirements and constraints

2. Use the worksheet for each location to assist you in creating your VPN remote access design (you can find completed sample design worksheets on the Supplemental Course Materials CD-ROM in the Completed Worksheets folder)

3. Create, eliminate, or replace existing networking devices and network segments when required

4. Ensure that your design fulfills the business requirements and constraints and technical requirements and constraints of the scenario by

   - Assigning the appropriate specifications for each VPN remote access server
   - Specifying the appropriate specifications for the remote access clients
   - Optimizing your design to provide the security, availability, performance, and affordability

Scenario

A chain of retail stores that caters to wireless telephone, paging, and other telecommunications services owns 3,200 locations throughout the United States. The retail stores provide both sales and post-sales customer support for the company's customers.

Each store transmits nightly financial information and orders for new inventory to the headquarters. The headquarters of the retail stores receives the orders, fills the orders, ships the product, and updates the order status. The store can check customer information and order status on a multitiered application that runs on Web and database servers located at the headquarters.

Within each store, the following computers are attached to the local network:

- Three point-of-sale computers that can invoice customers and check the status of customer accounts
- Two information kiosks that customers can use to find information about the services provided by the company and to inquire about their account
- Two computers used by the manager and assistant manager for reviewing financial information, checking inventory status, and e-mail communication

Each store has 25 sales representatives who are responsible for outbound sales to large corporate customers. These sales representatives must be able to access resources and run applications as though they were located at their respective store.

In addition, the manager and assistant manager must establish connectivity with the retail store chain's corporate network to access reports, marking information, employee benefits, and other human resource information.

Figure 12.17 is a diagram of the retail store chain. Currently, the retail stores connect to the headquarters by using dial-up modems. The headquarters of the retail store chain (shown in Figure 12.18) is installing multiple T1 connections to the Internet. Each retail store (shown in Figure 12.19) is installing an ISDN or DSL connection to the Internet.

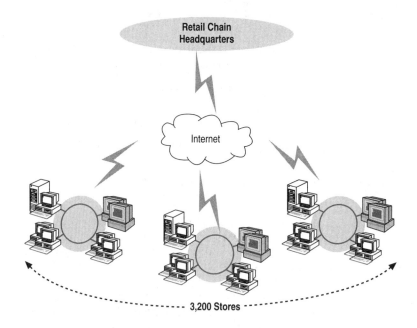

Figure 12.17   Diagram of the retail store chain

Business Requirements and Constraints

The retail store chain has a number of requirements and constraints based on the business model of the retail store chain. As you create your VPN remote access design, ensure that your design meets the business requirements and stays within the business constraints.

To achieve the business requirements and constraints, your design must

- Reduce the support required at each retail store by automating any configuration possible

- Allow only authorized users remote access to the headquarters' and retail store's private network

- Ensure that 25 percent of the computers used by the manager and assistant manager can simultaneously connect to resources in the headquarters' private network

- Ensure that all sales representatives can simultaneously connect to resources in their respective retail store's private network

- Protect any confidential data transmitted between the retail stores and the retail store chain's corporate network at headquarters

- Protect any confidential data transmitted between remote users and the headquarters' and retail store's private network

Technical Requirements and Constraints

The existing physical network, hardware, and operating systems place certain technical requirements and constraints on your design. As you create your VPN remote access design, ensure that your design meets the technical requirements and stays within the technical constraints.

In addition, the Web-based application that allows the retail store to check customer information and order status requires connectivity with each store and with the Internet. These Web-based applications are accessed on the manager's computer, the assistant manager's computer, and the kiosk computers.

To achieve the technical requirements and constraints, your design must

- Ensure that the firewalls at the headquarters and the Network Address Translation (NAT) servers at the retail stores protect the VPN remote access servers

- Support the NAT servers that provide Internet access

- Include a VPN remote access server for every 450 users so the desired performance, determined in pilot testing, is ensured

- Ensure that all remote users can access the network if an individual VPN remote access server fails
- Utilize the strongest possible security to protect confidential data
- Support the variety of operating systems running on the remote access clients, including Windows 95, Windows 98, Windows NT 4 Workstation, and Windows 2000 Professional

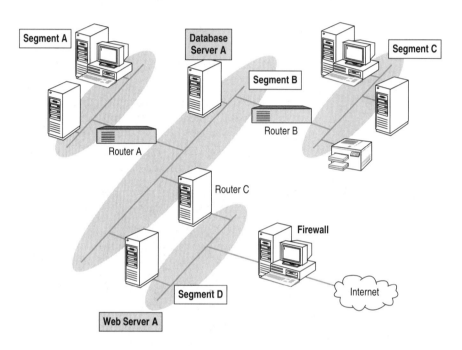

Figure 12.18   The existing network at the retail store chain headquarters

Design Worksheet – Figure 12.18
Retail Store Chain Headquarters – VPN Remote Access Server A

VPN Remote Access Server Specifications	Comments
VPN remote access server connects to segment: _____	
❑ Network Load Balancing cluster Cluster name: _____	
IP protocol support (Select the appropriate IP address configuration options)	
❑ Manually assigned ❑ DHCP assigned ❑ Include DHCP Relay Agent	
Security	
Authentication protocols (Select one or more authentication protocols)	
❑ MS-CHAP ❑ MS-CHAP v2 ❑ EAP ❑ CHAP ❑ PAP ❑ SPAP	
Encryption protocols (Select the appropriate data encryption protocols)	
❑ MPPE (Select the strength of MPPE encryption)	
❑ 40-bit ❑ 128-bit	
❑ IPSec (Select the IPSec protection to utilize)	

	Mode	Authentication	Identity	Protection	Encryption
	❑ Transport	❑ Kerberos	❑ MD5	❑ Identity (AH)	Not required
	❑ Tunnel	❑ X509	❑ SHA	❑ Identity and encryption (ESP)	❑ DES
		❑ Preshared key			❑ 56-bit DES
					❑ 3DES

VPN Remote Access Server Specifications (cont.)	Comments
❑ Remote access policies (Specify the remote access policy in the Comments column)	
❑ IP packet filters (Specify IP packet filter criteria in Comments column)	
Remote access to network resources	
❑ VPN remote access server only	
❑ Entire network	

Design Worksheet – Figure 12.18
Retail Store Chain Headquarters – VPN Remote Access Server B

VPN Remote Access Server Specifications	Comments
VPN remote access server connects to segment: _____	
❑ Network Load Balancing cluster Cluster name: _____	
IP protocol support (Select the appropriate IP address configuration options)	
❑ Manually assigned ❑ DHCP assigned ❑ Include DHCP Relay Agent	
Security	
Authentication protocols (Select one or more authentication protocols)	
❑ MS-CHAP ❑ MS-CHAP v2 ❑ EAP ❑ CHAP ❑ PAP ❑ SPAP	
Encryption protocols (Select the appropriate data encryption protocols)	
❑ MPPE (Select the strength of MPPE encryption)	
❑ 40-bit ❑ 128-bit	
❑ IPSec (Select the IPSec protection to utilize)	

Mode	Authentication	Identity	Protection	Encryption
❑ Transport	❑ Kerberos	❑ MD5	❑ Identity (AH)	Not required
❑ Tunnel	❑ X509	❑ SHA	❑ Identity and encryption (ESP)	❑ DES
	❑ Preshared key			❑ 56-bit DES
				❑ 3DES

❑ Remote access policies (Specify the remote access policy in the Comments column)	
❑ IP packet filters (Specify IP packet filter criteria in Comments column)	
Remote access to network resources	
❑ VPN remote access server only	
❑ Entire network	

Design Worksheet – Figure 12.18
Retail Store Chain Headquarters – VPN Remote Access Server C

VPN Remote Access Server Specifications	Comments
VPN remote access server connects to segment: _____	
❑ Network Load Balancing cluster Cluster name: _____	
IP protocol support (Select the appropriate IP address configuration options)	
❑ Manually assigned ❑ DHCP assigned ❑ Include DHCP Relay Agent	
Security	
Authentication protocols (Select one or more authentication protocols)	
❑ MS-CHAP ❑ MS-CHAP v2 ❑ EAP ❑ CHAP ❑ PAP ❑ SPAP	
Encryption protocols (Select the appropriate data encryption protocols)	
❑ MPPE (Select the strength of MPPE encryption)	
❑ 40-bit ❑128-bit	
❑ IPSec (Select the IPSec protection to utilize)	

Mode	Authentication	Identity	Protection	Encryption
❑ Transport	❑ Kerberos	❑ MD5	❑ Identity (AH)	Not required
❑ Tunnel	❑ X509	❑ SHA	❑ Identity and encryption (ESP)	❑ DES
	❑ Preshared key			❑ 56-bit DES
				❑ 3DES

	Comments
❑ Remote access policies (Specify the remote access policy in the Comments column)	
❑ IP packet filters (Specify IP packet filter criteria in Comments column)	
Remote access to network resources	
❑ VPN remote access server only	
❑ Entire network	

Design Worksheet – Figure 12.18
Retail Store Chain Headquarters – VPN Remote Access Server D

VPN Remote Access Server Specifications	Comments
VPN remote access server connects to segment: _____	
❏ Network Load Balancing cluster Cluster name: _____	
IP protocol support (Select the appropriate IP address configuration options)	
❏ Manually assigned ❏ DHCP assigned ❏ Include DHCP Relay Agent	
Security	
Authentication protocols (Select one or more authentication protocols)	
❏ MS-CHAP ❏ MS-CHAP v2 ❏ EAP ❏ CHAP ❏ PAP ❏ SPAP	
Encryption protocols (Select the appropriate data encryption protocols)	
❏ MPPE (Select the strength of MPPE encryption)	
❏ 40-bit ❏ 128-bit	
❏ IPSec (Select the IPSec protection to utilize)	

Mode	Authentication	Identity	Protection	Encryption
❏ Transport	❏ Kerberos	❏ MD5	❏ Identity (AH)	Not required
❏ Tunnel	❏ X509	❏ SHA	❏ Identity and encryption (ESP)	❏ DES
	❏ Preshared key			❏ 56-bit DES
				❏ 3DES

❏ Remote access policies (Specify the remote access policy in the Comments column)	
❏ IP packet filters (Specify IP packet filter criteria in Comments column)	
Remote access to network resources	
❏ VPN remote access server only	
❏ Entire network	

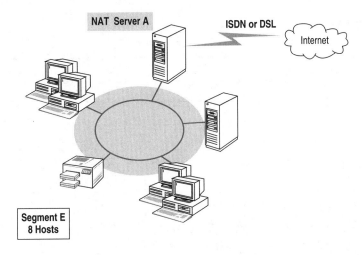

Figure 12.19   Existing network at one of the retail stores. For the purposes of this lab, assume that the stores have the same network configuration.

Design Worksheet – Figure 12.19
Retail Store – VPN Remote Access Server A

VPN Remote Access Server Specifications	Comments
VPN remote access server connects to segment: _____	
❏ Network Load Balancing cluster Cluster name: _____	
IP protocol support (Select the appropriate IP address configuration options)	
❏ Manually assigned ❏ DHCP assigned ❏ Include DHCP Relay Agent	
Security	
Authentication protocols (Select one or more authentication protocols)	
❏ MS-CHAP ❏ MS-CHAP v2 ❏ EAP ❏ CHAP ❏ PAP ❏ SPAP	
Encryption protocols (Select the appropriate data encryption protocols)	
❏ MPPE (Select the strength of MPPE encryption)	
❏ 40-bit ❏128-bit	
❏ IPSec (Select the IPSec protection to utilize)	

Mode	Authentication	Identity	Protection	Encryption
❏ Transport	❏ Kerberos	❏ MD5	❏ Identity (AH)	Not required
❏ Tunnel	❏ X509	❏ SHA	❏ Identity and encryption (ESP)	❏ DES
	❏ Preshared key			❏ 56-bit DES
				❏ 3DES

❏ Remote access policies (Specify the remote access policy in the Comments column)	
❏ IP packet filters (Specify IP packet filter criteria in Comments column)	
Remote access to network resources	
❏ VPN remote access server only	
❏ Entire network	

Design Worksheet – Figure 12.19
Retail Store – VPN Remote Access Server B

VPN Remote Access Server Specifications	Comments
VPN remote access server connects to segment: _____	
❑ Network Load Balancing cluster Cluster name: _____	
IP protocol support (Select the appropriate IP address configuration options) ❑ Manually assigned ❑ DHCP assigned ❑ Include DHCP Relay Agent	
Security	
Authentication protocols (Select one or more authentication protocols) ❑ MS-CHAP ❑ MS-CHAP v2 ❑ EAP ❑ CHAP ❑ PAP ❑ SPAP	
Encryption protocols (Select the appropriate data encryption protocols)	
❑ MPPE (Select the strength of MPPE encryption)	
❑ 40-bit ❑ 128-bit	
❑ IPSec (Select the IPSec protection to utilize)	

<table>
<tr><th>Mode</th><th>Authentication</th><th>Identity</th><th>Protection</th><th>Encryption</th></tr>
<tr><td>❑ Transport</td><td>❑ Kerberos</td><td>❑ MD5</td><td>❑ Identity (AH)</td><td>Not required</td></tr>
<tr><td>❑ Tunnel</td><td>❑ X509
❑ Preshared key</td><td>❑ SHA</td><td>❑ Identity and encryption (ESP)</td><td>❑ DES
❑ 56-bit DES
❑ 3DES</td></tr>
</table>

VPN Remote Access Server Specifications	Comments
❑ Remote access policies (Specify the remote access policy in the Comments column)	
❑ IP packet filters (Specify IP packet filter criteria in Comments column)	
Remote access to network resources	
❑ VPN remote access server only	
❑ Entire network	

Design Worksheet – Figure 12.19
Retail Store – VPN Remote Access Server C

VPN Remote Access Server Specifications	Comments
VPN remote access server connects to segment: _____	
❑ Network Load Balancing cluster Cluster name: _____	
IP protocol support (Select the appropriate IP address configuration options)	
❑ Manually assigned ❑ DHCP assigned ❑ Include DHCP Relay Agent	
Security	
Authentication protocols (Select one or more authentication protocols)	
❑ MS-CHAP ❑ MS-CHAP v2 ❑ EAP ❑ CHAP ❑PAP ❑SPAP	
Encryption protocols (Select the appropriate data encryption protocols)	
❑ MPPE (Select the strength of MPPE encryption)	
❑ 40-bit ❑ 128-bit	
❑ IPSec (Select the IPSec protection to utilize)	

Mode	Authentication	Identity	Protection	Encryption
❑ Transport	❑ Kerberos	❑ MD5	❑ Identity (AH)	Not required
❑ Tunnel	❑ X509	❑ SHA	❑ Identity and encryption (ESP)	❑ DES
	❑ Preshared key			❑ 56-bit DES
				❑ 3DES

❑ Remote access policies (Specify the remote access policy in the Comments column)	
❑ IP packet filters (Specify IP packet filter criteria in Comments column)	
Remote access to network resources	
❑ VPN remote access server only	
❑ Entire network	

Design Worksheet – Figure 12.19
Retail Store – VPN Remote Access Server D

VPN Remote Access Server Specifications	Comments
VPN remote access server connects to segment: _____	
❑ Network Load Balancing cluster Cluster name: _____	
IP protocol support (Select the appropriate IP address configuration options)	
❑ Manually assigned ❑ DHCP assigned ❑ Include DHCP Relay Agent	
Security	
Authentication protocols (Select one or more authentication protocols)	
❑ MS-CHAP ❑ MS-CHAP v2 ❑ EAP ❑ CHAP ❑ PAP ❑ SPAP	
Encryption protocols (Select the appropriate data encryption protocols)	
❑ MPPE (Select the strength of MPPE encryption)	
❑ 40-bit ❑ 128-bit	
❑ IPSec (Select the IPSec protection to utilize)	

Mode	Authentication	Identity	Protection	Encryption
❑ Transport	❑ Kerberos	❑ MD5	❑ Identity (AH)	Not required
❑ Tunnel	❑ X509	❑ SHA	❑ Identity and encryption (ESP)	❑ DES
	❑ Preshared key			❑ 56-bit DES
				❑ 3DES

VPN Remote Access Server Specifications	Comments
❑ Remote access policies (Specify the remote access policy in the Comments column)	
❑ IP packet filters (Specify IP packet filter criteria in Comments column)	
Remote access to network resources	
❑ VPN remote access server only	
❑ Entire network	

Review

The following questions are intended to reinforce key information in this chapter. If you're unable to answer a question, review the lesson and then try to answer the question again. You can find answers to the questions in the Appendix, "Questions and Answers."

1. An organization is considering VPN remote access solutions to provide remote access to users who work from home. The users are distributed across a number of geographic locations, but all report to a local office. As a consultant to the organization, what information do you need to obtain to assist the organization in creating the most appropriate solution?

2. Your organization wants to provide VPN remote access to users who travel extensively. The remote users travel internationally and must be able to connect to private network resources from any location. The network administrators want to ensure that minimal changes are made to the firewall rules. In addition, the solution must authenticate remote users and encrypt all data transmitted between the organization's private network and the remote users. What recommendations can you make to provide a VPN remote access solution?

3. An organization has retained you as a consultant to review a design that you created more than a year ago. The remote users are experiencing degradation in response times for applications they run. The response time has gradually degraded over a period of time. Without further examination, what suggestions can you make to the organization to restore remote access performance?

4. Remote users in your organization are reporting outages of remote access. The remote users are connecting properly to their ISP, but are unable to establish the VPN connection. How can you modify your design to reduce the number of remote access outages and improve overall remote access uptime?

CHAPTER 13

RADIUS in Remote Access Designs

About This Chapter

As discussed in previous chapters, many organizations have a significant number of users who must access their organizations' private network resources remotely. A significant portion of your networking services design must include remote access to the private network for these organizations.

For the organizations that require remote access, many of the solutions require the users to initially connect to a third-party remote access server, and then connect to the organizations' remote access servers. The organizations can control the security for their remote access servers but can't control the security for the third-party organization's remote access servers. Also, the remote users are required to remember two sets of user credentials (one set for the third-party organization's remote access server and one set for the organization's remote access server). Ideally, organizations want to control the security for the third-party organization's remote access servers while providing remote users with one set of user credentials.

Organizations that provide dial-up remote access for other organizations, such as Internet service providers (ISPs), want to track remote user connectivity for billing and accounting purposes. These organizations want to track remote user connectivity so they can charge the appropriate customer for connectivity charges.

Remote Authentication Dial-In User Service (RADIUS) is a collection of protocols that allows remote access, user authentication, auditing, and accounting of remote users. RADIUS enables you to create designs where an organization can outsource dial-up connectivity, while allowing you to enforce enhanced security (such as caller-ID identification or callback).

RADIUS also allows organizations, such as ISPs, to collect auditing and accounting information on remote user connectivity. The organization can use the auditing and accounting information for billing its customers.

You can include RADIUS in your design by using the Routing and Remote Access and Internet Authentication Server (IAS) features in Microsoft Windows 2000. RADIUS allows remote users to be authenticated by Active Directory directory services, Microsoft Windows NT 4 domains, or any RADIUS compatible server, such as a computer running UNIX.

This chapter answers questions such as:

- In what situations are the user authentication, auditing, and accounting services provided by RADIUS appropriate for your design?
- How can you integrate RADIUS in your network?
- How can you ensure the confidentiality of data between remote access clients, RADIUS clients, RADIUS servers, and remote access servers?
- What can you include in your design to ensure that RADIUS is always available to authenticate remote access users?
- How can you improve the performance of RADIUS solutions during peak periods of activity?

Before You Begin

Before you begin, you must have an overall understanding of

- The common transport protocol configuration for Internet Protocol (IP) and Internetwork Packet Exchange (IPX) (such as the IP address, subnet mask, or default gateway for IP)

- IP and IPX routed networks (including subnets, network segments, routers, and IP switches)

- Dial-up telephony technologies used by ISPs or other dial-up outsourcing (wholesale dial-up) organizations

- Tunneling protocols (including how packets are encapsulated in tunnels and how tunnels are established)

- The authentication, authorization, and accounting capabilities of RADIUS

Lesson 1: Designs That Include RADIUS

This lesson presents the requirements and constraints, both business and technical, which identify the user authentication, auditing, and accounting services in RADIUS as a solution.

After this lesson, you will be able to

- Identify the situation in which RADIUS is the appropriate solution in remote access designs
- Describe the relationship between RADIUS and Windows 2000
- Identify the business and technical requirements and constraints that must be collected to create a RADIUS design
- Identify the RADIUS design decisions
- Evaluate scenarios and determine which capabilities and features of Routing and Remote Access and IAS are appropriate in RADIUS solutions

Estimated lesson time: 30 minutes

RADIUS in Remote Access Designs

You can include RADIUS in remote access designs to provide remote user authentication, auditing, and accounting. To create successful remote access solutions, you must determine whether the solution requires RADIUS.

With RADIUS, you can provide remote access on one or more servers while providing user authentication, auditing, and accounting on other servers. RADIUS allows you to segregate remote access servers and user authentication servers. You can include RADIUS in dial-up remote access or virtual private network (VPN) remote access solutions when the remote access solution is

- Exclusively provided within an organization
- Divided between organizations

Although other remote access methods are available, RADIUS is the only method that allows the organization to control *all* security aspects of remote access connectivity for both internal and outsourced remote access solutions.

You can divide the RADIUS protocols into the

- **RADIUS client**   The RADIUS client provides remote access connectivity in a solution that includes RADIUS. The RADIUS client can be a dial-up or VPN remote access server, depending on the remote connectivity provided, and can be based on Windows 2000, UNIX, or other operating systems.

- **RADIUS server**   The RADIUS server provides authentication, auditing, and accounting in a solution that includes RADIUS. The RADIUS server can be based on Windows 2000, UNIX, or other operating systems.

Figure 13.1 illustrates the relationship between remote users, RADIUS clients, RADIUS servers, and remote access servers. The RADIUS clients may be owned by a different organization from the RADIUS servers and remote access servers.

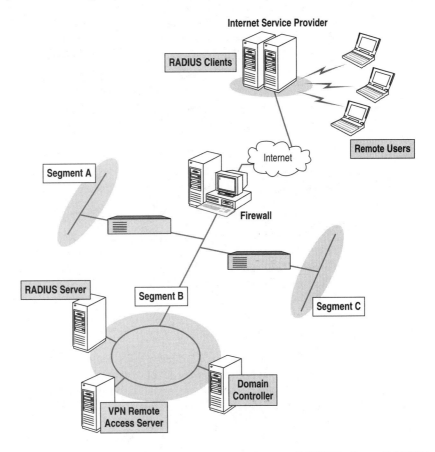

Figure 13.1   The relationship between remote users, RADIUS clients, RADIUS servers, and remote access servers

The following sequence further illustrates the relationship between remote users, RADIUS clients, RADIUS servers, and remote access servers.

1. A RADIUS client receives authentication requests and user credentials from remote users.
2. The RADIUS client forwards the authentication requests and user credentials to a RADIUS server.

3. The RADIUS server receives authentication requests from RADIUS clients and authenticates the user's credentials.

4. The RADIUS server validates the user credentials and sends a response to the RADIUS client.

5. The RADIUS client receives the response that notifies the RADIUS client to grant or deny the remote user's connection.

   The response sent to the RADIUS clients from the RADIUS servers instructs the RADIUS clients to grant or deny the remote user's remote access connection. The response sent to the RADIUS clients also includes *RADIUS attributes*. RADIUS attributes are similar to Routing and Remote Access remote access policies. RADIUS attributes can specify many of the same connection options found in remote access policies.

6. The remote user's connection is granted and the RADIUS client specifies the RADIUS attributes for the remote user's connection.

After the remote user's connection is granted, the remote user connects to the remote access servers. You can encrypt the remote user's data by establishing a VPN connection between one of the following:

- The remote user and the remote access servers
- The RADIUS client and the remote access servers

RADIUS solutions can utilize any of the protocols supported by dial-up or VPN remote access servers, such as Point-to-Point Protocol (PPP), Point-to-Point Tunneling Protocol (PPTP), and Layer 2 Tunneling Protocol (L2TP), to connect remote clients to the remote access server. Multiple vendors and operating systems support the RADIUS standards and protocols.

The primary difference between a VPN remote access solution and a RADIUS remote access solution is the level of integration with the dial-up remote access servers. In a VPN remote access solution, no service agreement exists with the third-party organization that provides dial-up remote access. In a RADIUS solution, a service agreement exists with the third-party organization that provides dial-up remote access.

This chapter discusses RADIUS remote access solutions provided by Routing and Remote Access and IAS. For more information on dial-up remote access solutions by using Routing and Remote Access, see Chapter 11, "Dial-Up Connectivity in Remote Access Designs." For more information on VPN client solutions by using Routing and Remote Access, see Chapter 12, "VPN Connectivity in Remote Access Designs."

RADIUS and Windows 2000

Routing and Remote Access and IAS are the Windows 2000 features that provide RADIUS solutions. As discussed in the previous section, you can create a variety of remote access solutions by using Routing and Remote Access. You can include IAS in any remote access solution that requires RADIUS.

The RADIUS support in Windows 2000 can be divided into

- **RADIUS client**   Routing and Remote Access in Windows 2000 provides the features of a RADIUS client in your remote access design. In RADIUS designs, the RADIUS client is responsible for providing all the equivalent features of a dial-up or VPN remote access server. You can include third-party RADIUS clients, also known as network access servers (NASs), in your remote access design.

  From the Windows 2000 perspective, Routing and Remote Access is a service that runs on Windows 2000. As a RADIUS client, Routing and Remote Access utilizes the Internet Protocol (IP), Internetwork Packet Exchange (IPX), and AppleTalk protocols of Windows 2000.

- **RADIUS server**   IAS in Windows 2000 can act as the RADIUS server in your remote access design. In addition, you can authenticate remote users by using local user accounts or user accounts in Active Directory. You can include third-party RADIUS servers in your remote access design.

Routing and Remote Access and IAS are available in Microsoft Windows 2000 Server, Microsoft Windows 2000 Advanced Server, and Microsoft Windows 2000 Datacenter Server. Routing and Remote Access and IAS aren't available in Windows 2000 Professional.

RADIUS Design Requirements and Constraints

Before you create your RADIUS design, you must gather the requirements and constraints, both business and technical, of the organization. As you create your design, you make design decisions based on the requirements and constraints that you collect.

The list of the design requirements and constraints that you collect will include

- The amount of data transmitted between the remote access clients and the remote access servers
- Connectivity and security capabilities of RADIUS clients or NASs
- Number of locations that require remote access and authentication
- Operating systems that contain the user accounts used for remote access authentication

- Strength of security to be enforced on remote users
- Number of simultaneous remote access client authentications
- Operating systems that the remote access clients, RADIUS clients, and RADIUS are running

RADIUS Design Decisions

After you determine the business and technical requirements and constraints, apply the information you gathered to make RADIUS design decisions. To create your RADIUS design, you must choose the

- Methods for integrating RADIUS into the existing network based on the
  - Connectivity between the RADIUS clients, RADIUS servers, and remote access servers
  - Existing RADIUS servers, RADIUS clients, remote access servers, or NASs
- Placement and number of RADIUS servers, RADIUS clients, and remote access servers
- Hardware requirements for the RADIUS clients, including the
  - Number of PPTP, L2TP, or dial-up ports required to support the maximum number of simultaneous remote access users
  - Data transmission rates of the RADIUS client's connections
- Methods for protecting confidential data that include
  - Isolating RADIUS servers
  - Identifying RADIUS servers and RADIUS clients
  - Authenticating remote access users
  - Encrypting confidential data
- Methods of ensuring that remote users are always authenticated
- Methods of optimizing the length of time required to authenticate remote users

The lessons that follow in this chapter provide the information required to make specific RADIUS design recommendations.

Outsourced Dial-Up Remote Access Designs

One of the most common remote access solutions that includes RADIUS is when the remote access design has outsourced dial-up connectivity. In outsourced dial-up remote access designs, the organization wants to delegate the dial-up remote access portion of the remote access design to a third-party organization.

Making the Decision

You must examine the requirements and constraints of the organization and then determine whether outsourced dial-up connectivity is an appropriate solution. Outsourced dial-up connectivity is an appropriate solution when the organization wants to

- Reduce the costs associated with dial-up remote access connectivity

- Provide a single set of logon credentials to the remote users

- Establish an agreement with the third-party organization that provides the dial-up remote access connectivity

- Provide enhanced security, such as remote user caller-ID identification or user callback

Applying the Decision

Figure 13.2 illustrates a scenario where RADIUS provides an outsourced dial-up remote access solution. The organization wants to reduce the costs associated with its remote access solution. The security requirements of the organization allow it to outsource the dial-up remote access portion of the remote access solution. In addition, the organization wants to provide a single set of logon credentials to remote users.

In the solution depicted in Figure 13.2, the RADIUS clients are owned and managed by the ISP. The RADIUS servers and remote access servers are owned and managed by the organization.

In-House Remote Access Designs

In some instances, the entire remote access design, either dial-up or VPN remote access, is owned totally by the organization. In in-house remote access designs, the organization wants to improve the security of the remote access design and to provide enhanced management of the remote access solution.

Making the Decision

To determine whether in-house remote access is an appropriate solution for an organization, you must examine the requirements and constraints of the organization. In-house remote access is an appropriate solution when the organization

- **Wants to or is willing to centralize the administration of the remote access servers and remote access policies**   Normally, remote access policies are stored locally on the remote access servers. In a RADIUS solution, the remote access policies are stored on the RADIUS server and shared by all the RADIUS clients. RADIUS allows you to centrally manage remote access policies.

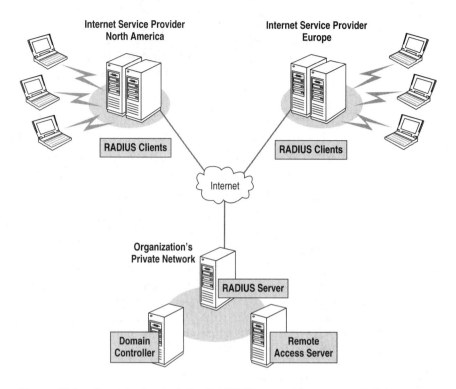

Figure 13.2   Scenario that includes RADIUS to provide outsourced dial-up remote access solutions

- **Wants to or is willing to place remote access servers outside the private network or on screened subnets**   Normally, the remote access servers that you place outside the private network, or on screened subnets, are member servers or domain controllers. As a result, placing a member server or a domain controller outside the *secured* portion of the private network *potentially* compromises the security of the network.

  In a RADIUS solution, you can place the RADIUS clients (remote access servers) that are *stand-alone* servers on unsecured network segments and place the RADIUS servers within the secured private network.

- **Wants to or is willing to retain ownership of all aspects of the remote access design (dial-up remote access solutions)**   As mentioned in Chapter 11, "Dial-Up Connectivity in Remote Access Designs," the most common reason for organizations to select a dial-up remote access solution is to control all aspects of the remote access design.

- **Doesn't want to establish an agreement with the third-party organization (VPN remote access solutions)**   As mentioned in Chapter 12, "VPN in Remote Access Designs," many organizations are unwilling to establish outsourced dial-up remote access agreements. Establishing an agreement with a third-party organization to provide outsourced dial-up remote access implies a long-term cost associated with the agreement. Because many users within these organizations already have Internet access, these organizations depend on the remote users to provide their own dial-up Internet access.

Applying the Decision

Figure 13.3 illustrates a scenario where RADIUS provides an in-house VPN remote access solution. The organization wants to reduce the costs associated with its remote access solution by utilizing third-party dial-up connectivity (by using ISPs). The security requirements of the organization allow it to outsource the dial-up remote access portion of the remote access solution. In addition, the organization is willing to allow a set of user credentials for the dial-up connectivity and a set of user credentials for VPN remote access.

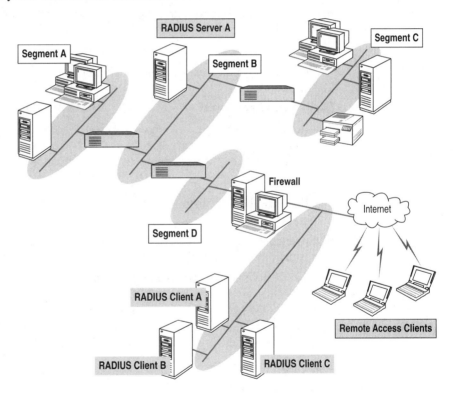

Figure 13.3   Scenario that includes RADIUS to provide an in-house VPN remote access solution

RADIUS Clients A, B, and C reside outside the private network and are directly accessible by remote users (authorized and unauthorized). RADIUS Server A resides within the private network and is protected from direct access by the remote users. In addition, RADIUS Clients A, B, and C share the same remote access policies stored on RADIUS Server A.

Partner Network Remote Access Designs

Many organizations are establishing relationships with business partners. Often these business partners exchange employees, ideas, concepts, or other resources to jointly develop new products or services.

In addition, many organizations have partner-type relations with their customers. In these types of partner relationships, some of the employees of the organization work onsite at the customer's location.

In partner network designs, the organization wants to

- Provide remote access connectivity for remote users working at the partner's network
- Improve the security of the remote access design
- Provide centralized management of the remote access solution

Making the Decision

To determine whether partner network remote access is an appropriate solution for an organization, you must examine the requirements and constraints of the organization. Partner network remote access is an appropriate solution when the organization wants to

- Centralize the administration of the remote access servers and remote access policies
- Enhance the security of the solution by ensuring that only users from the partner's private network can connect
- Place remote access servers in other organizations' private networks

    In a RADIUS solution, you can place the RADIUS clients (remote access servers) on the partner's private network segments and place the RADIUS servers within the organization's secured private network.

Applying the Decision

Figure 13.4 illustrates a scenario where RADIUS provides a partner network remote access solution. The organization wants to provide remote access connectivity only to remote users working in the partner's private network. In addition, the organization wants to control all aspects of the password policies (such as password length or password aging).

RADIUS Client A resides in the partner's private network and is directly accessible by users in the partner's private network (including the remote users). RADIUS Server A resides within the private network and is protected from direct access by users in the partner's private network.

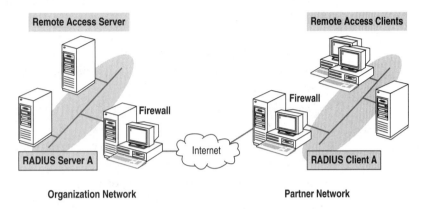

Figure 13.4   Scenario that includes RADIUS to provide a partner network remote access solution

Lesson 2: Essential RADIUS Design Concepts

This lesson discusses the requirements, constraints, and design decisions that are used in establishing the essential specifications in a RADIUS-based remote access design. This lesson covers the design concepts common to all RADIUS designs.

After this lesson, you will be able to

- Determine the number RADIUS clients and RADIUS servers to include in your design

- Determine the appropriate placement of RADIUS clients and RADIUS servers in your design

- Select the appropriate connections between RADIUS clients and RADIUS servers in your design

- Select the remote access client support

Estimated lesson time: 30 minutes

Determining the Number of RADIUS Clients and Servers

You must determine the number of RADIUS clients and servers required in your design. You can specify one or more RADIUS clients or RADIUS servers in addition to the remote access servers in your design.

Making the Decision

A single RADIUS client can potentially support hundreds of remote access client computers. A single RADIUS server can support many RADIUS clients. You can include multiple RADIUS clients or RADIUS servers in your design to support more remote access clients.

Radius Clients

The design decisions for determining the number of RADIUS clients is exactly like determining the number of dial-up or VPN remote access servers (depending on the types of remote access clients that the RADIUS clients must support). For more information on how to determine the number of dial-up (or VPN) remote access servers and, subsequently, RADIUS clients that support dial-up (or VPN) remote users, see Chapter 11, "Dial-Up Connectivity in Remote Access Designs," Lesson 2, "Essential Dial-Up Remote Access Design Concepts," or Chapter 12, "VPN Connectivity in Remote Access Designs," Lesson 2, "Essential VPN Remote Access Design Concepts."

Radius Servers

You must include at least one RADIUS server for each *unique* user account database that you want to use for remote user authentication. You can include additional

RADIUS servers to support additional RADIUS clients and subsequently additional remote access users.

One RADIUS server can provide RADIUS authentication and accounting in your design. However, you can segregate RADIUS authentication and accounting on different RADIUS servers. As a result, you can include one RADIUS server to provide RADIUS authentication and another RADIUS server to provide RADIUS accounting.

Applying the Decision

Figure 13.5 illustrates a network that includes RADIUS clients and RADIUS servers. The organizations illustrated want to provide outsourced dial-up remote access to remote users through ISP A and ISP B. You must calculate the number of RADIUS clients and RADIUS servers required in your design. For the purposes of this scenario, assume that

- There are two organizations and each has 1600 users who require remote access

- Up to 600 remote users *for each organization* may simultaneously access the remote access servers (RADIUS clients)

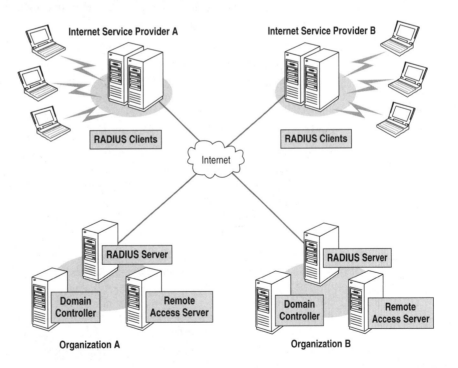

Figure 13.5 Scenario that illustrates existing networks that include RADIUS clients and RADIUS servers

- Acceptable application response times require a sustained data rate of 33.6Kbps or higher for each remote access client
- Each remote user connects to the dial-up remote access server (RADIUS client) by using a modem capable of at least 56Kbps
- Pilot tests confirm that the approved remote access servers (RADIUS client) can support 220 remote users with a sustained data rate of 56Kbps

Table 13.1 shows the calculations used in determining the number of remote access servers required in the design.

Table 13.1   Calculations for the Number of RADIUS Clients Required

Perform These Calculations		Using
A	Maximum number of simultaneous remote users	1200
B	Number of remote users that each RADIUS client can support	220
C	Number of RADIUS clients required ($C=A/B$)	5.45
D	Round up to the nearest even number of RADIUS clients	6

You must include 12 RADIUS clients in your design (6 for ISP A and 6 for ISP B) to ensure that either ISP can support the maximum number of simultaneous remote users.

A minimum of one RADIUS server is added to each organization's private network (additional RADIUS servers can be added to provide enhanced availability and improve performance). The RADIUS clients utilize each of the RADIUS servers for authentication, authorization, and accounting.

Determining the Placement of RADIUS Clients and Servers

You must determine where to place RADIUS clients and RADIUS servers in your design so that remote users can be authenticated. You place the RADIUS clients and RADIUS servers to centralize administration, reduce costs, and reduce the network traffic between locations.

Making the Decision

You place RADIUS clients close to remote client computers. You place RADIUS servers close to the servers that manage the user account database.

Radius Clients

As previously mentioned, you place RADIUS clients near the corresponding remote users. When the RADIUS clients provide dial-up remote access connectivity, place the RADIUS clients geographically close to the remote users. When the RADIUS clients provide VPN remote access connectivity, place the RADIUS clients near the Internet connection.

The design decisions for determining the placement of RADIUS clients are exactly like determining the placement of dial-up or VPN remote access servers (depending on the types of remote access clients that the RADIUS clients must support). For more information on how to determine the placement of dial-up (or VPN) remote access servers and, subsequently, RADIUS clients that support dial-up (or VPN) remote users, see Chapter 11, "Dial-Up Connectivity in Remote Access Designs," Lesson 2, "Essential Dial-Up Remote Access Design Concepts," or Chapter 12, "VPN Connectivity in Remote Access Designs," Lesson 2, "Essential VPN Remote Access Design Concepts."

Radius Servers

As previously mentioned, you place the RADIUS servers near the servers that manage the remote user accounts. When you're authenticating remote users by using Active Directory, place the RADIUS servers on network segments close to domain controllers.

To further reduce network traffic, you can run IAS on a domain controller. By running IAS (the RADIUS server in Windows 2000) on a domain controller, the RADIUS server can authenticate users without creating additional network traffic.

Applying the Decision

Figure 13.6 illustrates where to place RADIUS clients and RADIUS servers in your design. For the purposes of this scenario, assume that

- The ISP in the scenario has multiple locations throughout the world.
- Both organizations have remote users that connect through the respective ISP location.
- Both organizations authenticate remote users by using Active Directory.

For the scenario depicted in Figure 13.6, you place RADIUS clients at the ISP's locations. You place RADIUS servers and VPN remote access servers within each organization's private network.

Selecting the Connections Between RADIUS Clients and Servers

You must select the connections between each RADIUS client and RADIUS server. You must specify one or more RADIUS servers for each RADIUS client. Each RADIUS server must provide authentication or accounting for at least one or more RADIUS clients.

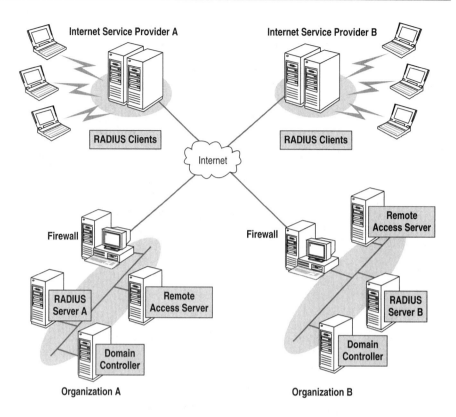

Figure 13.6   Scenario that illustrates where to place RADIUS clients and RADIUS servers in your design

Making the Decision

For each RADIUS client, you can specify

- At least one RADIUS server that provides RADIUS authentication and accounting
- Separate RADIUS servers that provide RADIUS authentication or accounting

You can specify multiple RADIUS servers for each RADIUS client. The following sequence describes how a RADIUS client can utilize multiple RADIUS servers.

1. The RADIUS client attempts to authenticate, or report accounting, with the first RADIUS server listed in the RADIUS client.
2. If the RADIUS client is unable to contact the first RADIUS server, the RADIUS client attempts to contact a subsequent RADIUS server.
3. The RADIUS client continues to attempt to contact a RADIUS server until a RADIUS server is contacted.

4. The RADIUS server that responds is automatically moved up in the list of RADIUS servers.

Conversely, each RADIUS server must provide RADIUS authentication, or accounting, for

- At least one RADIUS client
- More than one RADIUS client

Note   For a RADIUS client and a RADIUS server to communicate, you must specify the corresponding RADIUS server at the RADIUS client and the corresponding RADIUS client at the RADIUS server.

You can add additional RADIUS servers to distribute authentication and accounting traffic across the RADIUS servers. For more information on optimizing RADIUS designs, see Lesson 4, "RADIUS Design Optimization," later in this chapter.

Applying the Decision

Figure 13.7 illustrates the connections between RADIUS clients and RADIUS servers in your design. For the purposes of this scenario, assume that

- The ISP in the scenario has multiple locations throughout the world
- The organization has remote users that connect through their respective ISP location
- The organization wants to segregate RADIUS authentication and RADIUS accounting on different RADIUS servers

For the scenario depicted in Figure 13.7, RADIUS Clients A, B, C, and D must be specified to use RADIUS Server A for authentication and RADIUS Server B for accounting. RADIUS Servers A and B must be specified to allow authentication and accounting requests respectively from RADIUS Clients A, B, C, and D.

Selecting the Remote Access Client Support

You must determine the remote access client support to incorporate into your RADIUS remote access design. You must evaluate the applications run by the remote access clients and the resources accessed by the remote access clients.

Making the Decision

You can select the remote access client support by using the same method for selecting the remote access client support in dial-up and VPN remote access solutions. In addition, in RADIUS solutions you must specify the user account database (or *RADIUS realm*) to be used for remote user authentication.

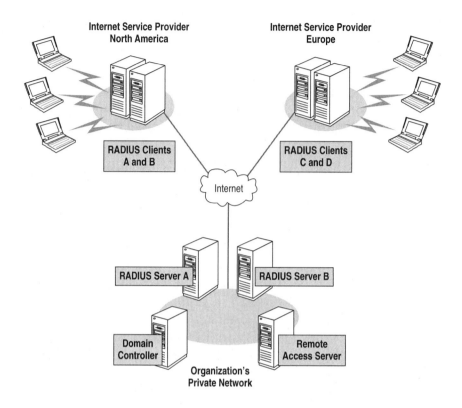

Figure 13.7   Scenario that illustrates the connections between RADIUS clients and RADIUS servers in your design

Applying Methods Used in Dial-Up and VPN Remote Access Solutions

For each remote access client that connects to the RADIUS, you must determine the

- Number and type of virtual ports to include for VPN remote access
- Number and type of modems, phone lines, and communications ports to include for dial-up remote access
- Transport protocols required
- Method of assigning network addressing

The design decisions for determining the remote access client support for a RADIUS solution is exactly like determining the remote access client support for a dial-up or VPN remote access solution (depending on the types of remote access clients that the RADIUS clients must support). For more information on how to determine the remote access client support of dial-up (or VPN) remote access servers and, subsequently, remote access client support for RADIUS clients that support dial-up (or VPN) remote users, see Chapter 11, "Dial-Up Connectivity in Remote Access Designs," Lesson 2, "Essential Dial-Up Remote Access Design Concepts," or Chapter 12, "VPN Connectivity in Remote Access Designs," Lesson 2, "Essential VPN Remote Access Design Concepts."

Specifying the RADIUS Realm

The RADIUS realm specifies the user account database to be used for remote user authentication. In Windows 2000 and Windows NT 4, the RADIUS realm is analogous to a domain. For other operating systems, the RADIUS realm can be any user account database accessible by the RADIUS server for authentication.

You can specify realm names that are prefixes (such as *realm/*) or suffixes (such as *@realm*). The realm name that you specify can include any separator characters, such as the at sign (@) or the slash (/).

You can specify a default realm for each RADIUS client (or NAS) in your RADIUS design. When remote users supply their user credentials without specifying a realm, the default realm is used. When remote users supply a realm with their user credentials, the realm specified by the remote user is used.

You must include RADIUS realms in your design when

- You want to direct remote user authentication requests to a specific RADIUS server
- More than one user account database (that contains a unique list of remote users) is used to authenticate remote users

Applying the Decision

Figure 13.8 illustrates the appropriate selection of remote access client support to include in your RADIUS design. For the purposes of this scenario, assume that

- All the remote access clients access File Transfer Protocol (FTP) and Web servers in the organization's private network
- Each virtual remote access port must support computers running Windows 2000 and other operating systems
- Some of the remote access clients require access to NetWare 4.2 file servers that use only the IPX protocol
- Up to 300 remote users must be able to simultaneously access the private network
- Dynamic Host Configuration Protocol (DHCP) must be used to assign all IP addresses and provide *total* IP configuration
- ISP supports only TCP/IP on RADIUS clients

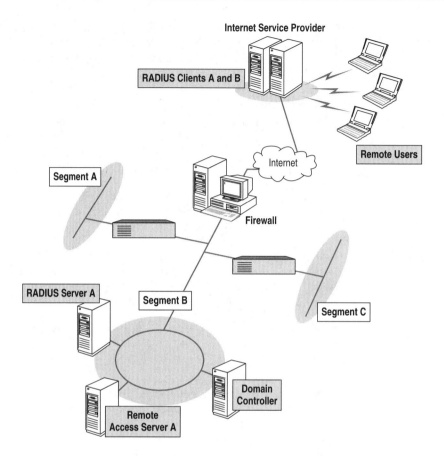

Figure 13.8   Scenario that illustrates the appropriate selection of remote access client support to include in your RADIUS design

To fulfill the requirements and constraints of the organization, you must include

- TCP/IP on all remote access clients to support access to the FTP and Web servers
- IPX and TCP/IP on the remote access clients that access the Netware 4.2 file servers and tunnel IPX through IP on the remote access clients to Remote Access Server A
- Manual network address ranges allocated for the IPX protocol
- DHCP configuration for IP
- DHCP Relay Agent installed on each remote access server
- Up to 300 PPTP virtual ports on Remote Access Server A to support the maximum number of simultaneous remote access clients

- Up to 300 phone lines, modems, and communications ports on RADIUS Clients A and B to support the maximum number of simultaneous remote access clients

Activity 13.1: Evaluating a RADIUS Design

In this activity, you're presented with a scenario. To complete the activity:

1. Evaluate the scenario and determine the design requirements

2. Answer questions and make design recommendations

In Figure 13.9, you see a map for a consortium of biotech companies. The biotech companies are participating in a joint research and development project to create new genetically engineered products. Each biotech company in the consortium has a facility where scientists and assistants conduct research and development.

As a member of the biotech consortium, each biotech company must provide a portion of its research and development facility for use by scientists from other consortium members. While working on the joint research and development project, scientists spend months at other consortium members' facilities.

Each research facility is connected to the Internet by using a combination of Integrated Services Digital Network (ISDN), Digital Subscriber Line (DSL), T1, and T3 connections.

Answer the following questions concerning your design recommendations. You can find answers to the questions in the Appendix, "Questions and Answers."

1. While working in other consortium member locations, scientists must access resources within their company's private network. The consortium members want to ensure that when the scientists access the company's resources, all data is encrypted. In addition, the director of information services for each consortium member wants to control the password characteristics (such as the frequency of password change, minimum password length, password aging, etc.). What recommendations can you make?

2. At a meeting of the directors of information services for the biotech companies, you're asked to participate in a question and answer session. At the session, one of the directors wants to know how the directors can ensure that each company's individual security requirements will be met. How do you respond?

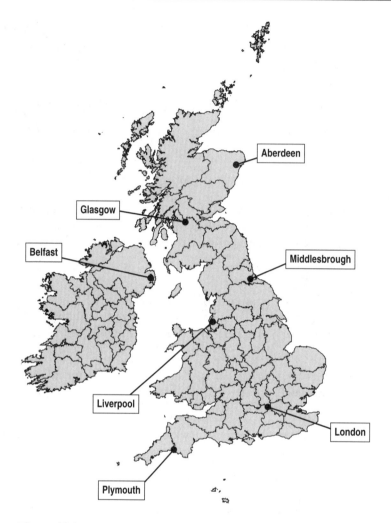

Figure 13.9   Map of a biotech consortium

3. During the same question and answer session in the previous question, another director asks about the ability of the scientists to access the biotech company's private network resources where they are conducting research. Because the scientist works for another biotech company, each company is concerned about loss of trade secrets. The director is concerned that RADIUS might compromise the security of the existing network at each biotech company. Each biotech company has standardized Active Directoryas their directory service. How do you respond?

Lesson 3: Data Protection in RADIUS Designs

This lesson discusses how to create designs that protect confidential data in remote access designs that include RADIUS. This lesson focuses on preventing unauthorized access to private network resources and protecting confidential data transmitted by remote users in your RADIUS design.

After this lesson, you will be able to

- Prevent unauthorized remote access to private network resources
- Protect confidential data transmitted between remote users and the private network

Estimated lesson time: 30 minutes

Preventing Access to Private Network Resources

When your design includes RADIUS, you must prevent unauthorized access to private network resources. Depending on the RADIUS solution you create, you may prevent access to private network resources at the RADIUS clients or the remote access servers within the private network.

Making the Decision

You can prevent unauthorized private network access by using the same method for preventing unauthorized private network access in dial-up and VPN remote access solutions. In addition, in RADIUS solutions you can prevent unauthorized access to private networks by identifying authorized RADIUS clients and RADIUS servers.

Applying Methods Used in Dial-Up and VPN Remote Access Solutions

You can prevent unauthorized access to private network resources in RADIUS designs by applying the same methods used in dial-up and VPN remote access solutions. These methods include

- Restricting remote user access to only the resources on the RADIUS clients or remote access servers
- Restricting the traffic transmitted through the RADIUS clients or remote access servers
- Placing RADIUS clients or remote access servers properly in relation to screened subnets or demilitarized zones (DMZs)

The design decisions for preventing access to private network resources through RADIUS clients (or remote access servers in the private network) are exactly like preventing access to private network resources through a dial-up or VPN remote access solution (depending on the types of remote access clients that the RADIUS clients must support).

For more information on how to prevent access to private network resources through dial-up (or VPN) remote access servers and, subsequently, through RADIUS clients (or remote access servers in the private network) that support dial-up (or VPN) remote users, see Chapter 11, "Dial-Up Connectivity in Remote Access Designs," Lesson 2, "Essential Dial-Up Remote Access Design Concepts," or Chapter 12, "VPN Connectivity in Remote Access Designs," Lesson 2, "Essential VPN Remote Access Design Concepts."

Identifying Authorized RADIUS Clients and RADIUS Servers

You can also prevent unauthorized access to private network resources by identifying authorized RADIUS clients and RADIUS servers using *RADIUS shared secrets*. A RADIUS shared secret is a text string that serves as a special password exchanged between RADIUS servers and corresponding RADIUS clients.

In addition to identifying authorized RADIUS clients and RADIUS servers, the RADIUS client and the RADIUS server use the shared secret to encrypt messages sent between them. You must configure both the RADIUS client and the RADIUS server to use the same shared secret.

As you specify RADIUS shared secrets in your design, create shared secrets that

- Are exactly the same on both RADIUS clients and RADIUS servers
- Are case-sensitive
- Include a combination of uppercase and lowercase letters, numbers, and special characters to make the shared secret more secure
- Are up to 255 characters in length (use longer shared secrets to make more secure shared secrets than shorter shared secrets)

Applying the Decision

Figure 13.10 illustrates the proper methods for preventing access to private network resources. For the purposes of this scenario, assume that

- You must restrict remote access network traffic to HTTP and FTP traffic
- Remote user accounts are stored in Active Directory
- The organization has outsourced the dial-up remote access portion of the design to an ISP
- Firewalls prevent unauthorized access to private network segments

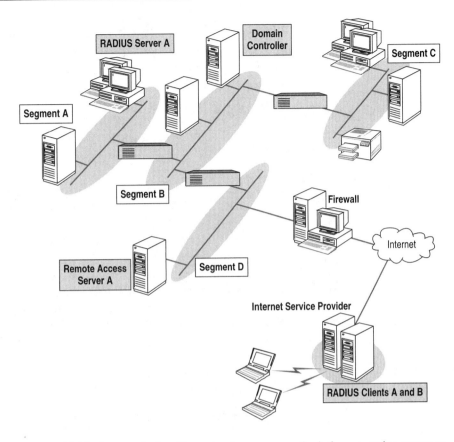

Figure 13.10 A scenario that illustrates the proper methods for preventing access to private network resources

To fulfill the requirements and constraints of the organization, you must specify that

- RADIUS clients that support dial-up remote access connection be placed at the ISP's locations
- The VPN remote access server be placed on Segment D behind the firewall
- The VPN remote access server IP filters allow *only* HTTP and FTP traffic
- RADIUS Server A be placed on Segment B
- RADIUS Clients A and B utilize RADIUS Server A for authentication and accounting
- RADIUS Server A allows authentication and accounting requests from RADIUS Clients A and B
- An identical RADIUS shared secret for each RADIUS client and RADIUS server

Protecting Confidential Remote Access Data

When your design includes remote access solutions based on RADIUS, remote users will access confidential data. You must ensure that the confidentiality of the data is protected at all times.

Making the Decision

You can protect confidential data transmitted between remote users and the private network by

- Authenticating remote users
- Encrypting confidential data
- Enforcing remote access policies

Authenticating Remote Users

In a RADIUS solution, you can authenticate remote users by using any methods previously discussed for dial-up or VPN remote access servers. The only difference in authenticating remote users by using RADIUS is that the user accounts used for remote user authentication can be stored in

- Active Directory
- Windows NT 4 domains
- Microsoft Commercial Internet System
- Any user account database utilized by RADIUS servers on other operating systems

For more information on remote user authentication for dial-up (or VPN) remote access servers and, subsequently, RADIUS, see Chapter 11, "Dial-Up Connectivity in Remote Access Designs," Lesson 3, "Data Protection in Dial-Up Remote Access Designs," and Chapter 12, "VPN Connectivity in Remote Access Designs," Lesson 3, "Data Protection in VPN Remote Access Designs."

Encrypting Confidential Data

You can use the same methods for encrypting confidential data in a RADIUS design that you can utilize in a dial-up or VPN remote access design. The only difference in encrypting confidential data in a RADIUS solution is that you can encrypt data between

- **Remote users and remote access servers within the private network (as shown in Figure 13.11)**   You can use VPN tunnels or IP Security (IPSec) to encrypt confidential data between the remote users and the remote access servers within the private network. The advantage to this solution is that the data encryption is independent of the RADIUS client. The disadvantage to this solution is that the firewall rules are more complex.

- **Remote users and the RADIUS clients and then between the RADIUS clients and the remote access servers within the private network (as shown in Figure 13.12)** You can use VPN tunnels (or IPSec) to encrypt confidential data between the remote users and the RADIUS client. You can further protect confidential data by an additional VPN tunnel (or IPSec connection) between the RADIUS client and the remote access servers within the private network.

The advantage to this solution is that the firewall rules are less complex. The disadvantage to this solution is that the data encryption depends on the capabilities of the RADIUS client. Some RADIUS clients from third-party vendors don't support VPN tunneling or IPSec.

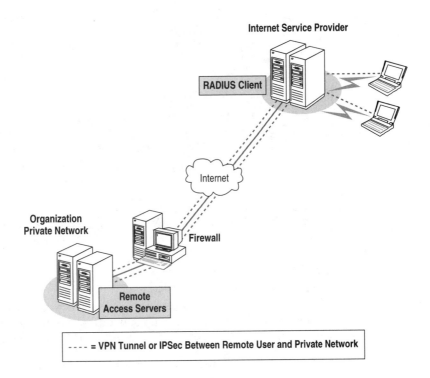

Figure 13.11   A scenario that illustrates using a single VPN tunnel between remote users and the remote access server in the private network

For more information on encrypting confidential data for dial-up (or VPN) remote access servers and, subsequently, RADIUS, see Chapter 11, "Dial-Up Connectivity in Remote Access Designs," Lesson 3, "Data Protection in Dial-Up Remote Access Designs," and Chapter 12, "VPN Connectivity in Remote Access Designs," Lesson 3, "Data Protection in VPN Remote Access Designs."

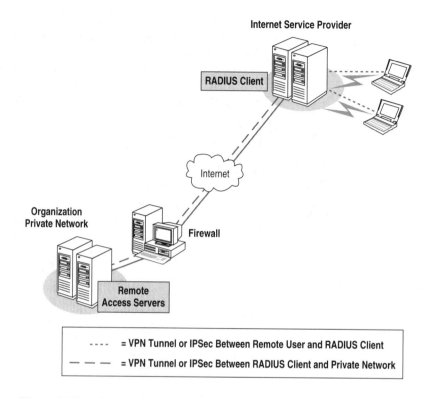

Figure 13.12   A scenario that illustrates using a VPN tunnel between remote users and the RADIUS client and a VPN tunnel between the RADIUS client and the remote access servers in the private network

Remote Access Policies

You can use the same methods for controlling remote user security (by using remote access policies) in a RADIUS design that you can utilize in a dial-up or VPN remote access design. The only difference in controlling remote user security in a RADIUS solution is that the remote access policies are

- **Called RADIUS attributes in a RADIUS design**
- **Managed and stored on the RADIUS servers**
- **Shared by all the RADIUS clients that utilize the same RADIUS server**
- **Replicated across all RADIUS servers that must have the same remote access policies**   Remote access policies are stored locally on each RADIUS server. You must specify the same remote access policies for all RADIUS servers that service the same RADIUS realm (same remote user accounts).
- **Different on RADIUS servers and RADIUS clients running on other operating systems**   RADIUS servers and RADIUS clients on other operat-

ing systems might not support every RADIUS attribute (remote access polices) included in Windows 2000.

For more information on encrypting confidential data for dial-up (or VPN) remote access servers and, subsequently, RADIUS, see Chapter 11, "Dial-Up Connectivity in Remote Access Designs," Lesson 3, "Data Protection in Dial-Up Remote Access Designs," and Chapter 12, "VPN Connectivity in Remote Access Designs," Lesson 3, "Data Protection in VPN Remote Access Designs."

For more information on remote access policies and RADIUS attributes, see the Windows 2000 help files.

Applying the Decision

Figure 13.13 illustrates the appropriate methods for protecting confidential data transmitted between remote users and the private network. For the purposes of this scenario, assume that

- All remote users must be authenticated
- Remote users can connect within and outside North America

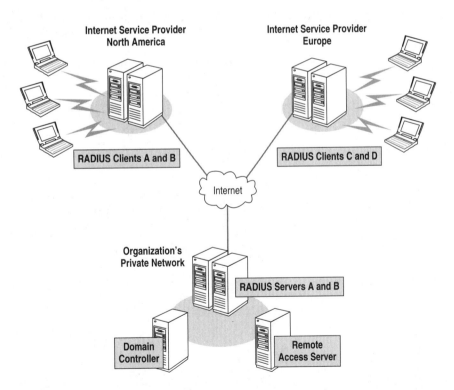

Figure 13.13   A scenario that illustrates the appropriate methods for protecting confidential data transmitted between remote users and the private network

- Remote access clients are running a variety of operating systems including Microsoft Windows 95, Microsoft Windows 98, Microsoft Windows Me, Windows NT 4, Windows 2000, UNIX, and Macintosh operating systems
- All remote users must encrypt all data transmitted between the remote access clients and the private network or be denied access to the private network
- RADIUS clients are running Windows 2000

To fulfill the requirements and constraints of the organization, you must specify that

- Remote access servers and remote access users within the North America must support PPTP tunnels that encrypt data by using 128-bit Microsoft Point-to-Point Encryption (MPPE)
- Remote access servers and remote access users outside North America must support PPTP tunnels that encrypt data by using 40-bit MPPE
- Extensible Authentication Protocol-Transport Level Security (EAP-TLS), Microsoft Challenge Handshake Authentication Protocol (MS-CHAP), or MS-CHAP v2 authenticates remote users
- RADIUS servers include remote access policies that deny remote access to remote users unable to meet the security requirements of the organization

Lesson 4: RADIUS Design Optimization

This lesson discusses how to optimize RADIUS designs to improve the availability and performance characteristics in your design. This lesson focuses on the strategies that increase the percentage of time that remote users can be authenticated and RADIUS accounting information can be reported. In addition, this lesson covers strategies that decrease any latency in authentication and reporting RADIUS accounting information.

After this lesson, you will be able to

- Select the appropriate method for enhancing the availability characteristics in your RADIUS design
- Select the appropriate methods for improving the performance characteristics in your RADIUS design

Estimated lesson time: 45 minutes

Enhancing RADIUS Availability

Once you have established the essential aspects and security aspects of your RADIUS design, you can optimize the design for availability. The business requirements of the organization may require your design to ensure RADIUS authentication and accounting at all times. Regardless of a single point of failure, your design must provide redundancy for each RADIUS server.

Making the Decision

You can improve the availability of your RADIUS designs by

- Using any of the strategies available to dial-up and VPN remote access servers for RADIUS clients
- Distributing RADIUS clients across multiple RADIUS servers

Strategies Used in Dial-Up and VPN Remote Access Solutions

You can improve the availability of your RADIUS solutions by applying the same strategies used in dial-up and VPN remote access solutions (depending on the types of remote access clients that the RADIUS clients must support).

For more information on how to improve the availability of dial-up (or VPN) remote access servers and, subsequently, RADIUS clients that support dial-up (or VPN) remote users, see Chapter 11, "Dial-Up Connectivity in Remote Access Designs," Lesson 2, "Dial-Up Remote Access Design Optimization," or Chapter 12, "VPN Connectivity in Remote Access Designs," Lesson 2, "VPN Remote Access Design Optimization."

Distributing RADIUS Clients Across Multiple RADIUS Servers

You can include multiple RADIUS servers in your design to provide redundancy and backup. You need to include a redundant RADIUS server for each existing RADIUS server in your design.

You can distribute RADIUS clients across the multiple RADIUS servers in your design by configuring RADIUS clients to use multiple RADIUS servers and by using Network Load Balancing. Configuring RADIUS clients and using Network Load Balancing to provide redundancy for RADIUS servers has specific advantages and disadvantages.

Table 13.2 lists the methods of improving RADIUS availability and the advantages and the disadvantages of including these methods in your design.

Table 13.2   Advantages and Disadvantages of Methods of Improving RADIUS Availability

Method	Advantages	Disadvantages
RADIUS configuration	Works on all operating system platforms Dynamically provides fault tolerance for all RADIUS clients and all RADIUS servers	Doesn't automatically remove failed RADIUS servers, so RADIUS client computers might experience time-out or other error messages RADIUS servers must be manually added or removed from the RADIUS configuration
Network Load Balancing	Automatically reconfigures a cluster if a RADIUS client fails Provides improved availability because the addition or removal of RADIUS servers is dynamic	Provides no load balancing for RADIUS servers, only RADIUS clients Requires extra processor and memory resources to run the Network Load Balancing service Doesn't work with RADIUS servers running on other operating systems, such as UNIX or Macintosh computers

The specifications for the RADIUS servers that provide redundancy must be *identical*. You must ensure that the same user account database and remote access policies exist on *all* servers.

For more information on Network Load Balancing, see the section, "Optimizing Private Network Resource Access," in Chapter 6, "Proxy Server in Internet and Intranet Designs," Lesson 4, "Proxy Server Design Optimization."

Applying the Decision

Figure 13.14 illustrates the proper methods for enhancing the availability of a RADIUS solution.

For the purposes of this scenario, assume that the business and technical requirements of the organization include

- Any failure of a RADIUS client or RADIUS server doesn't prevent authentication
- RADIUS clients are prevented from accessing failed RADIUS servers

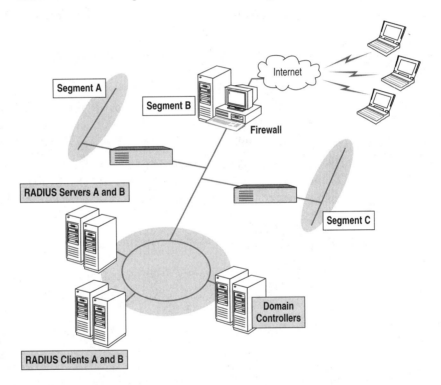

Figure 13.14 Scenario to illustrate the proper methods for enhancing the availability of a RADIUS solution

To provide the appropriate solution, multiple RADIUS clients and RADIUS servers must be included to achieve the business and technical requirements of the organization. RADIUS Clients A and B have the same specifications and belong to the same Network Load Balancing cluster. RADIUS Servers A and B also have the same specifications and belong to the same Network Load Balancing cluster.

Improving RADIUS Performance

Once you have established the essential aspects, the security aspects, and availability aspects of your RADIUS design, you can optimize the design for performance. The business requirements may include that RADIUS clients and RADIUS servers must support a sustained rate of authentication and accounting requests.

Making the Decision

You can improve RADIUS performance by

- Using any of the strategies available to dial-up and VPN remote access servers for RADIUS clients
- Distributing RADIUS clients across multiple RADIUS servers

Strategies Used in Dial-Up and VPN Remote Access Solutions

You can improve the performance of your RADIUS solutions by applying the same strategies used in dial-up and VPN remote access solutions (depending on the types of remote access clients that the RADIUS clients must support).

For more information on how to improve the performance of dial-up (or VPN) remote access servers and, subsequently, RADIUS clients that support dial-up (or VPN) remote users, see Chapter 11, "Dial-Up Connectivity in Remote Access Designs," Lesson 4, "Dial-Up Remote Access Design Optimization," or Chapter 12, "VPN Connectivity in Remote Access Designs," Lesson 4, "VPN Remote Access Design Optimization."

Distributing RADIUS Clients Across Multiple RADIUS Servers

When the existing RADIUS servers are saturated and you can't upgrade the hardware to improve performance, you can add additional RADIUS servers to your design.

You can distribute RADIUS clients and, subsequently, RADIUS authentication and accounting in your RADIUS design by configuring the RADIUS clients for multiple RADIUS servers or by using Network Load Balancing. In your RADIUS solutions, you can configure the RADIUS clients or Network Load Balancing to optimize RADIUS authentication and accounting performance.

Table 13.3 lists the methods for distributing RADIUS clients across multiple RADIUS servers and the advantages and the disadvantages of including these methods in your design.

Table 13.3   Advantages and Disadvantages of Methods for Distributing RADIUS Clients Across Multiple RADIUS Servers

Method	Advantages	Disadvantages
Network Load Balancing	Dynamically provides load balancing across all the RADIUS clients in the Network Load Balancing cluster Allows dynamic addition or removal of RADIUS clients in the cluster Automatically reconfigures a cluster if a RADIUS client fails Improves performance because the load balancing is dynamic and the addition or removal of RADIUS clients is performed dynamically	Provides no load balancing for RADIUS servers, only RADIUS clients Requires extra processor and memory resources to run the Network Load Balancing service Doesn't work with RADIUS servers running on other operating systems, such as UNIX or Macintosh computers
RADIUS configuration	Works on all operating system platforms Provides dynamic load balancing across all the RADIUS servers listed in the RADIUS client Improves performance for RADIUS authentication and accounting by load balancing across multiple RADIUS servers	Doesn't automatically remove failed RADIUS servers, so RADIUS clients might experience time-out or other error messages RADIUS servers must be manually added or removed from the RADIUS client configuration

For more information on Network Load Balancing, see the section, "Optimizing Private Network Resource Access," in Chapter 6, "Proxy Server in Internet and Intranet Designs," Lesson 4, "Proxy Server Design Optimization."

Applying the Decision

Figure 13.15 illustrates a RADIUS design prior to optimization for performance. For the purposes of this scenario, assume that the business and technical requirements of the organization include that the existing

- RADIUS clients and RADIUS servers can't be further upgraded
- RADIUS clients and RADIUS servers are running Windows 2000

Figure 13.16 illustrates a RADIUS design after optimization for performance. The following performance optimization changes were made to the design.

- RADIUS Client B is installed to distribute the remote access traffic between RADIUS Servers A and B.
- RADIUS Client A is assigned a unique bank of phone numbers.

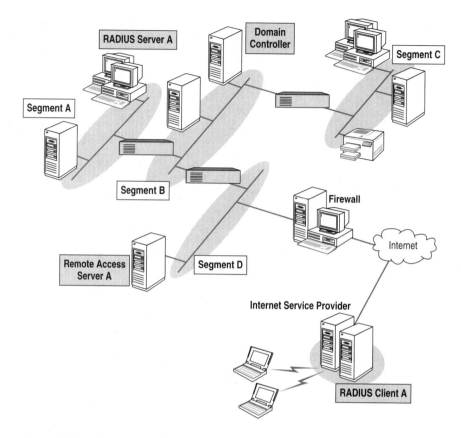

Figure 13.15   Scenario to illustrate a RADIUS design prior to optimization for performance

- RADIUS Client B is assigned a unique bank of phone numbers.
- Remote users are evenly distributed across RADIUS Clients A and B.
- RADIUS Server B is installed to distribute the authentication and accounting traffic between RADIUS Clients A and B.
- RADIUS Servers A and B belong to the same Network Load Balancing cluster

Activity 13.2: Completing a RADIUS Design

In this activity, you're presented with a scenario. To complete the activity:

1. Evaluate the scenario and determine the design requirements
2. Answer questions and make design recommendations

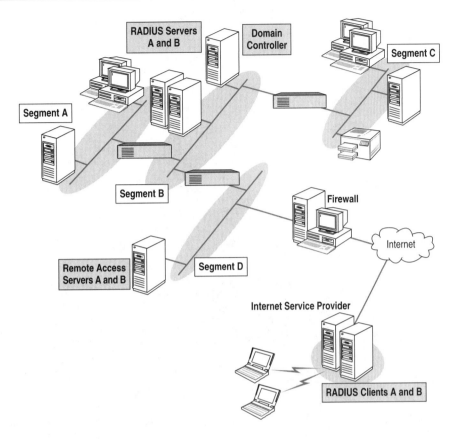

Figure 13.16   Scenario to illustrate a RADIUS design after optimization for performance

In Figure 13.17, you see a map for a consortium of biotech companies that was discussed in an earlier lesson. You're completing all aspects of the design that you started in the earlier lesson.

Answer the following questions concerning your design recommendations. You can find answers to the questions in the Appendix, "Questions and Answers."

1. The board of directors for the biotech consortium wants to ensure that only scientists who are working in the consortium's research facilities can access the private network resources within their respective biotech companies. How can you ensure that these requirements are met in your design?

2. The remote users run a variety of operating systems, including Windows 98, Windows NT 4.0 Workstation, and Windows 2000 Professional. The consortium

Figure 13.17   Map of a biotech consortium

wants all confidential data protected. How do you protect the confidential data accessed by the scientists working at other consortium research and development facilities?

3. One of the primary concerns of the consortium is that the scientists can access their resources at any time. In addition, the first phase of the deployment process occurred a few months ago. Since the initial deployment, remote users report that the length of time for authentication is increasing. How can you ensure that the scientists can always access their resources and reduce the length of time for authentication?

Lab: Creating a RADIUS Design

After this lab, you will be able to

- Evaluate a scenario and determine the design requirements
- Create a RADIUS design based on the design requirements

Estimated lab time: 45 minutes

In this lab, you're a consultant to an ISP and are responsible for the creation of a RADIUS design for the ISP. The ISP has 2600 point of presence (POP) locations throughout the world.

To complete this lab:

1. Examine the networking environment presented in the scenario, the network diagrams, the business requirements and constraints, and the technical requirements and constraints

2. Use the worksheet for each location to assist you in creating your RADIUS design (you can find completed sample design worksheets on the Supplemental Course Materials CD-ROM in the Completed Worksheets folder)

3. Create, eliminate, or replace existing networking devices and network segments when required

4. Ensure that your design fulfills the business requirements and constraints and technical requirements and constraints of the scenario by

   - Specifying the appropriate specifications for the RADIUS clients
   - Specifying the appropriate specifications for the RADIUS servers
   - Optimizing your design to provide security, availability, performance, and affordability

Scenario

An ISP provides Internet connectivity to remote users and outsourced dial-up remote access for other organizations. The ISP provides 2600 POP facilities (shown in Figure 13.19) throughout the world.

The ISP enters into SLAs with other organizations (shown in Figure 13.20) that provide outsourced dial-up remote access connectivity. These SLAs require the ISP to achieve specific performance and availability requirements for their customers.

The ISP must be able to provide customized levels of services for

- Various remote user contracts
- Outsourced dial-up remote access contracts

Each ISP POP facility manages the modems and phone lines that the remote users utilize to connect to the Internet.

Figure 13.18 is a diagram of the ISP. Currently, the ISP supports multiple types of connections to its customers that include dial-up modems, ISDN, DSL, T1, or T3 connections. The ISP maintains multiple T3 connections to the Internet at each POP facility.

ISP's POP Facilities

Figure 13.18   Diagram of the ISP

Business Requirements and Constraints

The ISP has a number of requirements and constraints based on the business model of the ISP. As you create your RADIUS design, ensure that your design meets the business requirements and stays within the business constraints.

To achieve the business requirements and constraints, your design must

- Track remote user connection time to provide billing information
- Authorize individual remote users by using user accounts managed by the ISP
- Authorize outsourced dial-up remote users by using user accounts managed by the outsourced dial-up remote access contract customers
- Protect any confidential data transmitted between remote users and the outsourced dial-up remote access contract customer's private network
- Provide enhanced security features for all remote users, such as caller-ID identification or user callback

Technical Requirements and Constraints

The existing physical network, hardware, and operating systems place certain technical requirements and constraints on your design. As you create your RADIUS design, ensure that your design meets the technical requirements and stays within the technical constraints.

To achieve the technical requirements and constraints, your design must

- Ensure that the firewalls at the outsourced dial-up remote access contract customer's private network protect private network resources

- Include a RADIUS server for each user accounts database

- Include a RADIUS client for every 450 users so that the desired performance, determined in pilot testing, is ensured

- Ensure that all remote users can be authenticated if an individual RADIUS client or RADIUS server fails

- Utilize the strongest possible security to protect confidential data

- Support the variety of operating systems running on the remote access clients, including Windows 95, Windows 98, Windows NT 4 Workstation, and Windows 2000 Professional

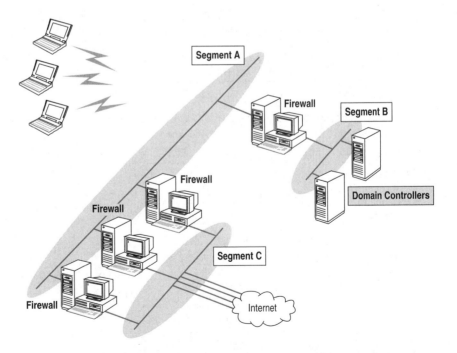

Figure 13.19 The existing network at one of the ISP's POP facilities. For the purposes of this lab, assume that the POP facilities have the same network configuration.

Design Worksheet – Figure 13.19
ISP POP Facility – RADIUS Client A

RADIUS Client Specifications	Comments
RADIUS client connects to segment: _____	

RADIUS server specifications

	Server name	RADIUS services provided	Shared secret
1		❑ Authentication ❑ Accounting	
2		❑ Authentication ❑ Accounting	
3		❑ Authentication ❑ Accounting	
4		❑ Authentication ❑ Accounting	

❑ Dial-up remote user support

Phone bank that connects to dial-up remote access server: _____

❑ VPN remote user support

❑ Network Load Balancing cluster   Cluster name: _____

IP protocol support (Select the appropriate IP address configuration options)

❑ Manually assigned   ❑ DHCP assigned   ❑ Include DHCP Relay Agent

Security

Authentication protocols (Select one or more authentication protocols)

❑ MS-CHAP ❑ MS-CHAP v2 ❑ EAP   ❑ CHAP   ❑ PAP   ❑ SPAP

Encryption protocols (Select the appropriate data encryption protocols)

❑ MPPE (Select the strength of MPPE encryption)

    ❑ 40-bit   ❑ 128-bit

❑ IPSec (Select the IPSec protection to utilize)

Mode	Authentication	Identity	Protection	Encryption
❑ Transport	❑ Kerberos	❑ MD5	❑ Identity (AH)	Not required
❑ Tunnel	❑ X509 ❑ Preshared key	❑ SHA	❑ Identity and encryption (ESP)	❑ DES ❑ 56-bit DES ❑ 3DES

Remote access to network resources

❑ RADIUS client resources only

❑ Entire network resources

Design Worksheet – Figure 13.19
ISP POP Facility – RADIUS Server A

RADIUS Server Specifications			Comments
RADIUS server connects to segment: _____			
RADIUS realm/domain name: _____			
RADIUS client specifications			

	Client name	RADIUS services provided	Shared secret
1		❑ Authentication ❑ Accounting	
2		❑ Authentication ❑ Accounting	
3		❑ Authentication ❑ Accounting	
4		❑ Authentication ❑ Accounting	
❑	Cluster name: _____		

Security

❑ Remote access policies (Specify the remote access policy in the Comments column)

Design Worksheet – Figure 13.19
ISP POP Facility – RADIUS Client B

RADIUS Client Specifications				Comments
RADIUS client connects to segment: _____				
RADIUS server specifications				
	Server name	RADIUS services provided	Shared secret	
1		❏ Authentication ❏ Accounting		
2		❏ Authentication ❏ Accounting		
3		❏ Authentication ❏ Accounting		
4		❏ Authentication ❏ Accounting		

❏ Dial-up remote user support

Phone bank that connects to dial-up remote access server: _____

❏ VPN remote user support

❏ Network Load Balancing cluster   Cluster name: _____

IP protocol support (Select the appropriate IP address configuration options)

❏ Manually assigned   ❏ DHCP assigned   ❏ Include DHCP Relay Agent

Security

Authentication protocols (Select one or more authentication protocols)

❏ MS-CHAP ❏ MS-CHAP v2 ❏ EAP   ❏ CHAP   ❏ PAP   ❏ SPAP

Encryption protocols (Select the appropriate data encryption protocols)

❏ MPPE (Select the strength of MPPE encryption)

❏ 40-bit   ❏ 128-bit

❏ IPSec (Select the IPSec protection to utilize)

Mode	Authentication	Identity	Protection	Encryption
❏ Transport	❏ Kerberos	❏ MD5	❏ Identity (AH)	Not required
❏ Tunnel	❏ X509 ❏ Preshared key	❏ SHA	❏ Identity and encryption (ESP)	❏ DES ❏ 56-bit DES ❏ 3DES

Remote access to network resources

❏ RADIUS client resources only

❏ Entire network resources

Design Worksheet – Figure 13.19
ISP POP Facility – RADIUS Server B

RADIUS Server Specifications				Comments
RADIUS server connects to segment: _____				
RADIUS realm/domain name: _____				
RADIUS client specifications				
	Client name	RADIUS services provided	Shared secret	
1		❑ Authentication ❑ Accounting		
2		❑ Authentication ❑ Accounting		
3		❑ Authentication ❑ Accounting		
4		❑ Authentication ❑ Accounting		
❑ Network Load Balancing cluster Cluster name: _____				
Security				
❑ Remote access policies (Specify the remote access policy in the Comments column)				

Design Worksheet – Figure 13.19
ISP POP Facility – RADIUS Client C

RADIUS Client Specifications	Comments
RADIUS client connects to segment: _____	
RADIUS server specifications	

	Server name	RADIUS services provided	Shared secret
1		❑ Authentication ❑ Accounting	
2		❑ Authentication ❑ Accounting	
3		❑ Authentication ❑ Accounting	
4		❑ Authentication ❑ Accounting	

❑ Dial-up remote user support

Phone bank that connects to dial-up remote access server: _____

❑ VPN remote user support

❑ Network Load Balancing cluster   Cluster name: _____

IP protocol support (Select the appropriate IP address configuration options)

❑ Manually assigned   ❑ DHCP assigned   ❑ Include DHCP Relay Agent

Security

Authentication protocols (Select one or more authentication protocols)

❑ MS-CHAP ❑ MS-CHAP v2 ❑ EAP ❑ CHAP ❑ PAP ❑ SPAP

Encryption protocols (Select the appropriate data encryption protocols)

❑ MPPE (Select the strength of MPPE encryption)

❑ 40-bit   ❑ 128-bit

❑ IPSec (Select the IPSec protection to utilize)

Mode	Authentication	Identity	Protection	Encryption
❑ Transport ❑ Tunnel	❑ Kerberos ❑ X509 ❑ Preshared key	❑ MD5 ❑ SHA	❑ Identity (AH) ❑ Identity and encryption (ESP)	Not required ❑ DES ❑ 56-bit DES ❑ 3DES

Remote access to network resources

❑ RADIUS client resources only

❑ Entire network resources

Design Worksheet – Figure 13.19
ISP POP Facility – RADIUS Server C

RADIUS Server Specifications	Comments
RADIUS server connects to segment: _____	
RADIUS realm/domain name: _____	
RADIUS client specifications	

	Client name	RADIUS services provided	Shared secret
1		❑ Authentication ❑ Accounting	
2		❑ Authentication ❑ Accounting	
3		❑ Authentication ❑ Accounting	
4		❑ Authentication ❑ Accounting	

❑ Network Load Balancing cluster   Cluster name: _____

Security

❑ Remote access policies (Specify the remote access policy in the Comments column)

Design Worksheet – Figure 13.19
ISP POP Facility – RADIUS Client D

RADIUS Client Specifications	Comments
RADIUS client connects to segment: _____	

RADIUS server specifications

		Server name	RADIUS services provided	Shared secret
	1		❑ Authentication ❑ Accounting	
	2		❑ Authentication ❑ Accounting	
	3		❑ Authentication ❑ Accounting	
	4		❑ Authentication ❑ Accounting	

❑ Dial-up remote user support

Phone bank that connects to dial-up remote access server: _____

❑ VPN remote user support

❑ Network Load Balancing cluster   Cluster name: _____

IP protocol support (Select the appropriate IP address configuration options)

❑ Manually assigned   ❑ DHCP assigned   ❑ Include DHCP Relay Agent

Security

Authentication protocols (Select one or more authentication protocols)

❑ MS-CHAP ❑ MS-CHAP v2 ❑ EAP   ❑ CHAP   ❑ PAP   ❑ SPAP

Encryption protocols (Select the appropriate data encryption protocols)

❑ MPPE (Select the strength of MPPE encryption)

❑ 40-bit   ❑ 128-bit

❑ IPSec (Select the IPSec protection to utilize)

Mode	Authentication	Identity	Protection	Encryption
❑ Transport	❑ Kerberos	❑ MD5	❑ Identity (AH)	Not required
❑ Tunnel	❑ X509	❑ SHA	❑ Identity and encryption (ESP)	❑ DES
	❑ Preshared key			❑ 56-bit DES
				❑ 3DES

Remote access to network resources

❑ RADIUS client resources only

❑ Entire network resources

Design Worksheet – Figure 13.19
ISP POP Facility – RADIUS Server D

RADIUS Server Specifications				Comments
RADIUS server connects to segment: _____				
RADIUS realm/domain name: _____				
RADIUS client specifications				
	Client name	RADIUS services provided	Shared secret	
1		❑ Authentication ❑ Accounting		
2		❑ Authentication ❑ Accounting		
3		❑ Authentication ❑ Accounting		
4		❑ Authentication ❑ Accounting		
❑ Network Load Balancing cluster Cluster name: _____				
Security				
❑ Remote access policies (Specify the remote access policy in the Comments column)				

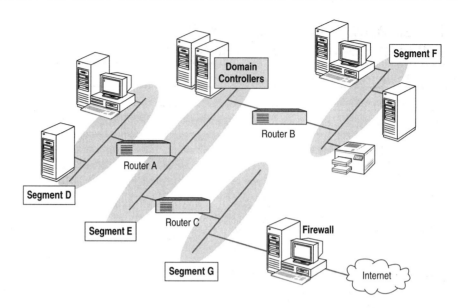

Figure 13.20 The existing network at one of the outsourced dial-up remote access customers. For the purposes of this lab, assume that the outsourced dial-up remote access customers have the same network configuration.

Design Worksheet – Figure 13.20
Outsourced Dial-Up Remote Access Customer – RADIUS Client A

RADIUS Client Specifications	Comments
RADIUS client connects to segment: _____	
RADIUS server specifications	

	Server name	RADIUS services provided	Shared secret
1		❑ Authentication ❑ Accounting	
2		❑ Authentication ❑ Accounting	
3		❑ Authentication ❑ Accounting	
4		❑ Authentication ❑ Accounting	

❑ Dial-up remote user support

Phone bank that connects to dial-up remote access server: _____

❑ VPN remote user support

❑ Network Load Balancing cluster   Cluster name: _____

IP protocol support (Select the appropriate IP address configuration options)

❑ Manually assigned   ❑ DHCP assigned   ❑ Include DHCP Relay Agent

Security

Authentication protocols (Select one or more authentication protocols)

❑ MS-CHAP ❑ MS-CHAP v2 ❑ EAP   ❑ CHAP   ❑ PAP   ❑ SPAP

Encryption protocols (Select the appropriate data encryption protocols)

❑ MPPE (Select the strength of MPPE encryption)

❑ 40-bit   ❑ 128-bit

❑ IPSec (Select the IPSec protection to utilize)

Mode	Authentication	Identity	Protection	Encryption
❑ Transport	❑ Kerberos	❑ MD5	❑ Identity (AH)	Not required
❑ Tunnel	❑ X509 ❑ Preshared key	❑ SHA	❑ Identity and encryption (ESP)	❑ DES ❑ 56-bit DES ❑ 3DES

Remote access to network resources

❑ RADIUS client resources only

❑ Entire network resources

Design Worksheet – Figure 13.20
Outsourced Dial-Up Remote Access Customer – RADIUS Server A

RADIUS Server Specifications				Comments
RADIUS server connects to segment: _____				
RADIUS realm/domain name: _____				
RADIUS client specifications				
	Client name	RADIUS services provided	Shared secret	
1	**RADIUS Client A**	❑ Authentication ❑ Accounting		
2	**RADIUS Client B**	❑ Authentication ❑ Accounting		
3	**RADIUS Client C**	❑ Authentication ❑ Accounting		
4	**RADIUS Client D**	❑ Authentication ❑ Accounting		
❑ Network Load Balancing cluster Cluster name: _____				
Security				
❑ Remote access policies (Specify the remote access policy in the Comments column)				

Design Worksheet – Figure 13.20
Outsourced Dial-Up Remote Access Customer – RADIUS Client B

RADIUS Client Specifications					Comments
RADIUS client connects to segment: _____					
RADIUS server specifications					
	Server name	RADIUS services provided		Shared secret	
1		❏ Authentication ❏ Accounting			
2		❏ Authentication ❏ Accounting			
3		❏ Authentication ❏ Accounting			
4		❏ Authentication ❏ Accounting			
❏ Dial-up remote user support					
Phone bank that connects to dial-up remote access server: _____					
❏ VPN remote user support					
❏ Network Load Balancing cluster Cluster name: _____					
IP protocol support (Select the appropriate IP address configuration options)					
❏ Manually assigned ❏ DHCP assigned ❏ Include DHCP Relay Agent					
Security					
Authentication protocols (Select one or more authentication protocols)					
❏ MS-CHAP ❏ MS-CHAP v2 ❏ EAP ❏ CHAP ❏ PAP ❏SPAP					
Encryption protocols (Select the appropriate data encryption protocols)					
❏ MPPE (Select the strength of MPPE encryption)					
❏ 40-bit ❏ 128-bit					
❏ IPSec (Select the IPSec protection to utilize)					

Mode	Authentication	Identity	Protection	Encryption
❏ Transport	❏ Kerberos	❏ MD5	❏ Identity (AH)	Not required
❏ Tunnel	❏ X509	❏ SHA	❏ Identity and encryption (ESP)	❏ DES ❏ 56-bit DES ❏ 3DES
❏ Preshared key				

Remote access to network resources					
❏ RADIUS client resources only					
❏ Entire network resources					

Design Worksheet – Figure 13.20
Outsourced Dial-Up Remote Access Customer – RADIUS Server B

RADIUS Server Specifications				Comments
RADIUS server connects to segment: _____				
RADIUS realm/domain name: _____				
RADIUS client specifications				
	Client name	RADIUS services provided	Shared secret	
1	**RADIUS Client A**	❑ Authentication ❑ Accounting		
2	**RADIUS Client B**	❑ Authentication ❑ Accounting		
3	**RADIUS Client C**	❑ Authentication ❑ Accounting		
4	**RADIUS Client D**	❑ Authentication ❑ Accounting		
❑ Network Load Balancing cluster Cluster name: _____				
Security				
❑ Remote access policies (Specify the remote access policy in the Comments column)				

Design Worksheet – Figure 13.20
Outsourced Dial-Up Remote Access Customer – RADIUS Client C

RADIUS Client Specifications					Comments
RADIUS client connects to segment: _____					
RADIUS server specifications					

	Server name	RADIUS services provided	Shared secret
1		❏ Authentication ❏ Accounting	
2		❏ Authentication ❏ Accounting	
3		❏ Authentication ❏ Accounting	
4		❏ Authentication ❏ Accounting	

❏ Dial-up remote user support

Phone bank that connects to dial-up remote access server: _____

❏ VPN remote user support

❏ Network Load Balancing cluster   Cluster name: _____

IP protocol support (Select the appropriate IP address configuration options)

❏ Manually assigned   ❏ DHCP assigned   ❏ Include DHCP Relay Agent

Security

Authentication protocols (Select one or more authentication protocols)

❏ MS-CHAP ❏ MS-CHAP v2 ❏ EAP   ❏ CHAP ❏ PAP   ❏ SPAP

Encryption protocols (Select the appropriate data encryption protocols)

❏ MPPE (Select the strength of MPPE encryption)

❏ 40-bit   ❏ 128-bit

❏ IPSec (Select the IPSec protection to utilize)

Mode	Authentication	Identity	Protection	Encryption
❏ Transport	❏ Kerberos	❏ MD5	❏ Identity (AH)	Not required
❏ Tunnel	❏ X509 ❏ Preshared key	❏ SHA	❏ Identity and encryption (ESP)	❏ DES ❏ 56-bit DES ❏ 3DES

Remote access to network resources

❏ RADIUS client resources only

❏ Entire network resources

Design Worksheet – Figure 13.20
Outsourced Dial-Up Remote Access Customer – RADIUS Server C

RADIUS Server Specifications			Comments
RADIUS server connects to segment: _____			
RADIUS realm/domain name: _____			
RADIUS client specifications			

	Client name	RADIUS services provided	Shared secret
1		❑ Authentication ❑ Accounting	
2		❑ Authentication ❑ Accounting	
3		❑ Authentication ❑ Accounting	
4		❑ Authentication ❑ Accounting	

❑ Network Load Balancing cluster   Cluster name: _____

Security

❑ Remote access policies (Specify the remote access policy in the Comments column)

Design Worksheet – Figure 13.20
Outsourced Dial-Up Remote Access Customer – RADIUS Client D

RADIUS Client Specifications			Comments
RADIUS client connects to segment: _____			
RADIUS server specifications			

	Server name	RADIUS services provided	Shared secret
1		❏ Authentication ❏ Accounting	
2		❏ Authentication ❏ Accounting	
3		❏ Authentication ❏ Accounting	
4		❏ Authentication ❏ Accounting	

❏ Dial-up remote user support

Phone bank that connects to dial-up remote access server: _____

❏ VPN remote user support

❏ Network Load Balancing cluster   Cluster name: _____

IP protocol support (Select the appropriate IP address configuration options)

❏ Manually assigned   ❏ DHCP assigned   ❏ Include DHCP Relay Agent

Security

Authentication protocols (Select one or more authentication protocols)

❏ MS-CHAP ❏ MS-CHAP v2 ❏ EAP   ❏ CHAP   ❏ PAP   ❏ SPAP

Encryption protocols (Select the appropriate data encryption protocols)

❏ MPPE (Select the strength of MPPE encryption)

❏ 40-bit   ❏ 128-bit

❏ IPSec (Select the IPSec protection to utilize)

Mode	Authentication	Identity	Protection	Encryption
❏ Transport ❏ Tunnel	❏ Kerberos ❏ X509 ❏ Preshared key	❏ MD5 ❏ SHA	❏ Identity (AH) ❏ Identity and encryption (ESP)	Not required ❏ DES ❏ 56-bit DES ❏ 3DES

Remote access to network resources

❏ RADIUS client resources only

❏ Entire network resources

Design Worksheet – Figure 13.20
Outsourced Dial-Up Remote Access Customer – RADIUS Server D

RADIUS Server Specifications			Comments
RADIUS server connects to segment: _____			
RADIUS realm/domain name: _____			
RADIUS client specifications			

	Client name	RADIUS services provided	Shared secret
1		❑ Authentication ❑ Accounting	
2		❑ Authentication ❑ Accounting	
3		❑ Authentication ❑ Accounting	
4		❑ Authentication ❑ Accounting	

❑ Network Load Balancing cluster   Cluster name: _____

Security

❑ Remote access policies (Specify the remote access policy in the Comments column)

Review

The following questions are intended to reinforce key information in this chapter. If you're unable to answer a question, review the lesson and then try to answer the question again. Answers to the questions can be found in the Appendix, "Questions and Answers."

1. An organization is considering outsourcing its dial-up connectivity to a third party to provide remote access to users who work from home. The users are distributed across a number of geographic locations, but all report to a local office. The organization wants to control all aspects of the remote user passwords (such as password length or password aging). As a consultant to the organization, what recommendation do you make to achieve the requirements of the organization?

2. You're the director of information services for an ISP and you want to provide outsourced dial-up remote access connectivity for organizations. Many of the organizations that your company provides connectivity for want a single set of user credentials and want to implement user callback to provide enhanced security. In addition, you have entered into an SLA with these organizations to provide specific authentication response times and ensure that the organizations' remote users can always access their private network resources. What recommendations can you make to these organizations?

3. An organization has an existing dial-up remote access solution that supports hundreds of remote users. The organization wants to control all aspects of its remote access solution and is unwilling to outsource any portion of the dial-up remote access solution. How can RADIUS provide improvements in the existing dial-up remote access solution?

4. The director of information services in your organization has reviewed your proposal to outsource the dial-up remote connectivity in the organization's remote access design. The director is confused about why your design includes remote access servers in addition to RADIUS clients and RADIUS servers. How do you respond to the director?

CHAPTER 14

Monitoring and Managing a Microsoft Windows 2000 Network

About This Chapter

Previous chapters discussed the implementation and deployment portions of your networking services design. After deployment, the operations staff must monitor and manage the networking services in your networking services design.

In many organizations, the team responsible for deployment is usually a different one from the team responsible for operations. The concerns and goals of these two teams are unique and completely distinct. However, both teams rely on your networking services design as a foundation for implementation and ongoing monitoring and management.

The majority of monitoring and managing networking services can be identified as policies and procedures that the operations staff must follow. You can optimize your networking services design to improve monitoring and management. You can also assist the operations staff in identifying appropriate methods for monitoring and managing your network design.

This chapter answers questions such as:

- What are the goals in monitoring and managing networking services?
- How can you optimize your networking services design to improve monitoring and management after deployment?

- Which methods can the operations staff employ to assist them in monitoring and managing networking services?

- How can you determine the appropriate networking services to monitor and manage?

Before You Begin

Before you begin, you must have an overall understanding of

- The relationship between applications and networking services

- The monitoring and management capabilities in Windows 2000, such as the Performance Logs and Alerts MMC snap-in, Windows Management Instrumentation (WMI), or Simple Network Management Protocol (SNMP)

- The responses that are utilized in monitoring and management designs

Lesson 1: Networking Services Monitoring and Management

This lesson presents the goals you want to achieve in monitoring and managing the networking services in your design. This lesson discusses the components of a management design. This lesson also presents how to identify the critical networking services that must be managed in your design.

After this lesson, you will be able to

- Identify the goals in monitoring and managing networking services
- Identify the components of a management design
- Identify the critical networking services to include in your management design

Estimated lesson time: 14 minutes

Goals of Monitoring and Managing Networking Services

Before you can create your management design, you must identify the goals the operations staff must achieve. The goal of the operations staff is to ensure that the network continues to run within the organization's requirements and constraints upon which your design is based.

Making the Decision

To identify the goals of monitoring and managing the networking services in your network, you must

- Identify the management design requirements and constraints
- Determine the complexity of the management design
- Select proactive or reactive networking services management

Identifying Management Design Requirements and Constraints

You use the same requirements and constraints you used to create your networking services design. Your management design must ensure that the requirements and constraints in your networking services design are achieved or exceeded.

As a part of the process, review each portion of your networking services design to ensure that you're achieving or exceeding all the requirements and constraints. The previous chapters grouped these requirements and constraints in your networking services design as

- Design essentials
- Security
- Optimization (including availability and performance)

Figure 14.1 illustrates the relationship between requirements and constraints, the networking services design, and the management design. The *same* requirements and constraints are the foundation for both the networking services design and the management.

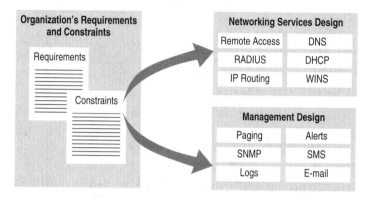

Figure 14.1   Illustration of the relationship between requirements and constraints, the networking services design, and the management design

For each of these facets to your networking services design, ensure that the requirements and constraints are achieved or exceeded.

Determining the Complexity of the Management Design

The complexity of the network and applications influences the complexity of your management design. You must design a management strategy that is appropriate for the

- **Size of the network**   You must customize your management design to the size of the network. As the size of your network increases

  - Your management design becomes more complex because there are more devices to manage

  - You must include more automatic management methods to reduce the amount of manual administration required to manage the network

- **Complexity of the applications that must be supported on the network** As the complexity of the applications increases, the requirements the applications place on networking services increases proportionally. As your networking services design becomes more complex, the management design must be capable of identifying the critical networking services required by these applications.

Selecting Proactive or Reactive Networking Services Management

The operations staff ensures that the network is running within the guidelines of your design by

- Proactively identifying and correcting potential problems before the actual problem occurs
- Reactively identifying and correcting problems once the actual problem occurs

Figure 14.2 illustrates the comparison of proactive and reactive management strategies. In an ideal situation, the operations staff identifies *all* potential problems before they occur and corrects the potential problem. In practice, identifying *all* potential problems before they occur is an impractical expectation.

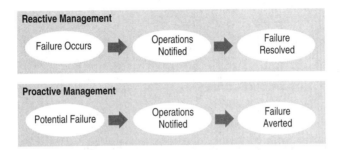

Figure 14.2   Comparison of proactive and reactive management strategies

You can consider your management design a success to the extent that it can proactively circumvent problems. To the extent that you must reactively identify and correct problems, your management design is less effective.

Note   As the size of your network and complexity of your applications increases, you must automate the management to reduce the manual intervention of the operations staff.

Applying the Decision

Figure 14.3 illustrates a scenario that you will use to identify the goals in monitoring and managing networking services. The organization in the scenario is deploying Distributed file system (Dfs) in its network. You're responsible for creating the networking services implementation design and assisting in creating the management design.

Note   The scenarios in this chapter use an example of an organization deploying Dfs. For more information on Dfs, see the Windows 2000 help files.

For the purposes of this scenario, assume

- The organization selected Active Directory as its directory services
- The organization wants to perform automatic replication of Dfs by using File Replication Service (FRS)

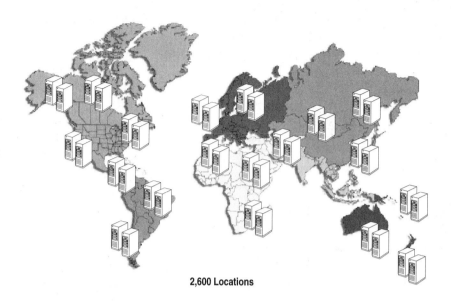

2,600 Locations

Figure 14.3   Scenario to identify the goals in monitoring and managing networking
services

- The organization operates from 2,600 locations throughout the world (as
  illustrated in Figure 14.3)

- Applications within the organization heavily depend on Dfs for proper operation

After evaluating the requirements and constraints of the organization, your networking services management design must

- Automate the management process to reduce the manual intervention of the
  operations staff

- Proactively manage the networking services to ensure that Dfs, and subsequently the applications that rely on Dfs, are always operational

Components of a Networking Services Management Design

After you identify the goals of your networking services management design,
you must identify how you can manage the networking services to achieve those
goals. To ensure that your management design covers all aspects of your networking
services, you must determine whether it includes the appropriate components.

Making the Decision

You can divide your networking services management design into the following
components.

- Collecting networking services status

- Analyzing networking services status
- Responding to changes in the networking services status

The length of time you want to wait before responding to changes in the networking services status determines how you must collect, analyze, and respond to networking services. You can collect, analyze, and respond to networking services

- **In real time**   When you want to respond to changes in the networking services immediately, you must collect and analyze the networking services in real time.
- **At scheduled intervals other than real time**   When you want to respond to changes in the networking services at scheduled intervals other than real time, you must collect and analyze the networking services many times, but at least once, during the scheduled interval.

Collecting Networking Services Status

You begin the management of the networking services in your network by collecting the status of the networking services. You can collect networking services status manually or automatically.

Tip   As you collect the status of networking services, save the status of the network services in a log file. You can use the archived log files to create historical analysis, or trend analysis, of the networking services.

Analyzing Networking Services Status

Once you have collected the status of the networking services, you can analyze the status of the networking services. As with collection, you can analyze the status of the networking services manually or automatically.

You can also analyze the status of the networking services in real time or over a period of time. Real-time analysis of the status allows you to identify potential problems before they occur.

By analyzing the status of the networking services over a period time, you can predict changes in the network services before they occur. In addition, by analyzing the status over a period of time, you can determine when network upgrades will be required.

Responding to Changes in the Networking Services Status

After you collect and analyze the networking services status, you must determine how to respond to changes in the networking services status. As with collection and analysis, you can respond to changes in the networking services status automatically or manually.

You can also respond to changes in the networking services status in real time or scheduled intervals. Responding in real time can notify operations staff immediately or can take actions to correct the potential problem. Responding to changes in the networking services status at scheduled intervals allows you to perform more complex responses or to ensure that networking services aren't interrupted.

From an operations perspective, you must collect the networking services status, analyze the status, and then respond to changes in the status. However, as the management designer, you create your design in the reverse sequence (determine the appropriate response to changes in status, specify how to analyze the status, and specify what status must be collected to perform the analysis).

The process for creating your networking services management design is discussed in Lesson 2, "Responding to Changes in the Networking Services Status," later in this chapter.

Applying the Decision

Figure 14.4 illustrates an example of how to identify the components in a networking services management design. For the purposes of this scenario, assume

- The organization selected Active Directory as its directory services

- The organization wants to perform automatic replication of Dfs by using FRS

- The organization operates from 2,600 locations within the United States (as illustrated in Figure 14.3)

- Applications within the organization heavily depend on Dfs for proper operation

- Users must be able to run the applications within the organization 24 hours a day, 7 days a week

- Only authorized users must be able to run the applications and subsequently access Dfs resources

- Many of the users must be able to run the applications remotely

- Applications must be able to respond to users within minimal lengths of time

By evaluating the requirements and constraints of the organization, your networking services management design must include

- Collecting status of the networking services required by the applications and Dfs

- Analyzing changes in the networking services status to determine whether critical networking services are close to failing or have failed

- Responding to the changes in networking services status to prevent the failure of critical networking services or to immediately notify operations staff of the changes

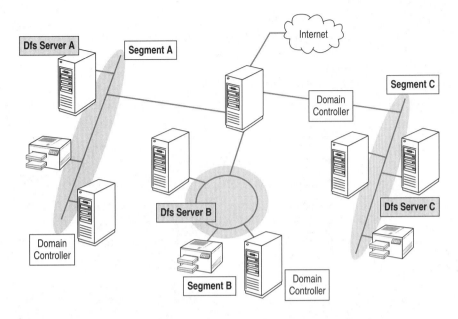

Figure 14.4   Scenario to identify the components in a networking services management design

Your networking services management design must proactively collect, analyze, and respond to the networking services to ensure that users can run the applications and access the Dfs resources. Because the organization's requirements require immediate notification of changes in the networking services, you must collect, analyze, and respond in real time.

Critical Networking Services

You must identify the critical networking services in your design to ensure that your management design can achieve the organization's requirements. You can identify the critical networking services by identifying the organization's critical applications.

These critical applications depend on the networking services in your design. The more these critical applications depend on an individual networking service, the more the networking service is critical in your design.

Making the Decision

To determine the critical networking services in your design, you must determine the

- Applications critical to the organization
- Servers that manage the resources critical to the applications
- Networking services critical to the servers and the applications

After you have determined the critical networking services in your design, you must ensure that your management design proactively monitors and manages these critical networking services.

Applying the Decision

Figure 14.5 illustrates an example of how to identify the critical networking services that support the applications and Dfs. For the purposes of this scenario, assume

- The organization selected Active Directory as its directory service
- The organization wants to perform automatic replication of Dfs by using FRS
- The organization operates from 2,600 locations within the United States (as illustrated in Figure 14.3)
- Applications within the organization heavily depend on Dfs for proper operation

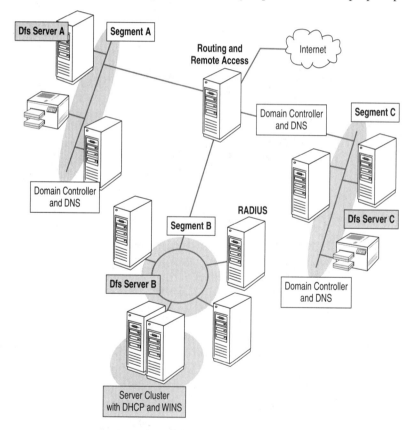

Figure 14.5   Scenario to identify the critical networking services that support the applications and Dfs

- Users must be able to run the applications within the organization 24 hours a day, 7 days a week

- Only authorized users must be able to run the applications and subsequently access Dfs resources

- Many of the users must be able to run the applications remotely

- Applications must be able to respond to users within minimal lengths of time

As you can see from Figure 14.6, the following dependencies exist.

- Remote users depend on remote access and Remote Authentication Dial-In User Service (RADIUS).

- Both local users and remote users rely on the applications and Dfs.

- Both the applications and Dfs depend on Domain Name System (DNS), Dynamic Host Configuration Protocol (DHCP), Internet Protocol (IP) routing, and Windows Internet Name Service (WINS).

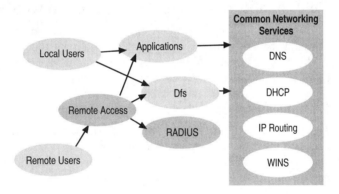

Figure 14.6   Scenario to identify the dependencies for networking services that support the applications and Dfs

Your networking services management design must proactively collect, analyze, and respond to remote access, RADIUS, DNS, DHCP, IP routing, and WINS. Because these networking services are critical to the applications and Dfs, you must provide real-time management and monitoring in your management design.

Lesson 2: Responding to Changes in the Networking Services Status

This lesson discusses the decisions you must make to determine how quickly your management design must respond to the changes in the networking services status. This lesson presents the methods you can include in your design to respond to changes in the networking services status.

After this lesson, you will be able to
- Determine how quickly your management design must respond to changes
- Select the type of response to changes in the networking services status
- Select the method of responding to changes in the networking services status

Estimated lesson time: 30 minutes

Determining How Quickly to Respond to Status Changes

Before you can make other decisions about your management design, you must determine how quickly your management design must respond to changes in the networking services status. You can customize your management design to respond to changes in the networking services based on the requirements of the organization.

Making the Decision

As mentioned in Lesson 1, you must determine the critical applications in your networking services design to determine the critical networking services. The applications in your network directly determine how quickly your management design must respond to changes in the networking services status changes.

To determine how quickly your management design must respond to changes in the networking services status changes, you must

- Determine the critical nature of each application that users run in your network
- Identify the critical networking services that support each application
- Identify the potential failures or resources shortages that can occur for each critical networking service
- Create a planned response for each of the potential failures or resource shortages that can occur

The remainder of this lesson focuses on Step 4—creating a planned response for each potential failure or resource shortage that occurs. You can divide the creation of the planned response into the following decision sequence.

1. Determine how quickly your management design must respond to the changes in the status of the networking services.

2. Identify the type of response for each potential failure or resource shortage.

3. Select the method for collecting, analyzing, and responding for each potential failure or resource shortage.

The more critical networking services are to the applications, the faster your management design must respond to changes in the status of the networking services. Figure 14.7 illustrates the relationship between the critical nature of a networking service and how quickly the management design must respond to the changes in the status of the networking services.

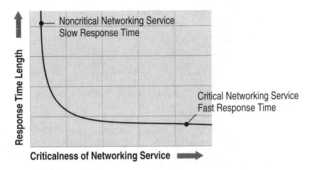

Figure 14.7   Relationship between the critical nature of networking services and how quickly the management design must respond

To respond to changes in the networking services immediately, your management design must collect and analyze the status of the networking services immediately. For example, to respond to changes in a networking service status within 30 seconds, you must collect, analyze, and respond to the changes in fewer than 30 seconds.

Your design will include responses to changes in the networking services that occur at various lengths of time. Each organization you create designs for might have existing severity levels or response time defined. You must consider any existing response times that are defined when creating your design.

Examples of possible response times include

- **Immediate (or real-time)**   Include immediate responses for the most critical failures or resource shortages. Immediate responses notify operations staff immediately when any failure or resource shortage occurs. Typically, you use automated processes to perform immediate responses.

    The advantage of immediate responses is that operations staff is aware of the failure or resource shortage as soon as the failure or resource shortage occurs. The disadvantage of immediate responses is that the system resources and financial costs to provide immediate response are higher than the other methods.

    Examples of immediate responses include paging, updates to a management console (such as SNMP consoles) notification, e-mail notification, restarting services, or other responses that provide immediate responses to operations staff.

- **Delayed (or near-time)**   Include delayed (or near-time) responses for failures or resource shortages that must be reported to operations staff, but a predefined delay is acceptable. This type of response is the most common response in your design. You can use automated or manual processes to perform delayed responses, based on the predefined delay. To reduce the administrative costs associated with manual processes, automate delayed responses when possible.

  The advantage of delayed responses is that operations staff is aware of the failure or resource shortage as within the predefined delay. The disadvantage of delayed responses is that the operations staff isn't notified immediately when the failure or resource shortage occurs.

  Examples of delayed responses include logging of events, e-mail notification, management console notification, or other responses that are performed on a specific, predefined interval.

- **Scheduled (or nonreal time)**   Include scheduled (or nonreal-time) responses for failures or resource shortages that are reviewed on longer intervals (usually measured in weeks or months) or when the analysis of the failure or resource shortage must be performed manually. The majority of scheduled responses are performed manually.

  The advantage of schedule responses is that operations staff is able to perform complex procedures that can't be performed otherwise. The disadvantage of scheduled responses is that the responses require a lot of operations staff time and that the operations staff isn't notified in a timely fashion when the failure or resource shortage occurs.

  Examples of scheduled responses include security audits, availability testing, or other responses that are performed manually or at longer, specific, predefined interval.

Applying the Decision

Figure 14.8 illustrates how to determine how quickly to respond to changes in the networking services. For the purposes of this scenario, assume

- All users in the organization run a mission-critical Web-based application
- The organization must support local and remote users
- The mission-critical Web-based application runs on a group of servers that all belong to the same Network Load Balancing cluster
- The mission-critical Web-based application depends on the following networking services:
  - DNS to provide name resolution
  - Routing and Remote Access to provide IP routing

- In addition to the networking services required by the mission-critical Web-based application, the networking services design includes
  - DHCP to provide IP configuration for local and remote client computers
  - Routing and Remote Access to provide remote user access
- The operations staff must be notified immediately of any failures or resource shortages for the networking services that support the mission-critical Web-based application
- The operations staff must be notified within 15 minutes of any failures or re-source shortages for all other networking services

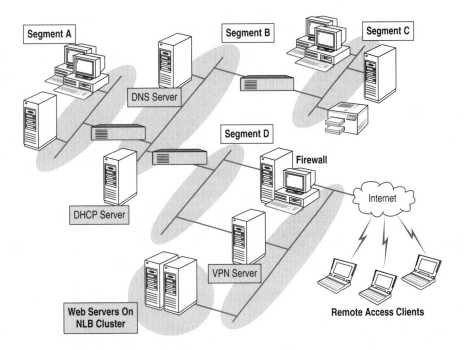

Figure 14.8 Scenario that illustrates how to determine how quickly to respond to status changes

The servers running DNS and providing IP routing are critical to the mission-critical Web-based application. Your management design must provide immediate responses to any failure or resource shortage on these servers that will affect DNS or IP routing.

The servers running DHCP and Routing and Remote Access are important for the client computers that access the mission-critical Web-based application. Your management design must provide delayed response (or immediate response if the resources permit) to any failure or resource shortage on these servers that will affect DHCP or Routing and Remote Access.

Your management design must also included scheduled tests of the Network Load Balancing cluster. You must ensure, in the event of a server failure, that the remaining servers in the Network Load Balancing cluster are capable of supporting the remote users.

Selecting the Type of Response to Changes

After you determine how quickly to respond to changes in the networking services status, you must select the type of response (such as paging, e-mail, logging, or manual processes) to include for each failure or resource shortage. The type of response you include in your management design must correspond to how quickly you must respond to changes in the networking services.

Making the Decision

You must select the type of response for each failure or resource shortage based on how quickly your management design must respond to changes in the networking services status.

Table 14.1 lists the possible response times, some examples of the types of immediate responses, and why you would include those responses in your management design. Your management design can include any combination of these immediate response types.

Table 14.1   Types of Immediate Responses to Include in Your Management Design

Immediate Response Type	Include This Response Type When You Want To
Paging	Notify operations staff regardless of their location. Paging is ideal for after-hours notification of critical failures or resource shortages.
E-mail	Notify operations staff at e-mail accounts. E-mail notification can include pagers or cellular telephones that are e-mail–enabled. E-mail is one of the most flexible response types because of the number of e-mail–enabled devices.
Console notification	Notify operations staff when the staff utilizes a network management console, such as a Simple Network Management Protocol (SNMP) console. Console notification is appropriate when the organization has a management console that is continually monitored by operations staff.
Service restarting	Attempt to restart networking services to correct failures or resource shortages. Service restarting allows automatic response that attempts to correct the failed service.
Running application	Run an application to notify operations, restart applications, or perform complex business logic. Select this method when you need to respond in ways that existing applications or other tools are unable to fulfill. This method also provides you with the greatest flexibility in responding to failed services or resource shortages.

Table 14.1 *(continued)*

Immediate Response Type	Include This Response Type When You Want To
Log status changes	Record failed services or resource shortages in a log file that can be analyzed at a later time. Although not used to create an immediate response, your design must log the failure or resource shortages for trend analysis.

Table 14.2 lists the possible response times, some examples of the types of delayed responses, and why you would include those responses in your management design. Your management design can include any combination of these delayed response types.

Table 14.2   Types of Delayed Responses to Include in Your Management Design

Delayed Response Type	Include This Response Type When You Want To
E-mail	Depending on the length of time to deliver e-mail messages, you can include e-mail for delayed response types. The reasons for including e-mail are the same for immediate response types.
Console notification	Depending on the length of time between console updates, you can include console notification for delayed response types. The reasons for including console notification are the same for immediate response types.
Running application	Depending on the length of time to collect and analyze the networking service status, you can include running applications for delayed response types. The reasons for including running applications are the same for immediate response types.
Log status changes	The reasons for including log status changes are the same for immediate response types.

Table 14.3 lists the possible response times, some examples of the types of scheduled responses, and why you would include those responses in your management design. Your management design can include any combination of these scheduled response types.

Table 14.3   Types of Scheduled Responses to Include in Your Management Design

Scheduled Response Type	Include This Response Type When You Want To
Auditing	Many aspects of your design, such as security or availability, may not be verified by automated methods. Include auditing in your management design as a method to verify specifications of your networking services design that can't be analyzed by automated methods.
Log status changes	The reasons for including log status changes are the same for immediate and delayed response types.

Applying the Decision

Figure 14.9 illustrates how to select the type of responses to changes in the net-working services. For the purposes of this scenario, assume

- All users in the organization run a mission-critical Web-based application
- The organization must support local and remote users
- The mission-critical Web-based application runs on a group of servers that all belong to the same Network Load Balancing cluster
- The mission-critical Web-based application depends on the following net-working services:
  - DNS to provide name resolution
  - Routing and Remote Access to provide IP routing
- In addition to the networking services required by the mission-critical Web-based application, the networking services design includes
  - DHCP to provide IP configuration for local and remote client computers
  - Routing and Remote Access to provide remote user access
- The operations staff must be notified immediately of any failures or resource shortages for the networking services that support the mission-critical Web-based application
- The operations staff must be notified within 15 minutes of any failures or resource shortages for all other networking services
- The operations staff monitors a management console 24 hours per day, 7 days per week

The servers running DNS and providing IP routing are critical to the mission-critical Web-based application and require immediate responses to any failure or resource shortage. Because the operations staff monitors a management console at all times, you can use console notification. Paging, service restarting, applications, or e-mail notification are also possibilities. Log all the DNS and IP routing failures or resource shortages.

The servers running DHCP and Routing and Remote Access are important for the client computers that access the mission-critical Web-based application and require delayed responses (or immediate responses if the resources permit) to any failure or resource shortages. You can use console notification, service restarting, paging, running applications, or e-mail to respond to failures or resource shortages. Log all the DHCP and Routing and Remote Access routing failures or resource shortages.

Your management design must also include scheduled tests of the Network Load Balancing cluster. You can use auditing to ensure that the Network Load Balancing cluster performs correctly in the event of a server failure.

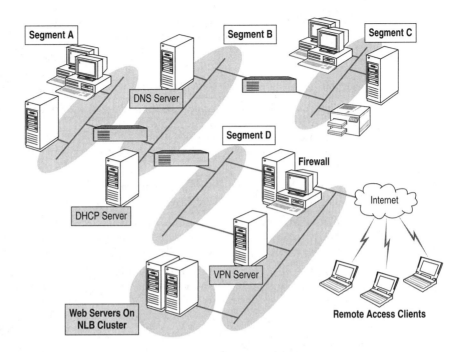

Figure 14.9   Scenario that illustrates how to select the type of responses to status changes

Selecting the Method of Responding to Changes

After you determine how quickly to respond to changes in the networking services status and the type of response, you must select the method (tools or procedures) that you will use to respond to the changes. You must also select a method of responding to changes in your management design that corresponds to how quickly you must respond to changes in the networking services.

Making the Decision

You must select the method for responding to each failure or resource shortage based on how quickly your management design must respond to changes in the networking services status. For example, if the business and technical requirements specify immediate response type (paging, e-mail, etc.) to a failure or resource shortage, the method you include in your design must be capable of providing immediate response of the specified type.

Table 14.4 lists some possible methods you can include in your management design, the types of responses the method can produce, and why you would include that method in your management design. Your management design can include any combination of these response methods.

Table 14.4   Possible Response Methods You Can Include in Your Management Design

Response Method	Provides	Include This Response Method When the Failures or Resource Shortages Are
Performance Logs and Alerts Microsoft Management Console (MMC) snap-in	Any of the immediate, delayed, or scheduled response types	Available as performance counters
Services MMC snap-in	Any of the immediate or delayed response types	Exhibited by causing services to fail
System Management Server (SMS)	Any of the immediate, delayed, or scheduled response types	Reported to SMS through hardware inventory, software inventory, or third-party software
Scripting or applications	Any of the immediate, delayed, or scheduled response types	Reported to Windows Management Instrumentation (WMI), Active Directory Service Interfaces (ADSI), or other Component Object Model (COM) objects
Manual processes or procedures	Any of the scheduled response types	Too complex for other methods or aren't reported to any other methods, but can be manually verified

The scripting and applications methods require programming expertise to create the appropriate responses. However, with scripting and applications methods, you can identify complex failures and critical application dependencies.

For example, an application depends on DNS for name resolution. In the networking services design, redundant DNS servers are installed to provide enhanced availability. By including a scripting or application method, you can identify that the failure of a single DNS server doesn't cause the application to fail, but rather can be issued as a critical warning (as opposed to an application offline situation).

The manual processes and procedures require the processes and procedures to be documented. At scheduled intervals, the operations staff must perform the processes and procedures to ensure that the network is functioning according to specifications.

For example, your design may require all traffic to be encrypted by using Triple Data Encryption Standard (3DES) encryption in Internet Protocol Security (IPSec). As a part of a comprehensive security audit, your management plan must include operations staff's manually examining network traffic (by using a protocol analyzer such as Network Monitor) to ensure that the appropriate traffic is being encrypted.

Applying the Decision

Figure 14.10 illustrates how to select the response method for changes in the networking services status. For the purposes of this scenario, assume

- All users in the organization run a mission-critical Web-based application
- The organization must support local and remote users
- The mission-critical Web-based application runs on a group of servers that all belong to the same Network Load Balancing cluster
- The mission-critical Web-based application depends on the following networking services:
  - DNS to provide name resolution
  - Routing and Remote Access to provide IP routing
- In addition to the networking services required by the mission-critical Web-based application, the networking services design includes
  - DHCP to provide IP configuration for local and remote client computers
  - Routing and Remote Access to provide remote user access

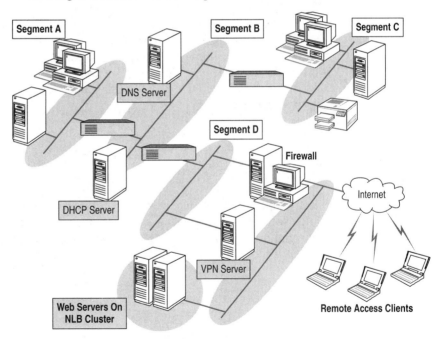

Figure 14.10   Scenario that illustrates how to select the response method for changes in the networking services status

- The operations staff must be notified immediately of any failures or resource shortages for the networking services that support the mission-critical Web-based application

- The operations staff must be notified within 15 minutes of any failures or resource shortages for all other networking services

- The operations staff monitors management consoles 24 hours per day, 7 days per week

- The operations staff is concerned about exhausting the DHCP-assigned IP addresses

The servers running DNS and providing IP routing are critical to the mission-critical Web-based application and require immediate responses to any failure or resource shortage. Because the operations staff monitors management consoles at all times, you can use the Performance Logs and Alerts MMC snap-in to generate alerts, page operations staff, or provide e-mail notification. In addition, you can use the Performance Logs and Alerts MMC snap-in to log all the DNS and IP routing failures or resource shortages.

The servers running DHCP and Routing and Remote Access are important for the client computers that access the mission-critical Web-based application and require delayed responses (or immediate responses if the resources permit) to any failure or resource shortages. You can use the Performance Logs and Alerts MMC snap-in to generate alerts, page operations staff, provide e-mail notification, and to log all the DHCP and Routing and Remote Access routing failures or resource shortages.

In addition, you can use scripting and WMI to periodically examine the number of available IP addresses in each DHCP scope and then notify the operations staff (by paging, sending an e-mail, or sending a management console notification) when the available IP addresses in a DHCP scope are almost exhausted.

Finally, you can use manual processes and procedures to perform scheduled tests of the Network Load Balancing cluster. You can use auditing to ensure that the Network Load Balancing cluster performs correctly in the event of a server failure.

Review

The following questions are intended to reinforce key information in this chapter. If you're unable to answer a question, review the lesson and then try to answer the question again. You can find answers to the questions in the Appendix, "Questions and Answers."

1. You're retained as a consultant to an organization to create the networking services portion of the organization's management design. The management design is in the early stages and you're attending a series of meetings to gather the organization's business and technical requirements and constraints. What type of information do you need to collect during the meetings?

2. An organization is evaluating its existing management design. The operations staff reports that many of the users are unable to access critical applications on a regular basis. The operations staff also reports that they aren't notified of any networking services failures until 30 minutes to an hour after the failure occurs. The organization wants to decrease the length of time between the time the failure occurs and the time the operations staff is notified. In the new management design, the operations staff wants to be immediately notified of any critical networking services failure. What recommendations can you make to these organizations?

3. You're creating a management design for an organization that runs a number of mission-critical applications. The mission-critical applications depend on the networking services within the organization. Some of the networking services that support these applications run on clusters and require high security to protect the applications. The organization's operations staff wants to ensure that they receive immediate responses to any critical networking services failures. What recommendations do you make in your networking services management design?

CHAPTER 15

Networking Services Design Optimization

About This Chapter

As discussed in previous chapters, the applications run by users in organizations ultimately determine the majority of the design decisions in your networking services design. The business and technical requirements of the organization assist in determining how the networking services can support the applications.

Many of the business and technical requirements affect the individual networking services. However, other business and technical requirements influence the networking services as a whole.

You must first evaluate the business and technical requirements that affect individual networking services to create your initial design. These requirements will assist you in determining the networking services that you must include in your design and the specifications for the networking services.

Then, you must evaluate the business and technical requirements that affect the networking services as a whole to optimize your design. These requirements will assist you in determining the

- Dependencies between applications running in the network and the networking services in your design

- Networking services you can combine to reduce the number of servers, and ultimately the total cost of ownership in your design

This chapter answers questions such as:

- How can you optimize your networking services design for applications?
- How can you optimize your networking services design to reduce the number of servers in your design?
- Which networking services can be combined on a single server?
- How can you improve the security, availability, or performance of your design by combining services onto a single server?
- How can you reduce the network traffic in your design?

Before You Begin

Before you begin, you must have an overall understanding of

- The integration of networking services, such as Domain Name System (DNS), Dynamic Host Configuration Protocol (DHCP), Windows Internet Naming Service (WINS), and Internet Authentication Service (IAS)
- Windows Clustering server cluster integration with networking services
- Network Load Balancing cluster integration with networking services

Lesson 1: Essential Networking Services Optimization

This lesson presents the design decisions you can make to optimize the essential portions of your networking design. This lesson discusses the essentials on how to optimize your design for applications and to reduce the number of servers.

After this lesson, you will be able to

- Optimize a networking services design for applications
- Optimize a networking services design to reduce the number of servers running networking services

Estimated lesson time: 14 minutes

Optimizing Designs for Applications

The most common goal in optimizing your networking services design is to optimize your networking services for the applications that must be supported by your design. Supporting the applications running in the organization is an *essential* part of your networking services design.

Making the Decision

To optimize the networking services in your network for applications, you must

- Identify the networking services required to support the application
- Select the optimal placement of servers running the networking services in relation to application servers
- Select the optimal specifications of the networking services

Identifying the Required Networking Services

Before you can optimize your networking services design for applications, you must determine the networking services required by the applications. For each application, you must identify the *dependencies* of the application on the networking services.

For example, consider an organization that runs Web-based applications. The Web-based applications require

- Transmission Control Protocol/Internet Protocol (TCP/IP) as the transport protocol
- IP routing to provide connectivity to other network segments
- Domain Name System (DNS) for name resolution

In addition, based on additional business and technical requirements, the Web-based applications might require

- Dial-up or virtual private network (VPN) remote access for users
- Vendor independent or outsourced user authentication by using Remote Authentication Dial-In User Service (RADIUS)
- Automatic IP configuration by using Dynamic Host Configuration Protocol (DHCP)
- Network Basic Input Output System (NetBIOS) name resolution by using Windows Internet Name Service (WINS) to support authentication of computers running Microsoft Windows 95, Microsoft Windows 98, or Microsoft Windows NT 4 operating systems

Selecting the Optimal Placement of Servers Running the Networking Services

After you have identified the networking services required by the applications, you must determine where to place the servers running the networking services. You determine the placement of the servers running the networking services in relation to the server and client computers running the applications.

Table 15.1 describes where to place the servers running the networking services in relation to the servers hosting the applications based on the requirements of the organization.

Selecting the Optimal Configuration of the Networking Services

After you have identified the networking services required to support the application and selected the optimal placement of the servers running the networking services, you must select the optimal configuration of the networking services.

The designs you create for each organization are based on the requirements and constraints (both business and technical) of the organization. Some of the organization's requirements and constraints that you identify will conflict with one another. In the instances where you're faced with conflicting requirements and constraints, you must work with the organization to prioritize the requirements and constraints.

For example, an organization requires that your design provide high security while providing high performance and a reduction in cost. Although possible in some scenarios, typically you can't create designs that provide higher security *and* higher performance at a *lower* cost.

To resolve conflicts in an organization's requirements and constraints, you must

- Determine the highest priority requirement of the organization
- Tailor your design to achieve the organization's highest priority requirement
- Prioritize all other organization requirements

- Incorporate the remaining requirements into your design without compromising a *higher* priority requirement

Table 15.1   How to Determine the Placement of the Servers Running the Networking Services

Place the Networking Services On	When The
The same server hosting the application. Example: Install DNS on an application server that performs a large number of DNS queries.	Security requirements of the organization allow the networking service to be installed on the server that hosts the application. System resources are capable of supporting the application and the networking service.
The same network segment as the server hosting the application. Example: An application server frequently queries Active Directory to authenticate users, however, the application server's system resources are unable to support the application and a domain controller.	Security requirements of the organization allow the networking service to be installed on the same network segment as the server that hosts the application. System resources of server hosting the application are unable to support the application and the networking service.
An adjacent network segment to the server hosting the application. Example: An application server in a screened subnet must authenticate users in Active Directory service, but the domain controller resides within the private network. The application server and the domain controller communicate through a VPN tunnel.	Security requirements of the organization require the networking service to be installed on a different network segment from the server that hosts the application. Other application servers on other network segments use the networking services, so the networking services are placed on a *centrally* located network segment (such as a backbone network segment).

Applying the Decision

Figure 15.1 illustrates a scenario prior to the optimization for applications. For the purposes of this scenario, assume that the organization

- Runs applications within the organization that depend on Distributed file system (Dfs) for proper operation
- Wants to perform automatic replication of Dfs by using File Replication Service (FRS), which requires Active Directory
- Requires that local and remote users must run the applications
- Includes desktop client computers running Windows 95, Windows 98, Microsoft Windows Me, Microsoft Windows NT 4 Workstation, and Microsoft Windows 2000 Professional

The networking services required for in the scenario include

- TCP/IP to support Active Directory, and Dfs
- TCP/IP routing to support TCP/IP
- DNS to support Active Directory and name resolution for network resources
- WINS to support NetBIOS name resolution for the desktop computer operating systems
- Routing and Remote Access to provide VPN remote access for remote users

To achieve the requirements and constraints of the organization, you must make the following changes to the design.

- Active Directory domain controllers are installed on Segments A, B, and C.
- DNS is installed on each domain controller.
- WINS server is installed on Segment B.
- VPN remote access server is installed between the Internet and Segment D.

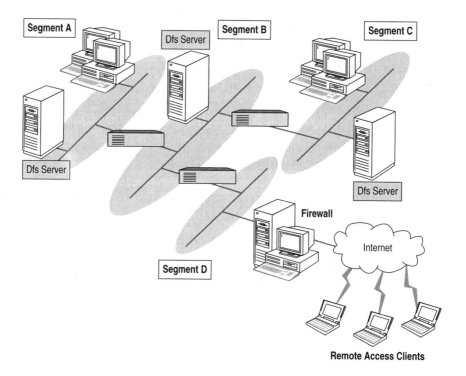

Figure 15.1   Scenario that illustrates a network prior to optimization for applications

Figure 15.2 illustrates a scenario after the optimization for applications.

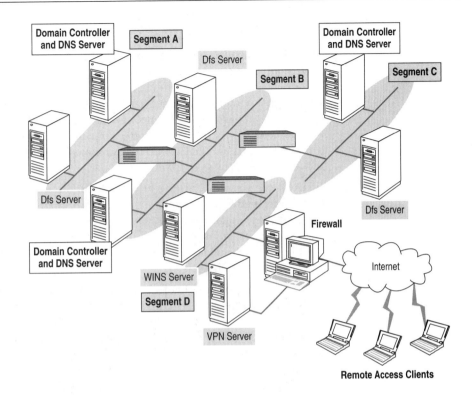

Figure 15.2 Scenario that illustrates a network after the optimization for
applications

Optimizing Designs to Reduce the Number of Servers

Another common goal in optimizing your networking services design is to
reduce the number of servers running networking services in your design. Typically, you reduce the number of servers in your design to reduce the *cost* associated with your design. Usually, organizations require you to create designs that
reduce the

- Initial cost of deploying the servers that run the networking services
- Long-term cost associated with managing and supporting the servers that run
  the networking services

Making the Decision

You can combine Microsoft Windows 2000 networking services on a server
because the networking services were designed to integrate with one another. As
a general rule, you can include any combination of networking services on a
computer.

You can combine Windows 2000 networking services on a server when the

- **Networking services utilize unique TCP or User Datagram Protocol (UDP) ports**   Each networking service you combine on a server must utilize a unique TCP or UDP port number. When networking services that utilize the same TCP or UDP port number (such as the DHCP Server service and the DHCP Relay Agent) are combined on the same server, both networking services attempt to receive traffic on the same port number. Because both networking services are contending for the same TCP or UDP port number, both networking services won't function properly.

- **Security requirements of the organization allow the networking services to be combined**   Before you combine networking services on a server, ensure that the combination of networking services supports the security requirements of the organization. For more information on combining networking services and security, see Lesson 2, "Data Protection and Optimization," later in this chapter.

- **Availability requirements of the organization allow the networking services to be combined**   As with security, before you combine networking services on a server, ensure that the combination of networking services supports the availability requirements of the organization. For more information on combining networking services and availability see Lesson 3, "Advanced Design Optimization," later in this chapter.

- **System resources are sufficient to support the combination of networking services**   Combining networking services on servers with sufficient system resources ensures that the performance of the networking services (and ultimately the response times of the applications) are optimized. For more information on combining networking services and performance, see Lesson 3, "Advanced Design Optimization," later in this chapter.

Applying the Decision

Figure 15.3 illustrates a scenario with a network prior to optimizing the design to reduce the number of servers. For the purposes of this scenario, assume

- The organization connects each location to the Internet through a firewall. (Note: Firewalls aren't shown in the diagram to reduce complexity of the diagram.)

- The organization connects locations to one another by using routers that communicate through the firewalls and across Internet. (Note: Routers aren't shown in the diagram to reduce the complexity of the diagram.)

- The organization has standardized on Active Directory as the directory service.

- The organization includes desktop client computers running Windows 95, Windows 98, Windows Me, Windows NT 4.0 Workstation, and Windows 2000 Professional.

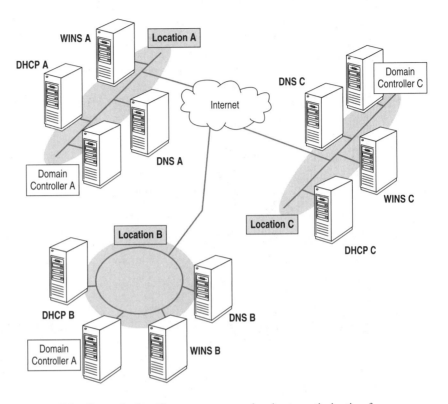

Figure 15.3   Scenario that illustrates a network prior to optimization for
reducing the number of servers

- WINS and DHCP services must be available for each location, regardless of
the failure of a single server.

Figure 15.4 illustrates a scenario after the optimization for reducing the number
of servers.

To achieve the requirements and constraints of the organization, you must make
the following changes to the design.

- **Active Directory domain controller and DNS are combined on one
server.**   Active Directory domain controllers perform a number of DNS queries in normal operation. Combining DNS on the Active Directory domain controller reduces the number of servers required and reduces the network traffic
(because DNS queries are resolved locally on the domain controller). Combining
networking services to reduce network traffic, and subsequently improve performance, is further discussed in Lesson 3, "Advanced Design Optimization,"
later in this chapter.

- **WINS and DHCP are combined on a Microsoft Windows Clustering server cluster.**   The combination of WINS and DHCP on a server cluster improves the availability and performance of the networking services design, *while maintaining the same number of servers*. Without server clusters, you must include *multiple* WINS and DHCP servers to provide improved performance and availability. Windows Clustering server clusters are discussed further in Lesson 3, "Advanced Design Optimization," later in this chapter.

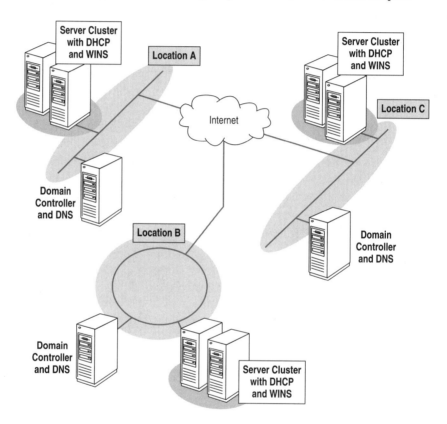

Figure 15.4   Scenario that illustrates a network after the optimization for reducing the number of servers

Lesson 2:   Data Protection and Optimization

This lesson discusses how you can optimize your design to improve the protection of confidential data and the networking service in your design. This lesson also discusses methods for improving protection of the servers running networking services within private networks, within screened subnets, or outside the private network.

After this lesson, you will be able to

- Identify the security requirements and constraints that affect the optimization of networking services
- Select the appropriate method for optimizing the security of networking services

Estimated lesson time: 15 minutes

Identifying the Security Requirements and Constraints

When you optimize your network for applications or to reduce the number of servers, you must consider the security requirements of the organization. Typically, the security requirements for servers within your private network are different from the security requirements for servers on screened subnets or completely outside the private network.

Making the Decision

In the networking services designs that you will optimize, you make your optimization decisions based on the types of users (or applications) accessing the server running the networking services. Your networking services design will include servers that are accessed by

- **Only authorized users**   Servers that are accessed by only authorized users typically exist within your private network. Usually the only security consideration is who can administer the server. You must ensure that the security requirements of the organization allow the same administrators (or network operators) to manage *all* the networking services running on the server.

- **Only unauthorized users**   Servers that are accessed by only unauthorized users typically exist within a screened subnet or outside your private network. These servers authenticate only administrators or network operators that manage the networking services running on the server. All other user access to these servers is unauthorized. You must ensure that the security requirements of the organization allow *all* the networking services running on the server to be utilized by unauthorized users.

- **A combination of authorized and unauthorized users**   Servers that are accessed by a combination of authorized and unauthorized users typically exist within a screened subnet and rarely outside your private network. As with servers that are accessed by only unauthorized users, you must ensure that the security requirements of the organization allow *all* the networking services running on the server to be utilized by unauthorized users.

Applying the Decision

Figure 15.5 illustrates how to determine how to identify the security requirements of your networking services design. For the purposes of this scenario, assume

- All users in the organization run a mission-critical Web-based application
- The organization must support local and remote users.
- The mission-critical Web-based application depends on
  - DNS to provide name resolution
  - Routing and Remote Access to provide IP routing
  - Internet Authentication Service (IAS) to provide authentication and accounting for the remote users
- Internet users aren't able to access any internal servers running the networking services (such as the DHCP server and Active Directory domain controllers)

To achieve the security requirements of the organization, the following configurations are appropriate.

- **The DNS server and remote access server on Segment D have the same security requirements.**   Internet users and private network users (accessing the network remotely) both must be able to access the DNS server and remote access server.

- **The server running DNS and IAS has the same security requirements as the DHCP server and the domain controllers.**   Only authorized users are allowed access to these networking services. However, IAS will receive authentication and accounting traffic from the remote access server (on Segment D).

- **Private network and Internet users access the servers running DNS and remote access.**   As a result, no confidential data can be stored on these servers. In addition, the namespace managed by the DNS servers must contain resource records that are accessed by Internet users. Because the DNS server and remote access server (on Segment D) have the same security requirements, you can combine DNS and routing and remote access on the same computer.

- **IAS and DNS (on Segment B) have the same security requirements.**   Because the security requirements for both networking services are the same, you can combine IAS and DNS on the same server.

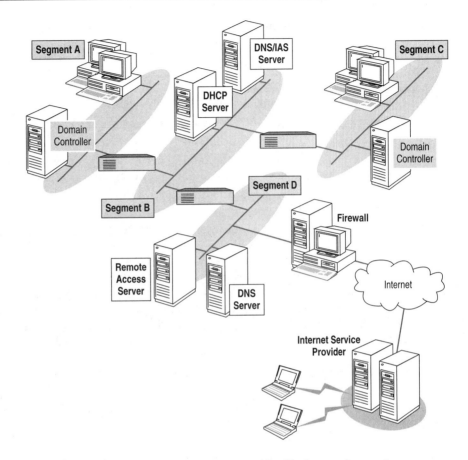

Figure 15.5   Scenario that illustrates how to identify the security requirements
of your networking services design

Selecting the Method of Security Optimization

After you have determined the security requirements of the organization, you
must select the appropriate method of security optimization. The method you
select must improve the security of the individual networking services without
compromising the security requirements of the organization.

Making the Decision

You can optimize the security of your networking services design by

- **Locating networking services on the same network segment (or on the
  same server) as the servers hosting the applications**   Applications might
  require the exchange of confidential information between the server hosting
  the application and networking services. You can improve the security by
  reducing (or eliminating) the number of network segments over which the
  confidential data must be transmitted.

- **Combining networking services onto a single server**   You can combine networking services onto a single server when
  - The security requirements of networking services are identical
  - The resources of the server are sufficient to support the networking services that are being combined on the server
- **Isolating the networking services onto separate servers**   Isolate the networking services onto separate server when
  - **The users accessing the networking services are different security levels**   You must isolate networking services that are utilized by users at one security level from networking services that are utilized by users at other security
  - **The networking services aren't used as firewalls, proxy servers, or secured routers**   You must isolate networking services, such as firewalls, proxy servers, Network Address Translation (NAT) servers, routers, or other devices that are used to create screened subnets, demilitarized zone (DMZ), or perimeter networks. By definition, the networking services that create screened subnets are at risk from a security perspective. Only combine networking services on servers that create screened subnets when the networking services are the same security risk.

Applying the Decision

Figure 15.6 illustrates the methods of optimizing the security of a networking services design. For the purposes of this scenario, assume

- All users in the organization run a mission-critical Web-based application
- The organization must support local and remote users
- The mission-critical Web-based application depends on the following networking services:
  - DNS to provide name resolution
  - Routing and Remote Access to provide IP routing
  - IAS to provide authentication and accounting for the remote users
- Internet users aren't able to access any internal servers running the networking services (such as the DHCP server and Active Directory domain controllers)

The DNS server and remote access server on Segment D must be isolated on separate servers because the remote access server is creating a virtual screened subnet.

In this scenario, DNS and IAS have the same security requirements. You can combine DNS and IAS on the same server. However, the remote access server on Segment D must communicate with the IAS server on Segment B. Establish a VPN tunnel between the remote access server and the IAS server.

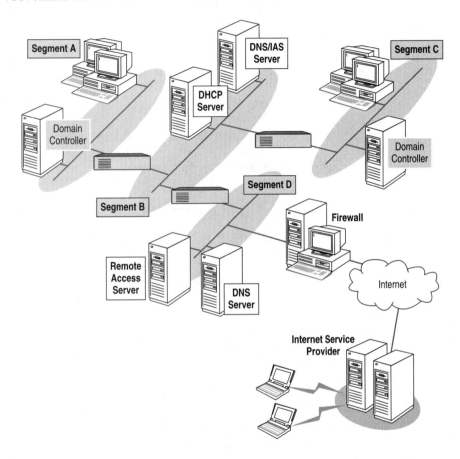

Figure 15.6   Scenario to illustrate the methods of optimizing the security of a networking services design

Lesson 3: Advanced Design Optimization

This lesson focuses on the advanced optimization techniques you can include in your networking service design. This lesson discusses methods for improving the availability and performance of the networking services running in your design.

After this lesson, you will be able to

- Include Microsoft Windows Clustering to improve the availability and performance of networking services
- Optimize the Windows 2000 configuration to improve the availability and performance of networking services
- Optimize the networking services design to reduce network traffic

Estimated lesson time: 15 minutes

Including Windows Clustering

When you optimize your network for applications or to reduce the number of servers, you must consider the availability and performance requirements of the organization. You can include Windows Clustering in your networking services design to improve the availability and performance for the networking services.

Making the Decision

All Windows Clustering solutions require two or more computers to provide fault tolerance and load balancing within the cluster. After you make the financial investment in Windows Clustering solutions, you can combine networking services on the clusters to

- Take advantage of the increased fault tolerance and load balancing
- Amortize the cost associated with the Windows Clustering solution across multiple networking services

With Windows Clustering, you can create two types of clusters—*Network Load Balancing clusters* and *server clusters*. You must determine which Windows Clustering solution is the most appropriate for the organization's business and technical requirements.

Network Load Balancing Clusters

You can create highly available and scalable solutions by combining two or more servers running Windows 2000 to form a Network Load Balancing cluster. Network Load Balancing clusters provide load balancing and fault tolerance with all servers in the cluster. The servers in the Network Load Balancing clusters share no resources other than a common IP address assigned to the cluster.

Include Network Load Balancing clusters in your design to provide

- **An alternative to round robin DNS solutions** You can substitute Network Load Balancing as an alternative to round robin DNS solutions. Table 15.2 compares the advantages and disadvantages of Network Load Balancing clusters and round robin DNS solutions.

Table 15.2   Comparison of Network Load Balancing Clusters and Round Robin DNS Solutions

Method	Advantages	Disadvantages
Network Load Balancing clusters	Dynamically provides load balancingacross all the servers in the Network Load Balancing cluster. Allows dynamic addition or removal of servers in the Network Load Balancing in the cluster Automatically reconfigures cluster in the event a server fails. Improves availability and performance because the load balancing is dynamic and the addition or removal of servers is dynamic	Requires extra processor and memory resources to run the service. Doesn't work with servers running on other operating systems, such as UNIX or Macintosh computers
Round robin DNS	Works on all operating system platforms Statically provides load balancing across all the servers listed in DNS Improves performance for private network access by load balancing network traffic across multiple servers.	Doesn't automatically remove failed servers, so client computers might experience time-out or other error messages.Servers must be manuallyadded or removed from the DNS entries. Doesn't improve the availability of the solution.

- **Application independent load balancing and fault tolerance** The load balancing and fault tolerance provided by Network Load Balancing clusters are transparent to the applications they support. After you have determined that the application is compatible with Network Load Balancing clusters, you can add and remove servers from the cluster as required without modification to the application.

- **Solutions that can utilize the "*share nothing*" clustering model** *Cluster nodes* (servers in the same Network Load Balancing cluster) in Network Load Balancing clusters follow the share nothing model Clusters that utilize the share nothing model have no physical resources that are *shared* between any of the cluster nodes (however, all cluster nodes share the same *logical* or *virtual* IP address assigned to the cluster).

Because Network Load Balancing cluster nodes share no common physical resources, no single point of failure can make the cluster inoperative. However, the share nothing clustering model requires that the same applications and data be replicated across all cluster nodes to provide fault tolerance and load balancing.

Server Clusters

You can create highly available and scalable solutions by combining two or more servers running Windows 2000 to form a server cluster. Server clusters provide fault tolerance with other servers in the cluster. The cluster nodes (servers) in the server cluster share common disk resources with the other cluster nodes.

To provide fault tolerance with server clusters, you must

- Install the corresponding networking service on two (or more) cluster nodes
- Designate one of the cluster nodes as the active node for the networking service

As one of the cluster nodes that is the active node for the networking service fails, the remaining cluster node starts the networking service. The configuration and any other pertinent networking services data (such as DHCP or WINS databases) are stored on the cluster's common disk resource.

Some networking services (such as DHCP and WINS) are *cluster-aware* networking services. Cluster-aware networking services make calls to the server cluster Application Programming Interfaces (APIs) to inform the cluster of the status of the networking service.

Networking services that are *cluster unaware* (such as DNS) can utilize server clusters by storing their configuration information on the cluster's common disk resource. If a cluster node fails, the remaining cluster node starts the cluster-unaware networking service.

Note   Cluster-aware networking services are designed to detect as many networking services failures as possible. Cluster-unaware networking services can fail in a manner that the cluster can't detect.

For more information on using server clusters for specific networking services, see the corresponding chapter in this book (for example, for DHCP and server clusters, see Chapter 8, "DHCP in IP Configuration Designs," Lesson 4, "DHCP Design Optimization").

To provide fault tolerance and load balancing with server clusters, you must

- Install multiple networking services, such as DHCP and WINS, on two (or more) cluster nodes

- Evenly distribute the load of the networking services across the cluster by designating different cluster nodes as the active node for the networking service

Figure 15.7 illustrates how to improve availability and performance with Windows Clustering solutions.

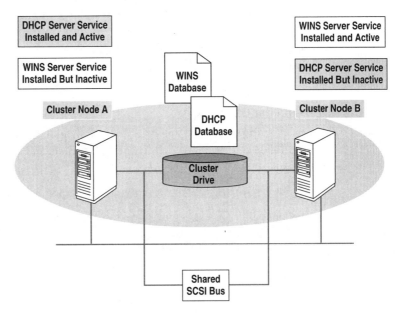

Figure 15.7   Scenario that illustrates how to improve availability and performance with Windows Clustering solutions

To provide the fault tolerance *and load balancing* for DHCP and WINS on a server cluster with two cluster nodes, you can

- Install DHCP and WINS on both cluster nodes
- Designate one cluster node as the active node for DHCP
- Designate the other cluster node as the active node for WINS

Because different cluster nodes are the active nodes for DHCP and WINS, you aren't forcing all the DHCP and WINS traffic to only one node in the cluster.

Include server clusters in your design to provide

- **Automatic fail over for networking services**   Many networking services have specific methods of providing fault tolerance (such as multiple DNS servers with primary and secondary zones or multiple WINS servers with replication). However, the methods that are specific to the networking service don't provide automatic failover in the event of a failure.

If a cluster node fails, the remaining cluster nodes automatically start the appropriate networking services.

■ **Minimal recovery time to restore a failed server**   For many of the networking services, a significant period of time might be required to recover a failed server. For example, if a WINS server fails, the replacement WINS server might take hours for the new WINS server's database to synchronize with the remaining WINS servers.

Because the networking services data is stored on the server cluster's common drive, the networking services data is current. When you replace the failed cluster node, no synchronization or restoration time is required.

Applying the Decision

Figure 15.8 illustrates a design prior to optimization by using Windows Clustering to provide improved availability and performance. For the purposes of this scenario, assume

■ All users in the organization run a mission-critical Web-based application

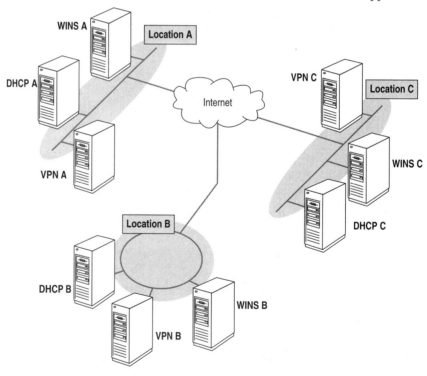

Figure 15.8   Scenario that illustrates a design prior to optimization by using Windows Clustering

- The organization must support local and remote users
- The organization's mission-critical applications depend on the following networking services:
  - WINS to provide NetBIOS name resolution
  - Routing and Remote Access to provide VPN remote access
  - DHCP to provide authentication and accounting for the remote users
- Internet users aren't able to access any internal servers running the networking services (such as the DHCP servers or WINS servers)
- Private network users must be able to access networking services regardless of the failure of a single server

Figure 15.9 illustrates a design after optimization by using Windows Clustering to provide improved availability and performance.

The VPN servers within each location belong to the same Network Load Balancing cluster. The combination of the VPN servers and Network Load Balancing clustering provide fault tolerance and load balancing. If a VPN server fails, the remaining VPN server continues to provide remote access. Because the remote access traffic is distributed across all VPN servers in the Network Load Balancing cluster, overall design performance is improved.

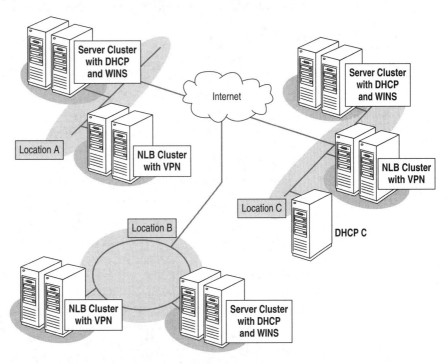

Figure 15.9   Scenario that illustrates a design after optimization by using Windows Clustering

The DHCP and WINS servers within each location run on server clusters. The DHCP Server service and WINS Server service are installed on both cluster nodes. The DHCP Server service is active on one of the cluster nodes. The WINS Server service is active on the other cluster node.

If one of the cluster nodes fails, the remaining cluster node continues to run both the DHCP Server service and the WINS Server service. The overall performance for WINS and DHCP is improved because each networking service is running on a cluster node dedicated to the networking service.

Optimizing the Windows 2000 Configuration

In addition to Windows clustering technologies, you can improve availability and performance by optimizing the configuration of Windows 2000. You can create servers that are reliable and have ample system resources by making the appropriate hardware decisions. In many instances, upgrading existing hardware or deploying new servers provides an improvement in availability and performance at less cost than monitoring, analyzing, and optimizing the design.

However, *even with optimal hardware*, the configuration of Windows 2000 affects the availability and performance of your networking services design. You must make the appropriate decisions regarding the configuration of Windows 2000 to ensure high availability and application response times in your design.

Making the Decision

In the networking services designs that you optimize, you must ensure that the configuration of Windows 2000 supports the availability and performance requirements of the organization.

To provide high availability and to improve performance, the servers that run the networking services in your design must

- Include only signed device drivers
- Run only reliable services or applications
- Run only the required services or applications
- Avoid running combinations of networking services that contend for limited resources

Signed Device Drivers

Windows 2000 device drivers run as an extension of the Windows 2000 operating system. A failure of a device driver can significantly impact the functions available to a computer running Windows 2000. For example, if a disk controller driver fails, the disks connected to the controller become unavailable. In more extreme examples, a device driver failure can make the entire operating system unstable.

You can improve the reliability of Windows 2000 by installing only *signed* device drivers. Signed device drivers are extensively tested and then certified by Microsoft to ensure that Windows 2000 runs reliably and requires no system restarts.

You can ensure the reliability of Windows 2000 by

- Including only signed device drivers on servers that require high availability
- Specifying Local Policies on the servers that require only signed device drivers or other software components

Reliable Services and Applications

In most of the designs you create, you must include software components (device drivers, services, and applications) that are developed by third-party vendors. The majority of these software components aren't signed or certified by Microsoft.

As part of your design, you must

1. Identify the uncertified software components required by the organization
2. Verify that these software components don't adversely affect the proper operation of Windows 2000
3. Ensure that the software components are tested and verified by the organization before you include them on any mission-critical server

Required Services and Applications

You can improve performance of your design by specifying only the required services and applications on servers that are resource constrained.

To ensure that the networking services in your design achieve optimal performance, you can:

- Dedicate a computer to running the networking service
- Segregate client server applications on servers other than the servers running the networking services
- Upgrade or replace existing hardware to support the networking services and the applications

Networking Services that Contend for Limited Resources

Many of the networking services you include in your design contend for the same type of resources (such as DHCP and WINS that contend for disk access). When your design includes networking services that contend for the same type of resources, you must ensure that the networking services don't affect the performance of one another.

You can improve the performance of networking services in your design by

- Segregating networking services that contend for the same limited resources You can specify that the networking services be segregated onto separate servers that have limited resources. In many instances, you can utilize existing or less expensive hardware.

- Combining networking services on servers that have an abundance of the resources required by the networking services You can specify enhanced hardware configuration, such as server clusters or Redundant Array of Inexpensive Disks (RAID) arrays, in your design. You can combine networking services that utilize the resources provided by the enhanced hardware.

Making the Decision

Figure 15.10 illustrates a design prior to the optimization of Windows 2000 for improved availability and performance. For the purposes of this scenario, assume

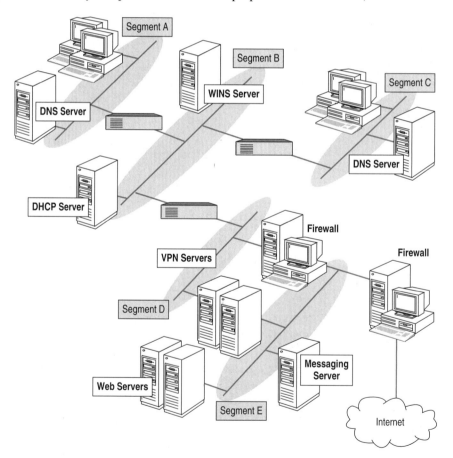

Figure 15.10   Scenario that illustrates a design prior to the optimization of Windows 2000

- All users in the organization run a mission-critical Web-based application
- The organization must support local and remote users
- Messaging server runs a third-party messaging application
- DNS servers on Segments A and C have disk controller device drivers that are unsigned
- WINS and DHCP servers require high-performance disk access to provide the appropriate performance

Figure 15.11 illustrates the scenario presented in Figure 15.10 after the optimization of Windows 2000. Make the following changes to the network design to improve the performance and availability of Windows 2000.

- No mission-critical networking services are run on the messaging server.

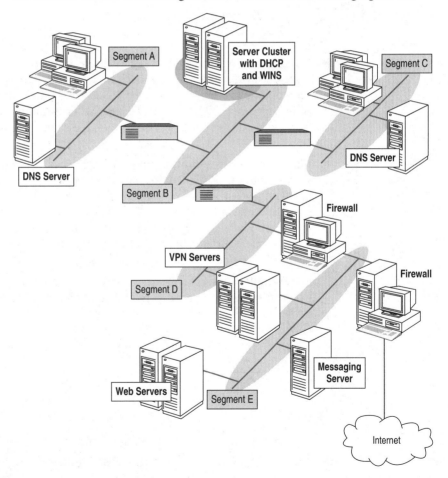

Figure 15.11   Scenario that illustrates a design after the optimization of Windows 2000

- Disk controller drivers on the DNS servers are updated with signed device drivers.
- WINS and DHCP servers are combined on a server cluster.

Optimizing to Reduce Network Traffic

In addition to Windows clustering technologies and Windows 2000 optimization, you can optimize your design to reduce network traffic. By reducing network traffic, you improve the performance by

- Reducing network utilization
- Preventing router saturation
- Reducing or eliminating time-outs due to slow response times

Making the Decision

To eliminate network traffic in your networking services design, you can

- **Combine networking services that interact with one another onto the same computer**   When your design includes networking services that interact with one another, such as DHCP and DNS with a dynamically updated zone, you can combine the networking services on the same computer. Because the networking services are on the same computer, no network traffic is generated.

- **Place the servers running the networking services on the appropriate network segments**   In many instances, the networking services can't be combined on the same computer because of security, system resource constraints, or constraints. When you can't combine the networking services on the same computer, place the servers running the networking services on the same network segment, or an adjacent network segment, as the applications or services that utilize the networking services.

  For example, consider a situation where an application server, such as Microsoft Exchange, makes frequent DNS queries. By placing a DNS server on the same network segment as the Microsoft Exchange server, you limit the network traffic between the Microsoft Exchange server and the DNS server to the local network segment.

Making the Decision

Figure 15.12 illustrates a design prior to the optimization of networking for improved performance. For the purposes of this scenario, assume

- All the users in the organization run a mission-critical Web-based application.
- The organization must support local and remote users.

- The DNS servers on Segments A, B, and C support the Active Directory domain controllers on each respective subnet.
- The server cluster on Segment B provides WINS and DHCP services for the organization.
- The Routing and Remote Access server on Segment B connects all private network segments to one another and to the Internet.
- The RADIUS server on Segment B provides authentication for the Routing and Remote Access server.
- The RADIUS server utilizes Active Directory to authenticate remote users.

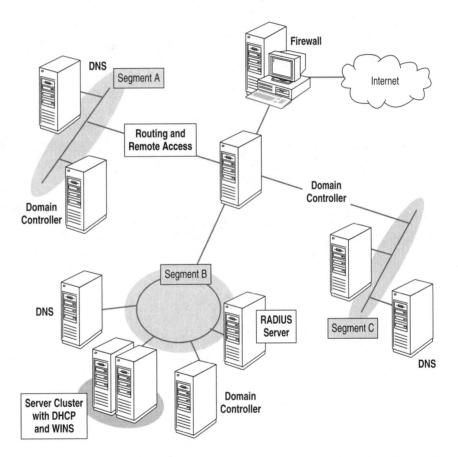

Figure 15.12   Scenario that illustrates a design prior to the optimization of network traffic

Figure 15.13 illustrates the scenario presented in Figure 15.12 after the optimization of the design to reduce network traffic. Make the following changes to the network design to reduce network traffic:

- Combine DNS and Active Directory domain controllers onto the same computer for each respective network segment.
- Combine RADIUS server, DNS, and Active Directory domain controller onto the same computer as DNS (RADIUS server utilizes Active Directory for user authentication).

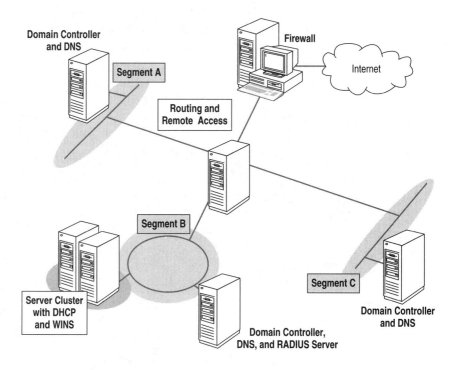

Figure 15.13   Scenario that illustrates a design after the optimization of network traffic

Lab: Creating an Optimized Networking Services Design

After this lab, you will be able to
- Evaluate a scenario and determine the design requirements
- Create and optimize a networking services design based on the design requirements

Estimated lab time: 45 minutes

In this lab, you're the director of information services for a domestic extended stay hotel chain with 15 locations throughout the United States. You're responsible for the creation and optimization of the networking services design for the chain.

To complete this lab:

1. Examine the networking environment presented in the scenario, the network diagrams, the business requirements and constraints, and the technical requirements and constraints

2. Use the worksheet(s) for each location to assist you in creating your networking services design (you can find completed sample design worksheets on the Supplemental Course Materials CD-ROM in the Completed Worksheets folder)

Note   The worksheets for each location include space to record your specification for up to eight servers. For designs that contain fewer than eight servers, leave the remaining worksheets blank. For designs containing more than eight servers, document the additional servers on additional sheets of paper.

---

3. Create, eliminate, or replace existing networking devices and network segments when required

4. Ensure that your design fulfills the business requirements and constraints and technical requirements and constraints of the scenario by

- Identifying the network devices, if any, replaced by the server (such as a Proxy Server replacing a router)

- Assigning the server's network interfaces to the appropriate network segments

- Specifying the appropriate networking services for each server

- Including the server in a Windows Clustering server cluster (when appropriate)

- Including the server in a Windows Clustering Network Load Balancing cluster (when appropriate)

Scenario

A chain of suite hotels (shown in Figure 15.14) that caters to extended stay business travelers owns 60 hotels located in 15 cities throughout the United States. The headquarters for the hotel chain (shown in Figure 15.15), is located in the hotel property in Atlanta. The hotel chain provides full business services to each guest's suite, including fax machines, photocopiers, and fax modem telephone connections.

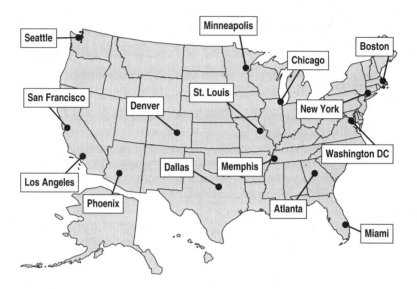

Figure 15.14   Map of the locations in the hotel chain

Each hotel location (shown in Figure 15.16) is managed as a separate business unit, but currently ships monthly financial information to the headquarters in Atlanta. The hotel chain has purchased a hotel reservation and accounting system that will allow each location to upload financial and room availability to headquarters. The newly purchased software is a Web-based application that will run on Web and database servers hosted by an Application Service Provider (ASP).

Figure 15.14 is a map of the locations where the hotel chain has locations. Currently, the hotel chain is installing T3 connections to the Internet at each location. The guest services personnel at each hotel will access the Web-based reservation and accounting system through the T3 connection. In addition, the hotel chain wants to provide high-speed Internet access to the hotel's guests.

Business Requirements and Constraints

The hotel chain has a number of requirements and constraints that are based on the business model of the hotel chain. As you create and optimize your networking services design, ensure that your design meets the business requirements and stays within the business constraints.

To achieve the business requirements and constraints, your design must

- Prevent hotel guests and Internet users from accessing the hotel chain's private networks

- Prevent Internet users from accessing the hotel guest's computers

- Prevent guest services representatives at the front desk from accessing any Web site other than the Web-based reservation and accounting system

- Ensure that connectivity between each hotel and the Internet is available 24 hours a day, 7 days a week

- Reduce the cost associated with the initial deployment and ongoing maintenance of the computers that run the networking services

Technical Requirements and Constraints

The existing physical network, hardware, and operating systems will place certain technical requirements and constraints on your design. As you create and optimize your networking services design, ensure that your design meets the technical requirements and stays within the technical constraints.

In addition, the Web-based application that is managed by the ASP requires connectivity with each hotel and with the Internet. These Web-based reservation and accounting applications are accessed on the computers used by the guest services representatives and by Internet users that want to make reservations.

To achieve the technical requirements and constraints, your design must

- Support Active Directory for only the guest services representatives, hotel guests, and Internet users who aren't authenticated

- Isolate the network segments that are designated for use by the guest services representatives from the Internet and the network segments designated for use by the hotel guests

- Support the private IP addressing scheme, 172.16.0.0/12, assigned within each hotel

- Utilize the assigned public IP addressing scheme, 10.133.25.0/24, allocated from an Internet registry

---

Note Although 10.133.25.0/24 is a private IP address range, assume the IP address range is a public IP address range for the purposes of this lab.

- Integrate with any existing IP routed network segments

- Utilize the existing IP routers that support DHCP forwarding

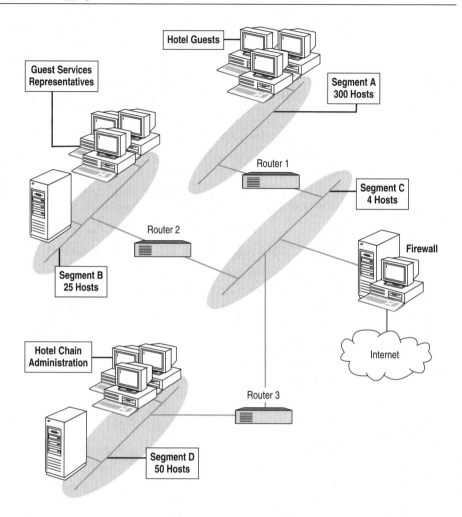

Figure 15.15   This is the existing network at the hotel chain headquarters in Atlanta.

Design Worksheet – Figure 15.15
Hotel Chain Headquarters – Server A

Server Specifications	Comments
❑ Replace existing device Device name: _____	
Connect server to the following network segments.	
❑ Network interface A connects to segment: _____	
❑ Network interface B connects to segment: _____	
Networking services to include	
❑ DHCP ❑ Routing and Remote Access	
❑ WINS ❑ Routing	
❑ DNS ❑ Remote Access	
❑ IAS ❑ NAT	
❑ Proxy Server 2.0	
Windows Clustering options	
❑ Install on server cluster node. Cluster name: _____	
❑ Install on NLB cluster node. Cluster name: _____	

Design Worksheet – Figure 15.15
Hotel Chain Headquarters – Server B

Server Specifications	Comments
❑ Replace existing device Device name: _____	
Connect server to the following network segments.	
❑ Network interface A connects to segment: _____	
❑ Network interface B connects to segment: _____	
Networking services to include	
❑ DHCP ❑ Routing and Remote Access	
❑ WINS ❑ Routing	
❑ DNS ❑ Remote Access	
❑ IAS ❑ NAT	
❑ Proxy Server 2.0	
Windows Clustering options	
❑ Install on server cluster node. Cluster name: _____	
❑ Install on NLB cluster node. Cluster name: _____	

Design Worksheet – Figure 15.15
Hotel Chain Headquarters – Server C

Server Specifications	Comments
❑ Replace existing device Device name: _____	
Connect server to the following network segments.	
❑ Network interface A connects to segment: _____	
❑ Network interface B connects to segment: _____	
Networking services to include	
❑ DHCP ❑ Routing and Remote Access ❑ WINS ❑ Routing ❑ DNS ❑ Remote Access ❑ IAS ❑ NAT ❑ Proxy Server 2.0	
Windows Clustering options	
❑ Install on server cluster node. Cluster name: _____ ❑ Install on NLB cluster node. Cluster name: _____	

Design Worksheet – Figure 15.15
Hotel Chain Headquarters – Server D

Server Specifications	Comments
❑ Replace existing device Device name: _____	
Connect server to the following network segments.	
❑ Network interface A connects to segment: _____	
❑ Network interface B connects to segment: _____	
Networking services to include	
❑ DHCP ❑ Routing and Remote Access	
❑ WINS ❑ Routing	
❑ DNS ❑ Remote Access	
❑ IAS ❑ NAT	
❑ Proxy Server 2.0	
Windows Clustering options	
❑ Install on server cluster node. Cluster name: _____	
❑ Install on NLB cluster node. Cluster name: _____	

Design Worksheet – Figure 15.15
Hotel Chain Headquarters – Server E

Server Specifications	Comments
❏ Replace existing device Device name: _____	
Connect server to the following network segments.	
❏ Network interface A connects to segment: _____	
❏ Network interface B connects to segment: _____	
Networking services to include	
❏ DHCP ❏ Routing and Remote Access	
❏ WINS ❏ Routing	
❏ DNS ❏ Remote Access	
❏ IAS ❏ NAT	
❏ Proxy Server 2.0	
Windows Clustering options	
❏ Install on server cluster node. Cluster name: _____	
❏ Install on NLB cluster node. Cluster name: _____	

Design Worksheet – Figure 15.15
Hotel Chain Headquarters – Server F

Server Specifications	Comments
❑ Replace existing device Device name: _____	
Connect server to the following network segments.	
❑ Network interface A connects to segment: _____	
❑ Network interface B connects to segment: _____	
Networking services to include	
❑ DHCP ❑ Routing and Remote Access ❑ WINS ❑ Routing ❑ DNS ❑ Remote Access ❑ IAS ❑ NAT ❑ Proxy Server 2.0	
Windows Clustering options	
❑ Install on server cluster node. Cluster name: _____	
❑ Install on NLB cluster node. Cluster name: _____	

Design Worksheet – Figure 15.15
Hotel Chain Headquarters – Server G

Server Specifications	Comments
☐ Replace existing device Device name: _____	
Connect server to the following network segments.	
☐ Network interface A connects to segment: _____	
☐ Network interface B connects to segment: _____	
Networking services to include	
☐ DHCP ☐ Routing and Remote Access	
☐ WINS ☐ Routing	
☐ DNS ☐ Remote Access	
☐ IAS ☐ NAT	
☐ Proxy Server 2.0	
Windows Clustering options	
☐ Install on server cluster node. Cluster name: _____	
☐ Install on NLB cluster node. Cluster name: _____	

Design Worksheet – Figure 15.15
Hotel Chain Headquarters – Server H

Server Specifications	Comments
❑ Replace existing device Device name: _____	
Connect server to the following network segments.	
❑ Network interface A connects to segment: _____	
❑ Network interface B connects to segment: _____	
Networking services to include	
❑ DHCP ❑ Routing and Remote Access	
❑ WINS ❑ Routing	
❑ DNS ❑ Remote Access	
❑ IAS ❑ NAT	
❑ Proxy Server 2.0	
Windows Clustering options	
❑ Install on server cluster node. Cluster name: _____	
❑ Install on NLB cluster node. Cluster name: _____	

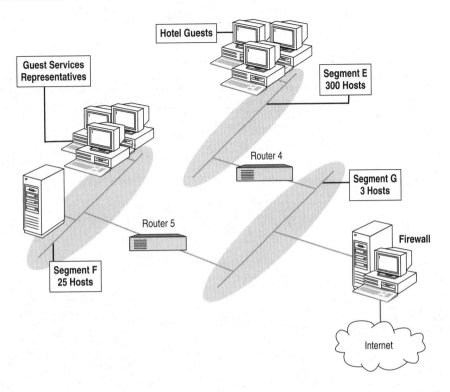

Figure 15.16   This is the existing network at one of the hotels. For the purposes of this lab, assume that the hotels have the same network configuration.

Design Worksheet – Figure 15.16
Hotel Property – Server A

Server Specifications	Comments
❏ Replace existing device Device name: _____	
Connect server to the following network segments.	
❏ Network interface A connects to segment: _____	
❏ Network interface B connects to segment: _____	
Networking services to include	
❏ DHCP ❏ Routing and Remote Access ❏ WINS ❏ Routing ❏ DNS ❏ Remote Access ❏ IAS ❏ NAT ❏ Proxy Server 2.0	
Windows Clustering options	
❏ Install on server cluster node. Cluster name: _____ ❏ Install on NLB cluster node. Cluster name: _____	

Design Worksheet – Figure 15.16
Hotel Property – Server B

Server Specifications	Comments
❑ Replace existing device Device name: _____	
Connect server to the following network segments.	
❑ Network interface A connects to segment: _____	
❑ Network interface B connects to segment: _____	
Networking services to include	
❑ DHCP ❑ Routing and Remote Access ❑ WINS ❑ Routing ❑ DNS ❑ Remote Access ❑ IAS ❑ NAT ❑ Proxy Server 2.0	
Windows Clustering options	
❑ Install on server cluster node. Cluster name: _____ ❑ Install on NLB cluster node. Cluster name: _____	

Design Worksheet – Figure 15.16
Hotel Property – Server C

Server Specifications	Comments
❑ Replace existing device Device name: _____	
Connect server to the following network segments.	
❑ Network interface A connects to segment: _____	
❑ Network interface B connects to segment: _____	
Networking services to include	
❑ DHCP ❑ Routing and Remote Access	
❑ WINS ❑ Routing	
❑ DNS ❑ Remote Access	
❑ IAS ❑ NAT	
❑ Proxy Server 2.0	
Windows Clustering options	
❑ Install on server cluster node. Cluster name: _____	
❑ Install on NLB cluster node. Cluster name: _____	

Design Worksheet – Figure 15.16
Hotel Property – Server D

Server Specifications	Comments
❏ Replace existing device Device name: _____	
Connect server to the following network segments.	
❏ Network interface A connects to segment: _____	
❏ Network interface B connects to segment: _____	
Networking services to include	
❏ DHCP ❏ Routing and Remote Access ❏ WINS ❏ Routing ❏ DNS ❏ Remote Access ❏ IAS ❏ NAT ❏ Proxy Server 2.0	
Windows Clustering options	
❏ Install on server cluster node. Cluster name: _____ ❏ Install on NLB cluster node. Cluster name: _____	

Design Worksheet – Figure 15.16
Hotel Property – Server E

Server Specifications	Comments
❏ Replace existing device Device name: _____	
Connect server to the following network segments.	
❏ Network interface A connects to segment: _____	
❏ Network interface B connects to segment: _____	
Networking services to include	
❏ DHCP ❏ Routing and Remote Access	
❏ WINS ❏ Routing	
❏ DNS ❏ Remote Access	
❏ IAS ❏ NAT	
❏ Proxy Server 2.0	
Windows Clustering options	
❏ Install on server cluster node. Cluster name: _____	
❏ Install on NLB cluster node. Cluster name: _____	

Design Worksheet – Figure 15.16
Hotel Property – Server F

Server Specifications	Comments
❏ Replace existing device Device name: _____	
Connect server to the following network segments.	
❏ Network interface A connects to segment: _____	
❏ Network interface B connects to segment: _____	
Networking services to include	
❏ DHCP ❏ Routing and Remote Access	
❏ WINS ❏ Routing	
❏ DNS ❏ Remote Access	
❏ IAS ❏ NAT	
❏ Proxy Server 2.0	
Windows Clustering options	
❏ Install on server cluster node. Cluster name: _____	
❏ Install on NLB cluster node. Cluster name: _____	

Design Worksheet – Figure 15.16
Hotel Property – Server G

Server Specifications	Comments
❑ Replace existing device Device name: _____	
Connect server to the following network segments.	
❑ Network interface A connects to segment: _____	
❑ Network interface B connects to segment: _____	
Networking services to include	
❑ DHCP ❑ Routing and Remote Access	
❑ WINS ❑ Routing	
❑ DNS ❑ Remote Access	
❑ IAS ❑ NAT	
❑ Proxy Server 2.0	
Windows Clustering options	
❑ Install on server cluster node. Cluster name: _____	
❑ Install on NLB cluster node. Cluster name: _____	

Design Worksheet – Figure 15.16
Hotel Property – Server H

Server Specifications	Comments
❑ Replace existing device Device name: _____	
Connect server to the following network segments.	
❑ Network interface A connects to segment: _____	
❑ Network interface B connects to segment: _____	
Networking services to include	
❑ DHCP ❑ Routing and Remote Access ❑ WINS ❑ Routing ❑ DNS ❑ Remote Access ❑ IAS ❑ NAT ❑ Proxy Server 2.0	
Windows Clustering options	
❑ Install on server cluster node. Cluster name: _____ ❑ Install on NLB cluster node. Cluster name: _____	

Review

The following questions are intended to reinforce key information in this chapter. If you're unable to answer a question, review the lesson and then try to answer the question again. You can find answers to the questions in the Appendix, "Questions and Answers."

1. You have been retained as consultant to review and evaluate a networking services design. The organization that retained you wants to ensure it reduces the cost associated with deploying and managing the design. What recommendations can you make to the organization?

2. You're creating a networking services solution for an organization that has a large Internet presence. The organization utilizes an e-commerce site to generate its revenue. The e-commerce site must be available to users 24 hours per day, 7 days per week. What recommendations can you make to the organization?

3. You're evaluating a networking services design that was created two years ago by an outside consulting firm. Since the initial deployment, the users report a gradual reduction in the overall network performance. The Chief Information Officer of the organization had given you the responsibility to review the design and to make suggestions for improving the performance. What general optimizations to the existing design can you utilize in your revision of the design?

APPENDIX

Questions and Answers

Chapter 1

Review Questions

1. You're participating in a meeting with other members of the information services department in your organization. The meeting is the first for a new deployment project that your organization is starting. The members of the team are introducing themselves and describing the part they will play in the deployment project. As the networking services designer, how do you define networking service and your role in the deployment project?

Networking services run on the physical network and protocols within the organization. Applications and users use these services to provide remote access, name resolution, IP configuration, routing, and Internet connectivity.

As the networking services designer, your primary role is the creation and management of the networking services design. Your primary responsibilities occur during the design phase of the deployment process.

During the implementation phase, you work with other members in the Information services department to conduct pilot tests, determine the sequence of networking services deployment, and answer specific questions about the design.

During the management phase, you work with administrators and the operations staff to identify the critical networking services that must be monitored, assist in the creation of management scripts, and provide the security, availability, and performance criteria that the design must achieve.

2. A multinational organization has locations in 22 countries around the world. Currently, the locations are connected via a network of point-to-point leased lines. You're responsible for creating a solution for the organization that will connect the locations over the Internet. The organization is very concerned about the confidentiality of the data transmitted between locations. The

organization will be using Active Directory as its directory services. In addition, the organization has a number of users who work remotely. Which Windows 2000 networking services do you include your design?

You can include Routing and Remote Access to provide routing between locations. Each router can use VPN tunnels to encrypt the data transmitted between locations.

You can include DHCP to provide automated IP configuration.

You can include DNS to provide name resolution and support Active Directory services deployment.

You can include Routing and Remote Access to provide remote access to the remote users.

3. You're creating a networking services design for an organization. The organization has mission critical e-commerce site that Internet-based users will access. The majority of the organization's revenue is derived from the e-commerce site. Customers make purchases on the site 24 hours per day, seven days per week. The sales department of the organization wants customers to complete a purchase in fewer than 30 seconds after they submit the purchase. What design aspects do you suspect are a high priority for the organization? Why are those design aspects important?

All networking services designs have the essential aspects of the design as a top priority.

Because the organization's revenue is tied to the site, security, availability, and performance are important.

Because financial transactions are occurring, security is a very high priority. Customers won't make purchases unless they can be reassured the site is secure.

Because customers are making purchase at all times, availability is also a high priority. As the designer, you need to determine the revenue that is lost when the site is unavailable for any length of time or reason. The organization will need to make cost trade-offs to ensure high availability.

Performance is important from the perspective of the sales department. However, the real performance threshold occurs when customers quit using the site because purchases take too long to complete. As the designer, you need to ensure that 30 seconds to complete the transaction is realistic and acceptable to the customers.

Chapter 2

Activity Questions

Lesson 2: Essential TCP/IP Design Concepts

Activity 2.1: Evaluating a TCP/IP Network Design

1. The field service firm is migrating from a Novell NetWare environment to Windows 2000. The firm plans on using Active Directory for directory services. The central office and regional offices communicate within each office and over the point-to-point connections by using the Internetwork Packet Exchange (IPX) protocol. Currently, the servers that support the Web site and the e-mail servers are the only computers that run TCP/IP. The central office and regional offices communicate with the Web site by using an IPX to TCP/IP gateway, such as Microsoft Proxy Server 2.0. What recommendations do you make to the firm?

   You can make the following recommendations:

   - **Migrate the existing network to TCP/IP for Windows 2000 and Active Directory support**

   - **Upgrade or replace the existing routers to support TCP/IP**

   - **Select an IP address range that supports the number of locations, subnets, and computers**

   - **After the migration is complete, remove the IPX protocol from the network**

2. The field service firm decided to use a public IP addressing scheme. You're in the process of obtaining public IP addresses for the firm. The preferred ISP can allocate you a block of IP addresses by using CIDR. How does the use of CIDR and public IP addressing affect your TCP/IP network design?

   CIDR and public IP addressing affect the design by

   - **Requiring the routers that connect to the ISP to support CIDR**

   - **Incurring an incremental charge for each of the public IP addresses obtained from the ISP**

3. After examining the proposal for the public IP addresses from the ISP, the field service firm is concerned about the associated costs. How can you modify your TCP/IP design to reduce the costs and how will the design modification affect your design?

   You can reduce the costs associated with the public IP addresses by

   - **Using private IP address within the field service firm**

   - **Allocating fewer public IP addresses for use by the firm**

The use of a private IP addressing scheme in the firm requires

- **A public IP address for each device not connected to the ISP through a network address translator**

- **Network address translators between the private network and the portion of the network connected to the ISP**

4. You want to reduce the number of unused IP addresses on each subnet within the firm. In addition, you want to reduce the routing information exchanged between offices over the point-to-point lines. How can you accomplish these design goals and how do these new goals affect your design?

You can reduce the number of unused IP addresses on each subnet and reduce the routing information by using VLSM within the firm's private network. VLSM allows you to adjust the subnet mask for each subnet to match the number of hosts on the subnets and reduce the number of unused IP addresses. VLSM also allows you to reduce the routing information by aggregating routing information for routers lower in the router hierarchy.

To use VLSM within the firm's private network, you must ensure that

- **All routers support VLSM by using OSPF or RIP version 2 routing protocols**

- **The routers are arranged hierarchically to allow aggregation of routing information**

Lesson 4: TCP/IP Optimization

Activity 2.2: Completing a TCP/IP Design

1. As the consultant, what recommendations do you make to migrate the firm from point-to-point connections to Internet-based connections?

You can make the following recommendations:

- **Add a network address translator at each location**

- **Allocate public IP addresses for all devices that don't communicate through a network address translator at each office**

2. The management of the field service firm is concerned about confidential data transmitted over the Internet. The firm wants to ensure that the strongest possible security is used. How can you address these security concerns?

You can make the following recommendations:

- **Establish VPN connections between the routers that connect the central office and the regional offices to the Internet**

- **Use L2TP, IPSec, and 3DES to provide encryption of data**

- **Use MS-CHAP v2 to provide mutual authentication of the routers**

3. An independent consulting firm has proposed the use of IPSec tunnel mode to protect the confidential data transmitted over the Internet. How do you respond to the recommendations proposed by the consulting firm?

   Although IPSec tunnel mode works, IPSec tunnel mode doesn't provide the additional level of authentication provided by VPN tunnel. VPN acts as an additional level of authentication to prevent unauthorized users from gaining access to the data.

   In addition, VPN tunnels, such as L2TP, are more broadly supported by third-party vendors.

4. After migrating to Internet-based connectivity between offices, the users in the regional offices are experiencing slower response time. The firm has verified that the Web servers aren't the source of the reduction in response time. How can you modify your design to improve the response time of the users in the regional offices?

   You can make the following recommendations:

   - **If the Internet connections are saturated, install additional Internet connections in each office**
   - **If the routers are saturated, install additional routers in each office**
   - **Distribute the traffic transmitted between offices across the additional Internet connection or routers**

Review Questions

1. An organization is preparing to migrate its network to Windows 2000. You're responsible for designing the networking services design for the organization. The organization has 3,200 users located in 25 offices throughout the world. What information do you need to collect to create your design?

   You must collect the following information to create the design:

   - **Amount of the data transmitted through each network segment**
   - **Confidentiality of the data transmitted through each network segment**
   - **Future network growth**
   - **Existing IP address range allocated to the organization**
   - **Number of existing network segments**
   - **Routing protocols in use**
   - **Response times for applications that access resources through the network**
   - **Availability of the network**

2. You're creating a networking services design for a multinational organization with locations in London, New York, Madrid, Paris, and Tokyo. The organization has recently connected the locations together over the Internet. As a result,

the organization is concerned about protecting data transmitted between locations. What can you do to ensure the integrity and confidentiality of the data transmitted over the network?

- **Each router can use VPN tunnels to encrypt the data transmitted between locations**
- **You can use up to 56-bit DES encryption for L2TP tunnels**
- **You can use 40-bit MPPE encryption for PPTP tunnels**
- **You can use MS-CHAP v2 to authenticate the VPN tunnels**

3. You're the director of information services for a university. The students, faculty, and the administration share the same physical TCP/IP-based network. However, the computers that contain the student registration, accounting, and budgetary information are connected to the same network segment. The faculty and administration must be able to access the confidential information. The students must not be able to access confidential data transmitted within the network. How do you ensure that these requirements are met in your design?

To protect the confidential data, you can

- **Use IPSec ESP to encrypt data if the servers and desktop computers both support IPSec.**
- **Replace the router that connects the network segment containing the servers with the confidential data with a Routing and Remote Access server.**
- **Establish a VPN tunnel between the desktop computers and the Routing and Remote Access server. Encrypt the VPN tunnel traffic to prevent unauthorized access to the confidential data.**

Chapter 3

Activity Questions

Lesson 2: IPX Design Concepts

Activity 3.1: Evaluating a Networking Protocol Design

1. As a consultant to the engineering firm, you're responsible for creating the networking services design. What network protocols must your design include and why are the network protocols required?

You might make the following recommendations:

- **Include TCP/IP to support the existing computers running Windows 2000 and Active Directory directory service**
- **Include IPX to support the existing NetWare 4.2 file and print servers**

2. The engineering firm wants to connect all locations to the Winnipeg central office so the engineers can access Web-based project management and time and billing software. However, the firm wants to migrate the new offices to IP over the next year. As the consultant, what recommendations do you make to the firm?

You might make the following recommendations:

- **Install Proxy Server at the Calgary, Edmonton, and Halifax offices**

- **Allocate a Classless Internet Domain Routing (CIDR) range from the Internet service provider (ISP) for each location to support the migration to IP over the next year**

- **Consider using private addressing for all private networks because Proxy Servers is already in place to act as IPX gateways**

3. The engineering firm transmits confidential customer information between offices. The offices are connected to each other by using the Internet. The engineering firm wants to use the strongest data encryption possible. What security recommendations do you make to the firm?

You might make the following recommendations:

- **Establish L2TP tunnels between the routers that connect the offices**

- **Tunnel IPX traffic through the L2TP tunnels that connect the offices**

- **Encrypt the data in the L2TP tunnels by using Internet Protocol Security (IPSec) with Triple Data Encryption Standard (3DES)**

- **Identify the routers by using Kerberos and Secure Hash Algorithm (SHA)**

Lesson 4: SNA Design Concepts

Activity 3.2: Completing a Network Protocol Design

1. The management at the Winnipeg office must access the applications running on the AS/400 in the Calgary office. Because the number of employees in Calgary is small, the network consists of a single, nonrouted Ethernet network segment. The users at the Calgary office connect to the AS/400 using DLC. How can you provide management access to the AS/400?

You might make the following recommendations:

- **Install a 3270/5250 gateway at the Calgary office**

- **Use DLC to communicate between the AS/400 and the gateway**

- **Use TCP/IP to communicate between the gateway and the users in the Winnipeg office**

2. While you're creating your design, you find out that a number of Macintosh-based computers and printers exist at the Halifax office. How does the presence of the Macintosh-based computers and printers affect your design?

You can make any one of the following recommendations to the firm:

- **Replace the Macintosh-based computers and printers with PC-based computers and LPR-based printers**
- **Add TCP/IP to the Macintosh computers and convert the Macintosh printers to LPR printers**
- **Ensure that the AppleTalk protocol is included in any final solution**

Review Questions

1. Your organization wants to integrate Windows 2000 into its existing network. Your organization uses Active Directory for directory services. The network is comprised of a variety of operating systems including Windows 95, Windows 98, Windows NT 4.0, NetWare 4.x, UNIX, and Macintosh operating systems. What information do you need to collect to determine the influence of these operating systems on your networking services design?

   Because the organization is deploying Windows 2000 and Active Directory, your design must include TCP/IP. Because of the diversity of operating systems, any TCP/IP data protection must be accomplished by using a PPTP VPN tunnel.

   The NetWare 4.x servers require IPX to access NetWare file and print resources. The routers in the organization must be able to provide IPX routing.

   The Macintosh computers may require the use of AppleTalk, however, the Macintosh computers may be configured to support TCP/IP.

2. You're creating a networking services design for your network that is comprised of Windows 2000 computers and Macintosh computers. Your organization has a number of locations. Each location has a number of networking segments. What information must you collect to determine the network protocol design?

   To create the network design, you must determine

   - **Whether any applications, such as Web servers or Active Directory, require TCP/IP**
   - **Whether the Macintosh computers require AppleTalk, TCP/IP, or both**
   - **The number of network segments**
   - **The number of network devices per network segment**

3. You're creating a networking services design for an organization. The organization is comprised of 15 locations. Each location has a number of network segments that are connected by Token Ring source routing bridges. The organization has a number of mission-critical applications that run on an AS/400. All desktop computers connect directly to the AS/400 by using DLC. The network operations and support staff informs you that as the network has

grown, the network utilization has increased dramatically. The organization plans to deploy Windows 2000 over the next 36 months. How can you address the network utilization concerns, while maintaining connectivity to the AS/400 and supporting the Windows 2000 deployment?

To address the network utilization, to maintain AS/400 connectivity, and to facilitate the Windows 2000 deployment

- **Place IP routers in parallel with each source routing bridge**
- **Install a 3270/5250 gateway to connect the IP-routed network to the AS/400 or add IP support to the AS/400**
- **Convert the network to a TCP/IP-only network**
- **Convert DLC-based printers, if any, to LPR-based printers**
- **Remove the source routing bridges when the TCP/IP migration is complete**

Chapter 4

Activity Questions

Lesson 2: Essential IP Routing Design Concepts

Activity 4.1: Evaluating an IP Routing Design

1. As the director of information services for the library system, you're responsible for creating the networking services design. You have decided to connect each of the remote branches to the Internet by using a T1 connection. Because all remote branches will be accessing resources in the main branch, you have decided to install a T3 Internet connection at the main branch. What do you recommend as a routing solution between the remote branches and the main branch?

   You can make the following recommendations:
   - **Install an edge of network router at each branch**
   - **Specify a demand-dial interface that will connect the corresponding router to the Internet**
   - **Use autostatic RIP routing at each branch that establishes a route path to the other branches**
   - **Schedule the autostatic RIP routing updates to occur each day at midnight**

2. After performing pilot testing, you have determined that you want to connect each network segment to a backbone segment within each branch. The backbone segment will be connected to the Internet. You have determined that the number of computers on each network segment won't increase significantly over the life of the new deployment. How do you provide routing between the network segments in each branch and to the Internet?

You can make the following recommendations:

- **Add a router for each network segment in each branch**
- **Specify that all the routers within each branch will connect to the backbone segment within each branch**
- **Add an additional interface in the edge of network routers to connect the router to the backbone segment**
- **Use RIP for IP version 2 at each location to manage routing tables**

3. You want to provide automatic IP address configuration for all desktop and laptop computers at each location by using DHCP. How can you modify your routing design to support DHCP configuration on all network segments within each branch?

You can support DHCP configuration by

- **Enabling the DHCP Relay Agent on each interface, except the T1, or T3, connection to the Internet**
- **Specify that each router interface has a fixed IP address**

4. The facilities and community relations director for the library system has funding to install a multimedia server at each branch. The multimedia server will be used to present streaming audio and video presentations within each branch. You want to reduce the amount of traffic used by the multimedia traffic. How can you modify your routing design to support the multimedia traffic while reducing the network utilization?

You can support the multimedia streaming content and reduce network utilization by

- **Locating the multimedia server on the backbone network segment within each branch**
- **Adding the IGMP protocol to each internal router within each branch**
- **Specifying that the internal router interface connected to the backbone network segment is the Proxy Mode interface**
- **Specifying that the other internal router interface is the Router Mode interface**

Lesson 4: IP Routing Design Optimization

Activity 4.2: Completing an IP Routing Design

1. The board of directors for the library system is concerned about library patrons and Internet-based users accessing the new Web-based application and the structured query language (SQL) server database that acts as the repository for application's data. You also want to reduce the risk of unauthorized access to the library confidential data. How can you address the concerns of the board of directors?

Your recommendations should include the following:

- Use RIP for IP peers to ensure that RIP routing updates are limited to known routers

- Use RIP for IP neighbors to send unicast RIP routing updates

- Use IPSec tunnels to identify routers and encrypt data between internal routers

- Use VPN tunnels to identify routers and encrypt data between edge of network routers

- Specify IP filter criteria on the edge of network routers that allow only Internet-based users access to the Web servers at the main branch

- Specify IP filter criteria on the internal routers that prevent Internet-based users from accessing any of the resources on the private network

2. The library personnel must be able to access the Web-based library application at all times. The facilities and community relations director requires that the meeting room computers access the Internet only during normal library branch hours. Internet-based library patrons must be able to reserve a book 24 hours a day, 7 days a week. How can you ensure that these design requirements and constraints are met?

You might make the following recommendations:

- Add redundant internal routers for the network segments that support the meeting rooms and the library personnel within each branch

- Add redundant edge of network routers at each branch

- Add a redundant T1, or T3, Internet connection at each branch in the event of a T1 connection failure

- Designate one of the redundant T1, or T3, connections as the primary connection

- Designate the other T1, or T3, connections as the backup connection

- Adjust the cost metric for the backup connection to be higher than the primary connection

3. The library system rents the meeting rooms to individuals and organizations. The proceeds from the meeting room rentals help fund future enhancements to the library system facilities and equipment. The facilities and community relations director wants to ensure that the people who rent the meeting rooms are satisfied with network response times. How can you optimize your design to ensure optimal response times?

You can improve the response times for the meeting rooms by performing the same design changes that you specified to improve the availability of the design.

Because you have optimized design for availability, no further changes are necessary in your design.

Review Questions

1. An organization has 35 locations throughout North and South America. The locations are connected over point-to-point communications links that include 56Kbps, T1, and T3 communications links. The organization wants to reduce the cost associated with these point-to-point communications links. The organization also wants to ensure that confidential data is protected in any new solution. As a consultant to the organization, what recommendations can you make?

   You can make the following recommendations:

   - **Provide comparable, or higher, speed connections to the Internet at each location**

   - **Install Routing and Remote Access-based routers at each location**

   - **Establish VPN tunnels between each of the locations**

   - **Use IPSec or MPPE to encrypt data transmitted between the locations over the Internet**

   - **Use MS-CHAP v2 to authenticate routers that establish the VPN tunnels because MS-CHAP v2 provides the highest security**

2. An organization has a number of Web-based services and applications that are provided to its customers. A computer running Windows 2000 and Routing and Remote Access provides the connectivity to the servers that host these services and applications. The majority of the revenue for the organization is derived from the Web-based services and applications. The board of directors is concerned about the ability of the customers to access the Web-based services and applications at all times. What recommendations can you make to ensure that customers can access the Web-based services and applications?

   You can make the following recommendations:

   - **Install additional connections to the Internet in the event an Internet connection fails**

   - **Install additional Routing and Remote Access-based routers in the event a router fails**

3. You're creating a routing design for your network. Your organization has a number of locations. Each location has a number of networking segments. What information must you collect to create your routing design?

   To create your routing design, you must determine the

   - **Quantity of data transmitted within each network segment**

   - **Confidentiality of data transmitted within each network segment**

   - **Routing protocols in use by existing routers**

   - **Response times for applications that access resources through the router**

   - **Acceptable percentage of time that users require access through the router**

4. You're creating a routing design for an organization that has 10 locations throughout the world. The existing network design has evolved over the last eight years, and needs to be redesigned. The organization has a range of IP addresses allocated from an ISP by using CIDR. The operations staff of the organization's information services department wants to ensure that the new network is easy to manage. What routing protocols do you include in your design, and what are the reasons for selecting the respective routing protocols?

Specify the following:

- **Default static route entries for edge of network routers to ensure packets destined for the Internet are forwarded to the ISP's routers.**

- **RIP for IP as the dynamic routing protocol if the router diameter is less than 15 hops. Additionally, RIP for IP requires that you**

  - **Select RIP for IP version 2 as the primary routing protocol because of the CIDR requirements**

  - **Specify autostatic RIP for IP routing to automatically update routing information between locations**

  - **Enable RIP neighbors for all routers to reduce, or eliminate, the number of broadcast, or multicast, packets on the network**

  - **Enable RIP for IP peer security on all edge of network routers to ensure that the routers accept updates only from other routers owned by the organization**

- **If RIP is inappropriate, select OSPF as the dynamic routing protocol if the organization has an infrastructure based on OSPF or significant financial and technological network support. Additionally, OSPF requires that you**

  - **Specify that all routers within the organization belong to the same Autonomous System**

  - **Specify an OSPF area to each location**

  - **Specify an OSPF network for each network segment**

Chapter 5

Activity Questions

Lesson 2: IPX Routing Design Concepts

Activity 5.1: Evaluating an IPX Routing Design

1. As an outside consultant hired to help the resort chain migrate to the X.25 network, you're responsible for creating the networking services design. The management of the vacation resort wants to ensure that the migration to X.25 won't disrupt the normal operation of business. What do you recommend as an IPX routing solution for the resort chain?

You might make the following recommendations:

- **Specify a demand-dial interface that connects the corresponding router to the existing dial-up modems**
- **Specify an interface that connects the corresponding router to the new X.25 network**
- **Use RIPX and SAP within each vacation resort**
- **Use autostatic RIPX and autostatic SAP at each vacation resort to establish a route path to the other vacation resorts**
- **Schedule autostatic updates to occur daily at midnight**

2. After subsequent meetings, the management of the vacation resort wants you to ensure that unauthorized users aren't able to view any data transmitted over the X.25 network. The management wants you to provide the strongest possible security. How do you protect the data transmitted over the X.25 network between each of the resort properties and the central office?

You can make the following recommendations:

- **Add IP to each edge of network router at each resort property and at the central office**
- **Specify a VPN tunnel between the resort properties**
- **Specify a VPN tunnel between each resort property and the central office**
- **Encrypt the data by using 56-bit Data Encryption Standard (DES)**
- **Authenticate routers by using Microsoft Challenge Handshake Authentication Protocol version 2 (MS-CHAP v2)**
- **Tunnel IPX traffic through the IP tunnel**

3. In another meeting, the management of the resort property chain wants to ensure that communications between resort properties and between the resort properties and the central office are always available during normal business hours. How can you ensure that these business requirements are met?

You can make the following recommendations:

- **Install redundant connections to the X.25 network at each resort property and at the central office**
- **Install redundant routers at each resort property and at the central office**
- **Specify routing path and route path cost metrics to ensure that redundant routers or connections are used in the event of a router or connection failure**

4. The director of information services for the vacation resort chain reviews the results of pilot test that have been run. The response time for some applications is less than the minimum response times in the vacation resort chain's requirements. After further investigation, the pilot test team discovers the

reduction in response time is due to network traffic congestion on the edge of network router at some of the locations. What recommendations can you make to reduce the network traffic congestion?

You can make the following recommendations:

- **Install additional connections to the X.25 network at each resort property and at the central office**

- **Install additional routers at each resort property and at the central office**

- **Specify routing path and route path cost metrics to ensure that the network traffic is load-balanced across the addition connections and routers**

Lesson 3: AppleTalk Routing Design Concepts

Activity 5.2: Evaluating an AppleTalk Routing Design

1. The chain of vacation resorts has retained you as a consultant to update the existing design that you created to integrate the Macintosh computers into the existing network. The management of the vacation resort wants to ensure that the integration of the Macintosh computers into the existing network won't disrupt the normal operation of business. What do you recommend as an AppleTalk routing solution for the resort chain?

You might make the following recommendations:

- **Specify the AppleTalk protocol be added to each router interface**

- **Specify the appropriate number of AppleTalk network numbers to each network segment**

- **Specify the appropriate zones for each network segment**

- **Specify one (or more) seed routers for each network segment**

2. Just as with IPX, the management of the resort property is concerned about the confidentiality of any data transmitted by using AppleTalk over the X.25 network. How do you protect the data transmitted over the X.25 network between each of the resort properties and the central office?

You can make the following recommendations:

- **Routing and Remote Access in Windows 2000 can't provide protection of confidential data**

- **Select a third-party routing solution to protect confidential data transmitted over the X.25 network**

3. In another meeting, the management of the resort property chain wants to ensure that communications between resort properties and between the resort properties and the central office are always available during normal business hours. In addition, the director of information services wants to ensure that the routers and network segments won't become saturated. How can you ensure that these business and technical requirements are met?

You can make the following recommendations:

- **Install redundant connections to the X.25 network at each resort property and at the central office**

- **Install redundant routers at each resort property and at the central office**

- **Specify routing path and route path cost metrics to ensure that redundant routers or connections are used in the event of a router or connection failure**

- **Specify routing path and route path cost metrics to ensure that the network traffic is load-balanced across the addition connections and routers**

Review Questions

1. You're creating an IPX routing design for an organization with 15 locations in Europe. The locations are connected over point-to-point communications links that include dial-up modems and ISDN communications links. The organization wants to reduce the cost associated with these point-to-point communications links. What recommendations can you make to the organization?

    You can make the following recommendations:

    - **Provide comparable, or higher, speed connections to the Internet at each location**

    - **Install Routing and Remote Access-based routers in each location**

    - **Establish VPN tunnels between each of the locations**

    - **Use IPSec or Microsoft Point-to-Point Encryption (MPPE) to encrypt data transmitted between the locations**

    - **Use MS-CHAP v2 to authenticate routers that establish the VPN tunnels**

    - **Route IPX through IPX over IP tunnels**

2. Your services as a consultant have been retained by an organization to resolve connectivity outages it is experiencing. The organization is comprised of a number of locations. During normal business hours, the connectivity between these locations must be maintained. What recommendations can you make to ensure that the connectivity between these locations isn't interrupted during normal business hours?

    You can make the following recommendations:

    - **Install additional WAN connections to each location in the event a WAN connection fails**

    - **Install additional Routing and Remote Access-based routers in the event a router fails**

    - **Specify IPX routing cost metrics that will enable the remaining router(s) to forward traffic in the event of a failure on the primary router**

3. You're creating an AppleTalk routing design for your network. The network is comprised of a number of locations. Each location contains numerous EtherTalk, TokenTalk and LocalTalk network segments. The AppleTalk network numbers and zones have been assigned to each network segment. What must you do to complete the AppleTalk routing design?

To create your routing design, do the following:

- **For each router interface, you must specify the AppleTalk network number, or range of numbers, assigned to the network segment to which the router interface is directly connected**

- **For each router interface, you must specify the AppleTalk zone(s) assigned to the network segment to which the router interface is directly connected**

- **For each network segment, you must specify one or more seed routers**

Chapter 6

Activity Questions

Lesson 2: Essential Proxy Server Design Concepts

Activity 6.1: Evaluating a Proxy Server Design

1. Currently, an IP router provides the Internet connectivity at each location. The organization wants to investigate other technologies that might improve the Internet connectivity services provided. As the director of information services for the shipping company, you're responsible for the networking services design. What recommendations can you make?

You might make the following recommendations:

- **Install a proxy server at each office**

- **Specify an interface that connects the proxy server to the private network**

- **Specify an interface that connects to the existing Internet connection that corresponds to the type of Internet connection**

- **Specify that the proxy servers provide Web content caching**

- **Enhance the existing router security by including Proxy Server security.**

2. A variety of operating systems, including Microsoft Windows 95, Windows 2000, Macintosh, and UNIX, are used within each office in the shipping company. A version of Internet Explorer 5.0 exists for each operating system. Currently, the shipping company is concerned only about HTTP and FTP traffic to the company's Web site. What client computer configurations are appropriate and why do you recommend the solution?

One solution might include

- **Proxy Server client software for the computers running Windows 95 and Windows 2000 to provide automatic updates of the LAT information**
- **SOCKS client software for the Macintosh and UNIX computers**

Another solution might include Internet Explorer 5.0 on all client computers because the organization is concerned only about HTTP and FTP traffic. However, if the organization becomes concerned about more than HTTP or FTP traffic, this solution won't work.

The least desirable solution might include specifying the IP address of the proxy server as the default router. This solution might increase network traffic because all unknown IP addresses are forwarded to the proxy server.

3. You find out in a later meeting that a number of the private networks in the offices are IPX-based. Currently, the customer representatives connect to the Internet by using dial-up modems connected to their computers. What recommendations can you make?

You can make the following recommendations:

- **Install a proxy server at each office that has an IPX-based private network**
- **Specify that the proxy server at each office provide IPX to IP gateway services**
- **Specify that the Proxy Server client software be installed on each desktop computer in the office**

Lesson 4: Proxy Server Design Optimization

Activity 6.2: Completing a Proxy Server Design

1. The management of the shipping company wants to restrict the customer representatives so they can access only the company's Web site. The chief information office of the company (CIO) wants to ensure that only HTTP and FTP traffic is sent to the company's Web site. The ASP that hosts the Web site might change—however, the impact on changing ASPs must be minimal in your design. Also, only authenticated users should be able to access the proxy server. As the director of information services, what Proxy Server solution do you recommend to management?

You might make the following recommendations:

- **Specify packet filters criteria to filter all traffic except HTTP and FTP traffic**
- **Specify a domain filter that allows communication with only the company's Web site**
- **Specify that the appropriate users or groups are granted access to the proxy servers**

2. Within each regional office, the marketing and sales team wants to host its own Web site that provides information and contact numbers for the customers of the

region. Although the board of directors strongly supports the initiative, the CIO is concerned about protecting private network resources. How do you protect private network resources while providing access to a Web server within each office?

You can make the following recommendations:

- **Specify packet filters criteria to filter all incoming traffic except HTTP and FTP traffic**

- **Specify a Web publishing entry in the Web publishing list for the URLs that point to the Web server in each location**

- **Specify that Web publishing will discard all URL requests that aren't in the Web publishing list**

3. After a few months of operation, certain offices are experiencing performance problems. Also, offices in remote countries are experiencing outages due to hardware and telecommunications failure. How can you improve the performance and increase the availability for these offices?

You can make the following recommendations:

- **Install redundant Internet connections at each office**

- **Install additional proxy servers at each office**

- **Specify that the proxy servers at each office belong to the same proxy array to improve the performance and availability of Internet access**

- **Specify that the proxy servers at each office belong to the same Network Load Balancing cluster to improve the performance and availability of private network access**

Review Questions

1. An organization with 35 locations throughout the world has retained your services as a consultant to create a Proxy Server design. Each of the locations is connected to a central office by using point-to-point communications links. The organization's Internet connection is comprised of multiple T3 connections. The organization wants to provide Internet access to the private network users. Also, the organization has Web servers located in the private network that must be accessed by Internet users. The client computers in the network run Windows 95, Microsoft Windows 98, Windows Me, and Windows 2000. What recommendations can you make to the organization?

You can make the following recommendations:

- **Install a proxy server at each location**

- **Specify Proxy Server packet filters to prevent unauthorized access to private network resources**

- **Specify the Proxy Server client software for each client computer**

- **Specify Web publishing to allow access to the Web servers on the private network**

2. As the director of information services for an international organization, you're responsible for evaluating your organization's Proxy Server design. The management of the organization is concerned about the unauthorized use of the organization's high-speed Internet connection and the accessing of unauthorized Internet sites. What recommendations can you make to ensure that the security requirements of the organization are achieved?

You can make the following recommendations:

- **Specify that only authenticated users can transmit data through proxy server**
- **Specify domain filters to restrict the Internet sites that private network users can access**
- **Specify packet filters to restrict the types of traffic that can be sent between the private network and the Internet**

3. You're optimizing an existing Proxy Server design. The network users report that response time for Internet access is slow. What changes to the design can you recommend to improve Internet access response time?

To create your routing design, you must

- **Specify additional proxy servers at each location**
- **Enable active caching on each proxy server**
- **Specify that the proxy servers be configured into appropriate proxy arrays**
- **Specify that the upstream connection for the proxy array that connects to the Internet is a direct Internet connection**
- **Specify that the upstream connection for all other proxy arrays or proxy servers is an upstream proxy server**

Chapter 7

Activity Questions

Lesson 2: Essential NAT Design Concepts

Activity 7.1: Evaluating a NAT Design

1. Currently the field engineers connect to the Internet to run the Web-based applications by using dial-up modems. The field service firm wants to upgrade the Internet connection for the field engineers for future applications and expansion. Also, the field server firm wants the field engineers to gain experience in Internet connectivity solutions. As a consultant to the field service firm, what recommendations can you make?

You can make the following recommendations:

- **Install a NAT server at each SOHO**

- Specify an interface that connects the NAT server to the SOHO network
- Specify an interface that connects to the Internet connection
- Specify that the NAT server provide automatic IP address assignment
- Specify that the NAT server provide DNS name resolution assignment

2. A variety of operating systems, including Windows 95, Windows 98, Windows Me, Windows 2000, and UNIX, must be supported by the field engineer's SOHO network. The field engineers change operating systems on the computers in the SOHO to gain experience in installation and support issues. How can you reduce the amount of time spent configuring the operating systems after installation?

You can make the following recommendations:

- **Ensure that all the client operating systems are configured to use DHCP for IP configuration**
- **Ensure that the automatic IP address assignment feature of the NAT server is enabled**

3. The director of customer services is evaluating new customer account management software specifically written for the electronics field service industry. The customer account management software is written as a multitier, client server application. The field engineers will run the client portion of the application on the SOHO network. What must you consider when selecting the new application?

You must determine the protocols that the customer account management software uses. Any protocols that aren't supported by NAT won't function properly in a NAT solution.

Lesson 4: NAT Design Optimization

Activity 7.2: Completing a NAT Design

1. The management of the field service firm wants the regional offices to transfer customer information between the servers at each regional office and computers within the field engineer's SOHO network. The data will be summarized in data files that will be exchanged by using FTP. As a consultant to the firm, what NAT solution do you recommend to management?

You can specify a NAT address mapping entry to provide access to the computer in the field engineer's SOHO network.

2. The management of the field engineering firm wants to ensure that only the regional office has access to the computer in the field engineer's SOHO network. In addition, because FTP transmits data in clear text, the organization wants to protect the confidential customer information transmitted over the Internet. How can you ensure that these security requirements are met?

You can make the following recommendations:

- Specify packet filters criteria to filter all incoming traffic except FTP traffic

- Specify packet filters criteria to filter all incoming traffic except for traffic originating from the regional office

- Establish VPN tunnels between the computer in the field engineer's SOHO network and a VPN server in the regional office

- Authenticate the field engineer, and encrypt all data in the VPN tunnel

3. After a few months of operation, certain field engineer SOHOs are experiencing performance problems. How can you improve the performance for these offices?

You can make the following recommendations:

- Upgrade the Internet connection to a higher speed connection

- Move any applications or services running on the NAT server in the field engineer's SOHO to other computers

Review Questions

1. An insurance company has agents who work from their homes. Currently, the agents connect to the insurance company's corporate network by establishing a dial-up Internet connection and then establishing a VPN tunnel. The insurance firm is in the process of upgrading the applications and services available to the agents. The applications and services will require the agents to upgrade their Internet connection to a high-speed connection such as ISDN or DSL. Many of the agents want to use the new high-speed Internet connection with other computers in their SOHO. As an independent consultant, what recommendations can you make to the organization?

If the new applications are compatible with NAT, you can make the following recommendations:

- Install a NAT server at each agent's SOHO

- Specify automatic IP addressing for all computers in the SOHO

- Specify automatic DNS assignment for all computers in the SOHO

- Specify VPNs to connect computers in the SOHO to VPN servers in the insurance company's corporate network

If the new applications aren't compatible with NAT, the agents should investigate

- Installing a proxy server at each agent's SOHO

- Acquiring additional IP addresses for the additional computers from the ISP used by the agent.

2. You're evaluating an existing NAT design for a franchised restaurant chain. Each of the restaurants has a database server located within the local restaurant. Nightly updates to financial and sales information are uploaded to regional franchise offices. However, the regional managers are unable to query the database server in any of the restaurants. What recommendations can you make that allow the managers to access information on the database servers?

You can make the following recommendations:

- **Specify a NAT address mapping entry or address pool entry to map the requests coming from the regional managers to the database servers in the restaurants**

- **Ensure that the Routing and Remote Access filters allow only the regional managers to access the restaurants network**

3. You're optimizing an existing NAT design. The network users report that response time for Internet access is slow. What changes to the design can you recommend to improve Internet access response time?

To create your routing design, you can make the following recommendations:

- **Specify a higher data rate Internet connection**

- **Migrate any unnecessary applications or services running on the NAT server to other computers in the SOHO network**

- **Specify a persistent Internet connection**

- **Upgrade the hardware configuration of the computer running NAT**

Chapter 8

Activity Questions

Lesson 2: Essential DHCP Design Concepts

Activity 8.1: Evaluating a DHCP Design

1. The library want to ensure that local administration of the network is minimized. In addition, the director of technology for the library wants to make certain that IP configuration errors are minimized as well. As a consultant to the library, what recommendations can you make?

You can make the following recommendations:

- **Install a DHCP server at each library**

- **Connect DHCP Relay Agents to all network segments not directly connected to the DHCP server**

- **Specify a DHCP scope for each IP address range to be automatically assigned**

- **Specify the appropriate DHCP scope options**

2. The director of technology for the library wants to reduce any costs possible in the design and isn't concerned about broadcast traffic within a location. How can you minimize the costs associated with the DHCP design?

You might make the following recommendations:

- **Place only one DHCP server within each library**
- **Enable DHCP/BOOTP forwarding on the routers that connect the network segments within each library**

3. The library has deployed Microsoft Internet Explorer 5.0 on all computers running Windows 2000. All other desktop computers are running older versions of Internet Explorer, but will be upgraded to Internet Explorer 5.0 as Windows 2000 is deployed to the respective computers. You want to enable the Internet Explorer 5.0 configuration option to automatically detect proxy server settings. How can you ensure that only Windows 2000 computers receive the Internet Explorer 5.0 configuration options?

You might make the following recommendations:

- **Create a DHCP class that contains only DHCP clients running Windows 2000**
- **Specify a DHCP scope option on the class to enable automatic proxy server setting detection**

Lesson 4: DHCP Design Optimization

Activity 8.2: Completing a DHCP Design

1. The library system is concerned about Internet users gaining access to the servers and resources in each library. What specifications can you include in your design to prevent Internet users from accessing DHCP servers?

You can specify that all DHCP servers be placed behind the firewall on each library's private network. Ensure that the firewall rules prevent Internet users from accessing the DHCP servers and prevent DHCP servers from providing IP configuration to Internet users.

2. DHCP servers running on Windows NT 4 Server currently manage the IP configuration for each library. You want to ensure that unauthorized DHCP servers aren't started within each library's private network. How do you ensure that these security requirements are met?

You can make the following recommendations:

- **Upgrade all existing DHCP servers running on Windows NT 4 Sever to Windows 2000**
- **Install at least one DHCP server on a domain controller or member server at each location**
- **Authorize the DHCP servers in Active Directory**

3. Each library has a local network administrator responsible for the operations within the respective library. In addition, the library system has three network administrators responsible for the operations of all the libraries. You want to ensure that only the local network administrator and the library system's network administrators can manage the DHCP servers in the design. How can you ensure that these requirements are achieved?

You can make the following recommendations:

- **Create a Windows 2000 group for each library that will manage the DHCP servers within the corresponding library**

- **Ensure that the local network administrator and the library system's network administrators are members of the Windows 2000 group**

- **Grant the Windows 2000 group that you created the permission to administer the DHCP servers within the corresponding library**

4. The existing design includes a single DHCP server within each library. At peak periods of activity, the DHCP server within many of the library becomes saturated with DHCP client requests. You want to ensure that if the DHCP server fails, DHCP automatic IP configuration occurs transparently to the users. In addition, you want to minimize any latency the DHCP client computers experience during DHCP automatic IP configuration. How can you ensure that these requirements are achieved?

You can make the following recommendations:

- **Place a Windows Clustering server cluster with two cluster nodes at each library**

- **Install the DHCP Server service on both nodes in the cluster**

- **Designate one of the nodes in the cluster as the active DHCP server**

- **Dedicate the two cluster nodes to running DHCP**

Review Questions

1. An organization currently administers the IP network configuration manually. The organization is comprised of 35 locations and each location has an average of 20 routed network segments. Each location contains a 100Mbps backbone segment that connects the other network segments to one another. The organization supports a variety of desktop operating systems. As an independent consultant, what recommendations can you make to the organization?

You can make the following recommendations:

- **Install a DHCP server on a Windows Clustering server cluster in each location**

- **On all network segments not directly connected to the DHCP server, install a DHCP Relay Agent or enable DHCP/BOOTP forwarding on routers connected to the corresponding network segment**

- Specify a DHCP scope for each IP address range defined within each location

- Specify the appropriate scope lease length

- Specify the appropriate scope options for each DHCP server, scope, class, or DHCP client

2. You're evaluating an existing DHCP design for a pharmaceutical company that has 230 research and development facilities throughout the world. The organization wants to ensure that all computers, those with manually assigned IP addresses and those with automatically assigned IP addresses, are listed in the organization's DNS servers. What recommendations can you make to the company?

You can make the following recommendations:

- Upgrade any existing DNS servers to Windows 2000–based DNS servers

- Specify the DNS zones to accept dynamic updates from the DHCP server

- Specify that the DHCP servers in each location automatically register the DHCP assigned IP addresses in DNS

3. You're evaluating an existing DHCP design for an international accounting firm that has locations throughout the world. The accounting firm is concerned about the ability of the Windows 2000–based DHCP servers to provide IP configuration at all times, regardless of a single point of failure. What changes to the design can you recommend to ensure that DHCP clients always receive the IP configuration *transparently*?

To ensure that the DHCP clients always receive the IP configuration transparently, your DHCP design must

- Specify a Windows Clustering server cluster at each location

- Specify that the DHCP Server service be installed on both cluster nodes

4. During the first 30 minutes of the business day, the users on your network notice a perceptible delay in DHCP configuration. You examine the network segment and router utilization and determine that the network segments and routers aren't the source of the DHCP configuration latency. You determine that the disk subsystem for the DHCP servers is unable to fulfill all the concurrent DHCP configuration requests. What changes to your DHCP design can you recommend to resolve these performance issues?

You can make the following recommendations:

- Specify an additional DHCP server at each location (or additional Windows Clustering server cluster)

- Specify that the existing DHCP traffic is distributed between the original DHCP server (or Windows Clustering server cluster) and the additional DHCP server (or Windows Clustering server cluster)

Chapter 9

Activity Questions

Lesson 2: Essential DNS Design Concepts

Activity 9.1: Evaluating a DNS Design

1. The consortium wants to allow the biotech firm's network support engineers to select the type of DNS servers in their own locations. As a consultant to the consortium, what recommendations can you make?

   You can make the following recommendations:

   - **Specify a DNS server at each consortium's research firm**

   - **Specify traditional DNS zones for each DNS server**

   - **Specify only RFC 1035–compliant domain names**

   - **Specify a unique namespace for the consortium**

   - **Specify an external and internal namespace for the consortium**

   - **Specify a subdomain within the internal namespace to contain the Active Directory DNS objects**

2. The director of information services for the consortium wants to reduce the administration for DNS zones. The director of technology is also concerned about the security of any automated updates to DNS zones. How can you minimize the DNS administration while ensuring integrity of DNS zones?

   You can make the following recommendations:

   - **Specify that all consortium research facilities deploy only DNS servers running Windows 2000**

   - **Specify Active Directory integrated zones on all DNS servers**

   - **Specify secured dynamically updated DNS zones on all DNS servers**

3. While collecting requirements from the biotech firms, you discover that many of the biotech firms have existing WINS servers. The biotech firms want to incorporate these WINS servers in their DNS designs (separate from the consortium's DNS design). What recommendations can you make to the biotech firms?

   You can make the following recommendations:

   - **Specify at least one DNS server running Windows 2000 in each biotech firm**

   - **Specify a subdomain in the internal namespace of each biotech firm's namespace design**

   - **Specify the WINS servers to include in the DNS zone that manages the WINS subdomain in each of the biotech firm's namespace**

Lesson 4: DNS Design Optimization

Activity 9.2: Completing a DNS Design

1. The biotech consortium is concerned about Internet users gaining access to the servers and resources in each research facility. What specifications can you include in your design to prevent Internet users from modifying the contents of consortium's DNS zones?

   You can make the following recommendations:

   - **Specify all DNS servers be placed behind the firewall at each biotech consortium research facility**
   - **Specify the DNS servers that manage the external namespace for the consortium is placed on screened subnets (or DMZs)**
   - **Specify the DNS servers that manage the external namespace for the consortium, placed on screened subnets (or DMZs), use only standard secondary DNS zones**
   - **Restrict the number of network administrators that can manage DNS servers**

2. Six months after the initial deployment of your DNS design, some of the research facilities are experiencing delays in domain name resolution. What recommendations can you make to improve the DNS query response times?

   You can make the following recommendations:

   - **Specify additional DNS servers at each research facility**
   - **Distribute the DNS clients evenly across the original and additional DNS servers**
   - **In instances where the number of resource records in a domain is excessive, divide the resource records into multiple delegated subdomains**

3. The director of research for the biotech consortium obtained a Web-based groupware application that allows research scientists to collaborate on their research. Because the research scientists are located throughout the world, the servers that host the groupware application must be accessible at all times. How can you ensure that these requirements are achieved?

   You can make the following recommendations:

   - **Place a Windows Clustering server cluster with two cluster nodes at each research facility**
   - **Install the DNS Server service on both nodes in the cluster**
   - **Designate one of the nodes in the cluster as the active DNS server**
   - **Dedicate the two cluster nodes to running DNS**

Review Questions

1. An organization is creating a design in preparation for the deployment of Windows 2000 and Active Directory. The organization has an existing DNS infrastructure based on BIND version 8.2.1 DNS servers. What additional information must you collect to determine the requirements and constraints for a DNS design?

   You must collect the following information:

   - **Existing internal and external domain namespace structure**

   - **Requirements for dynamically updated DNS zones**

   - **Character set to be used for domain names**

   - **Interoperability with existing BIND 8.2.1 DNS servers**

   - **Availability requirements of the design**

   - **Number of locations and types of WAN connections between locations**

   - **Number of computers at each location**

   - **DNS query response time requirements of the design**

2. You're creating a DNS design for an organization that has existing BIND DNS servers. The organization is deploying Active Directory and requires the DNS design to support the Active Directory deployment. The organization has an existing external and internal namespace and wants to reduce the administration of DNS by automatically populating the DNS zone resource records. However, the organization wants to protect the integrity of the DNS resource records. What recommendations can you make to the organization?

   You can make the following recommendations:

   - **Specify a subdomain within the internal namespace to contain the Active Directory domain namespace**

   - **Specify that the subdomain, and any subdomains beneath the subdomain, is dynamically updated DNS zones**

   - **For DNS clients running operating systems other than Windows 2000, specify that the DHCP servers within the organization automatically update the DNS zones**

   - **For DNS clients running Windows 2000, specify that either the DNS Client or the DHCP servers within the organization automatically update the DNS zones**

   - **Grant the appropriate permissions for the DHCP server, or DNS clients running Windows 2000, to update the DNS zones**

3. You're evaluating an existing DNS design for an Internet-based auction firm that has a significant e-commerce Web presence. The auction firm sells collectables, memorabilia, celebrity estate items, and other rare goods. The

director or information services for the auction firm is concerned about the ability of the Windows 2000–based DNS servers to provide name resolution at all times, regardless of a single point of failure. What changes to the design can you recommend to ensure that customers always *transparently* resolve domain names and subsequently access the e-commerce Web site?

To ensure that the customers are always able to resolve domain names and subsequently access the e-commerce Web site, your DNS design must

- **Specify a Windows Clustering server cluster for the DNS servers that manage the domain namespace for the Web site**
- **Specify that the DNS Server service be installed on both cluster nodes**
- **Specify that Internet registries point to the server cluster IP address to resolve domain names for the Web site**

4. An aerospace engineering firm that designs and builds satellite launch vehicles has retained your services to evaluate the existing DNS design. The firm started three years ago as a small entrepreneurial firm. In the last three years, the number of users, and corresponding computers, in the firm has tripled each year. Users are noticing a delay when initially accessing resources and accessing Active Directory. You determine that the DNS query response times are the root cause for the delays users are experiencing. After examining the network segment and router utilization, you determine that the network segments and routers aren't the source of the DNS query latency. What changes to your DNS design can you recommend to resolve these performance issues?

You can make the following recommendations:

- **Specify an additional DNS server at each location (or additional Windows Clustering server cluster)**
- **Specify that the existing DNS clients be distributed between the original DNS server (or Windows Clustering server cluster) and the additional DNS server (or Windows Clustering server cluster)**
- **If the number of resource records in any of the existing domains is excessive, you can divide the domains into delegated subdomains**

Chapter 10

Activity Questions

Lesson 2: Essential WINS Design Concepts

Activity 10.1: Evaluating a WINS Design

1. You're an outside consultant retained to create the networking services design for the resort chain. Each resort property has fewer than 3,500 computers within the location. The client computers at each resort property run various versions of Windows operating systems that include Windows 95, Windows 98,

Windows Me, Windows NT 4.0 Workstation, and Windows 2000 Professional. What do you recommend as a WINS solution for the resort chain?

You might make the following recommendations:

- **Specify at least one WINS server at each resort property**
- **Specify that the WINS Client (NetBT) be enabled on computers running Windows 2000 Professional**

2. While collecting the requirements and constraints for your design, you discover that a number of the computers at each location are non-WINS clients. How can you provide NetBIOS name resolution to these non-WINS clients?

For each network segment that contains non-WINS clients, you can make the following recommendations:

- **Specify at least one WINS client**
- **Specify that the WINS proxy be enabled on the WINS client**

3. The file and print resources accessed by the reservation and billing system at each resort property are located on network segments other than the WINS clients. The DNS zones at each resort property contain only external resource names. The director of information services for the resort chain wants to ensure that management of the name resolution is performed centrally. How can you ensure that these requirements are met?

You can make the following recommendations:

- **Specify a WINS node type of h-node to ensure that NetBIOS names are resolved by WINS first (p-node) and then b-node broadcasts**
- **Specify that DNS lookup for NetBIOS names be disabled**
- **Specify that LMHOSTS lookup be disabled**

Lesson 4: WINS Design Optimization

Activity 10.2: Evaluating a WINS Design

1. The marketing and sales representatives report that the length of time to start the computers has increased proportionally to the number of users added. You examine the network traffic and router statistics and determine that the increased time in starting the computers isn't related to network segment or router saturation. By examining the network traffic for a sampling of the computers exhibiting the performance problems, you determine the WINS servers are one of the primary reasons for the increased time in starting the computers. When you examine the WINS servers, you determine that during peak periods of activity, the WINS servers have as many as 1,000 NetBIOS registrations in the queue. What recommendations can you make to the vacation resort chain?

You can make one or more of the following recommendations:

- **Specify that burst handling be enabled**
- **Specify additional WINS servers be installed and distribute the WINS clients between the WINS servers**

- Specify that no other applications or services be running on the WINS servers

- Specify that the computers running the WINS servers be upgraded or replaced

2. Each resort property is concerned about security from within the resort property and from the public X.25 network that connects the resort properties. How do you protect WINS servers from access by unauthorized users through the X.25 network and within each resort property?

   You can make the following recommendations:

   - Specify that the WINS servers be placed on network segments that aren't accessible from the X.25 network, such as screened subnets (or DMZs) protected by firewalls

   - Specify that a limited number of authorized network administrators can administer the WINS servers

3. In another meeting, the management of the resort property chain wants to ensure that the marketing and sales representatives can access resources within the resort at all times (to accommodate the new hours of operation). How can you ensure that these business and technical requirements are met?

   You can make the following recommendations:

   - Specify that the WINS servers be installed on Windows Clustering server clusters within each resort property

   - Specify that the WINS clients at each resort property be configured to use the server cluster as the WINS server

4. The resort property chain's director of information services has reviewed the current utilization of the X.25 network that connects the locations. During peak periods of activity, the X.25 connections in many locations are at maximum utilization. The director of information services wants to eliminate traffic to ensure that the X.25 network segments don't become saturated. What modification can you make to your WINS design to ensure that these business and technical requirements are met?

   You can make the following recommendations:

   - Specify that pull partner replication occurs between the resort properties

   - Specify that the replication interval for the pull partner replication be increased to reduce network traffic

   - Specify that persistent connections are used on the pull partner replication between the resort properties

Review Questions

1. An organization is comprised of 130 locations and each location has an average of 35 routed network segments. Each location contains a 100Mbps backbone segment that connects the other network segments to one another. The

organization supports a variety of desktop operating systems. As an independent consultant to the organization, you're retained to create a WINS design. What recommendations can you make to the organization?

You can make the following recommendations:

- **Install WINS on a Windows Clustering server cluster in each location**

- **On all network segments that contain non-WINS clients, enable WINS proxies on at least two WINS clients**

- **Specify a hub-and-spoke replication topology for the WINS servers**

- **Specify push/pull replication between the WINS servers within each location**

- **Specify push replication between the hub WINS servers at each location**

- **Specify that authorized network administrators are the only users that can administer the WINS servers**

2. You're evaluating an existing WINS design for an international legal firm. The legal firm has 190 locations throughout the world. The desktop and laptop client computers in the legal firm run various network operating systems, including Windows 98, Windows Me, Windows NT 4.0, and Windows 2000. The legal firm wants to ensure that all networking services, including WINS, are protected from unauthorized users. Because the legal firm has locations worldwide, the users must be able to resolve NetBIOS names at all times. What recommendations can you make to the legal firm?

You can make the following recommendations:

- **Install WINS on a Windows Clustering server cluster in each location in the firm.**

- **Specify a hub-and-spoke replication topology for the WINS servers.**

- **Specify push/pull replication between the WINS servers within each location.**

- **Specify push replication between the hub WINS servers at each location.**

- **Specify that authorized network administrators are the only users that can administer the WINS serverss.**

- **Specify that WINS servers be placed on network segments that are inaccessible from the Internet or other public networks.**

3. You're evaluating an existing WINS design for an organization. The organization has 25 locations throughout Europe. Each location contains approximately 275 desktop computers, 15 file servers, and 25 print servers. Currently, the organization's WINS servers are running Windows NT 4.0 Server. The WAN network segments that connect the locations are saturated during peak periods of activity. What changes to the WINS design can you recommend to reduce the utilization of the WAN network segments during these peak periods of activity?

To reduce the utilization of the WAN network segments during these peak periods of activity, your WINS design must

- **Specify that existing WINS servers be upgraded to Windows 2000**
- **Specify that pull partner replication be utilized between WINS servers that replicate over the WAN network segments**
- **Specify that the pull partner replication interval be increased**
- **Specify that persistent connections be enabled on all WINS servers**

4. An organization is deploying Windows 2000 exclusively for all computers in the network. The existing network is running Windows 95, Windows 98, Windows NT, and other operating systems. The existing networking services are running on Windows NT 4 Server. The information services manager of the organization wants to eliminate NetBIOS traffic to reduce network traffic and remove the requirement for WINS servers. What must be done so you can achieve these business and technical requirements in your design?

To eliminate NetBIOS traffic and remove the requirement for WINS servers, the organization must

- **Finalize the deployment of Windows 2000 to *all* computers**
- **Ensure that no applications in the network require NetBIOS for peer-to-peer or client/server communication**
- **Ensure that Active Directory is deployed**
- **Ensure that DNS contains all the names of network resources that must be accessed**

Chapter 11

Activity Questions

Lesson 2: Essential Dial-Up Remote Access Design Concepts

Activity 11.1: Evaluating a Dial-Up Remote Access Design

1. As a consultant to the engineering firm, you're responsible for creating the dial-up remote access design. The field engineers work within the same city as the office where they report. The firm wants to ensure that long-term costs for the dial-up remote access solution are minimized. What recommendations can you make to the structural engineering firm?

You can make the following recommendations:

- **Specify that dial-up remote access servers be placed in each of the offices**
- **Specify that all dial-up remote access servers include TCP/IP**

- Specify that the dial-up remote access servers at the Calgary, Edmonton and Halifax offices include the IPX protocol

- Specify that the dial-up remote access servers at the Winnipeg, Vancouver, Toronto, and Montreal offices include the AppleTalk protocol

2. After conducting pilot tests on the computer platform selected to be remote access servers, you determine that each remote access server can support 90 simultaneous remote users at the minimum sustained data rate that provides acceptable application response time. Three-quarters of the remote users for each location must be able to simultaneously access the private network. How many remote access servers are required to fulfill the requirements of the organization?

You can make the following recommendations:

- **Specify five dial-up remote access servers at the Winnipeg, Vancouver, Toronto, and Montreal offices ((500 * 0.75)/90=4.167)**

- **Specify three dial-up remote access servers at the Calgary, Edmonton and Halifax offices ((300 * 0.75)/90=2.5)**

3. You're preparing the specifications for each remote access server. The vendor that supplies the remote access servers wants to know how many multiport communications adapters to include in each server. Each multiport communications adapter supports 32 communications ports. What specifications do you provide to the remote access server vendor?

Each remote access server can support a maximum of 90 remote users. You must include three multiport communications adapters to ensure that each remote access server can support 90 remote users (32*3=96).

4. You're finalizing the specifications for the dial-up remote access design and are allocating network addresses from the firm's IP, IPX, and AppleTalk network addresses. The network administrators want to minimize the administration of addresses assigned to remote access clients. The firm utilizes DHCP to provide automatic IP address configuration for computers within each office. How do you assign network addresses to the remote access clients?

You can make the following recommendations:

- **Specify that all dial-up remote access servers use DHCP to assign IP addresses**

- **Specify that an IPX network number be allocated for each dial-up remote access server at the Calgary, Edmonton and Halifax offices**

- **Specify that an AppleTalk network number be allocated for each dial-up remote access server at the Winnipeg, Vancouver, Toronto, and Montreal offices**

Lesson 4: Dial-Up Remote Access Design Optimization

Activity 11.2: Completing a Dial-Up Remote Access Design

1. The management for the consulting firm is concerned about the security associated with the new dial-up remote access design. What can you include in your design to ensure that private network resources and confidential data are protected?

   You can make the following recommendations:

   - **Specify that all dial-up remote access servers be placed only on screened subnets**
   - **Specify that the IP, IPX, and AppleTalk packet filters restrict access to private network resources**
   - **Specify that all remote users be authenticated**
   - **Specify that all remote access servers require the strongest authentication and encryption protocols possible**
   - **Specify that all remote access servers include remote access policies that enforce the organization's security requirements**

2. The consulting firm wants to provide a dial-up remote access server that customers can access anonymously. Your design must allow the customers to access only the resources on the dial-up remote access server, while protecting the consulting firm's private network resources. How can you provide access to the dial-up remote access server while protecting private network resources?

   One possible solution that you can create includes the following recom-mendations to the firm:

   - **Specify that all dial-up remote access servers be placed only on screened subnets**
   - **Specify that the IP, IPX, and AppleTalk packet filters restrict access to the dial-up remote access server's resources**

   Another possible solution that you can create includes the following rec-ommendations to the firm:

   - **Specify that all dial-up remote access servers be placed only on screened subnets**
   - **Specify that remote access to the entire network be disabled to restrict access to the dial-up remote access server's resources**

3. Construction on many of the projects managed by the consulting firm continues 24 hours per day, 7 days per week. A team of field engineers assigned to these projects is always onsite while construction occurs. The field engineers require remote access while onsite. What can you include in your design to ensure that the field engineers can always access the consulting firm's private network?

You can make the following recommendations:

- **Specify multiple dial-up remote access servers within each office**
- **Specify that a unique bank of phone numbers be assigned to each dial-up remote access server**
- **Specify that the field engineers utilize one bank of phone numbers as their primary remote access phone number**
- **Specify that the field engineers utilize a different bank of phone numbers as their backup remote access phone number**

4. A few months after deployment, the field engineers report that application response times through the remote access servers have decreased dramatically since the initial deployment. Upon investigation, you discover that the average data rate for each remote access connection has decreased accordingly. How can you modify your design to improve the application response times through the remote access servers?

You can make the following recommendations:

- **Specify additional dial-up remote access servers within each office**
- **Specify that a unique bank of phone numbers be assigned to each dial-up remote access server**
- **Specify that the field engineers be evenly distributed across the remote access servers**

Review Questions

1. An organization is considering remote access solutions to provide remote access to users that work from home. The users are distributed across a number of geographic locations, but all report to a local office. The director of information services is considering dial-up remote access solutions and VPN remote access solutions. As a consultant to the organization, what information do you need to obtain to assist the organization in determining the most appropriate solution?

You must determine the portions of the remote access design that the organization wants to directly control. When the organization wants to control all aspects of the remote access design, a dial-up remote access solution is the most appropriate. When the organization can outsource the dial-up remote access connections to ISPs or other third-party organizations, a VPN remote access solution is the most appropriate.

2. You're preparing a list of recommendations that you must present to the board of directors for a large international trading company. The trading company has retained your services to evaluate its current dial-up remote access solution. During your investigation and evaluation of the current dial-up remote access solution, you determine that remote users often experience poor phone

line quality. The poor phone line quality results in the users connecting at slower data rates and frequently disconnecting. Other than the poor phone line quality, the current remote access solution is meeting the trading company's requirements and constraints. What recommendations can you make to the trading company to resolve the slow data rates and frequent disconnections?

When the dial-up remote access servers are local to the remote access users (within the same metropolitan area or township), you can't modify your remote access solution to resolve these issues because the slow data rates and frequent disconnections are caused by the phone line quality. Contact the local telephone company to resolve the phone line quality issues.

When the remote users connect to remote access servers by using long distance, consider placing remote access servers local to the remote users (within the same metropolitan area or township).

3. An organization has retained you as a consultant to create a dial-up remote access solution. The organization has a number of remote users that connect to the private network resources by using a variety of operating systems, including Windows 95, Windows 98, Windows NT 4 Workstation, Windows 2000 Professional, and Macintosh operating systems. Within the organization, the remote users must access resources on servers running Windows 2000, NetWare 4.2, and Macintosh operating systems. What do you include in your design to create a dial-up remote access solution for the organization?

You can include the following in your design:

- **Specify that all dial-up remote access servers be placed only on screened subnets**

- **Specify that the IP, IPX, and AppleTalk protocols be included on all dial-up remote access servers**

- **Specify that all remote users be authenticated**

- **Specify that all remote access servers require the strongest authentication and encryption protocols possible**

- **Specify that all remote access servers include remote access policies that enforce the organization security requirements**

4. One year after the initial deployment of the dial-up remote access design that you created for your organization, remote users are reporting slow application response times. You were informed of the performance problems during a meeting with the chief information officer (CIO) of your organization. The CIO is concerned about the slow application response times and wants to know what strategy you'll use to resolve the application response issues. What strategies can you use to determine the source of the application response time problems and resolve the issue?

If remote users and *local users* are experiencing the degradation in application response time, consult with the group that manages the servers that host the applications experiencing the response times.

If only remote users are experiencing the degradation in application response time, you can

- Examine the average data rate experienced by remote users and determine whether the data rate is within the original specifications
- Specify additional dial-up remote access servers where appropriate
- Specify an additional phone line bank for each additional dial-up remote access server
- Specify that remote users are evenly distributed across the dial-up remote access servers

Chapter 12

Activity Questions

Lesson 2: Essential VPN Remote Access Design Concepts

Activity 12.1: Evaluating a VPN Remote Access Design

1. The shipping company's director of marketing and customer service has decided that the majority of the customer service representatives will work remotely at the shipping customer's location to provide better service. The customer service representatives must connect to the shipping company's private network to access the Web applications and resources. As the director of information services for the shipping company, you're responsible for the networking services design. What recommendations can you make?

   You can make the following recommendations:

   - Install a VPN remote access server at each office
   - Specify a PPTP, or L2TP, port for each simultaneous remote access client
   - Specify that DHCP provide IP configuration for remote access clients
   - Specify that a DHCP Relay Agent be installed on each VPN remote access server

2. The board of directors for the shipping company is reviewing the proposal you submitted for the VPN remote access design. One of the board members is also on the board of directors for another company. The other company selected dial-up remote access servers for its remote access solutions and the board member wants to know why you're recommending a VPN remote access design for this company. How do you respond?

The primary reason for selecting a VPN remote access design is to reduce the costs associated with the implementation and support of the dial-up connectivity of the remote access design. By allowing third-party organizations to provide the dial-up connectivity for the shipping company, the costs associated with the remote access solution.

Because the shipping company is willing to relinquish control of the dial-up connectivity portion of the design, a VPN remote access solution is the most appropriate.

The primary advantage to a dial-up remote access solution is that the organization retains control of all aspects of the remote access solution. The other organization that the board member referred to might not be willing to relinquish any control of any aspect of its remote access design.

3. The shipping company's director of marketing and customer service reports that the customer service representatives are confused by the credentials required to initiate dial-up connectivity and the credentials required to initiate the VPN connection. The director of marketing and customer service wants to know whether there is any way to consolidate the credentials so the customer service representatives are required to remember only one set of credentials. What recommendations can you make?

A RADIUS remote access solution allows the users to utilize only one set of user credentials, but requires a formal agreement with a third-party organization to provide dial-up remote access. A VPN remote access solution doesn't require a formal agreement with third-party organizations to provide dial-up remote access.

The shipping company must determine whether the costs associated in an agreement with a third-party organization offset the requirement for a single set of user credentials.

Lesson 4: VPN Remote Access Design Optimization

Activity 12.2: Completing a VPN Remote Access Design

1. The management of the shipping company wants to restrict the customer representatives so they can only access the company's Web site remotely. The chief information office of the company (CIO) wants to ensure that only HTTP and FTP traffic are sent to the company's Web site. Also, only authenticated users should be granted remote access. As the director of information services, what VPN remote access solution do you recommend to management?

You might make the following recommendations:

- **Specify that each VPN remote access server include packet filters criteria to filter all traffic except HTTP and FTP traffic**

- **Specify remote access policies that require all remote users to be authenticated**

- **Specify that remote users be granted access to the entire network**

2. The remote users run a variety of operating systems, including Windows 98, Windows NT 4 Workstation, and Windows 2000 Professional. All remote access traffic must be encrypted by using the strongest possible encryption protocol. How do you protect private network resources while providing access to the Web servers?

You can make the following recommendations:

- **Specify PPTP tunnels for the remote access clients running Windows 98 and Windows NT 4 Workstation**

- **Specify PPTP, or L2TP, tunnels for the remote access clients running Windows 2000**

- **Specify MS-CHAP as the authentication protocol**

- **Specify 128-bit MPPE as the encryption protocol for the PPTP tunnels**

- **Specify Triple Data Encryption Standard (3DES) as the encryption protocol for the L2TP tunnels**

- **Specify remote access policies that require all remote users to encrypt all traffic**

- **Specify that remote users be granted access to the entire network**

3. After a few months of operation, remote users are experiencing performance problems. The existing Internet connections are T1 connections. Also, some remote users are experiencing outages due to hardware and Internet connection failure. How can you improve the performance and increase the availability for these offices?

You can make the following recommendations:

- **Upgrade the existing Internet connections to T3 connections**

- **Specify redundant Internet connections**

- **Specify additional VPN remote access servers at each office**

- **Specify that the computers running Routing and Remote Access be dedicated to VPN remote access servers**

- **Specify that the VPN remote access servers at each office belong to the same Network Load Balancing cluster to improve the performance and availability of remote access**

Review Questions

1. An organization is considering VPN remote access solutions to provide remote access to users who work from home. The users are distributed across a number of geographic locations, but all report to a local office. As a consultant to the organization, what information do you need to obtain to assist the organization in creating the most appropriate solution?

You must collect the following information to create your VPN remote access design:

- **Number of remote users that require simultaneous remote access**
- **Operating systems running on remote access client computers**
- **Geographic location of remote users and remote access servers**
- **Strength of security required to protect confidential data and private network resources**
- **Percentage of time that remote users require remote access to the private network**
- **Response times that remote users require when accessing private network resources or running applications**

2. Your organization wants to provide VPN remote access to users who travel extensively. The remote users travel internationally and must be able to connect to private network resources from any location. The network administrators want to ensure that minimal changes are made to the firewall rules. In addition, the solution must authenticate remote users and encrypt all data transmitted between the organization's private network and the remote users. What recommendations can you make to provide a VPN remote access solution?

You can include the following in your design:

- **Specify that VPN remote access servers be placed outside the private network**
- **Specify that all traffic between the VPN remote access servers and the private network be protected by VPN or IPSec tunnels**
- **Specify that IP be included on all VPN remote access servers**
- **Specify that all remote users within North America be authenticated and their data encrypted by strongest possible security**
- **Specify that all remote users outside North America be authenticated and their data encrypted by the strongest possible security allowed by the local government**
- **Specify that all remote access servers include remote access policies that enforce the organization security requirements**

3. An organization has retained you as a consultant to review a design that you created more than a year ago. The remote users are experiencing degradation in response times for applications they run. The response time has gradually degraded over a period of time. Without further examination, what suggestions can you make to the organization to restore remote access performance?

You can make the following suggestions to design modifications:

- **Specify that additional VPN remote access servers be installed**
- **Specify that the appropriate VPN remote access servers belong to the same Network Load Balancing cluster**

- Specify that the existing Internet connections be upgraded

- Specify that additional Internet connections be installed

4. Remote users in your organization are reporting outages of remote access. The remote users are connecting properly to their ISP, but are unable to establish the VPN connection. How can you modify your design to reduce the number of remote access outages and improve overall remote access uptime?

You can make the following suggestions to design modifications:

- Specify that additional VPN remote access servers be installed

- Specify that the appropriate VPN remote access servers belong to the same Network Load Balancing cluster

- Specify that the existing Internet connections be upgraded

- Specify that additional Internet connections be installed

Chapter 13

Activity Questions

Lesson 2: Essential RADIUS Concepts

Activity 13.1: Evaluating a RADIUS Design

1. While working in other consortium member locations, scientists must access resources within their company's private network. The consortium members want to ensure that when the scientists access the company's resources, all data is encrypted. In addition, the director of information services for each consortium member wants to control the password characteristics (such as the frequency of password change, minimum password length, password aging, etc.). What recommendations can you make?

You might make the following recommendations:

- Specify new network segments at each biotech company that are designated for use by visiting scientists from other consortium

- Specify that a RADIUS client that supports VPN connections be placed on a network segment designated for use by consortium members

- Specify that a RADIUS server be placed within the private network at each biotech company

- Specify that each RADIUS client utilizes the RADIUS server at each respective biotech company for authentication and accounting

- Specify that each RADIUS server provides authentication and accounting for each RADIUS client

- Specify a unique RADIUS realm for each RADIUS server

2. At a meeting of the directors of information services for the biotech companies, you're asked to participate in a question and answer session. At the session, one of the directors wants to know how the directors can ensure that each company's individual security requirements will be met. How do you respond?

Because each biotech company manages its RADIUS server, the company can specify the appropriate RADIUS attributes (remote access policies). Because each RADIUS client authenticates by using the RADIUS server for the respective biotech company, the company's individual security requirements will be enforced.

3. During the same question and answer session in the previous question, another director asks about the ability of the scientists to access the biotech company's private network resources where they are conducting research. Because the scientist works for another biotech company, each company is concerned about loss of trade secrets. The director is concerned that RADIUS might compromise the security of the existing network at each biotech company. Each biotech company has standardized on Active Directory as their directory service. How do you respond?

RADIUS allows only the scientists to be authenticated by Active Directory in their respective company. RADIUS doesn't modify the trust relationships between the Active Directory domains for the consortium members.

Each biotech consortium member can still administer its own user accounts and resources independently of the other members. To allow scientists to access resources at other biotech companies, the members need to either create user accounts for the scientists or to create trust relationships between Active Directory domains for other members.

Lesson 4: RADIUS Design Optimization

Activity 13.2: Completing a RADIUS Design

1. The board of directors for the biotech consortium wants to ensure that only scientists who are working in the consortium's research facilities can access the private network resources within their respective biotech company. How can you ensure that these requirements are met in your design?

You can make the following recommendations:

- **Specify that each RADIUS client include IP packet filters criteria to filter all traffic that doesn't originate from other consortium members**

- **Specify remote access policies that require all remote users to be authenticated**

- **Specify RADIUS shared secrets for all the RADIUS clients and RADIUS servers in the biotech consortium**

2. The remote users run a variety of operating systems, including Windows 98, Windows NT 4 Workstation, and Windows 2000 Professional. The consortium wants all confidential data protected. How do you protect the confidential data accessed by the scientists working at other consortium research and development facilities?

You can make the following recommendations:

- **Specify PPTP tunnels between the remote users and the remote access servers for the remote access clients running Windows 98 and Windows NT 4 Workstation**

- **Specify PPTP, or L2TP, tunnels between the remote users and the remote access servers for the remote access clients running Windows 2000**

- **Specify MS-CHAP as the authentication protocol**

- **Specify 128-bit MPPE as the encryption protocol for the PPTP tunnels**

- **Specify Triple Data Encryption Standard (3DES) as the encryption protocol for the L2TP tunnels**

- **Specify remote access policies on the RADIUS servers that require all remote users to encrypt all traffic**

3. One of the primary concerns of the consortium is that the scientists can access their resources at any time. In addition, the first phase of the deployment process occurred a few months ago. Since the initial deployment, remote users report that the length of time for authentication is increasing. How can you ensure that the scientists can always access their resources and reduce the length of time for authentication?

You can make the following recommendations:

- **Specify additional RADIUS clients and RADIUS servers at each office**

- **Specify that the computers running RADIUS clients and RADIUS servers be dedicated to RADIUS**

- **Specify that the RADIUS clients at each office belong to the same Network Load Balancing cluster to improve the performance and availability of remote access**

- **Specify that the RADIUS servers at each office belong to the same Network Load Balancing cluster to improve the performance and availability of remote access**

Review Questions

1. An organization is considering outsourcing its dial-up connectivity to a third party to provide remote access to users who work from home. The users are distributed across a number of geographic locations, but all report to a local office. The organization wants to control all aspects of the remote user passwords (such as password length or password aging). As a consultant to the organization, what recommendation do you make to achieve the requirements of the organization?

You can make the following recommendations:

- **Specify that RADIUS servers be placed at each of the local offices**

- **Specify that the third-party RADIUS clients be configured to use the RADIUS servers for authentication and accounting**

- **Specify the same RADIUS shared secrets for all RADIUS clients and RADIUS servers**

2. You're the director of information services for an ISP and you want to provide outsourced dial-up remote access connectivity for organizations. Many of the organizations that your company provides connectivity for want a single set of user credentials and want to implement user callback to provide enhanced security. In addition, you have entered into a SLA with these organizations to provide specific authentication response times and ensure that the organizations' remote users can always access their private network resources. What recommendations can you make to these organizations?

You can make the following recommendations:

- **Specify that RADIUS servers be placed inside the private networks of these organizations**

- **Specify that all the RADIUS servers belong to the same Network Load Balancing cluster**

- **Specify that the RADIUS clients (or NASs) provided by your company be configured to use the organizations' RADIUS servers for authentication and accounting**

- **Specify that all the RADIUS clients belong to the same Network Load Balancing cluster**

- **Specify that the RADIUS servers provide authentication and accounting for the RADIUS clients**

- **Specify that the RADIUS clients and RADIUS servers have the same RADIUS shared secrets**

3. An organization has an existing dial-up remote access solution that supports hundreds of remote users. The organization wants to control all aspects of its remote access solution and is unwilling to outsource any portion of the dial-up remote access solution. How can RADIUS provide improvements in the existing dial-up remote access solution?

You can make the following suggestions to design modifications:

- **Specify that RADIUS servers be placed within the private network of the organization**

- **Specify that all RADIUS servers have the same remote access policies**

- **Specify that the existing dial-up remote access servers utilize RADIUS for authentication and accounting (and become RADIUS clients in the process)**

- Specify that the RADIUS clients belong to the same Network Load Balancing cluster

- Specify that the RADIUS servers belong to the same Network Load Balancing cluster

- Specify that the RADIUS clients and RADIUS servers have the same RADIUS shared secrets

4. The director of information services in your organization has reviewed your proposal to outsource the dial-up remote connectivity in the organization's remote access design. The director is confused about why your design includes remote access servers in addition to RADIUS clients and RADIUS servers. How do you respond to the director?

The remote access servers in the design are used to provide a VPN tunnel between the remote users (or RADIUS clients) and the remote access server. In addition, the remote access server provides a single entry point for all remote access traffic that you can use to protect private network resources.

Chapter 14

Review Questions

1. You're retained as a consultant to an organization to create the networking services portion of the organization's management design. The management design is in the early stages and you're attending a series of meetings to gather the organization's business and technical requirements and constraints. What type of information do you need to collect during the meetings?

You need to collect the following information:

- **The applications run by the organization's users**

- **The critical nature of each of the applications run by the organization's users**

- **The networking services critical to the operation of each application**

2. An organization is evaluating its existing management design. The operations staff reports that many of the users are unable to access critical applications on a regular basis. The operations staff also reports that they aren't notified of any networking services failures until 30 minutes to an hour after the failure occurs. The organization wants to decrease the length of time between the time the failure occurs and the time the operations staff is notified. In the new management design, the operations staff wants to be immediately notified of any critical networking services failure. What recommendations can you make to these organizations?

You can make the following recommendations:

- **Identify the networking services critical to the operation of the applications**
- **Determine the possible failures or resource shortages that can occur**
- **For each possible failure or resource shortage, you must determine how quickly the management design must respond, the type of response to be used, and the method that will be used to respond**
- **Ensure that the response to each possible failure for the critical networking services uses immediate responses**

3. You're creating a management design for an organization that runs a number of mission-critical applications. The mission-critical applications depend on the networking services within the organization. Some of the networking services that support these applications run on clusters and require high security to protect the applications. The organization's operations staff wants to ensure that they receive immediate responses to any critical networking services failures. What recommendations do you make in your networking services management design?

You can make the following recommendations:

- **Specify immediate response types for all critical networking services failures or resource shortages**
- **Specify delayed response types for the noncritical networking services failures or resource shortages**
- **Specify scheduled response types for the security and availability management of the networking services**

Chapter 15

Review Questions

1. You have been retained as consultant to review and evaluate a networking services design. The organization that retained you wants to ensure it reduces the cost associated with deploying and managing the design. What recommendations can you make to the organization?

   You can recommend that the organization combine networking services onto single computers. However, you must ensure that combining the networking services doesn't violate the security, availability, and performance aspects of the networking services design.

2. You're creating a networking services solution for an organization that has a large Internet presence. The organization utilizes an e-commerce site to generate its revenue. The e-commerce site must be available to users 24 hours per day, 7 days per week. What recommendations can you make to the organization?

You can make the following recommendations:

- Combine any networking servers that are cluster-aware onto server clusters

- Combine any networking servers that are cluster-unaware and that store networking services data on disk onto server clusters

- Include network load balancing on the servers running Internet Information Services (IIS) to provide load balancing and fault tolerance for the Web servers

- Ensure that only signed drivers and services are included on the server clusters

- Eliminate any unstable software from the server clusters

3. You're evaluating a networking services design that was created two years ago by an outside consulting firm. Since the initial deployment, the users report a gradual reduction in the overall network performance. The Chief Information Officer of the organization had given you the responsibility to review the design and to make suggestions for improving the performance. What general optimizations to the existing design can you utilize in your revision of the design?

You can include the following optimization techniques:

- Combine networking services onto single servers to reduce the costs by eliminating additional computers

- Combine networking services onto single server (or server clusters) to improve the security, availability, and performance of the design

- Place servers running networking services closer together in relation to servers hosting applications to improve the security, availability, and performance of the design

Glossary

3270 gateway A network device that translates local area network (LAN) protocols, such as Transmission Control Protocol/Internet Protocol (TCP/IP) or Internetwork Packet Exchange (IPX) to System Network Architecture (SNA) protocols. A 3270 gateway allows client computers to connect to IBM ES9000 mainframes or other IBM 370 architecture computers. Contrast 5250 gateway.

3DES *See* Triple DES (3DES).

40-bit DES An encryption scheme in which the sender and receiver of a message share a single, common key that is used to encrypt and decrypt the message. Developed in 1975 and standardized by the American National Standards Institute (ANSI) in 1981 as ANSI X.3.92, this version of Data Encryption Standard (DES) uses a 40-bit key and can be exported to most countries. Contrast Triple DES (3DES); 56-bit DES. *See also* DES.

5250 gateway A network device that translates local area network (LAN) protocols, such as Transmission Control Protocol/Internet Protocol (TCP/IP) or Internetwork Packet Exchange (IPX) to System Network Architecture (SNA) protocols. A 5250 gateway allows client computers to connect to IBM AS/400 computers. Contrast 3270 gateway.

56-bit DES An encryption scheme in which the sender and receiver of a message share a single, common key that is used to encrypt and decrypt the message. Developed in 1975 and standardized by the American National Standards Institute (ANSI) in 1981 as ANSI X.3.92, this version of Data Encryption Standard (DES) uses a 56-bit key and is illegal to export from the United States or Canada if you don't meet the Bureau of Export Administration (BXA) requirements. Contrast Triple DES (3DES); 40-bit DES. *See also* DES.

802.2 Institute of Electrical and Electronics Engineers (IEEE) designation for the Data Link Control (DLC) protocol. *See also* Data Link Control (DLC).

A

AARP *See* AppleTalk Address Resolution Protocol.

active caching A method of Web content caching included in Microsoft Proxy Server 2.0 that proactively updates the Web content cache during periods of inactivity. In addition to proactively updating Web content cache, active caching automatically updates the cache for any client requests (just like passive caching). *See also* passive caching; Web content caching.

active cluster node A server cluster node that is currently running an application or networking service. Another node within the cluster is acting as a redundant server in the event the active node fails. *See also* redundant cluster node; server cluster.

Active Directory The directory service included with Microsoft Windows 2000 Server. Active Directory stores information about objects on a network and makes this information available to users and network administrators. Active Directory gives network users access to permitted resources anywhere on the network using a single logon process. Active Directory provides network administrators with an intuitive hierarchical view of the network and a single point of administration for all network objects.

Active Directory integrated zone A zone type in Microsoft Windows 2000 DNS that stores a read-write copy of the DNS zone resource records in Active Directory. Active Directory integrated zones are replicated by using Active Directory replication. Active Directory integrated zones support secured, dynamic updates to the DNS zone resource records. To standard DNS zones, Active Directory integrated zones appear to be a standard primary zone. Contrast standard primary zone; standard secondary zone. *See also* DNS zone; Domain Name System (DNS).

Active Directory Service Interfaces (ADSI) A directory service model and a set of COM interfaces. ADSI enables Windows 95, Windows 98, Windows NT, and Windows 2000 applications to access several network directory services, including Active Directory. ADSI is described in the Windows 2000 Platform Software Developer's Kit (SDK).

Active Server Pages (ASP) A Web-oriented technology developed by Microsoft that is designed to enable server-side (as opposed to client-side) scripting. ASP are text files that can contain not only text and HTML tags as in standard Web documents, but also commands written in a scripting language (such as VBScript or JavaScript) that can be carried out on the server. This server-side work enables a Web author to add interactivity to a document or to customize the viewing or delivery of information to the client without worrying about the platform the client is running. All ASP are saved with an .asp extension and can be accessed like standard URLs through a Web browser, such as Microsoft Internet Explorer or Netscape Navigator. When an ASP is requested by a browser, the server carries out any script commands embedded in the page, generates an HTML document, and sends the document back to the browser for display on the requesting (client) computer. ASP can also be enhanced and extended with ActiveX components. *See also* Extensible Markup Language (XML); Open Database Connectivity (ODBC); Web-based applications.

Address Resolution Protocol (ARP) Determines hardware addresses (MAC addresses) that correspond to an Internet Protocol (IP) address.

ADSI *See* Active Directory Service Interfaces.

ADSL *See* Asymmetric Digital Subscriber Line.

Advanced Program-to-Program Communication (APPC) A specification developed as part of IBM's System Network Architecture (SNA) model and designed to enable application programs running on different computers to communicate and exchange data directly. *See also* System Network Architecture (SNA).

Advanced Research Projects Agency Network (ARPANET) A pioneering wide area network (WAN) commissioned by the Department of Defense, ARPANET was designed to facilitate the exchange of information between universities and other research organizations. ARPANET, which became operational in the 1960s, is the network from which the Internet evolved. *See also* Internet.

AFP *See* AppleTalk filing protocol.

AH *See* Authentication Header.

American National Standards Institute (ANSI) An organization of American industry and business groups dedicated to the development of trade and communications standards. ANSI is the American representative to the International Organization for Standardization (ISO). *See also* International Organization for Standardization (ISO).

American Standard Code for Information Interchange (ASCII) A coding scheme that assigns numeric values to letters, numbers, punctuation marks, and certain other characters. By standardizing the values used for these characters, ASCII enables computers and computer programs to exchange information.

API *See* application programming interface.

APPC *See* Advanced Program-to-Program Communication.

AppleShare The Apple network operating system. Features include file sharing, client software that is included with every copy of the Apple operating system, and the AppleShare print server, a server-based print spooler. *See also* AppleTalk filing protocol (AFP).

AppleTalk A transport protocol created by Apple Computer Co. that provides connectivity between Macintosh computers. Two versions of AppleTalk exist, AppleTalk Phase 1 and AppleTalk Phase 2; however, only AppleTalk Phase 2 is supported in Windows 2000. Contrast Internetwork Packet Exchange (IPX); Transmission Control Protocol/Internet Protocol (TCP/IP).

AppleTalk Address Resolution Protocol (AARP) A protocol found in AppleTalk networks that resolves AppleTalk addresses to Media Access Control (MAC) layer addresses. Similar to the Address Resolution Protocol found in Transmission Control Protocol/Internet Protocol (TCP/IP). *See also* AppleTalk.

AppleTalk filing protocol (AFP) Describes how files are stored and accessed on the network. AFP is responsible for the Apple hierarchical filing structure of volumes, folders, and files and provides for file sharing between Macintoshes and MS-DOS–based computers. It provides an interface for communication between AppleTalk and other network operating systems, allowing Macintoshes to be integrated into any network that uses an operating system that recognizes AFP. *See also* AppleShare; AppleTalk.

AppleTalk host ID An 8-bit decimal number that uniquely identifies a host computer within a network number. The host ID is automatically assigned within a network number. AppleTalk Phase 2 supports no more than 253 hosts within a network number.

AppleTalk network number A 16-bit decimal number that uniquely identifies an entire network segment or a portion of a network segment. Network numbers must be unique within your AppleTalk network. The AppleTalk network

number is also known as *network range* or *cable range.*

AppleTalk Phase 2 The second version of Apple Computer Co.'s transport protocol. AppleTalk Phase 2 is required to run Windows 2000 Server with AppleTalk network integration and is required to support Token Ring, Ethernet, and Fiber Distributed Data Interface (FDDI) in a network. *See also* AppleTalk.

AppleTalk zone A grouping of Macintosh computers and AppleTalk devices such that users can easily locate network resources and services. All the AppleTalk devices that belong to the same network number range must belong to the same zone. Contrast DNS zone. *See also* AppleTalk network number; network number.

AppleTalk zones Users locate network resources within an AppleTalk network by using AppleTalk zones. AppleTalk zones are very similar to Windows 2000 domains or workgroups.

application programming interface (API) A set of routines that an application program uses to request and carry out lower-level services performed by the operating system. Network Basic Input/Output System (NetBIOS), Active Directory Service Interfaces (ADSI), and Windows Management Instrumentation (WMI) are examples of APIs.

application server A midtier server in a multitier solution for providing end users with access back-end business applications. An application server translates browser-based requests from end users into a format supported by the back-end system such as a database management system, receives the reply from the back-end system, and formats the response as HTML before returning it to the end user's browser. Contrast file server; print server.

ARP *See* Address Resolution Protocol.

ARPANET *See* Advanced Research Projects Agency Network.

AS/400 computer A computer created by International Business Machines (IBM) that supports 5250 terminals and printers. In addition, the Advanced Program-to-Program Communication (APPC) peer-to-peer programming application programming interface (API) is supported by this type of computer. *See also* 5250 gateway.

ASBR *See* autonomous system boundary router.

ASCII *See* American Standard Code for Information Interchange.

ASP *See* Active Server Pages.

Asymmetric Digital Subscriber Line (ADSL) Technology and equipment allowing high-speed digital communication, including video signals, across an ordinary twisted-pair copper phone line, with speeds up to 8 Mbps (megabits per second) downstream (to the customer) and up to 640 Kbps (kilobits per second) upstream. ADSL access to the Internet is offered by some regional telephone companies, offering users faster connection times than those available through connections made over standard phone lines. Also called *asymmetric digital subscriber loop*. Compare Digital Subscriber Line (DSL); High-bit-rate Digital Subscriber Line (HDSL); Symmetric Digital Subscriber Line (SDSL).

asynchronous transfer mode (ATM) An advanced implementation of packet switching that provides high-speed data transmission rates to send fixed-size cells over LANs or WANs. Cells are 53 bytes—48 bytes of data with 5 additional bytes of address. ATM accommodates voice, data, fax, real-time video, CD-quality audio, imaging, and multi-megabit data transmission. ATM uses switches as multiplexers to permit several computers to put data on a network simultaneously. Most commercial ATM implementations transmit data at about 155 Mbps, but theoretically a rate of 1.2 gigabits per second is possible.

ATM *See* asynchronous transfer mode.

authentication Verification typically based on user name, password, and time and account restrictions.

Authentication Header (AH) An identity protocol that provides authentication, integrity, and antireplay for the entire packet (both the IP header and the data carried in the packet); AH signs the entire packet, but doesn't encrypt the data, so AH doesn't provide confidentiality. The data is readable, but protected from modification. AH uses the Hash-based Message Authentication Code (HMAC) algorithms to sign the packet. Contrast Encapsulating Security Payload (ESP). *See also* Internet Protocol Security (IPSec).

authorization A process that verifies that the user has the correct rights or permissions to access a resource.

autonomous system boundary router (ASBR) An Open Shortest Path First (OSPF) router that is used to connect to OSPF external routers. *See also* Open Shortest Path First (OSPF); OSPF autonomous system; OSPF external routes.

autostatic route entries Combine the best features of dynamic and static route entries. Autostatic route entries are periodically updated (like dynamic route entries) but require little network traffic, like static route entries). Contrast dynamic route entries; static route entries.

availability A measurement of system uptime that denotes the percentage of time applications and resources can be accessed by users. Contrast performance; security.

B

backbone The main cable, also known as the trunk segment, from which transceiver cables connect to computers, repeaters, and bridges.

back end In a client/server application, the part of the program that runs on the server.

bandwidth The amount of information that can be exchanged over a period of time. For computers and other digital devices, bandwidth is usually measured in bits per second or bytes per second. With analog devices, it is normally measured in cycles per second, or hertz (Hz). For example, a telephone operates between the frequencies of 300 and 3300 Hz, therefore its effective bandwidth is 3000 Hz. In computer networks, greater bandwidth indicates faster or greater data-transfer capability.

Berkeley Internet Name Domain (BIND) An implementation of DNS written and ported to most available versions of the UNIX operating system. The Internet Software Consortium maintains the BIND software.

Berkeley Software Distribution (BSD) UNIX A UNIX version developed at the University of California at Berkeley, providing additional capabilities such as networking, extra peripheral support, and use of extended filenames. BSD UNIX was instrumental in gaining widespread acceptance of UNIX and in getting academic institutions connected to the Internet. BSD UNIX is now being developed by Berkeley Software Design, Inc.

BGP *See* Border Gateway Protocol.

BIA *See* Burned In Address.

BIND *See* Berkley Internet Name Domain.

b-node WINS node type A method used by the Windows Internet Name Service (WINS) client in Windows 2000 for resolving NetBIOS names by sending IP broadcasts on the local network segment. B-node broadcasts aren't typically forwarded across IP-routed network segments unless the routers are specifically configured to route broadcast packets. Contrast h-node WINS node type; m-node WINS node type; p-node WINS node type.

BOOTP *See* bootstrap protocol.

bootstrap protocol (BOOTP) A protocol used on TCP/IP networks to provide IP protocol configuration for diskless workstations. Bootstrap protocol is used when the IP devices can't be configured by DHCP. DHCP is the configuration protocol that currently uses this protocol. The Microsoft DHCP service provides limited support for BOOTP service. Contrast Dynamic Host Configuration Protocol (DHCP).

Border Gateway Protocol (BGP) A routing protocol designed for use in connecting OSPF autonomous systems. As the name implies, BGP is utilized in OSPF networks to connect the borders of two or more OSPF autonomous systems. BGP is especially suited for detecting routing loops. *See also* Open Shortest Path First (OSPF).

bottleneck The limiting factor when analyzing performance of a system or network. Poor performance results when a device uses noticeably more CPU time than it should, consumes too much of a resource, or lacks the capacity to handle the load. Potential bottlenecks can be found in the processor, memory, network interface, and other components.

branch level domain name A hierarchical level in a domain namespace that contains other domain names (branch levels) or multiple DNS resource records (leaf levels). Contrast leaf level domain name.

broadcast IP address An IP address that has a destination of all computers. Broadcast IP addresses are utilized to send information from a computer to all computers on a network or network segment. Broadcast addressing is implemented to reduce network traffic and to locate devices without knowing the IP address. For example, Dynamic Host Configuration Protocol (DHCP) clients can locate a DHCP server by using a broadcast packet. Contrast multicast IP address; unicast IP address.

BSD *See* Berkeley Software Distribution.

burst handling WINS clients must register their NetBIOS names with the corresponding WINS servers. When a high volume of WINS clients attempt to simultaneously register their NetBIOS names, the WINS servers can become saturated and be unable to register names within the response time requirements of the organization. Burst handling allows WINS servers to postpone permanent registration of NetBIOS names. *See also* Windows Internet Name Service (WINS).

Burned In Address (BIA) The physical network address or Media Access Control (MAC) address used by network interface adapters. The BIA is typically stored in nonvolatile memory on the network interface adapter. *See also* business requirements; technical requirements.

business constraints Restrictions that set boundaries on the type of solution, based on an organization's business model, business practices, or other nontechnology-related issues. For example, budget restrictions may constrain the type of solution that can be created for an organization. Contrast technical constraints. *See also* business requirements; technical requirements.

business requirements Goals, expectations, customer model, organizational workflow, process flow, or other aspects of an organization's method of conducting day-to-day activities. For example, an organization may require that your solution work in different countries because the organization provides services, products, or has locations in those countries. Contrast technical requirements. *See also* business constraints; technical constraints.

C

CA *See* certificate authority.

caching-only DNS server A Domain Name System (DNS) server that doesn't contain a local copy of zone information on local disk. This type of DNS server places responses to DNS queries in memory for subsequent retrieval by DNS clients. Caching-only DNS servers can reduce network traffic by not requiring DNS zone replication.

callback A security method used by Routing and Remote Access to ensure that remote users are calling from a specific phone number. The remote access servers call the remote user back at a specified number. Contrast caller-ID.

caller-ID A security method used by Routing and Remote Access to ensure that remote users are calling from a specific phone number. This method uses the telephone companies' caller-ID technology to identify remote users. Contrast callback.

CCITT *See* ITU-T.

certificate A collection of data used for authentication and secure exchange of information on unsecured networks, such as the Internet. A certificate securely binds a public key to the entity that holds the corresponding private key. Certificates are digitally signed by the issuing certificate authority (CA) and can be managed for a user, computer, or service. The most widely accepted format for certificates is defined by ITU-T X.509 international standards. *See also* X509 version 3 certificate.

certificate authority (CA) A key component of public key encryption technology, a CA is responsible for issuing digital certificates used to create public-private key pairs and digital signatures. The CA guarantees the authenticity of one or both parties of a transaction, of the data within the transaction, and possibly the confidentiality of the transaction, depending on the application. *See also* X509 version 3 certificate.

Challenge Handshake Authentication Protocol (CHAP) An authentication protocol used by Microsoft Routing and Remote Access and Network and Dial-up Connections. Using CHAP, a remote access client can send its authentication credentials to a remote access server in a secure form. Microsoft has created a Windows–specific variant of CHAP called MS-CHAP. *See also* Extensible Authentication Protocol (EAP); Extensible Authentication Protocol – Message Digest 5 (EAP-MD5); Extensible Authentication Protocol – Transport Level Security (EAP-TLS); Microsoft Challenge Handshake Authentication Protocol (MS-CHAP); Microsoft Challenge Handshake Authentication Protocol version 2 (MS-CHAP v2); Password Authentication Pro-tocol (PAP); Shiva Password Authentication Protocol (SPAP).

CHAP *See* Challenge Handshake Authentication Protocol.

CIDR *See* classless interdomain routing.

class-based IP address An IP address that adheres to the classification of IP addresses as originally designated for Internet use. These classifications included Class A, Class B, Class C, Class D, and Class E. The increasing number of devices connecting to the Internet has resulted in Internet service providers (ISPs) and Internet registries utilizing classless IP addressing schemes by using classless interdomain routing (CIDR). Within a private network, organizations are using Variable Length Subnet Masks (VLSMs) to provide classless IP addressing. Contrast classless-based IP address. *See also* classless interdomain routing (CIDR); Variable Length Subnet Mask (VLSM).

classless-based IP address An IP address that supercedes the classification of IP addresses as originally designated for Internet use. The increasing number of devices connecting to the Internet has resulted in Internet service providers (ISPs) and Internet registries utilizing classless IP addressing schemes by using classless inter-domain routing (CIDR). Within a private network, organizations are using Variable Length Subnet Masks (VLSMs) to provide classless IP addressing. Classless IP addressing within an

organization results in a more efficient usage of the IP addresses available to an organization. Contrast class-based IP address. *See also* classless interdomain routing (CIDR); Variable Length Subnet Mask (VLSM).

classless interdomain routing (CIDR) A method of IP addressing that eliminates the traditional concept of Class A, Class B, and Class C network addresses. CIDR supports route aggregation where a single routing table entry can represent the address space of perhaps thousands of traditional classful routes. CIDR is typically utilized by Internet service providers (ISPs). Contrast Variable Length Subnet Mask (VLSM).

convergence time The length of time required for all databases in a distributed database system to synchronize and contain identical information. For example, the length of time taken by all WINS servers in a design to contain the same entries is the convergence time.

cryptography The processes and science of keeping messages and data secure. Cryptography is used to enable and ensure confidentiality, data integrity, authentication (entity and data origin), and nonrepudiation.

D

data encryption Preventing unauthorized viewing of the data.

Data Encryption Standard (DES) A grouping of encryption schemes that allow the sender and receiver of a message to share a single, common key that is used to encrypt and decrypt the message. In Windows 2000 these encryption schemes are used by Internet Protocol Security (IPSec) to provide data encryption of confidential data in IP packets. Contrast Microsoft Point-to-Point Encryption (MPPE). *See also* 40-bit DES; 56-bit DES; Triple DES (3DES).

data integrity Preventing data modification.

Data Link Control (DLC) A network protocol that operates at the data link layer in the Open Systems Interconnection (OSI) Network model. The protocols within DLC allow for peer-to-peer communication between any network devices by using the Media Access Control (MAC) address. In Windows 2000, the DLC protocol is utilized to communicate with IBM 370 architecture mainframe computers, IBM AS/400 computers, and some network attached printers. The DLC protocol was originally defined in IBM's System Network Architecture (SNA). Contrast Line Printer Remote (LPR); 3270 gateway; 5250 gateway. *See also* Internetwork Packet Exchange (IPX); System Network Architecture (SNA); Transmission Control Protocol/Internet Protocol (TCP/IP).

dedicated server A computer on a network that functions only as a server and is not also used as a client. In addition, dedicated servers typically provide only one network service or resource.

default gateway A router that is used by IP devices to forward IP packets when the IP device is unable to determine the appropriate route path. An entry in the IP routing table of 0.0.0.0 with a mask of 0.0.0.0 designates the default router for the IP device. *See also* default route entries.

default route entries A special type of static route entries that specify the route path for all destination networks that are unknown to the router. *See also* static route entries.

delayed (or near-time) response time A type of response for failures or resource shortages that must be reported to operations staff, but a predefined delay is acceptable. This type of response is the most common response in networking services management design. You can use auto-mated or manual processes to perform delayed responses, based on the predefined delay. To reduce the administrative costs associated with manual processes, automate delayed responses when possible. Contrast immediate (or real-time) response time; scheduled (or nonreal-time) response time.

demand-dial interface A type of logical interface supported by Routing and Remote Access used to initiate nonpersistent connections. Examples include dial-up modems, Integrated Services Digital Network (ISDN) connections, and virtual private network (VPN) connections.

Demilitarized Zone (DMZ) *See* screened subnet.

DES *See* Data Encryption Standard.

Dfs *See* Distributed file system.

Dfs replication The process of copying data from a data store or file system to multiple computers to synchronize the data. Active Directory provides multimaster replication of the directory between domain controllers within a given domain. The replicas of the directory on each domain controller are writeable. This allows updates to be applied to any replica of a given domain. The replication service automatically copies the changes from a given replica to all other replicas.

DHCP *See* Dynamic Host Configuration Protocol.

DHCP client An IP device whose IP configuration can be automatically updated by using Dynamic Host Configuration Protocol (DHCP). DHCP clients receive the IP configuration information from DHCP servers. DHCP clients can be desktop computers, remote computers, IP-based printers, Internet appliances, or other IP-based devices. Contrast DHCP server; DHCP Relay Agent. *See also* Dynamic Host Configuration Protocol (DHCP).

DHCP lease length How DHCP determines when an IP address assigned to computer, that has been subsequently removed from the network segment, is available for use by other computers on the network segment.

DHCP Relay Agent Forwards DHCP messages between DHCP clients and DHCP servers on different IP network segments. Routing and Remote Access includes the DHCP Relay Agent protocol to provide DHCP forwarding.

DHCP scopes A range of IP addresses to be managed by the DHCP server. DHCP scope options are assigned to a DHCP scope to provide IP configuration options that are specific to a specific IP address range. *See also* superscopes.

DHCP server An IP device that provides automatic IP configuration to other IP devices on the network by using Dynamic Host Configuration Protocol (DHCP). DHCP servers are configured with a range of IP addresses and other DHCP scope options. A DHCP server grants a DHCP client a lease for an IP address for a specific length of time. For the duration of the DHCP lease, the DHCP client is configured to use the IP address and other IP configuration parameters (such as default gateway, WINS server, DNS server, etc.). Contrast DHCP client; DHCP Relay Agent. *See also* Dynamic Host Configuration Protocol (DHCP).

DHCP/BOOTP forwarding A feature of an IP router that allows DHCP/BOOTP packets to be forwarded by the router. Contrast DHCP Relay Agent.

dial-up connection The connection to your network if you're using a device that uses the telephone network. This includes modems with a standard phone line, ISDN cards with high-speed ISDN lines, or X.25 networks. If you're a typical user, you might have one or two dial-up connections, perhaps to the Internet and to your corporate network. In a more complex server situation, multiple network modem connections might be used to implement advanced routing.

dial-up remote access A method of providing remote user access where the organization manages and supports the entire remote access

design, including the modems, phone lines, and remote access servers. Contrast virtual private network (VPN) remote access.

dial-up remote access client A remote computer that connects to the private network by using modems and phone lines. The remote computer is authenticated by utilizing user accounts managed by the organization that owns the dial-up remote access servers. Windows 2000 can support dial-up remote access clients that connect to the private network by using any Point-to-Point Protocol (PPP) supported transport protocol (such as TCP/IP, NWLink, and NetBEUI). Contrast VPN remote access client. *See also* dial-up remote access server; Point-to-Point Protocol (PPP).

dial-up remote access server A network access server that accepts Point-to-Point Protocol (PPP) connections from remote access clients and connects the remote access clients to the network segments connected to the network access server. In Windows 2000, Routing and Remote Access acts as a VPN remote access server. *See also* dial-up remote access client; Point-to-Point Protocol (PPP).

digital signature A means for originators of a message, file, or other digitally encoded information to bind their identity to the information. The process of signing information entails transforming the information, as well as some secret information held by the sender, into a tag called a signature. Digital signatures are used in public key environments and they provide nonrepudiation and integrity services.

Digital Signature Algorithm (DSA) The U.S. government standard for digital signatures, as specified by the National Institute of Standards and Technology, in FIPS 186, Digital Signature Standard (DSS). DSA is based on signature encryption based on a public and a private key. *See also* digital signature; Digital Signature Standard (DSS); hash algorithm; Secure Hash Algorithm (SHA).

Digital Signature Standard (DSS) A public key cryptographic standard issued in 1994 by the U.S. National Institute of Standards and Technology (NIST) to authenticate electronic documents. The DSS uses a Digital Signature Algorithm (DSA) to generate and verify digital signatures based on a public key, which is not secret, and a private key, which is known or held only by the person generating the signature. A digital signature serves to authenticate both the identity of the signer and the integrity of the transmitted information. *See also* digital signature; Digital Signature Algorithm (DSA); hash algorithm; Secure Hash Algorithm (SHA).

Digital Subscriber Line (DSL) A recently developed (late 1990s) digital communications technology that can provide high-speed transmissions over standard copper telephone wiring. DSL is often referred to as xDSL, where the x stands for one or two characters that define variations of the basic DSL technology. Compare Asymmetric Digital Subscriber Line (ADSL); High-bit-rate Digital Subscriber Line (HDSL); Symmetric Digital Subscriber Line (SDSL).

Distributed file system (Dfs) A Windows 2000 feature that make files distributed across multiple servers appear to users as if they reside in one place on the network. Users no longer need to know and specify the actual physical location of files to access them.

DLC *see* Data Link Control.

DMZ *See* Demilitarized Zone.

DNS *See* Domain Name System.

DNS zone A grouping of DNS resource records that reside within the same domain, subdomain, or delegated domain. A DNZ zone can be an Active Directory integrated zone, standard primary zone, or standard secondary zone. Contrast AppleTalk zone. *See also* Active Directory integrated zone; full zone transfer; incremental zone transfer; standard primary zone; standard secondary zone.

domain In Windows 2000 and Active Directory, a collection of computers defined by the administrator of a Windows 2000 Server network that share a common directory database. A domain has a unique name and provides access to the centralized user accounts and group accounts maintained by the domain administrator. Each domain has its own security policies and security relationships with other domains and represents a single security boundary of a Windows 2000 computer network. Active Directory is made up of one or more domains, each of which can span more than one physical location.

For DNS, a domain is any tree or subtree within the DNS namespace. Although the names for DNS domains often correspond to Active Directory domains, don't confuse DNS domains with Windows 2000 and Active Directory networking domains. *See also* Active Directory; domain namespace; Domain Name System (DNS).

domain filters A feature found in Microsoft Proxy Server 2.0 that restricts the Internet sites that private network users can access. Users can be restricted to any fully qualified domain name (FQDN), domain name, or subdomain. *See also* proxy server.

domain namespace The database used by the Domain Name System (DNS) to store computer names and IP address mappings. *See also* Domain Name System (DNS).

Domain Name System (DNS) A hierarchical name resolution service for Transmission Control Protocol/Internet Protocol (TCP/IP) devices. The DNS databases contain a list of host names and IP addresses. IP devices can locate other IP devices on the network sending a host name to DNS. DNS *resolves* the query and returns the IP address associated with the host name (forward DNS lookups). Also, devices can find the host name associated with an IP address by sending the IP address to DNS. DNS resolves the query and returns the host name associated with the IP address (reverse DNS lookups). Because of the hierarchical nature of DNS, the administration and management of DNS can be delegated. Contrast Windows Internet Name Service (WINS). *See also* DNS zone; domain; namespace.

domain root The highest portion of the domain namespace tree. The domain root is an unnamed portion of a domain name space that is designated by a trailing period ".". You must include the domain root to specify a fully qualified domain name (FQDN). *See also* host or resource name; second-level domain; subdomains; top-level domain.

downtime The amount of time a computer system or associated hardware remains nonfunctioning. Although downtime can occur because hardware fails unexpectedly, it can also be a scheduled event, such as when a network is shut down to allow time for maintaining the system, changing hardware, or archiving files. *See also* availability.

driver A software component that permits a computer system to communicate with a device. For example, a printer driver is a device driver that translates computer data into a form understood by the target printer. In most cases, the driver also manipulates the hardware to transmit the data to the device. *See also* signed software.

DSA *See* Digital Signature Algorithm.

DSL *See* Digital Subscriber Line.

DSS *See* Digital Signature Standard.

Dynamic Host Configuration Protocol (DHCP) A protocol that provides automatic configuration of IP on IP devices. As an Internet standard, DHCP is implemented on a variety of operating systems. All Windows 2000 operating systems can be automatically configured by using DHCP. Microsoft Windows 2000 Server, Microsoft Windows 2000 Advanced Server, and Microsoft Windows 2000 Datacenter Server can act as *DHCP servers* that configure *DHCP clients*. *See also* DHCP client; DHCP server.

dynamic route entry Used to automatically update the routing table information in a network. Dynamic routing table entries are created in routing tables by dynamic routing protocols. Contrast static route entries; autostatic route entries. *See also* dynamic routing protocols.

dynamic routing protocols Protocols used by routers to automatically build and maintain routing tables by communicating with other routers on the network that support dynamic routing. *See also* dynamic route entries.

dynamically assigned IP address An IP address that is automatically assigned to a network interface. Devices that access network resources can use dynamically assigned IP addresses. Contrast fixed IP address.

dynamically updated DNS zones A DNS zone that is updated by DHCP servers or Windows 2000 computers. Windows 2000 and BIND DNS servers support dynamically updated DNS zones. Only Windows 2000 supports secured dynamic updates. Contrast secured dynamically updated DNS zones.

E

EAP *See* Extensible Authentication Protocol.

EAP-MD5 CHAP *See* Extensible Authentication Protocol - Message Digest version 5 Challenge Authentication Protocol.

EAP-TLS *See* Extensible Authentication Protocol - Transport Level Security.

edge of network The portion of an organization's network that connects the private network to a public network. *See also* screened subnet.

edge of network router Connects an organization's private network to an unsecured public network, such as the Internet. *See also* external router.

Encapsulating Security Payload (ESP) A protocol used by IPSec that protects the network traffic. Using encryption ESP ensures the confidentiality and integrity of the data and protects against replay of the traffic. ESP is normally used to protect only the data portion of the packet (the IP header is usually protected through other methods). *See also* Authentication Header (AH); Internet Protocol Security (IPSec).

end-to-end data encryption A method where confidential data is protected between the originator and the *ultimate* recipient. All intermediary devices (such as routers, proxy servers, network address translators, or switches) can't view the confidential data. Internet Protocol Security (IPSec) provides this type of encryption between any devices that support IPSec. Contrast point-to-point data encryption. *See also* Internet Protocol Security (IPSec).

ESP *See* Encapsulating Security Payload.

EtherTalk The designation used by Apple Talk Phase 2 for Ethernet. *See also* TokenTalk.

Extensible Authentication Protocol (EAP) An extension of the Point-to-Point Protocol (PPP) that provides remote access user authentication by means of other security devices. These security devices can include smart cards, X509 certificates, Kerberos V5 tickets, and others. EAP works with remote access clients that connect by using PPP, PPTP, or L2TP. EAP provides stronger security (than other authentication methods such as CHAP) for remote access because it offers more security against brute force or dictionary attacks (where all possible combinations of characters are attempted), and password guessing. *See also* Challenge Handshake Authentication Protocol (CHAP); Microsoft Challenge Handshake Authentication Protocol (MS-CHAP); Password Authentication Protocol (PAP); Shiva Password Authentication Protocol (SPAP); X509 Version 3 certificate.

Extensible Authentication Protocol - Message Digest version 5 Challenge Authentication Protocol (EAP-MD5 CHAP) An authentication method that uses the same challenge handshake protocol as PPP-based CHAP, but the challenges and responses are sent as EAP messages. Contrast Extensible Authentication Protocol-Transport Level Security (EAP-TLS). *See also* Challenge Handshake Authentication Protocol (CHAP); Microsoft Challenge Handshake Authentication Protocol (MS-CHAP); Password Authentication Protocol (PAP); Shiva Password Authentication Protocol (SPAP); X509 Version 3 certificate.

Extensible Authentication Protocol - Transport Level Security (EAP-TLS) An authentication method that is used in certificate-based security environments, such as smart cards for remote access authentication. The EAP-TLS exchange of messages provides mutual authentication, negotiation of the encryption method, and secured private key exchange between the remote access client and the authenticator. EAP-TLS provides the strongest authentication and key exchange method. Contrast Extensible Authentication Protocol-Message Digest version 5 Challenge Handshake Authentication Protocol (EAP-MD5 CHAP). *See also* Challenge Handshake Authentication Protocol (CHAP); Microsoft Challenge Handshake Authentication Protocol (MS-CHAP); Password Authentication Protocol (PAP); Shiva Password Authentication Protocol (SPAP); X509 Version 3 certificate.

Extensible Markup Language (XML) A condensed form of SGML (Standard Generalized Markup Language). XML lets Web developers and designers create customized tags that offer greater flexibility in organizing and presenting information than is possible with the older HTML document coding system. The XML specification was published in draft form by a working group at the World Wide Web Consortium and supported by a number of leading companies in the computer industry.

external domain namespace The public domain namespace used by all Internet domain names and which is visible by users on the Internet. Contrast internal domain namespace.

external router Connects private network segments to public networks. In addition to providing IP routing, external routers prevent unauthorized access to private network resources, provide access to public network or Internet resources, protect confidential data transmitted over the public network or Internet, and connect to a variety of WAN technologies. Contrast internal router. *See also* edge of network router.

F

fast transfer method A DNS incremental transfer method that transfers multiple resource records at a time in a compressed format. Contrast slow transfer method.

fault tolerance The ability of a computer or an operating system to respond to an event such as a power outage or a hardware failure in such a way that no data is lost and any work in progress is not corrupted.

FDDI *See* Fiber Distributed Data Interface.

Federal Information Processing Standards (FIPS) A group of U.S. Government data processing standards managed by the National Institute of Standards and Technology (NIST). NIST is an agency of the U.S. Department of Commerce's Technology Administration and was established in 1901.

Fiber Distributed Data Interface (FDDI) A standard developed by the ANSI for high-speed, fiber-optic LANs. FDDI provides specifications for transmission rates of 100 Mbps on networks based on the Token Ring standard.

fibre channel A technology for 1-gigabit-per-second data transfer that maps common transport protocols such as SCSI and IP, merging networking and high-speed I/O into a single connectivity technology. Fibre Channel technology gives you a way to address the distance and the address-space limitations of conventional channel technologies. Contrast Small Computer System Interface (SCSI).

file replication service (FRS) Provides multimaster file replication for designated directory trees between Windows 2000 servers. The directory trees must be on disk partitions formatted with the version of NTFS file system used with Windows 2000. FRS is used by the Microsoft Distributed File System (Dfs) to automatically synchronize content between assigned replicas, and by Active Directory to automatically synchronize content of the system volume information across domain controllers.

file server A device that provides access to shared network disk resources. Contrast print server; application server.

File Transfer Protocol (FTP) The Transmission Control Protocol/Internet Protocol (TCP/IP) used to exchange files between two computers. FTP consists of an FTP client and FTP server component. The FTP client is authenticated by the FTP server and then sends or receives files.

FIPS *See* Federal Information Processing Standards.

firewall A combination of hardware and software that provides a secured barrier to prevent unauthorized access from outside a private network or intranet. A firewall prevents direct communication between private network and external computers by filtering traffic. A firewall determines whether it is safe to let a packet pass between the private network and the public network. Some proxy servers, such as Microsoft Proxy Server 2.0, provide enhanced features such as network address translation or Web content caching. *See also* Microsoft Proxy Server 2.0;

network address translator; proxy server; Routing and Remote Access.

firewall rules The criteria that determine the security provided by a firewall. A firewall receives a packet, examines the rules, and forwards or discards the packet based on the rules. Contrast IP packet filters.

fixed IP address An IP address that is manually assigned to a network interface. All network devices that manage network resources or run networking services typically require fixed IP addresses. Contrast dynamically assigned IP address.

forward lookup zone A type of DNS zone that is used by DNS to resolve fully qualified domain names (FQDNs) to IP addresses. Contrast reverse lookup zone.

FQDN *See* fully qualified domain name.

frame A single unit of data transmitted between devices on a synchronous network. A frame is typically found at the Media Access Control (MAC) layer, while packets are found at the network layer and above.

front-end processor A computer that resides between an IBM mainframe and the terminals that connect to the mainframe. Responsible for the management of session information and data transmission of all terminals, printers, or peer computers that communicate with a mainframe. A mainframe computer may communicate through multiple front-end processors for availability and load-balancing. Typically, 3270 gateways interface to these devices. *See also* 3270 gateway.

FRS *See* file replication service.

FTP *See* File Transfer Protocol.

full zone transfer A zone transfer method that transfers the complete contents of a DNS zone. DNS servers running Berkley Internet Domain

Name (BIND) versions prior to 8.2.1 can perform only full zone transfers. Contrast incremental zone transfer. *See also* zone transfer.

fully qualified domain name (FQDN) A DNS domain name that has been stated unambiguously so as to indicate with absolute certainty its location in the domain namespace tree. Fully qualified domain names differ from relative names in that they are typically stated with a trailing period (.), for example, "host.example.microsoft.com.", to qualify their position to the root of the namespace.

G

Generic Routing Encapsulation (GRE) Portion of an IP packet that maintains the sequencing and identification information for a virtual private network (VPN) tunnel. The IP or IPX datagram (including the original IP/IPX header and IP/IPX data) is encapsulated by GRE so that the packet can be forwarded through the tunnel. Once the tunneled packet exits the tunnel, the GRE header is removed and the IP (or IPX) datagram is forwarded to the destination address. Point-to-Point Tunneling Protocol (PPTP) and Layer 2 Tunneling Protocol (L2TP) both encapsulate IP and IPX datagrams by using GRE. *See also* Layer 2 Tunneling Protocol (L2TP); Point-to-Point Tunneling Protocol (PPTP); virtual private network (VPN).

GRE *See* Generic Routing Encapsulation.

H

hash algorithm A method for transforming data (for example, a password) in such a way that the result is unique and can't be changed back to its original form. This differs from encryption where the encrypted information can be transformed back to its original state by using the appropriate decryption method. For example, the CHAP authentication protocol uses challenge response with one-way Message Digest 5 (MD5) hashing algorithm on the response. *See also* Message Digest version 5 (MD5); Secure Hash Algorithm (SHA).

Hash-based Message Authentication Code (HMAC) A mechanism for message authentication using cryptographic hash functions. HMAC can be used with any iterative cryptographic hash function (for example, Message Digest version 5 (MD5), Secure Hash Algorithm (SHA)) in combination with a secret shared key. The cryptographic strength of HMAC depends on the properties of the underlying hash function. *See also* hash algorithm; Message Digest version 5 (MD5); Secure Hash Algorithm (SHA).

hashing scheme *See* hash algorithm.

HDSL *See* High-bit-rate Digital Subscriber Line.

hierarchical namespace A namespace, such as the Domain Name System (DNS) and Active Directory, that has a tiered structure allowing names and objects to be nested within each other. *See also* Active Directory; Domain Name System (DNS).

High-bit-rate Digital Subscriber Line (HDSL) A form of DSL, HDSL is a protocol for digital transmission of data over standard copper telecommunications lines (as opposed to fiber-optic lines) at rates of 1.544 Mbps in both directions. Also called High-data-rate Digital Subscriber Line. Compare Asymmetric Digital Subscriber Line (ADSL); Digital Subscriber Line (DSL); Symmetric Digital Subscriber Line (SDSL).

HMAC *See* Hash-based Message Authentication Code.

h-node WINS node type A method used by the Windows Internet Name Service (WINS) client in Windows 2000 for resolving NetBIOS names by first attempting to resolve by using p-node and then b-node methods. H-node WINS node type is the default node type when WINS is enabled. Contrast b-node WINS node type; m-node WINS node type; p-node WINS node type.

hop In routing through a mesh environment, the transmission of a data packet through a router.

host name The name of a device on a network. For a device on a Windows 2000 network, this can be the same as the computer name.

host number IP address that is used for identifying a specific host, or device, on a specific subnet.

host or resource name Name of computers or groups of computers (such as clusters) within the organization. You can specify any number of resource names within your design. *See also* domain root; second-level domain; subdomains; top-level domain.

host routing The routing that occurs between a source or destination computer and the router attached to the same network segment.

HOSTS A local text file in the same format as the 4.3 Berkeley Software Distribution (BSD) UNIX/etc/hosts file. This file maps host names to IP addresses. In Windows 2000, this file is stored in the *Systemroot*\System32\Drivers\Etc folder. *See also* LMHOSTS.

HTTP *See* Hypertext Transfer Protocol.

hub-and-spoke replication In the hub-and-spoke model, a centralized WINS server (that acts as the hub) replicates to all other WINS servers (that act as the spokes). The convergence time is minimized because WINS updates must be replicated only by a maximum of two WINS servers.

Hypertext Transfer Protocol (HTTP) A protocol used to transfer Web content between Web clients and Web servers. This protocol is used to transfer Hypertext Markup Language (HTML), Dynamic Hypertext Markup Language (DHTML), and graphic files, such as GIF or JPEG files.

I

IAB *See* Internet Architecture Board.

IANA *See* Internet Assigned Number Authority.

IAS *See* Internet Authentication Service.

ICANN *See* Internet Corporation for Assigned Names and Numbers.

identity checking The process of ensuring that only authorized remote users can access private network resources by authenticating remote users or remote routers. Identity checking can be performed by using user names and password, smart card certificates, or X509 version 3 certificates. *See also* smart card; X509 version 3 certificate.

IEEE *See* Institute of Electrical and Electronics Engineers.

IESG *See* Internet Engineering Steering Group.

IETF *See* Internet Engineering Task Force.

IGMP *See* Internet Group Messaging Protocol.

IGMP multicast proxy A device that forwards Internet Group Messaging Protocol (IGMP) multicast packets between network segments. To the multicast clients connected to the router mode interface, the devices appear to be a multicast router. To the multicast routers, or multicast data stream source, the device appears to be a multicast client. Contrast multicast router. *See also* Internet Group Messaging Protocol (IGMP); proxy mode interface; router mode interface.

immediate (or real-time) response time A type of response for the most critical failures or resource shortages. Immediate responses notify operations staff immediately when any failure or resource shortage occurs. Typically, you use automated processes to perform immediate responses. Contrast delayed (or near-time) response time; scheduled (or nonreal-time) response time.

incremental zone transfer A zone transfer method that transfers only the resource records of a DNS zone that change. DNS servers running Berkley Internet Domain Name (BIND) versions 8.2.1 and later can perform incremental zone

transfers. Contrast full zone transfer. *See also* zone transfer.

Institute of Electrical and Electronics Engineers (IEEE) An organization of engineering and electronics professionals; noted in networking for developing the IEEE 802.x standards for the physical and data-link layers of the OSI reference model, applied in a variety of network configurations.

Integrated Services Digital Network (ISDN) A high-speed digital communications network evolving from existing telephone services. The goal in developing ISDN was to replace the current telephone network, which requires digital-to-analog conversions, with facilities totally devoted to digital switching and transmission, yet advanced enough to replace traditionally analog forms of data, ranging from voice to computer transmissions, music, and video. ISDN is available in two forms, known as BRI (Basic Rate Interface) and PRI (Primary Rate Interface). BRI consists of two B (bearer) channels that carry data at 64 Kbps and one D (data) channel that carries control and signal information at 16 Kbps. In North America and Japan, PRI consists of 23 B channels and 1 D channel, all operating at 64 Kbps; elsewhere in the world, PRI consists of 30 B channels and 1 D channel. Computers and other devices connect to ISDN lines through simple, standardized interfaces.

intelligent communications adapter A wide area network (WAN) adapter that utilizes processors on the adapter to offload the processor(s) in the dial-up remote access server.

internal domain namespace The private domain namespace used by an individual organization and which is visible only to the users and computers within the organization. Contrast external domain namespace.

internal IPX network number The *logical* IPX network number used by applications (such as file servers, print servers, database servers, or other application servers) running on that computer. *See also* IPX network number.

internal router Connects network segments within a private network. Typically, internal routers require no features other than the ability to provide IP routing. Contrast external router.

International Organization for Standardization (ISO) An organization made up of standards-setting groups from various countries. For example, the United States member is the American National Standards Institute (ANSI). The ISO works to establish global standards for communications and information exchange. Primary among its accomplishments is development of the widely accepted OSI reference model. Note that the ISO is often wrongly identified as the International Standards Organization, probably because of the abbreviation ISO; however, ISO is derived from *isos*, which means equal in Greek, rather than an acronym.

Internet An IP-base public network created in the 1960s as a part of a research project funded by the United States Department of Defense. The network continues today to provide worldwide connectivity for government, military, educational, commercial, and other organizations. *See also* Advanced Research Projects Agency Network (ARPANET).

Internet Architecture Board (IAB) A technical advisory group of the Internet Society. Its responsibilities include

- **IESG Selection** The IAB appoints a new IETF chair and all other Internet Engineering Steering Group (IESG) candidates, from a list provided by the IETF nominating committee.

- **Architectural oversight** The IAB provides oversight of the architecture for the protocols and procedures used by the Internet.

- **Standards process oversight and appeal** The IAB provides oversight of the process used to create Internet Standards. The IAB serves as an

appeal board for complaints of improper execution of the standards process.

- **RFC series and IANA** The IAB is responsible for editorial management and publication of the Request for Comments (RFC) document series, and for administration of the various Internet assigned numbers.

- **External liaison** The IAB acts as representative of the interests of the Internet Society in liaison relationships with other organizations concerned with standards and other technical and organizational issues.

Internet Assigned Number Authority (IANA) An organization working under the auspices of the Internet Architecture Board (IAB) that is responsible for assigning new Internet-wide IP addresses. *See also* Internet Architecture Board (IAB); Internet Corporation for Assigned Names and Numbers (ICANN).

Internet Authentication Service (IAS) A Windows 2000 software service that provide security and authentication for remote users. Contrast RADIUS client. *See also* RADIUS server.

Internet Control Message Protocol (ICMP) Used by IP and higher-level protocols to send and receive status reports about information being transmitted.

Internet Corporation for Assigned Names and Numbers (ICANN) A technical coordination body for the Internet. Created in October 1998 by a broad coalition of the Internet's business, technical, academic, and user communities, ICANN is assuming responsibility for a set of technical functions previously performed under U.S. government contract by IANA and other groups. *See also* Internet Assigned Numbering Authority (IANA).

Specifically, ICANN coordinates the assignment of the following identifiers that must be globally unique for the Internet to function.

- Internet domain names
- IP address numbers
- protocol parameter and port numbers

Internet Engineering Steering Group (IESG)
The group within the Internet Society (ISOC) that, along with the Internet Architecture Board (IAB), reviews the standards proposed by the Internet Engineering Task Force (IETF). *See also* Internet Architecture Board (IAB); Internet Engineering Task Force (IETF).

Internet Engineering Task Force (IETF) A large open community of network designers, operators, vendors, and researchers concerned with the evolution of Internet architecture and the smooth operation of the Internet. Technical work is performed by working groups organized by topic areas (such as routing, transport, and security) and through mailing lists. Internet standards are developed in IETF Requests for Comments (RFCs), which are a series of notes that discuss many aspects of computing and computer communication, focusing on networking protocols, programs, and concepts.

Internet Group Messaging Protocol (IGMP) A protocol used by IP hosts to report their multicast group memberships to any immediately neighboring multicast routers. Defined in RFC 1112, IGMP is a standard for IP multicasting in the Internet. All hosts conforming to level 2 of the IP multicasting specification require IGMP. *See also* multicasting; multicast router.

Internet Information Services (IIS) Software services that support Web site creation, configuration, and management, along with other Internet functions. Microsoft Internet Information Services include Network News Transfer Protocol (NNTP), File Transfer Protocol (FTP), and Simple Mail Transfer Protocol (SMTP).

Internet Protocol (IP) The TCP/IP protocol for packet forwarding. *See also* Transmission Control Protocol/Internet Protocol (TCP/IP).

Internet Protocol Security (IPSec) A set of Internet standards that uses cryptographic security services to provide confidentiality, authentication, and data integrity. The Windows 2000 implementation of IPSec is based on industry standards in development by the Internet Engineering Task Force (IETF) IPSec working group. IPSec provides end-to-end security between any two computers. Other encryption technologies, such as Microsoft Point-to-Point Encryption (MPPE) protocol provides encryption only within a tunnel. IPSec can provide encryption for Layer 2 Tunneling Protocol (L2TP) tunnels or between any two IP devices running IPSec. IPSec support two modes of operation, IPSec transport mode and IPSec tunnel mode. Contrast Microsoft Point-to-Point Encryption (MPPE). *See also* IPSec transport mode; IPSec tunnel mode.

Internet registry An organization that is responsible for the administration and registration of IP Numbers. For example, American Registry of Internet Numbers (ARIN) is a nonprofit organization established for the purpose of administration and registration of IP numbers for the geographical areas of North America, South America, the Caribbean, and sub-Saharan Africa.

ARIN is one of the worldwide Internet registries that collectively provide IP registration services to all regions around the globe. The others are RIPE NCC (Europe, Middle East, parts of Africa) and APNIC (Asia Pacific).

Other registry organizations are separately responsible for registering and maintaining domain names, which are commonly used, unique identifiers translated into numeric addresses (IP numbers). IP numbers are globally unique, numeric identifiers that computers use to identify hosts and networks connected to the Internet.

Internet service provider (ISP) A company that provides individuals or companies with access to the Internet and the World Wide Web. When you sign a contract with an ISP, you're given a telephone number, a user name, a password, and other connection information so you can connect your computer to the ISP's computers. An ISP typically charges a monthly and/or hourly connection fees. Contrast Internet registry.

Internetwork Packet Exchange (IPX) The protocol in Novell NetWare that governs addressing and routing of packets within and between LANs. IPX packets can be encapsulated in Ethernet, FDDI, or Token Ring frames. IPX operates at ISO/OSI levels 3 and 4 but doesn't perform all the functions at those levels. In particular, IPX doesn't guarantee that a message will be complete (no lost packets); Sequenced Packet Exchange (SPX) is responsible for guaranteed delivery in an IPX network. Compare Sequenced Packet Exchange (SPX).

IP *See* Internet Protocol. *See also* Transmission Control Protocol/Internet Protocol (TCP/IP).

IP address A 32-bit address used to identify a node on an IP network. Each node on the IP network must be unique. An IP address consists of a network identifier and a host identifier. This address is typically represented in dotted-decimal notation, with the decimal value of each octet separated by a period, for example, 192.168.7.27. In Microsoft Windows 2000, you can configure the IP address statically or dynamically through DHCP.

IP forwarding *See* IP routing.

IP gateway *See* IP router.

IP network number The portion of an IP address that is used by routers to determine the appropriate route path. The IP subnet mask defines the portion of the IP address that is designated as the IP network number. Contrast IPX network number. *See also* Internet Protocol (IP); IP router.

IP packet filters Criteria used by Routing and Remote Access to prevent unwanted IP packets. Contrast IPX packet filters. *See also* packet filters.

IP router A network device that connects network segments in an IP network. An IP router is responsible for forwarding IP packets between network segments, ensuring that IP-based devices on different network segments can communicate. IP routers operate at the network layer of the Open Systems Interconnection (OSI) model. Contrast Media Access Control (MAC) layer bridge. *See also* IPX router.

IP routing The process of forwarding an Internet Protocol (IP) packet through a network via IP Routers. *See also* Internet Protocol (IP); IP router.

IP routing filter The definitions placed on an IP router indicating which types of traffic are allowed and disallowed on each network interface. *See also* IP router.

IP routing table A memory-based table that each IP device maintains to determine the appropriate path for IP packets. End hosts (such as servers, printers, desktop computers, etc.) maintain an IP routing table to determine when a destination address is on the same network segment or must be forwarded to a router. Intermediary devices (such as routers or switches) maintain an IP routing table to determine the appropriate route path when forwarding packets between network segments. *See also* route entries.

IPSec *See* Internet Protocol Security.

IPSec transport mode Used to provide security for Layer 2 Tunneling Protocol (L2TP) tunnels or for providing secured transmissions between a number of protocols. Contrast IPSec tunnel mode. *See also* Internet Protocol Security (IPSec); Layer 2 Tunneling Protocol (L2TP); Point-to-Point Tunneling Protocol (PPTP).

IPSec tunnel mode IPSec in tunnel mode provides IPSec protection between two specific IP addresses. IPSec tunnel mode provides encapsulation of IP traffic. Use IPSec tunnels for interoperability with other routers, gateways or end-systems that don't support L2TP/IPSec or

PPTP virtual private network (VPN) tunneling technology. IPSec tunnel mode is supported as an advanced feature, only in gateway-to-gateway tunneling scenarios and for server-to-server or server-to-gateway configurations. IPSec tunnels aren't supported for client remote access VPN scenarios. L2TP/IPSec or PPTP should be used for client remote access VPN. Contrast IPSec transport mode. *See also* Internet Protocol Security (IPSec); Layer 2 Tunneling Protocol (L2TP); Point-to-Point Tunneling Protocol (PPTP).

IPX *See* Internetwork Packet Exchange.

IPX direct hosting Communication protocol used between Microsoft Windows 95, Microsoft Windows 98, and Microsoft Windows Me client computers and Windows 2000 servers by using IPX without NetBIOS. All versions of Windows 2000 don't support IPX direct hosting as a client, only as a server (the IPX direct hosting protocol is bound to the file and print server services only). For compatibility across all platforms, utilize only NetBIOS over IPX (NBIPX). *See also* Internetwork Packet Exchange (IPX); NetBIOS over IPX (NBIPX).

IPX encapsulation IPX packets are placed in the datagram portion of an IP packet and then routed through an IP network, such as the Internet. IPX encapsulation allows IPX traffic to be sent through an intermediary IP network. Contrast IPX-to-IP gateway.

IPX frame type On Ethernet and Token Ring networks, Internetwork Packet Exchange (IPX) supports multiple formats of frame types. The NWLink protocol in Windows 2000 can automatically detect the IPX frame type used by the network adapters. For example, NWLink automatically sets the frame type to the 802.2 frame type for Ethernet networks when no network traffic is detected or multiple frame types, in addition to the 802.2, are detected. *See also* NWLink.

IPX host ID A 12-digit hexadecimal number that uniquely identifies a host computer on a net-

work segment. Host ID must be unique within an IPX network number. *See also* IPX network number.

IPX Internetwork address The combination of an IPX network number and an IPX host ID to uniquely identify an IPX-based device on a network. *See also* IPX host ID; IPX network number.

IPX network number An eight-digit hexadecimal number that uniquely identifies a network segment. Network numbers must be unique within an IPX internetwork. IPX network numbers must be assigned to each IPX frame type on each physical network segment, each file server, print server, or application server that advertises its services by Service Advertising Protocol (SAP) in the network. Contrast IP network number.

IPX packet filters Routing and Remote Access packet filters explicitly designated for IPX traffic. Contrast IP packet filters. *See also* packet filters.

IPX router A network device that connects network segments in an IPX network. An IPX router is responsible for forwarding IPX packets between network segments, ensuring that IPX-based devices on different network segments can communicate. IPX routers operate at the network layer of the Open Systems Interconnection (OSI) model. Contrast Media Access Control (MAC) layer bridge. *See also* IP router.

IPX-to-IP gateway A network device that receives Uniform Resource Locator (URL) requests in IPX packets and forwards the requests to IP-based networks (such as the Internet). The response to the URL request is received by the IPX-to-IP gateway and forwarded to the originator of the request in an IPX packet. Microsoft Proxy Server 2.0 can provide IPX-to-IP gateway features. *See also* Microsoft Proxy Server 2.0.

IPX tunneling IPX tunneling transmits Internetwork Packet Exchange (IPX) packets through a virtual private network (VPN) tunnel on IP routed networks. IPX tunneling doesn't provide Internet connectivity to the IPX-based computers within the private network. IPX tunneling transmits only IPX packets through VPN tunnels over the Internet. To provide Internet connectivity to IPX-based computers, use an IPX-to-IP gateway, such as Microsoft Proxy Server 2.0. Contrast IPX-to-IP gateway. *See also* virtual private network (VPN).

ISDN *See* Integrated Services Digital Network.

ISO *See* International Organization for Standardization.

ISP *See* Internet service provider.

ITU-T The sector of the International Telecommunication Union (ITU) responsible for telecommunication standards. ITU-T replaces the Comité Consultatif Internationale de Télégraphie et Téléphonie (CCITT). Its responsibilities include standardizing modem design and operations, and standardizing protocols for networks and facsimile transmission. ITU is an international organization within which governments and the private sector coordinate global telecom networks and services.

K

Kerberos version 5 An Internet standard security protocol for handling authentication of user or system identity. With Kerberos V5, passwords that are sent across network lines are encrypted, not sent as plaintext. Kerberos V5 includes other security features as well. Contrast preshared key; X509 version 3 certificates.

L

L2F *See* Layer 2 Forwarding.

L2TP *See* Layer 2 Tunneling Protocol.

LAN *See* local area network.

LAT *See* local address table.

Layer 2 Forwarding Cisco's tunneling protocol that is similar to Microsoft's PPTP. Cisco and Microsoft recently agreed to merge these two protocols into Layer 2 Tunneling Protocol (L2TP). *See also* Layer 2 Tunneling Protocol (L2TP).

Layer 2 Tunneling Protocol (L2TP) An industry-standard Internet tunneling protocol that can provide tunneling over IP networks, like Point-to-Point Tunneling Protocol (PPTP), or over packet-oriented point-to-point connectivity, such as ATM, Frame Relay, and X.25. L2TP requires Internet Protocol Security (IPSec) to provide protection of any confidential data. L2TP is based on the Layer 2 Forwarding (L2F) and PPTP specifications. Contrast Point-to-Point Tunneling Protocol (PPTP).

LDAP *See* Lightweight Directory Access Protocol.

leaf level domain name A hierarchical level in a domain namespace that contains the resource records in a domain that represent a specific resource. Contrast branch level domain name.

Lightweight Directory Access Protocol (LDAP) A set of protocols for accessing information directories. LDAP is based on the standards contained within the X.500 standard, but is significantly simpler. And unlike X.500, LDAP supports Transmission Control Protocol/Internet Protocol (TCP/IP). LDAP makes it possible for almost any application running on virtually any computer platform to obtain directory information, such as e-mail addresses and public keys. Because LDAP is an open protocol, applications need not worry about the type of server hosting the directory. LDAP is the primary access protocol for Active Directory. LDAP is documented in the Internet Engineering Task Force (IETF) RFC 2251.

Line Printer Daemon (LPD) A service on the print server that receives documents (print jobs) from Line Printer Remote (LPR) utilities running on client systems. Windows 2000 includes support for LPD. *See also* Line Printer Remote (LPR).

Line Printer Remote (LPR) A connectivity utility that runs on client systems and is used to print files to a computer running an LPD server. Windows 2000 includes support for LPR. *See also* Line Printer Daemon (LPD).

link state database Routing information table that is maintained by the Open Shortest Path First (OSPF) dynamic routing table protocol. OSPF maintains the status of each network segment (link) in the network by examining the status (active, inactive, etc.) of the network segment. Any changes in the link state database are propagated throughout the network. OSPF routers recalculate route paths when any change in the link state database occurs.

LMHOSTS A local text file that maps IP addresses to the computer names of Windows 2000 networking computers outside the local subnet. In Windows 2000, this file is stored in the *systemroot*\System32\Drivers\Etc folder. The primary difference between utilizing the LMOSTS file and the HOSTS file is that you can enable or disable the LMHOSTS file. The WINS client always utilizes the HOSTS file. Also, the HOSTS file doesn't contain the extended NetBIOS information (such as NetBIOS groups). *See also* HOSTS.

load balancing A technique used to scale the performance of a server-based program (such as a Web server) by distributing its client requests across multiple servers within the cluster. Typically, each host can specify the load percentage that it will handle, or the load can be equally distributed across all the hosts. If a host fails, the load is dynamically redistributed among the remaining hosts.

load-balancing The distribution of network traffic, users, or applications across multiple networking devices. For example, Network Load Balancing can distribute network traffic across multiple Internet Information Services (IIS) servers.

local address table (LAT) A list of IP addresses or IP address ranges that reside within an organization's private network. Network address translators (such as Microsoft Proxy Server 2.0) use this list to determine when a destination IP address resides inside or outside a private network. *See also* network address translator; proxy server.

local area network (LAN) A communications network that connects computers and computer peripherals located within well-defined locations such as an office or a building. Devices connected to a LAN are able to communicate with any other device on the network.

LocalTalk The Apple networking hardware built into every Macintosh computer. LocalTalk includes the cables and connector boxes that connect components and network devices that are part of the AppleTalk network system. LocalTalk was formerly known as the AppleTalk Personal Network. Contrast TokenTalk; EtherTalk. *See also* AppleTalk.

LPDv *See* Line Printer Daemon.

LPR *See* Line Printer Remote.

M

MAC address *See* Media Access Control (MAC) address.

MAC layer bridge *See* Media Access Control (MAC) layer bridge.

machine authentication An authentication method that verifies the identity of a network device (such as a server, router, remote access client, etc). Machine authentication requires a user account or certificate be assigned to the network devices (such as an X509 certificate for providing authentication for Internet Protocol Security (IPSec). *See also* user authentication.

MD5 *See* Message Digest version 5.

Media Access Control (MAC) address A globally unique address that is assigned to a physical network adapter. Also known as the physical network address or Burned In Address (BIA). The MAC address is utilized by the Media Access Control layer in the Open Systems Interconnection (OSI) model.

Media Access Control (MAC) layer bridge A network device that provides connectivity between network segments. MAC layer bridges operate at OSI layer 2, forward or drop frames based on the source and destination MAC address. Unlike routers, MAC layer bridges are protocol independent. Contrast router.

Message Digest version 5 (MD5) An industry-standard one-way, 128-bit hashing algorithm developed by RSA Data Security, Inc., and used by various Point-to-Point Protocol (PPP) vendors for encrypted authentication. For example, the CHAP authentication protocol uses challenge-response with one-way MD5 hashing on the response so that the user can be authenticated without actually sending the password over the network. Contrast Secure Hash Algorithm (SHA). *See also* hash algorithm.

Microsoft Challenge Handshake Authentication Protocol (MS-CHAP) An authentication protocol used by Microsoft Routing and Remote Access and Network and Dial-up Connections. Using CHAP, a remote access client can send its authentication credentials to a remote access server in a secure form. This is the Windows-specific variant of CHAP. Contrast Challenge Handshake Authentication Protocol (CHAP); Microsoft Challenge Handshake Authentication Protocol version 2 (MS-CHAP v2); Password Authentication Protocol (PAP); Shiva Password Authentication Protocol (SPAP).

Microsoft Challenge Handshake Authentication Protocol version 2 (MS-CHAP v2) An enhanced version of the Microsoft Challenge Handshake Authentication Protocol (MS-CHAP). In addition to the standard MS-CHAP features,

MS-CHAP v2 provides two-way authentication, uses separate cryptographic keys for transmitted and received data, and uses a different key for encryption each time the user logs on. Contrast Challenge Handshake Authentication Protocol (CHAP); Microsoft Challenge Handshake Authentication Protocol (MS-CHAP); Password Authentication Protocol (PAP); Shiva Password Authentication Protocol (SPAP).

Microsoft Management Console (MMC) A utility Microsoft developed for displaying all graphical management tools used in Windows environments. MMCs provide a consistent user interface that can be customized and extended. MMCs contain a console tree that can include containers such as folders, HTML documents, and other administrative objects. A MMC console contains one or more windows with views of the console tree and the properties, services, and events that are managed by the items in that console tree.

Microsoft Point-to-Point Encryption (MPPE) Provides for packet confidentiality (data encryption) between the remote access client and the remote access server or between two routers. Point-to-Point Tunneling Protocol (PPTP) uses MPPE to provide encryption for the PPTP tunnel. MPPE can be used when remote access clients or routers can't utilize Internet Protocol security (IPSec). MPPE supports either a 128-bit key or 40-bit key encryption algorithm. MPPE 40-bit keys are used to satisfy current North American export restrictions. MPPE is compatible with Network Address Translation. Contrast Internet Protocol Security (IPSec).

Microsoft Proxy Server 2.0 A Microsoft product that provides Web content caching, network address translation, firewall security, and IPX-to-IP gateway services. Typically, generic proxy servers provide only Web content caching. Microsoft Proxy Server 2.0 combines the features of a generic proxy server, a firewall, and connects Internetwork Packet Exchange (IPX) networks to Internet Protocol (IP) networks. Contrast Routing and Remote Access - NAT Protocol. *See also* firewall; IPX-to-IP gateway; network address translator; proxy server.

MMC *See* Microsoft Management Console.

m-node WINS node type A method used by the Windows Internet Name Service (WINS) client in Windows 2000 for resolving NetBIOS names by first attempting to resolve by using b-node and then p-node methods. Contrast b-node WINS node type; h-node WINS node type; p-node WINS node type.

MPPE *See* Microsoft Point-to-Point Encryption.

MS-CHAP *See* Microsoft Challenge Handshake Authentication Protocol.

MS-CHAP v2 *See* Microsoft Challenge Handshake Authentication Protocol version 2.

multicasting Sending network traffic to a set of hosts that belong to a multicast group. A broadcast message goes to all computers on a network, whereas a multicast message is sent to all computers on a network that belong to the multicast group. *See also* multicast IP address.

multicast IP address An IP address that has a destination of a grouping of multiple computers. Multicast IP addresses are utilized to send information from a computer to one or more computers on a network. Multicast addressing is implemented to reduce network traffic. A single multicast IP packet can be transmitted and simultaneously received by multiple devices. To accomplish the same task with unicast, IP packets would require sending individual IP packets to each device. Multicast IP addressing is often used to communicate between similar devices (such as routers). For example, routers running the Route Information Protocol (RIP) version 2 can utilize multicast packets to exchange routing information. Contrast broadcast IP address; unicast IP address.

multicast proxy Appears to multicast routers as a multicast client and appears to multicast clients as a multicast router. The Internet Group Messaging Protocol (IGMP) in Routing and Remote Access allows Windows 2000 to be a multicast proxy. Contrast multicast router. *See also* Internet Group Messaging Protocol (IGMP); proxy mode interface; router mode interface.

multicast router Forwards multicast IP packets between network segments. Multicast clients register with multicast routers to receive multicast traffic. The multicast router maintains a list of registered multicast clients and ceases to forward the multicast traffic when all registered clients are no longer registered. True multicast routers have routing protocols that allow multicast registrations to be propagated from the multicast clients to each intermediary multicast router. Contrast unicast router. *See also* Internet Group Messaging Protocol (IGMP); multicast proxy; proxy mode interface; router mode interface.

multicast routing table A memory-based structure maintained by a router to determine how to forward multicast packets. The multicast routing table is populated by multicast routing protocols, such as Internet Group Messaging Protocol (IGMP). The multicast routing table is repopulated each time the router is started. Contrast unicast routing table. *See also* Internet Group Messaging Protocol (IGMP); multicast proxy; multicast router.

multihomed A computer that has more than one network interface.

multimaster A type of data storage that can be updated in multiple places. For example, Active Directory supports the multimaster model because Active Directory objects (users, groups, organizational units, etc.) can be modified at any domain controller.

multinet Two or more IP address ranges on the same physical network segment.

N

name resolution The process of translating a name into some object or information that the name represents. A telephone book forms a namespace in which the names of the telephone subscribers can be resolved to telephone numbers. The Microsoft Windows NT file system (NTFS) forms a namespace in which the name of a file can be resolved to the file itself. Active Directory forms a namespace in which the name of an object in the directory can be resolved to the object itself.

namespace A set of unique names for resources or items used in a shared computing environment. For MMC, the namespace is represented by the console tree, which displays all the snap-ins and resources that are accessible to a console. *See also* Microsoft Management Console (MMC); resource; snap-in. For DNS, namespace is the vertical or hierarchical structure of the domain name tree. For example, each domain label, such as host1 or example, used in a fully qualified domain name, such as host1.example.microsoft.com, indicates a branch in the domain namespace tree. *See also* domain; Domain Name System (DNS); domain root.

NAS *See* network access server.

NAT *See* Network Address Translation.

NAT address mapping A feature of the NAT protocol in Routing and Remote Access that provides Internet users with access to resources in the SOHO network. Include NAT address mapping when you're assigned a single public IP address for use in the NAT design. The NAT server maps requests for the public IP address with a specific TCP or User Datagram Protocol (UDP) port number to a resource within the SOHO network. You can specify a NAT address map entry for each SOHO resource that you want Internet users to access. Contrast NAT address pools.

NAT address pools A feature of the NAT protocol in Routing and Remote Access that provides Internet users with access to resources in the SOHO network. Include NAT address pools when you're assigned multiple public IP addresses for use in the NAT design. The NAT server maps requests for one of the public IP addresses with a specific TCP or UDP port number to resources within the SOHO network. You can determine the combination of public IP address and TCP or UDP port number for each SOHO resource that you want Internet users to access. Contrast NAT address mapping.

NBIPX *See* NetBIOS over IPX.

NDIS *See* Network Driver Interface Specification.

NDS *See* NetWare Directory Service.

NetBEUI *See* Network Basic Enhanced User Interface.

NetBIOS *See* Network Basic Input/Output System.

NetBIOS over IPX (NBIPX) An implementation of the NetBIOS application programming interface (API) that communicates through Internetwork Packet Exchange (IPX). Contrast NetBIOS over TCP/IP (NetBT).

NetBIOS over TCP/IP (NetBT) An implementation of the NetBIOS application programming interface (API) that communicates through Transmission Control Protocol/Internet Protocol (TCP/IP). Contrast NetBIOS over IPX (NBIPX).

NetBT *See* NetBIOS over TCP/IP.

NetWare *See* Novell NetWare.

NetWare Directory Service (NDS) The directory service included with Novell NetWare. NDS stores information about objects on a network and makes this information available to NetWare users and network administrators. Active Directory, in Windows 2000, can integrate with NDS to provide a unified method of administration and management. Contrast Active Directory.

network access server (NAS) A device that accepts Point-to-Point Protocol (PPP) or Serial Line IP (SLIP) connections from remote access clients and connects the remote access clients to the network segments connected to the network access server. Routing and Remote Access acts as network access server for dial-up and virtual private network (VPN) remote access clients. *See also* dial-up remote access client; dial-up remote access server; RADIUS client; virtual private network (VPN); VPN remote access client; VPN remote access server.

Network Address Translation (NAT) A protocol that maps a number of private IP addresses to a limited number of public IP addresses. NAT protocol can be ran alone on a device or incorporated in other IP devices (such as routers, proxy servers, or firewalls). In Windows 2000, the NAT protocol is provided by Routing and Remote Access to provide network address translation. *See also* firewall; IP router; proxy server.

network address translator A generic network address translator hides internally managed IP addresses from external networks by translating private internal addresses to public external addresses. Network address translation reduces IP address registration costs by letting the organization use unregistered IP addresses internally, with translation to a small number of registered IP addresses externally. Network address translation also hides the internal network structure, reducing the risk of attacks against internal systems. Network address translator is often abbreviated NAT. Contrast network address translation. *See also* firewall; Microsoft Proxy Server 2.0; NAT Protocol; proxy server; Routing and Remote Access.

Network Basic Enhanced User Interface (NetBEUI) A network protocol native to Microsoft Networking. It is usually used in small, department-size local area networks (LANs) of 1 to 200 clients. NetBEUI can use Token Ring source routing as its only method of routing. NetBEUI is the Microsoft implementation of the NetBIOS standard. *See also* Network Basic Input/Output System (NetBIOS).

Network Basic Input/Output System (NetBIOS) An application programming interface (API) that can be used by programs on a network. NetBIOS provides programs with a uniform set of commands for requesting the lower-level services required to manage names, conduct sessions, and send datagrams between nodes on a network.

Network Driver Interface Specification (NDIS) A Microsoft/3Com specification establishing a common shared interface for Windows 2000 and other Microsoft operating systems to support protocol-independent transport of multiple network transport protocols (such as TCP/IP, NetBEUI, IPX/SPX, and AppleTalk). NDIS allows more than one transport protocol to be bound and to operate simultaneously over a single network adapter.

Network Load Balancing One of the Windows Clustering technologies that delivers high availability by redirecting incoming network traffic to working cluster hosts if a host fails or is offline. Existing connections to an offline host are lost, but the Internet services remain available. In most cases (for example, with Web servers), client software automatically retries the failed connections, and the clients experience only a few seconds delay in receiving a response. *See also* server cluster; Windows Clustering.

Network News Transfer Protocol (NNTP) A de facto protocol standard on the Internet used to distribute news articles and query news servers.

network number The portion of a network address that is used for determining route paths in routed networks. For IP-based networks, the network number is specified by the subnet mask. For IPX-based networks, the network number is assigned to network adapters, IPX frame types, and to internal IPX network numbers. For AppleTalk-based networks, a network segment may be assigned one network number or a range of network numbers (one network number for every 253 AppleTalk devices).

network prefix *See* network number.

NNTP *See* Network News Transfer Protocol.

nonpersistent connection A type of physical or logical network interface that is intentionally disconnected after a period of time. The connection must be reestablished after being disconnected. Examples include dial-up modems, virtual private network (VPN) connections, some Digital Subscriber Line (DSL) connections, some Integrated Services Digital Network (ISDN) connections, and any other connection that is intentionally disconnected. Contrast persistent connection.

Novell NetWare A network operating system created by Novell. NetWare utilizes NetWare Directory Service (NDS) to provide administration and management of users and resources. Windows 2000 supports the integration of NetWare and NDS. *See also* Active Directory; NetWare Directory Service (NDS).

NTFS file system An advanced file system designed for use specifically within the Windows 2000 operating system. It supports file system recovery, extremely large storage media, long file names, and various features for the POSIX subsystem. It also supports object-oriented applications by treating all files as objects with user-defined and system-defined attributes.

NWLink The Windows 2000 implementation of the Internetwork Packet Exchange (IPX),

Sequenced Packet Exchange (SPX), and NetBIOS protocols used in Novell networks. NWLink is a standard network protocol that supports routing and can support NetWare client-server applications, where NetWare-aware Sockets-based applications communicate with IPX/SPX Sockets-based applications. *See also* Internetwork Packet Exchange (IPX); NetBIOS over IPX (NBIPX); Sequenced Packet Exchange (SPX).

O

ODBC See Open Database Connectivity.

Open Database Connectivity In the Microsoft WOSA (Windows Open System Architecture) structure, an interface providing a common language for Windows applications to gain access to a database on a network. *See also* Active Server Pages (ASP); Extensible Markup Language (XML); Web-based applications.

Open Shortest Path First (OSPF) A routing protocol used in medium-sized and large networks. This protocol is more complex than Routing Information Protocol (RIP) for IP but allows better control and is more efficient in propagation of routing information. OSPF tracks only the changes in status for router network interfaces (and the corresponding network segments). As a result, the amount of network traffic to manage routing information is less than RIP. *See also* Routing Information Protocol (RIP).

Open Systems Interconnection (OSI) reference model A seven-layer architecture that standardizes levels of service and types of interaction for computers exchanging information through a network. It is used to describe the flow of data between the physical connection to the network and the end-user application. This model is the best known and most widely used model for describing networking environments.

OSI *See* Open Systems Interconnection (OSI) reference model.

OSPF *See* Open Shortest Path First.

OSPF area A grouping of routers that connect to contiguous network segments. *See also* OSPF; OSPF autonomous system; OSPF backbone area.

OSPF autonomous system All of the OSPF routers in an organization belong to the same autonomous system to automatically exchange routing information. Network segments outside your OSPF autonomous system can be reached through external routes. An OSPF autonomous system is comprised of one or more OSPF areas. *See also* Open Shortest Path First (OSPF); OSPF area; OSPF external routes.

OSPF backbone area A common area that connects all other areas within the same autonomous system. *See also* OSPF area; OSPF autonomous system.

OSPF external routes Any network segments that are outside an organization's autonomous system. OSPF external routes can include other OSPF autonomous systems, RIP for IP networks, static route entries, and route paths added by Simple Network Management Protocol (SNMP). You connect your OSPF autonomous system to external routes by using autonomous system boundary routers (ASBRs). *See also* autonomous system boundary router (ASBR); Open Shortest Path First (OSPF).

OSPF network A network segment that resides within and is managed by an OSPF area. OSPF areas are comprised of one or more OSPF networks. *See also* OSPF area.

outsourced dial-up remote access A method of providing remote access that allows an organization to eliminate the costs associated with dial-up remote access connectivity. Third-party organizations provide the dial-up remote access connectivity. The organization provides virtual private network (VPN) connectivity to ensure secured communications with their private network.

P

packet A unit of information transmitted as a whole from one device to another on a network. In packet-switching networks, a packet is defined more specifically as a transmission unit of fixed maximum size that consists of binary digits representing data; a header containing an identification number, source, and destination addresses; and sometimes error-control data. *See also* frame.

packet assembly and disassembly (PAD) An interface between nonpacket-switching equipment and a packet-switching network. *See also* packet switching.

packet filters Criteria used by a specific network interface in a computer running Routing and Remote Access to provide network security. The network interface receives a packet, examines the packet filter, and forwards or discards the packet based on the packet filter. Contrast firewall rules.

packet switching A message delivery technique in which small units of information (packets) are relayed through stations in a computer network along the best route available between the source and the destination. Data is broken into smaller units and then repacked in a process called packet assembly and disassembly (PAD). Although each packet can travel along a different path, and the packets composing a message can arrive at different times or out of sequence, the receiving computer reassembles the original message. Packet-switching networks are considered fast and efficient. Standards for packet switching on networks are documented in the CCITT recommendation X.25.

PAD *See* packet assembly and disassembly.

PAP *See* Password Authentication Protocol.

passive caching A method of Web content caching included in Microsoft Proxy Server 2.0 that retrieves and caches Web content cache when requested by client computers. *See also* active caching; Web content caching.

Password Authentication Protocol (PAP) An authentication protocol included in the Windows 2000 Routing and Remote Access feature. PAP has weak security because the user name and password are transmitted in *plain text*. However, PAP is supported on all operating systems and network access servers. Contrast Challenge Handshake Authentication Protocol (CHAP); Microsoft Challenge Handshake Authentication Protocol (MS-CHAP); Microsoft Challenge Handshake Authentication Protocol version 2 (MS-CHAP v2); Shiva Password Authentication Protocol (SPAP).

performance A measurement of system response times that denotes the length of time between the beginning of an event and the end of an event. For example, the response time can be a measurement of the length of time between a user's request (such as clicking a submit button on a Web form) and the response to the user's request (displaying of a Web page). Contrast availability; security.

perimeter network *See* screened subnet.

persistent connection A type of physical or logical network interface that is permanently connected. Examples include Ethernet, Token Ring, T1, or any other connection that is not intentionally disconnected. Contrast nonpersistent connection.

phone number bank A group of telephone numbers that reside within the same *hunt group*. The local telephone provider can create a hunt group by designating a primary phone number that the users call. When the first number in the hunt group is busy, the telephone provider automatically forwards another incoming call to the next telephone numbers in the hunt group.

PKI *See* public key infrastructure.

p-node WINS node type A method used by the Windows Internet Name Service (WINS) client in Windows 2000 for resolving NetBIOS names by sending the query to WINS servers. P-nodes are forwarded across IP-routed network segments because they utilize unicast packets. Contrast b-node WINS node type; h-node WINS node type; m-node WINS node type.

pointer (PTR) resource record A resource record used in a reverse lookup zone created within the in-addr.arpa domain to designate a reverse mapping of a host Internet Protocol (IP) address to a host Domain Name System (DNS) domain name.

point-to-point data encryption A method where confidential data is protected between two devices on a network (not necessarily the originator or the recipient). *Between the end points*, all intermediary devices (such as routers, proxy servers, network address translators, or switches) can't view the confidential data. Tunneling technologies, such as Point-to-Point Tunneling Protocol (PPTP) or Layer 2 Tunneling Protocol (L2TP), provide point-to-point data encryption. For example, two routers connected across the Internet may use an L2TP tunnel with Internet Protocol Security (IPSec) to protect confidential data between two locations. However, before entering the tunnel (from the originator) and after exiting the tunnel (to the recipient), the confidential data *may not be protected*. Contrast end-to-end data encryption. *See also* Internet Protocol Security (IPSec); Layer 2 Tunneling Protocol (L2TP); Point-to-Point Tunneling Protocol (PPTP).

Point-to-Point Protocol (PPP) A widely used data link protocol, defined in RFC 1661, for transmitting TCP/IP packets over dial-up telephone connections, such as between a computer and the Internet. PPP, which supports dynamic allocation of IP addresses, provides greater protection for data integrity and security and is easier to use than SLIP, at a cost of greater overhead. Contrast Serial Line Internet Protocol (SLIP).

See also Layer 2 Tunneling Protocol (L2TP); Point-to-Point Tunneling Protocol (PPTP).

Point-to-Point Tunneling Protocol (PPTP)
An industry-standard Internet tunneling protocol that can provide tunneling over IP networks. PPTP utilizes Microsoft Point-to-Point Encryption (MPPE) protocol to provide protection of any confidential data. PPTP is based on the Point-to-Point Protocol (PPP) specifications. Contrast Layer 2 Tunneling Protocol (L2TP). *See also* Point-to-Point Protocol (PPP).

PPP *See* Point-to-Point Protocol.

PPTP *See* Point-to-Point Tunneling Protocol.

preshared key A shared, secret key that is previously agreed upon by two administrators. Preshared keys are quick to use and don't require the client to run the Kerberos V5 protocol or have a public key infrastructure (PKI). Both administrators must manually configure IPSec to use this preshared key. Preshared keys are a simple method for authenticating computers that aren't based on Windows 2000, stand-alone computers, or any clients not running the Kerberos V5 protocol. Note that preshared keys are for authentication protection only. Contrast Kerberos version 5 protocol; X509 version 3 certificate.

print server A device that provides access to shared network printers. Contrast file server; application server.

private IP addresses A specific range of IP addresses that have been designated by the Internet Assigned Numbers Authority (IANA) for use within private networks. These addresses can be used by multiple organizations for *internal* use only. Any IP devices that connect to the Internet must be assigned a public IP address. A network address translator can be used to allow communication between the public IP addressing scheme and the private IP addressing scheme. Contrast public IP addresses. *See also* network address translation.

private network The portion of a network that is owned, managed, and maintained by an organization. The secured resources of the organization are directly connected to the private network. The private network is isolated from any public networks (such as the Internet). Contrast public network.

proxy array A grouping of proxy servers that distribute the cached Web content across all the servers in a proxy array. Because the Web content is distributed across all the proxy servers, the outbound traffic is load balanced across the proxy servers in proxy array and performance is improved. *See also* proxy server; Web content caching.

proxy mode interface Network interface in a multicast proxy that connects to a multicast router or the multicast source. Contrast router mode interface. *See also* multicast proxy.

proxy server Generic term for a computer that provides local Web content caching. Generic proxy servers are included in network designs to reduce the network traffic between network clients and the servers hosting the Web content. Some proxy servers, such as Microsoft Proxy Server 2.0, provide enhanced features such as network address translation or firewall security. *See also* firewall; Microsoft Proxy Server 2.0; network address translator.

PSTN *See* Public Switched Telephone Network.

public IP addresses A specific range of IP addresses that have been designated by the Internet Assigned Numbers Authority (IANA) for use within and outside private networks. These addresses can be used by only one organization for *internal or external* use. Any IP devices that connect to the Internet must be assigned a public IP address. Contrast private IP addresses. *See also* network address translation.

public key infrastructure (PKI) The term generally used to describe the laws, policies, standards, and software that regulate or manipulate certificates and public and private keys. In practice, it is a system of digital certificates, certification authorities, and other registration authorities that verify and authenticate the validity of each party involved in an electronic transaction. Standards for PKI are still evolving, even though they are being widely implemented as a necessary element of electronic commerce.

public network The portion of a network that is owned, managed, and maintained for the use of multiple organizations. The secured resources of an organization are isolated from the public network. Resources attached to public networks are for access by anonymous users or the servers that host the resources must provide their own security The Internet is an example of a public network. Contrast private network.

Public Switched Telephone Network (PSTN) The public telephone system.

pull partner replication A WINS service that pulls in replicas from its push partner by requesting them and then accepting the pushed replicas. Contrast push partner replication.

push partner replication A WINS service that sends replicas to its pull partner upon receiving a request from it. Contrast pull partner replication.

R

RADIUS *See* Remote Authentication Dial-In User Service.

RADIUS accounting A set of protocols used in RADIUS to record the remote user connection characteristics, such as length of time the user was connected, RADIUS client start up and shutdown, remote user connections authorized, remote user connections unauthorized, and other information. RADIUS accounting provides a method of centralizing the collection of the remote user connection characterizes by allowing multiple RADIUS clients to report RADIUS

accounting information to a centralized RADIUS server. Contrast RADIUS authentication; RADIUS authorization. *See also* Remote Authentication Dial-In User Service (RADIUS).

RADIUS attributes The criteria that determines when remote users should be granted remote access and the configuration of the connection established with the remote user. RADIUS attributes are similar to Routing and Remote Access remote access policies [Routing and Remote Access policies are a superset of the Request For Comment (RFC) RADIUS attributes]. RADIUS hardware/software from multiple vendors supports different RADIUS attributes. For example, a RADIUS attribute might specify the valid time that a remote user is granted access and require the remote user to connect by using only a VPN tunneled connection. Contrast remote access policies. *See also* Remote Authentication Dial-In User Service (RADIUS); RADIUS authorization.

RADIUS authentication A set of protocols used in RADIUS to verify the remote user log on credentials (such as user name and password) and realm (or domain) in which the user account resides. RADIUS authentication provides a method of centralizing the authentication of the remote users by allowing multiple RADIUS clients to request authentication from a centralized RADIUS server. Contrast RADIUS accounting; RADIUS authorization. *See also* Remote Authentication Dial-In User Service (RADIUS).

RADIUS authorization A set of protocols used in RADIUS to determine when remote users are granted or denied access to the RADIUS client. RADIUS authorization occurs immediately after RADIUS authentication. During RADIUS authentication, the remote user's logon credentials are validated. RADIUS authorization checks the RADIUS attributes to determine whether the remote user should be granted remote access. RADIUS attributes are very similar to remote access policies and can be based on security features such as caller-ID, callback, authorized remote access time, or other criteria. Authenticated remote users that meet the requirements of the RADIUS attributes are granted remote access. Otherwise, the RADIUS client is instructed to disconnect the remote user. Contrast RADIUS authentication; RADIUS accounting. *See also* RADIUS attributes; Remote Authentication Dial-In User Service (RADIUS); remote access policies.

RADIUS client The device in a RADIUS design that provides the same functionality as a remote access server. The RADIUS client is responsible for the remote user connectivity and for passing authentication requests and accounting information to RADIUS servers. In Windows 2000, RADIUS client functionality is provided by the Routing and Remote Access. Contrast Routing and Remote Access; network access server (NAS). *See also* RADIUS server; Remote Authentication Dial-In User Service (RADIUS).

RADIUS passwords *See* RADIUS shared secret.

RADIUS realms The authentication database to be used by RADIUS for authenticating a remote user's credentials. In Windows 2000, the RADIUS realm is a Windows 2000 domain that contains the remote user accounts.

RADIUS server The device in a RADIUS design that provides the authentication and accounting services for RADIUS clients. The RADIUS server is responsible for managing the RADIUS attributes, authenticating remote user credentials, and collecting the remote user connection historical information (such as length of time connected, RADIUS client startups and shutdowns, etc.). In Windows 2000, RADIUS server functionality is provided by the Internet Authentication Service (IAS). Contrast Internet Authentication Service (IAS). *See also* RADIUS accounting; RADIUS authentication; RADIUS authorization; RADIUS client; Remote Authentication Dial-In User Service (RADIUS).

RADIUS shared secret A set of passwords exchanged between RADIUS clients and RADIUS servers to mutually identify one another. The RADIUS secret must be the same for RADIUS clients and RADIUS servers to communicate.

redundant cluster node A server cluster node that is acting as a redundant server in the event the active node fails. *See also* active cluster node; server cluster.

remote access client A generic term for a remote computer that connects to the private network by using modems and phone lines or by virtual private network (VPN) connections. *See also* dial-up remote access client; VPN remote access client.

remote access policies The criteria that determine when remote users should be granted remote access and the configuration of the connection established with the remote user. Remote access policies are unique to Routing and Remote Access and Internet Authentication Service (IAS). In Routing and Remote Access, the remote access policies are applied to the remote users that connect to that specific server running Routing and Remote Access. In addition, in Routing and Remote Access the remote access policies are *stored locally* and must be *duplicated* across all the remote access servers in the design. In IAS, remote access policies are treated as RADIUS attributes and sent in RADIUS client request and responses. The RADIUS clients perceive the remote access policies as normal RADIUS attributes. In IAS, the remote access policies are *centrally* stored on the server running IAS. As a result, the RADIUS clients serviced by the *same* IAS server share the *same* remote access policies. Contrast RADIUS attributes. *See also* Internet Authentication Service (IAS); Remote Authentication Dial-In User Service (RADIUS).

remote access server A generic term for a device that provides connectivity to remote access clients by using either dial-up or virtual private networks (VPN). In Windows 2000, Routing and Remote Access acts as the remote access server for dial-up and virtual private network (VPN) remote access clients. Contrast network access server (NAS); dial-up remote access server; VPN remote access server. *See also* dial-up remote access client; RADIUS client; RADIUS server; virtual private network (VPN); VPN remote access client.

Remote Authentication Dial-In User Service (RADIUS) A security authentication protocol based on clients and servers and widely used by Internet service providers (ISPs) on non-Microsoft remote servers. RADIUS provides remote user authentication, authorization for remote access, and accounting of remote user access profile. *See also* Internet Authentication Service (IAS); RADIUS accounting; RADIUS authentication; RADIUS client; RADIUS server.

remote user A user who dials in to the server over modems and telephone lines from a remote location.

Request For Comments (RFC) The official documents of the Internet Engineering Task Force (IETF) that specify the details for protocols included in the TCP/IP family. *See also* Internet Engineering Task Force (IETF).

resource In Microsoft Management Consoles (MMCs), a portion of the operating system configuration that is managed by the MMC. Generally, any part of a computer system or network, such as a disk drive, printer, or memory, that can be allotted to a running program or a process.

resource record Standard database record types used in zones to associate Domain Name System (DNS) domain names to related data for a given type of network resource, such as a host Internet Protocol (IP) address. Most of the basic resource record types are defined in RFC 1035, but addi-

tional resource record types are defined in other RFCs and approved for use with DNS.

reverse lookup zone A type of DNS zone that is used by DNS to resolve an IP address to a fully qualified domain name (FQDN). Contrast forward lookup zone.

RFC *See* Request For Comments.

RIP *See* Routing Information Protocol (RIP) and Routing Information Protocol for IPX (RIPX).

RIP for IP *See* Routing Information Protocol (RIP).

RIP version 1 First version of the Routing Information Protocol (RIP) for IP. *See also* Routing Information Protocol (RIP) and RIP version 2.

RIP version 2 Second version of Routing Information Protocol (RIP) for IP. Provides enhanced support for Variable Length Subnet Masks (VLSM) and classless interdomain routing (CIDR). *See also* classless interdomain routing (CIDR); RIP Version 1; Routing Information Protocol (RIP); Variable Length Subnet Mask (VLSM).

RIPX *See* Routing Information Protocol for IPX.

round robin DNS A simple mechanism used by DNS servers to share and distribute loads for network resources. Round robin is used to rotate the order of resource record (data returned in a query answer when multiple resource records exist of the same resource record type for a queried DNS domain name.

For example, if a query is made for a multi-homed computer ("hostname") that uses three IP addresses, with each address specified in its own A-type resource record, as follows:

- hostname IN—A 10.0.0.1
- hostname IN—A 10.0.0.2
- hostname IN—A 10.0.0.3

The DNS server will round robin the order of the IP addresses when answering client requests.

In this example, the first client request will be answered with the addresses ordered 10.0.0.1, 10.0.0.2, and 10.0.0.3. The next client request for the same information will be answered with the order rotated to 10.0.0.2, 10.0.0.3, followed by 10.0.0.1. The rotation process continues until data from all of the same-type resource records associated with a name have been rotated to the top of the list returned to the clients. Then the process begins all over again.

route entries Are used by routers to determine the appropriate route paths between network segments. *See also* autostatic route entries; dynamic route entries; static route entries.

routed connection A connection to the Internet which requires that a public IP addressing scheme be used in the private network. Contrast translated connection.

router A network device that connects network segments in a routed network. A router is responsible for forwarding packets between network segments, ensuring that devices on different network segments can communicate. Routers operate at the network layer of the Open Systems Interconnection (OSI) model. Contrast Media Access Control (MAC) layer bridge. *See also* IP router; IPX router.

router mode interface Network interface in a multicast proxy that connects to the same network segments as the multicast clients. Listens for multicast registration requests and multicast traffic from the multicast clients. Contrast proxy mode interface. *See also* multicast proxy.

router routing The routing that occurs between the intervening routers between source or destination computers on different network segments.

Routing and Remote Access The feature in Windows 2000 that provides multiprotocol rout-

ing, dial-up remote access, and virtual private network (VPN) remote access.

Routing and Remote Access - NAT protocol The implementation of the Network Address Translation (NAT) protocol in Windows 2000. This feature allows private IP addressing schemes to connect to public IP networks (such as the Internet). *See also* Network Address Translation (NAT).

Routing Information Protocol (RIP) RIP for IP is a mature and well-documented dynamic IP routing protocol. Every IP router, and almost every operating system, supports some version of the RIP for IP routing protocol. Routing and Remote Access supports RIP versions 1 or 2 in IP routing design. RIP for IP can be used to enable autostatic RIP routing.

Routing Information Protocol for IPX (RIPX) Routing Information Protocol for IPX (RIPX) is a dynamic IPX routing protocol. Every IPX router, and almost every operating system, supports some version of the RIPX routing protocol. Routing and Remote Access Service supports RIPX. RIPX can be used to enable autostatic RIP for IPX routing.

routing table aggregation A method used by IP routers to reduce the amount of network traffic created by dynamic routing protocols. This method reduces the network traffic by combining multiple routing entries into a single route entry that represents all the routing entries. Both Open Shortest Path First (OSPF) and Routing Information Protocol version 2 (RIP v2) support routing table aggregation. *See also* route entries.

S

SA *See* security association.

scheduled (or nonreal-time) response time A type of response for failures or resource shortages that are reviewed on longer intervals (usually measured in weeks or months) or when the analysis of the failure or resource shortage must be performed manually. The majority of scheduled responses are performed manually. Contrast delayed (or near-time) response time; immediate (or real-time) response time.

screened subnet A network segment that is protected by a firewall, router, or proxy server. Access to this network segment is restricted to a specific type of traffic or users. Also known as a perimeter network or Demilitarized Zone (DMZ).

SCSI *See* Small Computer System Interface.

SDSL *See* Symmetric Digital Subscriber Line.

second-level domain Variable length domain names that designate the organization or individual for use on the Internet. You must obtain second-level domain names from Internet governing organizations (currently managed by Network Solutions, Inc.). *See also* domain root; host or resource name; subdomains; top-level domain.

Secure Hash Algorithm (SHA) A message digest hash algorithm that generates a 160-bit hash value. SHA-1 is used with the Digital Signature Algorithm (DSA) in the Digital Signature Standard (DSS), among other places. Contrast Message Digest version 5 (MD5). *See also* digital signature; Digital Signature Algorithm (DSA); Digital Signature Standard (DSS); hash algorithm.

secured dynamically updated DNS zones A DNS zone that is *securely* updated by DHCP servers or Windows 2000 computers. Unauthorized users, groups, or computers are unable to create, modify, or delete their corresponding DNS resource records. Only Active Directory integrated zones can be dynamically updated in a secure fashion. Contrast dynamically updated DNS zones.

security The aspect of a network that ensures that confidential data is protected from unautho-

rized users. Contrast availability; performance.

security association (SA) A session that is established between devices running Internet Protocol Security (IPSec). When these devices authenticate each other and agree upon the IPSec parameters, an IPSec SA is established. *See also* Internet Protocol Security (IPSec).

seed information The AppleTalk network numbers and zones managed by seed routers. *See also* seed router.

seed router The first AppleTalk on a network that establishes the network number range and the zones. Other AppleTalk seed routers (or nonseed routers) conform to the settings of the first seed router on the network.

segment The length of cable on a network between two terminators. A segment can also refer to messages that have been broken up into smaller units by the protocol driver.

Sequenced Packet Exchange (SPX) The transport level (ISO/OSI level 4) protocol used by Novell NetWare. SPX uses IPX to transfer the packets, but SPX ensures that messages are complete. Contrast Internetwork Packet Exchange (IPX).

Serial Line Internet Protocol (SLIP) A data link protocol that allows transmission of TCP/IP data packets over dial-up telephone connections, thus enabling a computer or a LAN (local area network) to be connected to the Internet or some other network. It is an older, less secure protocol than the Point-to-Point Protocol (PPP) and does not support dynamic allocation of IP addresses. Contrast Point-to-Point Protocol (PPP).

server cluster One of the Windows Clustering technologies that is a group of independent computer systems, known as nodes, running Microsoft Windows 2000 Advanced Server and working together as a single system to ensure that mission-critical applications and resources remain available to clients. Every node is attached to one or more cluster storage devices. Server clusters enable users and administrators to access and manage the nodes as a single system rather than as separate computers. *See also* Network Load Balancing; Windows Clustering.

service A program, routine, or process that performs a specific system function to support other programs, particularly at the hardware level. When services are provided over a network, they can be published in Active Directory, facilitating service-centric administration and usage. Some examples of Microsoft Windows 2000 services are Security Accounts Manager service, File Replication service, and Routing and Remote Access.

service (SRV) resource record A resource record used in a zone to register and locate well-known Transmission Control Protocol/Internet Protocol (TCP/IP) services. The SRV resource record is specified in RFC 2052 and is used in Microsoft Windows 2000 or later to locate domain controllers for Active Directory service.

SHA *See* Secure Hash Algorithm.

shared cluster drive A disk storage that is shared between all the nodes in a server cluster. The shared disk storage can be based on SCSI or fibre channel.

Shiva Password Authentication Protocol (SPAP) An authentication protocol implemented in the Routing and Remote Access feature in Windows 2000 that remote access can use to negotiate a connection. SPAP was developed by Shiva to provide access to the Shiva NetModem product. SPAP support in Windows 2000 allows computers running Windows 2000 to connect to Shiva NetModem servers or to allow Shiva NetModem clients to connect to remote access servers running Windows 2000. Contrast Challenge Handshake Authentication Protocol (CHAP); Microsoft Challenge Handshake Authentication Protocol (MS-CHAP); Microsoft Challenge Handshake Authentication Protocol

version 2 (MS-CHAPv2); Password Authentication Protocol (PAP).

signed software An extensively tested device driver, service, or other software that is certified by Microsoft to ensure that Windows 2000 runs reliably and requires no system restarts. Signed software ensures the reliability and integrity of Windows 2000 is maintained.

Simple Mail Transfer Protocol (SMTP) The network management protocol of TCP/IP. In SMTP, agents, which can be hardware as well as software, monitor the activity in the various devices on the network and report to the network console workstation. Control information about each device is maintained in a structure known as a management information block.

Simple Network Management Protocol (SNMP) A network protocol used to manage TCP/IP networks. In Windows 2000, the SNMP service is used to provide status information about the computer running Windows 2000.

SLIP *See* Serial Line Internet Protocol.

slow transfer method A DNS incremental transfer method that transfers a single resource record in an uncompressed format. Contrast fast transfer method.

Small Computer System Interface (SCSI) A standard high-speed parallel interface defined by the American National Standards Institute (ANSI). A SCSI interface is used for connecting microcomputers to peripheral devices such as hard disks and printers, and to other computers and local area networks (LANs). Contrast fibre channel.

small office or home office (SOHO) A type of organization that is categorized by a relatively small number of users (branch office) or users who work from home.

smart card A credit card–sized device used to securely store public and private keys, passwords, and other types of personal information. To use a smart card, you need a smart card reader attached to the computer and a personal identification number for the smart card. In Windows 2000, smart cards can be used to enable certificate-based authentication and single sign-on to the enterprise.

SMTP *See* Simple Mail Transfer Protocol.

SNA *See* System Network Architecture.

snap-in An object that can be added to a console tree within the Microsoft Management Console (MMC). A snap-in is used for management tasks. Each snap-in contains objects and actions related to a particular area of computer or directory management such as Disk Management or Event Viewer. A snap-in has one or more windows that display properties, services, and events with context-sensitive menus of actions relevant to each object. *See also* Microsoft Management Console (MMC); resource.

SNMP *See* Simple Network Management Protocol.

SOHO *See* small office or home office.

source-routing bridge A special type of Media Access Control (MAC) layer bridge that can incorporate multiple paths between endpoints in an extended network (transparent bridges require loop-free topologies). Source-routing bridges require source and destination computers to supply the bridging information needed to deliver a frame to a destination (transparent bridges use forwarding tables). Source-routing bridges are commonly used in Token Ring networks. Contrast router; transparent bridge.

SPAP *See* Shiva Password Authentication Protocol.

SPX *See* Sequenced Packet Exchange.

stand-alone server A computer that runs Microsoft Windows 2000 Server but doesn't par-

ticipate in a domain. A stand-alone server has only its own database of users, and it processes logon requests by itself. It doesn't share account information with any other computer and can't provide access to domain accounts.

standard primary zone A zone type in Windows 2000 and Berkley Internet Domain Name (BIND) DNS that stores a read-write copy of the DNS zone resource records in an operating system file. Standard primary zones are replicated by using DNS full or incremental zone transfers Standard primary zones support unsecured, dynamic updates to the DNS zone resource records. Contrast Active Directory integrated zone; standard secondary zone. *See also* DNS zone; Domain Name System (DNS); full zone transfer; incremental zone transfer.

standard secondary zone A zone type in Windows 2000 and Berkley Internet Domain Name (BIND) DNS that stores a read-only copy of the DNS zone resource records in an operating system file. Secondary primary zones are replicated from standard primary zones by using DNS full or incremental zone transfers. The resource records in a standard secondary zones can't be dynamically updated. Contrast Active Directory integrated zone; standard primary zone. *See also* DNS zone; Domain Name System (DNS); full zone transfer; incremental zone transfer.

static route entries Are considered *static* because once the entries are placed in the routing table, they don't change. Static routing entries are manually created in the routing table. Contrast autostatic route entries; dynamic route entries.

subdomains Additional variable length domain names that designate an organization's internal structure (for example geographic or departmental). You can specify any number and levels of subdomains within your domain namespace design. You must include the domain root to specify a fully qualified domain name (FQDN).

See also domain root; host or resource name; second-level domain; top-level domain.

subnet A portion of a network, which may be a physically independent network segment, that shares a classful network address with other portions of the network and is distinguished by a subnet number.

subnet mask The portion of IP configuration that is used to determine which portion of an IP address is the IP network number and the IP host address. The IP network number is used by IP devices and IP routers to determine route path. The IP host address uniquely identifies a host on a specific subnet. Subnetting allows the IP host address portion of the IP address to be further divided into two or more subnets. In subnetting, a part of the host address is reserved to identify the particular subnet. *See also* Variable Length Subnet Mask (VLSM).

subnet number The portion of your IP address that uniquely identifies a subnet within your private network.

superscopes A grouping of two or more DHCP scopes. You create superscopes when you want to support two IP address ranges on the same physical network segment. *See also* DHCP scopes.

Symmetric Digital Subscriber Line (SDSL) Acronym for symmetric (or single-line) digital subscriber line, a digital telecommunications technology that is a variation of HDSL. SDSL uses one pair of copper wire rather than two pairs of wires and transmits at 1.544 Mbps. Compare Asymmetric Digital Subscriber Line (ADSL); Digital Subscriber Line (DSL); High-bit-rate Digital Subscriber Line (HDSL).

System Network Architecture (SNA) A set of network protocols developed by IBM. Originally designed in 1974 for IBM's mainframe computers, SNA has evolved over the years so that it now also supports peer-to-peer networks of workstations.

T

T1 A dedicated telephony connection supporting a maximum data rate of 1.544Mbps. A T1 line actually consists of 24 individual 64Kbps channels. Each 64Kbps channel can be configured to carry voice or data traffic. In addition, individual channels can be purchases from telephone companies to provide fractional T1 access. Contrast Digital Subscriber Line (DSL); Integrated Services Digital Network (ISDN).

TCO *See* total cost of ownership.

TCP *See* Transmission Control Protocol.

TCP/IP *See* Transmission Control Protocol/Internet Protocol.

TCP/IP filters A feature of Windows 2000 that allows the filtering of IP traffic for applications. TCP/IP filters filter IP traffic at the Windows Sockets layer. The IP routing filters in Routing and Remote Access filter IP traffic at the data link layer. Contrast IP routing filter.

TDI Driver *See* Transport Driver Interface (TDI).

technical constraints Restrictions that set boundaries on the type of solution, based on an organization's existing hardware, existing software, future hardware, future software, or other technology-related issues. For example, when a solution must be provided by using existing hardware, the type of solution that can be created for an organization may be limited. Technical constraints limit a design while technical requirements set goals for the design. Technical constraints are often driven by or are a subset of business constraints. Contrast business constraints. *See also* business requirements; technical requirements.

technical requirements Conditions that establish goals that a solution must achieve based on an organization's existing hardware, existing software, future hardware, future software, or other technology-related issues. For example, when an organization requires that certain network resources must be accessible by users a given percentage of the time, the solution must achieve these goals. Contrast business requirements *See also* business constraints; technical constraints.

throughput A measure of the data transfer rate through a component, connection, or system. In networking, throughput is a good indicator of the system's total performance because it defines how well the components work together to transfer data from one computer to another. In this case, the throughput would indicate how many bytes or packets the network could process per second.

TokenTalk The designation used by Apple Talk Phase 2 for Token Ring. *See also* EtherTalk.

top-level domain Two or three letter names that designate the country, region, or type of organization using the name. You must obtain top-level domain names from Internet governing organizations (currently managed by Network Solutions, Inc.). *See also* domain root; host or resource name; second-level domain; subdomains.

total cost of ownership (TCO) The total amount of money and time associated with purchasing computer hardware and software and deploying, configuring, and maintaining the hardware and software. TCO includes hardware and software updates, training, maintenance, administration, and technical support.

translated connection A connection to the Internet that allows private IP addressing schemes to be used in the private network. Contrast routed connection.

Transmission Control Protocol (TCP) One of the primary protocols in the Transmission Control Protocol/Internet Protocol (TCP/IP) protocol suite. Whereas Internet Protocol (IP) deals only with IP packets and routing, TCP enables two IP-based devices to establish a connection and exchange streams of data. TCP provides guaranteed delivery of data and guarantees that packets will be delivered in the same order in which they were sent. Contrast Sequenced Packet Exchange (SPX); User Datagram Protocol (UDP). *See also* Transmission Control Protocol/Internet Protocol (TCP/IP).

Transmission Control Protocol/Internet Protocol (TCP/IP) A set of networking protocols used within private networks and on the Internet that provides communications across interconnected networks made up of computers with diverse hardware architectures and various operating systems. TCP/IP includes standards for how computers communicate and conventions for connecting networks and routing traffic. Contrast Internetwork Packet Exchange. *See also* Internet Protocol (IP); Transmission Control Protocol (TCP); User Datagram Protocol (UDP).

transparent bridge A type of Media Access Control (MAC) layer bridge that provides connectivity between network segments. Transparent bridges require loop-free topologies, dynamically learn the network topology, and forward or drop frames (Ethernet or FDDI) based on the source and destination MAC address. Contrast Media Access Control (MAC) layer bridge; router; source-routing bridge.

Transport Driver Interface (TDI) An application programming interface (API) at the OSI transport layer that allows application layer APIs to communicate directly with transport protocols. For example, the NetBIOS API communicates with the Internetwork Packet Exchange (IPX) protocol through TDI. Contrast Network Driver Interface Specification (NDIS).

Triple DES (3DES) An encryption scheme in which the sender and receiver of a message share a single, common key that is used to encrypt and decrypt the message. This version of Data Encryption Standard (DES) achieves a higher level of security by encrypting the data three times with three different, unrelated keys. 3DES is illegal to export out of the U.S. or Canada if you don't meet the Bureau of Export Administration (BXA) requirements. Contrast 56-bit DES; 40-bit DES. *See also* DES.

U

UDP *See* User Datagram Protocol.

unicast IP address An IP address that has a destination of only one computer. Unicast IP addresses are utilized to send information point-to-point between any two computers on a network. Contrast broadcast IP address; multicast IP address.

unicast router Forwards unicast (and potentially broadcast) IP packets between network segments. Routing and Remote Access allows Windows 2000 to be a unicast router. Contrast multicast router. *See also* Routing and Remote Access.

unicast routing table A memory-based structure maintained by a router to determine how to forward unicast packets. The unicast routing table is populated by static route entries, autostatic route entries, and dynamic route entries. The unicast routing table is repopulated each time the router is started. Contrast multicast routing table. *See also* autostatic route entries; dynamic route entries; static route entries.

user authentication An authentication method that verifies the identity of a user. User authentication requires user credentials (such as a user name and password). In addition, the security of user authentication can be enhanced by using smart card authentication (which requires a physical device). Contrast machine authentication.

User Datagram Protocol (UDP) One of the primary protocols in the Transmission Control Protocol/Internet Protocol (TCP/IP) protocol suite. Whereas Internet Protocol (IP) deals only with IP packets and routing, UDP enables two IP-based

devices to establish exchange streams of data without establishing a session. UDP provides best effort delivery of data. UDP doesn't guarantee that packets will be delivered in the same order in which they were sent. However, UDP creates less network traffic when communicating between two computers. Contrast Internetwork Packet Exchange (IPX); Transmission Control Protocol (TCP). *See also* Transmission Control Protocol/Internet Protocol (TCP/IP).

V

Variable Length Subnet Mask (VLSM) A method of IP addressing that assigns more than one subnet mask within a network. VLSM allows the subnet mask to be adjusted for network segments to reduce the number of unused IP addresses. In addition, VLSM supports route aggregation where a single routing table entry can represent the address space of perhaps thousands of traditional classful routes. VLSM is typically utilized within a private network. Contrast classless interdomain routing (CIDR).

virtual private network (VPN) An extension of a private network that provides encapsulated, encrypted, and authenticated virtualized connections across public networks. VPN connections can provide secured remote access and routed connections to private networks over the Internet. VPN connections can be created by using Layer 2 Tunneling Protocol (L2TP) or Point-to-Point Tunneling Protocol (PPTP) tunnels. *See also* Internet Protocol Security (IPSec); Layer 2 Tunneling Protocol (L2TP); Point-to-Point Tunneling Protocol (PPTP).

virtual private network (VPN) remote access A method of providing remote user access where the organization wants to outsource the dial-up portion of the remote access design. Contrast dial-up remote access.

VLSM *See* Variable Length Subnet Mask.

VPN remote access client A remote computer that connects to the private network by using a virtual private network (VPN). The remote computer is authenticated by using user accounts managed by the organization that owns the VPN remote access servers. Windows 2000 can support VPN remote access clients that connect to the private network by using the Point-to-Point Tunneling Protocol (PPTP) and Layer 2 Tunneling Protocols (L2TP) tunneling protocols. Contrast dial-up remote access client. *See also* Layer 2 Tunneling Protocol (L2TP); Point-to-Point Tunneling Protocol (PPTP); virtual private network (VPN); VPN remote access server.

VPN remote access server A network access server that accepts Point-to-Point Tunneling Protocol (PPTP) or Layer 2 Tunneling Protocol (L2TP) connections from remote access clients and connects the remote access clients to the network segments connected to the network access server. In Windows 2000, Routing and Remote Access acts as a VPN remote access server. *See also* dial-up remote access client; dial-up remote access server; RADIUS client; virtual private network (VPN); VPN remote access client.

VPN tunnel *See* virtual private network.

W

WAN *See* wide area network.

Web content caching A feature found in most proxy servers that allows the proxy server to store Web content on local disks to reduce the amount of traffic on Internet connections. *See also* proxy server.

Web publishing A feature in Microsoft Proxy Server 2.0 that allows users outside a private network to access resources that reside inside a private network. Network address translation prevents users outside the private network from directly accessing resources within the private network. Web publishing maps the private IP address of a resource to a public IP address. *See also* proxy server.

Web server A computer that is maintained by a system administrator or Internet service provider (ISP) and responds to requests from a user's Web browser.

Web-based applications A type of application written in Hypertext Markup Language (HTML), Dynamic Hypertext Markup Language (DHTML), or Active Server Pages (ASP). The users run the applications in a local Web browser and retrieve the applications from Web servers (such as Internet Information Services) by using the Hypertext Transfer Protocol (HTTP). Web-based applications can access data stored in Extensible Markup Language (XML) or any Open Database Connectivity (ODBC)–compatible data source (such as Microsoft SQL Server or Microsoft Access databases). *See also* Active Server Pages (ASP); Extensible Markup Language (XML); Open Database Connectivity (ODBC).

wide area network (WAN) A communications network connecting computers and computer peripherals separated geographically. A WAN allows any device to communicate with any other device on the network.

Windows Clustering A feature of Windows 2000 that provides high availability solutions for services and applications. Windows Clustering technologies include Network Load Balancing and server clusters. Windows Clustering technologies are available in Windows 2000 Advanced Server and Windows 2000 Datacenter Server. *See also* Network Load Balancing; server cluster.

Windows Internet Name Service (WINS) A software service that dynamically maps IP addresses to computer names (NetBIOS names). This allows users to access resources by name instead of requiring them to use IP addresses that are difficult to recognize and remember. WINS servers support clients that utilize NetBIOS name resolution to access network resources (such as Windows 2000 and earlier versions of Microsoft operating systems). Contrast Domain Name System (DNS). *See also* Network Basic Input/Output System (NetBIOS).

Windows Management Instrumentation (WMI) A management infrastructure in Windows 2000 that supports monitoring and controlling system resources through a common set of interfaces and provides a logically organized, consistent model of Windows operation, configuration, and status.

Windows Sockets (WinSocks) An application programming interface (API) standard for software that provides a TCP/IP interface under Windows. Contrast Network Basic Input/Output System (NetBIOS). *See also* Transmission Control Protocol/Internet Protocol (TCP/IP).

WINS *See* Windows Internet Name Service.

WINS Client An integral part of the IP protocol implemented in Windows 2000. The WINS Client receives requests for NetBIOS name resolution from applications running on the same computer and forwards the requests to WINS servers. Contrast WINS Proxies; WINS Server.

WINS persistent connections A feature in the WINS service in Windows 2000 that allows the WINS server to retain open connections with replication partners. Because connections between the WINS replication are already established, the network traffic associated with establishing the connection is eliminated.

WINS Proxies An integral part of the WINS Client, and subsequently the IP protocol implemented in Windows 2000. The WINS Client receives requests for NetBIOS name registration or resolution from non-WINS clients running on the same network segment and forwards the requests to WINS servers. Contrast WINS Proxies; WINS Server.

WINS Server The service in Windows 2000 that provides NetBIOS registration, resolution, and release to WINS clients. From the Windows 2000 perspective, WINS Server is a service that runs on Windows 2000. Contrast WINS Client; WINS Proxies.

WinSocks *See* Windows Sockets.

WMI *See* Windows Management Instrumentation.

X

X.25 A popular standard for packet-switching networks. The X.25 standard was approved by the CCITT (now the ITU) in 1976. It defines layers 1, 2, and 3 in the OSI Reference Model.

X509 certificate *See* X509 version 3 certificate.

X509 version 3 certificate Version 3 of the ITU-T recommendation X.509 for syntax and format. This is the standard certificate format used by Windows 2000 certificate-based processes. An X.509 certificate includes information about the person or entity to whom the certificate is issued, information about the certificate, plus optional information about the certificate authority (CA) issuing the certificate. Subject information may include the entity's name, public key, public-key algorithm, and an optional unique subject ID. *See also* certificate; certificate authority; ITU-T; preshared key; public key.

XML *See* Extensible Markup Language.

Z

zone *See* DNS zone or AppleTalk zone.

zone transfer The process by which Domain Name System (DNS) servers interact to maintain and synchronize authoritative name data for standard primary zones and standard secondary zones. When a DNS server is configured as a secondary master for a zone, it periodically queries another DNS server configured as its source for the zone. If the version of the zone kept by the source is different, the secondary master server will pull zone data from its source DNS server to synchronize zone data. Active Directory integrated zones utilize Active Directory replication to perform zone transfers. Contrast Active Directory integrated zone. *See also* full zone transfer; incremental zone transfer.

Index

A

N

Practical, *portable*
guides for
IT administrators

For immediate answers that will help you administer Microsoft products efficiently, get ADMINISTRATOR'S POCKET CONSULTANTS. Ideal at the desk or on the go from workstation to workstation, these hands-on, fast-answers reference guides focus on what needs to be done in specific scenarios to support and manage mission-critical products.

Microsoft® Windows NT® Server 4.0
Administrator's Pocket Consultant

U.S.A.	$29.99
U.K.	£20.99
Canada	$44.99

ISBN 0-7356-0574-2

Microsoft SQL Server™ 7.0
Administrator's Pocket Consultant

U.S.A.	$29.99
U.K.	£20.99
Canada	$44.99

ISBN 0-7356-0596-3

Microsoft Windows® 2000
Administrator's Pocket Consultant

U.S.A.	$29.99
U.K.	£20.99
Canada	$44.99

ISBN 0-7356-0831-8

Microsoft®

mspress.microsoft.com

Test *your* readiness *for the*
MCP**exam**

If you took a Microsoft Certified Professional (MCP) exam today, would you pass? With each READINESS REVIEW MCP exam simulation on CD-ROM, you get a low-risk, low-cost way to find out! The next-generation test engine delivers a set of randomly generated, 50-question practice exams covering real MCP objectives. You can test and retest with different question sets each time—and with automated scoring, you get immediate Pass/Fail feedback. Use these READINESS REVIEWS to evaluate your proficiency with the skills and knowledge that you'll be tested on in the real exams.

MICROSOFT LICENSE AGREEMENT
Book Companion CD

IMPORTANT—READ CAREFULLY: This Microsoft End-User License Agreement ("EULA") is a legal agreement between you (either an individual or an entity) and Microsoft Corporation for the Microsoft product identified above, which includes computer software and may include associated media, printed materials, and "online" or electronic documentation ("SOFTWARE PRODUCT"). Any component included within the SOFTWARE PRODUCT that is accompanied by a separate End-User License Agreement shall be governed by such agreement and not the terms set forth below. By installing, copying, or otherwise using the SOFTWARE PRODUCT, you agree to be bound by the terms of this EULA. If you do not agree to the terms of this EULA, you are not authorized to install, copy, or otherwise use the SOFTWARE PRODUCT; you may, however, return the SOFTWARE PRODUCT, along with all printed materials and other items that form a part of the Microsoft product that includes the SOFTWARE PRODUCT, to the place you obtained them for a full refund.

SOFTWARE PRODUCT LICENSE

The SOFTWARE PRODUCT is protected by United States copyright laws and international copyright treaties, as well as other intellectual property laws and treaties. The SOFTWARE PRODUCT is licensed, not sold.

1. **GRANT OF LICENSE.** This EULA grants you the following rights:

   a. **Software Product.** You may install and use one copy of the SOFTWARE PRODUCT on a single computer. The primary user of the computer on which the SOFTWARE PRODUCT is installed may make a second copy for his or her exclusive use on a portable computer.

   b. **Storage/Network Use.** You may also store or install a copy of the SOFTWARE PRODUCT on a storage device, such as a network server, used only to install or run the SOFTWARE PRODUCT on your other computers over an internal network; however, you must acquire and dedicate a license for each separate computer on which the SOFTWARE PRODUCT is installed or run from the storage device. A license for the SOFTWARE PRODUCT may not be shared or used concurrently on different computers.

   c. **License Pak.** If you have acquired this EULA in a Microsoft License Pak, you may make the number of additional copies of the computer software portion of the SOFTWARE PRODUCT authorized on the printed copy of this EULA, and you may use each copy in the manner specified above. You are also entitled to make a corresponding number of secondary copies for portable computer use as specified above.

   d. **Sample Code.** Solely with respect to portions, if any, of the SOFTWARE PRODUCT that are identified within the SOFTWARE PRODUCT as sample code (the "SAMPLE CODE"):

      i. **Use and Modification.** Microsoft grants you the right to use and modify the source code version of the SAMPLE CODE, *provided* you comply with subsection (d)(iii) below. You may not distribute the SAMPLE CODE, or any modified version of the SAMPLE CODE, in source code form.

      ii. **Redistributable Files.** Provided you comply with subsection (d)(iii) below, Microsoft grants you a nonexclusive, royalty-free right to reproduce and distribute the object code version of the SAMPLE CODE and of any modified SAMPLE CODE, other than SAMPLE CODE, or any modified version thereof, designated as not redistributable in the Readme file that forms a part of the SOFTWARE PRODUCT (the "Non-Redistributable Sample Code"). All SAMPLE CODE other than the Non-Redistributable Sample Code is collectively referred to as the "REDISTRIBUTABLES."

      iii. **Redistribution Requirements.** If you redistribute the REDISTRIBUTABLES, you agree to: (i) distribute the REDISTRIBUTABLES in object code form only in conjunction with and as a part of your software application product; (ii) not use Microsoft's name, logo, or trademarks to market your software application product; (iii) include a valid copyright notice on your software application product; (iv) indemnify, hold harmless, and defend Microsoft from and against any claims or lawsuits, including attorney's fees, that arise or result from the use or distribution of your software application product; and (v) not permit further distribution of the REDISTRIBUTABLES by your end user. Contact Microsoft for the applicable royalties due and other licensing terms for all other uses and/or distribution of the REDISTRIBUTABLES.

2. **DESCRIPTION OF OTHER RIGHTS AND LIMITATIONS.**

   • **Limitations on Reverse Engineering, Decompilation, and Disassembly.** You may not reverse engineer, decompile, or disassemble the SOFTWARE PRODUCT, except and only to the extent that such activity is expressly permitted by applicable law notwithstanding this limitation.

   • **Separation of Components.** The SOFTWARE PRODUCT is licensed as a single product. Its component parts may not be separated for use on more than one computer.

   • **Rental.** You may not rent, lease, or lend the SOFTWARE PRODUCT.

- **Support Services.** Microsoft may, but is not obligated to, provide you with support services related to the SOFTWARE PRODUCT ("Support Services"). Use of Support Services is governed by the Microsoft policies and programs described in the user manual, in "online" documentation, and/or in other Microsoft-provided materials. Any supplemental software code provided to you as part of the Support Services shall be considered part of the SOFTWARE PRODUCT and subject to the terms and conditions of this EULA. With respect to technical information you provide to Microsoft as part of the Support Services, Microsoft may use such information for its business purposes, including for product support and development. Microsoft will not utilize such technical information in a form that personally identifies you.

- **Software Transfer.** You may permanently transfer all of your rights under this EULA, provided you retain no copies, you transfer all of the SOFTWARE PRODUCT (including all component parts, the media and printed materials, any upgrades, this EULA, and, if applicable, the Certificate of Authenticity), **and** the recipient agrees to the terms of this EULA.

- **Termination.** Without prejudice to any other rights, Microsoft may terminate this EULA if you fail to comply with the terms and conditions of this EULA. In such event, you must destroy all copies of the SOFTWARE PRODUCT and all of its component parts.

3. **COPYRIGHT.** All title and copyrights in and to the SOFTWARE PRODUCT (including but not limited to any images, photographs, animations, video, audio, music, text, SAMPLE CODE, REDISTRIBUTABLES, and "applets" incorporated into the SOFTWARE PRODUCT) and any copies of the SOFTWARE PRODUCT are owned by Microsoft or its suppliers. The SOFT-WARE PRODUCT is protected by copyright laws and international treaty provisions. Therefore, you must treat the SOFTWARE PRODUCT like any other copyrighted material **except** that you may install the SOFTWARE PRODUCT on a single computer provided you keep the original solely for backup or archival purposes. You may not copy the printed materials accompanying the SOFTWARE PRODUCT.

4. **U.S. GOVERNMENT RESTRICTED RIGHTS.** The SOFTWARE PRODUCT and documentation are provided with RESTRICTED RIGHTS. Use, duplication, or disclosure by the Government is subject to restrictions as set forth in subparagraph (c)(1)(ii) of the Rights in Technical Data and Computer Software clause at DFARS 252.227-7013 or subparagraphs (c)(1) and (2) of the Commercial Computer Software—Restricted Rights at 48 CFR 52.227-19, as applicable. Manufacturer is Microsoft Corporation/One Microsoft Way/Redmond, WA 98052-6399.

5. **EXPORT RESTRICTIONS.** You agree that you will not export or re-export the SOFTWARE PRODUCT, any part thereof, or any process or service that is the direct product of the SOFTWARE PRODUCT (the foregoing collectively referred to as the "Restricted Components"), to any country, person, entity, or end user subject to U.S. export restrictions. You specifically agree not to export or re-export any of the Restricted Components (i) to any country to which the U.S. has embargoed or restricted the export of goods or services, which currently include, but are not necessarily limited to, Cuba, Iran, Iraq, Libya, North Korea, Sudan, and Syria, or to any national of any such country, wherever located, who intends to transmit or transport the Restricted Components back to such country; (ii) to any end user who you know or have reason to know will utilize the Restricted Components in the design, development, or production of nuclear, chemical, or biological weapons; or (iii) to any end user who has been prohibited from participating in U.S. export transactions by any federal agency of the U.S. government. You warrant and represent that neither the BXA nor any other U.S. federal agency has suspended, revoked, or denied your export privileges.

DISCLAIMER OF WARRANTY

MISCELLANEOUS

This EULA is governed by the laws of the State of Washington USA, except and only to the extent that applicable law mandates governing law of a different jurisdiction.

Should you have any questions concerning this EULA, or if you desire to contact Microsoft for any reason, please contact the Microsoft subsidiary serving your country, or write: Microsoft Sales Information Center/One Microsoft Way/Redmond, WA 98052-6399.

System Requirements

To get the most out of the *MCSE Training Kit: Designing a Microsoft Windows 2000 Network Infrastructure*, including the Supplemental Course Materials CD-ROM and the Microsoft Windows 2000 Advanced Server Evaluation Edition CD-ROM, you will need a computer equipped with the following minimum configuration:

- 133-MHz or higher Pentium-compatible CPU.

- 256 MB of RAM recommended minimum (128 MB minimum supported; 8 GB maximum).

- 2 GB hard disk with a minimum of 1.0 GB free space. (Additional free hard disk space is required if you are installing over a network.) Windows 2000 Professional supports single and dual CPU systems.

- 12*x* CD-ROM drive.

- Windows 2000 Advanced Server supports up to eight CPUs on one machine.

- Display system capable of 800 x 600 resolution or better.

To view the electronic version of the book on the companion CD, you will need a browser application such as Microsoft Internet Explorer 4.01 or later. These and other browser applications are available to download over the Internet. A version of Microsoft Internet Explorer 5 that allows you to view the electronic version of the book is supplied on the companion CD. See the README.TXT file on the companion CD for instructions on how to use this supplied version of the Internet Explorer browser to view the electronic version of the book.

For information about Microsoft Press®
products, visit our Web site at
mspress.microsoft.com

NO POSTAGE
NECESSARY
IF MAILED
IN THE
UNITED STATES

BUSINESS REPLY MAIL
FIRST-CLASS MAIL   PERMIT NO. 108   REDMOND WA

POSTAGE WILL BE PAID BY ADDRESSEE

MICROSOFT PRESS
PO BOX 97017
REDMOND, WA 98073-9830